UNITED NATIONS CONFERENCE ON TRADE AND DEVELOPMENT
Geneva

THE LEAST DEVELOPED COUNTRIES REPORT 2002

Prepared by the UNCTAD secretariat

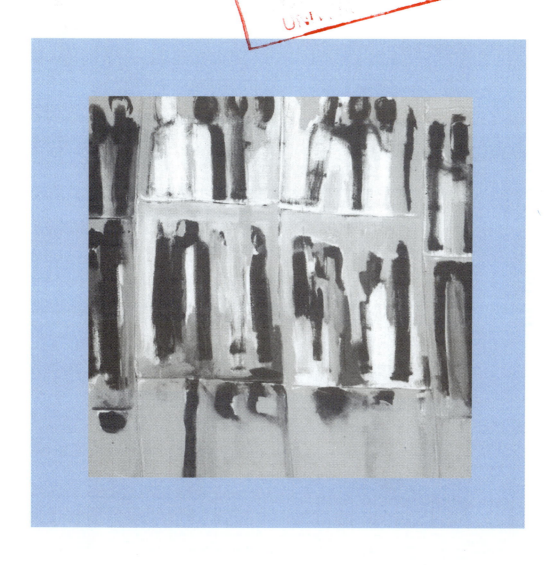

Note

Symbols of United Nations documents are composed of capital letters with figures. Mention of such a symbol indicates a reference to a United Nations document.

The designations employed and the presentation of the material in this publication do not imply the expression of any opinion whatsoever on the part of the Secretariat of the United Nations concerning the legal status of any country, territory, city or area, or of its authorities, or concerning the delimitation of its frontiers or boundaries.

Material in this publication may be freely quoted or reprinted, but full acknowledgement is requested. A copy of the publication containing the quotation or reprint should be sent to the UNCTAD secretariat at: Palais des Nations, CH-1211 Geneva 10, Switzerland.

The Overview from this Report can also be found on the Internet, in both English and French, at the following address:

http://www.unctad.org

UNCTAD/LDC/2002

UNITED NATIONS PUBLICATION

Sales No. E.02.II.D.13

ISBN 92-1-112562-6

ISSN 0257-7550

Acknowledgements

The Least Developed Countries Report 2002 was prepared by a team consisting of Charles Gore (team leader), Massoud Karshenas (principal consultant), Marquise David, Michael Herrmann, Zeljka Kozul-Wright and Utumporn Reungsuwan. Specific inputs were received from Mehmet Arda, Pierre Encontre, Joerg Mayer, Luca Monge-Roffarello, Marcel Namfua and Olle Ostensson. The staff of the Central Statistics Branch of the Division on Globalization and Development Strategies within UNCTAD fully supported the work on the Report, particularly Yumiko Mochizuki and Laurence Schlosser, who provided information on commodity price trends, Arunas Butkevicius, who provided much advice on international data issues, and Nelly Berthault, who worked on LDC trade statistics within the UN COMTRADE database. Makameh Bahrami and Erna Borneck also provided statistical advice. Lev Komlev and Taffere Tesfachew undertook a detailed review of the manuscript. Detailed comments were also received on specific chapters from Gabrielle Köhler, Joerg Mayer and Marcel Namfua. The work was completed under the overall supervision of Habib Ouane, Officer-in-Charge of the Office of the Special Coordinator for Least Developed, Land-locked and Island Developing Countries within UNCTAD.

The new poverty estimates on which Part Two of the Report is based were prepared using a methodology devised by Massoud Karshenas specifically for the Report. Background papers were prepared by Brian van Arkadie, Henrik Hansen, Paul Mosley, Felix Naschold, Graham Pyatt, David Sapsford and Ann Whitehead. Specific inputs for Part One of the Report were received from David Stewart (UNDP Human Development Report Office) and Rajesh Venugopal. Odd Gulbrandsen and Alf Maizels generously gave advice on estimating commodity terms of trade, and Samuel Wangwe provided information on latest developments in donor performance monitoring in the United Republic of Tanzania. Graham Pyatt also provided detailed comments on specific chapters.

The Report drew on the background papers prepared by FAO and UNIDO for the Third United Nations Conference on the Least Developed Countries, which address issues of building productive capacities in LDCs in agriculture and industry. Friedrich von Kirchbach (ITC) provided useful information and advice on the trade performance of LDCs, and fruitful discussions were maintained with José B. Figueiredo (ILO) on poverty and socio-economic security issues, and with Harmon Thomas (FAO) on issues of agricultural development in LDCs in the new global environment.

Secretarial support in the final production of the Report was provided by Corazon Alvarez, Sylvie Guy, Regina Ogunyinka and Sivanla Sikounnavong. Diego Oyarzun-Reyes designed the cover, and the text was edited by Graham Grayston. The overall layout, graphics and desktop publishing were done by Madasamyraja Rajalingam.

Contents

Part One
RECENT ECONOMIC TRENDS AND UNLDC III DEVELOPMENT TARGETS

Part Two
ESCAPING THE POVERTY TRAP

List of Boxes

List of Charts

Annex Chart

Box Charts

List of Tables

Annex Tables

Box Tables

Explanatory Notes

The term "dollars" ($) refers to United States dollars unless otherwise stated. The term "billion" signifies 1,000 million.

Annual rates of growth and changes refer to compound rates. Exports are valued f.o.b. (free on board) and imports c.i.f. (cost, insurance, freight) unless otherwise specified.

Use of a dash (–) between dates representing years, e.g. 1981–1990, signifies the full period involved, including the initial and final years. An oblique stroke (/) between two years, e.g. 1991/92, signifies a fiscal or crop year.

The term "least developed country" (LDC) refers, throughout this report, to a country included in the United Nations list of least developed countries.

In the tables:

Two dots (..) indicate that the data are not available, or are not separately reported.

One dot (.) indicates that the data are not applicable.

A hyphen (-) indicates that the amount is nil or negligible.

Details and percentages do not necessarily add up to totals, because of rounding.

Abbreviations

ACP	African, Caribbean and Pacific
AIDS	acquired immune deficiency syndrome
AGOA	African Growth and Opportunities Act
APQLI	Augmented Physical Quality of Life Index
ASEAN	Association of South-East Asian Nations
CDP	Committee for Development Policy
DAC	Development Assistance Committee
DC	developing country
EAA	external assistance to agriculture
EBA	Everything but Arms
ECA	Economic Commission for Africa
ECLAC	Economic Commission for Latin America and the Caribbean
ECOSOC	Economic and Social Council
EDI	Economic Diversification Index
ESAF	Enhanced Structural Adjustment Facility
ESCAP	Economic and Social Commission for Asia and the Pacific
EU	European Union
EVI	Economic Vulnerability Index
FAO	Food and Agriculture Organization of the United Nations
FDI	foreign direct investment
GATT	General Agreement on Tariffs and Trade
GDI	gross domestic investment
GDP	gross domestic product
GNI	gross national income
GNP	gross national product
GSP	Generalized System of Preferences
GSTP	Global System of Trade Preferences
HDI	Human Development Index
HIPC	heavily indebted poor country
HIV	human immunodeficiency syndrome
IBRD	International Bank for Reconstruction and Development
IDA	International Development Association
IF	Integrated Framework for Trade-Related Technical Assistance
IFIs	international financial institutions
ILO	International Labour Organization
IMF	International Monetary Fund
I-PRSP	Interim Poverty Reduction Strategy Paper
ITC	International Trade Centre UNCTAD/WTO
LDC	least developed country

MFA	Multi-Fibre Arrangement
MFN	most favoured nation
MISA	Minimum Income for School Attendance
NGO	non-governmental organization
NTBs	non-tariff barriers
ODA	official development assistance
OECD	Organisation for Economic Co-operation and Development
PFP	Policy Framework Paper
POA	Programme of Action
PRGF	Poverty Reduction Growth Facility
PRSC	Poverty Reduction Support Credit
PRSP	Poverty Reduction Strategy Paper
PPP	purchasing power parity
PV	present value
SAF	Structural Adjustment Facility
SMEs	small and medium-sized enterprises
SSA	sub-Saharan Africa
SPA	Special Programme of Assistance for Africa
TNCs	transnational corporations
UN	United Nations
UNAIDS	United Nations Joint Programme on HIV/AIDS
UNCTAD	United Nations Conference on Trade and Development
UNDESA	United Nations Department of Economic and Social Affairs
UNDP	United Nations Development Programme
UNESCO	United Nations Educational, Scientific and Cultural Organization
UNFPA	United Nations Population Fund
UNICEF	United Nations Children's Fund
UNLDC III	Third United Nations Conference on the Least Developed Countries
UNIDO	United Nations Industrial Development Organization
UNSD	United Nations Statistics Division
WDI	World Development Indicators (World Bank)
WHO	World Health Organization
WTO	World Trade Organization

Overview

A REAL TURNING POINT?

In his speech opening the Third United Nations Conference on the Least Developed Countries (UNLDC III), the Secretary-General of the United Nations, Kofi Annan, urged Governments to ensure that the meeting, unlike its two predecessors, would mark "a real turning point in the everyday life of poor people in the poorest countries". The purpose of this Report is to contribute to that vision by providing a better analytical basis for national and international policies designed to promote poverty reduction in the least developed countries (LDCs).

In recent years the international community has adopted poverty reduction as a central goal of international development cooperation. Within this context, an "overarching goal" of the Programme of Action for the Least Developed Countries for the Decade 2001–2010 agreed at UNLDC III is for the LDCs to make substantial progress towards halving the proportion of people living in extreme poverty by 2015. The Programme itself consists of a long list of actions that the LDCs and their development partners are urged to undertake. Implementing these actions in a way which supports the goal of poverty reduction will require a strategic perspective based on a better knowledge of the nature and dynamics of poverty in the LDCs, and also a more complete understanding of what policies can best reduce poverty in the particular yet diverse socio-economic conditions of these countries.

The inadequacy of the analytical foundations for effective poverty reduction in poor countries in general, and in the LDCs in particular, is not generally recognized. Current international poverty statistics are flawed in various ways and woefully inadequate in the LDCs. Yet calls are being made to allocate aid between countries according to the numbers of poor people. Analysis of the relationship between globalization and poverty is still at a rudimentary stage. Yet sweeping and simplistic policy conclusions are being drawn by anti-globalization activists, who are arguing that poor countries are getting too much globalization, and by pro-globalization zealots, who are arguing that they are getting too little. The world's foremost experts on poverty find it difficult to agree on the nature of the relationship between economic growth and poverty in developing countries and its place in an overall poverty reduction strategy. Yet over one billion people, including 400 million in LDCs, are now living in countries whose Governments are preparing Poverty Reduction Strategy Papers (PRSPs) as a condition for access to concessional aid and debt relief, a process which a World Bank official has described, with both honesty and accuracy, as "an experiment".

The idealistic impulse to improve the standard of living of the poor is the right one. But unless the actual policy solutions are well grounded in a deep understanding of the causes of poverty, and how those causes have been, and can be, effectively addressed, they could end up with worse results than in the past. As Simon Kuznets warned in the famous 1955 article in which he hypothesized that income inequality would increase in the early stages of economic development and subsequently decline, policies to help the poor that are "the product of imagination unrestrained by knowledge of the past" are likely to be "full of romantic violence". That is to say, in spite of the best intentions, policies based on inadequate knowledge are likely to increase rather than reduce poverty.

This Report aims to avoid romantic violence. Its central message is that there is a major, but currently underestimated, opportunity for rapid reduction in extreme poverty in the LDCs through sustained economic growth. However, this opportunity is not being realized in most LDCs because they are stuck in an international poverty trap. It should be possible through the PRSP approach to promote poverty reduction more effectively than in the past. But this requires: (a) a more complete transition to genuine national ownership and increased policy autonomy; (b) a shift from the adjustment-oriented poverty reduction strategies that are emerging in the initial phases of the PRSP approach to development-oriented poverty reduction strategies; and (c) a more supportive international environment. The Report proposes an alternative approach to the design of poverty reduction strategies that focuses on doubling average household living standards through growth-oriented macroeconomic policies, the building of domestic productive capacities and strategic integration into the global economy, whilst at the same time incorporating policies which reduce the risk of particular social groups and regions within the country being excluded from the benefits of economic growth. It also argues that international policy needs to give more attention to breaking the link between primary commodity dependence, pervasive extreme poverty and unsustainable external debt, and that policies to counter the increasing polarization of the global economy are necessary in order to reduce the socio-economic marginalization of the poorest countries. With improved national and international policies, a real turning point can occur.

THE NEW POVERTY ESTIMATES

This Report analyses the relationship between poverty and development in the LDCs in the context of increasing global interdependence. Before the present Report, such analysis was impossible. Internationally comparable poverty estimates that were publicly available covered too few LDCs over too few years. This Report overcomes this problem by using a new set of poverty estimates for 39 LDCs over the period 1965–1999. This data set has been constructed specially for the Report. But it has important implications for the global analysis of poverty and also for the achievement of Millennium Development Goals and International Development Targets, as well as the achievement of the UNLDC III development targets.

The new estimates are based on a simple notion of what poverty is. Poverty is understood in absolute terms as the inability to attain a minimally adequate standard of living. The standard of living is measured by the level of private consumption, and those who are poor are identified by adopting the $1-a-day and $2-a-day international poverty lines which are now conventionally used to make internationally comparable estimates of global poverty. These international poverty lines specify the level below which private consumption is considered inadequate, and are measured, again in line with current practice, using purchasing power parity (PPP) exchange rates, which seek to correct for differences in the cost of living between countries.

Many now argue that poverty is multidimensional, constituted by an interlocking web of economic, political, human and sociocultural deprivations, and characterized not simply by a lack of economic opportunity, but also by insecurity, vulnerability and powerlessness. The Report does not reject the multidimensional definition of poverty. Indeed, it is clear that this view offers an accurate description of the human experience of poverty. However, it uses a narrower definition as this enables greater analytical power, both to put national poverty dynamics in a global context and to understand the multidimensionality of the processes underlying these trends. The approach is best seen as complementary to approaches based on a multidimensional definition of poverty.

Although it uses a traditional definition of poverty, it innovates in the way in which the poverty estimates are derived. Current global and national poverty estimates which use the $1-a-day and $2-a-day international poverty lines are based on survey data of household income or consumption. The poverty estimates used in this Report are different. They are based on national-accounts-consistent poverty estimates which calculate the proportion of the population in a country who are poor using (i) average annual private consumption per capita as reported in national accounts data, and (ii) the distribution of private consumption amongst households as reported in household survey data.

It should be noted that national-accounts-consistent poverty estimates diverge from the World Bank's poverty estimates, which adopt the $1-a-day and $2-a-day international poverty lines but use household survey data to estimate both the average level and the distribution of private consumption. The nature of this divergence is important for global efforts to reduce extreme poverty. National-accounts-consistent poverty estimates suggest that the severity of poverty has been hitherto underestimated in the poorest countries, particularly in Africa, that the poverty-reducing effects of economic growth have equally been underestimated, and that the domain in which the $1-a-day international poverty line is most relevant is countries with a gross domestic product (GDP) per capita of less than $700.

The divergence between the household-survey-based and national-accounts-consistent poverty estimates should be a matter of concern for all engaged in more effective poverty reduction in developing countries. It implies that there is an urgent need to improve poverty statistics. This will require investment in statistical capacities for national accounts as well as household surveys, and a major effort is required in the LDCs in both respects. However, in the meantime, it is necessary to proceed with policy analysis.

This Report bases its analysis on national-accounts-consistent poverty estimates because these provide as plausible estimates for the international comparison of poverty as purely household-survey-based poverty estimates. Data from neither national accounts nor household living standard surveys are perfect. But it is likely that national accounts procedures are more standardized between countries than household surveys, and this is particularly important as the purpose here is international comparison of poverty. Preliminary research also shows that national-accounts-consistent poverty estimates are more highly correlated with some non-monetary indicators of poverty than current household-survey-based poverty estimates.

Finally, national-accounts-consistent poverty estimates are adopted for a pragmatic reason. With these estimates, the Report has found a close statistical relationship between the average level of private consumption per capita and the incidence of poverty. It is so close in fact that one can use national accounts data on private consumption, which are widely available, to make statistically robust estimates of the expected incidence and depth of poverty in countries and years in which there are no household survey data. It is these estimates which are used throughout this Report. They are the only way now available to describe levels of poverty in a large number of LDCs and to analyse their trends over time. The new poverty estimates open, for the first time, the opportunity to analyse empirically the relationship between poverty, development and globalization. The Report creates and seizes this opportunity.

THE NATURE OF POVERTY IN THE LDCs

The new poverty estimates prepared for this Report indicate seven major features of poverty in the LDCs.

Firstly, most LDCs are characterized by a situation in which absolute poverty is all-pervasive throughout society. During 1995-1999, for the group of LDCs for which we have data, 81 per cent of the population lived on less than $2 a day and the average level of consumption of these people was only $1.03 a day (in 1985 PPP dollars). Fifty per cent of the population in the LDCs lived in extreme poverty, that is on less than $1 a day, and their average level of consumption was just 64 cents ($0.64) a day. Extrapolating these patterns for LDCs for which we do not have data, it may be estimated that the total number of people living on less than $1 a day in all the 49 LDCs during 1995-1999 was 307 million, and that the total number of people living on less than $2 a day was 495 million. The total population of the LDCs at that time was 613 million.

Secondly, the incidence and the depth of poverty are particularly severe in African LDCs. In the second half of the 1990s, for the group of African LDCs for which we have data, 87 per cent of the population was living on less than $2 a day and the average consumption of these people was only 86 cents a day. Sixty-five per cent of the population in the African LDCs lived on less than a $1 a day, and the average consumption of these people was just 59 cents a day. In only 5 out of 29 African LDCs for which we have data are less than 80 per cent of the population living on less than $2 a day. These numbers suggest that the severity of the poverty problem in African LDCs has been hitherto underestimated.

Asian LDCs, in contrast, have poverty rates which, although extremely high in a global context, are relatively less severe. In the second half of the 1990s, for the group of Asian LDCs for which we have data, 68 per cent of the population were living on less than $2 a day and the average consumption of these people was $1.42 a day. Twenty-three per cent of the population were living on less than $1 a day, and the average consumption of these people, 90 cents a day, was much closer to the poverty line.

Thirdly, the incidence of extreme poverty is increasing in the LDCs as a whole. In the LDCs for which we have data, about 48 per cent of the population were living on less than $1 a day during 1965–1969, compared with 50 per cent during 1995–1999. This means that the number of people living in extreme poverty in the LDCs has more than doubled over the last thirty years, from 138 million in the second half of the 1960s to 307 million in the second half of the 1990s. The proportion of the population living on less than $2 a day was more or less the same in the second half of the 1990s as in the second half of the 1960s. This means that the number of people living on less than $2 a day in the LDCs has also more than doubled over the last thirty years.

Fourthly, the trends in extreme poverty in the LDCs contrast markedly with those in a sample of 22 other developing countries for which we have made national-accounts-consistent poverty estimates. The trends in the incidence of extreme poverty in the other developing countries, which are strongly influenced by what is happening in large, low-income Asian countries, particularly China, India and Indonesia, were sharply downward from the 1960s to the 1990s. As a corollary, the problem of extreme poverty in the world is increasingly becoming an LDC problem.

Indeed, according to the new poverty estimates, the LDCs have already become the primary locus of extreme poverty in the global economy.

Fifthly, there is a major contrast between trends in extreme poverty in Asian LDCs and African LDCs. The proportion of the population living in poverty in Asian LDCs for which we have data fell from 36 per cent during 1965–1969 to 23 per cent during 1995–1999. Over the same period, the depth of poverty also fell, with the average consumption of those people living on less than a $1 a day rising from 84 cents a day in the second half of the 1960s to 90 cents in the second half of the 1990s. Although not as impressive as the sample of other developing countries, this record in poverty reduction is far superior to what has been happening in the African LDCs. The proportion of the population living in extreme poverty there increased from 56 per cent during 1965–1969 to 65 per cent during 1995–1999. After an initial improvement, the depth of poverty has also increased in African LDCs since the mid-1970s. The average consumption of those living on less than $1 a day declined from $0.66 a day during 1975–1979 to $0.59 a day during 1995–1999.

Sixthly, amongst the LDCs, there is a close association between the incidence of extreme poverty and dependence on exports of primary commodities. Sixty-nine per cent of the population in non-oil commodity exporting LDCs were living on less than $1 a day during 1997-1999, and in mineral-exporting LDCs the proportion was over 80 per cent. The share of the population living on less than $1 a day was on average lower in service-exporting LDCs (43 per cent). It was even lower in LDCs that have managed to diversify into exporting manufactured goods (25 per cent), although excluding Bangladesh, which weighs heavily in the overall average, the share of the population living on less than a $1 a day in LDCs exporting manufactures was 44 per cent.

Seventhly, and lastly, in LDCs whose major exports are non-oil primary commodities, the share of the population living in extreme poverty increased from 63 per cent during 1981–1983 to 69 per cent during 1997–1999. The increase was particularly marked in mineral-exporting LDCs, in which the share of the population living in extreme poverty increased from 61 per cent to 82 per cent. In LDCs exporting services the incidence of poverty has also been rising, though more slowly than in the non-oil commodity exporting LDCs. In LDCs which have diversified into exporting manufactures, the incidence of extreme poverty has fallen from 30 per cent during 1981–1983 to 25 per cent during 1997–1999. The average incidence of poverty has fallen in this group of countries whether or not Bangladesh is included.

As a corollary of these trends, commodity-dependent LDCs are the predominant locus of extreme poverty in the LDC group. During 1997–1999, 79 per cent of the total number of people living in extreme poverty in the LDCs lived in countries which specialize in primary commodity exports. The number of people living in extreme poverty in commodity exporting LDCs increased by 105 million between 1981–1983 and 1997–1999, whilst the numbers living in extreme poverty in LDCs which have diversified into exporting manufactures and/or services increased by 10 million. The distinction between commodity-exporting LDCs and manufactures-exporting LDCs overlaps with the distinction between African and Asian LDCs, but is not completely identical.

THE INTERNATIONAL POVERTY TRAP

In most LDCs absolute poverty is generalized in the sense that the majority of the population live at or below income levels which are sufficient to meet their basic needs, and the available resources, even when equally distributed, are barely sufficient to cater for the basic needs of the population on a sustainable basis. Poverty is also generally persistent. *The central argument of this Report is that poverty is pervasive and persistent in most LDCs because they are caught in an international poverty trap.*

The overall argument can be summarized in five propositions:
*   In societies where there is generalized poverty, including the LDCs, sustained economic growth normally has strong positive effects in reducing poverty, particularly extreme poverty.
*   However, generalized poverty acts as a major constraint on economic growth, particularly through the way in which generalized poverty affects the domestic resources available for private investment and all public goods, including governance, and also affects environmental assets.
*   International economic relationships can play a key role in helping LDCs break the cycle of generalized poverty and economic stagnation.

- However, in many LDCs, particularly those dependent on primary commodity exports, an interrelated complex of international trade and finance relationships is reinforcing the cycle of generalized poverty and economic stagnation which is, in turn, reinforcing the negative complex of external relationships.
- The current form of globalization is tightening rather than loosening this international poverty trap.

The opportunity for rapid poverty reduction through sustained economic growth

In situations of generalized poverty, sustained economic growth normally has strong positive effects in reducing poverty, particularly extreme poverty. The typical pattern of change is evident in the relationship between average national levels of private consumption per capita and the proportion of the population living on less than $1 a day and less than $2 a day. The new poverty estimates indicate that the incidence of poverty falls in a regular and predictable way as the overall level of private consumption per capita rises. This relationship is much closer than was previously imagined on the basis of household-survey-based poverty estimates. The new poverty estimates also indicate that the incidence of extreme poverty will fall much more rapidly than was previously imagined. Current predictions of the potential for future poverty reduction are thus over-pessimistic.

For a country where average private consumption per capita is about $400 a year (in 1985 PPP dollars) one would typically expect that about 65 per cent of the population would be living on less than $1 a day. If the average private consumption per capita doubled to $800 a year, one would expect less than 20 per cent of the population to be living on less than $1 a day.

The potential for rapid poverty reduction in very poor societies through economic growth should not come as a surprise. One should expect that the growth–poverty relationship in situations of generalized poverty differs from that in rich countries where only a minor part of the population live in absolute poverty, or in middle-income countries which have already achieved a measure of prosperity, but where a significant proportion of the population have been left out of the development process. In the rich countries, economic growth is unlikely to be sufficient to reduce absolute poverty because, no matter how high an economy's per capita income may be, there will always be individuals or households that, because of their own special circumstances or because of sectoral shifts or cyclical fluctuations, fall below the poverty line. Poverty reduction in these circumstances necessarily involves income transfers, social welfare systems or targeted job creation programmes. In the middle-income countries, redistributive measures are also vital. But in situations of generalized poverty, where the available resources in the economy, even when equally distributed, are barely sufficient to cater for the basic needs of the population on a sustainable basis, poverty reduction can be achieved on a major scale only through economic growth which raises household living standards.

This conclusion follows necessarily from the typical relationship between the incidence of poverty and average levels of private consumption per capita which the Report identifies. The form of this relationship already includes within it the effects on poverty of increases in inequality which typically occur in low-income countries as average incomes and consumption rise. But, of course, the incidence of poverty will not fall if rising GDP per capita is not accompanied by increases in private consumption per capita.

The cycle of generalized poverty and economic stagnation

Although there is a major opportunity for rapid poverty reduction in conditions of generalized poverty, it is very difficult to realize that opportunity precisely because absolute poverty is generalized. In these circumstances, not only does economic growth affect the incidence of poverty, but also the incidence of poverty affects economic growth. In societies where there is generalized poverty, poverty itself acts as a major constraint on economic growth.

A major mechanism through which this occurs is the negative feedback effects of generalized poverty on domestic resources available to finance investment and public goods, including governance. Where the majority of the population earn less than $1 or $2 a day, a major part of GDP must be devoted to the procurement of the necessities of life. During the period 1995–1999, for example, the average per capita income in the LDCs when measured in terms of current prices and official exchange rates (rather than 1985 PPP dollars) was $0.72 a day and the average per capita consumption was $0.57 a day. This implies that on average, there were only 15 cents a day per person to spend on private capital formation, public investment in infrastructure and the running of vital public services, including health, education, administration and law and order.

With such limited domestic resources, it is difficult to finance new investment from domestic resources. Economic vulnerability is high as domestic resources are insufficient to cope with climatic and external shocks. Finally, there is an underfunding of public goods and services, including administration, law and order and the whole system of governance. Providing the necessary physical capital stock, education, health and other social and physical infrastructure to keep pace with population growth is a constant problem.

The higher the incidence of poverty is, the greater this constraint of domestic resource availability. Focusing on the LDCs in our sample where over 80 per cent of the population live on less than $2 a day, it is apparent that the domestic savings rate is on average no more than 2 to 3 per cent of GDP, total government consumption expenditure (which includes health and education) was on average $37 per person a year during the period 1995–1999, and health expenditure was on average $14 per person per year over this period.

These low levels of government expenditure per capita are primarily not the result of weak mobilization of resources by the public sector. For LDCs for which we have data, government revenue (excluding grants) as a share of GDP was on average about 16 per cent of GDP during the period 1995–1999, which was not much lower than in other developing countries. However, given the very small size of the GDP of most LDC economies, this average translates in real per capita terms into very low levels of public service provision.

The extremely limited availability of resources implies that Governments of LDCs are constantly faced with making difficult choices about the provision of different vital public services. Most of the public services such as health, education, agricultural support services, general administration and law enforcement, which form the foundations of modern economic development, are held back by serious supply constraints in the LDCs. No doubt there is room for improvements through reallocation of public expenditure. However, beyond that, what is required is the release of the constraint on domestic resource availability.

In many LDCs, not only are the domestic resources available to finance investment and public services pitifully low, but also a forced process of environmental degradation is taking place. This occurs when survival necessitates eating into the natural and environmental capital stock. In the poorest LDCs, "genuine domestic savings" — a measure of savings which subtracts from domestic savings the reduction in national wealth associated with the depletion of environmental resources and the depreciation of man-made capital stock — are on average minus 5 per cent of GDP. Many of these countries are not simply stuck in a low-level trap of underdevelopment, but have fallen into a downward spiral. Environmental assets on which most livelihoods depend are being eroded, and high population growth rates, environmental degradation and increasing poverty are mutually reinforcing each other.

The opportunity for economic growth through global integration

International economic relationships can play a key role in helping LDCs to break out of the domestic vicious circles which cause generalized poverty to persist.

Firstly, access to foreign savings can play a catalytic role in helping poor countries to break out of the low-level equilibrium of low incomes, low domestic savings and low investment. Once growth starts, foreign savings also permit a faster rate of growth of private consumption without the degree of belt-tightening which would be necessary if growth were financed wholly through domestic savings.

Secondly, generalized poverty implies that national demand is very limited, and national markets tend to be undynamic and usually segmented in ways which enable people to survive. Exporting to international markets enables land and labour resources, hitherto underutilized owing to domestic demand constraints, to be productively mobilized.

Thirdly, increased access to available modern technologies enables latecomer economies to realize significant productivity increases without having continually to reinvent. Exporting can facilitate this because a major channel for technology transfer to poor countries is through imports of machinery and transport equipment. Foreign direct investment can also serve as an important channel for technology acquisition under the right circumstances.

Fourthly, increased international migration enables poor people in poor countries to find employment even if opportunities are limited in their own country.

The fact that international relationships can play a major role in breaking the cycle of economic stagnation and generalized poverty has led some analysts to conclude that the key policy problem for LDCs is that they are not sufficiently integrated into the global economy. But this is a false inference.

International trade is already of major importance in the economies of LDCs. During 1997–1998, exports and imports of goods and services constituted on average 43 per cent of their GDP. The average level of trade integration for the LDCs is around the same as the world average, and also almost the same as the average for the group of countries which have been identified in the recent World Bank report *Globalization, Growth and Poverty* as "more globalized developing countries". The average level of trade integration is actually higher than that of high-income OECD countries.

Similarly, LDCs already rely very heavily on external finance to supplement their meagre domestic resources. During the period 1995–1999, the size of the external resource gap, measured as the net trade balance in goods and services, was equivalent to about 90 per cent of gross domestic investment and about 125 per cent of government consumption expenditure in the LDCs where over 80 per cent of the population was living on less than $2 a day. For the other LDCs, the proportions were somewhat lower. But the budgetary and accumulation processes are still dominated by external resources, particularly foreign aid inflows.

The problem for the LDCs is not the level of integration with the world economy but rather the form of integration. The current form of integration, which includes weak export capacities, is not supporting sustained economic growth and poverty reduction. Indeed, for many LDCs, external trade and finance relationships are an integral part of the poverty trap.

International trade, external finance and the cycle of poverty

The way in which international trade and finance relationships are an integral part of the poverty trap is most clear in those LDCs which depend on primary commodities as their major source of export earnings. As we have seen, it is in these countries that the problem of extreme poverty is most severe. It is also in these countries that the problem of socio-economic marginalization in the world economy is most dramatic. Weighted by population and estimated in PPP terms, the average income per capita in the world's 20 richest countries was 16 times greater than that in non-oil commodity exporting LDCs in 1960, but by 1999 it was 35 times greater. Trends in those LDCs which had by the end of the 1990s diversified into manufactures and/or services exports have been different. The average income per capita in the 20 richest countries was 8 times greater than that of this group of LDCs in 1960 and 12 times greater in 1999. During the 1990s, there was actually very slow convergence between income per capita in the richest countries and that in the manufactures and/or services exporting LDCs.

These income convergence trends mirror the poverty trends identified earlier. In the light of the importance of economic growth for poverty reduction, the persistence of extreme poverty can be properly seen as the result of the failure of commodity-dependent LDCs to share in global economic growth.

Within the commodity-dependent LDCs, the cycle of generalized poverty and economic stagnation is reinforced by a negative complex of external trade and finance relationships. This complex has three interrelated elements:

- Falling and volatile real primary commodity prices;
- Unsustainable external debt;
- A donor-driven aid/debt service system.

There has been a long-term downward trend in real non-fuel commodity prices since 1960. Comparative research shows that the commodity prices recession of the 1980s was more severe, and considerably more prolonged, than that of the Great Depression of the 1930s. In 2001, the UNCTAD combined non-fuel commodity price index, deflated by the price index of developed countries' manufactured exports, was at one half of its annual average for the period 1979–1981. Most commodity-dependent LDCs have been particularly exposed to the adverse consequences of these trends because productivity is low and they generally export a very narrow range of undynamic and low- value-added products. With very high rates of extreme poverty and low levels of education, it has been difficult to mobilize investment resources and know-how to upgrade production. Losses in market share have thus reinforced the effects of falling real commodity prices.

A further problem is that there is a close link between commodity dependence and the build-up of an excessive external debt burden. During 1998–2000, all except four of the commodity-dependent LDCs (Bhutan, Eritrea, Solomon Islands and Uganda) had an external debt burden which, according to international norms, is unsustainable. There are obviously many reasons for the build-up of the debt, including domestic mismanagement and corruption. But the degree of probability that commodity-dependent countries with generalized extreme poverty run up an unsustainable external debt is so high that the debt problem is properly regarded as systemic, rather than simply a national issue. Common factors are at work which affect all countries of this type.

Once a country has an unsustainable external debt, this has a number of negative features that further reinforce the trap of generalized poverty. First, as a very large proportion of the debt is owed by Governments rather than the private sector, debt servicing reduces resources available for public investment in physical and human capital. Second, the debt overhang acts as a deterrent to private investment, particularly because of uncertainty. Domestic interest rates may also be very high. Third, debt service payments tighten the foreign exchange constraint. Fourth, high levels of external debt also deter private capital inflows, contributing to a general perception of risk that discourages lenders and investors. Although highly indebted countries still receive foreign direct investment (FDI), they have been effectively marginalized from international capital markets. One important consequence of this is that it is difficult to access short-term loans in order to moderate the effects of external and climatic shocks.

Unsustainable external debt also undermines aid effectiveness. This is partly through the effects of external debt on private sector investment and on government capacities to provide public goods. But during the 1990s, the failure to put in place adequate debt relief for countries whose debt was mainly owed to official creditors led to the development of an aid/debt service system in which aid disbursements were increasingly allocated, implicitly or explicitly, to ensure that official debts could be serviced. This compromised the developmental effectiveness of aid, which has in turn reinforced and rationalized aid fatigue.

Globalization and the international poverty trap

Globalization — the increasing flows of goods and resources across national borders and the emergence of a complementary set of organizational structures to manage these flows — is tightening the international poverty trap of commodity-dependent LDCs and intensifying the vulnerabilities of LDCs which have managed to diversify out of primary commodity exports into exports of manufactures and/or services. This is happening directly, through the way in which globalization is changing the world commodity economy, and indirectly through the effects of globalization on more advanced developing countries which are then impinging on the development prospects of the LDCs.

Important changes in the world commodity economy which have occurred recently include: an increasing concentration of international trade, with a dramatic reduction in the number of firms with significant market shares, and vertical integration of large firms; an increase in the minimum requirements for capital resources, sophisticated technology and human skills for competing in more open but more sophisticated markets; the dismantling of marketing boards, trade barriers and restrictions on the operation of foreign firms in the LDCs; and the establishment of global commodity supply chains by supermarkets in developed countries. The full effects of these changes are not well known. But there is a danger of increasing exclusion of LDC producers from global markets as buyers within commodity chains upgrade their volume, reliability and quality criteria for purchasing, and as more stringent market requirements call for ever larger investments to meet buyers' quality requirements and specifications.

The current form of globalization is also affecting the relationships between LDCs and more advanced developing countries. These can be mutually supportive or competitive. But various asymmetries in the international system, together with global financial instability, are currently making it difficult for the more advanced developing countries to deepen industrialization and move up the technological ladder and out of simpler products being exported by the poorer countries. As the more advanced developing countries which have achieved a small measure of prosperity meet a "glass ceiling" which blocks their development, LDCs find it increasingly difficult to get on and move up the ladder of development.

It is significant in this regard that along with the marginalization of the poorest countries there is increasing polarization in the global economy. UNCTAD research has shown that the middle strata of developing countries, namely those with incomes of between 40 and 80 per cent of the average in the advanced countries, are thinner than in the 1970s. Also, the IMF has observed that "the forces of polarization seem to have become stronger since the early 1980s". In these circumstances, it is difficult for the LDCs to advance in a sustainable way.

Heightened competition with other exporters of low-skill manufactures is a major process increasing the vulnerability of those LDCs that have sought to escape the poverty trap by diversification out of commodities. Although these LDCs are doing better on average than the commodity-exporting LDCs, poverty levels are still unacceptably high when viewed on a global scale and the growth path and poverty reduction trajectory of those countries remain fragile. LDCs exporting manufactures have, like those exporting commodities, experienced the adverse effects of falling terms of trade in recent years. Moreover, they also tend to have a narrow export base which is concentrated in low-skill products with few backward linkages within the domestic economy and low levels of local value-added. Textiles and garments exports from LDCs have often expanded on the basis of special preferences, including in particular quotas within markets of industrialized countries under the Multi-Fibre Arrangement (MFA), which will be eroded in the near future. Although the international poverty trap is not as clear for LDCs which have diversified out of primary commodities into manufactures and/or services exports, they remain vulnerable, and the sustainability of poverty reduction processes associated with the expansion of manufacturing employment is still in question.

THE POTENTIAL AND LIMITS OF THE PRSP APPROACH

The point of delineating the international poverty trap is not to promote pessimism about the future prospects of the LDCs. It is rather to enable a better identification of the national and international policies which are required to promote poverty reduction in the diverse but particular circumstances of the 49 LDCs.

In recent years, concerns about persistent and unacceptably high poverty rates in the poorest countries have led to a rethinking of international development cooperation. The new approach, which has been developed by the IMF, OECD/DAC and the World Bank, had its origins in the broad consensus that unsustainable external debt was acting as a major impediment to growth and poverty reduction, and in the elaboration of the enhanced HIPC Initiative as a response to this problem. But it has gone far beyond debt relief now. National Governments have been asked to take responsibility for poverty reduction within their countries by developing nationally owned poverty reduction strategies. Donor countries are selectively focusing their aid and debt relief on those countries that have good poverty reduction strategies, and good systems of governance for formulating and implementing policies and mobilizing and managing public resources. Donors are seeking to work with these countries in a spirit of development partnership, keying their assistance to national priorities. There is also a move to increase the coherence of international policies to support poverty reduction in the poorest countries by providing greater market access for products from poor countries, increasing trade-related technical cooperation and, though this is much less developed, by encouraging developmental FDI and other beneficial private capital flows to the poorest countries.

The centrepiece of this new approach to international cooperation is the preparation and implementation of Poverty Reduction Strategy Papers (PRSPs). The PRSP is, simultaneously, the vehicle through which national Governments are expected elaborate nationally owned poverty-reducing policies, through which the IMF and the World Bank identify satisfactory policy environments, and through which bilateral donors are expected to align their assistance for poverty reduction. It is through the PRSP that national elements of the UNLDC III Programme of Action are being implemented in most LDCs. Effective poverty reduction will depend on how this experimental device works in practice, or rather, as the PRSP approach is not a blueprint but a process in the making, on how it can be made to work.

The analysis of this Report suggests that the potential of the PRSP approach is being undermined by three key problems:

- The incomplete transition from donor-driven policy to national ownership and policy autonomy;
- The policy content of the PRSPs;
- Resource constraints.

These problems are not an inevitable consequence of the approach, nor are they insoluble. However, if something is not done to address them, there is no reason to expect any better results than those produced by the policies of the past, and outcomes may even be worse.

The incomplete transition from donor-driven policy to national ownership and policy autonomy

Potentially the most important change which is occurring with the introduction of the PRSP approach is the transition from donor-driven policies to national ownership and policy autonomy. This transition is founded on the strengthening of the national ownership of policies. This means that policies should be domestically formulated and implemented, rather than driven by donors or imposed by the IMF or the World Bank, and that the Government should develop policies through participatory processes which involve national stakeholders and, more generally, civil society.

It is clear that with the introduction of the PRSP approach there is increasing national leadership in the technical processes of policy formulation and there is increasing, though usually circumscribed, dialogue with civil society organizations. However, enhancing national ownership and policy autonomy is proving extremely difficult. The ever-present possibility of withdrawal of concessional assistance and debt relief makes it very difficult for government officials to take the risks which would enable the full potential of the PRSP approach to be realized, and is inhibiting what national authorities feel they can say.

The transition to policy autonomy is also being hampered owing to the dearth of national capacities in key areas, including understanding the complex relationships between poverty, development and globalization, and the translation of these relationships into concrete policies. Confidence in the room for independent action is also undermined by the fact that in the initial stages of the PRSP approach, there has been a wide divergence between Interim PRSPs and conditionalities for HIPC completion point. This may well reflect the early phases of the application of the PRSP approach, but the symbolic message is that if the PRSP does not conform to what the IMF and the World Bank consider right, then what are considered the appropriate conditionalities will be established anyway.

The policy content of the PRSPs

In these circumstances, the poverty reduction strategies which are emerging in the initial stages of the PRSP approach are tending to be adjustment-oriented poverty reduction strategies. They seek to integrate pro-poor public expenditure patterns with deeper and broader structural reforms and the macroeconomic policies adopted in earlier structural adjustment programmes. Past experience suggests that for countries where productive capacities, markets and the entrepreneurial class are all underdeveloped, and where absolute poverty is generalized, such programmes are not going to be sufficient to escape the poverty trap. The policy model is wrong for achieving that particular purpose.

A large number of LDCs undertook structural adjustment programmes in the 1990s and as a result the policy environment in many LDCs changed significantly. This has had some positive macroeconomic effects, notably in reducing excessively high rates of inflation and by correcting overvalued exchange rates, and exports have also often increased. But domestic investment and savings rates have generally not increased much, private capital inflows have not been attracted, and although the decline in market share in traditional exports has often been halted, there has been no progressive structural change towards more dynamic exports. In fact, rather than an upgrading of primary commodity exports, there has been a collapse of local processing of commodities before export and also, in some cases, a decline in quality.

In general, the implementation of adjustment policies has not been followed by a steady downward trend in the incidence of poverty. For the LDCs undertaking Enhanced Structural Adjustment Facility (ESAF) structural adjustment programmes, the proportion of the total population living on less than $1 a day rose from 51 per cent in the three years before the adoption of a programme to 52 per cent in the first three years after and 53 per cent in the next three years. Given rising total population, this means that the people living in extreme poverty increased under these programmes.

The new poverty reduction strategies seek to make economic growth more pro-poor when the problem is that adjustment policies generally have not delivered, and cannot deliver, sustainable economic growth at rates sufficient to make a significant dent in poverty. As a result, there is a danger that the PRSP approach could leave countries with the worst of all worlds. The policies adopted in the new poverty reduction strategies will increase exposure to intensely competitive global markets but without facilitating the development of the productive and supply capacities necessary to compete. At the same time, there will be increased arm's length regulation and administrative guidance of social welfare through international development cooperation.

Resource constraints

The scope for poverty reduction through the PRSP approach is also being hampered by severe resource constraints. These are rooted in: (i) the failure to resolve the external debt problem, (ii) low levels of aid and the emergence of poverty reduction financing gaps, and (iii) the "one-eyed" approach to aid effectiveness. These issues will be taken up in the last section of the Overview, which deals with international policies.

NATIONAL DEVELOPMENT STRATEGIES AND POVERTY REDUCTION

From the foregoing analysis, as well as the understanding of the nature of the international poverty trap, one must conclude that there is excessive optimism with regard to the likely impact of the new national and international policies which are being put in place with the introduction of the PRSP approach. But equally there is excessive pessimism with regard to the opportunity for rapid poverty reduction through pragmatic and practical alternatives. It should be possible, through the PRSP approach, to elaborate poverty reduction strategies that provide a real and improved alternative to past economic reforms and adjustment policies. But this will require genuine national ownership and policy autonomy based on a rebuilding of State capacities, a real break in national policies which moves beyond the adjustment policies of the 1990s, and more supportive international policies.

A central recommendation of this Report is that *it is necessary to shift from adjustment-oriented poverty reduction strategies to development-oriented poverty reduction strategies*.

This can be achieved if poverty reduction strategies are anchored in long-term development strategies rather than elaborated as extensions of past adjustment policies. In this approach priority policy actions within the PRSP, including trade issues, which currently are not treated in depth, would be derived from the overall development strategy. Private enterprise should play the leading role in the achievement of the goals of such strategies. But the development process should be catalysed and guided by a pragmatic developmental State which, through good governance of markets, harnesses the profit motive for the purposes of national development and poverty reduction. Creating capable and effective States, and also a dynamic domestic entrepreneurial class willing to commit its resources to domestic investment rather than to luxury consumption or holding private wealth abroad, is a central institutional issue which also must be addressed in a developmental approach to poverty reduction.

It is for individual Governments themselves to make their strategic choices. But the analysis of generalized poverty in the present Report suggests four general policy orientations that are likely to have wide, though contextually specific, application. These are:

- The central importance of promoting rapid and sustained economic growth;
- The establishment of a dynamic investment-export nexus;
- The elaboration of productive development policy options;
- The adoption of policies to ensure that social groups and regions are not left behind as growth takes place.

The overall approach seeks to reduce poverty through economic growth and sustained development based on building productive capacities.

The importance of rapid and sustained economic growth

Governments need to give priority to promoting rapid and sustained economic growth. Given that the average level of private consumption per capita is so low, the primary goal must be, quite simply, to *double the average household living standards as quickly as possible.*

What is required for this to occur is not simply expansion of GDP, but a type of economic growth which is founded on the accumulation of capital and skills and productivity growth, and the expansion of sustainable livelihoods and employment opportunities, and which thereby expands the consumption possibilities of households and individuals.

The new Programme of Action for the LDCs has a set a 7 per cent GDP growth target. This is ambitious. But if it were achieved, and if private consumption grows in line with GDP, the number of people living in extreme poverty in 2015 in the LDCs could be 200 million lower than if current trends persisted.

The paramount importance of economic growth for poverty reduction in the LDCs does not mean that inequality and exclusion can be ignored. Efficiency-expanding redistributions of assets and income are important for sustained economic growth and poverty reduction in situations of generalized poverty. The behaviour of the small proportion of the population who are rich is also relevant. Sustained economic growth depends on them using their high incomes and wealth in ways such as reinvesting profits in domestic production, which support capital accumulation, productivity growth and employment expansion. Respect for rights also matters. But the simple priority should be to double average household living standards.

The need to establish a dynamic investment–export nexus

It is necessary to establish a sustainable growth mechanism which supports a doubling of the average household living standard. The Programme of Action envisages increased rates of investment as a basis for higher growth rates. But experience suggests that a sustainable growth process requires mutually reinforcing interactions between investment growth and export growth. Moreover, although external finance, usually aid, is vitally important in the initial stages of building an investment–export nexus, particularly to jump-start the process, the sustainability of growth will be best ensured if domestic savings start to grow along with investment and exports, and over time increasingly drive the process.

Establishing a dynamic investment–export nexus requires the creation of profitable investment opportunities, reducing the risks and uncertainty of investment activity, and ensuring the availability of finance so that entrepreneurs are able to invest in expanding production. Policy interventions of various kinds must play a key role in setting the general conditions for a faster pace of capital accumulation and in correcting specific market failures which impede access to finance and technology. It is also necessary to give export activity a special push with special incentives. There are a range of well-tried export promotion measures, which for LDCs are still WTO-compatible, including: tariff rebates, so that export companies have access to imported goods at international prices; tax exemptions; preferential credits allowing exporters access to finance at internationally competitive rates; export credit insurance; the provision of information through export promotion agencies; and subsidized infrastructure. Important strategic issues which must be addressed are: whether trade expansion is best founded on upgrading primary commodity exports, or on labour-intensive manufactures, or on services such as tourism, or on some combination of these; the role of import substitution in the investment–export nexus (through backward linkages and the development of exports out of import-substitution industries); and any potential conflicts between export activity and food security.

Productive development policy options

Sound macroeconomic policies are an essential element of long-term development strategies. But short-term macroeconomic objectives of internal and external balance should be pursued through means which are consistent with long-tem development objectives and which do not require investment levels which are so low as to compromise future growth. Too tight credit ceilings can effectively undermine the ability of local firms to obtain the finance they need to expand production and improve supply capabilities. Low and stable interest rates to finance productive investment and competitive exchange rates are ingredients of a growth-oriented approach. Fiscal measures can also be used to increase corporate profitability and to encourage retention in order to accelerate capital accumulation.

Alongside growth-oriented macroeconomic policies it is important to adopt mesoeconomic and microeconomic policies that are designed specifically to improve supply capabilities and productive capacities. This is the third basic element of the policy orientation here. Such policies, which are called productive development policies in Latin America, include financial policy, technology policy, human resource development and physical infrastructure development. They are designed to accelerate capital accumulation, productivity growth and learning in specific sectors, and thereby throughout the economy, and to manage the dynamic complementarities, both between sectors and between productive enterprises, which can block profitable investment in any single one. Improving agricultural productivity is likely to be a particularly important initial sectoral focus in many LDCs as most of the population derive their livelihoods from farming.

The Government must ensure that any subsidies or rents which are provided as part of productive development policies are designed to encourage the development of supply capabilities. It is possible to do this by making subsidies or rents conditional on investment, exports, technological learning and productivity targets, by making them temporary, by focusing them on overcoming specific market failures, and by establishing "contests" amongst the private sector as an allocation mechanism. This is not a matter of hand-outs to business, but creating rent opportunities that induce economically efficient developmental actions that private markets would not otherwise undertake.

Policies to prevent marginalization within LDCs

As economic growth occurs, it is highly likely that some groups or regions will be left behind in poverty. The fourth element of the approach advocated here is therefore the adoption of policies to prevent marginalization within countries. The surest way to ensure that economic growth is more inclusive is through the wide distribution of assets, the expansion of productive employment, creating linkages that incorporate marginal sectors into the space of productivity growth, and linking import substitution with export promotion.

Particular policies are best identified through a structural approach to poverty analysis which directs attention to the generation and sustainability of livelihoods, their location within the structure of the economy and the way in which they are affected by the relations of the national economy with the rest of the world, as well as to the vulnerability of individuals and groups to impoverishment. Gender relations are included in a structural approach as an intervening variable in all economic activities, influencing the ways in which factor and product markets work, the productivity of inputs and the economic behaviour of agents, and the joint determination of the growth and distribution of income. Policies which may be important to prevent marginalization within countries include: agrarian reform and rural development policies (land tenure, agricultural productivity growth, rural industries and rural labour markets); micro-credit; support for small and medium-sized enterprises; promotion of backward linkages from export activity; broad-based human resource development through investment in education and health; establishment of profit-related pay systems; and decentralization. Application of principles of good governance can also help to ensure inclusion through greater accountability.

INTERNATIONAL POLICIES FOR EFFECTIVE POVERTY REDUCTION

Good national policies are a sine qua non for effective poverty reduction in the LDCs. But a major implication of the conclusion that the poverty trap is international, and that the current form of globalization is tending to tighten it, is that international policies are equally important. A multi-level approach is thus required.

The analysis in this Report reaffirms long-standing concerns of the LDCs regarding aid, aid effectiveness, debt relief and market access, which are major elements of the Programme of Action for the Least Developed Countries for the Decade 2001–2010. But the interdependencies identified in the analysis of the poverty trap also suggest that greater attention should be paid to two key policy issues:

- How to break the link between primary commodity dependence and the debt problem;
- How to break the link between the polarization of the world economy and the socio-economic marginalization of the poorest countries.

Increasing levels of aid

In real per capita terms, net ODA disbursements to the LDCs dropped by 46 per cent between 1990 and 2000. Aid inflows have been falling whether or not countries have what is regarded as a good policy environment. Net ODA disbursement per capita to HIPC-LDCs that have reached decision point (which requires a good policy track record in terms of the IMF and the World Bank) fell by 35 per cent in real terms between 1990 and 2000, and has fallen by 25 per cent since 1995, the year before the HIPC Initiative. There is also evidence that debt service reductions have been financed through reduction in levels of aid.

One of the major potential benefits of the PRSP approach is that it will facilitate a reversal of these trends. But countries are currently expected to submit PRSPs which are "realistic" in terms of external financing projections. This derives from a major aim of the PRSP approach, which is to ensure that government revenue and aid are used more effectively for poverty reduction, and are shown to be used more effectively. This is certainly a vital aim. However, in the context of low levels of aid, the requirement of realism results in a loss of opportunity for poverty reduction and of the ability to explore that opportunity.

Much greater poverty reduction could be achieved by increasing the resources available for poverty reduction as well as by improving the poverty-reducing efficiency of public expenditure. If prior commitments of substantial donor assistance are obtained as programmes are being formulated, higher public spending, compatible with a prudent fiscal stance, could be built in at the outset. But in practice, this is not happening. Poverty reduction financing gaps are thus emerging as Governments prepare their PRSPs. The pace of poverty reduction is then being scaled back to ensure that the PRSP is deemed realistic and thus worthy of donor support.

Donor countries' agreement within the Programme of Action to provide, within a menu of options, ODA equivalent to 0.15 per cent or 0.20 per cent of their GNP to LDCs could have powerful positive effects given the domestic resource constraints on poverty reduction. It is important that donor countries clarify what their commitments actually are and move speedily to implement them. Simple scenarios indicate that assuming the same pattern of commitments which prevailed after UNLDC II continues, and assuming that donors move to achieving the targets by 2007, a 63 per cent increase in aid flows over the 2000 level could be achieved by 2005. A doubling of aid flows, which UNCTAD has estimated is essential for accelerated growth and reduced aid dependence in the medium term, and which, according to the World Bank, would be necessary for achieving international poverty targets, could be achieved only if Japan and the United States, which are the largest donors to the LDCs in absolute terms, but which have not committed to either the 0.15 per cent or 0.2 per cent of GNP target, also come on board.

Increasing aid effectiveness

It is widely agreed that more effective aid is required as well as more aid. However, current efforts to increase aid effectiveness are based on a "one-eyed" approach which locates the problem of ineffective aid in recipient country policies, but is largely blind to the weaknesses of donor country policies. This "one-eyed" approach is the basis for the belief that the way to increase aid effectiveness is through increased selectivity, that is to say focusing aid disbursements on countries which have the right national policy environment. It is of course certainly true that aid will be more effective if national policies are right. But the emphasis placed on selectivity simply leaves out of the frame of analysis the ways in which donor policies also reduce aid effectiveness.

The introduction of the PRSP approach can potentially bring significant benefits in this regard. In the 1980s and 1990s, the process of structural adjustment, as it was carried out, itself undermined aid effectiveness. In that period, there was no mechanism for coordinating aid inflows and thus the aid delivery system was characterized by a multiplicity of fragmented aid-funded programmes and projects that generated high transaction costs for recipient countries and were weakly integrated into national economic and administrative structures. Donor alignment behind nationally owned PRSPs would effectively resolve this problem. However, progress in donor alignment has thus far been uneven, across donor countries and recipient countries.

Donor assistance should be delivered through government systems unless there are compelling reasons to the contrary; where this is not possible, any alternative mechanisms must be time-limited, and develop and build, rather than undermine or bypass, government systems. Aid effectiveness will also be enhanced through (i) increased stability and predictability of aid inflows, (ii) expeditious implementation of the OECD/DAC recommendation to untie aid to the LDCs, and (iii) the use of aid to promote technical progress and to rectify the adverse consequences of international capital market failures. Articulating the relationship between ODA and FDI is important in the last regard. Aid should also not only be concerned with social sectors, on the grounds that these are easily monitorable as being pro-poor. In the context of increasing aid disbursements, more attention needs to be given to using aid to support production sectors, particularly agriculture, and to improve economic infrastructure.

An important institutional innovation which can promote increased aid effectiveness in the context of the principle of partnership is the introduction of donor performance monitoring indicators at the recipient country level. The approach developing in the United Republic of Tanzania may provide a working model for this.

Improved market access and its effectiveness

An important thrust of the new Programme of Action is to improve market access for LDCs and to provide trade-related technical assistance through the Integrated Framework to help LDCs take advantage of these opportunities. But improving market access for the LDCs is not simply a matter of providing quota- and duty-free access, but also of making trade preferences commercially meaningful. For example, in 1999, before the "Everything but Arms" Initiative, 99 per cent of total imports into the European Union from non-ACP (African, Caribbean and Pacific) LDCs were eligible for General System of Preferences (GSP) treatment in the EU, but only 34 per cent of the imports eligible for preferential treatment actually received it. Making trade preferences commercially meaningful requires attention in particular to the security of preferences, product coverage, rules of origin and supply capacities. It is clear that trade preferences should not be seen as a substitute for aid inflows in countries where supply capacities are weak. The Integrated Framework (IF) can help if trade-related technical assistance activities are broadly defined and focused on strengthening export supply capacities, if the principle of ownership is fully respected in the mainstreaming of trade issues into PRSPs, and if both financial assistance and technical assistance are provided. After five years of existence, the IF must now move speedily to implementing concrete capacity-building projects and demonstrating tangible benefits for the LDCs. The "disconnect" between the accumulated knowledge in providing technical assistance for commodity-dependent economies and the work of the IF needs to be speedily bridged.

Re-enhanced debt relief

Unsustainable external debt is a central ingredient of the cycle of stagnation and generalized poverty in poor countries. The HIPC Initiative was introduced following recognition of this relationship. But the debt relief provided within the framework of the HIPC Initiative, even after the latter's enhancement in 1999, opens little extra fiscal space for poverty reduction and is insufficient to enable a durable exit from the debt problem. Out of 20 HIPC-LDCs which have already reached HIPC decision point, four countries will have annual debt service payments due in 2003–2005 which will actually be higher than annual debt service paid in 1998–2000 and annual debt service payments will be reduced by less than $15 million in a further 6. In only three countries will annual debt service payments due in 2003–2005 be over $50 million less than those paid in 1998–2000.

Increased and accelerated debt relief is an important requirement for effective poverty reduction in many LDCs. As the members of the Panel which prepared the Zedillo Report emphasized, a re-enhanced HIPC Initiative merits serious consideration. This requires serious attention to be given to the problem of financing further debt relief, as it is this, rather than the needs of the countries in relation to promoting economic growth and poverty reduction, that is dictating the scale of debt relief which is being provided. In order to avoid future debt problems, it is also necessary to explore ways and means of breaking the link between falling and volatile commodity prices and the build-up of unsustainable external debt.

International commodity policy

For more than a decade after 1974, price-stabilizing international commodity agreements were the focus of international commodity policy. The success of this approach has been mixed at best, and its revival appears unlikely. The need to address the specific problems faced by commodity-exporting countries, however, is evident. Three issues are central to an international commodity policy which is concerned to promote development and poverty reduction. The first is the availability in producing countries of exportable products in sufficient volumes that would interest buyers and that meet the consumers' increasingly stringent requirements. Second, exporting countries need to enter supply chains for these products at points where higher degrees of value added are generated. The third issue is world primary commodity prices. Excessive instability in primary commodity prices, at least its negative impacts, needs to be mitigated and the problem of a continual downward trend in these prices must be addressed.

Given the abundance of supplies in world markets of many commodities of interest to LDCs, improvement of supply capacities should be interpreted to mean provision of better-quality and higher-valued products, possibly in their processed forms, rather than an outright increase in the quantities put on world markets. Technical assistance needs to be provided towards this end, and financing can be mobilized by increasing the resources available through the Common Fund for Commodities (CFC) or directly through the relevant international organizations. In areas such as research and development, quality control and assurance, a subregional approach may be adopted.

The new structure of supply chains leads to the generation of increasingly high proportions of value added at the marketing and distribution stages. The new approach to international commodity policy must include measures that would enable developing countries, particularly LDCs, to participate more fully at these stages of the supply chain. Research by international organizations, in cooperation with international commodity bodies (ICBs), is required in order to understand better the structure of supply chains, to identify the specific stages of high-value-added generation, to assess exporting countries' potential for entering these activities, and then to develop appropriate policies to enable LDCs to capture a higher proportion of the value added of the final products.

Mitigating excessive instability in world primary commodity prices, at least its negative impacts, and dealing with the problem of the continual downward trend of these prices also require concerted action by international commodity bodies and international organizations, supported by governmental policies. Past efforts to mitigate excessive instability through economic measures in international commodity agreements (ICAs) have been successful only for limited periods of time. In view of this mixed record and the current lack of political will to implement such economic measures, their reintroduction into ICAs appears unlikely. One possible approach in this respect seems to be the promotion of arrangements between buyers and sellers that are based on longer-term commitments rather than on daily dealings. All parties must accept, however, that attaining some degree of stability may mean forgoing short-term gains. The introduction of at least some aspects of "fair trade" principles into mainstream trade may be an avenue to explore in this connection. For this to happen, incentives need to be provided by Governments and there needs to be cooperation between the NGO community and large business concerns.

Price risk management instruments are a way to limit the incidence of instability for producers and traders. But for risk management instruments to be used successfully in the LDCs, innovative organizational forms will be needed to reach small farmers. A considerable investment in training will also be required and there is a need to establish the requisite institutional and legal frameworks. Ongoing application of these instruments in some LDCs is likely to reveal both the problems and the potential of this approach.

Compensatory financing is another means of mitigating some of the negative impacts of instability in prices and earnings. The international community, in discussing a new developmental approach to international commodity policy, must urgently reconsider the use of compensatory financing for export earnings shortfalls as part of an effort to address what the new Programme of Action calls "the structural causes of indebtedness".

Tackling the long-term decline in world commodity prices is perhaps the most difficult issue. International commodity policy should include modalities whereby regular consultations among international organizations, ICBs and Governments, as well as improved transparency, would help in directing efforts to increase production away from crowded markets to more dynamic products. In this connection, support is needed to assist high-cost producers in overcoming exit barriers that may prevent them from reacting rationally to declining prices, and to help those producers for whom the exit barriers cannot be eliminated. International commodity policy should also consider mechanisms for voluntary supply management schemes. In considering such mechanisms it is necessary to evaluate carefully the different objectives (elimination of accumulated stocks and reduction of production) and different instances of supply control (discouragement of new entrants, of increased production or of exports, and encouraging exit from production), as well as what is expected of consumers. In relation to declining prices, international commodity policy must also accord sufficient importance to increasing consumption of commodities, both through generic promotion and through new and innovative uses.

South–South cooperation and the problem of polarization of the global economy

Effective poverty reduction in the LDCs also requires enhanced South–South cooperation. The new Programme of Action recognizes that it can play an important role in the development of the LDCs, and encourages the use of "triangular mechanisms", through which "successful South–South cooperation may be attained using financial contributions from one or more donors, and taking advantage of economic complementarities among developing countries".

Increasing differentiation among developing countries should be seen as an opportunity for mutually beneficial interactions. Possible areas for South–South cooperation noted in the Programme of Action include the encouragement of regional trade and investment dynamics, which, as is evident in this Report, can be an important element in the development of new export capacities in the LDCs, as well as technical assistance and exchange of best practices in a range of areas (such as the Minimum Income for School Attendance Initiative based on Brazil's Bolsa Escola scheme). A number of LDCs are landlocked or transit countries, and for these countries a regional approach to transport infrastructure financing and to the development and management of transit systems is likely to be a particularly important aspect of building a dynamic investment–export nexus.

It is important that South–South cooperation be a complement, and not a substitute for North–South cooperation. It is also important that enhanced South–South cooperation takes place in a context in which the various asymmetries in the international system that are making it difficult for the more advanced developing countries to deepen industrialization and move up the technological ladder are addressed. It will be difficult for the LDCs to get on and move up the ladder of development if the more advanced developing countries face a "glass ceiling" which blocks their development.

In the end, addressing the socio-economic marginalization of the LDCs will require addressing the polarization in the global economy. Gains from differentiated treatment will be particularly strong for LDCs if an approach is adopted which enables all developing countries to advance. Indeed, this may very well be essential in order to prevent more developing countries from slipping into the LDC category.

Rubens Ricupero
Secretary-General of UNCTAD

Part One
RECENT ECONOMIC TRENDS AND UNLDC III DEVELOPMENT TARGETS

Recent Economic Trends

Chapter
1

A. Overall growth trends

The real GDP of the LDCs as a group grew by an annual average of 4.5 per cent over the three years from 1997 to 2000. This represents an improvement over the period 1990–1996, when LDCs grew at an annual average of 2.8 per cent, and it compares favourably with the average of 3.3 per cent for other developing countries (table 1). The overall growth rate of the LDCs during the late 1990s is somewhat lower when Bangladesh, which accounts for about a quarter of the economic size of the LDC group, is omitted. But excluding Bangladesh, the increase in the real growth rate between 1990–1996 and 1997–2000 is actually greater — from 2.0 per cent to 4.2 per cent per annum. The improvement in the overall growth rate is particularly marked in African LDCs.[1]

This improved growth performance for the LDCs as a whole is encouraging. However, recent growth rates are less adequate when viewed in real per capita terms, as population growth rates are very high in most LDCs. Real GDP per capita in the LDCs grew at 2.1 per cent per annum during 1997–2000. This was higher than the average for other developing countries (1.9 per cent). But excluding Bangladesh, real GDP per capita in the LDCs as a group grew at only 1.6 per cent per annum during 1997–2000. This implies that the gap in per capita incomes between LDCs and other developing countries was not reduced during 1997–2000. Furthermore, real GDP per capita grew at only 1.5 per cent per annum in African LDCs plus Haiti, and at only 0.8 per cent per annum in island LDCs (table 1).

Real GDP per capita in the LDCs grew at 2.1 per cent per annum during 1997–2000... but the performance of the LDCs was very mixed.

The performance of the LDCs was also very mixed. Focusing on trends in real GDP per capita by country, it is apparent that during 1997–2000, real GDP per capita actually declined in 13 out of 42 LDCs for which data are available (table 2). There are three Pacific small island States in this group, as well as a number of countries that have experienced armed conflict. There are a further 11 LDCs in which growth in real GDP per capita was less than 2 per cent per annum. Eighteen grew at 2 per cent per annum or more during 1997–2000, and 11 of these achieved growth rates of over 3 per cent per annum. Per capita GDP growth is by far the highest in Equatorial Guinea, where it is based on expansion

TABLE 1. LDCs' REAL GDP AND PER CAPITA GDP GROWTH RATES, 1990–1996 AND 1997–2000
(Annual average growth rate, percentage)

	Real GDP growth		Real GDP per capita growth	
	1990–1996	*1997–2000*	*1990–1996*	*1997–2000*
Least developed countries	2.8	4.5	0.3	2.1
LDCs (excluding Bangladesh)	2.0	4.2	-0.2	1.6
African LDCs	1.5	4.1	-0.7	1.5
Asian LDCs	4.5	5.0	2.6	3.0
Island LDCs	3.9	3.6	1.9	0.8
Other developing countries	3.5	3.3	2.3	1.9

Source: UNCTAD secretariat estimates based on World Bank, *World Development Indicators 2001*, CD-ROM, and *2002*, on-line data.

Note: Real GDP is measured in constant 1995 dollars. No data available for Afghanistan, Democratic Republic of the Congo, Liberia, Myanmar, Somalia, Sudan and Tuvalu.

TABLE 2. REAL GDP AND REAL GDP PER CAPITA GROWTH RATES IN THE LDCS, BY COUNTRY, 1997–2000
(Annual average growth rate, percentage)

	Real GDP growth	Real GDP per capita growth
High-growth economies (11)		
Equatorial Guinea	19.4	16.2
Maldives	8.4	5.7
Mozambique	7.6	5.4
Samoa	5.3	4.7
Rwanda	6.9	4.2
Bhutan	7.0	3.9
Cape Verde	7.0	3.9
Bangladesh	5.2	3.4
Burkina Faso	5.9	3.3
Lao People's Democratic Republic	5.7	3.2
Uganda	6.0	3.1
Moderate-growth economies (7)		
Senegal	5.3	2.4
Yemen	5.2	2.4
Gambia	5.5	2.3
Central African Republic	4.1	2.3
Mali	4.7	2.2
United Republic of Tanzania	4.6	2.1
Benin	4.8	2.1
Slow-growth economies (11)		
Nepal	4.1	1.7
Madagascar	4.5	1.3
Angola	4.1	1.2
Guinea	3.4	1.0
Mauritania	4.3	1.0
Cambodia	3.2	0.9
Malawi	3.0	0.8
Niger	4.2	0.7
Ethiopia	3.1	0.6
Sao Tome and Principe	2.7	0.4
Haiti	2.2	0.1
Regressing economies (13)		
Chad	2.6	-0.2
Djibouti	1.3	-0.6
Burundi	1.3	-0.6
Lesotho	0.8	-0.7
Kiribati	1.9	-0.9
Zambia	1.2	-1.0
Vanuatu	1.8	-1.4
Togo	1.2	-1.8
Comoros	0.6	-1.8
Sierra Leone	-2.1	-4.1
Eritrea	-1.6	-4.3
Guinea-Bissau	-5.6	-7.5
Solomon Islands	-5.2	-8.3

Source: UNCTAD secretariat estimates based on World Bank, *World Development Indicators 2002,* on-line data.

of oil production and exports. There are also three Asian LDCs in the high growth group (Bangladesh, Bhutan and Lao People's Democratic Republic), four African LDCs (Burkina Faso, Mozambique, Rwanda and Uganda), and three island LDCs (Cape Verde, Maldives and Samoa).

A key issue is the sustainability of the recent improvement in economic performance. Economic growth rates in the LDCs have been quite volatile in the past. During the period 1990–2000, the standard deviation of the annual real per capita GDP growth rates of the LDCs for which data are available was, on average, 20 per cent higher than in other developing countries.[2] Amongst the LDCs, economic growth rates were much more volatile in the African LDCs than in the Asian LDCs. The standard deviation of the annual real per capita growth rates during 1990–2000 in the former group of countries was three time higher than in the latter. Volatility in the island LDCs was also higher, but somewhat lower than in the African group.

While aggregate exports of LDCs are at record levels, more than one third of the LDCs actually experienced a sharp contraction of their trade during 1997–2000.

The latest data show that GDP declined in real terms in 4 out of 42 LDCs for which data are available, between 1999 and 2000. But this finding, which is based on World Bank on-line data, is very sensitive to the GDP deflator used, and this has been subject to revision in many LDCs during the late 1990s. In nominal terms, GDP declined between 1999 and 2000 in 29 out of 42 LDCs.

B. Trends in external trade

External factors remain an important determinant of economic trends in LDCs. Merchandise exports of LDCs as a group were at a record level in 2000. They stood at $31.3 billion in that year, up from $23 billion in 1997, an increase of 36 per cent.[3] Imports increased as well, but less sharply. They rose from $36.7 billion in 1997 to $40 billion in 2000, an increase of 9 per cent (table 3).

However, behind this impressive overall trade performance, there are significant differences amongst the LDCs. In fact, while aggregate exports of LDCs are at record levels, a closer look reveals that more than one third of them actually experienced a sharp contraction of their trade during 1997–2000.

TABLE 3. LDCs'[a] MERCHANDISE EXPORTS AND IMPORTS, 1997–2000

($ millions)

	1997	1998	1999	2000	Change from 1997 to 2000	
			Value		*Value*	*%*
Exports by:						
Total LDCs	23 045	22 183	24 720	31 337	8 291	36.0
Oil exporters	6 432	5 518	8 116	12 400	5 969	92.8
Non-oil commodity exporters	9 915	9 558	9 151	9 169	-746	-7.5
Manufactures and/or services exporters	6 699	7 107	7 453	9 768	3 069	45.8
Imports by:						
Total LDCs	36 667	37 555	38 233	39 954	3 287	9.0
Oil exporters	5 933	6 328	6 168	6 969	1 037	17.5
Non-oil commodity exporters	14 144	14 325	14 221	14 202	58	0.4
Manufactures and/or services exporters	16 590	16 903	17 844	18 783	2 193	13.2

Source: UNCTAD secretariat estimates based on UN COMTRADE data.

a Not including Eritrea and Tuvalu.

For analytical purposes, it is useful to distinguish: (i) oil-exporting LDCs (which at the end of the 1990s comprised Angola, Equatorial Guinea, Sudan and Yemen); (ii) non-oil commodity exporters, which comprise over half of all LDCs (mostly in Africa); and (iii) exporters of manufactures and/or services, which include garment exporters (e.g. Bangladesh).[4] With this disaggregation, it is apparent that the increase in merchandise exports of the LDC group is concentrated in oil exporters and manufactures and/or services exporters.

It is apparent that the increase in merchandise exports of the LDC group is concentrated in oil exporters and manufactures and/or services exporters... Exports dropped in 19 of the 26 non-oil commodity exporters between 1997 and 2000.

Exports of the LDC oil exporters increased by 92.8 per cent between 1997 and 2000. As a consequence, the four oil-exporting LDCs together accounted for 40 per cent of total LDC exports in 2000. The increase was partly due to the surge in oil prices in 2000, and partly due to increased production capacity related to recent investments in Equatorial Guinea and Sudan. Equatorial Guinea started producing oil at the beginning of the 1990s. Oil exports are estimated to have been $320 million in 1998 and $490 million in 1999, and production is estimated to have doubled between 1999 and 2000. Sudan became a net oil-exporting country with the opening of a 1,600 km pipeline in August 1999. Oil exports are estimated to have been $200 million in 1999 and $1 billion in 2000 (ITC, 2001).

Merchandise exports from the LDCs that export mainly manufactures and/or services increased by 46 per cent between 1997 and 2000, and by as much as 30 per cent from 1999 to 2000. This continued a positive upward trend which was apparent throughout the 1990s in the LDCs that export textiles and garments. By 2000, exports from this group of countries constituted almost a third of total LDC exports. Asian LDCs are prominent in this group. The growth of manufactured exports in the 1990s in Bangladesh, Cambodia, the Lao People's Democratic Republic, Myanmar and Nepal has been helped by low labour costs and proximity to other East Asian developing countries which have served as both a source of investment and end markets.

In contrast to these groups, the export performance of the primary commodity exporters, located mainly in Africa, was erratic and uncertain. Between 1997 and 2000, the value of merchandise exports for this group dropped by 7.5 per cent (table 3). Overall, exports dropped in 19 of the 26 non-oil commodity exporters between 1997 and 2000.

Trends in world commodity prices are an important factor leading to this weak performance. Between 1997 and 2001, copper prices fell by 27 per cent, cotton prices by 39 per cent and coffee prices by 66 per cent.

Trends in world commodity prices are an important factor leading to this weak performance. Between 1997 and 2001, copper prices fell by 27 per cent, cotton prices by 39 per cent and coffee prices by 66 per cent (table 4); the price of gold declined by around 18 per cent, the price of food declined by 31 per cent, the price of agricultural raw materials declined by 20 per cent, and the price of minerals, ores and metals declined by 17 per cent.

The adverse economic consequences of falling world non-fuel primary commodity prices in net oil-importing LDCs was initially offset by low oil prices during the period 1997–1999. Moreover, food prices have been falling along with the general fall in primary commodity prices, which has also helped to cushion the blow of declining prices as many LDCs are net food importers (Herrmann and David, 2001). But after oil prices reached an extreme low in 1999 (approximately $10 a barrel), they climbed sharply in 2000, averaging over $30 in the first three quarters of that year. Although oil prices have since fallen back, there has not been a return to the low levels of oil prices that prevailed in the period 1997–1999 and helped underpin economic growth in that period.

TABLE 4. CHANGE IN PRICE INDICES OF SELECTED PRIMARY COMMODITIES OF IMPORTANCE TO THE LDCs, 1997–2001

	1997 Index	1998	1999	2000	2001
All foods	100	87	71	69	69
Cocoa	100	104	71	56	70
Coffee	100	82	64	48	34
Fish meal	100	109	65	68	80
Rice	100	101	82	67	57
Sugar	100	79	55	72	76
Tea	100	104	97	104	83
Wheat	100	79	74	76	80
All agricultural raw materials	100	89	80	82	80
Cotton	100	82	66	74	61
Tobacco	100	94	88	85	85
Minerals, ores and metals	100	84	82	92	83
Copper	100	72	70	83	73
Gold	100	89	84	84	82
Memo item: Crude petroleum	100	68	95	147	127

Source: UNCTAD secretariat estimates based on UNCTAD *Commodity Price Bulletin*.

C. Trends in external finance

1. OVERALL PICTURE

Economic performance in LDCs is also affected by trends in external finance. Trends in the 1990s were dominated by two major tendencies: declining levels of aid and rising levels of private capital inflows, in particular FDI. Previous World Bank estimates indicated a significant decline in total long-term capital inflows into LDCs as a whole during the decade as aid had been falling faster than private capital flows had been rising. But estimates of private capital flows to some LDCs in the late 1990s were revised upwards in the latest version of Global Development Finance statistics.

According to these new estimates, long-term capital flows to the LDCs as a whole in 1999 were $15 billion. This was the highest level of any year in the 1990s. They fell by 11 per cent in 2000 to $13.3 billion. But taking the two years together, average annual long-term net capital inflows into the LDCs were higher in nominal terms in 1999–2000 than the average annual inflows in 1989–1993 and in 1994–1998 (table 5).

The driving force for higher capital inflows for the group as a whole has been increasing private capital inflows. Official net resource flows (including both concessional and non-concessional finance) to the LDCs have continued to decline. According to World Bank statistics, they were 22 per cent less in nominal terms in 2000 than during the period 1989–1993. However, private capital inflows in the period 1997–2000 were more than double the levels of the early 1990s, with a particularly strong surge in 1999. As a consequence, private capital flows to the LDCs constituted as much as 35 per cent of aggregate net resource flows to the group as a whole in 1999 and 28 per cent in 2000. Net FDI

Private capital inflows in the period 1997–2000 were more than double the levels of the early 1990s, with a particularly strong surge in 1999.

TABLE 5. LONG-TERM NET CAPITAL FLOWS TO LDCS,[a] BY TYPE OF FLOW, AND AGGREGATE NET TRANSFERS,
1989–1993, 1994–1998, 1999 AND 2000
(Current $ millions, annual average)

	1989–1993	1994–1998	1999	2000
Aggregate net resource flows	13 933	13 308	15 039	13 331
Official net resource flows	12 396	10 719	9 817	9 630
Grants, excluding technical cooperation	8 392	7 958	7 753	7 578
Official debt flows	4 004	2 761	2 064	2 053
Bilateral	1 009	-36	-439	-327
Multilateral	2 995	2 797	2 503	2 379
Private net resource flows	1 538	2 589	5 222	3 701
Foreign direct investment, net inflows	1 132	2 432	5 276	4 315
Portfolio equity flows	0	40	4	3
Private debt flows	406	666	-58	-617
Private, publicly guaranteed	419	686	-78	-598
Private non-guaranteed	-13	-20	20	-19
Aggregate net transfers	12 162	11 396	12 979	11 358
Interest payments on long-term debt	1 110	1 150	1 149	980
Profit remittances on FDI	661	762	910	993
Memo item:				
IMF, net concessional and non-concessional flows	-57	210	-6	-152

Source: UNCTAD secretariat estimates based on World Bank, *Global Development Finance 2002,* on-line data.

a All LDCs, except Afghanistan, Kiribati and Tuvalu, for which no data are available.

CHART 1. COMPOSITION OF LONG-TERM CAPITAL FLOWS TO LDCS, 1989–1993, 1994–1998, 1999 AND 2000
(Percentage of aggregate net resource flows)

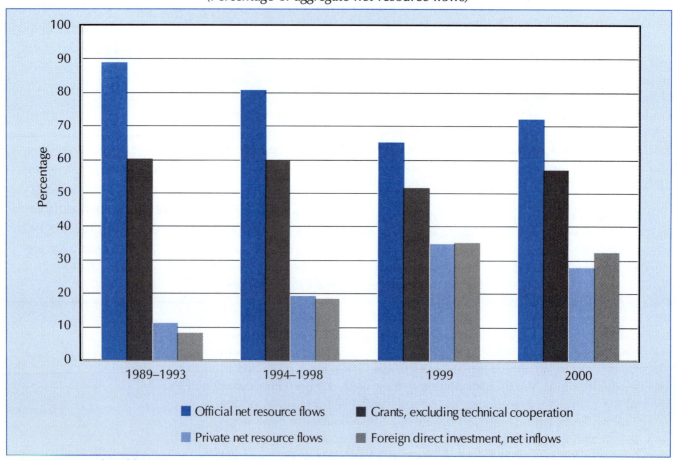

Source: Same as for table 5.
Note: Same as for table 5.

is estimated to have comprised 35 per cent of aggregate net resource flows in 1999 and 32 per cent in 2000 (chart 1).

Four qualifications must be made to place this overall picture in perspective. Firstly, in real per capita terms long-term net capital flows to the LDCs continue to decline. Using the index of manufactured exports from industrial countries as a deflator, real long-term capital inflows per capita to LDCs fell by 21 per cent between 1990 and 2000.

However, real long-term capital inflows per capita to LDCs fell by 21 per cent between 1990 and 2000.

Secondly, although they have been receiving more FDI, the LDCs remain excluded from international bank finance and bond issues. Private debt flows to LDCs have been negative for every year since 1995 except 1999, thus indicating that repayments of existing debt to private creditors have been in excess of new loan disbursements.

Thirdly, as with the external trade trends, there are major variations amongst the LDCs, and the increase in capital flows is highly concentrated. If one looks at trends in individual countries, it is apparent that aggregate net resource flows were lower in 1999–2000 than in 1994–1998 in 33 out of 46 countries for which data are available. In only nine LDCs were the levels of capital inflows higher in both 1999 and 2000 than in 1994–1998 — Angola, Bangladesh, Burkina Faso, Equatorial Guinea, Eritrea, Mozambique, Sudan, Uganda and the United Republic of Tanzania. It is also apparent that, in 2000, 47 per cent of net FDI flows to all LDCs went to the four oil-exporting LDCs — Angola, Equatorial Guinea, Sudan and Yemen. It is also worth noting that the major source of the upward revision of private capital flows to the LDC group in 1999 is Angola, where private capital flows are revised upwards in the latest Global Development Finance database by $2.5 billion from the previous estimates. This statistical adjustment is equivalent to 17 per cent of total capital inflows to the LDCs in 1999.

As with the external trade trends, there are major variations amongst the LDCs, and the increase in capital flows is highly concentrated. If one looks at trends in individual countries, it is apparent that aggregate net resource flows were lower in 1999–2000 than in 1994–1998 in 33 out of 46 countries for which data are available.

Fourthly, the LDCs still attract a relatively low share of aggregate net resource flows going to all developing countries. This occurs in spite of high levels of aid. In 2000, they received 28 per cent of the official net resource flows going to all developing countries, but only 1.7 per cent of the private resource flows and 2.6 per cent of the net FDI inflows. Overall, they received 5.2 per cent of aggregate net resource flows to the developing countries (table 6).

TABLE 6. LDCS' SHARE OF NET RESOURCE FLOWS TO ALL DEVELOPING COUNTRIES, BY TYPE OF FLOW,1989–1993, 1994–1998, 1999 AND 2000

(Percentage)

	1989–1993	1994–1998	1999	2000
Aggregate net resource flows	10.3	4.6	5.6	5.2
Official net resource flows	23.2	24.0	20.8	27.5
Private net resource flows	1.9	1.1	2.4	1.7
Foreign direct investment, net inflows	2.9	1.8	2.9	2.6

Source: As for table 5.

Note: The sample of LDCs is the same as in table 5.

2. TRENDS IN AID FLOWS

The sharp decline in aid flows to LDCs which began at the start of the 1990s was halted during the period 1998–2000. Indeed net ODA disbursements to LDCs from all donors rose slightly in 2000 to $12.5 billion.

Nevertheless, in real per capita terms, aid from all donors in 2000 was 30 per cent lower than in 1994.

A more detailed account of aid flows to the LDCs can be obtained from statistics compiled by the OECD's Development Assistance Committee (DAC).[5] These data show that the sharp decline in aid flows to LDCs which began at the start of the 1990s was halted during the period 1998–2000. Indeed estimates for 2000 show that net ODA disbursements to LDCs from all donors rose slightly in that year to $12.5 billion. But, nevertheless, in nominal terms, aid to LDCs was 26 per cent lower in 2000 than in 1994. In real per capita terms, aid from all donors in 2000 was 30 per cent lower than in 1994 (table 7).

The main source of aid to LDCs is DAC member countries, which together supplied 98 per cent of net ODA disbursements to the LDCs in 2000. Aid flows from DAC member countries is mainly in the form of bilateral grants (which are estimated to have constituted 66 per cent of net ODA disbursements to LDCs in 2000) and contributions to multilateral organizations. Data on bilateral aid commitments by DAC member countries indicate that the trend away from providing aid for economic infrastructure and services (particularly transport and communications, and energy) and production sectors (agriculture, industry, trade and tourism) on the one hand, and towards social infrastructure and services (particularly education, and government and civil society) on the other, continued in the late 1990s. Indeed, in 1998–2000, bilateral aid commitments for social infrastructure and services constituted one third of total bilateral aid commitments to the LDCs, exceeding the commitments to economic infrastructure and services, production sectors, and multisectoral and cross-cutting initiatives such as gender and environment (table 8), which together received only 23 per cent of total bilateral aid commitments. This is a significant shift from the early 1980s, when only 11 per cent of total bilateral aid commitments were focused on social infrastructure and services, and 45 per

TABLE 7. NET ODA INFLOWS INTO LDCS FROM ALL DONORS, 1994–2000

	1994	1995	1996	1997	1998	1999	2000
Net ODA (current $, million)	16 825.5	17 241.7	14 084.6	13 035.8	12 806.2	12 325.0	12 477.8
Net ODA per capita (current $)	29.3	29.3	23.5	21.2	20.4	19.2	19.0
Real net ODA (1999 $, million)	16 652.3	15 404.7	12 827.9	12 884.8	12 896.2	12 325.0	13 256.4
Real net ODA per capita (1999 $)	29.0	26.2	21.4	21.0	20.5	19.2	20.2

Source: UNCTAD secretariat estimates based on OECD/DAC Statistical Reporting System, on-line data.

TABLE 8. BILATERAL ODA COMMITMENTS FROM DAC DONORS TO LDCS BY SECTOR AS A PERCENTAGE OF TOTAL BILATERAL ODA COMMITMENT
(Percentage)

	1994–1997	1998–2000
Social infrastructure and services	32.1	34.3
Economic infrastructure and services, production sectors and multisectoral/cross-cutting issues	31.4	23.2
Commodity aid/ general programme assistance	12.6	13.9
Action relating to debt	11.7	15.7
Emergency assistance	7.9	9.1
Other	4.3	3.8
Total	100.0	100.0

Source: UNCTAD secretariat estimates based on OECD *International Development Statistics 2002,* CD-ROM.

cent on economic infrastructure, production sectors, and multisectoral and cross-cutting issues.[6] Emergency assistance and debt relief have also become significant elements of bilateral aid commitments, constituting 25 per cent of total aid commitments by DAC member countries in 1998–2000.

Closer analysis of the pattern of emergency aid and debt relief disbursements in 2000 indicates that 41 LDCs received some form of emergency aid in that year. Moreover, for 10 LDCs, emergency aid exceeded 15 per cent of net ODA from all donors. Those countries were the following: Afghanistan, Angola, Burundi, the Democratic Republic of the Congo, Eritrea, Ethiopia, Mozambique, Sierra Leone, Somalia and Sudan. Net debt forgiveness by DAC member countries in 2000 was equivalent to 15 per cent or more of net ODA disbursements in seven LDCs — Central African Republic, Guinea-Bissau, Mozambique, Myanmar, Togo, the United Republic of Tanzania and Zambia.

Finally, it is worth stressing that technical cooperation remains an important form of aid to the LDCs. Technical cooperation provided by DAC member countries is estimated at $2.1 billion in 2000.

Emergency assistance and debt relief have become significant elements of bilateral aid, constituting 25 per cent of total aid commitments by DAC member countries in 1998–2000.

3. TRENDS IN FOREIGN DIRECT INVESTMENT

The UNCTAD FDI/TNC database also provides a more detailed picture of FDI inflows. Over the past decade, global FDI flows have been steadily increasing — from $209 billion in 1990 to more than $1.3 trillion in 2000. A number of developing countries have participated in this surge. However, according to latest estimates, only 0.5 per cent of global FDI flows have been invested in the 49 LDCs (UNCTAD, 2000; UNCTAD, 2001).

Absolute levels of FDI inflows to the LDCs rose in the 1990s, particularly between 1994 and 1999. However, as noted above, there has been a strong concentration in a small number of countries. The top 10 recipient LDC countries in 1999 were Angola, Bangladesh, Cambodia, Lesotho, Mozambique, Myanmar, Sudan, Uganda, the United Republic of Tanzania and Zambia. Together these countries accounted for over 86 per cent of FDI inflows into all LDCs in the period 1998–2000 (table 9). This is even more concentrated than the pattern in all developing countries, where, for example, in 2000, 73 per cent of all FDI inflows were concentrated in the top 10 recipient developing countries (UNCTAD, 2001). Moreover, the UNCTAD FDI/TNC database indicate that the four oil-exporting LDCs accounted for over 50 per cent of all FDI in LDCs in both 1999 and 2000.

The top 10 LDC recipients of FDI accounted for over 86 per cent of FDI inflows into all LDCs in the period 1998–2000.

TABLE 9. FDI INFLOWS INTO LDCs BY GROUP, 1997–2000
($ millions and percentage)

	1997	1998	1999	2000
Total LDCs	2 976.3	3 678.7	5 176.3	4 414.3
Oil-exporting LDCs	391.1	1 242.5	2 633.1	2 046.0
Top ten recipient LDCs[a]	2 115.0	3 165.2	4 495.1	3 764.4
Rest of LDCs	861.3	513.5	681.2	649.8
Share of top ten recipient LDCs (%)	71.1	86.0	86.8	85.3
Share of rest of LDCs (%)	28.9	14.0	13.2	14.7

Source: UNCTAD, FDI/TNC database.

a Based on the top ten recipients in 1999: Angola, Sudan, Uganda, Myanmar, Lesotho, Zambia, United Republic of Tanzania, Bangladesh, Cambodia and Mozambique.

There was a global downturn in FDI inflows in 2000, and LDCs were not immune to this trend. According to UNCTAD statistics, there was a 15 per cent decline in FDI inflows to LDCs, from $5.2 billion in 1999 to approximately $4.4 billion in 2000 (ibid.). Different groups of countries were, however, affected differently. FDI inflows to African LDCs declined by 18.4 per cent in 2000, although FDI inflows remained high in the oil-exporting African LDCs — Angola, Equatorial Guinea, and Sudan — in that year. LDCs in South and South-East Asia with export-oriented manufacturing sectors have also continued to attract FDI, although there was a sharp fall after the financial crisis of 1997. Overall, FDI flows to Asia increased by 35.5 per cent in 2000, mainly in textiles and garments and in some services sectors. FDI inflows declined by 56 per cent in Haiti, the only LDC in the Latin American and Caribbean region. In the Pacific, there was a 44 per cent increase in FDI inflows in 2000, associated with increased investment in tourism in some island LDCs (table 10).

There was a global downturn in FDI inflows in 2000, and LDCs were not immune to this trend. There was a 15 per cent decline in FDI inflows to LDCs in 2000.

D. Trends in external debt

High levels of external debt continue to impede economic performance in many LDCs. As at the end of 2000, the LDCs as a group had a total debt stock of $143.2 billion. This was a reduction of $4.4 billion from the beginning-of-year balance, and a reduction of $9.3 billion (or 6.1 per cent) from the debt stock at the beginning of 1999. Debt stocks fell owing to debt forgiveness grants (which were particularly important in 1999), and changes due to cross-currency valuation (which were particularly important in 2000) which together counterbalanced a small increase in debt owing to new loans. The major source of new debt in the LDCs is official loans, particularly multilateral loans. Excluding IMF credit, multilateral loans were equivalent to 115 per cent of net official debt flows in 2000. Net bilateral debt flows were negative in that year.

The external debt burden is falling. But at the end of 2000, the LDCs as a group had a total debt stock of $143.2 billion. Debt service payments amounted to $4.6 billion in 2000.

The levels of debt stocks are lower in relation to GDP and exports as well as in absolute terms. Total debt stocks for the LDCs as a group were equivalent to 105 per cent of GDP in 1995, but fell to 84 per cent in 1999 and 78 per cent in 2000. There was little change in the level of debt service payments. For all LDCs, they amounted to $4.7 billion in 1999, and $4.6 billion in 2000. As a ratio of exports of goods and services, debt service payments were 9.6 per cent in 2000, down from 11.8 per cent in 1999 (see table 11).

Behind these aggregate statistics, there is a much more mixed situation. Between 1999 and 2000, for a sample of 42 LDCs for which data are available,

TABLE 10. FDI INFLOWS INTO LDCs, BY REGION ,1990–2000

($ millions)

	1990	1997	1998	1999	2000	Annual average % change 1990–2000	Annual average % change 1999–2000
Total LDCs	573.5	2 976.3	3 678.7	5 176.3	4 414.3	18.0	-14.7
Africa	482.5	2 170.3	3 206.7	4 773.8	3 893.5	23.2	-18.4
Asia	52.6	717.0	428.5	340.0	460.6	6.3	35.5
West Asia	-130.9	-138.5	-266.1	-328.7	-200.9	..	..
South, East and South-East Asia	183.5	855.5	694.6	668.7	661.5	17.2	-1.1
Latin America and the Caribbean	8.0	4.0	10.8	30.0	13.2	..	-56.0
Pacific	30.5	85.1	32.7	32.5	46.9	0.9	44.2

Source: UNCTAD, FDI/TNC database.

TABLE 11. EXTERNAL DEBT BURDEN INDICATORS FOR THE LDCS, 1995, 1999 AND 2000

(Percentage)

	Total debt stocks/ GDP			Total debt service paid/exports[a]			Total debt stock/ exports[a]			Present value of debt/exports[b]
	1995	1999	2000	1995	1999	2000	1995	1999	2000	1998–2000
Afghanistan	..	..	..	..	..	..	..	..	..	..
Angola	219.4	178.0	114.9	12.0	18.7	15.1	295.4	206.7	127.4	170
Bangladesh	42.0	36.0	33.1	14.2	9.2	9.1	290.1	211.2	180.3	120
Benin	80.3	72.4	73.7	6.8	10.0	12.6	221.0	242.0	263.4	253
Bhutan	34.4	42.1	40.7	10.9	5.1	4.2	117.3	132.6	126.5	111
Burkina Faso	53.8	61.7	60.8	11.2	15.5	17.3	292.1	387.8	421.8	210
Burundi	115.7	158.4	159.7	27.6	45.6	37.2	828.5	1791.9	1910.9	985
Cambodia	69.3	75.1	74.1	0.7	2.9	2.0	205.8	197.9	152.5	158
Cape Verde	43.7	55.7	58.6	5.0	10.0	7.5	112.0	163.5	152.2	128
Central African Republic	84.3	86.5	90.6	7.8	12.1	9.0	471.5	589.4	556.4	356
Chad	62.7	73.0	79.3	4.1	11.0	9.3	235.0	388.8	394.3	222
Comoros	99.5	102.6	114.8	1.6	5.7	5.0	347.5	421.8	428.9	296
Dem. Rep. of the Congo	234.6	..	..	1.4	..	..	747.9	..	..	797
Djibouti	57.4	51.2	47.4	5.5	4.1	5.5	133.0	112.4	106.9	71
Equatorial Guinea	177.9	31.1	18.5	2.2	0.4	0.2	309.7	19.2	10.5	13
Eritrea	6.4	39.0	51.2	0.1	1.6	1.1	12.3	121.8	104.0	75
Ethiopia	178.3	85.5	85.8	19.1	16.4	13.9	1276.3	586.7	548.1	343
Gambia	111.8	107.5	111.7	14.7	8.6	7.0	235.9	185.9	176.2	217
Guinea	87.8	102.7	112.5	25.0	15.6	15.3	454.3	428.6	389.4	286
Guinea-Bissau	353.7	416.2	436.9	51.7	15.7	8.6	3035.8	1608.9	1305.1	1321
Haiti	31.0	29.0	28.9	50.2	8.8	8.0	424.1	209.2	224.4	132
Kiribati	..	..	..	..	..	..	..	..	..	..
Lao People's Dem. Rep.	122.8	174.2	146.2	6.3	7.7	8.1	521.5	527.8	484.1	243
Lesotho	73.7	80.3	79.6	6.1	10.9	12.1	102.4	135.0	131.9	91
Liberia	..	..	..	..	..	..	..	..	..	..
Madagascar	136.8	127.8	121.2	7.6	17.1	7.7	564.9	510.9	388.4	333
Malawi	157.0	152.0	160.1	25.6	12.7	11.7	484.8	506.7	543.3	314
Maldives	57.2	39.1	37.2	3.4	4.0	4.3	48.1	49.4	44.2	32
Mali	119.9	123.8	128.7	13.3	13.7	12.1	455.2	413.6	367.7	209
Mauritania	219.9	263.9	267.4	22.9	28.4	25.9	459.8	681.3	645.1	319
Mozambique	311.8	175.2	190.1	34.5	18.5	11.4	1585.5	1092.1	927.8	187
Myanmar	..	..	..	19.2	6.0	4.7	441.5	371.8	327.6	248
Nepal	55.1	59.0	51.4	7.05	7.9	6.5	200.5	219.4	184.7	113
Niger	84.4	81.3	89.7	16.7	11.2	9.2	475.9	545.7	534.6	345
Rwanda	80.0	66.8	70.8	20.4	25.9	24.7	1040.9	1063.8	896.2	628
Samoa	110.0	80.6	83.6	4.2	5.1	10.8	157.2	151.6	250.8	115
Sao Tome and Principe	539.7	683.1	679.6	23.4	29.1	31.7	2493.8	2168.2	2273.2	1307
Senegal	85.8	78.0	77.1	16.7	14.3	14.4	228.7	224.0	213.4	151
Sierra Leone	136.0	187.3	200.2	61.5	29.5	48.0	912.8	1686.4	1434.7	800
Solomon Islands	48.5	51.6	56.6	3.83	4.82	6.72	75.1	72.9	114.8	53
Somalia	..	..	..	..	..	..	..	..	..	..
Sudan	244.7	160.9	136.7	10.0	6.7	3.2	2551.6	1897.7	829.8	1319
Togo	112.7	107.4	117.6	6.0	8.9	6.1	302.1	302.5	294.7	199
Tuvalu	..	..	..	..	..	..	..	..	..	..
Uganda	62.1	53.9	55.2	20.0	22.1	23.7	523.3	445.1	506.1	138
United Rep. of Tanzania	141.1	95.0	82.5	17.9	16.2	16.2	571.7	658.1	555.7	395
Vanuatu	20.4	30.2	32.4	1.5	1.1	1.4	37.3	36.0	42.3	20
Yemen	165.7	74.1	65.8	3.1	3.9	3.8	203.0	135.3	95.7	99
Zambia	200.3	188.6	196.8	181.6	45.8	18.7	481.3	611.8	578.1	537
LDCs[c]	104.6	83.9	78.4	20.1	11.8	9.6	414.5	332.0	264.9	234

Source: UNCTAD secretariat estimates based on World Bank, Global Development Finance 2002, on-line data, and World Development Indicators 2001, CD-ROM.
a Exports of goods and services.
b The ratio is based on the net present value of debt in the year 2000 and average annual exports of goods and services during 1998–2000.
c Weighted average based on 43 LDCs. No data are available for Afghanistan, Democratic Republic of the Congo, Kiribati, Liberia, Somalia and Tuvalu.

Twenty-nine LDCs had an unsustainable external debt in 2000.

the ratio of debt stocks to GDP declined in 18. Total arrears on long-term debt declined in only 8 LDCs between 1999 and 2000. Moreover, 29 LDCs had an unsustainable external debt in 2000, if sustainability is measured according to one of the criteria of the enhanced HIPC Initiative, namely a ratio of the net present value of debt stocks to exports of 150.

Most of the debt is owed to official creditors, and multilateral debt remains particularly important. It is for this reason that the Enhanced HIPC Initiative is so important to the LDCs with unsustainable external debts. Some of the improvements in the debt situation of LDCs are related to actions taken in

TABLE 12. RATIO OF DEBT SERVICE PAID TO GOVERNMENT REVENUE AND
SOCIAL EXPENDITURE IN SELECTED HIPC-LDCs,[a] 1998, 1999 AND 2000
(Percentage)

Country	Date of decision point	Debt service paid/govt. revenue (%)			Debt service paid/social exp. (%)	
		1998[b]	1999[b]	2000[c]	1999[b]	2000[c]
Countries reaching decision point in first half of 2000						
Mauritania	Feb. 00	35	30	39	95	100
Mozambique	Apr. 00	23	12	5	23	8
Senegal	Jun. 00	27	18	18	57	63
Utd. Rep. of Tanzania	Apr. 00	29	20	16	67	44
Uganda	May 00[d]	16	13	13	32	22
Simple average		*26*	*19*	*18*	*55*	*47*
Countries reaching decision point in third quarter of 2000						
Benin	Jul. 00	17	17	14	57	50
Burkina Faso	Jul. 00	18	15	17	38	40
Mali	Sep.00	17	20	18	82	65
Simple average		*17*	*17*	*16*	*82*	*65*
Countries reaching decision point in end 2000, 2001 and 2002						
Chad	May 01	29	23	29	16	17
Ethiopia	Nov. 01	9	11	10	47	21
Gambia	Dec. 00	12	25	16	83	59
Guinea	Dec. 00	34	35	36	155	167
Guinea-Bissau	Dec. 00	63	15	32	9	15
Madagascar	Dec. 00	42	25	19	68	46
Malawi	Dec. 00	22	21	27	31	49
Niger	Dec. 00	9	11	12	18	20
Rwanda	Dec. 00	7	25	17	63	42
Sao Tome and Principe	Dec. 00	84	21	53	25	63
Sierra Leone	Mar. 02	18	77	44	247	213
Zambia	Dec. 00	24	23	24	76	99
Simple average		*29*	*26*	*27*	*70*	*68*

Source: UNCTAD secretariat estimates based on IMF/IDA (2001).

Notes: a The list includes all HIPC-LDCs which had reached decision point/completion point by the end of September 2001.
b Debt service paid.
c Debt service due after the full use of traditional debt service mechanism and assistance under the Enhanced HIPC Initiative.
d Completion point.

the context of that Initiative. However, the full effects of the Initiative had still not been achieved in the year 2000, even for countries that had reached decision point in that year. Estimates of debt service payments in 2000 for 20 HIPC-LDCs which have reached decision point or completion point show that debt service exceeded 20 per cent of government revenue in 8, and exceeded 20 per cent of social expenditure in 7. Indeed, in 14 of these countries, debt service payments in 2000 were equivalent to 40 per cent or more of government social expenditure (table 12).

E. Conclusion

The economic performance of LDCs as a group was much better in the late 1990s than in the early 1990s. Economic growth for the whole group was higher in 1996–2000 than it was in the period 1990–1997, and exports in 2000 were at a record level. Private capital inflows, though they slumped in 2000, remain at higher levels than the early 1990s.

However, within this positive aggregate picture, economic trends have been very diverse. Divergence is increasing amongst the LDCs, particularly between LDCs which export manufactures and services, and LDCs which export non-fuel primary commodities. The latter have been particularly adversely affected by the recent decline in commodity prices. The level of merchandise exports and of private capital flows to the LDCs as a group in 1999 and 2000 was also highly dependent on the situation of the four LDCs which export oil — Angola, Equatorial Guinea, Sudan and Yemen.

Important concerns must also be expressed regarding the sustainability of recent trends. Growth in the LDCs remains highly dependent on commodity prices and trends in external finance. The year 2001 is likely to have been a difficult year in many LDCs. Global economic conditions deteriorated in the first part of the year and the events of 11 September added much uncertainty to an already weak global economy. World trade, which grew by 12 per cent in volume terms in 2000 slowed down sharply in 2001, some initial estimates suggesting that it grew by only 2 per cent (WTO, 2001). This was due to a major slowdown of demand in Western Europe and stagnation of imports into the United States. The travel and tourism industry, which is important for a number of LDCs, particularly island LDCs, was especially hard hit in the aftermath of the events of 11 September. Preliminary estimates also suggest that FDI inflows to developing countries declined steeply in 2001 (UNCTAD, forthcoming).

Demand for primary commodities is not expected to increase substantially in 2002–2003. Moreover, the experience of Yemen, where there was a surge of net FDI inflows in the early 1990s, suggests that there is a danger that aggregate FDI flows to LDCs could fall sharply in future as known oil resources are exploited. The consequences of the current economic and political conjuncture for future aid flows to the LDCs remain unclear. But the most likely trend is towards increased concentration of aid flows amongst the LDCs. If recent commodity price trends persist, and assuming that other things are equal, there is a danger that growth rates in many LDCs in the near future will return to the weak performance of the early 1990s, a period when the commodity terms of trade also fell sharply.

In 14 out of 20 HIPC-LDCs which have reached decision point or completion point, debt service payments in 2000 were equivalent to 40 per cent or more of government social expenditure.

The economic performance of LDCs as a group was much better in the late 1990s than in the early 1990s... But growth in the LDCs remains highly dependent on commodity prices and trends in external finance.

If recent commodity price trends persist, there is a danger that growth rates in many LDCs will return to the weak performance of the early 1990s, a period when the commodity terms of trade also fell sharply.

Notes

1. Throughout this report (unless otherwise specified) African, Asian and island LDCs are as follows: African LDCs: Angola, Benin, Burkina Faso, Burundi, Central African Republic, Chad, Democratic Republic of the Congo, Djibouti, Equatorial Guinea, Eritrea, Ethiopia, Gambia, Guinea, Guinea-Bissau, Lesotho, Liberia, Madagascar, Malawi, Mali, Mauritania, Mozambique, Niger, Rwanda, Senegal, Sierra Leone, Somalia, Sudan, Togo, Uganda, United Republic of Tanzania and Zambia. Haiti is normally included in the African LDC group unless otherwise stated. Asian LDCs: Afghanistan, Bangladesh, Bhutan, Cambodia, Lao People's Democratic Republic, Myanmar, Nepal and Yemen; island LDCs: Cape Verde, Comoros, Kiribati, Maldives, Samoa, Sao Tome and Principe, Solomon Islands, Tuvalu and Vanuatu.
2. This is based on 43 LDCs using data from IMF World Economic Outlook on-line database, December 2001.
3. These statistics are based on UN COMTRADE data. They diverge slightly from WTO estimates, which indicate the same pattern and trend, but estimate the total merchandise exports of LDCs in 2000 at $34 billion.
4. The countries classified as exporters of manufactures and/or services are: Bangladesh, Cambodia, Cape Verde, Comoros, Djibouti, Gambia, Haiti, Lao People's Democratic Republic, Lesotho, Madagascar, Maldives, Mozambique, Myanmar, Nepal, Samoa, Senegal, Tuvalu and Vanuatu. For further details on classification, see Part Two, annex to chapter 3.
5. OECD/DAC estimates of aid flows diverge somewhat from World Bank estimates of official resource flows (see UNCTAD, 2000: box 2). Trends are similar, but the OECD/DAC statistics suggest that the decline in aid since the early 1990s has been more marked than the World Bank estimates imply.
6. For discussion of long-term trends, see UNCTAD (2000, table 14).

References

Herrmann, M. and David, M. (2001). Recent price changes in primary commodities, 1998–2000: Implications for least developed countries, background report for *The Least Developed Countries Report 2002*, Geneva.

IMF/IDA (2002). Heavily Indebted Poor Countries (HIPC) Initiative: Status of implementation, 12 April, Washington DC.

International Trade Centre UNCTAD/WTO (ITC) (2001). LDC trade: an analytical note, report prepared for the Business Sector Round Table, Third United Nations Conference on Least Developed Countries, Brussels 16 May 2001.

UNCTAD (2000). *The Least Developed Countries 2000 Report*, United Nations publication, sales no. E.00.II.D.21, Geneva.

UNCTAD (2001). *World Investment Report 2001*. United Nations publication, sales no. E.01.II.D.12, Geneva.

UNCTAD (forthcoming). *World Investment Report 2002*, New York and Geneva.

WTO (2001). *Annual Report 2001*, Geneva.

The UNLDC III Development Targets

A. Introduction

A new Programme of Action for the Least Developed Countries for the Decade 2001–2010 was agreed at the Third United Nations Conference on the Least Developed Countries (UNLDC III), held in Brussels in May 2001. The Programme of Action is intended as "a framework for a strong global partnership to accelerate sustained economic growth and sustainable development in LDCs, to end marginalization by eradicating poverty, inequality and deprivation in these countries, and to enable them to integrate beneficially into the global economy" (United Nations, 2001). Partnership is founded on mutual commitments by LDCs and their development partners to undertake concrete actions in seven areas:

(i)   Fostering a people-centred policy framework;

(ii)   Good governance at national and international levels;

(iii)   Building human and institutional capacities;

(iv)   Building productive capacities to make globalization work for LDCs;

(v)   Enhancing the role of trade in development;

(vi)   Reducing vulnerability and protecting the environment;

(vii) Mobilizing financial resources.

An important feature of the Programme of Action is that it includes a number of quantified, time-bound development targets. The inclusion of these targets is important as it is now easier to monitor the success of the Programme. Indeed, "results-orientation" is one of the key considerations which LDCs and their partners are meant to be guided by in the implementation of the Programme of Action. The Programme stresses that "the process of identifying, assessing and monitoring progress on process and concrete outcomes will be a key aspect of the implementation of the Programme of Action" (para. 21e).

An important feature of the Programme of Action for the Least Developed Countries for the Decade 2001–2010 is that it includes a number of quantified, time-bound development targets.

This chapter assesses the extent to which it is possible to describe where the LDCs now stand in relation to the quantified, time-bound targets specified in the Programme of Action. The targets considered are:

(i)   Growth and investment targets;

(ii)   Poverty reduction targets;

(iii)   A range of human development targets in relation to population, education and training, and health, nutrition and sanitation;

(iv)   A range of infrastructure development targets in relation to transport and communications;

(v)   Official development assistance (ODA) flows to LDCs equivalent to 0.15 per cent or 0.2 per cent of donor countries' gross national product (GNP) for most donor countries;

(vi)   Progress towards graduation from the category of LDC, for which there are defined and quantified thresholds.

The description is provided, firstly, in relation to current levels of achievement according to the most recently available international data. These levels indicate shortfalls in relation to the desired goals. It is provided, secondly, in relation to trends during the 1990s. These show the extent to which countries have been on track towards the achievement of the UNLDC III development goals, and establish the "business-as-usual" trajectory of change, which will generally have to be modified if the desired goals are to be achieved.

In seeking to describe the current situation in relation to the targets quantified in the Programme of Action, various technical and data problems arise. Data are not readily available for some of the targets. For others, it is necessary to specify the precise indicators which would desirably be used to monitor progress. Furthermore, for some of the quantifiable targets there is some degree of ambiguity in their specification, including their time horizon. A pragmatic principle which is used to deal with some of these problems is to build on the work to measure progress towards the achievement of International Development Goals and the Millennium Development Goals.[1] This makes sense, since the Programme of Action is based, *inter alia*, "on the international development targets…and on the values, principles and objectives of the Millennium Declaration" (para. 5), and its success will be judged, *inter alia*, by "its contribution to progress towards achieving international development targets" (para. 21e). However, even with the application of this principle, difficulties remain. The present chapter should thus be regarded as a preliminary description of the baseline from which, over time, the outcomes of the new Programme of Action can be assessed.

Finally, it must be stressed that the Programme of Action encompasses more objectives than the quantified time-bound targets discussed here. For example, important goals are to reverse the socio-economic marginalization of LDCs in the global economy and to promote good governance. However, these wider objectives have not been specified in the Programme of Action in a way that enables precise and time-bound monitoring to be carried out, and they are thus excluded from consideration here.[2]

B. Growth and investment targets

The Programme of Action for the LDCs for the Decade of 2001–2010 states that "LDCs, with the support of their development partners, will strive to attain a GDP growth rate of at least 7 per cent per annum and increase the ratio of investment to GDP to 25 per cent per annum" (para. 6).

Current levels of achievement fall far short of this goal. International data on growth rates for the 1990s are available for 43 LDCs. During 1997–1999, only five LDCs — Bhutan, Cape Verde, Equatorial Guinea, Mozambique and Rwanda — achieved the target growth rate. For the period 1990–1999, only Equatorial Guinea and Uganda exceeded the target. Over the same period, the growth rate was less than half the target rate in 23 out of 43 LDCs, and was declining in 7 out of 43.

International data on investment rates are available for the period 1990–1999 in 37 LDCs. Amongst these countries, nine achieved the 25 per cent target during 1997–1999, namely Bhutan, Burkina Faso, Cape Verde, Eritrea, Equatorial Guinea, the Lao People's Democratic Republic, Lesotho, Mozambique and Sao Tome and Principe. For the 1990s as whole, average annual investment rates exceeded the target in all these countries except Burkina Faso and Mozambique, plus Guinea-Bissau. For 12 out of the 37 LDCs the investment rate was on average under 15 per cent of GDP during the period 1990–1999.

The Programme of Action states that "LDCs, with the support of their development partners, will strive to attain a GDP growth rate of at least 7 per cent per annum and increase the ratio of investment to GDP to 25 per cent per annum". Current levels of achievement fall far short of this goal.

C. Poverty reduction goals

The Programme of Action states that "The overarching goal of the Programme of Action is to make substantial progress toward halving the proportion of people living in extreme poverty and suffering from hunger by 2015 and promote sustainable development of the LDCs" (para.6). However, identifying where the LDCs stand now, and how they have been performing in the past, in relation to the poverty reduction goal is very difficult.

The proportion of the population living in "extreme poverty" is usually defined as the proportion of the population living on less than a $1 a day. Descriptions of the distribution of world poverty, as well as projections of future trends, are currently based on the Chen/Ravallion database at the World Bank. However, there are only 20 LDCs in the data set. Only 12 LDCs have poverty estimates in more than one year, which is necessary to track change over time, and only 4 LDCs have poverty estimates in more than two years (table 13).

Another possible source of information on poverty is use of inequality measures in the Deininger/Squire dataset, and focus on the bottom 20 per cent or 40 per cent of the population. However, as in the case of the Chen/Ravallion dataset, there are few LDCs in this data set. It is possible to examine trends in income distribution over time in only five LDCs using this data set (table 13).

Statistical techniques can be used to make aggregate estimates of future levels of poverty in the LDC group as a whole on the basis of the limited available data. Work of this type indicates that whilst developing countries as a whole are on course to reduce the proportion of the people living on less than $1 a day by 2015, the LDCs are not (Naschold, 2001). According to the available Chen/Ravallion poverty estimates, the incidence of poverty in the LDCs was almost the same in 1998 as in 1990. But in other low-income countries it had fallen by 67 per cent below the 1990 level, and in middle-income countries by 51 per cent. These last two groups of countries are thus well on track to reduce the incidence of poverty by half by 2015 whilst LDCs are not. On the basis of past trends and regional growth forecasts, it has thus been concluded that "the prospects for reducing poverty in the LDCs are bleak. They are far from meeting the poverty Millennium Development Goals under any growth or inequality scenario" (p. 8).

In Part Two of this Report, the nature and dynamics of poverty are analysed on the basis of a new data set of poverty estimates for 39 LDCs, which has been constructed specially for this Report. These new poverty estimates give a much more detailed and differentiated view of levels of poverty in the LDCs, and also a better picture of long-term trends and more reliable forecasts. The new estimates do not give such a bleak picture of future prospects for the LDCs, as they indicate that there is a major opportunity for rapid poverty reduction based on sustained economic growth. They also imply that the methodology on which existing forecasts of the achievement of the poverty reduction targets in the Millenium Development Goals and International Development Targets, which are the same as those in Naschold (2001), may not be fully reliable.[3] However, the new poverty estimates also indicate that whilst developing countries as a whole are on track to achieve the goal of reducing the incidence of extreme poverty by half by 2015, the LDCs as a group are not.

"The overarching goal of the Programme of Action is to make substantial progress toward halving the proportion of people living in extreme poverty and suffering from hunger by 2015 and promote sustainable development of the LDCs".

Whilst developing countries as a whole are on track to achieve the goal of reducing the incidence of extreme poverty by half by 2015, the LDCs as a group are not.

TABLE 13. AVAILABILITY OF DATA ON POVERTY AND INCOME DISTRIBUTION IN LDCs

	Frequency of appearance in:	
	Chen/Ravallion data set[a]	*Deininger and Squire data set*[b]
Countries with 3 or more observations	Bangladesh (1984, 1985, 1988, 1992, 1996) Madagascar (1980, 1993, 1997) Mauritania (1988, 1993, 1995) Zambia (1991, 1993, 1996)	Bangladesh (1963, 1967, 1973, 1977, 1978, 1981, 1983, 1986, 1989, 1992) United Republic of Tanzania (1969, 1977, 1993) Zambia (1976, 1991, 1993, 1996)
Countries with 2 observations	Ethiopia (1981, 1995) Lesotho (1986, 1993) Mali (1989, 1994) Nepal (1985, 1995) Niger (1992, 1995) Senegal (1991, 1994) Uganda (1989, 1992) Yemen (1992, 1998)	Mauritania (1988, 1995) Uganda (1989, 1992)
Countries with 1 observations	Burkina Faso (1994) Central African Republic (1993) Gambia (1992) Lao People's Democratic Republic (1992) Mozambique (1996) Rwanda (1984) Sierra Leone (1989) United Republic of Tanzania (1991)	Burkina Faso (1995) Central African Rep. (1992) Djibouti (1996) Ethiopia (1996) Gambia (1992) Guinea (1995) Guinea-Bissau (1991) Lao People's Democratic Republic (1991) Lesotho (1987) Madagascar (1993) Malawi (1993) Mali (1994) Nepal (1984) Niger (1992) Rwanda (1983) Senegal (1991) Sierra Leone (1968) Sudan (1968)
Countries with no observations	Afghanistan Angola Benin Bhutan Burundi Cambodia Cape Verde Chad Comoros Democratic Republic of the Congo Djibouti Equatorial Guinea Eritrea Guinea Guinea-Bissau Haiti Kiribati Liberia Malawi Maldives Myanmar Samoa Sao Tome and Principe Solomon Islands Somalia Sudan Togo Tuvalu Vanuatu	Afghanistan Angola Benin Bhutan Burundi Cambodia Cape Verde Chad Comoros Democratic Republic of the Congo Equatorial Guinea Eritrea Haiti Kiribati Liberia Maldives Mozambique Myanmar Samoa Sao Tome and Principe Solomon Islands Somalia Togo Tuvalu Vanuatu Yemen

Source: UNCTAD secretariat estimates.

a   Chen and Ravallion (2000).
b   http://www.worldbank.org/research/growth/dddeisqu.htm

D. Human development targets[4]

The Programme of Action includes 13 human development targets that are sufficiently specified to be measured in quantitative terms. Box 1 suggests 20 indicators, with associated baseline years, which can be used to monitor these 13 goals. Tables 14, 15 and 16 show current levels of achievement in the LDCs, and progress in the 1990s, in relation to these 13 goals, using the 20 listed indicators. Following the approach to monitoring targets proposed by the UNDP Human Development Report Office, countries are classified, according to their progress in the 1990s, into five categories: "Achieved" (the country has already achieved the target, or 95 per cent of it); "On-track" (the country has attained 95 per cent or more of the rate of progress needed to achieve the target); "Lagging" (the country has achieved 75–94 per cent of the required rate of progress to achieve the target); "Far behind" (the country has achieved 0–74 per cent of the required rate of progress to achieve the target); and "Slipping back" (the country's level of achievement is at least five percentage points worse in 1999 than in 1990).

Three major observations may be made from these tables: Firstly, it is apparent that recent levels of human development in most LDCs are extremely low. Over one quarter of the children are undernourished in 33 out of 43 LDCs for which data are available. Nineteen out of 33 African LDCs have maternal mortality rates above 1 per 100 live births. The chance of a child dying under the age of 5 is more than 1 in 10 in 38 out of 49 LDCs. On average, under 50 per cent of the adult female population is literate in LDCs. For 22 LDCs for which data on net primary school enrolment are available from UNESCO statistics, less than half the children are in school in 10 of them.

Secondly, only a minority of the LDCs are on track to achieve any of the UNLDC III human development targets.

- For undernutrition, only 13 of the 34 LDCs with data are on track to achieve the goal of halving malnourishment by 2015. Over 64 per cent of the LDC population are living in countries which are regressing or are far behind in accomplishing the target of reducing hunger.

- For infant mortality and under-5 mortality, 10 countries representing 27 per cent of the LDC population are on track, 30 countries (65 per cent of the LDC population) are far behind and 3 countries are actually slipping back. Over 75 per cent of the LDC population are living in countries which are either regressing or are far behind in accomplishing the target of reducing the infant and under-5 child mortality rate.

- In terms of access to safe drinking water, 11 countries, representing one third of the LDC population, are on track, while 13 (a further third) are lagging or are far behind.

- For primary school enrolment, only one third of the countries are on track. Over 40 per cent of the LDC population are living in countries which are regressing or are far behind in accomplishing the target of increasing primary school enrolment.

- Notifications for tuberculosis and malaria are increasing, as well as for HIV/AIDS, particularly female infection rates.

The main area of progress is in terms of female literacy goals.

Thirdly, it is clear that, as with the poverty reduction target, data availability is a critical problem in monitoring human development targets in the LDCs. There is an urgent need for greater coverage, and more high-quality data, and particularly more timely data, on key issues of human development. For 11 of

Over one quarter of the children are undernourished in 33 out of 43 LDCs for which data are available. Nineteen out of 33 African LDCs have maternal mortality rates above 1 per 100 live births. The chance of a child dying under the age of 5 is more than 1 in 10 in 38 out of 49 LDCs. On average, under 50 per cent of the adult female population is literate in LDCs.

Box 1. Suggested indicators for monitoring of UNLDC III human development goals

1. Education

a. *Ensuring that by 2015 all children, particularly girls, children in difficult circumstances and those belonging to ethnic minorities, have access to a complete, free and compulsory primary education of good quality (para. 36a)*

Key indicators are: (i) net primary school enrolment ratio (the ratio of the number of children of official school age, as defined by the national education system, who are enrolled in school to the population of the corresponding official school age); and (ii) percentage share of the children enrolled in primary school who eventually reach Grade 5.

b. *Achieving a 50 per cent improvement in levels of adult literacy by 2015, especially for women, and equitable access to basic and continuing education for all adults (para. 36b)*

This is assumed to be a 50 per cent improvement over 1999 levels. Literacy is defined, according to UNESCO norms, as the ability of a person to understand, read, and write a short statement on their everyday life, and key indicators are: (i) total adult literacy; (ii) male adult literacy; and (iii) female adult literacy. The baseline year for the target is 1999.

c. *Eliminating gender disparities in primary and secondary education by 2005, and achieving gender equality in education by 2015, with a focus on ensuring girls' full and equal access to and achievement in basic education of good quality (para. 36c)*

Key indicators are: (i) ratio of girls to boys in primary school; (ii) ratio of girls to boys in secondary school; and (iii) ratio of young (15–24) literate females.

2. Population and health

a. *Making accessible, through the primary health care system, reproductive health to all individuals of appropriate ages as soon as possible and no later than the year 2015 (para. 34a)*

This is measured in the International Development Goals by: (i) the contraceptive prevalence rate, the percentage of women (usually married women aged 15–49) who are practising, or whose sexual partners are practising, any form of contraception; and (ii) the percentage of females aged 15–24 infected with HIV.

b. *Reducing the infant mortality rate to below 35 per 1,000 live births by 2015 (para. 38a)*

Although this diverges from the International Development Goal, which is to reduce the infant mortality rate by two thirds of the 1990 level by 2015, it can be measured in the same way as the number of infants dying before reaching 1 year of age per 1,000 births in a given year.

c. *Reducing the under-5 mortality rate to below 45 per 1,000 live births by 2015 (para. 38b)*

This similarly diverges from the International Development Goal, which is to reduce the under-5 mortality rate by two thirds of the 1990 level by 2015. But it can be measured in the same way as the probability that a newborn baby will die before reaching the age of 5, if subject to current age-specific mortality rates. The probability is expressed as a rate per 1,000.

d. *Reducing the maternal mortality rate by three quarters of the current rate by 2015 (para. 38c)*

The key indicator is the number of women who die during pregnancy and childbirth, per 1,000 live births.

e. *Increasing the percentage of women receiving maternal and prenatal care by 60 per cent (para. 38g)*

The key indicator is the percentage of deliveries attended by skilled health staff.

f. *Reducing HIV infection rates in persons 15–24 years of age by 2005 in all countries and by 25 per cent in the most affected countries (para. 38f)*

This is assumed to be a reduction from current levels and is measured as the total infection rate (men and women).

g. *Substantially reducing infection rates from malaria, tuberculosis and other killer diseases in LDCs by the end of the decade; reducing TB deaths and prevalence of the disease by 50 per cent by 2010; and reducing the burden of disease associated with malaria by 50 per cent by 2010 (para. 38i)*

This is assumed to be a reduction from 1990 levels as suggested by WHO, and can be measured in terms of (i) TB cases notified, and (ii) malaria cases notified.

3. Nutrition

a. *Reducing the number of undernourished people by half by 2015 (para. 38d)*

This is assumed to be a reduction from the 1996 level, as specified at the 1996 World Food Summit. The key indicator is the percentage of population undernourished as estimated by the FAO method.

b. *Halving malnutrition among pregnant women and among pre-school children in LDCs by 2015 (para. 38h)*

Box 1 (contd.)

There do not appear to be any specific data on pregnant women. A key indicator for the second part of this goal is the percentage of children under 5 whose weight for age is less than minus two standard deviations from the median for the international reference population, ages 0–59 months. The time frame for this, which is also used as an indicator for monitoring the International Development Goals, is assumed to be 1990 to 2015.

4. Sanitation

a. *Reducing by half by 2015 the proportion of people who are unable to reach or afford safe drinking water (para. 38e)*

The time frame for this goal, which is also an International Development Goal, is assumed to be from 1990 to 2015. The key indicator for this is the percentage of the population with reasonable access to an adequate amount of water from an improved source, such as household connection, public standpipe, borehole, protected well or spring, and rainwater collection. Reasonable access is defined as the availability of at least 20 litres per person per day from a source within one kilometre of the dwelling (see WHO, UNICEF and WSSCC, 2000).

the 20 indicators, progress in the 1990s cannot be monitored in over 25 per cent of the LDCs. Data on malaria and tuberculosis prevalence are based on reported cases, and are thus not ideal. Some question the accuracy of the data on undernutrition (Svedberg, 1999).

E. Transport and communications infrastructure development targets

The Programme of Action (para. 43) includes five quantifiable goals regarding improvement of the physical infrastructure in the area of transport and communications. These are:

(a) Increasing road networks and connections in LDCs to the current level of other developing countries and urban road capacities, including sewerage and other related facilities, by 2010;

(b) Modernizing and expanding railway connections and facilities, increasing their capacities to the level of those in other developing countries by the end of the decade;

(c) Increasing LDCs' communication networks, including telecommunication and postal services, and improving access of the poor to such services in urban and rural areas to reach the current levels in other developing countries;

(d) Increasing computer literacy among students in higher institutions and universities by 50 per cent and in junior and high schools by 25 per cent by 2015;

(e) Increasing average telephone density to 5 main lines per 100 inhabitants and Internet connections to ten users per 100 inhabitants by the year 2010.

For 11 of the 20 human development indicators, progress in the 1990s cannot be monitored in over 25 per cent of the LDCs.

For the last of these goals, data are available for 36 LDCs and estimation is relatively straightforward. The data suggest that the current situation is far from satisfactory. Only 10 have more than one telephone mainline per 100 inhabitants. Cape Verde and Maldives have achieved the target, and the only other LDC which is on track is Kiribati. Information is readily available on road and railway connections, but it is necessary to develop ways to standardize this information so as to make any comparisons meaningful. For example, it would be unreasonable to expect sparsely populated countries to have the same road density as densely populated countries. Moreover, for monitoring purposes, it is necessary to clarify whether the precise target for these goals is to aim by 2010 to bring LDCs up to the level of other developing countries in 2001 or to their level in 2010. Data on Internet users are not widely available and information on computer literacy is similarly lacking.

TABLE 14. UNLDC III HUMAN DEVELOPMENT GOALS: WHERE DO LDCS STAND?

	Education								Nutrition	
	Universal enrolment and completion of primary education (of school age population)		Adult literacy rate (% of total population)			Gender inequality in education (female rate as % of male rate)				
	Net primary enrolment rate	Children reaching Grade 5	Total	Female	Male	Primary enrolment (by 2005)	Secondary enrolment (by 2005)	Youth literacy	Under-nourished people	Mal-nourished children
	1994–1998	1995–1997	1999	1999	1999	1995–1997	1995–1997	1999	1996–1998	1995
Afghanistan	..	..	36	20	50	50	38	57	70	48
Angola	34	..	..	..	..	92[a]	..	..	43	42
Bangladesh	..	..	41	29	52	86[a]	52[a]	65	38	56
Benin	64	55[a]	39	24	55	58	42	48	14	29
Bhutan	..	..	..	..	..	..	..	..	..	38[b]
Burkina Faso	33	70[a]	23	13	33	65	56[a]	50	32	36
Burundi	29	..	47	39	56	84	57[a]	93	68	37[b]
Cambodia	100	49	39	21	59	85	55	55	33	52
Cape Verde	..	..	74	65	85	98	104	93	..	14[b]
Central African Republic	..	..	45	33	59	64[a]	41[a]	76	41	27
Chad	52	59	41	32	50	51	27	80	38	39
Comoros	..	..	59	52	66	72[a]	79	84	..	26
Dem. Rep. of the Congo	61	55[a]	60	49	72	74[a]	..	83	61	34
Djibouti	32	79	63	53	75	75	71	89	..	18
Equatorial Guinea	..	..	82	73	92	..	..	97	..	..
Eritrea	30	70	53	39	67	81	71	76	65	44
Ethiopia	35	51	37	32	43	55	71	96	49	47
Gambia	65	..	36	29	43	77	63	74	16	26
Guinea	42	59[a]	..	..	..	60	35	..	29	..
Guinea-Bissau	..	..	38	18	58	..	..	40	..	23[b]
Haiti	56	..	49	47	51	94[a]	95[a]	100	62	28
Kiribati	..	95	..	..	..	..	..	..	..	13[b]
Lao People's Dem. Rep.	76	55	47	32	63	82	68	69	29	40[b]
Lesotho	66	71[a]	83	93	72	112	144	120	29	16
Liberia	..	..	53	37	69	..	..	64	46	..
Madagascar	61	22[a]	66	59	73	99	100	91	40	40
Malawi	..	64[a]	59	45	74	91	57	74	32	30
Maldives	..	..	96	96	96	98	106	101	..	43
Mali	31	84	40	33	47	69	47	82	32	40
Mauritania	61	64	42	31	52	89	52	67	13	23
Mozambique	40	33[a]	43	28	59	71	56	60	58	26
Myanmar	..	..	84	80	89	97[a]	100[a]	99	7	39
Nepal	..	..	40	23	58	74	65	54	28	47
Niger	25	73	15	8	23	64	56	42	46	50
Rwanda	..	60[a]	66	59	73	99[a]	78[a]	95	39	27
Samoa	96	85	80	79	81	99	112	101	..	..
Sao Tome and Principe	..	..	..	..	..	..	..	..	..	16
Senegal	60	87	36	27	46	83	60	69	23	22
Sierra Leone	..	..	..	..	..	68[a]	59[a]	..	43	29[b]
Solomon Islands	..	85[a]	..	..	..	86[a]	65[a]	..	..	21[b]
Somalia	..	..	..	..	..	..	..	..	75	26
Sudan	..	94[a]	57	45	69	85	87	85	18	34[b]
Togo	83	..	56	40	74	71	35	66	18	25
Tuvalu	..	..	..	..	..	..	..	..	..	..
Uganda	..	..	66	56	77	84	60	84	30	26
United Rep. of Tanzania	48	81	75	66	84	99	83	94	41	27
Vanuatu	..	..	..	..	..	96[a]	74[a]	..	..	20[b]
Yemen	..	..	45	24	67	40	26	53	35	46
Zambia	75	..	77	70	85	95	..	94	45	24

Table 14 (contd.)

	Population and health									Sanitation
	Child mortality		Maternal health		Reproductive health		Disease prevalence			
	Infant mortality rate (POA) (per 1,000 live births)	Under-5 mortality rate (POA) (per 1,000 live births)	Maternal mortality rate (per 100,000 live births)	Births attended by skilled health staff (%)	Contraceptive prevalence (%)	Female HIV/AIDS-prevalence in age group 15-24 (by 2015) (%)	HIV/AIDS prevalence in age group 15-24 by 2005 (%)	Malaria prevalence (per 100,000 people)	Tuberculosis prevalence (per 100,000 people)	Access to safe water (%)
	1999	1999	1995	1995–1999	1992–2000	1999[c]	1999[c]	1997	1998	2000
Afghanistan	165	257	819	9[a]	..	..	..	1 533[h]	14	13
Angola	172	295	1 308	17[d]	..	3	2	1 381[i]	102	38
Bangladesh	58	89	596	14[a]	54	1	0	53	58	97
Benin	99	156	884	60[e]	..	2	2	11 561	41	63
Bhutan	80	107	502	16[a]	..	..	..	470	64	62
Burkina Faso	106	199	1 379	27[f]	12	6	4	4 878[i]	18	53[e]
Burundi	106	176	1 881	20[e]	..	12	9	15 344[i]	101	65[e]
Cambodia	86	122	590	31[a]	..	4	3	950	158	30
Cape Verde	54	73	188	..	..	..	..	5	50	74
Central African Rep.	113	172	1 205	46[f]	..	14	11	2 513[i]	140	60
Chad	118	198	1 497	11[a]	..	3	2	4787	38	27
Comoros	64	86	573	52[f]	..	..	..	2 472[h]	22[h]	96
Dem. Rep. of the Congo	128	207	939	..	..	5	4	29[e]	120	45
Djibouti	104	149	520	..	..	14	11	747	597	100
Equatorial Guinea	105	160	1 404	..	..	1	0	3 136[i]	97	43
Eritrea	66	105	1 131	21	..	..	..	2 545[i]	218	46
Ethiopia	118	176	1 841	10[f]	8	12	10	666[j]	116	24
Gambia	61	75	1 071	44[a]	..	2	2	27 320	114[l]	62
Guinea	115	181	1 224	35[d]	6	1	1	10 400	65	48
Guinea-Bissau	128	200	914	..	..	2	2	15 494[k]	156[h]	49
Haiti	83	129	1 122	20[f]	28	3	4	..	124[d]	46
Kiribati	53	72	..	..	..	..	..	..	333	47
Lao People's Dem. Rep.	93	111	653	..	..	0	0	1 101	42	90
Lesotho	93	134	529	40[f]	..	26	19	..	272[l]	91
Liberia	157	235	1 016	..	..	2	1	..	66	..
Madagascar	95	156	583	47[d]	19	0	0	2 882[e]	97	47
Malawi	132	211	576	50[a]	22	15	11	47 855[j]	220	57
Maldives	60	83	385	55[a]	..	..	..	4	65	100
Mali	143	235	630	24	7	2	2	3 681	39	65
Mauritania	120	183	874	58[g]	..	1	0	9 428[i]	154[l]	37
Mozambique	127	203	975	44	..	15	11	..	104	60
Myanmar	79	112	165	57[a]	33	2	1	246	33	68
Nepal	75	104	826	10[e]	29	0	0	31	106	81
Niger	162	275	923	18[d]	8	1	1	10 037	34	59
Rwanda	110	180	2 318	22[f]	..	11	8	21 103	93	41
Samoa	21	26	15	52[a]	..	..	..	..	13	99
Sao Tome and Principe	59	76	..	..	..	..	..	62 685[e]	32[j]	..
Senegal	68	118	1 198	47[f]	13	2	1	7 577[i]	94	78
Sierra Leone	182	316	2 065	..	..	3	2	..	72	28
Solomon Islands	22	26	59	85[e]	..	..	..	..	71	71
Somalia	125	211	1 582	..	..	..	..	42[k]	44	..
Sudan	67	109	1 452	69	8	..	..	5 018	80	75
Togo	80	143	983	51[g]	24	6	4	8 765[j]	28	54
Tuvalu	40	56	..	..	..	..	..	..	180	100
Uganda	83	131	1 056	38[f]	15	8	6	3 285[e]	142	50
United Rep. of Tanzania	90	141	1 059	35[f]	24	8	6	3 468	160	54
Vanuatu	37	46	32	70[g]	..	..	..	..	98	88
Yemen	86	119	850	22[d]	21	..	..	..	73	69
Zambia	112	202	867	47[a]	25	18	13	34 000[h]	482[h]	64

Sources: UNCTAD secretariat estimates based on UNESCO (2000); FAO (2000); Kenneth, Abou Zahr, Wardlaw (2001); UNICEF (2001); WHO/ UNICEF/ WSSCC (2001); World Bank, World Development Indicators, CD-ROM; WHO global database on coverage of maternal care, Department of Productive Health and Research, January 2001; and UNAIDS (www.unaids.org/epidemic_update/report/ Final_Table_Eng_Xcel.xls).

Notes: For definition of indicators see box 1. The target fulfilment year for the reduction of HIV/AIDS in young women differs from the target fulfillment year of HIV/AIDS reduction in young persons overall, because the target for young women is part of the reproductive health goal which is set for 2015, whereas the overall target for young persons is a specific health goal that is set for 2005. Values correspond with headline years and periods, unless otherwise specified. If the value does not correspond with the specified year or period, the corresponding year or period is specified with a lower-case letter, where a 1990; b data refers to a year or period other than that specified, differs from the standard definition or refers to only part of the country; c late 1999; d 1992; e 1991; f 1989; g 1988; h 1996; i 1995; j 1994; k 1993; l 1997.

TABLE 15. UNLDC III HUMAN DEVELOPMENT GOALS: PROGRESS IN THE 1990S

	Education								Nutrition	
	Universal enrolment and completion of primary education (of school age population)		Adult literacy rate (of total population)			Gender inequality in education (female rate as % of male rate)				
	Net primary enrolment rate	Children reaching Grade 5	Total	Female	Male	Primary enrolment (by 2005)	Secondary enrolment (by 2005)	Youth literacy	Under-nourished people	Mal-nourished children
Baseline years	1990	1990	1999	1999	1999	n.a.	n.a.	n.a	1996	1990
Afghanistan	..	..	Lagging	On track	Lagging	Far behind	..	Lagging	Slipping back	..
Angola	..	..	..	..	..	..	..	..	On track	..
Bangladesh	..	..	Far behind	Lagging	Far behind	..	..	Far behind	Far behind	..
Benin	On track	..	On track	On track	On track	Far behind	Far behind	Far behind	On track	..
Bhutan	..	..	..	..	..	..	..	..	..	..
Burkina Faso	Far behind	..	On track	On track	Lagging	Far behind	..	Far behind	Far behind	..
Burundi	Slipping back	..	Lagging	On track	Far behind	Far behind	..	On track	Slipping back	..
Cambodia	..	..	Lagging	On track	Far behind	..	Far behind	Far behind	On track	..
Cape Verde	..	..	Lagging	Far behind	On track	..	..	On track	..	..
Central African Republic	..	..	On track	On track	Lagging	..	..	On track	On track	..
Chad	Far behind	Far behind	On track	On track	On track	Far behind	Far behind	On track	On track	..
Comoros	..	..	Far behind	Far behind	Far behind	..	On track	Far behind	..	..
Dem. Rep. of the Congo	Lagging	..	Lagging	On track	Lagging	..	..	On track	Slipping back	..
Djibouti	Far behind	Slipping back	Far behind	Lagging	Far behind	Far behind	Far behind	On track	..	..
Equatorial Guinea	..	..	Lagging	Lagging	On track	..	..	Achieved	..	..
Eritrea	Far behind	..	Far behind	On track	Far behind	..	..	On track	..	..
Ethiopia	Far behind	..	Lagging	On track	Far behind	Slipping back	Slipping back	Achieved	..	..
Gambia	On track	..	On track	On track	On track	Lagging	Lagging	Far behind	On track	..
Guinea	Far behind	..	..	..	..	Far behind	Far behind	..	On track	..
Guinea-Bissau	..	..	Lagging	On track	Lagging	..	..	Far behind	..	..
Haiti	On track	..	Lagging	Lagging	Far behind	..	..	Achieved	Far behind	..
Kiribati	..	On track	..	..	..	..	..	..	..	..
Lao People's Dem. Rep.	On track	..	Lagging	On track	Far behind	Far behind	Far behind	On track	Far behind	..
Lesotho	Slipping back	..	Far behind	On track	Far behind	Achieved	Achieved	Achieved	Far behind	..
Liberia	..	..	Lagging	On track	Lagging	..	..	Far behind	Far behind	..
Madagascar	Slipping back	..	Far behind	Far behind	Far behind	Achieved	Achieved	On track	Slipping back	..
Malawi	..	..	Far behind	Lagging	Far behind	On track	Far behind	Far behind	On track	..
Maldives	..	..	Achieved	Achieved	Achieved	..	..	Achieved	..	..
Mali	Far behind	On track	On track	On track	On track	Far behind	Slipping back	On track	Slipping back	..
Mauritania	On track	Slipping back	Far behind	Far behind	Far behind	On track	Far behind	Far behind	On track	..
Mozambique	Slipping back	..	Lagging	On track	Far behind	Far behind	Far behind	Far behind	On track	..
Myanmar	..	..	Far behind	Far behind	Far behind	..	..	Achieved	On track	..
Nepal	..	..	Lagging	On track	Far behind	Lagging	Lagging	Far behind	Slipping back	..
Niger	Far behind	On track	Lagging	On track	Lagging	Far behind	Far behind	Far behind	Far behind	..
Rwanda	..	..	Lagging	Lagging	Far behind	..	..	On track	Far behind	..
Samoa	..	..	Far behind	Far behind	Far behind	Achieved	Achieved	Achieved	..	..
Sao Tome and Principe	..	..	..	..	..	..	..	..	..	..
Senegal	On track	Far behind	Lagging	On track	Far behind	Lagging	Far behind	Far behind	Far behind	..
Sierra Leone	..	..	..	..	..	..	..	..	Far behind	..
Solomon Islands	..	..	..	..	..	..	..	..	..	..
Somalia	..	..	..	..	..	..	..	..	Slipping back	..
Sudan	..	..	Lagging	On track	Far behind	On track	On track	On track	On track	..
Togo	On track	..	Far behind	On track	Far behind	Far behind	Far behind	Far behind	On track	..
Tuvalu	..	..	..	..	..	..	..	..	..	..
Uganda	..	..	Far behind	Lagging	Far behind	Far behind	Far behind	Lagging	Slipping back	..
United Rep. of Tanzania	Far behind	Far behind	Lagging	Lagging	Lagging	Achieved	On track	On track	Slipping back	..
Vanuatu	..	..	..	..	..	..	..	..	..	..
Yemen	..	..	On track	On track	Far behind	..	..	Lagging	Far behind	..
Zambia	Slipping back	..	Lagging	Lagging	Lagging	..	..	On track	Slipping back	..

Table 15 (contd.)

	Population and health									Sanitation
	Child mortality		Maternal health		Reproductive health		Disease prevalence			
	Infant mortality rate (POA) (per 1,000 live births)	Under-5 mortality rate (POA) (per 1,000 live births)	Maternal mortality rate (per 100,000 live births)	Births attended by skilled health staff (%)	Contraceptive prevalence (%)	Female HIV/AIDS-prevalence in age group 15–24 (by 2015) (%)	HIV/AIDS prevalence in age group 15–24 by 2005 (%)	Malaria prevalence (per 100,000 people)	Tuberculosis prevalence (per 100,000 people)	Access to safe water (%)
Baseline years	1990	1990	1990	1990	n.a.	1990	1990	1990	1990	1990
Afghanistan	Far behind	Far behind	..	..			..	On track	Achieved	..
Angola	Far behind	Far behind	..	..			..	On track	Far behind	..
Bangladesh	On track	On track	..	Far behind	Lagging		..	Slipping back	Slipping back	Achieved
Benin	Far behind	Far behind	..	On track			..	Slipping back	Far behind	..
Bhutan	On track	On track	..	..			..	Lagging	Far behind	..
Burkina Faso	Far behind	Far behind	..	Far behind	Far behind		..	Lagging	Far behind	..
Burundi	Far behind	Far behind	..	..			..	Slipping back	Slipping back	..
Cambodia	Far behind	Far behind	..	Slipping back			..	On track	Slipping back	..
Cape Verde	Far behind	Far behind	..	..			..	Achieved	On track	..
Central African Republic	Far behind	Far behind	..	Slipping back			..	Achieved	Slipping back	Far behind
Chad	Far behind	Far behind	..	Far behind			..	Slipping back	Lagging	..
Comoros	On track	On track	..	On track			..	..	On track	Achieved
Dem. Rep. of the Congo	Far behind	Far behind	..	..			..	..	Slipping back	..
Djibouti	Far behind	Far behind	..	..			..	Slipping back	Slipping back	Achieved
Equatorial Guinea	Far behind	Lagging	..	..			..	Achieved	Slipping back	..
Eritrea	On track	On track	..	..			..	..	Slipping back	..
Ethiopia	Far behind	Far behind	..	..	Far behind		..	Slipping back	On track	Far behind
Gambia	On track	On track	..	..			..	Slipping back	..	..
Guinea	Lagging	Lagging	..	Far behind	Far behind		..	Slipping back	Slipping back	Far behind
Guinea-Bissau	Far behind	Far behind	..	..			..	Slipping back	Slipping back	..
Haiti	Lagging	Far behind	..	Slipping back	Far behind		..	..	Lagging	Far behind
Kiribati	On track	On track	..	..			..	..	Slipping back	..
Lao People's Dem. Rep.	Lagging	On track	..	..			..	Slipping back	Far behind	..
Lesotho	Far behind	Far behind	..	..			..	..	Slipping back	..
Liberia	Far behind	Far behind	..	..			..	..	On track	..
Madagascar	Far behind	Far behind	..	Slipping back	Far behind		..	..	Slipping back	Far behind
Malawi	Far behind	Far behind	..	..	Far behind		..	Slipping back	Slipping back	Lagging
Maldives	On track	On track	..	..			..	Achieved	Far behind	Achieved
Mali	Far behind	Far behind	..	..	Far behind		..	Slipping back	Slipping back	On track
Mauritania	Far behind	Far behind	..	On track			..	Slipping back	On track	Far behind
Mozambique	Far behind	Far behind	..	..			..	..	Far behind	..
Myanmar	Far behind	Far behind	..	On track	Lagging		..	On track	Far behind	Far behind
Nepal	On track	On track	..	Far behind	Far behind		..	Achieved	Slipping back	On track
Niger	Far behind	Far behind	..	Far behind	Far behind		..	Slipping back	Achieved	Far behind
Rwanda	Far behind	Far behind	..	..			..	Slipping back	Far behind	..
Samoa	Achieved	Achieved	..	..			..	..	Achieved	Achieved
Sao Tome and Principe	Lagging	Lagging	..	..			..	..	Slipping back	..
Senegal	On track	Lagging	..	Far behind	Far behind		..	Slipping back	Slipping back	On track
Sierra Leone	Far behind	Far behind	..	..			..	..	Slipping back	..
Solomon Islands	Achieved	Achieved	..	..			..	..	On track	..
Somalia	Far behind	Far behind	..	..			..	Achieved	Slipping back	..
Sudan	Far behind	Far behind	..	..	Far behind		..	Slipping back	Slipping back	On track
Togo	Far behind	Far behind	..	Lagging	Far behind		..	Achieved	On track	Far behind
Tuvalu	Far behind	Far behind	..	..			..	..	On track	Achieved
Uganda	Far behind	Lagging	..	Far behind	Far behind		..	..	Far behind	Far behind
United Rep. of Tanzania	Far behind	Far behind	..	Slipping back	Far behind		..	Achieved	Slipping back	Far behind
Vanuatu	On track	On track	..	..			..	..	Slipping back	..
Yemen	Far behind	Far behind	..	Far behind	Far behind		..	..	..	Far behind
Zambia	Far behind	Far behind	..	Far behind	Far behind		..	Slipping back	Slipping back	On track

Source: As for table 14.

Note: See text for definition of "achieved", "on track", "lagging", "far behind" and "slipping back".

TABLE 16. UNLDC III HUMAN DEVELOPMENT GOALS: SUMMARY OF PROGRESS IN THE 1990S

		Number of LDCs according to progress categories[a]					
		Achieved	On track	Lagging	Far behind	Slipping back	No data
Education	Net primary enrolment	0	7	1	9	5	27
		(0)	(6)	(8)	(23)	(8)	(56)
	Children reaching Grade 5	0	3	0	3	2	41
		(0)	(3)	(0)	(8)	(0)	(88)
	Adult literacy rate — total	1	7	19	12	0	10
		(0)	(9)	(48)	(37)	(0)	(6)
	Adult literacy rate — female	1	23	9	6	0	10
		0)	(49)	(35)	(10)	(0)	(6)
	Adult literacy rate — male	1	6	9	23	0	10
		(0)	(4)	(22)	(68)	(0)	(6)
	Gender equality in primary enrolment (by 2005)	4	3	3	13	1	25
		(8)	(7)	(5)	(20)	(9)	(50)
	Gender equality in secondary enrolment (by 2005)	3	3	2	13	2	26
		(3)	(10)	(4)	(18)	(11)	(54)
	Gender equality in youth literacy	7	14	3	15	0	10
		(18)	(29)	(9)	(38)	(0)	(6)
Nutrition	Undernourished people	0	13	0	11	10	15
		(0)	(25)	(0)	(33)	(31)	(11)
	Malnourished children	0	0	0	0	0	49
		(0)	(0)	(0)	(0)	(0)	(100)
Population and health	Infant mortality rate (POA)	2	10	4	33	3	0
		(0)	(27)	(3)	(70)	(5)	(0)
	Under-5 mortality rate (POA)	2	10	5	32	4	0
		(0)	(26)	(6)	(68)	(7)	(0)
	Maternal mortality rate	0	0	0	0	0	49
		(0)	(0)	(0)	(0)	(0)	(100)
	Births attended by skilled health staff	0	4	1	10	5	29
		(0)	(9)	(1)	(39)	(11)	(40)
	Contraceptive prevalence	0	0	2	16	0	31
		(0)	(0)	(28)	(44)	(0)	(28)
	Female HIV/AIDS prevalence in age group 15–24 (by 2015)	0	0	0	0	0	49
		(0)	(0)	(0)	(0)	(0)	(100)
	HIV/AIDS prevalence in age group 15–24 (by 2005)	0	0	0	0	0	49
		(0)	(0)	(0)	(0)	(0)	(100)
	Malaria prevalence (per 100,000 people)	8	4	2	0	18	17
		(11)	(14)	(2)	(0)	(50)	(22)
	Tuberculosis prevalence (per 100,000 people)	3	8	2	10	24	2
		(5)	(11)	(2)	(17)	(62)	(3)
Sanitation	Access to safe water	6	5	1	12	0	25
		(21)	(13)	(2)	(36)	(0)	(29)

Source: As for table 14.

a For definition of categories see text. Numbers in brackets represent percentage of LDC population in category.

F. ODA targets for donor countries

Under commitment 7 of the Programme of Action, "Mobilizing financial resources", it is stated that "Donor countries will implement the following actions that they committed to at the second United Nations Conference on the Least Developed Countries as soon as possible:

(a) Donor countries providing more than 0.20 per cent of their GNP as ODA to LDCs: continue to do so and increase their efforts;

(b) Other donor countries which have met the 0.15 target: undertake to reach 0.20 per cent expeditiously;

(c) All other donor countries which have committed themselves to the 0.15 per cent target: reaffirm their commitment and undertake either to achieve the target within the next five years or to make their best efforts to accelerate their endeavours to reach the target;

(d) During the period of the Programme of Action, the other donor countries: exercise individual best efforts to increase their ODA to LDCs with the effect that collectively their assistance to LDCs will significantly increase" (para. 83).

One feature of the way in which this target was originally formulated at UNLDC II was that it allows donor countries some flexibility in deciding what they are committed to. However, a problem in ascertaining whether this goal is being met is that it is unclear which countries have committed to what options. For the future monitoring of aid targets, it is important that donor countries clarify where precisely they stand in relation to this goal and also specify, if possible, the time frame for the realization of this goal.

Chart 2 shows net ODA flows to LDCs as a percentage of individual donors' GNI in 1999 and 2000.[5] The situation in 2000 was such that only five donor countries surpassed the target of making net ODA disbursements more than 0.2 per cent of their GNI. These were: Denmark (0.34 per cent), Norway (0.27 per cent), Luxembourg (0.25 per cent), Sweden (0.24 per cent) and the Netherlands (0.21 per cent). All the other countries were below the 0.15 per cent of GNI target. In absolute terms, Japan and USA remained the largest donors to the LDCs in 2000, with net ODA flows, including imputed flows through multilateral channels, equivalent to $2.1 billion and $2.0 billion respectively.

In 2000, only five donor countries surpassed the target of making net ODA disbursements more than 0.2 per cent of their GNP. All the other countries were below the 0.15 per cent of GNP target.

G. Progress towards graduation from LDC status

The Programme of Action for the Least Developed Countries for the Decade 2001–2010 states that its success will be judged, *inter alia*, by its contribution to "their graduation from the list of LDCs" (para. 21e). With this in view, assessment of progress towards graduation may provide a useful further way of assessing the results of the Programme of Action.

The Committee for Development Policy (CDP) of the United Nations Economic and Social Council (ECOSOC) is responsible for recommendations about inclusion in and graduation from the list of least developed countries, as well as for establishing appropriate criteria and thresholds. Statistics, produced every three years, provide the basis for a somewhat complex judgement by the CDP on the extent to which particular LDCs have made sufficient and sustainable progress in overcoming structural weaknesses and handicaps such that they should graduate from the list. Tracking progress towards graduation as an aspect of monitoring the Programme of Action should not prejudice these judgements, which are the proper preserve of the CDP, nor judgements about criteria and thresholds, which are also its concern.

In absolute terms, Japan and USA remained the largest donors to the LDCs in 2000.

Box 2 sets out the criteria and thresholds for possible graduation from the list of LDCs as used in the 1990s, as well as the revised methodology used since the year 2000. At the present time, the criteria for inclusion within and graduation from the list of LDCs are the following: the income level, as measured by GDP per capita; the level of human resource development, as measured by the Augmented Physical Quality of Life Index (APQLI); and the level of economic

CHART 2. NET ODA DISBURSEMENTS TO LDCs FROM DAC MEMBER COUNTRIES,[a] 1999 AND 2000
(As percentage of donor's GNI)

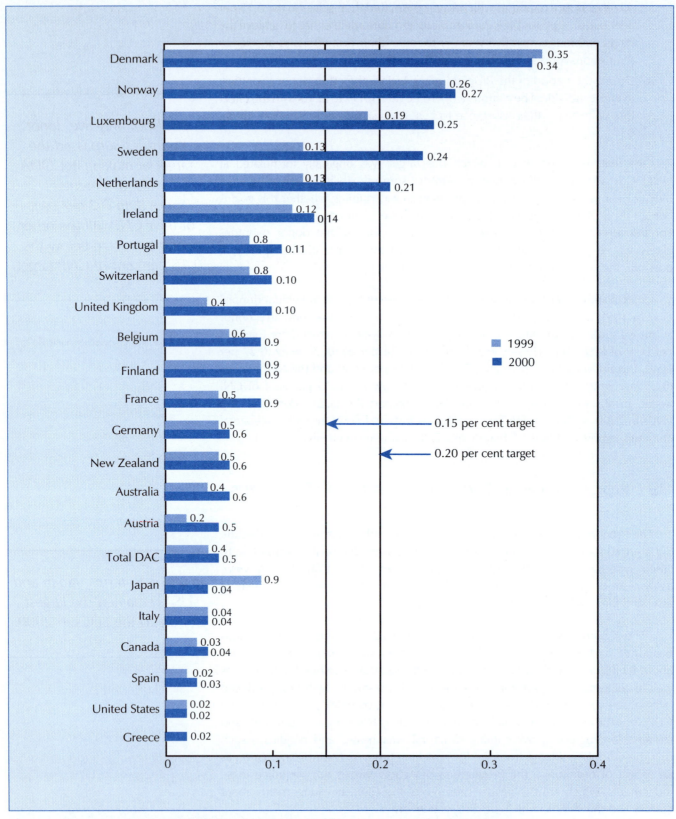

Source: UNCTAD secretariat estimates based on OECD Development Co-operation 2001 Report.

a   Including imputed multilateral flows, i.e. making allowance for contributions through multilateral organizations, calculated
       using the geographical distribution of multilateral disbursements for the year of reference.

BOX 2. CRITERIA AND INDICATORS FOR GRADUATION FROM THE LIST OF THE LDCs

Criteria used in determining the list of LDCs during the 1990s	Revised criteria for determining the list of LDCs since 2000
1. Per capita GDP:	**1. Per capita GDP:**
Three-year average, converted at each year's official exchange rate. Threshold for graduation: above $700 (1991), above $800 (1994), above $900 (1997)	Three-year average, converted at each year's official exchange rate. Threshold for graduation: above $1,035
2. Augmented Physical Quality of Life Index (APQLI):	**2. Augmented Physical Quality of Life Index (APQLI):**
calculated as a simple average of four component indices based on the following indicators:	calculated as a simple average of four component indices based on the following indicators:
a. *Health: life expectancy at birth*	a. *Health: child mortality rate (under age 5)*
b. *Nutrition: per capita daily calorie intake as a percentage of daily requirement*	b. *Nutrition: per capita daily calorie intake as a percentage of daily requirement*
c. *Education: combined primary and secondary school enrolment ratio*	c. *Education: combined primary and secondary school enrolment ratio*
d. *Education: adult literacy rate*	d. *Education: adult literacy rate*
Threshold for graduation: greater than 52 (1991, 1994 and 1997)	Threshold for graduation: greater than 68
3. Economic Diversification Index (EDI):	**3. Economic Vulnerability Index (EVI):**
Calculated as a simple average of four component indices based on the following indicators:	Calculated as a simple average of five component indices based on the following indicators:
a. *Share of manufacturing in GDP*	a. *Share of manufacturing and non-government services in GDP*
b. *Share of industry in the labour force*	b. *UNCTAD's merchandise export concentration index*
c. *Annual per capita commercial energy consumption*	c. *An indicator of instability of agricultural production*
d. *UNCTAD's merchandise export concentration index*	d. *An indicator of instability of exports of goods and services*
	e. *Population size (in logarithm)*
Threshold for graduation: greater than 25 (1991), greater than 29 (1994 and 1997)	Threshold for graduation: less than 31
	4. Supplementary (qualitative) considerations:
	If any of the three criteria (per capita income, quality of life, vulnerability) is near its graduation threshold, a vulnerability profile of the country is called for to enable the Committee for Development Policy members to make a sound judgement on graduation out of the list of LDCs.

vulnerability, as measured by the Economic Vulnerability Index (EVI). The current thresholds for graduation from the list of LDCs are the following: per capita GDP greater than $1,035; an APQLI greater than 68; and an EVI lower than 31. The CDP applies the decision rule that it is necessary for at least two of the three graduation criteria to be met for the relevant country to be found eligible for graduation, and that it must meet at least two criteria in two consecutive reviews.[6]

Charts 3, 4 and 5 show where the LDCs stood in the second half of the 1990s in terms of their position relative to these graduation thresholds, the estimates being based on the CDP's review of the list for GDP per capita, APQLI and EVI conducted in 2000 (UNCDP, 2000). It is apparent from the chart that only ten countries met either one or two of the thresholds for graduation. For 40 out of the 49 LDCs, their GDP per capita performance was less than two thirds of the threshold for graduation, while for 33 the APQLI was less than two thirds of the benchmark.

Progress in the 1990s towards eligibility for graduation is examined on a case-by-case basis in UNCTAD (2002). Botswana is the only country that has so far graduated from the LDC category. There have also been three cases of full eligibility for graduation from least developed country status (i.e. eligibility pronounced after relevant criteria were met in two consecutive reviews): Cape Verde and Vanuatu in 1997, and Maldives in 2000. But in practice none of these have yet graduated.[7] The countries that currently have the greatest potential for graduation in the coming decade are those three, plus Samoa. However, they face major structural handicaps as a result of their geographical situation and also, in the case of Maldives, specific vulnerabilities as regards the prospect of rising sea-levels. Generally, they remain highly vulnerable, although they have made progress under the income and human resource criteria for graduation, largely through tourism development.

If the trends of the 1990s persist, the graduation prospects of most LDCs during the 2001–2010 decade are limited.[8] The reality may, of course, turn out to be better or worse. Indeed, a prime purpose of the Programme of Action for the LDCs during 2001–2010 is to ensure that this dismal scenario does not occur. It is towards creating this better future that the concrete efforts by LDCs and their development partners in implementing the new Programme of Action should be directed.

H. Conclusion

The data which are internationally available for monitoring the progress towards the quantified and time-bound targets in the Programme of Action for the Least Developed Countries for the Decade 2001–2010 are woefully inadequate in terms of their coverage of LDCs, their quality and their timeliness. It is essential to improve national statistical systems in the LDCs, not simply for the UNLDC III development targets, but also for national accounts and trade statistics.

The data problem is particularly acute in relation to the overarching goal of the Programme of Action, which is to make substantial progress towards halving by 2015 the proportion of people living in extreme poverty. It is currently impossible to monitor achievement of this target in most LDCs on the basis of internationally comparable data. This situation must be speedily rectified if results-oriented progress monitoring is to be a meaningful activity.

The data which are internationally available for monitoring the progress towards the quantified and time-bound targets in the Programme of Action are woefully inadequate in terms of their coverage of LDCs, their quality and their timeliness.

This situation must be speedily rectified if results-oriented progress monitoring is to be a meaningful activity.

CHART 3. AVERAGE GDP PER CAPITA IN LDCs, 1995–1997: RATIO TO GRADUATION THRESHOLD

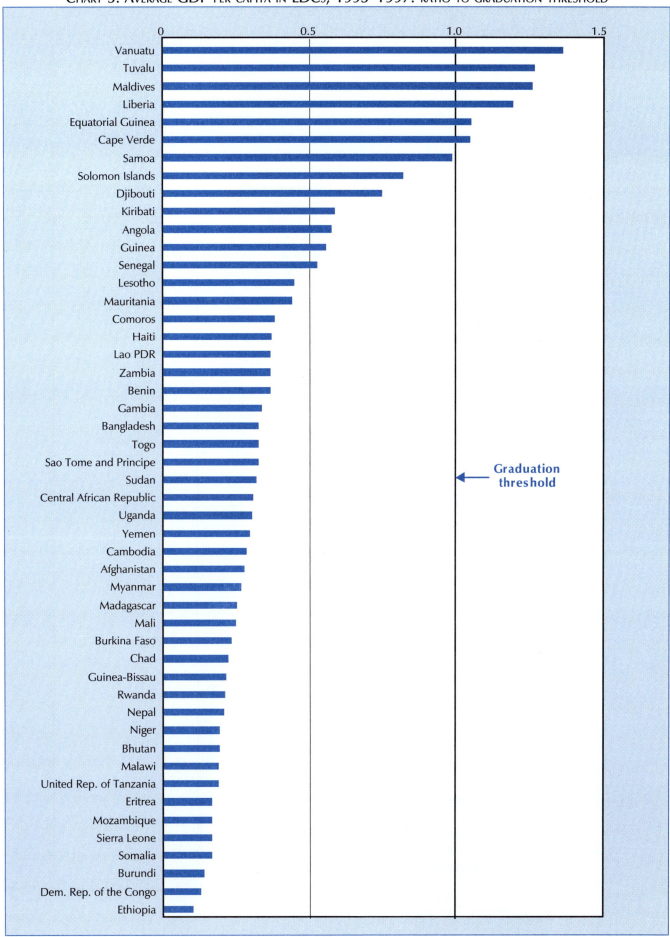

Source: United Nations Committee for Development Policy (2000).

CHART 4. AUGMENTED PHYSICAL QUALITY OF LIFE INDEX IN LDCS, 1997: RATIO TO GRADUATION THRESHOLD

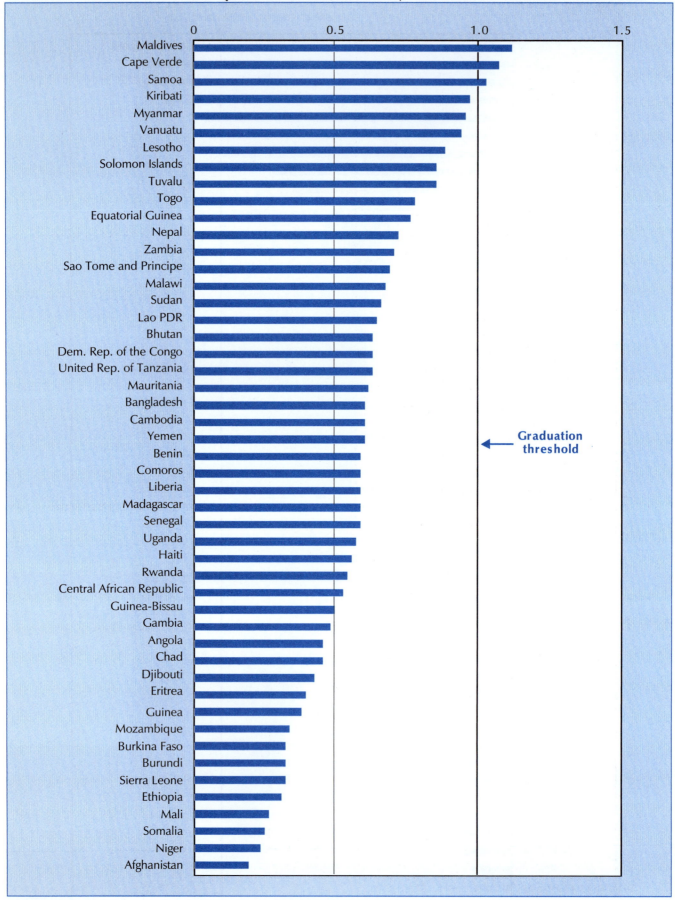

Source: United Nations Committee for Development Policy (2000).

CHART 5. ECONOMIC VULNERABILITY INDEX IN LDCS, 1997–1998: RATIO TO GRADUATION THRESHOLD

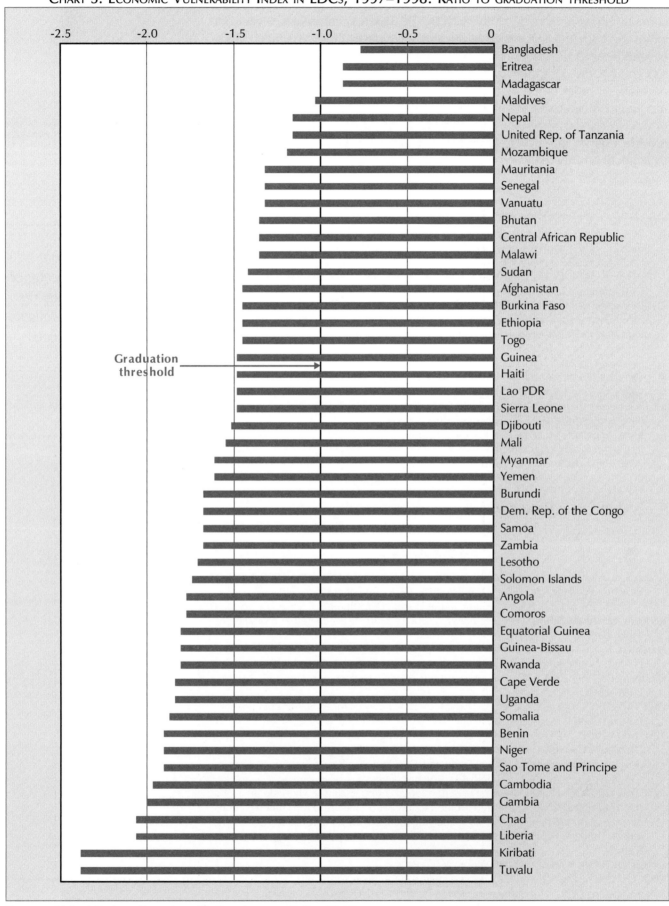

Source: United Nations Committee for Development Policy (2000).

Note: All countries with less than -1.0 have economic vulnerability exceeding the graduation threshold. The instability components of the Economic Vulnerability Index are based on data from 1979 to 1997 or to 1998, and the other components on data for 1997 or 1998. See box 2 for components of this index.

Where data are available, it is apparent that the majority of the LDCs are currently off track in terms of the UNLDC III development targets. Significant efforts by both the LDCs themselves and their development partners, going beyond those of the 1990s and, where appropriate, building on experiences of success and diverging from specific policies pursued in that decade, will be necessary in order to ensure that greater progress is made. The second part of this Report is dedicated to supporting this effort. It seeks to rectify the problem of data availability in relation to the incidence of poverty in the LDCs, and to provide a better analytical basis for national and international policies designed to promote poverty reduction in these countries.

Notes

1. This includes information at www.developmentgoals.org and the outcome of the meeting of the representatives of the Secretary-General's Office, UNDESA, UNDP, UNFPA, UNICEF, UNSD, DGO, IMF, OECD and the World Bank held in New York on 21 June 2001 to map the Millennium Development Goals and the International Development Goals.
2. Discussion of UNCTAD (2001), which provides the basis for this chapter, in the 48th session of the Trade and Development Board emphasized the desirability of identifying indicators for monitoring the Programme of Action comprehensively . But how to do this requires further intergovernmental discussion.
3. See box 7, p.74.
4. The tables in this section are based on work in UNDP's Human Development Report Office by David Stewart.
5. The targets are now measured as ODA/GNI rather than ODA/GNP as all DAC Members have adopted the 1993 System of National Accounts.
6. It should be noted that the thresholds for inclusion in the list of LDCs do not correspond to the thresholds for graduation from the list. In the CDP review of the list of LDCs in 2000, the inclusion thresholds were set at: GDP per capita, $900; APQLI, 59; and EVI, 36.
7. For discussion of these cases, see UNCTAD (2002). pp. 4–5.
8. See UNCTAD (2000, table 4) for the GDP per capita criterion.

Where data are available, it is apparent that the majority of the LDCs are currently off track in terms of the UNLDC III development targets.

References

Chen, S. and Ravallion, M. (2000). How did the world's poorest fare in the 1990s?, Policy Research Working Paper No. 2409, World Bank, Washington DC.

FAO (2000). *The State of Food Insecurity in the World 2000*, Rome.

Kenneth, H., Abou Zahr, C. and Wardlaw, T. (2001). Estimates of maternal mortality for 1995, *Bulletin of the WHO*, 79 (3): 182–193.

Naschold, F. (2001). Growth, distribution and poverty reduction: LDCs are falling further behind, background report for The Least Developed Countries Report 2002, Geneva.

Svedberg, P. (1999). 841 million undernourished? *World Development*, 1999, 27 (12): pp. 2081–2098.

UNCTAD (2000). The Least Developed Countries 2000 Report, United Nations publication, sales no. E.00.II.D.21, Geneva.

UNCTAD (2001). The development goals of the Programme of Action for the Least Developed Countries for the Decade 2001–2010: Towards a set of indicators to monitor progress, report prepared for the Trade and Development Board, forty-eight session, Geneva 1 October 2001, TD/B/48/14, 3 August, Geneva.

UNCTAD (2002). Graduation from the least developed countries status: where do the LDCs stand? Background note, prepared for the Expert Group Meeting of the United Nations Secretariat on the methodology for identifying the Least Developed Countries, 16–17 January, and the Fourth Session of the Committee for Development Policy, 8–12 April, Geneva.

UNESCO (2000). *World Education Report 2000*, Paris.

UNICEF (2001). *The State of the World's Children 2001*, New York.

United Nations (2001). Programme of Action for the Least Developed Countries for the Decade 2001–2010, 8 June, A/CONF.191/11.

United Nations Committee for Development Policy (2000). Report on the second session (3–7 April 2000), ECOSOC Official Records, 2000, supplement no. 13 (E/2000/33).

WHO/UNICEF/WSSCC (2001). *Global Water Supply and Sanitation Assessment 2000 Report*, Geneva and New York, NY.

Part Two

ESCAPING THE POVERTY TRAP

The nature and dynamics of poverty in the least developed countries

Chapter

1

A. Introduction

This Part of the Report examines the relationship between poverty and development in the LDCs in the context of increasing global interdependence. The nature and dynamics of poverty in the LDCs have never been analysed in an international comparative perspective. The poverty statistics that are required in order to do this have hitherto been so limited in their coverage that international comparisons amongst the LDCs, and between LDCs and other countries, have been impossible. This chapter outlines the approach that the Report adopts to defining and measuring poverty, and describes the nature and dynamics of poverty in the LDCs. The analysis is founded upon a new data set of poverty estimates for LDCs that has been specially constructed for this Report. These estimates are not only relevant for the LDCs, but also have important implications for the global map of poverty and international commitments to reduce extreme poverty.

The most distinct aspect of poverty in the LDCs is that poverty is generalized.

The nature of poverty in the LDCs differs from poverty in other countries in various ways. This chapter identifies the most distinct aspect of poverty in the LDCs, which is that poverty is generalized in most LDCs. "Generalized poverty" is defined here as a situation in which a major part of the population lives at or below income levels sufficient to meet their basic needs, and in which the available resources in the economy, even when equally distributed, are barely sufficient to cater for the basic needs of the population on a sustainable basis. The causes of this situation, including the relationship between international trade and poverty, as well as the implications of generalized poverty for economic development and for poverty reduction strategies, are discussed in the subsequent chapters of the Report.

B. The approach of the Report and its rationale

The main features of the way in which this Report defines and measures poverty can be summarized as follows:

- Poverty is defined as the inability to achieve minimally adequate levels of consumption.

- Poverty is measured using the $1-a-day and $2-a-day international poverty lines.

- The poverty estimates are anchored in national accounts estimates of private consumption.

- For countries where there are no data on the distribution of consumption amongst households, poverty is estimated by extrapolating the close relationship that is found to exist between annual average levels of private consumption per capita and both the incidence and depth of poverty.

"Generalized poverty" is defined here as a situation in which a major part of the population lives at or below income levels sufficient to meet their basic needs, and in which the available resources in the economy, even when equally distributed, are barely sufficient to cater for the basic needs of the population on a sustainable basis.

The Report's approach is based on three key choices: the focus on consumption poverty; the use of the $1-a-day and $2-a-day poverty lines; and the anchoring of poverty estimates in the national accounts statistics. This section looks more closely at the rationale for each of these choices.[1]

1. THE FOCUS ON CONSUMPTION POVERTY

Poverty is defined in this Report as the inability to attain a minimally adequate standard of living. What is considered "minimally adequate" includes necessities for physical survival (food, water, clothing, shelter, and so on), plus what is required for participation in the everyday life of society. Some argue that the latter element of an adequate standard of living is more relevant in rich countries. But there is absolutely no reason to assume that social participation is less important in poor countries than in rich ones. As Adam Smith (1776: 351–352) famously put it, "necessaries" include "not only the commodities which are indispensably necessary for the support of life, but whatever the custom of the country renders it indecent for creditable people, even the lowest orders to be without". In these terms, an adequate living standard should encompass not simply access to commodities which ensure the physical ability to survive, but also access to commodities which enable a person to live with dignity in the society to which he or she belongs.

The incidence of poverty and the depth of poverty are identified by the specification of a poverty line. This line represents, in monetary terms, the level of consumption that is regarded as minimally adequate. The monetary value of household consumption includes both purchased goods and the imputed value of consumption from a household's own production. The incidence of poverty is calculated as the proportion of the total population living below the poverty line, i.e. on less than a minimally adequate amount. The depth of poverty is calculated by estimating, in monetary terms, the average level of consumption of the poor, namely those people living below the poverty line.

This Report does not reject the multidimensional view. However, it uses a narrower definition of poverty as this enables greater analytical power in addressing the relationship between poverty, development and globalization.

In recent years, it has been argued that a focus on consumption poverty defined using a monetary metric is too simple. Poverty, according to this view, is multidimensional, constituted by an interlocking web of economic, political, human and sociocultural deprivations, and characterized by insecurity, vulnerability and powerlessness.[2] This Report does not reject the multidimensional view; indeed, this view offers an accurate description of the experience of poverty.[3] However, it uses a narrower definition of poverty as this enables greater analytical power in addressing the relationship between poverty, development and globalization.

Understanding this relationship, which is vital for the formulation of poverty reduction strategies in the LDCs and other developing countries, is not impossible with a multidimensional definition of poverty that includes economic, social and political dimensions of deprivation. But the complexity of the task can overwhelm adequate understanding. It is easy for the multidimensional approach to definition and measurement to lead to a complex but static view of poverty in which the focus of anti-poverty strategy is on targeting symptoms (what people lack) rather than on tackling causes (why they lack these things). In short, increased descriptive fidelity to the human experience of poverty is gained at the expense of the capability to analyse the causes of poverty and develop effective policies to reduce poverty. With a focus on consumption poverty, it is also possible to build on useful insights of past work that have often been forgotten, or put aside as redundant, in the shift to a multidimensional approach (box 3).

BOX 3. LEARNING IN THE INTERNATIONAL ANALYSIS OF POVERTY

A weak feature of international analysis of poverty is the tendency for fads and fashions, with new approaches being introduced and old ones falling out of favour. One consequence of this for policy analysts in developing countries is that there is a process of de-skilling. With the traditional approach to poverty analysis it is possible to reverse this process of unlearning even though that approach will not provide such a complex description of poverty.

In seeking to link poverty with development and globalization, it is also possible to learn from many insightful past studies. These include *Redistribution with Growth* (Chenery et al., 1974), and also the World Bank's *World Development Report 1990* (World Bank, 1990). The former sought to link poverty trends to national growth–inequality relationships and national processes of capital accumulation, structural transformation and productivity growth, whilst the latter attempted in a pioneering and innovative way to situate the problem of poverty reduction within the context of integration into the global economy, postulating links between efficient resource allocation in open economies and labour-intensive growth.

The approach of each of these studies was flawed in its own way. The former failed to place national poverty analysis in a global context, whilst the latter had a much too simple view of growth processes in developing economies, which ignored structural heterogeneities and dynamics of accumulation, an excessive faith in the beneficial effects of liberalization in all countries at all times, and a benign view of the working of the global economy. But jettisoning the insights of this work, because it uses a definition of poverty which is not multidimensional, entails the loss of important intellectual capital.

A way forward now to improve poverty analysis and develop more effective poverty reduction strategies is to link the insights of the 1970s approach with those of the 1990s approach. That is to say, national poverty trends need to be analysed in relation to processes of capital accumulation, structural transformation, productivity growth and employment generation (as in Chenery et al., 1974), but in a global context (as in World Bank, 1990). This is what the present Report seeks to do.

It must be emphasized, as the OECD/DAC Guidelines on Poverty Reduction helpfully point out, that a money-metric approach to defining and measuring poverty such as that adopted in the present Report is best regarded as complementary to more complex multidimensional approaches (OECD, 2001). The latter may just entail adding the benefits that people receive from freely provided public goods to estimates of private consumption. However, it could also involve the construction of composite indicators of the nature of the lives people lead, such as the UNDP's human development index and the human poverty index, or discrete indicators of specific deprivations, such as food deprivation or housing deprivation (chart 6). Also, it must be stressed that the focus on monetary indicators of poverty does not mean that the causes of poverty can be simply located in the economic sphere. Processes underlying consumption poverty trends are thoroughly multidimensional, as later chapters show.

CHART 6. ALTERNATIVE INDICATORS FOR MEASURING POVERTY

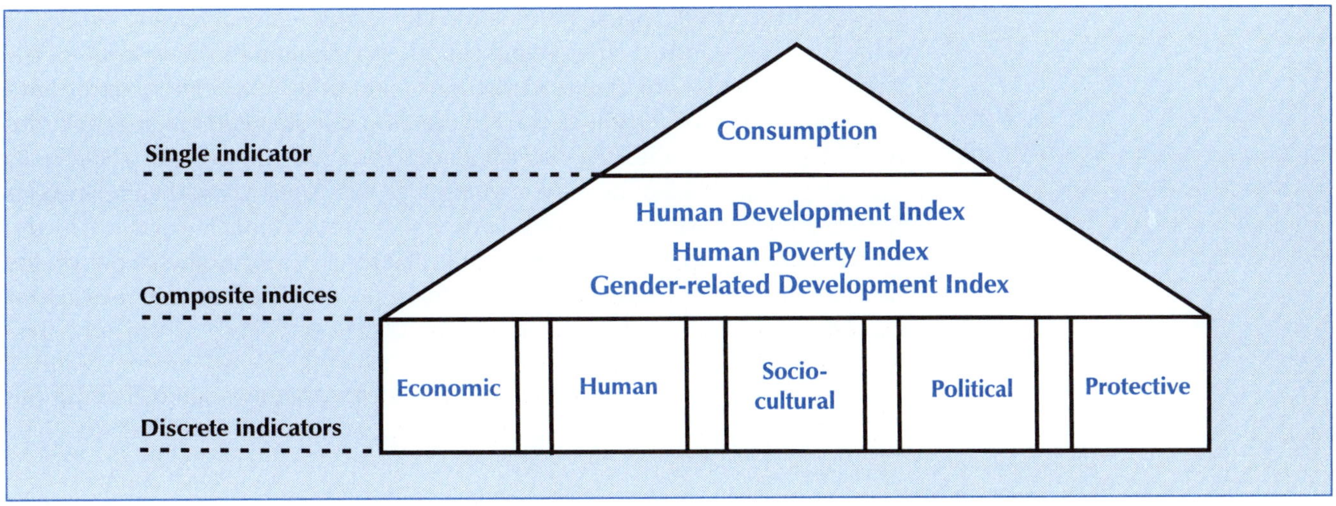

Source: OECD (2001: figure 2).

2. THE CHOICE OF $1-A-DAY AND $2-A-DAY
INTERNATIONAL POVERTY LINES

The Report uses consumption levels of $1 a day and $2 a day as the standards by which to identify minimally adequate levels of poverty in the LDCs. In line with current practice, each of these poverty lines is estimated using purchasing power parity (PPP) exchange rates, which seek to make comparable the purchasing power of one dollar in different countries at different times.[4] The $1-a-day international poverty line is the focal concern of the International Development Goal and the Millennium Development Goal of reducing the incidence of extreme poverty by half between 1990 and 2015, and is also a primary objective of the Programme of Action for the Least Developed Countries for the Decade 2001–2010. It may be argued, therefore, that it is sufficient to limit analysis to this single standard.

The two poverty lines were chosen following close examination of the rationale for the $1-a-day line. This standard has its origins in pioneering World Bank research on the way in which nationally defined poverty lines vary between countries according to their level of development. This research found that:

The Report uses consumption levels of $1 a day and $2 a day as the standards by which to identify minimally adequate levels of poverty in the LDCs.

- There is a marked tendency for countries with higher GNP per capita and with higher levels of private consumption per capita to define higher national poverty lines.

- A consumption level of $31 per month (measured in 1985 PPP exchange rates), i.e. $1 a day, is a "common poverty line for the dozen or so low-income countries for which poverty lines have been calculated" (Ravallion, Datt and van de Walle, 1991: 27).

The $1-a-day poverty line was then chosen as the standard for the international comparison of poverty. The minimum adequacy of consumption in all countries was thus equated with the typical standard of minimally adequate consumption in the poorest countries.[5]

Re-examination of these data shows that, even amongst the LDCs and low-income countries, there is a tendency for countries with higher national GNP per capita and with higher average annual levels of private consumption per capita to define higher national poverty lines (chart 7). However, focusing on countries whose annual levels of private consumption are in the same range as those of the LDCs makes it is possible to identify two clusters. The first cluster, those countries where levels of per capita consumption are below $1,000 per annum (in 1985 PPP dollars), have defined their own national poverty lines close to the $1-a-day standard. The second cluster, those countries where levels of per capita consumption are above $1,000 per annum (in 1985 PPP dollars), have nationally defined poverty lines close to the $2-a-day standard. Increasingly, the World Bank is using the $2-a-day standard (along with the $1-a-day line) in its international analyses of poverty, arguing that this "upper poverty line" reflects more closely the national poverty lines which are commonly used in "lower-middle-income" countries (World Bank, 2000: 17). Re-examination of the national poverty lines suggests that both these poverty lines are also relevant for the LDCs.

The use of these two poverty lines, nevertheless, requires some clarifications and qualifications.

CHART 7. THE RELATIONSHIP BETWEEN NATIONAL POVERTY LINES AND ANNUAL PER CAPITA PRIVATE CONSUMPTION
(In 1985 PPP $ a year)

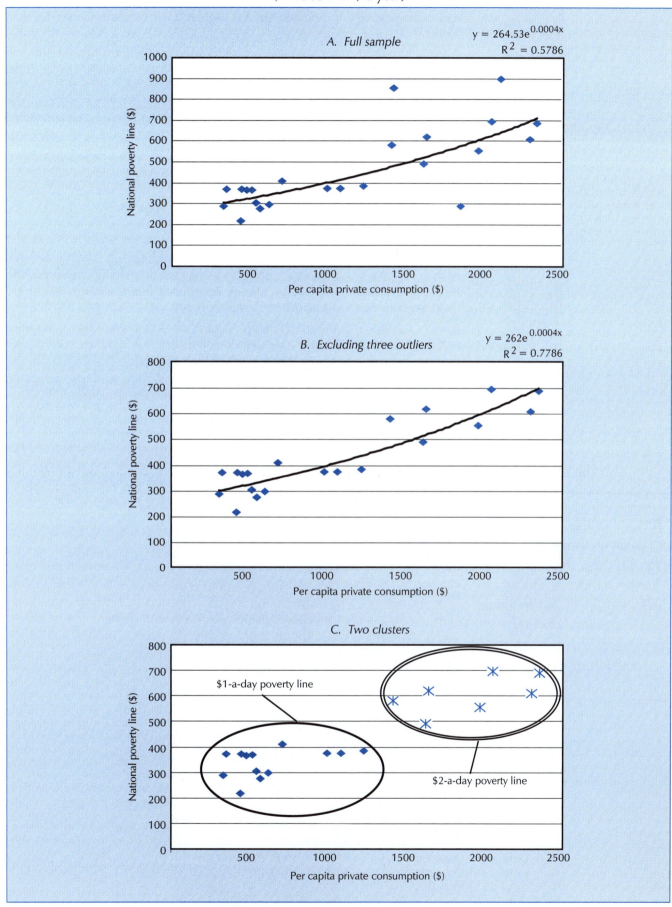

Source: Karshenas (2001), based on Ravallion, Datt and van de Walle (1991).

First, both these poverty lines define situations of great austerity. It is widely agreed that the $1-a-day poverty line depicts a situation of "extreme poverty", and that language is retained in this Report. This consensus has focused international and national efforts to eradicate extreme poverty on the $1-a-day poor. However, it may reasonably be asked whether the $2-a-day poverty line could also be said to identify a situation of "extreme poverty" in a global context. Confirming this judgement ideally entails finding out what level of consumption a person can actually achieve given $2 a day (in 1985 PPP terms).[6] But some notion of the austerity of these poverty lines in global terms can be gained by knowing that at current prices and official exchange rates, the $1-a-day poverty line in 1985 international prices translates into 51 cents a day for an average African LDC, and 31 cents a day for the average Asian LDC. The $2 poverty line for the average African and Asian LDCs translates into $1.02 and 61 cents respectively at current prices and official exchange rates.[7]

It is widely agreed that the $1-a-day poverty line depicts a situation of "extreme poverty", and that language is retained in this Report.

Second, the use of the $1-a-day and $2-a-day poverty lines in this Report does not imply that higher standards should be excluded in the international analysis of poverty, particularly in more advanced developing countries. The World Bank research on national poverty lines shows that poverty standards are related to the societies of which individuals are members. There is a clear tendency for the minimally acceptable levels of consumption to rise as societies become richer and average consumption increases.[8] In making international poverty comparisons on the basis of the typical standards of a few countries, there is no logical reason not to use the typical standard of minimally adequate consumption in richer countries rather than the poorest countries. Indeed, as globalization occurs, the consumption standards which people aspire to are defined not simply by national norms, but also by global norms. Thus what people consider to be minimally acceptable is shifting with globalization. But this is not downwards to the standards of living in the poorest countries, but rather upwards to the standards of living, and also the command of consumer goods available, in the richest countries.

The use of the $1-a-day and $2-a-day poverty lines in this Report does not imply that higher standards should be excluded in the international analysis of poverty, particularly in more advanced developing countries.

Third, the Report relies on publicly available purchasing power parity exchange rates to estimate poverty. The PPP exchange rates, which are used to ensure that the purchasing power of a dollar is comparable between countries, can potentially distort poverty estimates. Recently, a number of leading analysts have pointed out that in the revision of PPP estimates in 1993 disconcertingly large changes in the incidence of poverty occurred (Lipton, 1996; Deaton, 2000; Milanovic, 2001). The problem of PPP estimates is exacerbated in the case of the LDCs as there are few LDCs in the database from which PPP estimates are derived. The Report does not tackle this problem.[9] But it is worth noting that, according to available PPP estimates, the cost of living is much higher in African LDCs than in Asian LDCs.[10] The magnitude of the difference is such that if the costs of living which the PPP conversion rates suggest for Asian LDCs were actually closer to those which they suggest for African LDCs, poverty rates in the Asian LDCs would be as much as two thirds higher.

Finally, the use of the $1-a-day and $2-a-day international poverty lines in the present Report does not reduce the relevance of national poverty lines. National authorities should have discretion to define poverty in their own way.[11] One advantage of country-specific poverty lines is that the problems of PPP exchange rates can be avoided. But the use of such poverty lines was not possible in the present Report as its concern is to derive policy insights from international comparative analysis of poverty. It is most likely that the poverty estimates that are presented in this Report using international poverty lines diverge from current national poverty estimates based on country-specific poverty lines in a number of countries. This should not be a surprise. It should also not be used to argue that the "true" incidence and depth of poverty in any particular country are actually higher or lower than national estimates suggest. Poverty estimates vary depending on where the poverty line is drawn. International and national poverty estimates will necessarily differ if they are based on different poverty lines. But the international estimates in the present Report are valuable for international comparisons as they are derived in a consistent way across countries and also over time.

3. THE USE OF NATIONAL-ACCOUNTS-CONSISTENT POVERTY ESTIMATES

National poverty estimates using the $1-a-day and $2-a-day poverty lines are generally based on surveys that use questionnaires to estimate household income, or household consumption expenditure, for a representative sample of the national population. The poverty estimates used in this Report are different. They are anchored in national accounts data. Almost all countries in the world have national income and product accounts, and these serve as the basis for estimates of gross domestic product (GDP), gross national product (GNP), and so on. They generally include estimates of macroeconomic aggregates such as private and public savings, gross domestic investment and private consumption. It is this last aggregate that is used in calculating the national-accounts-consistent poverty estimates of this Report. The incidence and depth of poverty in each LDC for which there are data are calculated by combining estimates of average private consumption per capita from the national accounts with estimates of the distribution of consumption amongst individuals and households from household survey data. The method of estimating poverty is exactly the same as the purely survey-based approach.[12] But the national-accounts-consistent estimates are based on estimates of the total population's average per capita private consumption of the total population using national accounts data rather than the mean consumption level of the sample derived from the household survey data.

It is most likely that the poverty estimates that are presented in this Report using international poverty lines diverge from current national poverty estimates based on country-specific poverty lines. This should not be a surprise.

Anchoring poverty estimates in national accounts statistics is not without precedent. National-accounts-consistent poverty estimates of the type used in this Report have been made in India. Moreover, the World Bank, whose national poverty estimates are based on household surveys, uses estimates of the consumption growth rate from national accounts to align its survey-based national poverty estimates (which refer to different years in different countries) to obtain global estimates of poverty in, say, 1990 or 1996 (World Bank, 2000: 23). However, household-survey-based and national-accounts-consistent poverty estimates do not tally well. Amongst the LDCs, in countries such as the United Republic of Tanzania (1991), Ethiopia (1981, 1995) and Mali (1989), average consumption figures according to the household surveys are between two and nearly three times higher than the national accounts estimates (see table 17). On the other hand, in Bangladesh, the survey estimates are much lower than the national accounts consumption data. Similar inconsistencies are apparent in trends over time. According to the household survey data, average private consumption per capita increased by over 17 per cent in Ethiopia between 1981 and 1995. But according to national accounts data, average private consumption per capita fell by over 13 per cent between these two years. In Bangladesh in contrast, household surveys suggest that average private consumption per capita fell by over 13 per cent between 1984 and 1991, whilst the national accounts data indicate a growth in average private consumption per capita of over 13 per cent in the same period.

National poverty estimates using the $1-a-day and $2-a-day poverty lines are generally based on household surveys... The poverty estimates used in this Report are different. They are anchored in national accounts data.

TABLE 17. ALTERNATIVE ESTIMATES OF THE INCIDENCE OF POVERTY
AND ANNUAL PRIVATE CONSUMPTION PER HEAD IN LDCs

	Year	Share of population living on less than $1 a day (%)		Share of population living on less than $2 a day (%)		Annual private consumption per head (1985 PPP $)	
		Household-survey-based estimates	National-accounts-consistent estimates	Household-survey-based estimates	National-accounts-consistent estimates	Household-survey-based estimates	National-accounts-consistent estimates
African LDCs							
Burkina Faso	1994	61.2	68.5	85.5	89.5	477.9	401.7
Central African Rep.	1993	66.6	70.3	84.0	86.4	455.3	402.8
Ethiopia	1981	32.7	89.5	82.9	96.8	558.4	231.8
	1995	31.3	89.9	76.4	97.1	657.8	228.8
Gambia	1992	53.7	42.9	84.0	76.6	504.7	623.0
Lesotho	1986	30.9	47.7	55.5	73.2	1132.6	696.0
	1993	43.1	56.4	65.7	76.8	890.7	599.7
Madagascar	1980	49.2	28.9	80.3	62.5	557.1	856.1
	1993	60.2	48.9	88.8	83.3	434.1	528.7
Mali	1989	16.5	55.6	55.4	88.7	852.8	426.6
	1994	72.3	67.2	90.6	92.7	360.8	353.9
Mauritania	1988	40.6	37.6	78.9	76.1	534.4	567.4
	1993	49.4	42.7	81.9	78.1	605.9	680.0
	1995	31.0	32.7	70.8	72.4	661.1	642.3
Mozambique	1996	37.9	37.7	78.4	78.7	588.7	589.9
Niger	1992	41.7	76.1	84.1	95.6	523.0	312.7
	1995	61.4	69.0	85.3	89.6	401.9	331.1
Rwanda	1984	35.7	25.4	84.6	78.5	518.1	592.1
Senegal	1991	45.4	38.1	73.0	66.3	707.8	851.2
	1994	26.3	23.8	67.8	64.0	754.1	801.7
Sierra Leone	1989	56.8	53.2	74.5	69.4	544.1	644.7
Uganda	1989	39.2	55.1	72.9	84.4	639.7	465.8
	1992	36.7	57.7	77.2	85.8	598.4	443.1
United Rep. of Tanzania	1991	48.5	78.2	72.5	91.9	735.8	303.6
	1993	19.9	78.0	59.7	95.2	814.0	291.3
Zambia	1991	58.6	66.7	81.5	87.3	434.3	348.0
	1993	69.2	75.6	89.5	93.0	318.9	269.5
	1996	72.6	80.5	91.7	94.6	345.7	279.0
Asian LDCs							
Bangladesh	1984	26.2	10.4	84.0	61.0	535.1	729.6
	1985	22.0	8.0	79.9	61.1	586.0	753.9
	1988	33.8	10.0	85.4	60.5	518.7	765.8
	1991	35.9	8.9	86.4	55.7	498.7	796.0
	1995	29.1	7.2	77.8	54.3	613.3	885.8
Nepal	1985	40.4	57.4	86.0	92.5	491.9	393.1
	1995	37.7	51.2	82.5	89.2	584.4	489.1

Source: UNCTAD secretariat estimates based on Karshenas (2001).

Note: This table covers LDCs and years in which there are household surveys of consumption expenditure.

The discrepancy between household-survey-based and national-accounts-consistent estimates of private consumption has long been known (Pyatt, 2000). But it is only recently, following debate on the effects of economic reform on poverty in India, that much more attention has been given to the issue, its causes and the implications for international comparisons of poverty (Deaton, 2000; Pyatt, 2000; Ravallion, 2000a, 2001; Karshenas, 2001). In this work, it has been argued that for a large sample of countries there is no statistically significant difference between estimates of average consumption expenditure from national accounts and from household surveys (Ravallion, 2000a, 2001). It has also been argued that the most likely form of any discrepancy is the underestimation of average levels and growth of consumption in household surveys, which is the Indian case. But the argument of "no statistically significant difference" has been shown to be unsound (Karshenas, 2001). Moreover, it is clear from charts 8 and 9 that, for the $1-a-day and $2-a-day poverty lines, the discrepancy is related to how poor a country is (measured in terms of average levels of consumption in international PPP terms). If the national-accounts-consistent poverty estimates are accepted as correct, there is an overestimation of average private consumption per capita levels (and thus underestimation of the incidence of poverty) in household surveys in the very poorest countries, and an underestimation of private consumption per capita levels (and thus overestimation of the incidence of poverty) in household surveys in developing countries that are less poor. The national-accounts-consistent poverty estimates also suggest that poverty in sub-Saharan Africa is also greater than current estimates based on household surveys imply.

These differences are not only relevant for the LDCs, but also have important implications for the global map of poverty (see box 4). A critical question is: Which estimates provide a more accurate view of the situation on the ground? Ideally, this question should be resolved by looking closely, on a country-by-country basis, at the accuracy of national accounts and household survey data, and reconciling the discrepancies.[13] This requires further investment in statistical capacities for national accounts as well as household surveys, and also in methods, such as the construction of social accounting matrices, which necessarily require that efforts be made to reconcile the statistical discrepancies. However, in the meantime, it is necessary to proceed with poverty analysis and poverty monitoring, and to develop more effective poverty reduction policies.

This Report is based on national-accounts-consistent poverty estimates for various reasons. Firstly, they offer as plausible poverty estimates as purely household-survey-based estimates. Both the national accounts data and the household survey data are flawed (see box 5). The approach adopted here combines elements of each type of data in a way that seeks to minimize their disadvantages. It focuses on household surveys of consumption, rather than of income, as it is generally agreed that household consumption data are more accurate than household income data.[14] Moreover, it limits the information derived from the household surveys to information on distribution of consumption among households. This is because the primary purpose of household surveys is not the estimation of average levels of household income or consumption of the population, but rather the estimation of the distribution of income or consumption amongst the population.

The case for using national-accounts-consistent poverty estimates is reinforced as our purpose is the international comparison of poverty. National accounts procedures are likely to be more standardized between countries than household surveys, and this should enable greater international comparability. Preliminary research also shows that the national-accounts-consistent poverty estimates are more highly correlated with some non-monetary indicators of poverty than the purely household-survey-based estimates (Karshenas, 2001). More work of this nature is required. However, these preliminary results suggest that national-accounts-consistent poverty estimates could even be more plausible indicators of material deprivation than the household-survey-based poverty estimates.

If the national-accounts-consistent poverty estimates are correct, the incidence and depth of poverty have been hitherto underestimated in the very poorest countries and in sub-Saharan Africa.

Preliminary research shows that the national-accounts-consistent poverty estimates are more highly correlated with some non-monetary indicators of poverty than the purely household-survey-based estimates

CHART 8. DISCREPANCY BETWEEN NATIONAL-ACCOUNTS-CONSISTENT AND HOUSEHOLD-SURVEY-BASED ESTIMATES OF THE INCIDENCE OF POVERTY IN THE LDCS AND OTHER DEVELOPING COUNTRIES

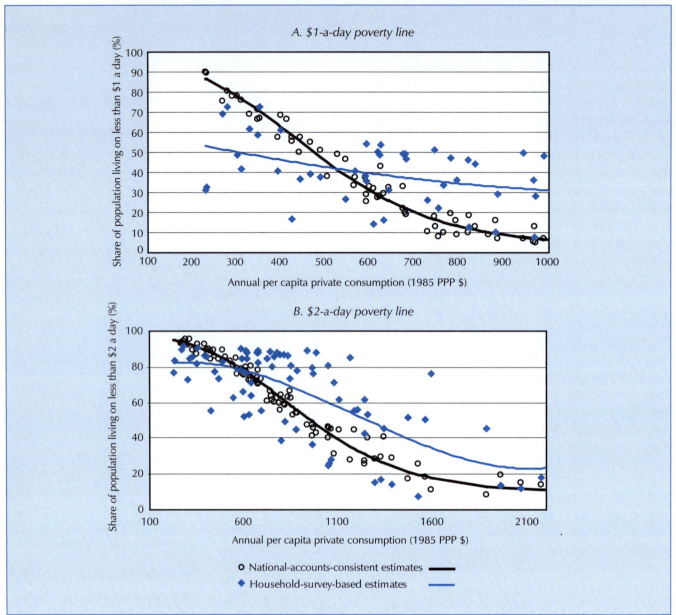

Source: Karshenas (2001).

A final advantage of the national-accounts-based approach is that it can provide a way to make poverty estimates for countries and years for which none currently exist. This possibility exists because there is a very close relationship between average private consumption per capita (estimated from national accounts) and the incidence of consumption poverty in those countries for which household survey data on the distribution of consumption expenditure are available. The expected incidence of poverty in countries where distribution data are not available can thus be extrapolated on the basis of the trend lines in countries where such data are available.[15]

This is of major importance for understanding and tackling poverty in the LDCs. Without these statistics, the international analysis of poverty in the LDCs is virtually impossible.[16] Moreover, as this method can be used to estimate expected levels of poverty in years for which no distribution data exist, it is also possible to describe the long-term dynamics of poverty change. This is potentially of major importance for national and international policy formulation as current data on poverty change in developing countries are limited to the

CHART 9. DISCREPANCY BETWEEN NATIONAL-ACCOUNTS-CONSISTENT AND HOUSEHOLD-SURVEY-BASED ESTIMATES OF THE DEPTH OF THE POVERTY IN THE LDCS AND OTHER DEVELOPING COUNTRIES
(1985 PPP $ a year)

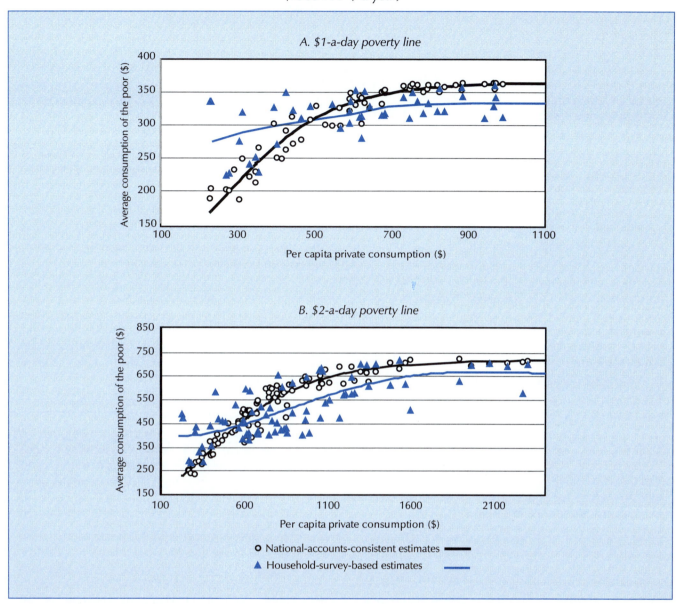

Source: As for chart 8.

period of time between the years when household surveys were conducted. With the exception of all but a few developing countries, notably India, these periods are short. Poverty estimates anchored in national accounts thus make it possible to understand the analytical links between poverty and economic growth, macroeconomic change and structural transformation. They enable examination of the relationship between poverty and development as a policy issue.

C. The poverty situation in the LDCs in the late 1990s

This Report is based on a new data set of national-accounts-consistent estimates of poverty. These estimates are used in the rest of this chapter, and throughout the Report. The details of how the estimates were derived are summarized in the annex at the end of this chapter (see also Karshenas, 2001).

Box 4. Implications of national-accounts-consistent poverty estimates for the global map of poverty

The discrepancy between household-survey-based and national accounts estimates of private consumption, and its implications for poverty estimates, have recently become the subject of lively debate in India (Bhalla, 2000; Ravallion, 2000b). According to national-accounts-consistent poverty estimates, economic reforms in that country have been associated with much more rapid poverty reduction than appears when poverty is estimated on the basis of household surveys. A question which must be asked now at the start of any serious international analysis of poverty is whether this is purely an Indian issue, or whether it matters globally. The national-accounts-consistent poverty estimates produced for this Report suggest that the discrepancy has significant effects on the global map of poverty, and also on forecasts about the achievement of Millennium Development Goals and International Development Goals.

The poverty estimates produced for this Report reveal systematic deviations between household-survey-based poverty estimates and national-accounts-consistent poverty estimates. If one accepts the national-accounts-consistent poverty estimates as the correct estimates:

- Current international poverty statistics, which are calculated on the basis of household sample survey data, underestimate both the incidence and depth of $1-a-day poverty in the very poorest countries, and also in sub-Saharan Africa.

- Current international poverty statistics equally underestimate the major opportunity for the rapid reduction of extreme poverty in the poorest countries if higher rates of economic growth can be attained and sustained.

Poverty is underestimated in the poorest countries according to national-account-consistent poverty estimates as there is an overestimation of average private consumption levels in household surveys in the very poorest countries. Equally, there is an underestimation of consumption levels (and thus overestimation of the incidence of poverty) in household surveys in less poor developing countries. The opportunity for poverty reduction associated with sustained economic growth is underestimated as household-survey-based poverty estimates lead to a much less close relationship between the incidence of poverty and average levels of private consumption per capita, and also, generally, to a lower rate of poverty change consequent upon the growth of average levels of consumption.

It is difficult to say exactly why these systematic biases arise. Two major possible sources of bias leading to the overestimation of average consumption (and the underestimation of the incidence of poverty) in the poorest countries are the under-representation of the poorest in the surveys, and over-inflation of the value of home-produced consumption. As chart 8A shows, there is a tendency for household-survey-based estimates of $1-a-day poverty to lie within the range 25–55 per cent, no matter what the average level of consumption of the population. It is, however, very surprising to find that two countries, one with an average per capita GDP of close to $1 per day (in 1985 PPP dollars) and the other with an average per capita GDP of above $3 per day, both have about 40 per cent of their population living below an international poverty line of $1 per day.

Close examination of the poverty curves which describe the relationship between average levels of private consumption per capita and national-accounts-consistent estimates of the incidence of $1-a-day and $2-a-day poverty also has important implications for forecasts of future poverty. Such forecasts are generally made by assuming a single aggregate estimate of the change in poverty that occurs together with a change in consumption (or GDP), which is assumed to pertain in a heterogeneous group of developing countries (see, for example, Collier and Dollar, 2001; Naschold, 2001). But although there is certainly a very close relationship between the growth of consumption and the incidence of poverty, the relationship is non-linear, and for any given country, the growth–poverty relationship depends on where the poverty line is set. The important implication of this is that if one accepts the national-accounts-consistent estimates as the correct ones:

- Current international forecasts of the map of poverty in the year 2015, which are based on household survey data, need to be revisited.

It is difficult to say whether current forecasts are over-optimistic or too conservative. As noted above, the national-accounts-consistent poverty estimates suggest that the incidence and depth of poverty in the very poorest countries are underestimated. But the new poverty estimates may actually provide a more optimistic view about reaching the international target of reducing $1-a-day poverty by 2015, because poverty can fall faster with rising levels of average private consumption per capita.

Moreover — and this is the final important implication of the national-accounts-consistent poverty estimates for the international map of poverty — if one accepts these estimates as accurate:

- The set of countries to which the $1-a-day international poverty line is most relevant is limited to the LDCs and other low-income countries.

Box 4 (contd.)

By implication, the geographical domain to which the international commitment to reduce the incidence of extreme poverty (measured using the $1-a-day poverty line) by 2015 is relevant is the LDCs and other low-income countries.

The domain to which the $1-a-day poverty line is relevant can be seen precisely from the position of the poverty curve. As average consumption levels rise, $1-a-day poverty becomes much more of a residual phenomenon, affecting a very small proportion of the population. In fact, according to the poverty curve, this occurs at annual private consumption levels of about $1,000 per capita in 1985 PPP, or $500 per capita in current dollars at current exchange rates. With the national-accounts-consistent poverty estimates, the upper limit of average private consumption per capita at which the $1-a-day poverty line generates a significant incidence of poverty is $3 a day (in 1985 PPP dollars). This corresponds to an annual per capita private consumption of $451 at current prices and exchanges rates, which is roughly equivalent to an annual per capita GDP of $550 to $600.

When the position of the $1-a-day and $2-a-day poverty curves is compared, it is also apparent that the national-accounts-consistent poverty estimates suggest that as the average consumption per capita becomes even higher, the share of the population living on less than $2 a day also becomes very small. This is likely to be part of the reason why one observes that nationally defined poverty lines tend to rise with increasing income.

These four findings are of immense importance for the international analysis of poverty and for international action for poverty reduction. Given the commitment of the international community to poverty reduction, further research to examine the international dimensions of the discrepancy between national-accounts-consistent and household-survey-based poverty estimates, and to explore how it may be resolved, should be a high priority.[1]

[1] This call for research is also evident in Pyatt (2000), World Bank (2000: box 1.8) and Deaton (2000).

Box 5. Some problems with national-accounts-consistent and
household-survey-based poverty estimates

National accounts estimates of private consumption are not conceptually exactly the same as those of household consumption, as they implicitly include spending by non-profit organizations (NGOs, charities, religious organizations, and even political parties). Private consumption is also calculated within the national accounts as a residual from estimates of other macroeconomic aggregates, that is after calculation of aggregate output, imports, purchases by firms and government, inventory changes, and so on. It is thus far from an error-free number.

However, household surveys are also not error-free.[1] Best-practice consumption measures use very long lists of specific items to estimate household consumption, while widely used short-cut methods lead to underestimation of consumption. Imputing the monetary value of consumption based on self-provisioning rather than market purchases is always complex. Bias also arises in sample selection, in which there is generally an under-representation of the poor, and in response patterns, with a tendency towards underestimation of non-wage income and a higher non-response tendency in the higher-income strata. A major problem is to ensure consistency between surveys in different countries. Indeed, the ways in which poverty estimates derived from surveys vary from year to year indicate that, even within the same country, it is difficult to ensure comparability from year to year. For example, according to household-survey-based estimates, 16.5 per cent of the population of Mali was living in poverty in 1989 and 72.3 per cent in 1994, and 48.5 per cent of the population of the United Republic of Tanzania was living in poverty in 1991 and 19.9 per cent in 1993.[2]

A final important aspect of household surveys of living standards is that the primary purpose of these surveys is not the estimation of average levels of household income or consumption for the population, but rather the estimation of the distribution of income or household expenditure amongst the population. Deaton and Grosh (forthcoming, p. 5) state that "LSMS surveys [Living Standard Measurement Surveys] are rarely the instrument of choice for estimating mean income or mean consumption". However, they also note the problems of national-accounts estimates of consumption, and argue that it is wrong to assume that discrepancies between national accounts and household surveys derive solely from the latter.

[1] For a full discussion of methods of measuring consumption in living standard surveys, see Deaton and Grosh (forthcoming). This can be downloaded from http://www.wws.princeton.edu/~rpds/deatongrosh.pdf
[2] These data are from www.worldbank.org/research/povmonitor/index.htm

1. Average levels of poverty in LDCs in a comparative perspective

An overview of the state of poverty in the LDCs using these new poverty estimates is provided in table 18, which shows average per capita income and private consumption in current dollars and in 1985 PPP dollars, as well as indicators of the incidence and depth of poverty for African and Asian LDCs in the latter half of the 1990s.[17] The table also shows per capita income and consumption for selected high-income OECD countries for comparative purposes.

The data cover 91 per cent of the total population in the LDCs. Focusing on the average incidence and depth of poverty, weighted by population, table 18 shows that during 1995–1999:

- 81 per cent of the population in the LDCs for which we have data lived on less than $2 a day.

- 50 per cent of the population in the LDCs lived in extreme poverty, that is on less than $1 a day.

- The average private consumption per capita of the 50 per cent of the LDC population that live below the $1 poverty line is 64 cents a day (in 1985 PPP dollars).

- The average private consumption per capita of the 81 per cent of the LDC population living below the $2 poverty line is only $1.03 a day (in 1985 PPP dollars).

When most of the population in a country live below the international poverty line, poverty assumes a totally new dimension as compared with the conventional conception of poverty, where the main interest is in the relatively

During 1995–1999: 81 per cent of the population in the LDCs for which we have data lived on less than $2 a day; 50 per cent of the population in the LDCs lived in extreme poverty, that is on less than $1 a day.

TABLE 18. AVERAGE INCOME, PRIVATE CONSUMPTION AND THE INCIDENCE AND DEPTH OF POVERTY IN AFRICAN AND ASIAN LDCs AND SELECTED OECD COUNTRIES, 1995–1999

| | GDP per capita per day | | Per capita private consumption per day | | | | | | Percentage share of population living on less than: | |
| | | | Total population | | Poor (living below $1 a day) | | Poor (living below $2 a day) | | | |
	Current $	1985 PPP $	Current $	1985 PPP $	Current $	1985 PPP $	Current $	1985 PPP $	$1 a day	$2 a day
Weighted averages										
LDCs[a]	0.72	2.50	0.57	1.39	0.29	0.64	0.44	1.03	50.1	80.7
African LDCs	0.65	1.51	0.52	1.01	0.30	0.59	0.44	0.86	64.9	87.5
Asian LDCs	0.88	4.59	0.69	2.21	0.28	0.90	0.45	1.42	23.0	68.2
Selected OECD countries[b]					*Poorest 10%*		*Poorest 20%*			
United States	90.1	57.9	58.2	41.4	10.5	7.5	15.1	10.8	..	..
Switzerland	99.3	44.6	61.9	28.2	16.1	7.3	21.4	9.7	..	..
Sweden	73.8	43.7	37.3	23.5	13.8	8.3	17.9	10.8	..	..
Japan	94.1	43.4	50.5	24.2	24.2	11.6	26.7	12.8	..	..
France	66.9	41.9	36.7	25.4	10.3	7.0	13.2	9.0	..	..
United Kingdom	66.4	41.6	43.7	29.9	11.4	7.4	14.4	9.4	..	..

Source: UNCTAD secretariat estimates based on World Bank, *World Development Indicators 2001*, CD-ROM, and Karshenas (2001).

a Thirty-nine countries, including 4 island LDCs. For exhaustive country list, see table 19.

b Data on individual OECD countries refer to 1998. The share of the bottom deciles in OECD countries is calculated by applying per capita consumption averages to decile income distribution.

small share of the population in the bottom "tail" of the income distribution. As the proportion of the total population living in poverty increases beyond 50 per cent, the economy is in a situation of generalized poverty. Most LDCs are characterized by a situation in which poverty is generalized. A major part of the population lives at or below income levels sufficient to supply their basic needs, and the available resources in the economy, even when equally distributed, are barely sufficient to cater for the basic needs of the population on a sustainable basis.

In order to better understand the extent and the implications of generalized poverty in various LDCs, it would be helpful to further explore the intensity of poverty in those countries by examining the standards of living of those who fall below the poverty line. A polar extreme that can help bring the picture into sharp relief is provided by the comparison with the standards of living in the high-income OECD countries. As shown in table 18, per capita GDP in high-income OECD countries in current dollars and in official exchange rate is on average more than 100 times higher than in the African and Asian LDCs. At PPP exchange rates, however, as expected, the differences between the LDCs and the high-income countries are less pronounced. Nevertheless, per capita income in the high-income OECD countries is still on average about 30 times higher than in the average African LDCs and close to 10 times higher than in the Asian LDCs at 1985 PPP exchange rates. Similar ratios apply to the differences between the average per capita consumption of the LDCs and the high-income OECD countries.

The average private consumption per capita of the 81 per cent of the LDC population living below the $2 poverty line is only $1.03 a day (in 1985 PPP dollars).

The average consumption of the poor in the LDCs is of course well below the overall average consumption in those countries. As mentioned above, for example, close to 80 per cent of the population in the LDCs — those living below the $2-a-day poverty line — have an average consumption of $1.03 a day. This implies that even if the income of the bottom 80 per cent of population in the LDCs is equally distributed amongst them, they still barely manage a per capita consumption level above the international extreme poverty line. This average consumption level also compares with the average per capita private consumption of $7 to $10 a day for the poorest 10 to 20 per cent of the population in high-income OECD countries at 1985 international prices (table 18).

Although these per capita consumption figures are in real purchasing power terms — that is, they take into account cross-country variations in consumer price levels — one should not conclude that the extremely poor and the poor in the high-income countries, who can be roughly defined as the bottom 10 and 20 per cent consumption groups respectively, are exactly 7 or 10 times better off than the poor in the LDCs. The PPP exchange rates are intended to ensure that in comparing living standards between countries a dollar in one country commands the same basket of goods and services as in another country. However, the same basket of goods and services may mean different degrees of hardship in different countries and over time owing to differences in institutions, social norms and practices, and differences in available goods and services.[18] Nevertheless, the comparison of the levels of consumption of the poor in the high-income countries and the LDCs does put the nature of generalized poverty in the LDCs into a broader perspective.

The current dollar estimates of average per capita income and consumption in the table are also of significant interest. These are not measures of living standards, but they indicate the purchasing power of nations or the poor within the nations in terms of current international prices. As various LDCs over the past two decades have eased current account trade and exchange restrictions, the current dollar figures may have become more relevant to people's lives. As can be seen from the table, in terms of current prices and official exchange rates during 1995–1999:

- The average per capita income in the LDCs for which we have data is about 72 cents a day, and the average per capita private consumption is 57 cents a day.

- In African LDCs, the average per capita income is 65 cents a day, and the average per capita private consumption is 52 cents a day. In Asian LDCs, the average per capita income is 88 cents a day and the average per capita private consumption is 69 cents a day.

- The average per capita private consumption of those living in LDCs below the $2-a-day international poverty line is 44 cents a day. The average per capita consumption of those living in LDCs below the $1-a-day international poverty line is 29 cents a day.

- The poorest 10 per cent of the population in the industrialized countries have an average private consumption per head of about $13 a day.

In terms of current prices and official exchange rates during 1995–1999, the average per capita private consumption of those living in LDCs below the $2-a-day international poverty line is 44 cents a day. The poorest 10 per cent of the population in the industrialized countries have an average private consumption per head of about $13 a day.

These extremely low levels of per capita income and consumption at official exchange rates and in current dollars are indicative of the very low levels of labour productivity and the meagre resource availability in the LDCs, with far-reaching implications for the nature of required poverty reduction policies and strategies in those countries (see chapter 5). This also provides one of the important underlying reasons for the persistence of generalized poverty over time, which is a central feature of the trends in poverty discussed in section D of this chapter.

2. A POVERTY MAP FOR THE LDCs IN 1995–1999

There are of course variations between the LDCs. On the basis of estimates of the incidence of poverty at the internationally defined $1-a-day and $2-a-day poverty lines, one can sketch a poverty map for the LDCs (chart 10). The horizontal axis of the map shows the incidence of poverty for the $1 international poverty line and the vertical axis shows the incidence of poverty for the $2 line. The closer a country is to the north-east corner on the poverty map the worse the poverty situation in that country is, and the closer a country is to the south-west corner the lower the incidence of poverty.

The poverty estimates shown in chart 10 are sensitive to the errors in national accounts estimates of consumption as well as errors in PPP exchange rates. However, even if we allow for a 20 to 30 per cent margin of error, the chart suggests an alarming poverty profile for the LDC countries.

- In three-quarters of the LDCs, including most of those located in sub-Saharan Africa, over 80 per cent of the population live on less than $2 a day.

- In all African LDCs, and all Asian LDCs with the exception of one, the share of the population living on less than $2 a day was close to and often well over 60 per cent in the late 1990s.

- In 30 LDCs, more than 25 per cent of the population live below the $1-a-day poverty line and in 20 countries the share of the population living in extreme poverty is above 50 per cent.

CHART 10. A POVERTY MAP FOR LDCs, 1995–1999[a]

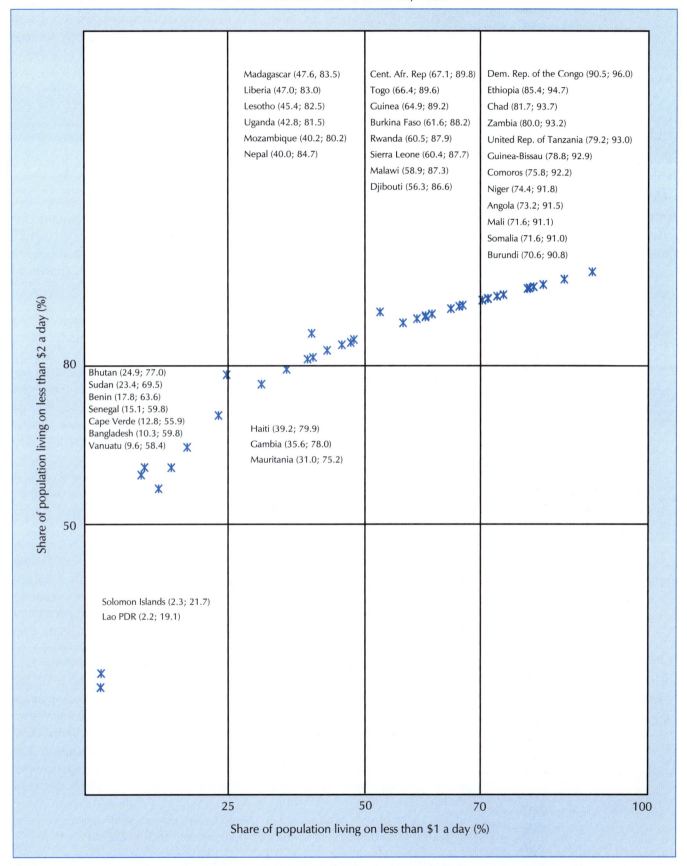

Madagascar (47.6, 83.5)
Liberia (47.0; 83.0)
Lesotho (45.4; 82.5)
Uganda (42.8; 81.5)
Mozambique (40.2; 80.2)
Nepal (40.0; 84.7)

Cent. Afr. Rep (67.1; 89.8)
Togo (66.4; 89.6)
Guinea (64.9; 89.2)
Burkina Faso (61.6; 88.2)
Rwanda (60.5; 87.9)
Sierra Leone (60.4; 87.7)
Malawi (58.9; 87.3)
Djibouti (56.3; 86.6)

Dem. Rep. of the Congo (90.5; 96.0)
Ethiopia (85.4; 94.7)
Chad (81.7; 93.7)
Zambia (80.0; 93.2)
United Rep. of Tanzania (79.2; 93.0)
Guinea-Bissau (78.8; 92.9)
Comoros (75.8; 92.2)
Niger (74.4; 91.8)
Angola (73.2; 91.5)
Mali (71.6; 91.1)
Somalia (71.6; 91.0)
Burundi (70.6; 90.8)

Bhutan (24.9; 77.0)
Sudan (23.4; 69.5)
Benin (17.8; 63.6)
Senegal (15.1; 59.8)
Cape Verde (12.8; 55.9)
Bangladesh (10.3; 59.8)
Vanuatu (9.6; 58.4)

Haiti (39.2; 79.9)
Gambia (35.6; 78.0)
Mauritania (31.0; 75.2)

Solomon Islands (2.3; 21.7)
Lao PDR (2.2; 19.1)

Share of population living on less than $2 a day (%)

80

50

25   50   70   100

Share of population living on less than $1 a day (%)

Source: UNCTAD secretariat estimates based on Karshenas (2001).

Note: The numbers in parentheses indicate the share of the population living on less than $1 a day and $2 a day, respectively during the period 1995–1999.

a Based on international poverty line in 1985 PPP dollars. These estimates do not conform to estimates based on a national poverty line.

Individual country data during 1995–1999 for those LDCs where data are available are presented in table 19. It shows national-accounts-consistent estimates of the incidence of poverty, the number of poor and their average consumption, based on international poverty lines of $1 a day and $2 a day in constant 1985 PPP dollars. The total number of people living on less than $1 a day in the LDCs as a whole in the later 1990s is estimated to be 307 million, and the total number of people living on less than $2 a day is estimated to be 495 million.

The total number of people living on less than $1 a day in the LDCs as a whole in the later 1990s is estimated to be 307 million, and the total number of people living on less than $2 a day is estimated to be 495 million.

D. The dynamics of poverty in the LDCs

Average poverty trends in the LDCs, and 22 other developing countries for which we have data during the past four decades, are shown in tables 20 and 21 and chart 11.[19] The key pattern which the tables and chart reveal is that poverty in the LDCs as a group, in contrast to the other developing countries, appears to be persistent and even growing over time.

The incidence of poverty for the LDC group is estimated to have increased from about 48 per cent during 1965–1969 to over 50 per cent during 1995–1999 for the $1 poverty line. For the $2 poverty line, the incidence of poverty for the LDC group as a whole seems to have been fluctuating at around 80 per cent over the past few decades. These figures are in sharp contrast to the trends in the sample of other developing countries, which are driven by trends in large low-income Asian countries, particularly China, India and Indonesia. In the group of other developing countries, the incidence of poverty using a $1-a-day poverty line is estimated to have declined from about 45 per cent during 1965–1969 to just over 8 per cent during 1995–1999. Using a $2-a-day poverty line, it is estimated to have declined from about 83 per cent to nearly 35 per cent over the same period. Similar contrasting trends are shown with regard to the average consumption of the poor.

On the basis of these figures, it is apparent that the LDCs have become the primary locus for extreme poverty in the global economy.

On the basis of these figures, it is apparent that the LDCs have become the primary locus for extreme poverty in the global economy.[20] Of course, there are wide variations in the performance of different LDCs as there are variations amongst the other developing countries. Asian LDCs seem to have performed much better than African LDCs with regard to poverty trends over time. The average incidence of poverty in the Asian LDCs for the $1-a-day poverty line fell from 35.5 per cent in the late 1960s to about 23 per cent in the late 1990s, and the same indicator for the $2-a-day poverty line declined from about 79 per cent to 68 per cent in those countries. These trends are not as impressive as for other developing countries, but are still considerable improvements relative to trends in the African LDCs. In the African LDCs in fact, the incidence of poverty appears to have been increasing over time during the past few decades. The proportion of the population living below $1 a day is estimated to have increased from about 56 per cent during 1965–1969 to about 65 per cent during 1995–1999 in the African LDCs as a group. Over the same period, the incidence of poverty with regard to the $2-a-day poverty line appears to have increased from 82 per cent to over 87 per cent for African LDCs as a whole.

Similar trends are observable with regard to depth of poverty in the African and Asian LDCs relative to the other developing countries. In African LDCs, after an initial improvement, the depth of poverty seems to have been increasing since the mid-1970s. The average consumption of those living on less than $1 a day in those countries declined from an average of $0.66 a day to $0.59 a day between 1975–1979 and 1995–1999. The average consumption of the poor

TABLE 19. THE INCIDENCE AND DEPTH OF POVERTY IN THE LDCs, 1995–1999

	Population living on less than $1 a day[a]			Population living on less than $2 a day[a]		
	Incidence of poverty (%)	Number of poor ('000)	Average consumption of poor (1985 PPP $ a day)	Incidence of poverty (%)	Number of poor ('000)	Average consumption of poor (1985 PPP $ a day)
African LDCs[b]	**64.9**	**233 454.1**	**0.59**	**87.5**	**315 060.1**	**0.86**
Angola	73.2	8 535.1	0.63	91.5	10 668.0	0.81
Benin	17.8	1 029.1	0.96	63.6	3 674.9	1.45
Burkina Faso	61.6	6 446.3	0.73	88.2	9 244.5	0.94
Burundi	70.6	4 531.3	0.65	90.8	5 824.6	0.84
Central African Republic	67.1	2 294.9	0.69	89.8	3 068.8	0.88
Chad	81.7	5 791.8	0.53	93.7	6 643.0	0.70
Dem. Rep. of the Congo	90.5	42 340.6	0.38	96.0	44 915.4	0.55
Djibouti	56.3	351.8	0.77	86.6	540.5	0.99
Ethiopia	85.4	51 011.1	0.47	94.7	56 523.7	0.65
Gambia	35.6	420.3	0.89	78.0	921.3	1.21
Guinea	64.9	4 491.5	0.70	89.2	6 173.5	0.90
Guinea-Bissau	78.8	896.8	0.56	92.9	1 056.3	0.74
Lesotho	45.4	912.0	0.84	82.5	1 661.2	1.11
Liberia	47.0	1 365.6	0.82	83.0	2 397.3	1.09
Madagascar	47.6	6 731.6	0.82	83.4	11 821.4	1.08
Malawi	58.9	6 031.0	0.75	87.3	8 966.4	0.97
Mali	71.6	7 229.2	0.64	91.1	9 192.6	0.83
Mauritania	31.0	762.6	0.91	75.2	1 851.5	1.27
Mozambique	40.2	6 649.6	0.86	80.2	13 292.7	1.16
Niger	74.4	7 301.3	0.62	91.8	9 007.7	0.80
Rwanda	60.5	4 507.4	0.74	87.9	6 573.8	0.95
Senegal	15.1	1 320.5	0.97	59.8	5 256.2	1.50
Sierra Leone	60.4	2 874.2	0.73	87.7	4 157.9	0.95
Somalia	71.6	6 307.2	0.64	91.0	8 002.0	0.83
Sudan	23.4	6 486.5	0.94	69.5	19 275.5	1.36
Togo	66.4	2 878.3	0.69	89.6	3 889.0	0.89
Uganda	42.8	8 681.3	0.85	81.5	16 556.6	1.13
United Rep. of Tanzania	79.2	24 785.3	0.56	93.0	29 121.2	0.74
Zambia	80.0	7 546.6	0.55	93.2	8 799.1	0.73
Haiti	39.2	2 943.6	0.87	79.9	5 983.6	1.17
Asian LDCs	**23.0**	**44 843.7**	**0.90**	**68.2**	**133 295.8**	**1.42**
Bangladesh	10.3	12 681.5	0.99	59.8	73 996.7	1.6
Bhutan	24.9	183.1	0.95	77.0	567.5	1.4
Lao PDR	2.2	105.9	1.00	19.1	924.8	1.9
Myanmar	52.3	22 957.2	0.86	88.6	38 912.8	1.1
Nepal	40.0	8 915.9	0.91	84.7	18 894.0	1.2
Island LDCs	**31.3**	**470.7**	**0.66**	**59.5**	**896.1**	**1.18**
Cape Verde	12.8	51.4	0.98	55.9	225.5	1.5
Comoros	75.8	392.7	0.60	92.2	477.3	0.8
Solomon Islands	2.3	9.3	1.00	21.7	88.1	1.9
Vanuatu	9.6	17.4	0.99	58.5	105.2	1.6
39 LDCs[c]	**50.1**	**278 768.5**	**0.64**	**80.7**	**449 252.0**	**1.03**
All LDCs[d]	**50.1**	**306 937.5**	**0.64**	**80.7**	**494 625.7**	**1.03**

Source: UNCTAD secretariat estimates based on Karshenas (2001).

a Based on international poverty line in 1985 PPP dollars. These estimates do not conform to estimates based on a national poverty line.
b Including Haiti.
c Refers to LDCs listed in the table.
d Estimated on the assumption that the incidence and depth of poverty in the LDCs for which we have no data are the same as for the 39 LDCs.

with regard to the $2-a-day poverty line declined from $0.96 a day to $0.86 a day over the same period. The Asian LDCs, on the other hand, have shown a continuous improvement, with the average consumption of those living below the $1-a-day poverty line increasing from about $0.84 a day during 1965–1969 to $0.90 a day during 1995–1999. The average consumption of those living below the $2-a-day poverty line in Asian LDCs increased from $1.27 a day to $1.42 a day during the same period. Other developing countries have, on the other hand, exhibited a much sharper increase as regards the average consumption of the poor relative to the Asian LDCs and particularly relative to the LDC average as a whole (tables 20 and 21).

An important difference between the LDCs and other developing countries which is worth highlighting is the difference in the depth of poverty between the two, as indicated by the average level of consumption of the poor. During 1965–1969, the average private consumption of the population living on less than $1 a day is estimated to have been at about $0.70 a day in the LDCs, compared with $0.86 a day for other developing countries. By 1995–1999, the gap between the two had increased to $0.64 a day and $0.93 a day respectively. With regard to the $2-a-day poverty line, the average private consumption per capita of the poor declined in the LDCs from $1.07 a day to $1.03 a day between 1965–1969 and 1995–1999, whilst in other developing countries it rose from $1.17 and $1.65 a day.

The extremely adverse initial conditions in the LDCs, particularly the African LDCs, with respect to the depth of poverty are an important handicap which needs to be taken into account in any realistic poverty reduction strategies.

The situation in the Asian LDCs, though lagging behind that of the other developing countries, was relatively better. The African LDCs, however, substantially lag behind other developing countries with respect to the depth of poverty. The average consumption of the poor in the African LDCs is estimated at $0.59 for the $1-a-day poverty line and only $0.86 for the $2-a-day poverty line during 1995–1999, which contrasts with $0.93 and $1.65 for the other developing countries. According to these figures, more than 87 per cent of the population of the African LDCs living below $2 a day have an average consumption that is even lower than the average consumption of those living below $1 a day in other developing countries and indeed other LDCs. The extremely adverse initial conditions in the LDCs, particularly the African LDCs, with respect to the depth of poverty are an important handicap which needs to be taken into account in any realistic poverty reduction strategies.

The regional poverty trends of course hide individual country variations. In order to examine the trends in poverty for various individual LDCs, the trends in the incidence of $1-a-day poverty for individual countries for the decade of the 1980s and the decade of the 1990s are plotted in chart 12. The change in the incidence of poverty during the 1980s is depicted on the horizontal axis of the chart, and the change for the 1990s is shown on the vertical axis. The line AB divides the LDCs into two broad groupings. Countries that have shown an overall increase in headcount poverty during the two decades as a whole are located above AB, and those where the overall headcount poverty has declined are located below this line. As can be seen, 23 out of the 37 LDCs for which poverty estimates are available over the two decades show an increase in poverty over the period as a whole.

The chart can be used to make a further classification of the LDCs in relation to poverty trends. The countries in the north-east quadrant of the chart are countries where the poverty situation was deteriorating during both the 1980s and the 1990s. Twelve countries are in this quadrant, showing persistent deterioration throughout the two decades. Eleven of these countries are African LDCs. At the other extreme, in the south-west quadrant there are nine countries

TABLE 20. POVERTY TRENDS IN LDCS AND OTHER DEVELOPING COUNTRIES, 1965–1999[a]

(1985 PPP $1-a-day international poverty line)

	1965–1969	1975–1979	1985–1989	1995–1999
Population living on less than $1 a day *(%)*				
39 LDCs[b]	48.0	48.5	49.0	50.1
African LDCs	55.8	56.4	61.9	64.9
Asian LDCs	35.5	35.9	27.6	23.0
22 other developing countries[c]	44.8	32.5	15.0	7.5
Number of people living on less than $1 a day *(millions)*				
39 LDCs[b]	125.4	164.0	216.0	278.8
African LDCs	89.6	117.4	170.5	233.5
Asian LDCs	35.6	46.5	45.2	44.8
22 other developing countries[c]	760.0	697.0	389.3	229.2
Average daily consumption of those living below $1 a day *(1985 PPP $)*				
39 LDCs[b]	0.70	0.71	0.69	0.64
African LDCs	0.64	0.66	0.64	0.59
Asian LDCs	0.84	0.85	0.89	0.90
22 other developing countries[c]	0.86	0.91	0.96	0.93

Source: UNCTAD secretariat estimates based on World Bank, *World Development Indicators 2001* CD-ROM, and Karshenas (2001).

a   Country group averages are weighted averages.
b   For LDCs sample composition see LDCs listed in table 19.
c   Other developing countries are: Algeria, Cameroon, China, Congo, Côte d'Ivoire, Dominican Republic, Egypt, Ghana, India, Indonesia, Jamaica, Kenya, Morocco, Namibia, Nigeria, Pakistan, Philippines, Sri Lanka, Thailand, Tunisia, Turkey and Zimbabwe.

TABLE 21. POVERTY TRENDS IN LDCS AND OTHER DEVELOPING COUNTRIES, 1965–1999[a]

(1985 PPP $2-a-day international poverty line)

	1965–1969	1975–1979	1985–1989	1995–1999
Population living on less than $2 a day *(%)*				
39 LDCs[b]	80.8	82.1	81.9	80.7
African LDCs	82.0	83.7	87.0	87.5
Asian LDCs	78.8	79.6	73.4	68.2
22 other developing countries[c]	82.8	76.5	61.6	35.3
Number of people living on less than $2 a day *(millions)*				
39 LDCs[b]	211.1	277.5	360.5	449.3
African LDCs	131.7	174.4	239.5	315.1
Asian LDCs	79.1	102.9	120.3	133.3
22 other developing countries[c]	1 405.0	1 639.7	1 599.0	1 084.2
Average daily consumption of those living below $2 a day *(1985 PPP $)*				
39 LDCs[b]	1.07	1.07	1.06	1.03
African LDCs	0.95	0.96	0.90	0.86
Asian LDCs	1.27	1.27	1.37	1.42
22 other developing countries[c]	1.17	1.30	1.53	1.65

Source: Same as for table 20.

a   Country group averages are weighted averages.
b   For LDCs sample composition see LDCs listed in table 19.
c   Other developing countries are: Algeria, Cameroon, China, Congo, Côte d'Ivoire, Dominican Republic, Egypt, Ghana, India, Indonesia, Jamaica, Kenya, Morocco, Namibia, Nigeria, Pakistan, Philippines, Sri Lanka, Thailand, Tunisia, Turkey and Zimbabwe.

CHART 11. POVERTY TRENDS IN LDCs, BY REGION, AND IN OTHER DEVELOPING COUNTRIES, 1965–1999[a]

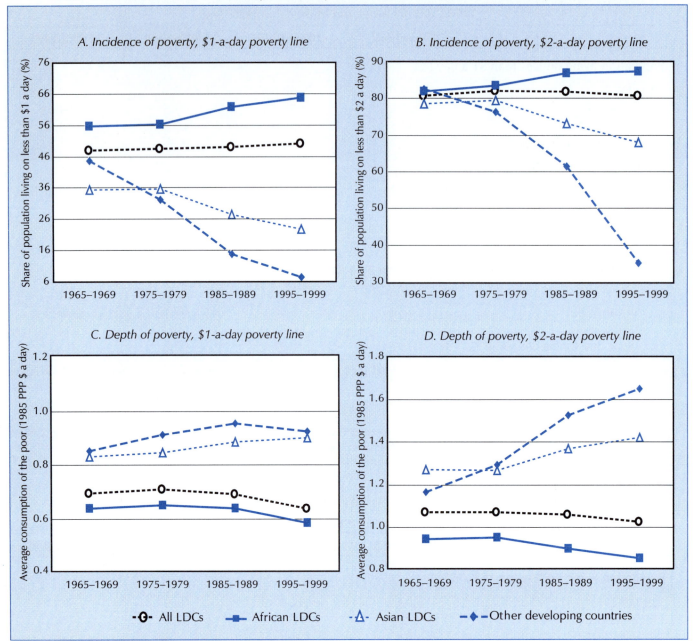

Source: UNCTAD secretariat estimates based on Karshenas (2001).

a   Based on 39 LDCs and 22 other developing countries. See table 19 for list of LDCs, and table 20, note c, for list of developing
        countries.

that showed persistent poverty reduction during both the 1980s and the 1990s.
With the exception of one island (Cape Verde) and three African LDCs (Burkina
Faso, Mauritania and Uganda), all these countries are Asian LDCs. In fact, all
Asian LDCs for which data are available are in this quadrant. A third group of
countries in the south-east quadrant are those that had increased poverty during
the 1980s, but showed improvement over the 1990s. The nine countries listed
in that quadrant can be further classified into two groups, namely those falling
above the AB line and those falling below. Five African countries (Benin,
Gambia, Liberia, Mozambique and United Republic of Tanzania) in the former
group are those where the reduction in poverty during the 1990s was not
sufficient to neutralize the deterioration that occurred during the decade of the
1980s, and hence show an overall deteriorating trend. On the other hand, four
countries in the south-east quadrant (Ethiopia, Guinea, Malawi and Sudan)

CHART 12. CHANGE IN PERCENTAGE OF POPULATION LIVING ON LESS THAN $1 A DAY IN THE LDCs, 1980s AND 1990s[a]

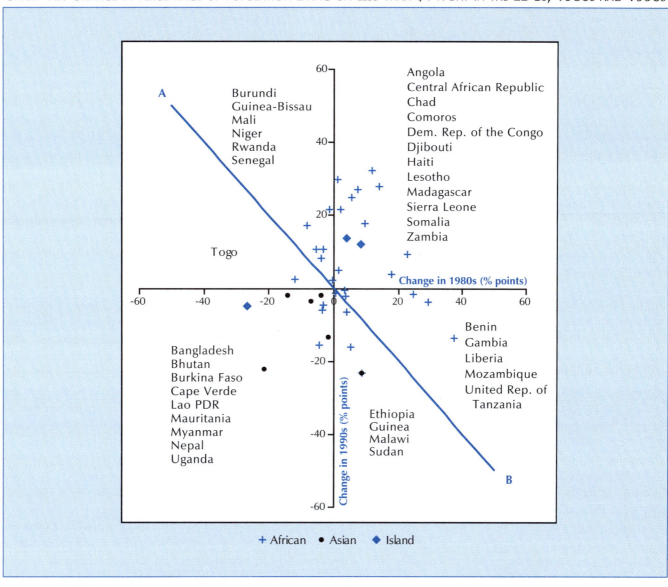

Source: UNCTAD secretariat estimates based on Karshenas (2001).

a   Change in the 1980s refers to the difference in the share of the population living on less than $1 a day between 1975–1979
      and 1985–1989, in percentage points (horizontal axis). Change in 1990s refers to the same difference between 1985–1989
      and 1995–1999 (vertical axis). Solomon Islands and Vanuatu are not included owing to lack of data during the 1980s.

managed to compensate for the increasing poverty trends during the 1980s by relatively larger improvements during the 1990s. Seven LDCs (Burundi, Guinea-Bissau, Mali, Niger, Rwanda, Senegal and Togo) witnessed improvements in the 1980s but worsening poverty in the 1990s. All of these countries are African LDCs. Amongst all of them except Togo, the deterioration during the 1990s reversed all the poverty reduction gains achieved during the 1980s.

It is significant that only three LDCs managed to reduce the incidence of poverty with respect to the $1 poverty line by more than 20 per cent during the 1980s and the 1990s. Of these three countries, only two (namely, Cape Verde and the Lao People's Democratic Republic) had a consistent reduction in poverty during those two decades. The third country (Sudan) achieved this by a spurt in the rate of poverty reduction in the 1990s, which reversed the 1980s deterioration. In the majority of the LDCs, therefore, poverty is not only generalized. It is also persistent.

Only three LDCs managed to reduce the incidence of poverty with respect to the $1 poverty line by more than 20 per cent during the 1980s and the 1990s.

Annex to Chapter 1

METHODOLOGY OF POVERTY MEASUREMENT USED IN THIS REPORT

This Report describes and analyses poverty in the LDCs on the basis of a new data set of poverty estimates for 39 LDCs and 22 other developing countries (Karshenas, 2001). The data set covers all LDCs and developing countries for which, given the methodology used, it was possible to obtain estimates of the incidence and depth of poverty using $1-a-day and $2-a-day poverty lines. The LDCs for which poverty estimates have been made cover 91 per cent of the total population of the LDCs in the year 2000.

The poverty estimates are national-accounts-consistent estimates of poverty in the sense that they are anchored in national macroeconomic estimates of aggregate private consumption. The incidence and the depth of poverty are calculated using the normal procedures of poverty estimation. But instead of relying on household survey data for estimating both the mean and the distribution of private consumption, the new measures combine the average per capita private consumption of the population as reported in national accounts data with estimates of the distribution of consumption across households from the sample surveys of living standards.

The poverty data created by Karshenas are not only anchored in national accounts, but also consist of statistical estimates of "expected poverty". It is possible to make these estimates because there is a regular relationship between average levels of private consumption per capita and the incidence and depth of poverty among countries. This relationship has been established by focusing on those LDCs and other developing countries that have survey data available for directly estimating the distribution of consumption across households, and examining how the national-accounts-consistent estimates of the incidence and depth of $1-a-day and $2-a-day poverty vary with the average level of private consumption per capita in each country. The results cover 92 observations for 32 countries over three decades. The sample is confined to African and Asian developing countries as Latin American household surveys focus on income rather than consumption expenditure.

In the present Report, the poverty estimates for LDCs are derived using regression analysis. This is done by fitting "poverty curves" which specify the regular relationship between average levels of private consumption per capita and poverty in the sample of countries for which we have data. Various functional forms were applied to find the best fit between average private consumption per capita and the incidence and depth of poverty. In all cases the logistic (s-shaped) curve was preferred, with consumption per capita accounting for 95 per cent of the variation in the incidence of $1-a-day poverty in the sample, and 96 per cent of the variation in the incidence of $2-a-day poverty. A time dummy variable (distinguishing observations in the 1990s from the other decades) and a regional dummy variable (distinguishing African from non-African observations) were also introduced to determine whether they might further reduce the standard error of the fitted curve. The time dummy variable had no impact on the results, whilst the regional dummy slightly improved the predictive power of the regression model for $1-a-day poverty and was incorporated into the final estimates. Other variables related to the structure of the economy could have been included, but were not included since the predictive power of the model was already high.

Annex table 1 below shows the regression results for estimating the incidence of poverty using the $1-a-day and $2-a-day international poverty lines. Regression equation II in the top panel of the table corresponds to the fitted line in chart 8A, and regression equation IV was used in estimating the expected incidence of poverty in the LDCs and other developing countries for the $1-a-day poverty line. Regression equation II in the bottom panel of the table corresponds to the fitted line in chart 8B, and was also used in estimating the expected incidence of poverty for the $2-a-day poverty line.

The close fit of the model implies that one may be confident, in statistical terms, that the estimates of expected poverty made without household survey distribution data are very close to actual (national-accounts-consistent) poverty estimates made with household distribution data. Indeed, in all cases there is a 95 per cent probability that the expected incidence of poverty is within one percentage point of the actual incidence of poverty for countries where household survey data enable such actual estimates to be made. Annex chart 1 shows, for countries where there are data on the distribution of consumption, the difference between actual national-accounts-consistent poverty estimates and the estimates of expected poverty which are derived from the regression model.

ANNEX TABLE 1. ESTIMATED STATISTICAL RELATIONSHIP BETWEEN INCIDENCE OF POVERTY
AND AVERAGE PRIVATE CONSUMPTION PER CAPITA AND OTHER VARIABLES

| | Dependent variable: logistic transformation of proportion of population below $1 a day | | | | | | | | | | | |
| | (I) | | | (II) | | | (III) | | | (IV) | | |
Variable	Coeff.	S.E.	t-Statistic	Coeff.	S.E.	t-Statistic	Coeff.	S.E.	t-Statistic	Coeff.	S.E.	t-Statistic
Constant	2.9376	0.14	21.29379	3.93	0.31	12.71	3.63	0.31	11.61	3.66	0.29	12.71
C (consumption)[a]	-0.006	0.00	-24.30974	-0.009743	0.00	-8.48	-0.0084	0.00	-7.83	-0.0087	0.00	-8.70
C^2 (consumption sq.)				3.09E-06	0.00	3.19	2.47E-06	0.00	2.90	2.68E-06	0.00	3.41
Region[b]							-0.388	0.09	-4.29	-0.435	0.08	-5.39
D90[c]							-0.138	0.08	-1.69			
No. of observations	58			58			58			58		
R-squared	0.934			0.946			0.967			0.965		
Adjusted R-squared	0.933			0.944			0.964			0.963		
SE of regression[d]	0.342			0.315			0.250			0.256		
Mean dependent var.	-0.665			-0.665			-0.66459			-0.66459		
SD dependent var.	1.326			1.326			1.326024			1.326024		

| | Dependent variable: logistic transformation of proportion of population below $2 a day | | | | | | | | | | | |
| | (I) | | | (II) | | | (III) | | | (IV) | | |
Variable	Coeff.	S.E.	t-Statistic	Coeff.	S.E.	t-Statistic	Coeff.	S.E.	t-Statistic	Coeff.	S.E.	t-Statistic
Constant	2.7362	0.13	20.26838	4.07	0.15	27.31	4.05	0.15	26.31	4.05	0.15	26.42
C (consumption)[a]	-0.003	0.00	-15.1782	-0.005372	0.00	-16.68	-0.00529	0.00	-15.63	-0.00529	0.00	-15.77
C^2 (consumption sq.)				1.17E-06	0.00	8.07	1.15E-06	0.00	7.72	1.15E-06	0.00	7.79
Region[b]							-0.062	0.05	-1.17	-0.060	0.05	-1.16
D90[c]							0.010	0.05	0.19			
No. of observations	90			90			90			90		
R-squared	0.878			0.962			0.962			0.962		
Adjusted R-squared	0.877			0.961			0.960			0.961		
SE of regression[d]	0.466			0.262			0.264			0.263		
Mean dependent var.	0.533			0.533			0.533			0.533		
SD dependent var.	1.328			1.328			1.328			1.328		

Source: Karshenas (2001).

Note: The total sample is: Algeria (1988, 1995), Bangladesh (1984,1985, 1988, 1991, 1995), Burkina Faso (1994), Ethiopia (1981, 1995), Egypt (1991), Gambia (1992), Ghana (1987, 1989, 1992), Guinea-Bissau (1991), India (1965, 1970, 1983, 1986, 1987, 1988, 1989, 1990, 1992, 1995, 1996, 1997), Indonesia (1976, 1984, 1987, 1990, 1993, 1996, 1998), Côte d'Ivoire (1985, 1986, 1987, 1988, 1993, 1995), Kenya (1992, 1994), Lesotho (1986, 1993), Madagascar (1980, 1993), Mali (1989, 1994), Mauritania (1988, 1993, 1995), Morocco (1985, 1990), Mozambique (1996), Nepal (1985, 1995), Niger (1992, 1995), Nigeria (1986, 1992, 1993, 1996), Pakistan (1969, 1979, 1987, 1990, 1993, 1996), Philippines (1985, 1988, 1991, 1994, 1997), Rwanda (1984), Senegal (1991, 1994), Sri Lanka (1985, 1995), Thailand (1992, 1998), Tunisia (1985, 1990), Turkey (1987, 1994), Uganda (1989, 1992), United Republic of Tanzania (1991, 1993) and Zambia (1991, 1993, 1996).

a   Consumption (C) is per capita private consumption expenditure in 1985 PPP dollars.
b   Region is an Africa(0)/non-Africa(1) dummy variable.
c   D90 is dummy variable for the 1990 decade.
d   Standard errors are White heteroskedasticity-consistent standard errors.

    The $1-a-day and $2-a-day poverty lines, and also estimates of average private consumption per capita of the total population and of the poor in each country, are calculated in constant 1985 PPP dollars using publicly available PPP exchange rates to convert consumption in local currency units into an internationally comparable money-metric. This is how global poverty estimates were originally made, but the World Bank has recently changed the base year from 1985 to 1993. The two international poverty lines in World Bank statistics have correspondingly changed to $1.08 and $2.15 in 1993 prices. They are, nevertheless, still referred to as the $1-a-day and $2-a-day poverty lines respectively. Since the change of the base year, if correctly done, should not make any difference to the poverty estimates, this Report continues to use the 1985 base year and sets the poverty lines at exactly one and two dollars.

ANNEX CHART 1. NATIONAL-ACCOUNTS-CONSISTENT POVERTY ESTIMATES IN LDCS AND OTHER DEVELOPING COUNTRIES, ACTUAL VS. EXPECTED ESTIMATES OF THE INCIDENCE OF POVERTY AND AVERAGE CONSUMPTION OF THE POOR

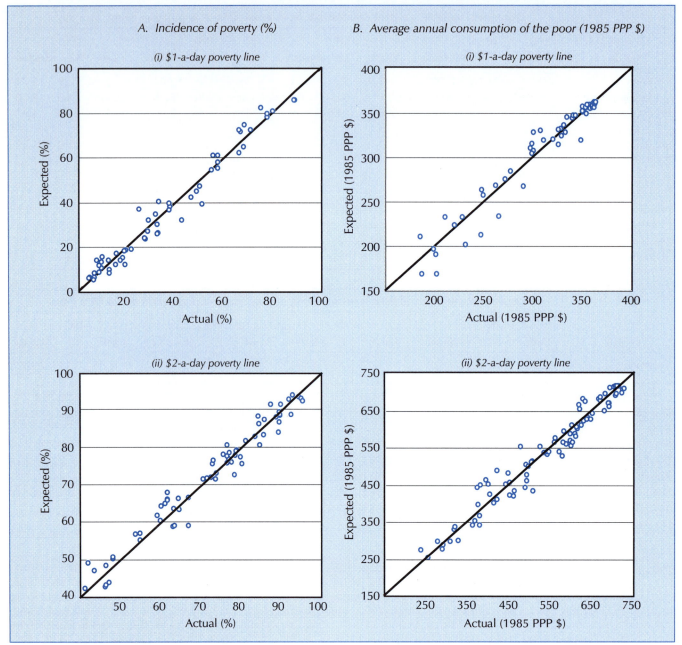

Source: Karshenas (2001).

The 1985 base year is preferred since the final year of the Summers and Heston data set, which is the source of PPP exchange rate estimates, is 1992, and hence it is difficult to check the consistency of the new World Bank poverty lines with the old ones. It appears that in addition to the change in the base year, the World Bank 1993 PPP rates have re-estimated some of the earlier measures in Penn World Tables version 5.6 (see, e.g., Chen and Ravallion, 2000). Since there is no official documentation on this and the data are not also available publicly, this Report has used PPP exchange rates from the latest Penn World Tables (version 5.6) with a 1985 base year.

The last date for the Summers and Heston estimates of private consumption in 1985 PPP dollars is 1992. Values of private consumption per capita in PPP terms in the 1990s have been estimated by applying the growth rates of real private consumption per capita to the 1992 figures. In a few cases and years where data on the growth rate of real consumption were not available, the growth rate of real GDP per capita has been used to extend the latest estimates of consumption.[21] This assumes that the share of private consumption in GDP remains constant.

Full details of the methods used in constructing the data set are available in Karshenas (2001).

Notes

1. It should be noted that in setting the poverty lines as a fixed real amount (either $1 a day or $2 a day in 1985 PPP $) this Report focuses on absolute poverty rather than relative poverty. With the latter notion of poverty, the part of the population that is poor is identified in relation to the average income of the total population. For example, the poor may be identified as those who have 50 per cent or less of the mean income in the country. The term "absolute poverty" is not used in the main text in order to avoid excessive terminology. In line with current international conventions, the term "extreme poverty" is defined throughout the Report on the basis of the $1-a-day international poverty line.

2. There are different approaches to the multidimensionality of poverty. See World Bank (2000), UNDP (1997), and Rodgers, Gore and Figueiredo (1995).

3. For a vivid description of the multidimensionality of poverty, see Narayan et al. (2000).

4. At the PPP exchange rate, one international dollar has the same purchasing power over domestic GNP that the United States dollar has over United States GNP.

5. For discussion of some of the problems of international comparisons of poverty, see Atkinson (1991), Chen, Datt and Ravallion (1994), and Chen and Ravallion (2000), and for an alternative approach to international poverty comparison, see Townsend (1993). Vandemoortele (2001) also provides an insightful discussion of some limits of the $1-a-day poverty line.

6. Work of this nature in Latin America, which empirically examined the relationship between the $1-a- day and $2-a-day poverty lines and the costs of differently defined minimally acceptable baskets of goods and services, shows that in that context the $2-a-day poverty line can be interpreted as a measure of malnutrition or physical survival. The research also suggests that the $1-a-day poverty line in that context "has no meaning" since, given the costs of securing the bare prerequisites for physical survival, "people with this level of income would be technically dead" (Boltvinik, 1996: 254).

7. These are weighted averages. It should be noted that estimates of the levels of consumption are not simply market purchases, but include goods produced and consumed by the household itself.

8. Historical research also shows the same phenomenon. In the United States, the minimum subsistence budget rose by about 0.75 per cent for every 1 per cent increase in disposable per capita income of the general population over the period 1905–1960 (Fisher, 1997, cited in Vandemoortele, 2001). This reflects amongst other things the fact that certain goods and services which made it possible to live on less in the earlier period were no longer available later on.

9. However, the Report specifies the international poverty lines using 1985 as a base year; see the annex to this chapter. For some suggestions on how to deal with the PPP problem, as well as a major critique of the way in which PPP conversion rates are used in the World Bank's global poverty estimates, see Reddy and Pogge (2002).

10. The difference in price levels between average African and average Asian LDCs is likely to be due to the relatively lower wage rates and hence price levels (particularly of non-tradable goods and services) in the densely populated Asian LDCs. Furthermore, the imported component of consumption expenditure is likely to be greater in African LDCs than in large Asian LDCs such as Bangladesh. Some of the African LDCs are also landlocked economies with sparse populations spread over large expanses of land, and this adds to both the internal and the external cost of transportation as compared with the densely populated Asian LDCs. See Karshenas (2001) for further discussion of this issue.

11. It is pertinent in this regard that in the current guidelines for Poverty Reduction Strategy Papers (PRSPs) it is recognized that appropriate indicators and specific targets will vary between countries, even though the inclusion of indicators related to the International Development Goals is considered to be desirable.

12. The estimates were made using the World Bank's very useful POVCAL programme. See Datt, Chen and Ravallion (1994).

13. This entails the type of analysis that has been undertaken in India — see World Bank (2000: box 1.8) — and also in Latin America (Altimir, 1987).

14. The World Bank also argues that consumption is the preferred indicator, "for practical reasons of reliability and because consumption is thought to better capture long-run welfare levels than current income" (World Bank, 2000: 17). However, in making its global poverty estimates the World Bank uses both consumption and income data collected through household surveys. Where survey data are available on incomes but not on consumption, consumption is "estimated by multiplying all incomes by the share of aggregate private consumption in national income based on national accounts data", a procedure which "scales back income but leaves the distribution unchanged" (ibid.: 17). This type of adjustment was not undertaken in the present analysis.

15. See Karshenas (2001), and the annex to this chapter, for more details. Confidence intervals and validation tests for estimated poverty measures indicate that the error involved in this estimation procedure is relatively low. No estimates are made for Latin American countries owing to the lack of household survey data on the distribution of consumption.

16. The term "international analysis of poverty" is used here to refer to an approach to poverty analysis that identifies differences in the nature and dynamics of poverty between countries, and which includes the effects of both domestic factors and international relationships in the analysis of poverty within countries.

17. National accounts consumption data for most island LDCs are not available at 1985 PPP exchange rates. Poverty estimates for a few island LDCs that have available data are reported in table 19.

18. Also, the private consumption figures do not take into account the much greater magnitude and quality of public services that the poor in high-income OECD countries benefit from.

19. The sample of other developing countries excludes Latin American countries and upper-middle-income countries. It also excludes developing countries with private consumption of more than $2,400 a year (in 1985 PPP dollars) as this is the upper limit at which it is possible to make estimates of the incidence and depth of poverty for the $2-a-day poverty line. Other developing countries for which there are data on average private consumption per capita (in 1985 PPP dollars) from the 1960s to the 1990s are included. The 22 other developing countries are listed in table 20.

20. The upper limit of private consumption per capita beyond which $1-a-day poverty becomes a residual phenomenon is about $1,000 (in 1985 PPP dollars). Apart from the developing countries included in table 20, the only other developing countries with annual private consumption per capita below $1,200 (in 1985 PPP dollars) in the late 1990s for which data are available are: Guyana, Honduras, Nicaragua and Papua New Guinea. No data on private consumption per capita (in 1985 PPP dollars) are available for the following economies classified as low- and lower-middle-income in the World Bank statistics: Albania, Armenia, Azerbaijan, Belarus, Bosnia and Herzegovina, Cuba, Democratic People's Republic of Korea, Georgia, Kyrgyzstan, Latvia, Lithuania, Marshall Islands, Micronesia (Federated States of), Moldova, Tajikistan, The Former Yugoslav Republic of Macedonia, Turkmenistan, Ukraine, Uzbekistan, West Bank and Gaza, and Yugoslavia (Serbia and Montenegro).

21. The countries and years in which this was done are: Bhutan (1986–1999), Democratic Republic of the Congo (1998–1999), Djibouti (1988–1999), Lao People's Democratic Republic (1992–1999), Liberia (1987–1999), Solomon Islands (1989–1999), Somalia (1990–1999), Sudan (1993–1999) and Vanuatu (1991–1999).

References

Altimir, O. (1987). Income distribution statistics in Latin America and their reliability, *Review of Income and Wealth*, 33 (2): 111–156.

Atkinson, A.B. (1991). Comparing poverty rates internationally: lessons from recent studies in developed countries, *World Bank Economic Review*, 5: 3–22.

Bhalla, S.S. (2000) Growth and poverty in India: myth and reality, mimeo (http://www.oxusresearch.com/economic/asp).

Boltvinik, J. (1996). Poverty in Latin America: a critical analysis of three studies, *International Social Science Journal*, 148: 245–260.

Chen, S., Datt, G. and Ravallion, M. (1994). Is poverty increasing in the developing world?, *Review of Income and Wealth*, 40(4): 359–377.

Chen, S. and Ravallion, M. (2000). How did the world's poorest fare in the 1990s?, Policy Research Working Paper No. 2409, World Bank, Washington DC.

Chenery, H.B., Ahluwalia, M.S., Bell, C.L.G., Duloy, J.H. and Jolly, R. (1974). *Redistribution with Growth*, Oxford University Press, London.

Collier, P. and Dollar, D. (2001). Can the world cut poverty in half? How policy reform and effective aid can meet International Development Goals, *World Development*, 29 (11): 1727–1802.

Datt, G., Chen, S. and Ravallion, M. (1994). POVCAL: a program for calculating poverty measures for grouped data, mimeo, World Bank, Washington DC.

Deaton, A. (2000). Counting the world's poor: problems and possible solutions, mimeo, Princeton University, Princeton, New Jersey.

Deaton, A. and Grosh, M. (forthcoming). Consumption. In: Grosh, M. and Glenwe, P. *Designing Household Survey Questionnaires for Developing Countries: Lessons from Ten Years of LSMS Experience*, World Bank, Washington DC.

Fisher, G. (1997). Poverty lines and measures of income inadequacy in the United States since 1870: collecting and using a little-known body of historical material, paper presented at the 22nd meeting of the Social Science History Association, Washington DC.

Karshenas, M. (2001). Measurement and nature of absolute poverty in least developed countries, background report for *The Least Developed Countries Report 2002*, Geneva.

Lipton, M. (1996). Emerging Asia, the Penn Tables, and poverty measurement, Poverty Research Unit at Sussex University, *Newsletter*, pp. 1–2.

Milanovic, B. (2001). True world income distribution, 1988 and 1993: first calculation based on household surveys alone, *Economic Journal*, 112: 51–92.

Narayan, D., Chambers, R., Shah, M.K. and Petesch, P. (2001). *Voices of the Poor: Crying Out for Change*, Oxford University Press, New York.

Naschold, F. (2001). Growth, distribution and poverty reduction: LDCs are falling further behind, background report for *The Least Developed Countries Report 2002*, Geneva.

Organisation for Economic Co-operation and Development (OECD) (2001). *DAC Guidelines on Poverty Reduction*, OECD, Paris.

Pyatt, G. (2000). The distribution of living standards within countries: some reflections on an evolving international data base, mimeo, Institute of Social Studies, The Hague.

Ravallion, M. (2000a) Do national accounts provide unbiased estimates of survey-based measures of living standards?, mimeo, Development Research Group, World Bank, Washington DC.

Ravallion, M. (2000b). Should poverty measures be anchored to the national accounts?, *Economic and Political Weekly*, 26 August – 2 September: 3245–3252.

Ravallion, M. (2001). Measuring aggregate welfare in developing countries: how well do national accounts and surveys agree?, mimeo, Development Research Group, World Bank, Washington DC.

Ravallion, M., Datt, G. and van de Walle, D. (1991). Quantifying absolute poverty in the developing world, *Review of Income and Wealth*, 37(4): 345–361.

Reddy, S.G. and Pogge, T.W. (2002). How *not* to count the poor, mimeo, Colombia University, New York. Available at www.socialanalysis.org

Rodgers, G., Gore, C.G. and Figueiredo, J.B. (1995). *Social Exclusion: Rhetoric, Reality, Responses*, International Institute for Labour Studies, ILO, Geneva.

Smith, A. (1776). *An Inquiry into the Nature and Causes of the Wealth of Nations*, Everyman Edition (1910), Home University Library, London.

Townsend, P. (1993). *The International Analysis of Poverty*, Harvester Wheatsheaf, Hertfordshire.

United Nations Development Programme (UNDP) (1997). *Human Development Report 1997*, Oxford University Press, New York.

Vandemoortele, J. (2001). Questioning some norms, facts and findings on global poverty, mimeo, UNDP Bureau for Development Policy, New York.

World Bank (1990). *World Development Report 1990 – Poverty*, Oxford University Press, New York.

World Bank (2000). *World Development Report 2000/2001 — Attacking Poverty*, Oxford University Press, New York.

Generalized poverty, domestic resource availability and economic growth

Chapter 2

A. Introduction

The existence of generalized poverty in most LDCs has important implications for the relationship between economic growth and poverty. In situations of generalized poverty, sustained increases in the level of per capita income and of per capita private consumption have particularly large effects in reducing the incidence and depth of poverty. But generalized poverty itself acts as a major constraint on the sustained economic growth and structural transformation that are necessary for such increases to occur. In short, most LDCs are stuck in a poverty trap. The central policy problem in the LDCs is how to break the cycle of economic stagnation and generalized poverty, and to realize the great opportunity for fast poverty reduction that can occur through sustained economic growth and development.

The fact that many poor countries are caught in a poverty trap is widely acknowledged. The IMF has described "the persistent failure to break the cycle of stagnation and poverty in the poorest countries" as "perhaps the most striking exception to the otherwise remarkable economic achievements of the twentieth century" (IMF, 2000: 36). Similarly, the OECD/World Bank, in their paper on the problem of financing development in the LDCs prepared for the Third United Nations Conference on the Least Developed Countries, has argued that LDCs are caught in a "low-level equilibrium trap" (OECD/World Bank, 2001: 3). It is also increasingly recognized that this problem is of global significance. The despair and anger associated with persistent generalized poverty are an incubator of violence that, as the events of 11 September 2001 show, can have a global reach.

This chapter identifies the magnitude of the opportunity for poverty reduction in the LDCs, and examines some of the national-level cause-effect relationships through which generalized poverty itself acts as a constraint on the realization of this opportunity. It begins by looking more closely at how the incidence of poverty can be expected to decline in the LDCs as per capita private consumption and per capita incomes rise (section B). It then goes on to examine (in section C) a central mechanism through which generalized poverty undermines the conditions for economic development, namely the effects of generalized poverty on domestic resource availability. The chapter discusses how the incidence of poverty affects the domestic resources available to finance private capital formation and public investment, as well as to provide vital public services (section D). It also examines the complex inter-relationships between generalized poverty, population growth and environmental degradation, which in a number of LDCs are leading to a downward spiral in which the natural resource base, on which the livelihood of the majority of the population depends, is being eroded (section E).

In situations of generalized poverty, sustained increases in the level of per capita income and of per capita private consumption have particularly large effects in reducing the incidence of poverty.

But generalized poverty itself acts as a major constraint on the sustained economic growth and structural transformation that are necessary for such increases to occur. In short, most LDCs are stuck in a poverty trap.

It must be stressed at the outset that generalized poverty affects institutions and incentives, as well as domestic resource availability, and that these relationships are also important mechanisms through which generalized poverty constrains growth and development in the LDCs. In this regard, the relationships between generalized poverty and the nature of market institutions, between generalized poverty and domestic corporate capacities, and between generalized poverty and systems of governance, are all relevant. Some LDCs are also caught in a downward spiral in which generalized poverty is interacting with political instability and armed conflict. These relationships, though important, are largely left aside here in order to focus on the resource issue properly. The chapter also leaves aside for the moment the effects of international relationships on the cycle of economic stagnation and generalized poverty in the LDCs, although these are integral to the poverty trap (box 6). Chapters 3 and 4 take up the question of how international trade may reinforce, or help countries to break out of, the poverty trap.

BOX 6. THE NOTION OF A POVERTY TRAP

A poverty trap can be said to exist when poverty has effects which act as causes of poverty. The causes of poverty can be identified at different levels of aggregation, running from the micro level (the characteristics of the household and community), up to the national level (characteristics of the country) and up to the global level (the nature of the international economy and the institutional structures which govern international relationships) (see box 18). It is thus possible to identify poverty traps at different levels of aggregation.

Box Chart 1 sets out elements of a poverty trap which can occur at the individual level. Within this pattern of circular causation, there are a number of feedback loops. Very poor people tend to be hungry, sick and weak. Being hungry makes one prone to being sick and being weak. People are thus able to cultivate less and work less, and as a result they have less money to buy food or can produce less food, and so they are hungry. They also have less money for medical treatment, and so they are more likely to be sick and weak. Becoming HIV-positive can be an integral part of this poverty trap, and as AIDS becomes more prevalent in a population, it has important consequences throughout society.

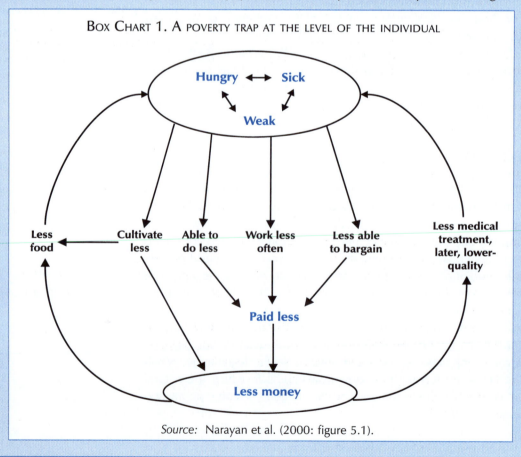

BOX CHART 1. A POVERTY TRAP AT THE LEVEL OF THE INDIVIDUAL

Source: Narayan et al. (2000: figure 5.1).

Box 6 (contd.)

When one moves up to a higher level of aggregation, it is evident that regions within countries can also be stuck in a poverty trap. An aspect of this may be isolation from the main centres of economic activity within a country. Profitable business opportunities may be few, and thus productive employment lacking, owing to poor transport and communication links with those centres. But the low level of economic activity in the isolated region means that transport services are inadequate and that improved transport infrastructure cannot be economically justified, thus perpetuating the isolation.

At the national level, similar circles of causation can occur and make poverty persist. Low income leads to low savings; low savings lead to low investment; low investment leads to low productivity and low incomes. Poverty leads to environmental degradation, which in turn undermines the assets of the poor and exacerbates poverty. Poverty can lead to violence and conflict, and the associated destruction of physical, human, social and organizational capital in turn causes poverty to intensify.

An international poverty trap exists when international relationships are implicated in the process of circular causation which makes poverty persist at the national level. This does not mean that it is only international relationships that are the causes of poverty. Rather, it means that international relationships reinforce, instead of helping to break, the vicious circles of cumulative causation within countries which make poverty persist there.

Saying that there is an international poverty trap does not necessarily mean that globalization is causing poverty. Globalization, understood as increasing interrelationships between countries, is important as it implies that it is logically impossible to explain persistent poverty at the national level solely by national factors. By definition, globalization implies that what is happening within countries is increasingly related to what is happening elsewhere. Globalization thus necessitates a shift in the framework of analysis so that the poverty trap at the national and local levels is put into a global perspective.

Saying that a country is caught in a poverty trap does not imply that the future prospects for that country are hopeless. Rather, identifying the key relationships within a poverty trap is important for policy purposes. They indicate the interlocking constraints that must be addressed by national and international policies in order to have sustained poverty reduction. The elements of a poverty trap do not necessarily provide a complete analysis of the causes of poverty in the country, which would require analysis of how the poverty trap originally arose. But they do provide a sufficient basis for identifying the policies that are necessary for escaping the poverty trap.

In general, in countries suffering from generalized poverty, which are trapped either in a low-level equilibrium or a downward spiral, an orchestrated policy package consisting of the simultaneous deployment of various policies and measures in several areas is likely to be necessary. The unifying idea behind such a policy package should be to break the downward economic spiral or to shift the economy out of its low-level equilibrium. If the poverty trap is international, adequate policy must encompass both national and international policies. Neither national nor international policies can break the poverty trap on their own.

B. The long-run relationship between economic growth and poverty reduction[1]

If there is a sustained increase in average levels of private consumption in the LDCs, the incidence of poverty will normally fall sharply. This expectation is founded on the close relationship that this Report finds to exist between average private consumption per capita and the incidence of $1-a-day and $2-a-day poverty in countries in which the annual private consumption per capita is less than $2,400 (in 1985 PPP dollars).

The precise nature of that relationship is set out in chart 13. The chart depicts two "poverty curves", which define how the share of the population, living on less than $1 a day and on less than $2 a day respectively, varies with the level of annual private consumption per capita for a sample of developing countries in which the average private consumption per capita ranges between $270 a year and $2,400 a year (in 1985 PPP dollars).[2] The observations on which the poverty curves are based are national-accounts-consistent poverty estimates. As explained in the annex in the last chapter, it is these poverty curves that have

CHART 13. $1-A-DAY AND $2-A-DAY POVERTY CURVES[a]

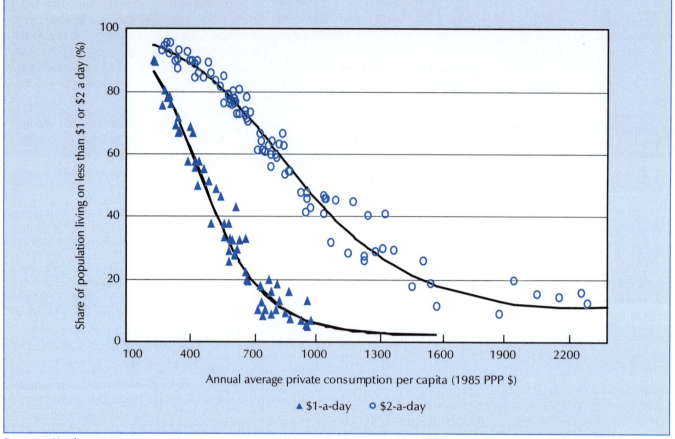

Annual average private consumption per capita (1985 PPP $)

▲ $1-a-day   ○ $2-a-day

Source: Karshenas (2001).

a   The poverty curves show the relationship between average annual private consumption per capita and the share of the population living on less than $1 or $2 a day in a sample of LDCs and other low- and lower-middle income countries. For sample composition, see annex table.

been used to estimate expected poverty in countries and years where there are no survey data on the distribution of consumption. But the poverty curves themselves are founded on actual poverty estimates for countries and years where household survey data of consumption expenditure are available.[3]

As the observations relate to different countries at different levels of development, the poverty curves in the chart can be regarded as depicting the "normal" long-term relationship between average levels of private consumption per capita and the incidence of $1-a-day and $2-a-day poverty. It is the normal relationship in the sense that it is a historically observed empirical regularity. It is reasonable to infer that the poverty curves depict the typical pattern of change in the incidence of poverty that occurs as development takes place.[4] That is to say, in the long run countries which are emerging from a situation of generalized poverty as average private consumption per capita rises are expected to follow these paths of change.

> *The poverty curves depict the "normal" long-term relationship between average levels of private consumption per capita and the incidence of $1-a-day and $2-a-day poverty... In the long run, countries which are emerging from a situation of generalized poverty as average private consumption per capita rises are expected to follow these paths of change.*

The poverty estimates in the chart are based on both average private consumption per capita and the distribution of private consumption expenditure amongst households, and thus the long-run paths of poverty change, which are expressed by the poverty curves, incorporate the effects of "normal" changes in the inequality of private consumption per capita which historically have occurred as the average level of private consumption per capita and income per capita rise. The pattern of change is actually such that inequality can usually be expected to increase within countries in the early stages of development (Karshenas, 2001). But despite increasing inequality, the poverty curves indicate that in conditions of generalized poverty, rising average private consumption per capita is not only necessary for poverty reduction on a major scale, but in normal conditions can also be sufficient.

There are certainly exceptions to the pattern. But the exceptional historical experiences of countries such as South Africa and Zimbabwe, and the lack of political and economic sustainability of the historical inequalities and exclusionary practices in those experiences, indicate that these may be exceptions that indeed prove the rule. Although there is no guarantee that the future trajectories of growth in average private consumption per capita and the incidence of poverty will follow those of the past, it is highly likely that there will always be a strong relationship between the two in conditions of generalized poverty.

The strength of the relationship between average private consumption per capita and the incidence of poverty is apparent in the closeness of the scatter of the observations around the average poverty curve. Indeed, the close fit of the national accounts-consistent poverty estimates to the poverty curve is an important finding of the present Report. However, the relationship depicted is non-linear. This means that the relationship between the rate of growth of private consumption per capita and the rate of poverty reduction varies according to a country's average level of private consumption per capita. In fact, for any given $10 increase in average annual private consumption per capita, the reduction in the share of the population living on less than $1 a day will be greatest when a country has an annual private consumption per capita of around $400 (in 1985 PPP dollars), and the reduction in the share of the population living on less than $2 a day will be greatest when annual private consumption per capita is around $750 (in 1985 PPP dollars). A further consequence of the shape of the poverty curves is that elasticity of poverty reduction with respect to private consumption growth (i.e. the percentage change in the incidence of poverty for an increase in average private consumption of 1 per cent) varies according to where the poverty line is set and according to the average private consumption per capita within a country. This is a very different picture from that usually assumed in discussions of the relationship between economic growth and poverty (see box 7).

The poverty curves in chart 13 indicate the magnitude of the opportunity for poverty reduction in the LDCs if increases in average private consumption per capita can be sustained over a period of time. The curves show that:

- For a country where average private consumption per capita is about $400 a year, one would expect about 65 per cent of the population to be living on less than $1 a day. If the average private consumption per capita doubled to $800 a year, one would expect less than 20 per cent of the population to be living below the $1-a-day international poverty line.

- For an average African LDC where close to 88 per cent of the population live on less that $2 a day, and where average private consumption per capita is on average $1.01 a day, a doubling of the average private consumption per capita would reduce the incidence of $2-a-day poverty to around 60 per cent. However, if average private consumption per capita increased to about $4 a day or about $1,400 a year (in 1985 PPP dollars), one would expect the incidence of $2-a-day poverty to fall to 24 per cent.

- For an average Asian LDC where 68 per cent of the population live on less than $2 a day and where the average private consumption per capita is $2.21 a day, a doubling of the average private consumption per capita should reduce the incidence of $2-a-day poverty to 21 per cent.

For a country where average private consumption per capita is about $400 a year, one would expect about 65 per cent of the population to be living on less than $1 a day. If the average private consumption per capita doubled to $800 a year, one would expect less than 20 per cent of the population to be living on less than $1 a day.

BOX 7. THE ELASTICITY OF POVERTY REDUCTION WITH RESPECT TO ECONOMIC GROWTH

Aggregate estimates of the elasticity of poverty reduction with respect to economic growth are central in current discussions of the growth–poverty relationship in developing countries and also in attempts to analyse whether international poverty targets will be met. Such elasticity estimates generally measure the percentage change in the share of the population living below the poverty line following an increase of 1 per cent in the average income or private consumption per capita of the population as a whole. Most of the elasticity estimates are based on observations of the percentage change in the incidence of poverty and the percentage change of per capita private consumption or income during "spells" defined by the periods of time spanning two successive household surveys of the distribution of income or consumption in a country. Such observations are made for a large number of spells and countries, and the elasticity is then estimated through a regression analysis that specifies the average relationship for the sample as a whole. The results are generally presented as a fixed- or single-value elasticity for the whole sample. These results, however, vary substantially, depending on the particular sample of countries chosen, and the poverty lines and poverty measures adopted.

For example, Ravallion and Chen (1997) provide estimates of the income growth elasticity of the incidence of poverty ranging from -0.53 to -3.12 for various poverty lines and samples, based on consumption averages from household surveys. In everyday language, this means that with every 1 per cent increase in average private consumption, the proportion of the population living in poverty will fall by between one-half (0.53) and three (3.12) per cent. With similar methdologies, UNECA (1999) provides measures of income growth elasticity of headcount poverty for Africa of -0.92 and -0.85. Ravallion, Datt and van de Walle (1991), on the other hand, calculate elasticities of poverty reduction of -2.2 for the developing countries and -1.5 for sub-Saharan Africa, based on per capita consumption growth. And the list goes on. In general, if growth has a weak effect on poverty, it is assumed that this is due to high inequality or a worsening income distribution, and thus poverty reduction policies should focus more on inequality than on growth.

But the question that arises in the light of the form of the $1-a-day and $2-a-day poverty curves in chart 13 is: what meaning can one give to an aggregate elasticity estimate for a heterogeneous group of countries with different levels of private consumption per capita? The highly non-linear shape of the relationship between the incidence of poverty and the average level of private consumption per capita which is apparent in the long-run poverty curves indicates that one should be wary of aggregate measures that assume a fixed elasticity (e.g. Collier and Dollar, 2001).

Box chart 2 below focuses on the incidence of $1-a-day and $2-a-day poverty and estimates the expected poverty reduction elasticities with respect to growth in average private consumption per capita on the basis of the long-run poverty curve. It is apparent that the elasticity is critically dependent on the poverty line chosen as well as on the average level of private consumption per capita in the country concerned. From the chart it can be seen that, for the $1 poverty line, the growth elasticities of poverty can range from -0.5 to about -3.0. In everyday language this means that if average private consumption per capita goes up by 1 per cent, the share of the population living on less than $1 a day will fall by between 0.5 per cent and 3 per cent. For the $2 poverty line it can vary between -0.5 and just over -2.0.

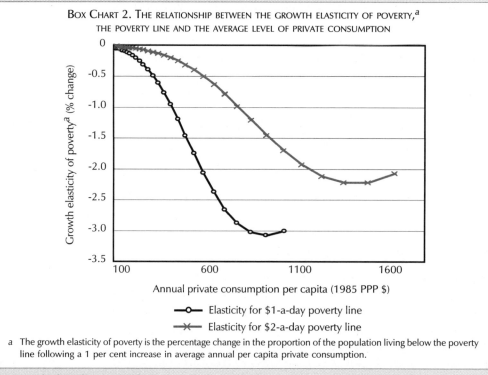

BOX CHART 2. THE RELATIONSHIP BETWEEN THE GROWTH ELASTICITY OF POVERTY,[a] THE POVERTY LINE AND THE AVERAGE LEVEL OF PRIVATE CONSUMPTION

Annual private consumption per capita (1985 PPP $)

—o— Elasticity for $1-a-day poverty line
—✕— Elasticity for $2-a-day poverty line

a The growth elasticity of poverty is the percentage change in the proportion of the population living below the poverty line following a 1 per cent increase in average annual per capita private consumption.

The range of estimates, which is the inevitable consequence of the shape and position of the poverty curves, may explain the apparent instability in the elasticity estimates and the wide variation in different estimates reported in different studies since the country sample and the poverty line adopted vary. This indicates that a single-value aggregate elasticity applied to heterogeneous groups of developing countries, as has become customary, is bound to be misleading. As shown above, cross-country data indicate significant variations in elasticity estimates, depending on the choice of the poverty line and the average level of private consumption per capita of individual countries.

Source: Karshenas (2001).

One important implication of these findings is that sustained and rapid economic growth which raises average levels of income and consumption in the LDCs can be expected to have a major impact in reducing the share of the population living on less than $1 or $2 a day. The magnitude of the effects is due to the fact that poverty is generalized.

The reason this is so can be understood if a situation of generalized poverty is compared with the typical situation in a rich country where poverty is not all-pervasive, but rather where a minor proportion of the population are poor. In rich countries where poverty affects only a minor part of the population, economic growth is neither necessary nor sufficient for poverty reduction. It is not necessary, because the economy already has sufficient resources to introduce poverty reduction programmes. It is not sufficient, because no matter how high an economy's per capita income level may be, there will always be individuals or households that, because of their own special circumstances or because of sectoral shifts or cyclical fluctuations in the economy, fall below the poverty line. Poverty reduction in these circumstances depends on social and political processes and necessarily involves a redistribution of income. The introduction of different types of social welfare system in the European countries after the Second World War is an example of this type of poverty reduction. The differences in observed rates of extreme poverty in different European countries in the post-war period are explained more by their social and political institutions than by their per capita income levels. High rates of economic growth may ease the acceptance of redistribution policies, but there is no necessary empirical relationship linking high growth rates to the introduction of more adequate welfare systems in those countries.

In situations of generalized poverty, in contrast, since the majority of the population fall below the poverty line, growth and poverty reduction are necessarily linked. Redistributive transfers can play a direct role in alleviating the worst aspects of poverty. However, generalized poverty, as we understand it, is a situation where the available resources in the economy, even when more equally distributed, are barely sufficient to cater for the basic needs of the population on a sustainable basis. In these circumstances, poverty reduction can be achieved on a major scale only through economic growth. What is possible is indicated by the dramatic effects of rapid and sustained economic growth on the incidence of poverty in those low-income countries, particularly in East Asia, which, beginning from a situation of generalized poverty, have managed to achieve sustained growth.

Nevertheless various qualifications are necessary to complete the picture of the long-run relationship between economic growth and poverty.

First, growth in GNP per capita and in GDP per capita are less closely related to poverty reduction than growth in average private consumption per capita. Although average private consumption per capita generally increases as GNP per capita rises, there are variations around the normal trend (chart 14). As a consequence, the relationship between increases in average incomes, as measured by GNP per capita, and poverty reduction is less close than the relationship between increases in private consumption per capita and poverty reduction. When one examines the relationship between increases in average GDP per capita (rather than average private consumption per capita) and poverty, the growth–poverty relationship will become even more blurred. It is possible, for example, to imagine economies in which the bulk of the GDP is produced in foreign-owned mining enclaves whose growth can have little effect on the population's average levels of private consumption, and hence little effect on poverty.

The magnitude of the effects of sustained and rapid economic growth on the incidence of poverty is due to the fact that poverty is generalized.

Growth in GNP per capita and in GDP per capita are less closely related to poverty reduction than growth in average private consumption per capita.

CHART 14. THE RELATIONSHIP BETWEEN PRIVATE CONSUMPTION GROWTH AND
GNP GROWTH IN THE LDCS DURING THE 1970S, 1980S AND 1990S

(Per capita, in real terms)

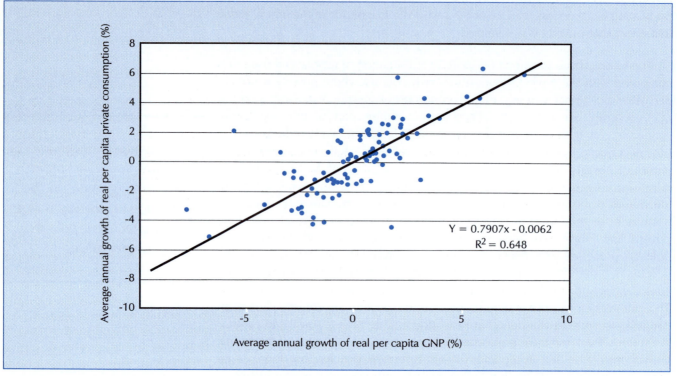

Source: UNCTAD (2000: chart 18).
Note: Annual growth rates refer to average 10-year trends during the 1970s, 1980s and 1990s.

For any given rate of income growth, the faster the growth of savings, the slower the growth of consumption, and thus poverty reduction.

Second, for any given rate of income growth, the faster the growth of savings, the slower the growth of consumption, and thus poverty reduction. UNCTAD (2000: 33–37) shows that there is a strong savings effort in the LDCs when economic growth occurs. This effort reduces the amount by which private consumption increases as the average income increases. An important corollary of this relationship is that the more the growth process depends on domestic resource mobilization as countries emerge from generalized poverty, the slower will be the rate of poverty reduction associated with rising GNP per capita. The short-term trade-off between the mobilization of domestic resources for investment on the one hand, and the growth of private consumption and poverty reduction on the other hand, is lessened if countries do not have to rely totally on national savings, but have access to foreign savings as well.

Sustainable increases in living standards and average levels of private consumption depend on the accumulation of capital and skills, productivity growth and the expansion of employment opportunities.

Third, sustainable increases in living standards and average levels of private consumption depend on the accumulation of capital and skills, productivity growth and the expansion of employment opportunities. It is these proximate causes and effects of economic growth that are important for poverty reduction. This can be seen by looking at the sources of living standards when viewed from the perspective of the household (see box 8). The inability to achieve minimally adequate levels of consumption is, within this micro-level approach, rooted in a lack of household assets that serve as the basis for livelihoods, and in the low productivity and low remunerability of those assets. This is a far from complete picture of the causes of poverty. But it is sufficient to show that economic growth will not reduce poverty unless it releases these constraints on consumption possibilities. It is this type of growth that is important for poverty reduction.

Fourth, inequality and social exclusion still matter. The fact that, in situations of generalized poverty, poverty reduction on a major scale can be achieved only through economic growth does not mean that redistribution of income and assets has no role to play in such circumstances. It has been shown empirically that the redistribution of income is more important for poverty reduction in middle-income countries than in poor countries (Hagdeviren, van der Hoeven and Weeks, 2001). Nevertheless, efficiency-enhancing redistributions of assets and income can be important for poverty reduction in situations of generalized poverty. Moreover, the behaviour of the small proportion of the population in the LDCs who are rich is also very relevant. As UNCTAD (1997: 151–176) argues, when viewed from a dynamic perspective, what matters more than inequality per se is whether the rich use their high incomes and wealth, and in particular reinvest profits, in ways which support accumulation of capital and skills, productivity growth and technical progress, and the creation of employment opportunities for the majority of the population.

As the average levels of income and private consumption of the population as a whole rise, there is a high probability that certain regions and social groups will be left behind. This will be more likely to happen to the extent that discrimination on the basis of gender, ethnicity, race or social status prevents people from enjoying the potential benefits of assets and skills, or denies them the opportunity to acquire those assets and skills. The danger of certain groups being left behind can be lessened through policies that are undertaken to reduce their marginalization. Also, particular attention should be paid to gender relations and the special needs of economically dependent groups such as the disabled, children and old people.

The fact that, in situations of generalized poverty, poverty reduction on a major scale can be achieved only through economic growth does not mean that redistribution of income and assets has no role to play in such circumstances.

C. Generalized poverty, domestic resource mobilization and low-level equilibrium

In situations of generalized poverty, economic growth that raises average levels of household income and consumption should normally lead to major reductions in poverty. However, another implication of generalized poverty is that poverty of this type also affects the prospects for growth. Indeed, in these situations the promise of rapid poverty reduction, which is evident in poverty curves that define the normal relationship between average private consumption per capita and the incidence of poverty, cannot be realized precisely because generalized poverty can have a negative impact on growth.

A major way in which generalized poverty constrains economic growth is through its effects on domestic resource availability.

A major way in which generalized poverty constrains economic growth is through its effects on domestic resource availability. In conditions of generalized poverty, domestic resources available to finance capital formation and provide for vital public services are extremely limited. As a consequence, the available resources are barely sufficient to provide the necessary physical capital stock, education, health, and other social and physical infrastructure to keep pace with population growth. Many LDC economies are caught in this situation, which the development economists of the 1950s described as a "low-level equilibrium trap" (Liebenstein, 1957; Nelson, 1956).

Where the majority of the population earn less than $1 or $2 a day, a major part of GDP is expected to be devoted to the procurement of the basic necessities of life. The domestic resources which are available for financing investment, both private and public, and public services, including administration and law and order, would under these circumstances inevitably

Box 8. A household model of the generation of living standards

Pyatt (2001) develops a useful way of understanding the factors affecting poverty seen from the perspective of an individual household, which is summarized in box chart 3. At the base of the diagram in the chart are household assets, and human and property rights. Household assets include: (a) physical assets owned individually or jointly by household members, such as land, workshop tools, livestock, housing, transport vehicles and domestic appliances; (b) human assets, such as capacity for basic labour, skills and organizational abilities, educational attainment, and good health; (c) financial assets in various forms; and (d) social assets, such as networks of contacts. These assets are the basis of livelihoods. But for assets to matter, rights of various kinds must be respected. Benefits which can flow from owning land or tools or dwellings cannot be fully realized if property rights are not respected. Similarly, human capital depends on human rights in order to be fully functional, as discrimination on the basis of gender, ethnicity, race or social status can negate the potential benefits of abilities and skills.

Household assets are translated into consumption possibilities through production activities, and also reproductive activities, which in the present context refer to the raising of children and supporting an older generation that is no longer able to sustain itself without some help. If the household is self-sufficient, the key factors affecting the set of consumption possibilities are the size of the household and its dependency ratio, the physical assets which the household commands through private ownership or access to common property resources, and the productivity of those assets. But in more complex circumstances, markets and Governments as institutions critically affect the returns and productivity of assets.

As households engage in the cash economy, productivity gains from trade and specialization become possible. This can be a potent mechanism for poverty reduction in situations where the division of labour is rudimentary, which is often the case with generalized extreme absolute poverty. But the gains depend on access to markets for those goods and services that the household can produce and wishes to sell, as well as on the ways in which those markets function.

Access to employment is critical for many households since their basic asset is their labour power, and thus the availability of employment and the organization of labour markets are central factors affecting the relationship between the assets and productive activities of households. Access to credit markets is also vital for expanding financial assets and obtaining more productive forms of informal employment. In addition, access to services provided by Governments, including health care and education services — the basis for improved human capital — is also important, as is the availability of physical and administrative infrastructure. Communities may also play a role in provision of those services.

Once households are engaged in market transactions, including the purchase of public services, the terms of trade of the household become an important proximate determinant of the household's living standards. This is likely to be different for households with different occupations. For farmers, what matters is the price of the goods that they produce as against the price of final consumption goods and services that they purchase, as well as the cost of fertilizer and seed. For the wage earner the wage rate in relation to the price of food and other basic goods is central.

Finally, the consumption possibilities available to a household depend on transfers. They can be significantly extended if the household becomes a net recipient of transfers, but conversely they can contract if net payments are made, for example in paying a debt.

The factors discussed so far are proximate determinants of the set of consumption possibilities. But it is apparent from box chart 3 that the actual consumption standards of members of the household depend on choices made within the constraints of the feasible set of consumption possibilities. Complex issues of intra-household distribution may arise at this point. Moreover, the size and composition of the household will matter for individual living standards.

Poverty can be explained, within the framework of the diagram in box chart 3, as the result of various constraints and circumstances which limit the feasible set of consumption possibilities to an extremely low level. Although individual choices enter the picture, and transfers can modify the pattern, the basic causes of poverty are identified here as the large size and composition of the household, lack of skills and abilities, lack of physical and financial assets, low productivity, limited access to markets, inadequate wage employment, poor public services and common property resources, and unfavourable terms of trade for the goods and services which the household buys and sells.

These factors are "causes" of poverty in the sense that if they improve, the consumption possibilities of the household can expand so that actual consumption levels are above the poverty line. Economic growth is very closely related to poverty reduction in situations of generalized poverty because it is necessary for such improvements to occur. Economic growth shifts the factors limiting consumption when it is underpinned by the processes of accumulation of physical and human capital, increasing specialization and the division of labour, productivity growth through technical progress or structural change, and more widespread and improved public service provision as well as infrastructure development.

This household model makes possible an intuitive view of the congruence between the growth process for a national economy and poverty reduction at the household level. But it must be stressed that as an explanation of the causes of poverty the household model is limited. It is a partial equilibrium approach that takes prices, access to market, and so

Box 8 (contd.)

on, as given. Furthermore, it does not take account of the broader social externalities that arise from individual household decisions. A broader view of the determinants of low consumption standards requires an economy-wide framework in which households, companies, non-governmental organizations and government are all key actors. It is the combined behaviour of each of these that determines household living standards within the context of international trade and other aspects of international economic relationships.

BOX CHART 3. A SCHEMATIC REPRESENTATION OF THE GENERATION OF LIVING STANDARDS

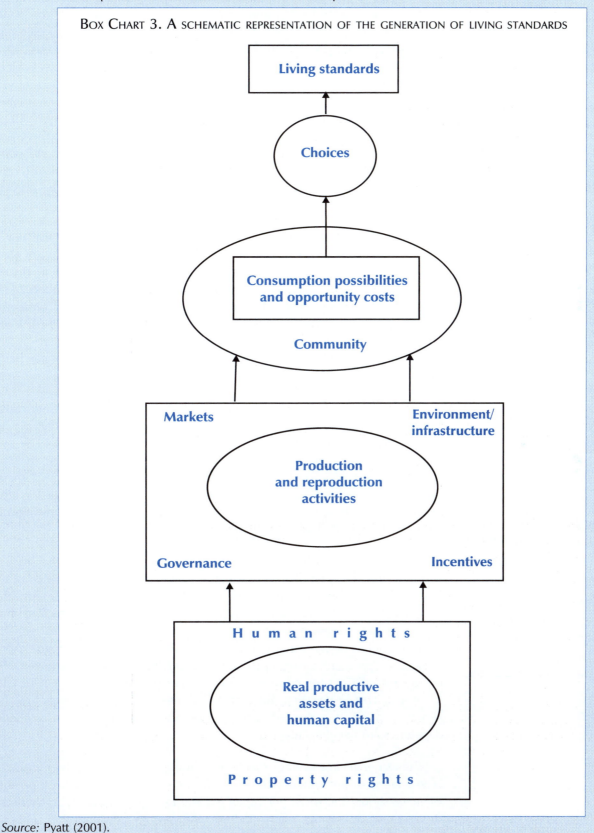

Source: Pyatt (2001).

be very low. Furthermore, in the prevailing living conditions for the majority of the population in such economies there is little potential for expanding the domestic resources available for financing investment and public services without an initial period of sustained growth in the domestic economy.

Estimates of the domestic resources available for financing investment and public services for the LDCs and other developing countries[5] for the period 1995–1999 are shown in chart 15. They are calculated as the difference between GDP and private consumption, expressed as a percentage of GDP. In order to show how the severity of poverty affects domestic resources available for financing investment and public services, the LDCs are subdivided into the poor LDCs and the poorest LDCs. The poorest LDCs are those countries where over 40 per cent of the population live on less than $1 a day and over 80 per cent live on less than $2 a day. The remaining LDCs are referred to as poor LDCs.[6] The domestic resources available for financing investment and public services in these different groups are compared with the sample of other developing countries for which poverty trends were described in the previous chapter.

The average domestic resources available to finance investment and public services for other developing countries are about 35 per cent of GDP. The average domestic resources available to finance investment and public services in the poor LDCs are, in contrast, around 24 per cent of GDP. In the poorest LDCs, they are less than 15 per cent.

As can be seen from chart 15, the average domestic resources available to finance investment and public services for other developing countries are about 35 per cent of GDP.[7] The average domestic resources available to finance investment and public services in the poor LDCs are, in contrast, around 24 per cent of GDP. In the poorest LDCs, they are less than 15 per cent. Considering that the provision of basic public services such as education, health, law and order, agricultural extension services and public administration absorb at least 10 to 15 per cent of GDP in any modern economy, all these activities can barely be properly funded out of domestic resources.

The low levels of domestic resources available for financing private capital formation, public infrastructure and public services reflect the fact that average savings rates are very low in the LDCs. This can be seen more directly by a comparison of the average savings rates in the LDCs with those in other developing countries in chart 16. For the poor LDCs, the average domestic savings rate is around 12 per cent, almost half of the average rate for other developing countries. In the case of the poorest LDCs, the domestic savings rate is on average no more than 2 to 3 per cent.

For the poor LDCs, the average domestic savings rate is around 12 per cent of GDP. In the case of the poorest LDCs, the domestic savings rate is on average no more than 2 to 3 per cent.

Such low savings rates are not even sufficient to keep intact the stock of wealth in the LDCs, let alone to generate economic growth.   Evidence of this can be seen by comparing the "genuine savings" rates in the LDCs and other developing countries. Genuine savings rates are net estimates which subtract from domestic savings the reduction in national wealth associated with the depletion of environmental resources and the depreciation of man-made capital stock. The "genuine" savings rates for the poor LDCs are barely above zero. For the poorest LDCs, genuine savings are on average minus 5 per cent of GDP (chart 17). This implies that not only are domestic savings extremely low, but also the natural and created capital stock, the assets on which livelihoods depend, is not being maintained.

The extremely low average savings rate in these countries is rather the result of low levels of per capita income, or the prevalence of generalized poverty. Evidence shows that when per capita income increases in the LDCs, there is a strong domestic savings effort. Indeed, the savings effort in the LDCs, as measured by the degree to which extra income is saved, is at least as strong as in other developing countries (see UNCTAD, 2000: 36–37). Thus if growth can be started and sustained, and the LDCs emerge from generalized poverty,

CHART 15. DOMESTIC RESOURCES AVAILABLE FOR FINANCE[a] AS A SHARE OF GDP
IN LDCS AND OTHER DEVELOPING COUNTRIES, 1995–1999
(Percentage)

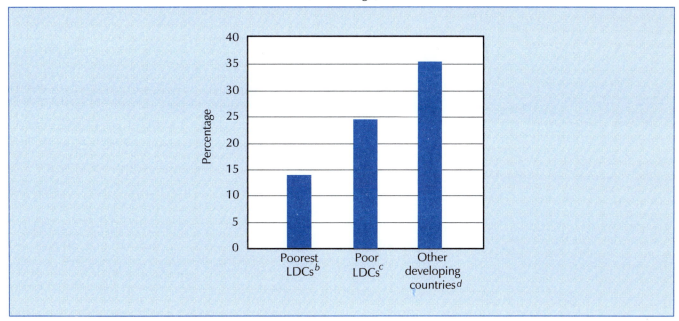

Source: UNCTAD secretariat estimates based on World Bank, *World Development Indicators 2001*, CD-ROM.

Note: The figures are simple averages. No data are available for Angola, Liberia, Solomon Islands, Somalia and Sudan.

a Domestic resources available for finance is estimated as the difference between GDP and private consumption.

b The "poorest LDCs" group comprises: Angola, Burkina Faso, Burundi, Central African Republic, Chad, Comoros, Democratic Republic of the Congo, Djibouti, Ethiopia, Guinea, Guinea-Bissau, Haiti, Lesotho, Liberia, Madagascar, Malawi, Mali, Mozambique, Niger, Rwanda, Sierra Leone, Somalia, Togo, Uganda, United Republic of Tanzania and Zambia.

c The "poor LDCs" group comprises: Bangladesh, Benin, Bhutan, Cape Verde, Gambia, Lao People's Democratic Republic, Mauritania, Myanmar, Nepal, Senegal, Solomon Islands, Sudan and Vanuatu.

d The "other developing countries" comprises: Cameroon, China, Congo, Côte d'Ivoire, Dominican Republic, Egypt, Ghana, India, Indonesia, Jamaica, Kenya, Morocco, Namibia, Nigeria, Pakistan, Philippines, Sri Lanka, Thailand, Tunisia, Turkey and Zimbabwe.

significant increases in domestic resource mobilization can be expected. But with sluggish growth, economic stagnation and even economic regression, this potential cannot be realized. With many people living hand to mouth, and with a weakly developed corporate sector, domestic savings are necessarily very low. This not only limits domestically financed economic growth, but also is a fundamental source of vulnerability of LDC economies.

During the period 1995–1999, the domestic resources available to finance investment and public service in the LDCs, when measured at current prices and exchange rates, were on average no more than 0.15 dollars per person per day. In other words, on average there were only 15 cents a day available per capita to spend on private capital formation, public investment in infrastructure, and the running of vital public services such as health, education and administration, as well as law and order. The implications of this situation for investment and growth, and also for the provision of public services and governance, are serious.

In terms of GDP share, government revenue and final consumption expenditure[8] in the LDCs do not appear to be significantly different from what they are in other developing countries (see charts 18A and 18B). Government revenue as a share of GDP during the period 1995–1999 in the LDCs as a whole was on average about 16 per cent, compared with 19 per cent in other developing countries. Government consumption expenditure of about 12 per cent average share of GDP in the LDCs also compares with about 13 per cent for other developing countries. This indicates that in terms of mobilization and use

In LDCs during the period 1995–1999, there were on average only 15 cents per person per day available to spend on private capital formation, public investment in infrastructure, and the running of vital public services such as health, education and administration, as well as law and order.

CHART 16. GROSS DOMESTIC SAVINGS AS A SHARE OF GDP IN LDCS
AND OTHER DEVELOPING COUNTRIES, 1995–1999

(Percentage)

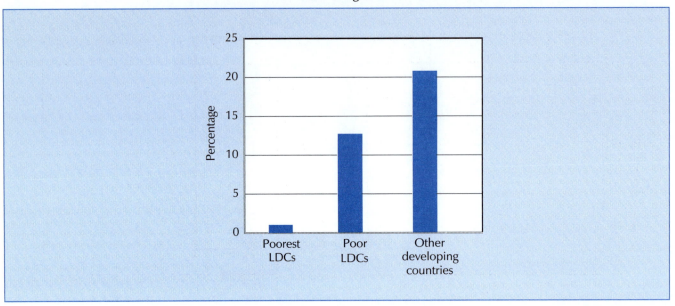

Source: Same as for chart 15.

Note: The country groups are the same as for chart 15. The figures are simple averages. No data are available for Liberia, Solomon
Islands, Somalia, Sudan and Vanuatu.

CHART 17. GENUINE DOMESTIC SAVINGS AS A SHARE OF GDP IN LDCS
AND OTHER DEVELOPING COUNTRIES, 1995–1999[a]

(Percentage)

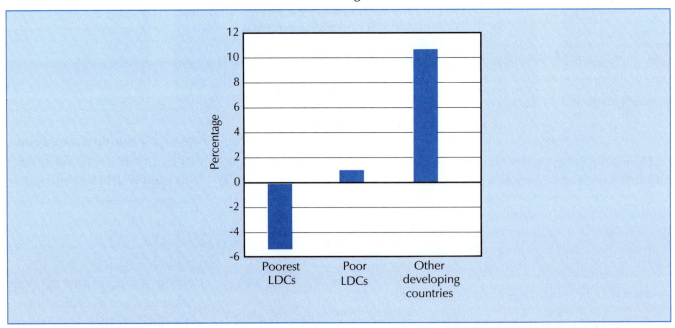

Source: Same as for chart 15.

Note: The country groups are the same as for chart 15. The figures are simple averages. No data are available for Angola, Bhutan,
Cape Verde, Comoros, Djibouti, Liberia, Myanmar, Solomon Islands, Somalia, Sudan and Vanuatu.

   a   Genuine savings rates are net estimates which subtract from domestic savings the reduction in national wealth associated
with the depletion of environmental resources and depreciation of man-made capital stock.

CHART 18. CURRENT GOVERNMENT REVENUE AND FINAL CONSUMPTION EXPENDITURE AS
A SHARE OF GDP IN LDCs AND OTHER DEVELOPING COUNTRIES, 1995–1999
(Percentage)

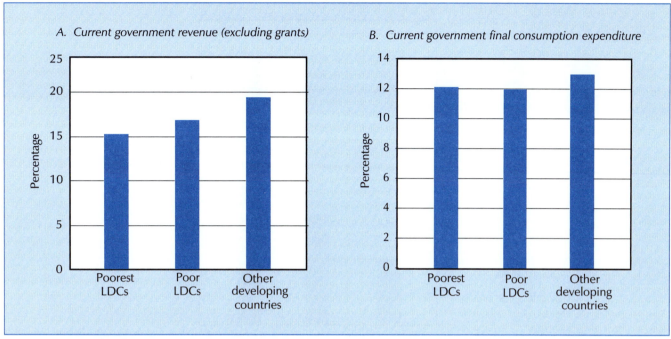

Source: Same as for chart 15.

Note: The country groups are the same as for chart 15. The figures are simple averages. Chart 18A is based on a small sample of LDCs for which data are available — Bhutan, Burundi, Democratic Republic of the Congo (1995–1997), Guinea (1998–1999), Lesotho (1995–1998), Madagascar (1995–1996), Nepal, Sierra Leone (1995–1997) and Vanuatu. In the sample of other developing countries, no data are available for Ghana, Jamaica, Namibia and Nigeria in chart 18A. No data are available for Liberia, Myanmar, Solomon Islands, Somalia, Sudan and Vanuatu in chart 18B.

of resources in the public sector, the development effort in the LDCs was not significantly below that of other developing countries.

However, under the conditions of generalized poverty in the LDCs these average government revenue and expenditure shares, once translated into real per capita terms, highlight the extreme resource constraints facing public sector service provision in the LDC economies (chart 19). Government consumption expenditure in the poorest LDCs was on average about $37 per person per year over the period 1995–1999. For the poor LDCs group the average per capita government consumption was about $64 per year for the same period. These figures compare with over $160 on average for the sample of other developing countries.

The extremely limited availability of resources implies that the Governments of LDCs are constantly faced with making difficult choices about the provision of different vital public services. Most of the public services such as health, education, agricultural support services, general administration and law enforcement, which form the foundations of modern economic development, are held back by serious supply constraints in the LDCs.

The example of health expenditure, where comparable data for other developing countries are available, highlights this point (see chart 20). Health expenditure per capita in the poorest LDCs during the period 1995–1998 was about $14 per year, which was one sixth of the average $84 per head in other developing countries. Over the same period the average per capita health expenditure in the poor LDCs was about $25 a day.[9] The low rate of per capita expenditure on essential public services such as health and education in the

Health expenditure per capita in the poorest LDCs during the period 1995–1998 was about $14 per year.

CHART 19. ANNUAL GOVERNMENT FINAL CONSUMPTION EXPENDITURE PER HEAD
IN LDCs AND OTHER DEVELOPING COUNTRIES, 1995–1999

(Current $)

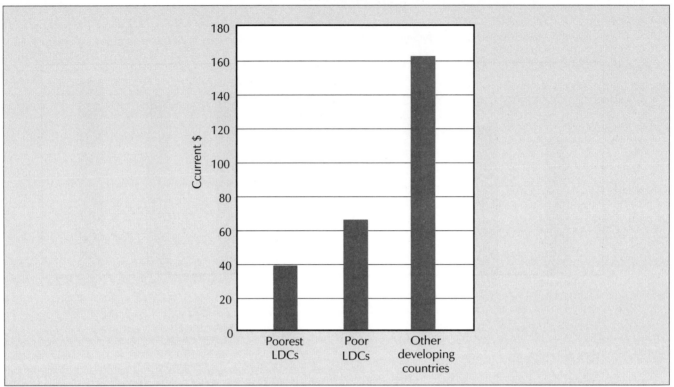

Source: Same as for chart 15.

Notes: The country groups are the same as for chart 15. The figures are simple averages. No data are available for Liberia, Myanmar, Solomon Islands, Somalia, Sudan and Vanuatu.

CHART 20. ANNUAL HEALTH EXPENDITURE PER CAPITA IN LDCs AND OTHER DEVELOPING COUNTRIES, 1995–1998

(Current $)

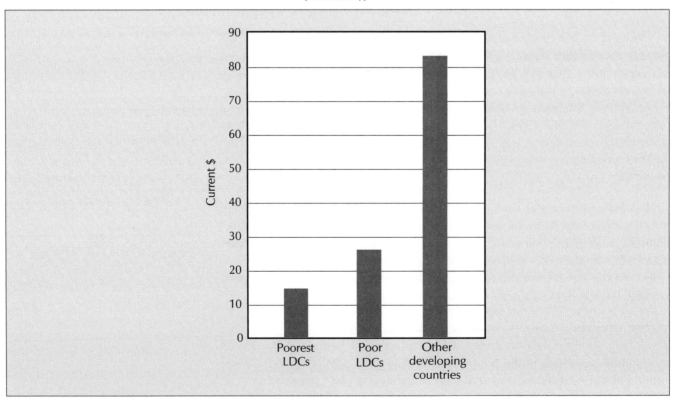

Source: Same as for chart 15.

Note: The country groups are the same as for chart 15. The figures are simple averages. No data are available for Angola, Comoros, Democratic Republic of the Congo, Djibouti, Guinea-Bissau, Lesotho, Liberia, Somalia and Vanuatu.

LDCs does not result from different public expenditure priorities in those countries: it is essentially due to the extremely low overall resource availability in countries with generalized poverty. Under conditions of generalized poverty, poverty reduction strategies thus need to go beyond simple reallocation of public expenditure.

The paucity of domestic resources is one reason why very low levels of human development persist in many LDCs. Chart 21 shows levels of human development as measured by the UNDP's Human Development Index (HDI), and levels of real GDP per capita (in 1999 PPP dollars) in 1985 and 1999 for LDCs and other low-income and middle-income countries.[10] It is clear, as has been noted in past LDC Reports, that the island LDCs are somewhat different from other LDCs. They have higher GDP per capita and also a higher HDI level. The majority of the LDCs are, however, clustered in the bottom left-hand corner of the chart, with an HDI level of less than 0.5 and GDP per capita of less than $1,600 (in 1999 PPP dollars). Some other low-income countries are also in this part of the chart. But when the situation in 1985 is compared with that in 1999, it is apparent that there was a much greater overlap between LDCs and other low-income countries in 1985. By 1999, many of the other low-income countries had managed to achieve higher levels of HDI and GDP per capita. At the same time, the LDCs are generally stuck in the bottom left-hand corner of the chart with relatively low GDP per capita and low levels of human development.

Under conditions of generalized poverty, poverty reduction strategies thus need to go beyond simple reallocation of public expenditure.

The low-level equilibrium trap in the LDCs facing generalized poverty, therefore, does not solely imply low levels of savings and investment, which were the focus of the development economists of the 1950s, but also involves inadequate and low-grade public services. These can negatively affect economic efficiency and also human development. In extreme cases this lack of access to resources can undermine the basic mechanisms of governance and lead to political disintegration and open social conflict. Armed conflicts are on the rise worldwide and many are taking place in poor countries (Stewart and Fitzgerald, 2000; Messer and Cohen, 2001; SIPRI, 2000). When they occur there can be a massive destruction of capital stocks. A growing number of LDCs experienced disruptive civil wars and armed conflicts during the 1990s.[11]

Another implication of the extremely low levels of domestic resources available for finance in the LDCs is that these countries have had to rely on external resources in order to supplement their meagre domestic resources. In the late 1990s, the size of the external resource gap, measured as the net trade balance in goods and services, was equivalent to about 90 per cent of investment in the poorest LDCs on average, and about 50 per cent in the poor LDCs. This contrasts with just over a 10 per cent average for the sample of other developing countries (see chart 22A). Similarly, the external resource gap was equivalent to over 100 per cent government consumption expenditure in the case of the poorest LDCs in contrast to an average of about 17 per cent for the other developing countries (chart 22B). These ratios, which in the case of the LDCs have remained at very high levels since the early 1980s, indicate that external resources have not been adequate to pull the LDCs out of their low-level equilibrium trap.

In the late 1990s, the size of the external resource gap, measured as the net trade balance in goods and services, was equivalent to about 90 per cent of investment in the poorest LDCs on average, and about 50 per cent in the poor LDCs.

Another important feature of the LDCs is that the external resources that cover their domestic resource gap are entirely composed of foreign aid and grants. Most LDCs do not have access to private capital markets, and the extent of foreign direct investment in those economies during the past two decades has been very limited (UNCTAD, 2000: 81–100). The budgetary and accumulation

CHART 21. HUMAN DEVELOPMENT INDEX AND GDP PER CAPITA IN LDCs AND
OTHER LOW-INCOME AND MIDDLE-INCOME COUNTRIES, 1985 AND 1999

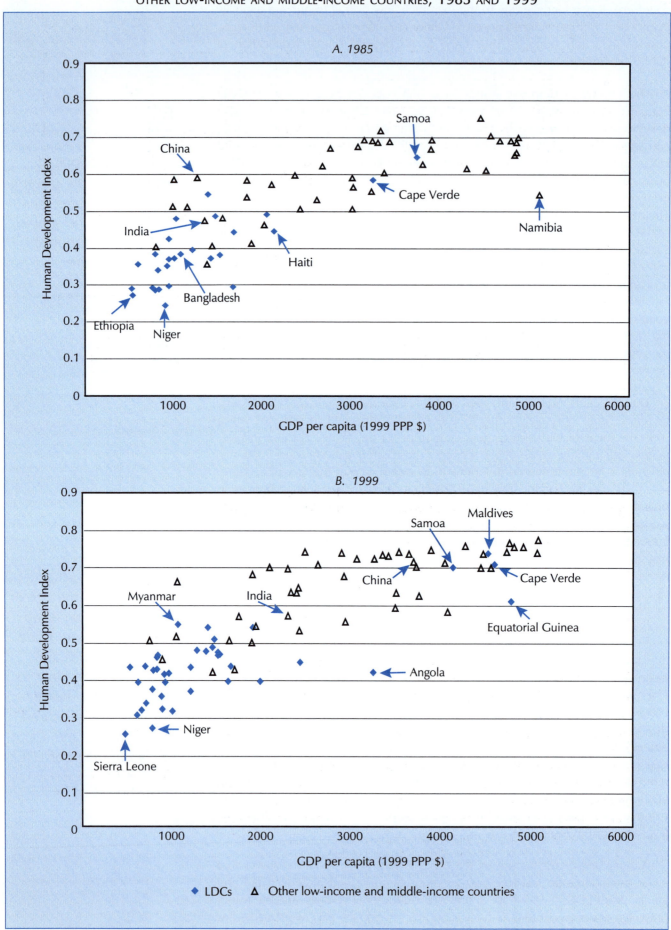

Source: UNDP Human Development Office.

CHART 22. EXTERNAL RESOURCE GAP IN LDCS AND OTHER DEVELOPING COUNTRIES, 1995–1999

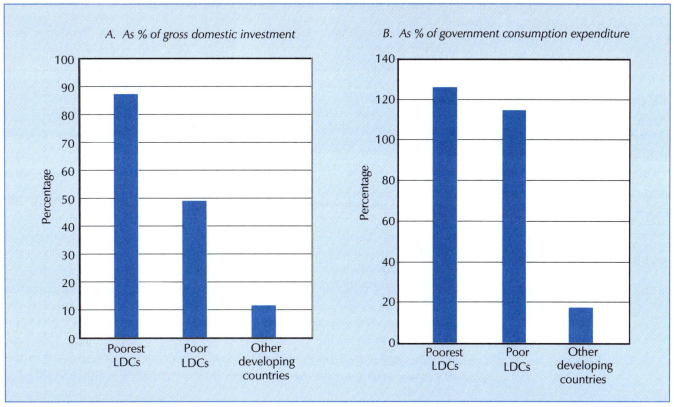

Source: Same as for chart 15.

Notes: The country groups are the same as for chart 15. The figures are simple averages. No data are available for Liberia, Myanmar, Solomon Islands, Sudan and Vanuatu.

processes in the LDCs over the past two decades have therefore been dominated by foreign aid. The nature of foreign aid and the aid delivery system has hence played a critical role in economic management and development possibilities in the LDCs facing generalized poverty.

D. Generalized poverty, population growth and environmental degradation

The problems facing many LDCs also go beyond those perceived in traditional low-level equilibrium trap models because a large number of the LDC economies have experienced not only economic stagnation, but also a long-term sustained downward spiral. This is evident in the poverty trends discussed in the previous chapter. In order to examine the underlying mechanisms that give rise to downward spiral processes, one needs to go beyond the conventional low-level equilibrium trap theories. In these conventional theories, population growth is taken as an exogenous factor and environmental resources are ignored or treated as unlimited free gifts of nature. In generalized poverty, however, important interactions can take place between growth, environment and demographic factors, which lead to complex dynamic processes not envisaged in the low-level equilibrium models.

A growing body of empirical evidence over the past two decades has highlighted the importance of interactions between poverty, environment and population growth for economic development. The evidence suggests that in poor countries, poverty, environmental degradation and population growth are

A large number of the LDC economies have experienced not only economic stagnation, but also a long-term sustained downward spiral.

interlinked. As a result, rather than being caught in a low-level equilibrium trap, the economy can fall into a downward spiral where higher population growth, greater environmental degradation and increasing poverty reinforce one another. Before the relevance of this for the LDC economies is examined, it would be helpful to highlight some of the stylized facts about the relationship between poverty and demographic and environmental factors in the LDCs at an aggregate level.

1. PATTERNS OF POVERTY, POPULATION GROWTH AND ENVIRONMENTAL RESOURCE USE

By the late 1990s on average more than 75 per cent of the LDC labour force were engaged in the agricultural sector as compared with less than 35 per cent in other developing countries. Over 70 per cent of the LDC population live in rural areas.

The first set of issues that need to be clarified are the nature of the environmental resource dependence of the LDC economies, the type of environmental resources on which they are most dependent, and the nature of the activities in which the bulk of the population are engaged. The LDC economies are dependent on ecological and natural resources, particularly of the agricultural type, to a much larger extent than other developing countries and, a fortiori, industrialized countries. One indicator of this is the much larger share of the LDC population living in rural areas and engaged in agricultural activities compared with other developing countries. By the late 1990s on average more than 75 per cent of the LDC labour force were engaged in the agricultural sector as compared with less than 35 per cent in other developing countries. Over 70 per cent of the LDC population live in rural areas as compared with under 44 per cent for other developing countries on average (table 22). A further indicator of this phenomenon is the LDC economies' reliance on wood and charcoal as the main sources of energy. In the late 1990s, wood fuel and charcoal constituted over 75 per cent of the total energy consumption in the LDCs as compared with just over 10 per cent in other developing countries.

Wood fuel and charcoal constituted over 75 per cent of the total energy consumption in the LDCs as compared with just over 10 per cent in other developing countries.

Another related indicator is the much greater share of primary commodities in LDC merchandise exports as compared with other developing countries. As will be discussed in the next chapter, there are a number of LDCs that have managed to diversify their exports away from unprocessed primary commodities towards manufactures and services. But on average close to 70 per cent of overall LDC merchandise exports consist of primary commodities as compared with an average of about 30 per cent for other developing countries. Even in LDCs that are not mainly specialized as primary commodity exporters, services and manufacturing exports such as tourism and textiles have close links with ecological and natural resources. In general, economic activity in the LDCs seems to be much more immediately dependent on natural resources, particularly agriculture-based ones, than in other developing countries. This has important implications for the type of linkages between poverty, environment and population growth that matter most in these countries.

Birth rates are falling much more slowly in the LDCs, particularly in African LDCs, than in other developing countries.

Table 23 shows demographic indicators for the LDCs over the period 1970–1999. It is clear that birth rates are falling much more slowly in the LDCs, particularly in African LDCs, than in other developing countries. Moreover, the age dependency ratio, which measures the ratio of dependants (people younger than 15 and older than 64) to the working age population, is more than 45 per cent higher in the LDCs than in other developing countries. While many other developing countries are completing their population transition phase and on average have shown rapidly declining population growth and dependency rates over the past few decades, the LDCs have in fact witnessed an acceleration in the rate of population growth with increasing dependency rates. This, amongst

TABLE 22. POPULATION GROWTH AND SHARE OF RURAL POPULATION
IN LDCs AND OTHER DEVELOPING COUNTRIES, 1970–1999
(Percentage per annum)

	Population growth (total)		Population growth (urban)		Population growth (rural)		Share of rural population (%)	
	1970–1979	*1990–1999*	*1970–1979*	*1990–1999*	*1970–1979*	*1990–1999*	*1970*	*1999*
All LDCs	2.5	2.4	6.1	4.6	2.1	1.8	88.1	76.0
African LDCs	2.7	2.7	5.7	4.9	2.2	1.9	87.0	74.2
Asian LDCs	2.4	2.1	6.6	4.1	1.9	1.6	89.7	78.5
Island LDCs	2.0	2.5	4.2	4.5	1.5	1.4	84.0	68.2
Other DCs	2.2	1.6	3.6	3.2	1.6	0.6	61.4	44.0

Source: UNCTAD secretariat estimates based on World Bank, *World Development Indicators 2001*, CD-ROM.

Note: Group averages are weighted by population. The sample includes all LDCs except Tuvalu, for which no data are available, and 79 other developing countries. Haiti is included with African LDCs.

TABLE 23. DEMOGRAPHIC INDICATORS IN LDCs AND OTHER DEVELOPING COUNTRIES, 1970–1999

	Crude birth rate (per 1000 people)		Crude death rate (per 1000 people)		Birth minus death rate (per 1000 people)		Age dependency ratio (percentage)	
	1970	*1999*	*1970*	*1999*	*1970*	*1999*	*1970*	*1999*
All LDCs	47.5	38.0	21.4	14.6	26.1	23.4	0.90	0.86
African LDCs	48.3	42.6	21.9	17.2	26.4	25.3	0.91	0.95
Asian LDCs	46.4	31.2	20.8	10.8	25.6	20.4	0.89	0.74
Island LDCs	40.3	32.8	13.5	6.6	26.8	26.2	1.00	0.84
Other DCs	37.8	22.3	12.4	8.0	25.3	14.3	0.83	0.59

Source: UNCTAD secretariat estimates based on World Bank, *World Development Indicators 2001*, CD-ROM.

Note: Same as for table 22.

other things, has important implications for savings generation, and for the provision of education, health and other basic needs.

At the aggregate level, different patterns can be observed in poverty trends, the behaviour of demographic variables and environmental resource depletion in the LDCs and other developing countries, and also within sub-groups of the LDCs, if they are grouped according to whether the incidence of poverty was higher during late 1990s than during the late 1970s, or lower. Average trends in poverty, a number of demographic indicators and genuine savings are shown in chart 23 for 23 LDCs where the incidence of poverty has increased since the late 1970s (the LDC I group), for 14 LDCs where the incidence of poverty has decreased somewhat (the LDC II group),[12] and also for a sample of other developing countries. Both groups of LDCs can be characterized as countries with generalized poverty. But while countries in the LDC II group are in a low-level equilibrium, with the incidence of poverty falling either slowly or during certain periods over the last 30 years in most cases, countries in the LDC I group seem to be caught in a downward spiral as attested by their high and increasing poverty rates (see chart 23A and B). The poverty trends in both LDC groups are, it should be noted, in sharp contrast to those in the sample of other developing countries.

CHART 23. POVERTY TRENDS, DEMOGRAPHIC INDICATORS AND GENUINE DOMESTIC SAVINGS
IN LDCs AND OTHER DEVELOPING COUNTRIES

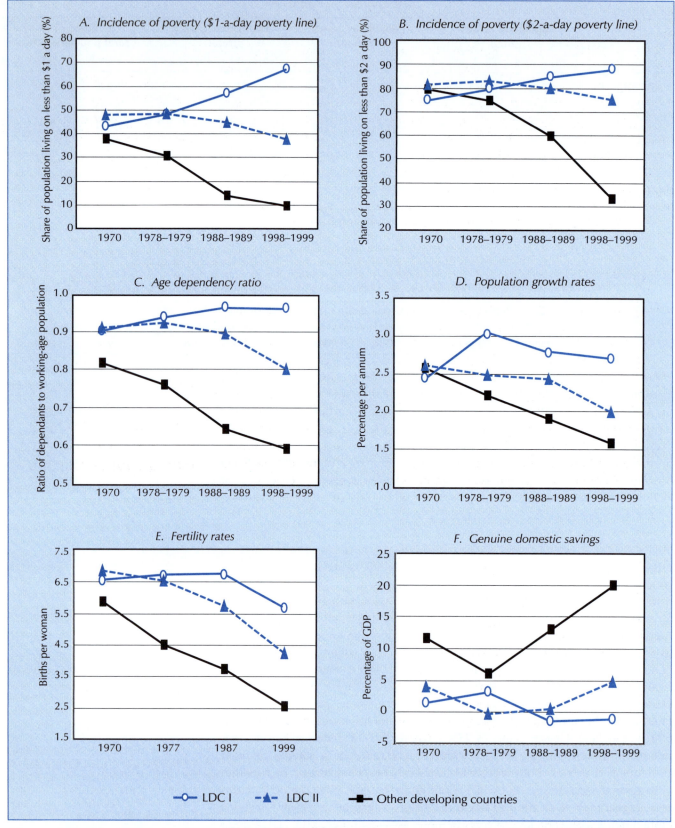

Source: Same as for chart 15.

Note: The "LDC I" group consists of the following 23 LDCs: Angola, Benin, Burundi, Central African Republic, Chad, Comoros, Democratic Republic of the Congo, Djibouti, Gambia, Guinea-Bissau, Haiti, Lesotho, Liberia, Madagascar, Mali, Mozambique, Niger, Rwanda, Senegal, Sierra Leone, Somalia, United Republic of Tanzania and Zambia.

The "LDC II" group consists of the following 14 LDCs: Bangladesh, Bhutan, Burkina Faso, Cape Verde, Ethiopia, Guinea, Lao People's Democratic Republic, Malawi, Mauritania, Myanmar, Nepal, Sudan, Togo and Uganda.

The other developing countries are the same as for chart 15.

There is a remarkable correspondence between demographic trends and poverty trends in the two LDC groups and other developing countries. Population growth rates were on average similar in the three country groups in the early 1970s, as were the average poverty levels. By the late 1990s, however, poverty in the LDC I group had increased substantially, and correspondingly the population growth rates and age dependency ratio in this group of countries had on average increased. The annual population growth rate increased from an average of 2.4 per cent in 1970 to 2.7 per cent by the late 1990s in this group of LDCs, and the age dependency ratio increased from 0.90 to 0.96 over the same period. This was because fertility rates remained high while the death rates were declining in this group of LDCs. Fertility rates fell moderately from 6.5 in 1970 to 5.7 in 1999. This is in sharp contrast to the experience of other developing countries, where along with declining poverty the demographic trends also showed considerable improvements. Population growth declined from 2.6 per cent in 1970 to 1.6 per cent in the late 1990s in other developing countries, and dependency ratios fell from an average of 0.8 to 0.6 during the same period. In other developing countries, fertility rates also followed a steep downward trend. They fell from 5.9 in 1970 to 2.5 in 1999. As shown in chart 23, the demographic trends in the LDC II group, where poverty declined, fall between the trends in the LDC I group and those in other developing countries.

There is also a remarkable correspondence between the average poverty and demographic trends and the average trends in genuine savings among the three groups of countries. Genuine savings are a measure of net domestic savings that in addition to the depreciation of the man-made capital stock takes into account the depreciation of natural capital stock and net additions to human resources (see Kunte et al., 1998; Hamilton and Clemens, 1999). As shown in chart 23F, the other developing countries exhibited a rapid increase in genuine savings during the 1980s and the 1990s along their trajectory of rapidly declining poverty. Genuine savings increased from just over an average of 6 per cent of GDP in the late 1970s for this group of countries to over 20 per cent in the late 1990s. On the other hand, the LDC I group experienced a decline in their genuine savings rates from an average of over 3 per cent to minus 1 per cent during the same period. Throughout the 1980s and the 1990s genuine savings rates in the LDC I group were indeed negative, a fact which indicates that this group of countries were depleting their national wealth or eating up their stock of assets over this period. The LDC II group, on the other hand, exhibited moderate increases in average genuine savings rates during the 1980s and the 1990s. Nevertheless, at about 5 per cent of GDP, the genuine savings rate in the late 1990s in this group of countries was not much more than in the early 1970s.

Although it is difficult to provide aggregate indicators of environmental degradation at national or regional levels, the low or negative genuine savings rates give some indication of environmental degradation processes in the LDCs. One aggregate indicator which is also suggestive of this phenomenon is the trend in net forest depletion in the LDCs as compared with other developing countries during the past three decades. As shown in chart 24, the average rate of net forest depletion in the LDCs experienced a sharp increase during the 1980s and the 1990s. It is estimated that in the late 1990s it was equivalent to more than 2 per cent of LDCs' GDP. This is over three times the rates of deforestation in other developing countries. Indeed, the average rate of forest depletion as a share of GDP for the LDC group as a whole in the late 1990s was more than 90 per cent of their average rate of genuine savings.

There is a remarkable correspondence between demographic trends and poverty trends in the two LDC groups and other developing countries.

There is also a remarkable correspondence between the poverty and demographic trends and the trends in genuine savings among the three groups of countries.

The average rate of net forest depletion in the LDCs experienced a sharp increase during the 1980s and the 1990s, and in the late 1990s it was equivalent to more than 2 per cent of LDCs' GDP.

CHART 24. NET FOREST DEPLETION AS A SHARE OF GDP IN LDCs AND OTHER DEVELOPING COUNTRIES, 1970–1999
(Percentage)

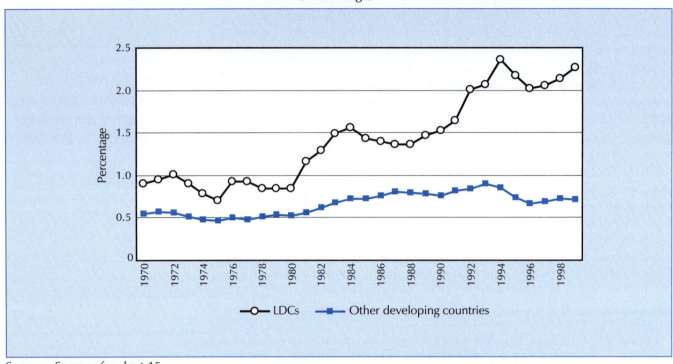

Source: Same as for chart 15.

Note: The sample of other developing countries is the same as for chart 15. The sample of LDCs includes all countries in the
"poorest LDCs" and "poor LDCs" groups in chart 15 except Cape Verde, Comoros, Djibouti, Liberia, Solomon Islands,
Somalia and Vanuatu, for which no data are available.

2. THE DOWNWARD SPIRAL OF IMPOVERISHMENT AND ENVIRONMENTAL DEGRADATION

Cross-country research shows that fertility rates are particularly closely related to per capita GDP, higher GDP per capita being associated with lower fertility rates and with female education. Historically, it is also clear that fertility rates have declined with increases in female employment and wages.

It would be, of course, too simplistic to envision a linear causal chain running from generalized poverty to demographic and environmental factors. The above evidence, however, is in conformity with the assumed interlinkages between poverty, population and environment discussed in the downward spiral theories in which these three factors can reinforce each other in a vicious spiral. Chart 25 can help one to envision the complex feedback loops involved in such a downward spiral. However, it should be noted that in practice the effect of some factors depends on, or is mediated by, the presence of other factors. For example, the impact of demographic factors on economic growth and the environment depends on the nature of poverty in the economy. Alternatively, the implications of poverty for population growth can be strongly influenced by environmental and other factors. The behaviour of complex interacting systems of the type depicted in the chart is hard to predict, and the overall trajectories will always be context-specific rather than general. An examination of some of these channels of interaction, however, would be useful in shedding light on the nature of policy problems facing LDCs that are caught in downward spirals.

We shall start with the population growth circle in the chart and proceed to the other two factors in turn. The determinants and effects of population growth have been subject to debate amongst demographers, economists and other scientists for many decades. Cross-country research shows that fertility rates are particularly closely related to per capita GDP, higher GDP per capita being associated with lower fertility rates and with female education (Barro, 2000).

CHART 25. FEEDBACK LOOPS BETWEEN GENERALIZED POVERTY, ENVIRONMENTAL DEGRADATION AND POPULATION GROWTH

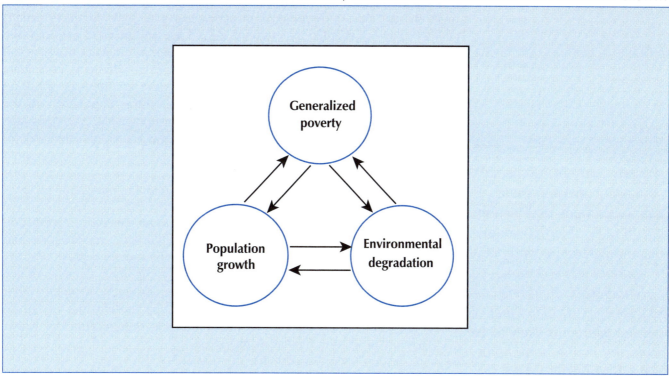

Historically, it is also clear that fertility rates have declined with increases in female employment and wages (Schultz, 2002). When the opportunity costs of women's time is higher, fertility rates tend to be lower. Additionally, improvements in child health technologies have increased children's survival rates, which put downward pressure on high birth rates. The availability of family planning services can also be important. But historically the existence of such services was not a necessary condition for the fertility transition.

In order to go beyond these general associations between fertility and population growth, however, it may be useful to pose the question in terms of the determinants of demand for children by households. Once the question is posed in this fashion it will become clear that, for example, the existence of contraceptives and family planning services can be less effective where there is a high demand by households for children and a desire for larger families. Also, female education, age of marriage and the number of children are likely to be joint decisions rather than the latter being caused by female education. Factors that determine demand for children are likely to also influence the decision about the education of female children. It is within this framework that most of the recent studies draw on the linkages between population, poverty and environmental resources to explain the persistence of high fertility and population growth rates. This type of analysis is mainly relevant to poor agrarian economies of the LDC type where the majority of the population live in the countryside and are engaged in low-productivity agricultural production. The labour intensity of agricultural work under these circumstances is said to lead to a high demand for extra hands in the form of large families. In particular, with the receding of water and wood fuel sources as a result of environmental degradation the demand for children's work increases as more time needs to be spent on fetching water, wood fuel and other materials for domestic energy consumption (see Bledso, 1994; Cleaver and Schreiber, 1994; Filmer and Prichett, 1996).

Another reason for the high fertility rates in poor agrarian economies is said to be the fact that in the absence of access to capital and insurance markets children may be regarded as insurance for old age and times of hardship (see Cain, 1981; Cox and Jimenez, 1992). For example, in his study of villages in Bangladesh and India, Cain (1981) argues that the diversity of fertility experiences can be explained by the differences in the environment of risk on the one hand, and the adequacy of risk insurance on the other hand. As the poor agrarian economies in increasingly fragile environmental conditions face increasing volatility in income and consumption, he argues, the demand for children, particularly boys, rises as a means of consumption smoothing and old age insurance. Under these conditions, public employment schemes that reduce income volatility are advocated as a possible tool of population policy.

The above, of course, should not be regarded as an exhaustive explanation of high fertility rates in the LDCs. Various institutional, sociocultural and historical elements need to be included in the specific country context. Poverty and environmental fragility, however, are evidently important elements of any explanation of high rates of fertility in low-income agrarian economies. Under such economic conditions, children's education, particularly that of female children, is likely to be neglected by the households, even in situations where the necessary facilities in rural areas may exist.

Another important feedback loop relates to the implications of high population growth rates for income growth and poverty. The empirical evidence on this issue is mixed: some have observed a negative correlation between population, economic growth and poverty, while others have observed positive links (see National Research Council, 1986; Mauro, 1995; Eastwood and Lipton, 1999). One reason for this type of contradictory result is that the studies do not differentiate between situations of generalized poverty and residual poverty. Under generalized poverty, where the economy is characterized by low productivity, low levels of capital stock and low savings, it is more likely that high population growth rates will lead to lower per capita income and a higher degree of poverty. As observed above in the context of the LDCs, high fertility rates also lead to high rates of age dependency and that further undercuts the saving capacity of the economy and its potential growth. On the other hand, in a technologically dynamic economy with high labour productivity, well-developed capital markets, use of capital-intensive production techniques and high savings rates, population growth is likely to act as a stimulus to economic growth. Such a result can be, for example, easily derived from the new models of endogenous growth, where higher population growth can be shown to be a stimulus to economic growth by increasing the demand for goods and services. Under conditions of generalized poverty, however, this would be a highly unlikely outcome.

The next feedback loop is the impact of population growth on environmental resources. A prominent thesis in the existing literature is that high fertility in low-income countries leads to rapidly growing population pressure on the resource base, which is said to be the main cause of both environmental degradation and marginalization or poverty (see, for example, Repetto and Holmes, 1983, and Perrings, 1991). This is supposed to take place both directly and indirectly. It takes place directly when rapid population growth directly leads to marginalization and environmental degradation as the supply of labour increases faster than demand and population pressure on environmental resources increases. It takes place indirectly when population growth leads to greater demand for food, which in turn leads to the adoption of policies mainly concerned with the maximization of food production to the possible detriment

Poverty and environmental fragility are important elements of any explanation of high rates of fertility in low-income agrarian economies. Under such economic conditions, children's education, particularly that of female children, is likely to be neglected by the households, even in situations where the necessary facilities in rural areas may exist.

In the context of the LDCs, high fertility rates also lead to high rates of age dependency and that further undercuts the saving capacity of the economy and its potential growth.

of the environment. It is important to note, however, that in both versions of this argument the link between population growth on the one hand and environmental degradation and poverty on the other is mediated through broader economic factors. As in the case of economic growth discussed above, the impact is likely to depend on initial economic conditions and in particular on whether the economy is characterized by generalized poverty or not. In a technologically dynamic developing economy, where rapid processes of capital accumulation and structural change lead to rapid rates of employment generation in the non-agricultural sectors and at the same time rapid rates of agricultural productivity growth, population growth need not necessarily have detrimental environmental and poverty implications. On the other hand, in an economy where the conditions of generalized poverty prevail, with low savings, low labour productivity and stagnant technology, population growth is bound to have detrimental environmental consequences. Once again, it is the combination of generalized poverty and population growth that is likely to have serious consequences for environmental degradation.

The above point is worth emphasizing, because it is often mistakenly assumed that the environmental problems of the LDCs are due to a paucity of environmental resources relative to the size of the population. For example, in the context of sub-Saharan African LDCs, Pearce and Turner (1990: 47) maintain that "In the Sahel, it is difficult to envisage development without natural resource augmentation". On the contrary, the existing evidence suggests that developmental problems in the LDCs in general, and in sub-Saharan African LDCs in particular, are less to do with the paucity of environmental resources as such. As shown in chart 26, the main difference between the LDCs and other, more successful developing countries lies not in the low levels of environmental resources per head; rather, it is the extremely low levels of per capita man-made capital and human resources that distinguish the LDCs from other developing countries. This is even more clearly shown in table 24, where arable land per person is compared with investment indicators and land productivity in agriculture in the LDCs and other developing countries in the latter half of the 1990s. As can be seen, in terms of arable land per person, both the LDC I and the LDC II groups of countries are on average better endowed than other developing countries. However, in terms of investment indicators such as fertilizer use, irrigation and tractor use the LDCs, particularly the LDC I group, are well behind other developing countries. Another indicator of the under-investment in LDC agriculture is the very low level of value added per hectare of arable land in LDCs as compared with other developing countries (see table 24).

The environmental problems of the LDCs therefore are not due to their low levels of per capita environmental resources. They are rather the combined result of generalized poverty, manifested in low levels of, and low rates of addition to, man-made capital stock, and high population growth rates, which are in turn both exacerbated by environmental degradation itself. The environmental degradation processes in the LDCs can best be characterized by what in the literature has been referred to as the "forced environmental degradation" process (Karshenas, 1995). Forced environmental degradation is said to take place where "inadequate man-made capital stock, stagnant technology, lack of employment opportunities and the inability to cater for basic human needs, combined with a growing population, force the economy into a state where survival necessitates eating into the natural or environmental capital stock in order to survive" (ibid.: 754). Many instances of environmental degradation in LDC agriculture — for example, deforestation, desertification and soil degradation — are closely associated with this phenomenon.

Forced environmental degradation takes place where inadequate man-made capital stock, stagnant technology, lack of employment opportunities and the inability to cater for basic human needs, combined with a growing population, force the economy into a state where survival necessitates eating into the natural or environmental capital stock in order to survive.

Many instances of environmental degradation in LDC agriculture — for example, deforestation, desertification and soil degradation — are closely associated with this phenomenon.

CHART 26. PER CAPITA WEALTH IN LDCs AND OTHER DEVELOPING COUNTRIES IN 1994

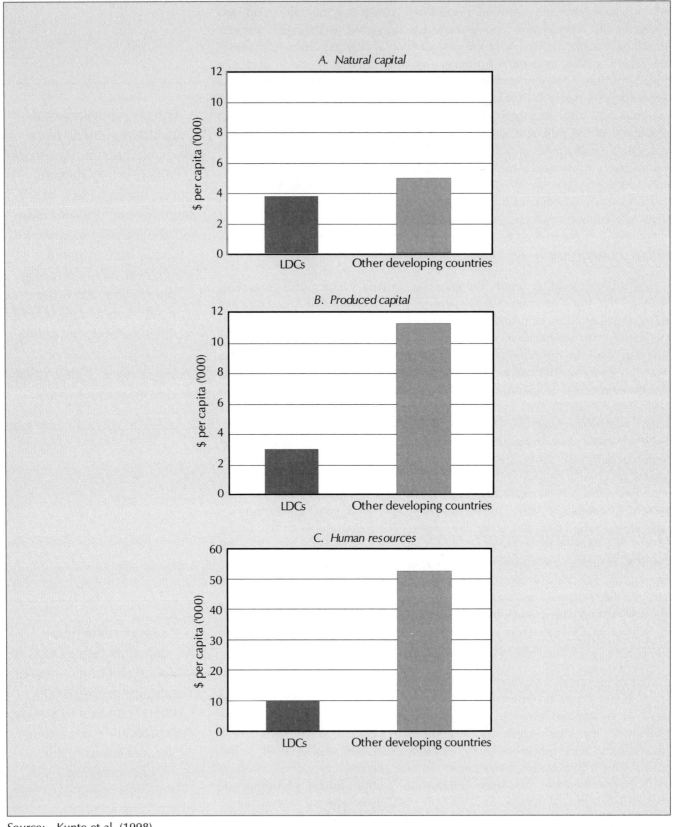

Source: Kunte et al. (1998).

Note: Based on a sample of 24 LDCs and 46 other developing countries for which data are available.

TABLE 24. AGRICULTURAL INVESTMENT AND PRODUCTIVITY INDICATORS
IN LDCs AND OTHER DEVELOPING COUNTRIES, 1995–1998

	Fertilizer consumption[a]	Irrigated land % cropland	Tractors per hectare of arable land	Arable land per person (hectares)	Agricultural value-added per hectare of agricultural land[b]
Total LDCs[c]	115	8.5	0.09	0.24	203.8
LDC I group	57	5.3	0.10	0.24	155.7
LDC II group	206	13.0	0.07	0.23	291.2
Other DCs	1 011	19.4	0.85	0.21	551.8

Source: UNCTAD secretariat estimates based on World Bank, *World Development Indicators 2001*, CD-ROM.

Note: Figures are simple averages. LDC I and LDC II groups are the same as in chart 23. The other developing countries group is the same as for chart 15. No data are available for Bhutan (tractors), Central African Republic (irrigated land), Comoros (tractors and irrigated land), Djibouti (all variables), Ethiopia (agricultural value-added), Lesotho (irrigated land), Liberia (agricultural value-added), Myanmar (agricultural value-added), Somalia (agricultural value-added) and Sudan (agricultural value-added).

a 100 grams per hectare of arable land.
b Data for 1994 (the latest available year) in 1995 constant US dollars.
c 39 LDCs, comprising all countries in LDC I and LDC II groups.

Finally, it must be stressed that not only is generalized poverty implicated in processes of environmental degradation, but also environmental degradation has important consequences for poverty. The poor are more seriously affected by environmental degradation, because owing to lack of assets they are less capable of defending themselves against environmental damage, while being more exposed to environmental pollution. Also, in low-income agrarian economies the poor are more immediately dependent on poor-quality and fragile natural resources. Unfortunately, when poverty is generalized and when the bulk of the population in a country consists of poor peasants and agricultural workers, who lack access to capital and alternative sources of employment, poverty and environmental degradation become the two sides of the same coin.

E. Conclusion

In most LDCs, a major part of the population live at or below income levels sufficient to meet their basic needs, and the available resources in the economy, even when equally distributed, are barely sufficient to cater for the basic needs of the population on a sustainable basis. In societies where poverty is generalized in this way, the causes and effects of poverty need to be understood in a different way from the way they are understood in societies where absolute poverty is not all-pervasive, but rather affects only a minor part of the population. This chapter has identified three key features of the relationship between economic growth and poverty that are characteristic of situations of generalized poverty. Firstly, in societies where there is generalized poverty, economic growth has particularly strong positive effects in reducing poverty, particularly extreme poverty. Secondly, in societies where there is generalized poverty, the relationship between growth and poverty is two-way. Economic growth affects the incidence and depth of poverty; at the same time the incidence and depth of poverty affect economic growth. Thirdly, in societies where there is generalized poverty, poverty acts as a major constraint on economic growth.

Generalized poverty constrains economic growth in diverse ways. These include, but go beyond, those examined by development economists who identified in the 1950s a low-level equilibrium trap which was related to the lack

In societies where there is generalized poverty, the relationship between growth and poverty is two-way.

of domestic resources available for financing investment. Two further important channels of influence are the relationship between generalized poverty and environmental degradation, and the relationship between generalized poverty and the underfunding of public goods and services, including administration, law and order and the whole system of governance.

As a result of these relationships, there has been a tendency for generalized poverty to persist, or to decline very slowly, in most LDCs. In some cases, countries are pushed into a downward spiral of economic regression, social stress and environmental degradation. Political instability and conflict can easily become part of this downward spiral.

Notes

1. There is large literature on the way in which economic growth affects poverty. The recent debate on the subject, including the much-cited paper by Dollar and Kraay (2001), focuses on the relationship between economic growth and selected indicators of poverty in "spells" defined by the periods of time spanning two successive household surveys for a given country. Such work generally examines the short-term relationship between growth and poverty, rather than the long-term relationship which is the concern here. These different foci can give different results (see Ahluwalia, 1976). Also, in the light of the discussion in the last chapter, it should be noted that conclusions from the spell analysis are likely to be questionable if the growth of mean private consumption per capita is estimated from national accounts data and the incidence of poverty from household surveys. For an even-handed review of recent literature of the growth-poverty relationship using spell analysis, see Ravallion (2001).

2. The term "poverty curve" is not in current usage in national and international analysis of poverty. However, Anderson (1964) uses the term to refer to the curve defining the proportion of families in the United States with incomes below $3,000 as a function of the log of median income for the period 1947–1960. His paper is of interest as it also shows poverty curves for sub-groups of the American population — rural and urban, white and non-white — over this period, indicating how specific sub-groups may not follow the overall trend. See also Smolensky et al. (1994) for a discussion of the relationship between growth and poverty in the United States over the period 1963–1991 in terms of Anderson's poverty curve.

3. The chart includes all available observations, covering 32 countries in Africa or Asia over three decades. Two clearly outlying countries — South Africa and Zimbabwe — have been omitted. The sample is set out in annex table 1 in the last chapter.

4. This inference is in the same tradition as economic work to identify long-run patterns of development that includes Chenery and Syrquin (1975), Chenery, Robinson and Syrquin (1986), and Syrquin and Chenery (1989). The relationship between income distribution and development was a central issue in these studies, but the long-run relationship between poverty and development, which is defined in this Report using the poverty curve, was not analysed.

5. The sample of other developing countries includes all low- and lower-middle-income countries for which it is possible to make national-accounts-consistent estimates of poverty using the $1-a-day and $2-a-day international poverty lines, and for which other data used in this chapter are available. The list of other developing countries is given in chart 15.

6. It should be noted that this classification is for analytical rather than policy purposes. For the list of LDCs in each group, see chart 15. Two Asian LDCs, Myanmar and Nepal, are included in the group of poor LDCs, although their $2-a-day poverty indicators are higher than those of other members of this group.

7. This is about the same as the average ratio of domestic resources available for finance to GDP over the period 1995–1999 for other developing countries in general. The ratio for 90 developing countries, excluding the LDCs, was 34.9 per cent.

8. Government final consumption expenditure is defined, as in World Bank *World Development Indicators*, to include all government current expenditures for purchases of goods and services (including compensation of employees).

9. These are in official exchange rates appreciably at current prices. Translating these figures into PPP exchange rates does not change the gap between the LDCs and the sample of other developing countries, as the exchange rate deviations between the PPP and the official exchange rates are not very different between the two groups of

countries. The ratio of PPP for services to official exchange rate in the LDCs on average is only 20 to 30 per cent over that of the sample of other developing countries, which is of a totally different order of magnitude compared with their per capita expenditure gaps discussed in the text above.

10. We are grateful to the UNDP Human Development Office in New York for supplying these data.

11. For a recent discussion which deals with this phenomenon, see Nafziger and Auvinen (2002). They identified range of causal factors, but note that "a major factor responsible for the increase in emergencies in the 1990s is the developing world's stagnation and protracted decline in incomes, primarily in the 1980s, and its contribution to state decay and collapse" (p. 159).

12. The classification into two LDC groups is based on chapter 1, chart 12. The sample excludes the Solomon Islands and Vanuatu, for which no data are available on poverty levels in the late 1970s.

References

Ahluwalia, M.S. (1976). Inequality, poverty and development, *Journal of Development Economics*, 3: 307–342.

Anderson, W.H.L. (1964). Trickling down: the relationship between economic growth and the extent of poverty among American families, *Quarterly Journal of Economics*, 78 (4): 511–524.

Barro, R. (2000). Human capital and growth, *American Economic Review*, 91 (2): 12–17.

Bledso, C. (1994). Children are like young bamboo trees: potentiality and reproduction in sub-Saharan Africa. In: Lindahl-Keissling, K. and Landberg, H., eds., *Population, Economic Development and Environment*, Oxford University Press, Oxford.

Cain, M. (1981). Risk and insurance: perspectives on fertility and agrarian change in India and Bangladesh, *Population and Development Review*, 7 (3): 435–474.

Chenery, H.B. and Syrquin, M. (1975). *Patterns of Development, 1950–1975*, Oxford University Press, London.

Chenery, H.B., Robinson, S. and Syrquin, M. (1986). *Industrialization and Growth*, Oxford University Press, New York.

Cleaver, K.M. and Schreiber, G.A. (1994). *Reversing the Spiral: the Population, Agriculture, and Environment Nexus in sub-Saharan Africa*, World Bank, Washington DC.

Collier, P. and Dollar, D. (2001). Can the world cut poverty in half? How policy reform and effective aid can meet International Development Goals, *World Development*, 29 (11): 1727–1802.

Cox, D. and Jimenez, E. (1992). Social security and private transfers in developing countries: the case of Peru, *World Bank Economic Review*, 6 (1): 155–169.

Dollar, D. and Kraay, A. (2001). Growth is good for the poor, Policy Research Working Paper No. 2587, World Bank, Washington DC.

Eastwood, R. and Lipton, M. (1999). The impact of changes in human fertility on poverty. Department of Economics, University of Sussex.

Filmer, D. and Prichett, L. (1996). Environmental degradation and the demand for children, Policy Research Working Paper No. 1623, Policy Research Department, World Bank, Washington DC.

Hagdeviren, H., van der Hoeven, R. and Weeks, J. (2001). Redistribution does matter: redistribution for poverty reduction, paper presented at the WIDER Development Conference on Growth and Poverty, 25–26 May 2001, Helsinki, Finland.

Hamilton, K. and Clemens, M. (1999). Genuine savings rates in developing countries, *World Bank Economic Review*, 13 (2): 333–356.

IMF (2000). *World Economic Outlook, May 2000*, IMF, Washington DC.

Karshenas, M. (1995). Environment, technology and employment: towards a new definition of sustainable development, *Development and Change*, 25 (4): 723–756.

Karshenas, M. (2001). Measurement and nature of absolute poverty in least developed countries, background report for *The Least Developed Countries Report 2002*, UNCTAD, Geneva.

Kunte, A., Hamilton, K., Dixon, J. and Clemens, M. (1998). Estimating national wealth: methodology and results, Environmental Department Working Paper No. 57, World Bank, Washington DC.

Liebenstein, H. (1957). *Economic Backwardness and Economic Growth: Studies in the Theory of Economic Development*, John Wiley, New York.

Mauro, P. (1995). Corruption and growth, *Quarterly Journal of Economics*, 110 (3): 681–712.

Messer, E. and Cohen, M.J. (2001). Shaping globalization for poverty alleviation and food security: conflict and food insecurity, mimeo, International Food Policy Research Institute (IFPRI), Washington DC (http://www.ifpri.org/2020/focus08/focus08_12.htm).

Nafziger, E.W. and Auvinen, J. (2002). Economic development, inequality, war, and state violence, *World Development*, 30 (2): 153–163.

Narayan, D., Chambers, R., Shah, M.K. and Petesch, P. (2001). *Voices of the Poor: Crying out for change*, Oxford University Press, New York.

National Research Council (1986). *Population Growth and Economic Development: Policy Questions,* National Academy of Sciences Press, Washington DC.

Nelson, R.R. (1956). A theory of the low-level equilibrium trap, *American Economic Review*, 46: 48–90.

OECD/World Bank (2001). *New Partnerships for Financing Development in the Least Developed Countries*, background paper for the Thematic Session on financing Growth and Development, Third United Nations Conference on the Least Developed Countries, Brussels,14–20 May, 2001.

Pearce, D.W. and Turner, R.K. (1990). *The Economics of Natural Resources and the Environment,* Harvester-Wheatsheaf, London.

Perrings, C. (1991). Incentives for the ecologically sustainable use of human and natural resources in the drylands of sub-Saharan Africa: a review, World Employment Programme Research Working Paper, ILO, Geneva.

Pyatt, G. (2001). An alternative approach to poverty analysis, with particular reference to poverty reduction strategies being developed in the context of the HIPC Initiative, background paper for *The Least Developed Countries Report 2002*, UNCTAD, Geneva.

Ravallion, M. (2001). Growth, inequality and poverty: looking beyond the averages, *World Development*, 29 (11): 1803–1816.

Ravallion, M. and Chen, S. (1997). What can new survey data tell us about recent changes in distribution and poverty?, *World Bank Economic Review*, 11(2): 358–382.

Ravallion, M., Datt, G. and van de Walle, D. (1991). Quantifying absolute poverty in the developing world, *Review of Income and Wealth*, 37: 345–361.

Repetto, R. and Holmes, J. (1983). The role of population in resource depletion in developing countries, *Population and Development Review*, 9 (4): 155–172.

Schultz, T.P. (2002). Why governments should invest more to educate girls, *World Development*, 30 (2): 207–225.

Smolensky, E., Plotnick, R., Evenhouse, E. and Reilly, S. (1994). Growth, inequality, and poverty: a cautionary note, *Review of Income and Wealth*, Series 40 (2): 217–222.

Stewart, F. and Fitzgerald, E.V.K. (eds.) (2000). *War and Underdevelopment,* vols. 1 and 2, Oxford University Press, Oxford.

Stockholm International Peace Research Institute (SIPRI) (2000). *SIPRI Yearbook 2000 — Armaments, Disarmament and International Security*, Oxford University Press, Oxford.

Syrquin, M. and Chenery, H.B. (1989). Patterns of development, 1950–1983, World Bank Discussion Paper No. 41, World Bank, Washington DC.

UNCTAD (1997). *Trade and Development Report — Globalization, Distribution and Growth*, United Nations publication, sales no. E.II.D.8, Geneva.

UNCTAD (2000). *The Least Developed Countries 2000 Report*, United Nations publication, sales no. E.00.II.D.21, Geneva.

United Nations Economic Commission for Africa (UNECA) (1999). *Economic Report on Africa, 1999*, E/ECA/CM.24/3, Addis Ababa.

Patterns of trade integration and poverty

A. Introduction

The previous chapter identified various cause-and-effect relationships that work within many LDCs to cause generalized poverty to persist and even intensify. International economic relationships were not included in the discussion. But these relationships affect any country that is not completely isolated from the world economy, and with the globalization of production systems and finance, and liberalization of economic activities, they are becoming even more closely implicated in national processes of accumulation, productivity growth, and trends in inequality and poverty. This chapter and the next one focus on the relationship between international trade and poverty in the LDCs, examining whether the current pattern of trade is reinforcing the poverty trap or helping countries to break out of it.

At the present time much international policy advice, as well as the policy conditionality which governs access to concessional finance, is founded on the argument that a major reason why poverty persists in the least developed countries is their low level of integration into the global economy through trade, which in turn is due to the failure of LDCs to adopt sufficiently open trade regimes.[1] This argument is clouded by conceptual weaknesses and semantic confusions surrounding the key notion of "integration" (see box 9). It is also not well grounded empirically, partly owing to problems with specifying in a quantitative way the nature of national trade regimes and partly owing to a lack of adequate poverty statistics. The present chapter uses the new data set of poverty estimates for the LDCs to rectify this last deficiency. It describes some key features of LDCs' international trade (section B), distinguishing the level of trade integration, the form of trade integration (defined by the composition of exports and imports of goods and services), the extent of marginalization within global trade flows and the degree of trade liberalization. It then goes on to establish, as far as possible, the precise nature of the relationships between poverty and (a) trade liberalization (section C), (b) export orientation (section D) and (c) export structure (section E). Section F discusses some of the factors that influence the different poverty-reducing effects of exports of primary commodities, manufactures and services.

The main message of the chapter is that the current conventional wisdom that persistent poverty in LDCs is due to their low level of trade integration and insufficient trade liberalization is grossly simplistic. The persistence of generalized poverty is less related to a low level of integration into the global economy, and to insufficient trade liberalization, than to the form of trade integration. Amongst the LDCs, there is a clear link between dependence on primary commodity exports and the incidence of extreme poverty, defined by the proportion of the population living on less than a dollar a day. The next chapter takes up in more detail the question of the precise nature of this relationship, and also considers some of the new vulnerabilities which pose a downside risk for the LDCs exporting manufactures and services, where extreme poverty tends to be less pervasive and, more often than not, declining. The analysis extends the discussion of the poverty trap within which most LDCs are caught, arguing that the poverty trap is international in scope and that the current form of globalization is tending to reinforce it.

The current conventional wisdom that persistent poverty in LDCs is due to their low level of trade integration and insufficient trade liberalization is grossly simplistic.

The persistence of generalized poverty is less related to a low level of integration into the global economy, and to insufficient trade liberalization, than to the form of trade integration.

BOX 9. SOME CONCEPTUAL AND SEMANTIC WEAKNESSES IN THE POLICY DEBATE
ON THE RELATIONSHIP BETWEEN TRADE AND POVERTY

The current debate on international trade and poverty, both for developing countries in general and the least developed countries in particular, is characterized by a number of serious weaknesses which together prevent effective policies for poverty reduction.

Firstly, there is a semantic looseness in the use of key terms such as "outward-orientation", "openness", "integration" and "marginalization". The goal of "integrating" LDCs into the world economy can be, and is, understood as increasing their share of total global trade (the opposite of marginalization), increasing the trade orientation of their economies (measured by the ratio of total imports and exports to GDP), or increasing their institutional integration into the multilateral trading system embodied in the rules and procedures of the WTO. The "openness" of a national economy in trade terms is measured using either an indicator of trade orientation (the ratio of trade to GDP) or an indicator of trade restrictions (such as tariff or non-tariff barriers). Often it has been assumed that the former is a good proxy of the latter. But this assumption effectively forecloses discussion of: (a) what is the relationship between trade policies and trade orientation, and of each to growth?; and (b) what are the trade and other policies which countries should adopt to integrate into the world economy in a way which promotes their sustained development? Similarly, the term "outward-oriented" has been used as an adjective to describe both a type of trade policy regime (one in which there is an absence of bias against exports) and the degree of export orientation or trade orientation (measured by the export/GDP or trade/GDP ratio) of an economy. Also, an "outward-oriented" trade regime has been equated with the removal of trade barriers, even though it is correctly understood as one which establishes incentives that are neutral between production for external markets and production for domestic markets, and can be achieved not only by trade liberalization but also through a judicious mix of export incentives and import restrictions (Bhagwati, 1988).

Secondly, the discussion of trade and poverty is often abstracted from the types of goods and services which are being traded. But the relationship between exports, growth and poverty is likely to be different if the exports in question are products with a high income elasticity of demand or a high potential for productivity growth and linkage effects. One should not expect the relationship to be the same for primary commodity-exporting economies as it is for exporters of manufactured goods.

Thirdly, the discussion of trade and poverty is analytically separated from questions of financing trade development. But the way in which investment in tradables, either export activities or import substitutes, can take place in situations of generalized poverty, as well as how trade itself is financed, is a vital issue in most LDCs. Aid must play a central role in trade development in those countries. Moreover, the two-way relationships between export growth and the build-up of unsustainable external debt, with slow export growth contributing to the emergence of a debt problem and the debt burden in turn making it more difficult to achieve faster export growth, must be taken into account in discussing the trade–poverty relationship in poor countries.

Fourthly, the policy debate often fails to distinguish between the problems and needs of countries at different levels of development. The argument that outward-oriented economies grow faster was initially put forward over 30 years ago for what were then described as "semi-industrial economies" (Balassa, 1970). It was in the 1980s that the geographical scope of this argument was widened to include all developing countries. But whether it is correct to extend the field of application of the argument (whose meaning itself needs to be clarified in the light of the semantic caveats above) in this way is an issue which requires empirical validation. It is a priori unlikely that trade liberalization will have the same effects in a country where there are few domestic corporate capacities as in one where there is well-developed corporate sector. The question which must be asked is: What effects does trade liberalization have in a typical LDC where, at official exchange rates and current prices, average private consumption per capita is only 57 cents ($0.57) a day?

Finally, there are increasing differences in the trade structures and export capabilities of the least developed countries. Appropriate national measures to promote trade need to take these differences into account, and the potential of international policy measures, such as improvements in market access, to reverse the marginalization of LDCs in global trade flows needs to be seen in the light of those differences.

B. Trade integration, marginalization and liberalization: patterns and trends in the LDCs

Discussion of international trade relations of the LDCs tends to be characterized by a number of accepted stylized facts that do not necessarily reflect current realities (Kirchbach, 2001). These include such propositions as "Trade/GDP ratios are low in the LDCs"; "All LDCs export primary commodities"; "All LDCs suffer from marginalization from global trade flows, and this tendency is inexorably increasing"; and "All LDCs have closed trade regimes". The present section examines the validity of those propositions as a basis for the subsequent discussion of the relationship between trade and poverty.[2]

1. LEVEL OF TRADE INTEGRATION

International trade is of major importance in the economies of LDCs. During 1997–1998, exports and imports of goods and services constituted on average 43 per cent of their GDP (table 25). For 22 out of 39 LDCs for which data are available on this indicator, the trade orientation of their economies was higher than 50 per cent. The average level of trade integration for the LDCs is around the same as the world average, and also almost the same as the average for the group of countries which have been identified in a recent World Bank policy research report as "more globalized developing countries" (World Bank, 2002b: 51). The average level of trade integration is actually higher than that of high-income OECD countries, and there are only eight LDCs for which data are available in which the integration of the national economy with the rest of the world through trade, as measured by the share of trade in GDP, is at a level lower than the average level in advanced economies. But the level of trade integration for the LDC group is lower than that of low-income and low- and middle-income countries.[3]

International trade is of major importance in the economies of LDCs. During 1997–1998, exports and imports of goods and services constituted on average 43 per cent of their GDP

The average level of LDCs' trade integration was comparatively high at the beginning of the 1980s, particularly relative to the low-income countries as a group, but after falling in the 1980s, it increased in the 1990s. Measured in current prices, exports and imports of goods and services as a share of GDP for the LDCs as a whole increased by 25 per cent between 1987–1989 and 1997–1998. This was a larger proportionate increase in the trade/GDP ratio than the world average. But it was less than that in other developing countries and much less than that of the "more globalized developing countries", which are defined as such because of the growing importance of trade in their economies and which started in the early 1980s with the lowest average level of trade integration.

Imports of goods and services were equivalent to 26 per cent of GDP on average in LDCs in 1997–1998. In 29 out of 39 LDCs import dependence is even higher than this level. But the export orientation of LDC economies is generally lower than import dependence. Exports of goods and services constituted 17 per cent of GDP in the LDCs as a group in 1997–1998. This level is below the average level of low-income countries (24 per cent), low- and middle-income countries (26 per cent), high-income OECD countries (21 per cent) and the world average (23 per cent).

Even though one would expect export orientation to vary systematically between countries with both income per capita levels and size of population, the relatively low export/GDP ratios are indicative of weak export capacities in

TABLE 25. TRADE AS A SHARE OF GDP IN LDCS AND OTHER COUNTRY GROUPS,
1981–1983, 1987–1989 AND 1997–1998

(Percentage)

	1981–1983	1987–1989	1997–1998
LDCs			
A. Total trade (B+C)	36.4	34.4	42.9
B. Exports of goods and services	12.1	12.6	17.0
C. Imports of goods and services	24.4	21.8	25.9
D. Trade balance (B-C)	-12.3	-9.2	-8.9
Low-income			
A. Total trade (B+C)	32.0	31.5	50.8
B. Exports of goods and services	14.1	14.5	24.1
C. Imports of goods and services	17.9	17.0	26.7
D. Trade balance (B-C)	-3.7	-2.5	-2.7
Low- and middle-income countries			
A. Total trade (B+C)	37.3	38.3	52.3
B. Exports of goods and services	18.3	19.7	26.1
C. Imports of goods and services	19.1	18.6	26.2
D. Trade balance (B-C)	-0.8	1.1	-0.1
High-income OECD countries			
A. Total trade (B+C)	35.1	32.3	40.2
B. Exports of goods and services	17.5	15.8	20.5
C. Imports of goods and services	17.7	16.5	19.7
D. Trade balance (B-C)	-0.2	-0.6	0.8
World			
A. Total trade (B+C)	38.7	37.2	44.6
B. Exports of goods and services	19.2	18.6	22.6
C. Imports of goods and services	19.5	18.5	22.0
D. Trade balance (B-C)	-0.3	0.1	0.6
More globalized developing countries[a]			
A. Total trade (B+C)	25.4	29.3	43.5
B. Exports of goods and services	12.3	15.0	21.7
C. Imports of goods and services	13.1	14.3	21.9
D. Trade balance (B-C)	-0.8	0.7	-0.2

Source: UNCTAD secretariat estimates based on World Bank, *World Development Indicators 2001,* CD-ROM.

Note: The figures in the table, except for more globalized developing countries, are calculated using the country group averages reported by the World Bank for exports and imports of goods and non-factor services as a percentage of GDP.

   a   More globalized developing countries — defined as "the top-third of developing countries in terms of increased trade to GDP between the 1970s and the 1990s" — are Argentina, Bangladesh, Brazil, China, Colombia, Costa Rica, Dominican Republic, Haiti, Hungary, India, Côte d'Ivoire, Jamaica, Jordan, Malaysia, Mali, Mexico, Nepal, Nicaragua, Paraguay, Philippines, Rwanda, Thailand, Uruguay and Zimbabwe (World Bank, 2002b: 51).

CHART 27. MERCHANDISE EXPORTS AS A SHARE OF GDP IN THE LDCS, BY COUNTRY, 1997–1999

(Percentage)

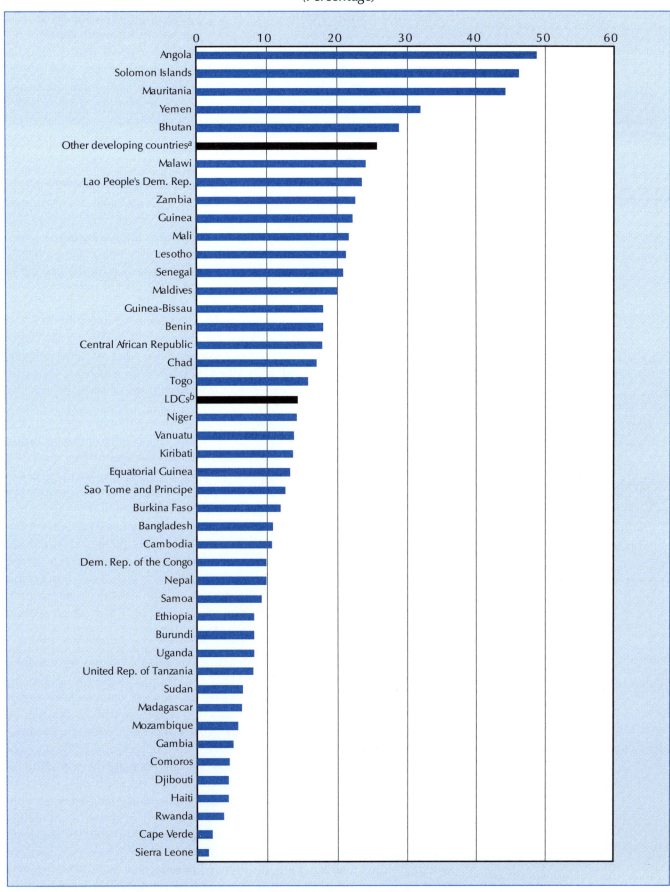

Source: UNCTAD secretariat estimates based on World Bank, *World Development Indicators 2001*, CD-ROM.

a Weighted average for 104 other developing countries.

b Weighted average for 43 LDCs.

many LDCs. In 17 LDCs merchandise exports account for less than 10 per cent of GDP (chart 27). Moreover, exports of goods and services do not cover imports of goods and services in most LDCs. The balance of trade for the group as a whole improved slightly in the 1990s, but there was a negative balance of 8.9 per cent of GDP in 1997–1998, a deficit which far exceeds that of all other country groups. This pattern persisted throughout the 1980s and 1990s, although the magnitude of the deficit of the LDCs at the end of the 1990s was somewhat lower than in the early 1980s.

2. FORM OF TRADE INTEGRATION

In the late 1990s, unprocessed primary commodities constituted 62 per cent of the total merchandise exports of the LDCs as a group (table 26). Processed primary commodities made up a further 8 per cent of merchandise exports, and manufactured exports were equivalent to 30 per cent of merchandise exports. According to UNCTAD data, service exports were also important for LDCs, constituting 19 per cent of total exports of goods and services in the late 1990s in the 35 LDCs for which data are available.

These group averages mask considerable differences amongst the LDCs in terms of the composition of their exports. There are 31 LDCs whose major source of export earnings are primary commodities, and of these Angola, Equatorial Guinea, Yemen and, after 1999, Sudan, are oil exporters. There are 18 LDCs that predominantly export either manufactures or services, or some combination of these.[4]

The main feature that distinguishes the LDCs which predominantly export primary commodities from the LDCs exporting manufactures and/or services is that the latter group have generally experienced, during the last 20 years, a transformation in their export structure in which the proportion of primary commodities in total exports has declined (relatively or absolutely), and either manufacturing or service activities have become the major export activities.[5] The most important exports of manufactures are textiles and clothing, whilst the key service export is tourism, although business services are important in a few island LDCs. It is possible to identify eight LDCs in which there has been a significant expansion in exports of labour-intensive manufactures since the early 1980s and particularly in the 1990s, and another eight LDCs in which services are now particularly important (see annex to this chapter).

Focusing on the merchandise export structure, table 27 shows the extent of this change in export structure for the LDCs as a whole and also for sub-groups: oil exporters, non-oil commodity exporters, exporters of manufactures and/or services, and exporters of manufactures. It is apparent that in the non-oil commodity exporters, between the early 1980s and late 1990s, unprocessed primary commodities increased in importance from 65 per cent to 74 per cent of total merchandise exports. There was a slight increase in the share of manufactured exports in total merchandise exports — from 10 per cent to 14 per cent. But downstream processing of commodities collapsed, declining from just over one quarter of the total merchandise exports of non-oil commodity-exporting LDCs in 1981–1983 to about one eighth in 1997–1999. For the group of LDCs classified as exporters of manufactures and/or services, manufactures constituted a much higher share of merchandise exports in 1981–1983, namely 30 per cent, and this share had increased to 70 per cent of their total merchandise exports in 1997–1999. An important factor in this shift is the performance of Bangladesh. But the increase in the share of manufactured

There are 31 LDCs whose major source of export earnings are primary commodities, and of these Angola, Equatorial Guinea, Yemen and, after 1999, Sudan, are oil exporters.

TABLE 26. EXPORT COMPOSITION IN LDCs, BY COUNTRY, IN THE LATE 1990s

	Type[a]	Share of primary commodities and manufactures in total merchandise exports, 1997–1999[b] (%)							Share of service exports in total exports of goods and services,
		Primary commodities			Manufactures			Total	1995–1999 (%)
		Unprocessed	Processed	Total	Low-skill	High-skill	Total		
Afghanistan	C	66.0	8.5	74.5	21.2	4.3	25.5	100	..
Benin	C	89.6	6.6	96.3	3.0	0.8	3.7	100	22.3
Bhutan	C	..	..	..	..	..	..	..	..
Burkina Faso	C	87.9	1.6	89.5	8.4	2.1	10.5	100	..
Burundi	C	..	..	..	..	..	..	..	5.0
Central African Rep.	C	90.7	6.8	97.5	1.2	1.2	2.5	100	..
Chad	C	94.9	1.4	96.3	0.6	3.2	3.7	100	..
Dem. Rep. of the Congo	C	84.2	12.1	96.2	3.1	0.7	3.8	100	..
Eritrea	C	..	..	..	..	..	..	..	..
Ethiopia	C	82.7	6.5	89.2	5.7	5.1	10.8	100	41.1
Guinea	C	82.0	10.3	92.3	0.5	7.2	7.7	100	5.6
Guinea -Bissau	C	97.5	0.7	98.3	0.8	1.0	1.7	100	8.4
Kiribati[c]	C	95.0	0.1	95.1	3.8	1.1	4.9	100	..
Liberia	C	..	..	..	..	..	..	..	..
Malawi	C	85.4	1.7	87.1	12.0	0.9	12.9	100	..
Mali	C	97.3	1.2	98.5	0.9	0.6	1.5	100	12.2
Mauritania	C	86.4	10.5	96.9	1.7	1.5	3.1	100[d]	4.1
Niger	C	85.4	4.6	90.1	4.6	5.4	9.9	100	4.1[e]
Rwanda	C	71.5	15.0	86.5	5.5	7.9	13.5	100	23.3
Sao Tome and Principe	C	..	..	..	..	..	..	..	..
Sierra Leone	C	..	..	..	..	..	..	..	44.3[e]
Solomon Islands	C	80.6	17.9	98.5	0.9	0.6	1.5	100	24.2
Somalia	C	92.5	3.6	96.1	1.7	2.2	3.9	100	..
Sudan[f]	C	84.5	10.3	94.8	3.0	2.2	5.2	100	7.0
Togo	C	74.7	12.6	87.3	12.0	0.7	12.7	100	14.7
Uganda	C	90.8	4.8	95.6	1.6	2.8	4.4	100	22.6
United Rep. of Tanzania	C	82.6	6.3	88.9	5.0	6.1	11.1	100	45.6
Zambia	C	..	..	..	..	..	..	..	..
Angola	Oil	97.6	1.9	99.4	0.2	0.3	0.6	100	5.3
Equatorial Guinea	Oil	94.7	2.7	97.4	2.0	0.6	2.6	100	3.3
Yemen	Oil	91.4	8.1	99.4	0.2	0.3	0.6	100[g]	6.4
Bangladesh	M	9.5	0.3	9.9	87.8	2.4	90.1	100	7.7
Cambodia	M	..	..	..	..	..	..	..	14.6
Haiti	M	14.5	1.2	15.7	75.7	8.6	84.3	100[h]	52.5
Lao People's Dem. Rep.	M	..	..	..	..	..	..	..	20.8
Lesotho	M	..	..	..	..	..	..	..	19.4
Madagascar[i]	M	52.6	10.6	63.2	30.5	6.3	36.8	100	46.8
Myanmar	M	59.5	9.1	68.6	29.5	1.9	31.4	100	33.2
Nepal	M	6.3	1.8	8.1	88.7	3.2	91.9	100	54.8
Cape Verde	S	15.6	6.8	22.4	77.5	0.1	77.6	100[h]	88.1
Comoros	S	46.1	0.2	46.3	4.9	48.8	53.7	100	61.5[e]
Djibouti	S	..	..	..	..	..	..	..	62.1[e]
Gambia	S	80.5	7.4	87.9	7.0	5.1	12.1	100	79.1
Maldives	S	32.2	16.1	48.4	48.7	2.9	51.6	100	82.4
Samoa	S	..	..	..	..	..	..	..	80.2
Tuvalu	S	..	..	..	..	..	..	..	..
Vanuatu	S	..	..	..	..	..	..	..	74.5
Mozambique	MMS	75.5	8.5	84.0	7.8	8.2	16.0	100	56.0
Senegal	MMS	18.3	49.4	67.6	8.0	24.3	32.4	100	25.9
LDCs [j]		62.4	7.8	70.1	26.9	3.0	29.9	100	19.3

Source: UNCTAD secretariat estimates based on UN COMTRADE data and UNCTAD data for commercial service exports.

a   Non-oil commodity exporting LDC (C); oil exporting LDC (Oil); manufactures exporting LDC (M); services exporting LDC (S); and mixed manufactures and services exporting LDC (MMS). See annex 3.1 for details of country classification.
b   For product classification, and also sub-groups within primary commodities and manufactures, see annex to this chapter.
c   The main source of export earnings of Kiribati is licensing fees and royalties from fishing.
d   1997–1998.
e   1993–1995.
f   After 1999, Sudan is best classified as an oil exporter.
g   1998.
h   1997.
i   For Madagascar, UN COMTRADE data excludes exports from the Export Processing Zone. With these exports, manufactures constitute over 50 per cent of total merchandise exports (see ITC, 2001).
j   Weighted average based on all LDCs, except Cambodia, Eritrea, Lao People's Democratic Republic and Lesotho.

TABLE 27. COMPOSITION OF MERCHANDISE EXPORTS OF LDCS AND LDC SUB-GROUPS,[a]
1981–1983, 1987–1989 AND 1997–1999
(Percentage of total merchandise exports)

	Non-oil commodity exporting LDCs			Oil exporters			Manufactures and/or services exporting LDCs			Manufactures exporting LDCs			Total LDCs		
	1981–1983	1987–1989	1997–1999	1981–1983	1987–1989	1997–1999	1981–1983	1987–1989	1997–1999	1981–1983	1987–1989	1997–1999	1981–1983	1987–1989	1997–1999
Primary commodities															
Unprocessed	64.6	63.9	73.6	91.0	94.1	96.0	47.3	38.3	23.5	47.3	35.5	20.3	66.0	64.4	62.4
Processed	25.7	27.2	12.2	7.8	4.5	2.8	23.2	14.5	6.0	15.1	4.8	2.5	21.4	18.8	7.8
Total	90.3	91.2	85.8	98.8	98.5	98.8	70.5	52.8	29.6	62.4	40.3	22.8	87.5	83.2	70.1
Manufactures															
Low-skill	8.6	7.2	11.2	0.7	0.7	0.7	25.5	42.4	65.6	33.8	56.1	74.6	10.9	14.6	26.9
High-skill	1.1	1.7	3.0	0.5	0.7	0.5	4.0	4.8	4.9	3.8	3.6	2.6	1.6	2.3	3.0
Total	9.7	8.8	14.2	1.2	1.5	1.2	29.5	47.2	70.4	37.6	59.7	77.2	12.6	16.8	29.9
Total	100.0	100.0	100.0	100.0	100.0	100.0	100.0	100.0	100.0	100.0	100.0	100.0	100.0	100.0	100.0

Source: UNCTAD secretariat estimates based on UN COMTRADE data.

Note: Weighted averages based on all LDCs, except Cambodia, Eritrea, Lao People's Democratic Republic and Lesotho.

a For the countries in each sub-group, see annex table 2.

exports in total merchandise exports is a more general tendency in this group of countries, and includes LDCs which predominantly export services.

Whether or not they are mainly primary commodity exporters or exporters of manufactures or exporters of services, a further feature of the LDCs' form of trade integration into the world economy is that their export structure tends to be concentrated on a narrow range of products. For the group as a whole, export concentration has remained about the same over the last 20 years. The three leading products accounted on average for 78 per cent of total exports in 1981–1983, and for 76 per cent in 1997–1999 (table 28).

Turning to the import side, it is worth underlining two significant features of the composition of LDCs' imports. The first is their relatively high dependence on food imports (chart 28). In 1997–1999, food imports accounted for 18 per cent of total merchandise imports of the LDCs as against 6 per cent in other developing countries. As a share of merchandise imports, food imports were increasing in the 1990s in almost half of the LDCs for which there are data (21 out 44 countries). In a longer-term perspective, it is apparent that the ratio of food exports to food imports fell from more than 100 per cent in 1970 to around 40 per cent in the mid-1980s, and to as low as 20 per cent in 1999. The trend contrasts markedly with that of other developing countries' into the global food economy. In those countries on average, food exports have stabilized at around 80–100 per cent of food imports since the mid-1980s (chart 29).

The second feature of the composition of LDCs' imports is that machinery and equipment imports are much lower than in other developing countries. Such imports constituted just 1.2 per cent of GDP in 1996–1998, compared with 2.6 per cent in other low-income countries and 3.8 per cent in other developing countries. As chart 30 shows, machinery and equipment imports have been falling for LDCs as a whole since the early 1980s, a pattern which contrasts markedly with that in other developing countries (although for the latter there has been a sharp downturn since the Asian financial crisis). The low level of machinery and equipment imports in LDCs is significant as such imports can act as a central channel of technology transfer for low-income countries (see

A further feature of the LDCs' form of trade integration into the world economy is that their export structure tends to be concentrated on a narrow range of products. The three leading products accounted on average for 78 per cent of total exports in 1981–1983, and for 76 per cent in 1997–1999.

TABLE 28. MERCHANDISE EXPORT CONCENTRATION IN LDCS, BY COUNTRY, 1981–1983
AND 1997–1999, AND LEADING MERCHANDISE EXPORT ITEMS IN THE LATE 1990S
(Percentage)

	Share of 3 leading export products in total merchandise exports of LDCs[a]		Leading merchandise export items[b]
	1981–1983	1997–1999	
Afghanistan	67.7	43.5	Grapes, furs and skins and wool carpets
Angola	96.5	97.6	Petroleum and diamonds
Bangladesh	60.3	53.2	Men's and women's clothing
Benin	52.9	86.1	Cotton, palm oil and cashew nuts
Bhutan	83.8	60.0	Electrical energy, calcium carbide, portland cement and ferro-silicon
Burkina Faso	77.5	81.8	Cotton, sugar and meat products
Burundi	81.4	98.0	Coffee, tea and gold
Cambodia	64.4	61.3	Garments, footwear and wood
Cape Verde	82.2	76.0[c]	Fish and garments
Central African Republic	74.4	79.5	Diamonds, tropical wood and coffee
Chad	95.6	97.0	Cotton, gum arabic and livestock
Comoros	93.0	93.2	Vanilla beans and cloves
Dem. Rep. of the Congo	68.4	79.6	Diamonds, petroleum, cobalt, wood and coffee
Djibouti	38.0[d]	28.6	Live animals and agricultural products
Equatorial Guinea	84.9	93.0	Oil and wood
Eritrea	..	70.1	Salt, semi-processed leather goods, flowers, livestock and textiles
Ethiopia	80.2	81.1	Coffee, sesame seeds and leather
Gambia	74.4	69.1	Octopi and groundnuts
Guinea	96.9	80.1	Aluminium, bauxite and diamonds
Guinea-Bissau	58.5	79.8	Cashew nuts and fish products
Haiti	39.6	42.9[c]	Garments
Kiribati	92.9	90.6	Fish products
Lao People's Dem. Rep.	70.2	40.5	Garments, wood and wood products, hydroelectric power and coffee
Lesotho	..	76.5	Garments and diamonds
Liberia	84.6	92.2	Diamonds, rubber and timber
Madagascar	70.7	40.5	Garments, shellfish and coffee
Malawi	82.9	78.8	Tobacco, sugar, tea and coffee
Maldives	70.1	73.2	Garments and fish products
Mali	81.6	92.9	Diamonds, gold, cotton and livestock
Mauritania	93.3	89.7[e]	Fish products and iron ore
Mozambique	55.6	59.8	Prawns and cotton
Myanmar	57.6	44.8	Garments and prawns
Nepal	39.6	61.7	Carpets and garments
Niger	94.7	83.3	Uranium and live animals
Rwanda	91.2	84.4	Tea and coffee
Samoa	68.2	80.5	Ignition wiring sets and fishery
Sao Tome and Principe	94.1	77.3	Cocoa beans and fishery
Senegal	52.2	49.5	Fish and fertilizers
Sierra Leone	63.2	75.3	Diamonds, footwear and cocoa beans
Solomon Islands	74.9	80.0	Fishery
Somalia	94.8	79.4	Live animals
Sudan	59.0	52.6	Oil (recent addition), cotton, sesame seeds and livestock
United Rep. of Tanzania	54.9	51.3	Coffee and cashew nuts
Togo	70.8	76.5	Calcium phosphates and cotton
Tuvalu	100.0	49.5	Stamps, copra and handicrafts
Uganda	97.5	69.9	Coffee and fish
Vanuatu	90.6	62.1	Copra
Yemen	94.0	94.1	Oil and fish
Zambia	93.8	89.3	Copper and cobalt
LDCs[f]	78.2	76.0	

Source: UNCTAD secretariat estimates and ITC (2001).

    a   Based on UN COMTRADE data at SITC 3 Rev 2.
    b   ITC (2001). c 1997. d 1982. e 1997–1998.
    f   Weighted averages based on all LDCs, except Cambodia, Eritrea, Lao People's Democratic Republic and Lesotho.

CHART 28. FOOD IMPORTS[a] AS A SHARE OF TOTAL MERCHANDISE IMPORTS IN THE LDCS, BY COUNTRY, 1997–1999
(Percentage)

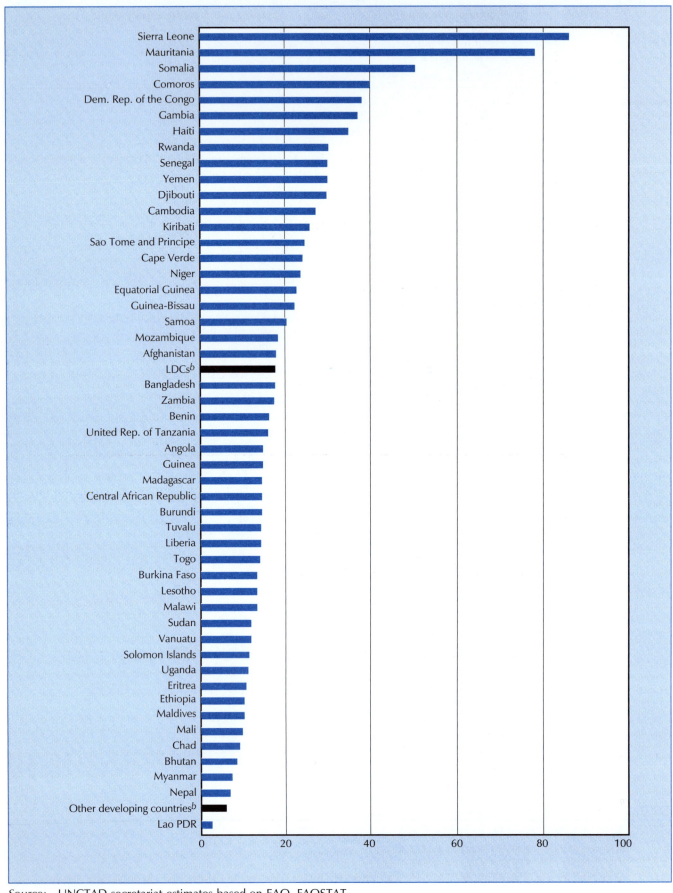

Source: UNCTAD secretariat estimates based on FAO, FAOSTAT.
  a   Excluding fish.
  b   Weighted averages.

CHART 29. RATIO OF FOOD EXPORTS TO FOOD IMPORTS FOR LDCS AND OTHER DEVELOPING COUNTRIES, 1971–1999[a]

(Percentage)

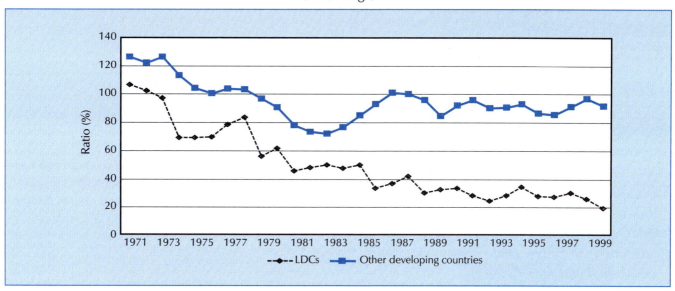

Source: UNCTAD secretariat estimates based on FAO, FAOSTAT.

  a   Food exports and food imports exclude fish.

CHART 30. MACHINERY AND EQUIPMENT IMPORTS AS A SHARE OF GDP IN LDCS
AND OTHER DEVELOPING COUNTRIES, 1970–1998

(Percentage)

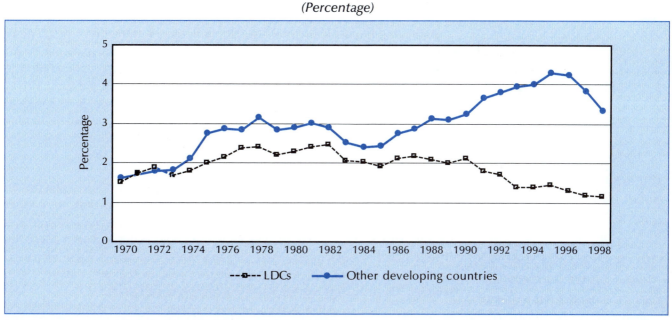

Source: UNCTAD secretariat estimates based on Mayer (2001).

Note: The sample includes 35 LDCs and 56 other developing countries for which data are available.

Mayer, 2000, 2001), and their level is also correlated with economic growth (Mazumdar, 2001).

3. PARTICIPATION IN GLOBAL TRADE FLOWS

Although trade is of central importance to LDCs, the smallness of LDC economies in global terms means that their participation in global trade flows is limited. In 2000, LDCs' total merchandise exports amounted to around $31.5 billion. This was equivalent to 0.5 per cent of world merchandise exports and equal to only 8 per cent of low-income countries' total merchandise exports. The total merchandise exports of all the LDCs was equivalent to about half those of Austria. Moreover, in 2000, about 52 per cent of total merchandise exports of the LDCs were accounted for by three countries — Angola and Yemen (both oil exporters), and Bangladesh. About 74 per cent of total LDC merchandise exports came from just 10 countries — Angola, Bangladesh, Cambodia, Guinea, Myanmar, Nepal, Senegal, Sudan, Yemen and Zambia.

Over time, the share of LDCs in world exports and imports has been declining. This phenomenon, which reflects the fact that LDC exports and imports, although they are growing, are growing less quickly than world exports and imports, is often described as the marginalization of LDCs in the world economy. The share of LDCs in world exports of goods and services declined by 47 per cent between 1980 and 1999, and stood at only 0.42 per cent of total world trade in the latter year. The share of LDCs in world imports of goods and services declined by 40 per cent over the same period and stood at 0.7 per cent of world imports in 1999.[6]

Within this broad picture of marginalization, there is, however, a much more differentiated story (chart 31). A closer look at the trend of participation in world trade over time shows that for exports of goods and services as a whole the process of marginalization (as defined above) bottomed out in the early 1990s. That is to say, since 1992 the share of LDCs in global trade has ceased to decline. But this important break in the trends has so far not become a turning point, in that a significant upturn and reversal of the marginalization process for the LDCs as a whole have yet to appear (chart 31A).

Disaggregating by type of export (chart 31B) reveals that the marginalization process is strongest for non-fuel primary commodity exports and, to a lesser extent, services, and that in each case there was a bottoming out in the 1990s. But the share of LDCs in world oil exports rose in the 1980s and since 1988 the share of world manufactures exports has also risen significantly. These increased from 0.1 per cent of the world total in that year to 0.2 per cent in 1999. Although still small, this represents a doubling of market share.

When one disaggregates by type of exporter (chart 31C) and focuses on the more limited number of LDCs for which it is possible to get data for the period 1980–1999, it becomes apparent that for the LDCs classified as exporters of manufactured goods or services there is no process of marginalization. Services exporters increased their share of world exports of goods and services in the early 1980s and although there have been significant ups and downs since then, they have maintained their increase in market share. Manufactured goods exporters were being marginalized in global trade flows in the mid-1980s, but since 1990 they have significantly increased their global market share. In contrast, it is the non-oil commodity exporters that have experienced a strong process of marginalization. This slowed down in the 1990s, but their market share is still declining. In fact, in 1999 the share of non-oil commodity exporting

The share of LDCs in world exports of goods and services declined by 47 per cent between 1980 and 1999.

In 1999 the share of non-oil commodity exporting LDCs in global trade had declined by more than 60 per cent below its level in 1980. During the same period, LDCs exporting manufactures and services had increased their share of global trade by about 40 per cent above their level in 1980.

CHART 31. LDCs' SHARE IN WORLD EXPORTS OF GOODS AND SERVICES, 1980–1999

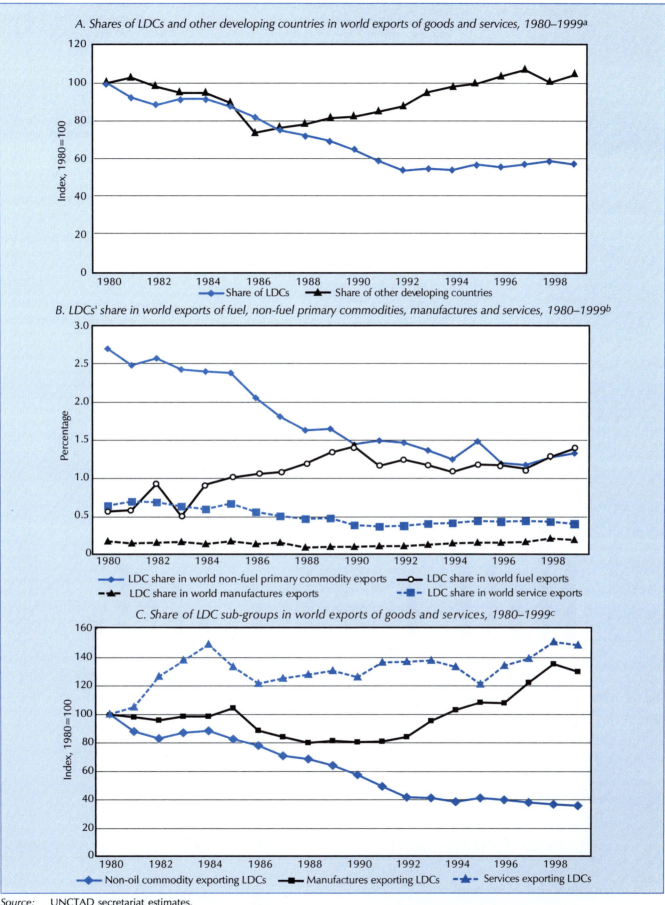

A. Shares of LDCs and other developing countries in world exports of goods and services, 1980–1999a

B. LDCs' share in world exports of fuel, non-fuel primary commodities, manufactures and services, 1980–1999b

C. Share of LDC sub-groups in world exports of goods and services, 1980–1999c

Source: UNCTAD secretariat estimates.

a   Based on balance-of-payments estimates of exports of goods and services in current dollars, World Bank, *World Development Indicators 2001*, CD-ROM. The sample consists of 36 LDCs and 72 other developing countries.

b   Based on UN COMTRADE data and UNCTAD data on commercial service exports.

c   The data, source and LDC sample are the same as in chart 31A, although Mozambique and Senegal are not included as they are classified as mixed manufactures and services exporters. For the countries in each sub-group, see annex to this chapter. The chart includes all LDCs, except: Afghanistan, Angola, Burundi, Cambodia, Djibouti, Equatorial Guinea, Guinea, Lao People's Democratic Republic, Liberia, Somalia, Tuvalu and Yemen.

LDCs in global trade had declined by more than 60 per cent below its level in 1980. During the same period, LDCs exporting manufactures and services had increased their share of global trade by about 40 per cent above their level in 1980. It must be stressed, however, that despite the positive upward trend, the share of these countries in world trade remains very low, constituting around one half of 1 per cent of total world exports of goods and services at the end of the 1990s.

The trade regimes of the LDCs at the end of the 1990s were much more open than at the end of the 1980s.

4. EXTENT OF TRADE LIBERALIZATION

Many least developed countries have been intensively engaged in structural adjustment programmes since the late 1980s. As shown in UNCTAD (2000: 102–108), this has involved significant policy changes, including widespread trade liberalization. As a result, the trade regimes of the LDCs at the end of the 1990s were much more open than at the end of the 1980s.

Using the IMF index of trade restrictiveness as a measure, it is apparent that although a few LDCs have not been vigorously engaged in trade liberalization, LDCs have actually gone further than other developing countries in dismantling trade barriers.[7] In 1999, of the 43 LDCs for which data are available, over one third had average tariff rates of under 20 per cent coupled with no or minor

CHART 32. TRADE RESTRICTIVENESS FOR COMMODITY EXPORTING LDCS
AND MANUFACTURES AND/OR SERVICES EXPORTING LDCS, 1999

(Index)

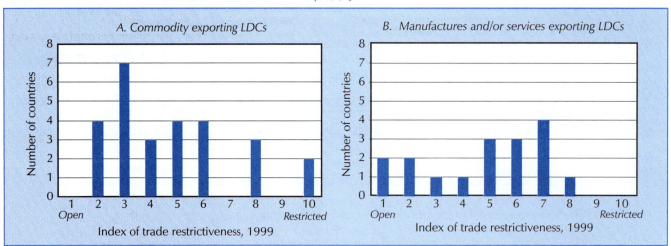

Source: UNCTAD secretariat estimates based on IMF index of trade restrictiveness.

Note: The index is based on the following classification scheme:

Tariffs	Open	Moderate	Restrictive
Open	1	4	7
Relatively open	2	5	8
Moderate	3	6	9
Relatively restrictive	4	7	10
Restrictive	5	8	10

Tariffs are classified as follows:

Open, average tariff range 0≤t<10 per cent. Relatively open, average tariff range 10≤t<15 per cent. Moderate, average tariff range 15≤t<20 per cent. Relatively restrictive, average tariff range 20≤t<25 per cent. Restrictive, average tariff range 25 per cent or over.

Non-tariff barriers are classified as follows:

Open, NTBs are either absent or minor. Less than 1 per cent of production or trade is subject to NTBs. Moderate, NTBs are significant covering at least one important sector of the economy but not pervasive. Between 1 per cent and 25 per cent of production or trade is subject to NTBs. Restrictive many sectors or entire stages of production are covered by NTBs. More than 25 per cent of production or trade is subject to NTBs.

non-tariff barriers, and three fifths had average import tariffs of below 20 per cent and non-tariff barriers which were either minor or moderate, covering less than 25 per cent of production or trade. This process of liberalization has gone further in the commodity exporters than in the manufactures and/or services exporters (chart 32).

C. Trade liberalization, growth and poverty

In recent years, arguments linking trade liberalization and poverty have moved away from grand theorization to identifying possible mechanisms through which trade liberalization can influence poverty (see Winters, 1999, 2001; Cirera, McCulloch and Winters, 2001). These mechanisms include the effects of trade liberalization on:

- The prices of goods and services that the poor consume and produce, benefiting those who are net consumers of goods that become cheaper and those who can obtain higher prices for their products on international markets;

- The demand for, and returns to, factors of production that the poor have to offer, notably unskilled labour;

- Government revenue and the resources available to promote growth and poverty reduction, which, given the high dependence on trade taxes, can be at risk during trade liberalization in poor countries;

- Risks and volatility, which can tend to increase as economies become more exposed to global forces.

Increasing attention is also being paid to both transitional adjustment costs, which occur as previously protected uncompetitive domestic activities are exposed to international competition, and long-term growth effects. The overall effect of trade liberalization reflects the balance of all these mechanisms, which are different in different contexts as well as for different groups, and also affect men and women differently (see box 10). As the African Development Bank et al. (2001: 1) has put it, "These effects vary significantly across countries, regions and groups within countries, which makes it difficult to generalize about the effects of trade liberalization on poverty".

This process of trade liberalization has gone further in the commodity exporters than in the manufactures and/ or services exporters

For the least developed countries, available evidence shows that trade liberalization has so far not been closely associated with poverty reduction. Chart 33 indicates changes in the share of the population living on less than $1 a day during the 1990s in a sample of 36 LDCs, classified according to the degree of trade restrictiveness at the end of the 1990s. It must be stressed that this is not a comparison of the situation before trade liberalization with the situation after such liberalization. However, it is not unrealistic to assume that these countries generally had much more restrictive trade regimes at the end of the 1980s. Thus the chart shows differences in poverty trends during the 1990s in countries grouped according to how far they went in the process of trade liberalization during that period.

The chart shows that poverty is increasing unambiguously in those economies that have adopted the most open trade regime and in those that have continued with the most closed trade regime. But in between these extremes, there is a tendency for poverty to be declining in those countries that have liberalized their trade regime to a lesser extent, and for poverty to be increasing in those countries that have liberalized their trade regime more.

Box 10. Trade liberalization, gender and rural poverty in African LDCs

In his analysis of the relationships between trade liberalization and poverty, Winters (1999) identifies a number of important channels through which trade policy changes may be expected to have an impact on poverty. He argues that gender issues are likely to affect the results, but he states that "it is difficult to know how to proceed" (p. 47). Ann Whitehead (2001) puts forward a framework for rectifying this deficiency. She applies a gender perspective to some of the main channels of influence that Winters identifies, so as to show how trade liberalization can be expected to influence the living standards of rural women in African LDCs.

She argues that the best approach for including a gender perspective in the analysis of economic processes is to see gender relations as an intervening variable in all economic activities, influencing the ways in which factor and product markets work, the productivity of inputs and the economic behaviour of agents, and the joint determination of the growth and distribution of income. The economy of monetized production and the non-monetized economy of reproductive work should also be seen as interdependent.

There is a growing literature that argues that rural women have not been benefiting from trade liberalization, nor from agricultural reforms more generally, owing to the nature of intra-household relations. In particular, the incomplete pooling of household resources between men and women is said to be leading to weak incentives to increase production and to allocative inefficiencies; and obligations to produce traditional food crops, and a simple lack of time due to household work burdens, are supposed to be making it difficult for women to respond to new production opportunities.

Whitehead agrees that there are certainly major constraints on women's ability to respond positively to any higher producer prices and any better employment opportunities that might result from trade liberalization. But she argues that the key constraints are not a matter of intra-household relations between men and women, but rather arise from the gendered nature of labour markets and markets for agricultural goods and the gendered nature of property and land access regimes. She identifies women's lack of investment capital as the central factor that reinforces women's poverty. As she puts it,

"Capital is needed to farm subsistence as well as cash crops, although cash crops usually require considerably more cash resources than growing family food supplies… Most crop innovations are predicated on the purchase of inputs and may also require new technology. It is because they are farming in a resource-starved environment that poor rural men and women are effectively socially excluded from growth. For women ability to participate in agricultural innovation is limited by the extreme scarcity of these resources. The sums may be quite small, but they are often beyond the reach of many women, through whose hands pitifully little cash may pass during the normal year. Women's lack of investment capital is exacerbated by two factors: public and private policy with respect to credit, input schemes and crop markets and the extent to which they get off-farm incomes and the level of these incomes" (Whitehead, 2001: 24).

Whitehead argues that the problem of women's access to land is properly understood as a question of lack of working capital, although a significant emerging question is the way in which the relatively strong claims of women to land in land-abundant areas turn into much weaker claims in land-scarce areas. She also argues that women's lack of capital is closely related to the segmentation of rural labour markets and of off-farm employment opportunities, whereby women get stuck in casual and poorly remunerated activities as a complement to farming. Labour market segmentation is due to the high entry costs of more remunerative activities and also the gendered nature of social capital and risk-reducing institutions. Formal education is less relevant in the segmentation of rural labour markets.

Women's lack of working capital thus becomes part of a vicious circle in which they are restricted with regard to the type of off-farm employment they take up, and so they cannot save enough from low-return off-farm incomes to invest in agricultural innovation and improvement. Women's reserve price of labour in off-farm activities is also low where the income potential of their own production is low, where the income-generating opportunities off-farm are few, and where, given the low returns to their labour, the need is urgent. Young women become particularly vulnerable to an informal market for sex, and thus to HIV infection. This whole process of gender disadvantage is reinforced by public and private institutions.

The key policy conclusion to emerge from this analysis is that rural women will not necessarily benefit from any positive price and employment effects that might stem from trade liberalization unless there are a range of measures to address the gender-intensified disadvantages and gender-imposed constraints which permeate the operation of production and factor markets. The surest way to ensure that rural women are not socially excluded from the benefits of economic growth is to address their lack of capital. This is a matter of improving access to credit and also expanding remunerative off-farm employment activities by "thickening" rural labour markets. The focus on intra-household relations as a cause of disadvantage is excessive, directing attention towards more intractable issues and distracting policy makers from measures that can make a real difference to women's lives.

Source: Whitehead (2001).

CHART 33. TRADE LIBERALIZATION AND POVERTY TRENDS IN LDCs DURING THE 1990s

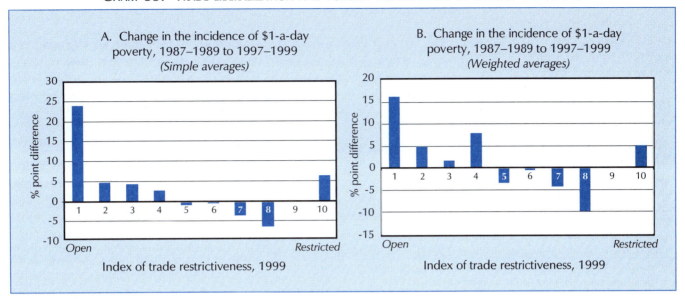

A. Change in the incidence of $1-a-day
poverty, 1987–1989 to 1997–1999
(Simple averages)

B. Change in the incidence of $1-a-day
poverty, 1987–1989 to 1997–1999
(Weighted averages)

Source: As for chart 32.

Note: See chart 32.

It would not be correct to conclude from this evidence that trade liberalization is causing increased poverty in least developed countries. For this conclusion to be drawn, it would be necessary to construct a counter-factual which would show what would have happened in the absence of trade liberalization. But the chart does not support the equally stark alternative view that trade liberalization reduces poverty. Indeed, what it shows is that rapid and deep trade liberalization has been associated, at least in the short run, with a rising incidence of poverty.[8]

In the face of evidence such as this, it has become increasingly common to argue that the positive effects of trade liberalization on poverty depend on the implementation of "complementary measures" (see, for example, World Bank, 2001: chapter 2) or will make themselves felt in the long run, despite increasing poverty and unemployment in the short run. The effects of the full package of economic reforms associated with structural adjustment programmes in the LDCs are discussed in detail in chapter 5. But here it may be noted that the evidence that will be presented there suggests that the incidence of poverty in the years after the implementation of the reform packages was, in most cases, similar to what it was in the years before.

The chart shows that poverty is increasing unambiguously in those economies that have adopted the most open trade regime and in those that have continued with the most closed trade regime.

As for long-run effects, there is a large literature of cross-country empirical studies on openness and growth. In the past it was common to assert that these purportedly demonstrated that economies with open trade regimes grow faster and experience greater poverty reduction. But this view is being increasingly challenged (see, in particular, Rodriguez and Rodrik, 1999). Even the proponents of trade liberalization are now more cautious. Thus, for example, Winters (1999: 59) has concluded: "Overall the fairest assessment of the evidence is that, despite the clear plausibility of such a link, open trade alone has not yet been unambiguously and universally linked to subsequent economic growth", although he adds that "it certainly has not been identified as a hindrance".

D. Export orientation, growth and poverty

The fact that there is no clear relationship between trade liberalization and poverty reduction does not mean that there is no relationship between trade and poverty reduction. Indeed, an important lesson from recent development experience is that those developing countries which have been growing most rapidly in the last 20 years, and which have also been experiencing rapid poverty reduction, have generally also experienced an increase in the share of domestic output which is exported (Rodrik, 1999: chapter 2). It is wrong, however, to assume that this is due to trade liberalization. Moreover, the relationship between exports and growth is complex. Close study of the most successful developing countries by UNCTAD in a series of Trade and Development Reports and associated research (UNCTAD, 1994, 1996, 2002) shows that:

- The countries that grew the fastest were not simply characterized by an increase in their export/GDP ratios, but also investment and savings grew as a proportion of GDP in tandem (chart 34).

- These macroeconomic changes occurred as part of a process of late industrialization, in which manufacturing activities and manufacturing exports became increasingly important, and there was a progressive shift in production from less to more skill-, technology- and capital-intensive activities both within and between sectors.

- At the micro level domestic enterprises imitated and adapted internationally available technologies in order to reduce costs, improve quality and introduce goods and services not existing in the country, and the diffusion of best practice from more advanced to less advanced enterprises within a country took place, including from foreign to domestic firms.

CHART 34. INVESTMENT TRANSITION,[a] SAVINGS AND EXPORTS IN EAST ASIA

Year relative to investment transition

— Investment   - - - Exports   — Savings

Source: Akyüz and Gore (2001: figure 1).

a   Following Rodrik (1999), a country is said to undergo an investment transition at year T if (a) the three-year moving average of its investment rate over an eight-year period starting at T+1 exceeds the five-year average of its investment rate prior to T by 5 percentage points or more, and (b) the post-transition investment rate remains above 10 per cent. Savings are defined as: gross domestic fixed investment plus exports minus imports. The figures are unweighted averages of the following countries and dates of transition year: Indonesia (1969), Republic of Korea (1965) and Thailand (1966). These are derived from Rodrik (1999: table 3.2). The transition year on the graph is year 0.

- Poverty reduction occurred as part of this process, particularly through agricultural growth, the expansion of employment opportunities and extension of productivity improvements to marginal sectors.

Increases in export orientation thus certainly played an essential role in accelerated development in the most successful countries. Given this role, it is not surprising to find changes in export orientation correlated with both economic growth and poverty reduction. But if changes in export orientation occur without the concomitant changes in investment, savings and technology imports, one should not expect the same results.

For the least developed countries, the available data show that, as for developing countries as a whole, the LDCs that grew in the 1990s almost invariably experienced an increase in the share of national output which is exported. As table 29 shows, during the period 1987–1999 only 2 out of 16 growing national economies (Guinea and Mauritania) experienced declines in export/GDP ratios. Of those in which real GDP per capita (in 1985 PPP dollars) grew at over 2 per cent per annum over the period, all exhibited increasing export orientation. But although economic growth in LDCs is almost invariably associated with increasing export orientation, this does not mean that increasing export orientation is almost invariably associated with growth. In fact, in 8 out of 22 LDCs with increasing export orientation during 1987–1999, GDP per capita was stagnant or declined during the same period. Moreover, in over half (13) of the LDCs with increasing export orientation, annual GDP per capita growth was less than 1 per cent per annum during 1987–1999. Thus, although LDCs which grow fast tend to experience rising export/GDP ratios, LDCs which experience rising export/GDP ratios do not necessarily grow fast.

Similarly, LDCs in which poverty rates fell in the 1990s have also almost invariably experienced an increase in the share of national output that is exported. The incidence of poverty fell in 16 LDCs in the sample during 1987–1999, and only four of those LDCs (Gambia, Guinea, Mauritania and Togo) experienced declines in export/GDP ratios. But although LDCs in which the incidence of poverty fell generally experienced increasing export orientation, LDCs in which export orientation increased did not generally experience a reduction in the incidence of poverty. In fact, in 10 out of 22 LDCs with increasing export orientation during 1987–1999, poverty rates increased during the same period (table 29).

LDCs in which poverty rates fell in the 1990s have also almost invariably experienced an increase in the share of national output that is exported. But LDCs in which export orientation increased did not generally experience a reduction in the incidence of poverty. In fact, in 10 out of 22 LDCs with increasing export orientation during 1987–1999, poverty rates increased during the same period

As argued in the last chapter, the key to poverty reduction in LDCs is rapid and sustained economic growth. Thus if we focus on the 16 LDC economies in the sample in which GDP per capita is rising, we see that poverty rates are rising in just two — Lesotho, where trends are influenced by the return of miners from South Africa, and Mali. There are only two LDCs (Guinea and Mauritania) which experienced economic growth and falling export orientation over the period 1987–1999. But in both cases, poverty rates declined.

In LDCs which have grown, there is also generally an increase in the share of investment in GDP. Only 3 out of 15 growing LDCs for which there are investment data during the period 1987–1999 had falling investment/GDP ratios. Poverty-reducing LDCs also tend to have increasing investment/GDP ratios. Only 4 out of 15 poverty-reducing LDCs for which data are available had falling investment/GDP ratios during 1987–1999 (table 29). The LDCs with rising investment rates are not all characterized by growth and poverty reduction over the same period. For 18 LDCs with rising investment/GDP ratios, annual GDP per capita growth rates are negative in 5, and poverty is rising in 7. However, for LDCs in which per capita income is growing, investment/GDP

TABLE 29. ECONOMIC GROWTH, EXPORTS, INVESTMENT AND TRENDS IN POVERTY IN THE LDCs,
FROM LATE 1980s TO LATE 1990s

	Annual GDP per capita growth[a]	Exports of goods and services		Gross capital formation			Share of the population living on less than $1 a day		
	%	% GDP	% point difference	% GDP		% point difference	% total population		% point difference
	1987–1999	1987–1989 1997–1999		1987–1989 1997–1999			1987–1989 1997–1999		
LDCs with increasing export/ GDP ratio and increasing GDP/ capita									
Lao People's Dem. Rep.	3.5	9.8[b]	29.6[c]	19.8	11.4[b]	26.4[c]	15.0	4.1	2.1	-2.0
Bangladesh	3.3	5.6	12.9	7.2	17.0	21.5	4.6	13.4	10.0	-3.4
Uganda	3.1	7.9	11.5	3.6	10.5	15.8	5.3	57.6	41.5	-16.1
Bhutan	3.0	27.9	33.0	5.1	32.7	48.0	15.3	42.2	23.0	-19.2
Cape Verde	2.9	14.9	24.0	9.1	24.7	37.3	12.6	18.2	11.9	-6.3
Mozambique	2.5	7.6	11.0	3.4	13.9	25.1	11.1	40.5	36.8	-3.6
Nepal	2.4	11.4	24.1	12.7	20.6	23.4	2.8	52.6	38.4	-14.3
Solomon Islands[d]	1.4	47.7	65.9	18.2	32.4	..	..	6.5	2.4	-4.1
Benin	1.0	14.2	16.8	2.6	13.5	17.7	4.2	22.4	16.4	-6.1
Malawi	0.9	22.9	27.2	4.3	18.8	13.3	-5.4	76.2	55.8	-20.4
Ethiopia	0.8	8.6	15.2	6.6	15.8	17.4	1.6	86.8	85.5	-1.2
Lesotho	0.7	17.9	27.4[c]	9.5	44.5	50.6[c]	6.1	19.5	41.8	22.3
Burkina Faso	0.4	10.7	12.2	1.5	20.8	28.3	7.5	66.6	60.1	-6.5
Mali	0.1	16.5	25.2	8.6	21.3	20.9	-0.4	63.0	71.7	8.7
Group, simple average	*1.9*	*16.0*	*24.0*	*8.0*	*21.3*	*26.6*	*6.2*	*40.7*	*35.5*	*-5.2*
LDCs with increasing export/ GDP ratio and decreasing or stagnant GDP/ capita									
Senegal	0.0	24.5	33.2	8.7	12.4	18.5	6.2	13.3	14.1	0.8
Central African Rep.	-0.8	16.1	17.6	1.4	11.4	12.3	0.9	45.6	68.9	23.3
Chad	-1.3	14.7	18.2	3.5	8.0	13.8	5.8	79.1	81.6	2.5
Vanuatu[b]	-1.3	39.2	55.0	15.8	34.3	..	..	6.3	9.8	3.5
Guinea-Bissau	-1.6	10.7	20.5	9.8	39.5	16.9	-22.6	56.0	80.9	25.0
Madagascar	-1.8	17.1	22.7	5.6	12.2	12.4	0.2	42.2	46.7	4.5
Comoros	-3.5	16.1	23.5	7.5	21.5	15.6	-5.9	64.6	76.4	11.8
Angola	-3.8	33.2	56.8[e]	23.6	13.2	24.0[e]	10.8	70.4	71.9	1.5
Group, simple average	*-1.8*	*21.4*	*30.9*	*9.5*	*19.1*	*16.2*	*-0.7*	*47.2*	*56.3*	*9.1*
LDCs with decreasing export/ GDP ratio and increasing GDP/ capita									
Mauritania	1.6	49.7	39.2	-10.5	24.9	18.1	-6.8	36.2	30.0	-6.2
Guinea	0.8	29.2	21.6	-7.6	16.5	17.7	1.2	71.5	64.1	-7.4
Group, simple average	*1.2*	*39.5*	*30.4*	*-9.1*	*20.7*	*17.9*	*-2.8*	*53.8*	*47.1*	*-6.8*
LDCs with decreasing export/ GDP ratio and decreasing or stagnant GDP/ capita									
Gambia	-0.9	51.8	48.9	-2.9	18.1	17.8	-0.2	52.0	35.8	-16.3
Togo	-2.0	41.6	31.8	-9.8	16.7	14.0	-2.7	64.8	63.0	-1.7
Niger	-2.0	18.6	16.7	-1.9	14.8	10.8	-4.1	69.3	74.4	5.1
Rwanda	-2.9	6.7	6.2	-0.5	14.5	15.0	0.5	45.5	58.5	13.1
Burundi	-3.4	10.7	9.0	-1.7	18.1	8.6	-9.5	60.2	71.2	11.0
Haiti	-3.5	15.1	11.1	-4.0	14.0	10.7	-3.3	26.1	41.0	14.9
Sierra Leone	-5.7	15.8	13.7[f]	-2.2	8.6	2.8[f]	-5.8	30.2	67.4	37.2
Group, simple average	*-2.9*	*22.9*	*19.6*	*-3.3*	*15.0*	*11.4*	*-3.6*	*49.7*	*58.8*	*9.0*

Source: UNCTAD secretariat estimates based on World Bank, *World Development Indicators 2001*, CD-ROM.

a In 1985 PPP dollars.
b 1988–1989.
c 1997–1998.
d Based on balance-of-payments estimates of exports of goods and services.
e 1998.
f 1998–1999.

rates are rising and export orientation is increasing, there is a very strong probability of poverty reduction. In only 1 country (Lesotho) out of 11 countries does poverty increase in this situation. The greatest poverty reduction, in terms of percentage reduction in poverty rates, is also apparent in LDCs in which per capita income is growing, investment/GDP rates are rising and export orientation is increasing.

The main conclusion that may be drawn from this is that what is central to poverty reduction is economic growth. Export growth is critical for poverty reduction because it supports the overall growth process. In growing economies increasing export orientation enables exports to grow faster than income. But in the 1990s increasing export orientation occurred in some LDCs along with stagnation and decline. In those countries changes in export orientation have not been associated with poverty reduction. Our findings thus indicate that unless accompanied by economic growth, greater export orientation was not associated with poverty reduction.

E. Export structure, growth and poverty

A much more refined view of the relationship between international trade and poverty can be achieved if the discussion is not abstracted from the types of goods and services being traded. Amongst the LDCs, there is a close relationship between long-term growth performance and export structure. Moreover, the incidence of poverty in the least developed countries, and also recent poverty trends, vary significantly between countries according to their export structure.

This section considers these patterns, using the classification of countries according to their export structure, set out earlier in the chapter and in the annex below. There are insufficient poverty data to treat oil-exporting LDCs in any systematic way. The analysis thus focuses on: (a) non-oil commodity exporting LDCs, which are subdivided into agricultural and mineral exporters; and (b) manufactures and/or services exporting LDCs, within which exporters of manufactured goods and exporters of services are separated out.

Two caveats should be entered at the outset. First, the classification is made on the basis of export structure at the end of the 1990s and not the initial export structure. The data thus compare growth and poverty trends in LDCs whose export composition remains focused on primary commodities with trends in LDCs that have, during the last 20 years, experienced a transformation in the composition of their exports in which the proportion of primary commodities in total exports has declined (relatively or absolutely), and either manufacturing and/or service activities have become the major exports. Nevertheless, as was apparent in section B, many of those countries classified as manufactured goods exporting LDCs started in the early 1980s with a higher proportion of manufactured goods in total exports. Second, as with any exercise of this nature, the results are affected by the classification of the countries and some difficult judgements had to be made in deciding in which group a few marginal cases should be placed (see annex to this chapter). However, it is believed that this does not have a bearing on the overall tendencies identified.

1. EXPORT STRUCTURE AND INCOME CONVERGENCE WITH RICH COUNTRIES

Table 30 shows the average income per capita between 1960 and 1999 in the world's richest 20 countries, 31 LDCs for which data are available, and non-

The main conclusion that may be drawn from this is that what is central to poverty reduction is economic growth. Export growth is critical for poverty reduction because it supports the overall growth process. Our findings indicate that unless accompanied by economic growth, greater export orientation was not associated with poverty reduction.

A much more refined view of the relationship between international trade and poverty can be achieved if the discussion is not abstracted from the types of goods and services being traded.

oil commodity exporting LDCs and manufactures and/or services exporting LDCs. GDP is estimated in 1985 PPP terms, which makes the income gap smaller than if GDP is calculated at current official exchange rates. Moreover, the results for each group are shown as simple averages, or weighted by the population of each country. The income gaps between the richest countries and the LDCs, based on the weighted averages, are shown in chart 35.

From table 30 and chart 35, it is apparent that the dominant trend over the last 40 years has been increasing divergence between the average income per capita of LDCs and that of the world's 20 richest countries. Weighted by population, the income per capita of the 20 richest countries was 11 times higher than that of the LDCs in 1960, and 19 times higher in 1999. However, there are major differences in the trends between LDCs that have diversified out of commodities, and those that have not done so.

The simple average of income per capita in the non-oil commodity exporting LDCs was almost the same in 1999 as it was in 1960. It was lower in 1999 than in 1990, lower in 1990 than in 1980, and lower in 1980 than in 1970. On the basis of averages weighted by population, the income per capita of the richest 20 countries was 16 times greater than that of the non-oil commodity exporting LDCs in 1960. In 1999, it was 35 times greater. A strong divergence between the richest countries and the non-oil commodity exporting LDCs has also been associated with convergence amongst this group of LDCs, particularly from 1970 to 1990. However, there was an increasing divergence in average per capita incomes amongst this group of LDCs in the 1990s.

On the basis of averages weighted by population, the income per capita of the richest 20 countries was 16 times greater than that of the non-oil commodity exporting LDCs in 1960. In 1999, it was 35 times greater.

TABLE 30. TRENDS IN GDP PER CAPITA IN THE WORLD'S 20 RICHEST COUNTRIES, LDCS AND LDC SUB-GROUPS,[a] 1960–1999

(GDP per capita, in PPP 1985 $)

	1960	1970	1980	1990	1999
World's 20 richest countries[b]					
Simple average	6 535.1	9 124.2	11 851.1	13 636.4	16 723.5
Weighted average	7 591.7	10 008.6	12 584.0	15 316.9	17 880.0
Standard deviation	1 529.7	1 736.8	1 500.5	2 673.0	1 767.4
LDCs[c]					
Simple average	661.1	771.9	843.8	760.0	779.8
Weighted average	685.0	857.3	766.7	813.9	948.0
Standard deviation	264.7	326.2	491.2	338.5	446.1
Non-oil commodity exporting LDCs[d]					
Simple average	594.5	673.5	668.6	609.2	587.5
Weighted average	477.7	553.4	535.4	499.7	515.7
Standard deviation	219.2	298.1	236.8	164.4	197.6
Manufactures and/or services exporting LDCs[e]					
Simple average	780.1	905.6	1 161.6	1 028.0	1 136.4
Weighted average	933.7	1 194.0	1 042.8	1 211.1	1 545.5
Standard deviation	290.3	324.5	671.3	414.3	556.2

Source: UNCTAD secretariat estimates based on Summers and Heston International Comparison Programme and World Bank, *World Development Indicators 2001*, CD-ROM.

Note: a The sub-groups are defined according to their export composition in the late 1990s. For country classification, see annex table 2.
b The set of the world's 20 richest countries varies over time.
c Based on 31 LDCs for which data are available. The countries listed in d and e plus Angola.
d Benin, Burkina Faso, Burundi, Central African Republic, Chad, Democratic Republic of the Congo, Ethiopia, Guinea, Guinea-Bissau, Malawi, Mali, Mauritania, Niger, Rwanda, Sierra Leone, Togo, Uganda, United Republic of Tanzania and Zambia.
e Bangladesh, Cape Verde, Comoros, Gambia, Haiti, Lesotho, Madagascar, Mozambique, Nepal, Samoa and Senegal.

CHART 35. TRENDS IN THE INCOME GAP[a] BETWEEN THE WORLD'S 20 RICHEST COUNTRIES AND LDCs, 1960–1999

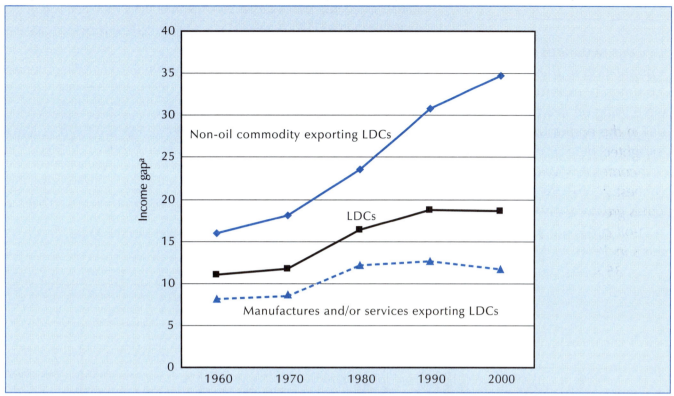

Source: See table 30.

Note: The sample is the same as for table 30. The sub-groups are defined according to their export composition in the late 1990s. For country classification, see annex table 2.

a The income gap is the ratio of the average GDP per capita (in 1985 PPP dollars) in the world's 20 richest countries to that in the LDCs and LDC sub-groups. The sample of the world's 20 richest countries varies over time. The averages are weighted by population.

Initial per capita incomes in the LDCs that have diversified into manufactures and/or services exports were much higher in 1960 than those in non-oil commodity exporting LDCs, and over time these countries have done better than the latter group. The weighted average of income per capita in the manufactures and/or services exporting LDCs was almost twice as high as that in the non-oil commodity exporting LDCs in 1960, and by 1999 it was almost three times higher. As shown in chart 35, the ratio between income per capita in the 20 richest countries and that in the manufactures and/or services exporting LDCs increased between 1960 and 1999. But the income gap is smaller than that between the richest countries and the non-oil commodity exporting LDCs and the increase much less. Weighted by population, the average income per capita in the 20 richest countries was 8 times that of the manufactures and services exporting LDCs in 1960. In 1999, it was 12 times greater. During the 1990s there was actually a slow convergence between the weighted average income per capita in the manufactures and/or services exporting LDCs, although this result is strongly dependent on the economic performance of Bangladesh.[9]

Weighted by population, the average income per capita in the 20 richest countries was 8 times that of the manufactures and services exporting LDCs in 1960. In 1999, it was 12 times greater.

2. EXPORT STRUCTURE AND THE INCIDENCE OF POVERTY

Differences in poverty trends are associated with differences in long-term growth performance. Chart 36 shows the trends in the incidence of poverty, using the $1-a-day and $2-a-day poverty lines, over the period 1981–1999 in LDCs grouped according to their export structure. From chart 36, it is apparent that:

Over two thirds of the population in the non-oil commodity exporting LDCs were living on less than $1 a day at the end of the 1990s.

- Over two thirds of the population in the non-oil commodity exporting LDCs were living on less than $1 a day at the end of the 1990s, and within the mineral-exporting LDCs the incidence of extreme poverty was over 80 per cent.

- The incidence of extreme poverty increased in non-oil commodity exporting LDCs between the early 1980s and late 1990s, and this increase was particularly marked (21 percentage points) in mineral-exporting LDCs.

- The share of the population living on less than $1 a day was on average lower in the services exporting LDCs (43 per cent). It is even lower in the exporters of manufactured goods (25 per cent), although excluding Bangladesh, the share of the population living on less than a $1 a day in LDCs exporting manufactures was 44 per cent.

CHART 36. THE INCIDENCE OF POVERTY IN LDCS GROUPED ACCORDING TO EXPORT SPECIALIZATION, 1981–1983, 1987–1989 AND 1997–1999

(Share of total population)

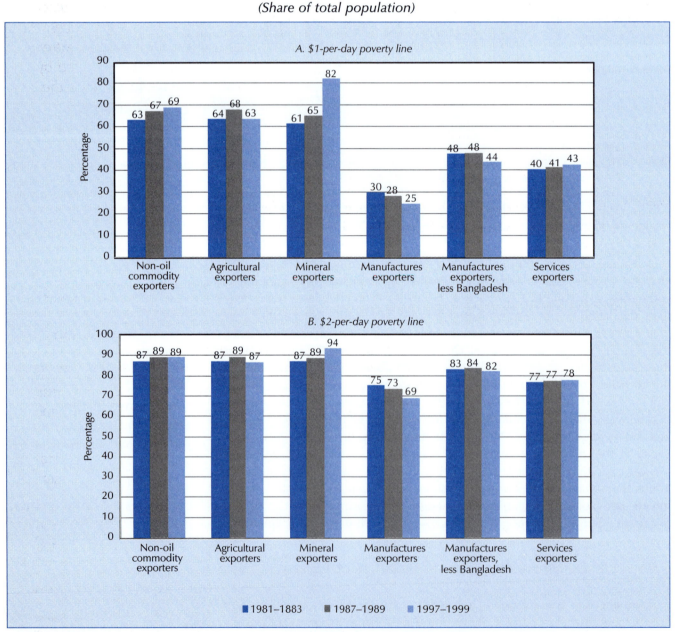

Source: UNCTAD secretariat estimates.

Note: The countries are grouped according to their export composition in the late 1990s. For country classification, see annex table 2. No data are available for Afghanistan, Cambodia, Equatorial Guinea, Eritrea, Kiribati, Maldives, Samoa, Sao Tome and Principe, Tuvalu and Yemen. Angola is also excluded as there are insufficient data to include oil exporters.

- The incidence of extreme poverty was increasing between the early 1980s and the late 1990s in the LDCs exporting services, although more slowly than in the non-oil commodity exporting LDCs.

- The incidence of extreme poverty has on average been falling in LDCs exporting manufactures. This result is unchanged whether or not Bangladesh is included or excluded.

When one focuses on the share of the population living on less than $2 a day, similar patterns and trends are evident, but the differences are less marked. It is also clear that despite their better performance, the poverty problem remains severe in LDCs exporting manufactures and services. In 1997–1999, the share of the population living on less than $2 a day was over 75 per cent in 8 out of the 12 LDCs exporting manufactures and services for which data are available.

Despite this qualification, there is a clear association between dependence on primary commodities and the incidence of extreme poverty in the LDCs. Table 31 estimates levels and trends in the numbers of poor within LDCs, grouped into primary commodity-exporting LDCs and LDCs exporting manufactures or services, or some combination of these. Overall, it is estimated that 79 per cent of the total population living on less than $1 a day within LDCs were living in primary commodity-exporting LDCs in 1997–1999, and that around 21 per cent were living in LDCs exporting manufactures and/or services. The increase in the numbers of poor is also greatest in the primary commodity-exporting LDCs. It is estimated that in these countries the number of people living in extreme poverty (on less than $1 a day) increased by 105 million between 1981–1983 and 1997–1999, reaching a total of 251 million in the late 1990s. Within the LDCs exporting manufactured goods and/or services, the number of people living in extreme poverty increased by 10 million, reaching 67 million in the late 1990s.

In commodity-exporting LDCs, the number of people living in extreme poverty increased by 105 million between 1981–1983 and 1997–1999... Within the LDCs exporting manufactured goods and/or services, the number living in extreme poverty increased by 10 million over the same period.

TABLE 31. DISTRIBUTION OF THE POOR AMONGST LDCS GROUPED ACCORDING TO EXPORT SPECIALIZATION,[a]
1981–1983 TO 1997–1999

	Primary commodity exporters		Manufactures and/or services exporters		All LDCs	
	1981–1983	1997–1999	1981–1983	1997–1999	1981–1983	1997–1999
Population *(millions)*	230	365	189	263	419	628
Population *(% of LDC total)*	55	58	45	41	100	100
Number of poor[b] *(millions)*						
People living on less than $1 per day	146	251	57	67	203	318[c]
People living on less than $2 per day	201	324	142	183	343	507[c]
Distribution of poor amongst LDCs *(% of total number of poor in LDCs)*						
People living on less than $1 per day	72	79	28	21	100	100
People living on less than $2 per day	59	64	41	36	100	100

Source: UNCTAD secretariat estimates.

a The countries are grouped according to their export composition in the late 1990s. For country classification, see annex table 2.

b Poverty estimates are not available for Afghanistan, Cambodia, Equatorial Guinea, Eritrea, Kiribati, Maldives, Samoa, Sao Tome and Principe, Tuvalu and Yemen. The total number of poor in these countries has been estimated on the assumption that the incidence of poverty is the same as the incidence of poverty in the export groups to which they belong. Oil-exporting LDCs are assumed to have the same incidence of poverty as non-oil commodity exporting LDCs.

c These numbers differ slightly from table 19, chapter 1, owing to the different method of estimating missing data and also the different time-period.

F. The poverty-reducing impact of different types of export growth

Differences in the poverty trends in the different types of LDCs are related to different economic growth rates. As the earlier discussion indicated, export growth is one factor which is part of a sustained growth process, and there are clear differences amongst LDCs exporting primary commodities, manufactures and services in terms of their export growth rates. Chart 37 shows, for a sample of 26 LDCs for which data are available, real export growth rates in the 1980s and 1990s. It is clear that export growth rates have been relatively slow within non-oil commodity exporting LDCs. The difference was particularly marked in the 1990s. During that decade, the real export growth rate in the non-oil commodity exporting economies was only 2.3 per cent per annum, compared with 11.2 per cent per annum in the LDCs exporting manufactured goods, and 10.7 per cent in the LDCs exporting manufactures or services, or some combination thereof. Some Asian LDCs exporting manufactures achieved particularly high rates of growth (see box 11). The mineral-exporting LDCs did worst in the 1990s, with real exports for the LDCs in the sample declining by 1.9 per cent per annum over the period 1990–1999. The LDCs exporting agricultural commodities in contrast improved their export growth from 1.7 per cent per annum in the 1980s to 6.3 per cent in the 1990s.

Assuming that resources employed in export production were unutilized or under-utilized before, the faster the export growth rate, the faster the economic growth rate and hence potential poverty reduction. This applies equally no matter what the type of exports. Export production can further contribute to economic growth by engendering positive external effects, notably by reducing the foreign exchange constraint, and promoting learning and technology

Export growth rates have been relatively slow within non-oil commodity exporting LDCs.

CHART 37. REAL EXPORT GROWTH RATE IN ALL LDCS AND LDCS GROUPED ACCORDING TO EXPORT SPECIALIZATION,[a] 1980–1989 AND 1990–1999

(Percentage per annum)

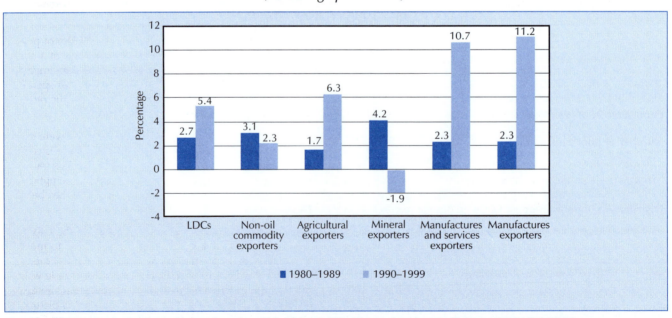

Source: UNCTAD secretariat estimates based on World Bank, *World Development Indicators 2001*, CD-ROM.

Note: Growth rates of exports of goods and services are in constant 1995 dollars.

a   The countries are grouped according to their export composition in the late 1990s. For country classification, see annex table 2. No data are available for Afghanistan, Angola, Bhutan, Cambodia, Cape Verde, Central African Republic, Djibouti, Equatorial Guinea, Guinea, Kiribati, Lao People's Democratic Republic, Liberia, Maldives, Myanmar, Samoa, Sao Tome and Principe, Solomon Islands, Somalia, Sudan, Tuvalu, United Republic of Tanzania, Vanuatu and Yemen.

Box 11. Trade policy in some Asian LDCs exporting manufactures

The growth of manufactured exports in Asian LDCs was supported by "export-push strategies", which provided extra incentives to promote exports, and in the case of the South-East Asian LDCs — Cambodia, the Lao People's Democratic Republic and Myanmar — their integration into regional trading arrangements has also been a critical factor.

The production of export-quality garments in Bangladesh started on the basis of a collaboration agreement between a company from the Republic of Korea and a Bangladeshi company, established for this purpose in 1979. Before that date Bangladesh had not been exporting garments because of a lack of domestic production technology and marketing know-how. The Republic of Korea company was attracted to Bangladesh by its low wages and, in particular, by its unused quota for exporting textiles and apparel to the markets of the United States and the EU. Marketing was initially handled by the Republic of Korea company, thus creating a reputation for the Bangladeshi company as a producer of quality garments and a reliable counterpart, and the Government of Bangladesh also provided basic export incentives. The agreement ended in June 1981, but export activities continued as Bangladeshis themselves mastered the production and marketing know-how (UNCTAD, 1995).

After this breakthrough, textiles and garments have become the engine of export growth in Bangladesh. The Government of Bangladesh has actively promoted this expansion. Its trade policy has over time encouraged exports through various policies such as duty-free and restriction-free regimes for imported inputs, including capital machinery, easy access to financing for exporters, interest rate subsidies for exporters, and enabling exporters to exchange 100 per cent of their foreign currency earnings through any authorized dealer. To encourage private investment in the export sector, government bonds have been offered to attract resources for industrial investment. FDI was also used strategically to develop capabilities complementing domestic capabilities in this sector. Furthermore, Bangladesh has established several highly successful export processing zones (EPZs), in which investors from the Republic of Korea have been particularly active. Trade liberalization has taken place, but it has been in a gradual and sequenced manner. Foreign aid has also supported the process (Bhattacharya, 2000).

Trade policies in other Asian LDCs developing a capability to export manufactures have also been characterized by an export-push strategy within the context of regional linkages, with special incentives for foreign investors. Two notable examples are Cambodia and the Lao People's Democratic Republic, where very high export growth rates of 20 per cent per annum and 21 per cent per annum, respectively, were achieved in the context of a transition from a centrally planned in economy (Martin, 2001). In the Lao People's Democratic Republic, the adoption of the New Economic Mechanism (NEM) in 1986 began the shift to a market system. Since then public enterprises have been given operating autonomy, and the private sector has been authorized to participate in economic activities. In 1988, the country abandoned the multiple exchange rate system and moved to a single rate close to that previously prevailing in the parallel market.

Trade liberalization has been part of the economic reform process, but the approach of the Government has been gradual rather than a "big bang" approach. Average tariff rates are relatively low. However, tariffs on "luxury" consumption goods (motor vehicles, motorcycles, beer, tobacco and household appliances) have been kept higher. Moreover, various non-tariff barriers exist. There are licensed trading companies, whose number was reduced to six in 1999. Each importer is licensed to import no more than the allocated quantity, and individual shipments need to be licensed by the Ministry of Commerce and Transport. Quotas apply to the importation of fuel and lubricants, steel bars used in construction, all types of cement, and all types of motor vehicles and motorcycles. The authorities have used administrative measures to allocate foreign exchange (Martin, 2001).

Special privileges are granted to foreign firms. Foreign investors are required to pay import duties for the importation of production equipment and facilities, spare parts and other equipment used in project or business operations at the rate of 1 per cent of the import value. Raw material and intermediate components imported for export processing are exempt from import duties. Raw material and intermediate components imported for the purpose of import substitution are also eligible for special duty reductions. In addition, some companies have obtained a convention that clears them to import or export specific products free of all taxes. Ad hoc tariff exemptions are often granted for imports by State enterprises (Martin, 2001).

In Cambodia, trade policy reform was faster than in the Lao People's Democratic Republic. Important early reforms were the unification of exchange rates, tariff reform and the abolition of many non-tariff barriers. Tariffs are fairly low, but there is considerable variation between products as in the Lao People's Democratic Republic. An important feature of Cambodia's transition strategy is a very liberal investment regime designed to attract foreign investment. This regime includes liberal exemptions on investment goods and inputs used in the production of exports, as well as income-tax concessions. This regime has been successful in attracting investment in clothing exports.

In both Cambodia and the Lao People's Democratic Republic, regional linkages have been an important part of the export growth dynamic. Meeting the requirements of accession to the ASEAN Free Trade Area has helped those countries to modernize their trade procedures and required wide-ranging preferential trade liberalization. Trading links amongst ASEAN member States have been increasing strongly over the last decade. ASEAN has promoted economic cooperation through trade with the objective of creating a single ASEAN market and also to enable member States to strengthen their competitive advantage vis-à-vis the rest of the world through greater intraregional trade. Increasingly, Asian LDCs are becoming part of this picture, although their participation up to now has not been very significant. In June 2000 the Prime Ministers of Thailand and Cambodia agreed to formulate an integrated plan for cooperation, including the development of industrial zones along their border. Thai manufacturers are interested in relocating their production operations as Cambodia has preferential market access under the Generalized System of Preferences (GSP), and labour costs are less than half those in Thailand.

upgrading, economies of scale and production linkages. The impact of manufacturing exports on economic growth is likely to be greater than the impact of primary commodity exports because the former can generate much greater externalities and learning effects.[10] These external effects are not absent in commodity exporting economies, but they are likely to be particularly small in economies with low-value, low-productivity commodity exports.

The impact of manufacturing exports on economic growth is likely to be greater than the impact of primary commodity exports because the former can generate much greater externalities and learning effects.

In mineral-exporting economies, the relationship between export growth and economic growth has often been tenuous. Several explanations for the relationship have been put forward, notably the "Dutch disease" phenomenon, where surges in mineral export revenue lead to appreciating real exchange rates and consequently to reduced competitiveness in other tradable sectors. However, exchange rate variability and the failure to reinvest mineral rents could be more important (Auty and Evans, 1994). Problems of governance are also evident. Rents from mining activities may be easily be appropriated by the central government and give rise both to political rivalries over rent income and to the establishment of clientelist systems. It would appear that poor mineral-rich economies, including the LDCs, have become particularly prone to armed conflict caused by the struggle over resource rents by domestic and external actors. Mineral exports nevertheless can have a powerful potential to serve as a base for rapid growth and economic diversification, as the case of Botswana, the only country ever to "graduate" from LDC status, illustrates. Translating this into poverty reduction requires careful policy as production is often capital-intensive (Modise, 2000).

Expansion of manufactures and services exports can have relatively strong poverty-reducing effects because it leads to an increase in employment opportunities, particularly for unskilled labour. In situations of surplus labour, real wages are unlikely to rise and thus at early stages of the expansion of manufactured exports there can be increasing inequality (UNCTAD, 1997). But poverty falls owing to expansion of jobs. Employment of female labour has often been important in this process. But there is no inevitable connection between the expansion of manufactures and services exports and poverty reduction.

Expansion of manufactures and services exports can have relatively strong poverty-reducing effects because it leads to an increase in employment opportunities, particularly for unskilled labour. In situations of surplus labour, real wages are unlikely to rise and thus at early stages of the expansion of manufactured exports there can be increasing inequality. But poverty falls owing to expansion of jobs.

This is apparent if one looks behind the average trends in poverty in LDCs exporting manufactures and services described above. It is clear that there are major variations between countries. The overall trend for LDCs exporting services is the product of two countries experiencing rapidly falling poverty rates (Cape Verde and Gambia), two experiencing rising rates (Comoros and Djibouti) and one where little change is evident (Vanuatu). Amongst the LDC exporters of manufactures, there is a more pervasive downward trend, but poverty rates are increasing in Lesotho, Haiti and Madagascar. In the latter country, the trend in the poverty rate reflects the fact that expansion of exports of manufactures is very recent. Conflict and political instability are key factors that can lead to growing poverty in exporters of manufactures and services.

In LDCs which export agricultural commodities, the situation is very complex. The poverty impact of export growth depends on the organization of production (plantations versus smallholder production organized by households), access by farmers to production inputs (credit, land, labour), trends in productivity and prices, the bargaining power of farmers in relation to traders and processors, and the relationship between export crop expansion and food prices. In most LDCs household production is predominant and the way in which these factors operate is affected by gender relationships.

Agricultural expansion which brings hitherto unutilized or underutilized land and labour resources into use can also be poverty-reducing through the same vent-for-surplus mechanism as expansion of manufacturing and service employment. But the effects of this mechanism on poverty can be less for agro-exports than for manufacturing and services exports for two main reasons. Firstly, as will be discussed in more detail in the next chapter, there has been a tendency for international primary commodity prices to fall. This implies that there will be constant downward pressure on real returns at the producer level. Secondly, where land ownership patterns are very unequal, it is possible for small farmers to be excluded from agro-export booms (see Barham, Carter and Sigelko, 1995; and Carter and Barham, 1996, for Latin America). Expansion of agricultural exports can also have perverse effects on levels of poverty if it leads to higher food prices and declining food entitlements. However, in LDCs in which there has been a transition in which the role of plantations or State farms in agricultural export production has declined relative to the role of smallholders, export growth has become less exclusionary than in the past and this can promote poverty reduction. Notable cases in this regard are those of Ethiopia, Malawi and Mozambique.

One problem with upgrading into more dynamic agricultural exports is that this can exclude smallholders. Fresh fruit and vegetable chains once started with smallholder producers in Africa are now supplied by large-scale farms with on-site packing houses, mostly ones under the direct control of export companies. There is also increasing differentiation amongst these large farms. This is associated with the buyer-drivenness of the supply chain, with supermarkets choosing to coordinate this supply chain not directly, but through externalizing a wide range of functions to preferred suppliers. To qualify, the suppliers have to be able to deliver phytosanitary-tested, prepared and packaged, and bar-coded products within 24 hour of an order. The result has been a shake-out of suppliers (Gibbon, 2001).

Turning to service exports, the poverty-reducing effect of international tourism is expected to take place through a wide income-multiplying impact of tourist expenditure, which should be filtered through the local economy as a result of a significant local input into the tourism industry, through participation in ownership in the industry or in the employment generated by it, and also through local supply of goods and services. There are, however, practical limitations to the income-multiplying impact of tourism in the LDCs. These limitations are usually analysed in terms of "leakages" from the tourism economy: the smaller the local input into the tourism product, the greater will be the magnitude of financial leakages. Leakages essentially occur through the repatriation of profit to the country of origin of the foreign investor in the industry, remittances sent abroad by expatriate workers in the sector, and the imports resulting from the obligation to bring in goods and services in the absence of an adequate supply of such inputs in the host country.

The magnitude of leakages is generally expected to decrease after a first stage of successful tourism development has been completed, if local capacities to participate in tourism operations have increased. However, no correlation has been found, among LDCs, between the degree of maturity of the tourism industry and reductions in leakages. The latter can indeed remain substantial. As the case of Maldives illustrates, a sophisticated tourism product offered in a structurally handicapped country often involves multifaceted leakages and limited linkages with the local population, thereby contributing little to poverty reduction. Specific national policies, which develop relevant human resources and encourage tourism-specific entrepreneurship through financial and technical support, in particular for small tourism enterprise development, are necessary to increase in order the pro-poor impact of the sector.

In LDCs in which there has been a transition in which the role of plantations or State farms in agricultural export production has declined relative to the role of smallholders, export growth has become less exclusionary than in the past and this can promote poverty reduction. Notable cases in this regard are those of Ethiopia, Malawi and Mozambique.

As the case of Maldives illustrates, a sophisticated tourism product offered in a structurally handicapped country often involves multifaceted leakages and limited linkages with the local population, thereby contributing little to poverty reduction.

G. Conclusion

This review of the patterns of trade integration and poverty within LDCs suggests that trade is as important in the economic life of the LDCs as it is in the economic life of other developing countries, but that export capacities are underdeveloped. This problem is particularly important in those LDCs that predominantly export primary commodities. Generalized poverty is characteristic of almost all LDCs. But the countries where the incidence of extreme poverty, defined by the $1-a-day poverty line, is highest are those LDCs whose export structures are dominated by primary commodities. These countries tend to be well integrated into the global economy in terms of their trade/GDP ratios and also to have undertaken more trade liberalization than LDCs that export manufactures and/or services. But they also have slower rates of export growth, they are becoming increasingly marginalized in global trade flows, and the incidence of poverty tends to be rising rather than falling.

The conventional wisdom that persistent poverty is due to the low level of trade integration of LDCs with the global economy, and insufficient trade liberalization, must be reassessed. The grip of the doctrine of inadequate integration and liberalization on policy thinking is founded on the prioritization of the goal of global integration over the goal of national development. These goals are, of course, not unrelated. But the way in which they are related should be an empirical issue, not an article of faith, nor, still less, founded on the assumption that integration is development, rather than a means to an end.

It is clear that the LDCs must integrate into the world economy. But they must manage their integration in a way that supports growth and poverty reduction.

International trade is of immense importance for growth and poverty reduction in the least developed countries. Poverty is decreasing in those LDCs in which both GDP per capita and export orientation are increasing. It is clear that the LDCs must integrate into the world economy. But they must manage their integration in a way that supports growth and poverty reduction. The critical policy issue for most is not their low level of integration into the global economy, understood in terms of their trade/GDP ratio, but rather how to build competitive and dynamic export capacities and how to ensure that export growth is an integral element of a sustained development process. Improvement in production and supply capacities is a necessary condition for deriving benefits from globalization of markets.

How and when trade liberalization fits into a development strategy which promotes growth and poverty reduction must take account of the structural constraints in LDCs, particularly lack of social and economic infrastructure, weakness of market development, the thinness of the entrepreneurial class and low private sector production capabilities.

Trade liberalization within the LDCs has a role to play in this process of managed integration. But it is wrong to conflate the role that trade can play in poverty reduction with the role that trade liberalization can play. Moreover, how and when trade liberalization fits into a development strategy which promotes growth and poverty reduction must take account of the structural constraints in LDCs, particularly lack of social and economic infrastructure, weakness of market development, the thinness of the entrepreneurial class and low private sector production capabilities. The lesson from some of those LDCs that have developed competitiveness in manufactures is that a proactive export-push strategy, encompassing special incentives for export production, is vital for building up new export capabilities. Trade liberalization has generally been gradual, and regional arrangements have been an important part of the supportive trade regime. There has been a process of strategic integration into the world economy geared to supporting national development priorities.

Annex to Chapter 3

PRODUCT CLASSIFICATION AND COUNTRY CLASSIFICATION USED IN THE ANALYSIS OF THE EXPORT STRUCTURE OF LDCs

Product classification

The product classification used in the analysis of the merchandise export structure of LDCs in this chapter is based on the work of Wood and Mayer (1998). Data on merchandise exports were taken from the United Nations COMTRADE database and divided into two broad groups — primary products and manufactures — by classifying as manufactures all items in categories 5–9 of the Standard International Trade Classification (SITC) except phosphorous pentoxide and phosphoric acids (522.24), aluminium hydroxide (522.56), radioactive and associated material (524), pearl, precious and semi-precious stones, other than diamonds (667 other than 667.29), non-ferrous metals (68), live animals not elsewhere specified (941) and non-monetary gold (971).

Manufactures are further subdivided into low-skill and high-skill manufactures as follows: (a) low-skill manufactures: leather and leather manufactures (61); rubber articles (62); cork and wood manufactures, paper and paperboard (63–64); textiles, clothing, travel goods and footwear (65, 83, 84, 85); non-metallic mineral products, excluding precious stones (66 less 667); iron and steel (67); fabricated metal products (69); sanitary and plumbing equipment (81); transport equipment other than road motor vehicles and aircraft (78 less 781–784 + 79 less 792); furniture and parts thereof (82); miscellaneous manufactured articles (89); commodities and manufactures not classified elsewhere other than live animals and non-monetary gold (9 less 941, 971); (b) high-skill manufactures: chemicals and pharmaceutical products (5 less 522.24, 522.56, 524); diamonds, cut or otherwise worked but not mounted or set (667.29); non-electrical machinery (71–74); computers and office equipment (75); communication equipment and semiconductors (76, 776); electrical machinery (77 less 776); road motor vehicles (781–784); aircraft and associated equipment (792); scientific instruments, watches and photographic equipment (87, 88).

Primary products are then subdivided into unprocessed and processed primary products using the definition of manufactures in the International Standard Industrial Classification (ISIC). Processed primary products are those products that the ISIC classifies as manufactures but the SITC classifies as primary products. These include goods which are produced in factories, but which use large inputs of local raw materials — for example, canned tuna, wine, cigarettes, paper and aluminium ingots.

Primary products are further subdivided into minerals, metals and fuels on the one hand, and agricultural products on the other hand. Agricultural products are then subdivided into static and dynamic products on the basis of high unit values or an income elasticity of demand greater than one. The full listing of the sub-groups of primary products is set out in Wood and Mayer (1998).

Country classification

The LDCs are classified into different types of exporters on the basis of the share of primary products and manufactures, as defined above, and of the share of services, in total exports of goods and services in the late 1990s. Total exports of goods and services were estimated by adding merchandise exports from the United Nations COMTRADE database to UNCTAD estimates of exports of commercial services. The latter are based largely on balance-of-payments statistics. The classification also drew on other sources, mainly ITC (2001) and country reports by the Economist Intelligence Unit (EIU).

The subdivision between exporters of primary commodities and exporters of manufactures and/or services is based on whether or not primary commodities or manufactures and services constituted over 50 per cent of total exports of goods and services. Ethiopia and the United Republic of Tanzania are borderline cases that are both classified as commodity-exporting LDCs.

The primary-commodity-exporting LDCs are further subdivided into oil-exporting LDCs and non-oil commodity exporting LDCs. The former group comprises Angola, Equatorial Guinea and Yemen, but excluded Sudan. Oil is now the major export of the latter country, but the classification is based on the composition of merchandise exports during the period 1997–1999.

The LDCs exporting manufactures and services are further subdivided into exporters of manufactures, exporters of services, and mixed manufactures and services exporters. This subdivision is difficult to make as the merchandise and services export data are not totally compatible.

LDCs exporting manufactures are identified as those economies in which there has been a significant expansion of labour-intensive manufactured exports since the early 1980s. Both Madagascar and Myanmar are included in the group, even though their manufactured exports are less than 50 per cent of merchandise exports. The group corresponds to the WTO (2001) classification of LDCs exporting manufactures, but includes Haiti.

LDCs exporting services are identified as those in which services constituted over 60 per cent of total exports of goods and services. If a strict 50 per cent criterion were used, Haiti, Nepal and Mozambique would be classified as exporters of services. But their economies are very different from those of the other exporters of services, and in the first two cases, manufactures constitute over 75 per cent of merchandise exports.

Finally, Senegal and Mozambique are included as mixed manufactures and services exporters as these two categories of exports constitute over 50 per cent of their total exports of goods and services, but they do not fall into the subdivisions above.

The classification of countries is shown below in annex table 2.

ANNEX TABLE 2. CLASSIFICATION OF LDCs BY MAJOR SOURCE OF EXPORT EARNINGS, LATE 1990s

Exporters of primary commodities (31)			Exporters of manufactures and/or services (18)		
Non-oil commodity exporters		Oil exporters	Manufactures exporters	Services exporters	Mixed manufactures and services exporters
Agricultural exporters	*Mineral exporters*				
Afghanistan	Central African Republic	Angola	Bangladesh	Cape Verde	Mozambique
Benin	Dem. Rep. of the Congo	Equatorial Guinea	Cambodia	Comoros	Senegal
Bhutan	Guinea	Yemen	Haiti	Djibouti	
Burkina Faso	Liberia		Lao PDR	Gambia	
Burundi	Niger		Lesotho	Maldives	
Chad	Sierra Leone		Madagascar	Samoa	
Eritrea	Zambia		Myanmar	Tuvalu	
Ethiopia			Nepal	Vanuatu	
Guinea-Bissau					
Kiribati					
Malawi					
Mali					
Mauritania					
Rwanda					
Sao Tome and Principe					
Solomon Islands					
Somalia					
Sudan[a]					
Togo					
Uganda					
United Rep. of Tanzania					

Source: UNCTAD secretariat estimates based on UN COMTRADE data, UNCTAD data on commercial services exports, ITC (2001) and various EIU country reports.

a   Sudan should be classified as an oil exporter after 1999.

Notes

1. Some examples of this view are: "Countries with the highest levels of integration tended to exhibit the fastest output growth, as did countries that made the greatest advances in integration. Many low-income countries are among the least integrated, however, and some became even more marginalized during this period experiencing falling incomes and reduced integration" (World Bank, 1996: 20); "Countries that align themselves with the forces of globalization and embrace the reforms needed to do so, liberalizing markets and pursuing disciplined macroeconomic policies, are likely to put themselves on a path of convergence with advanced economies, following the successful Asian newly industrializing economies (NIEs). These countries may be expected to benefit from trade, gain global market share and be increasingly rewarded with larger private capital flows. Countries that do not adopt such policies are likely to face declining shares of world trade and private capital flows, and to find themselves falling behind in relative terms" (IMF, 1997: 72); "Open trade regimes lead to faster growth and poverty reduction in poor countries" (Dollar and Kraay, 2001: 27); "Globalization generally reduces poverty because more integrated economies tend to grow faster and this growth is usually widely diffused" (World Bank, 2002a:1); and "*Problem* — Countries that are not involved in globalization may become increasingly marginalized and mired in poverty. *Policy response* — This calls for poverty reduction strategies and policies to promote the integration of low-income countries into world markets. Rich countries need to open their markets to exports from developing countries" (Finance and Development, 2002). For a non-technical critique of the integrationist perspective, see Rodrik (2001).

2. Trade data available for this task are not ideal. This chapter uses United Nations COMTRADE data for analysis of the composition of exports, including mirror statistics in group aggregates where necessary, and it also uses World Bank *World Development Indicators 2001* for information on total exports and imports of goods and services. In each chart, the sample is based on the maximum available number of countries. For a country-by-country overview of export composition, as well as the data problems in analysing trade of LDCs, see ITC (1999, 2001).

3. The reader should be aware that different trade indicators can be used to estimate trade integration (for example, balance-of-payments statistics versus trade statistics, constant prices versus current prices, local currency units versus dollars, trade ratios which estimate GDP at PPP exchange rates). The statistics chosen here are the most straightforward — World Bank group averages for exports and imports of goods and services as a percentage of GDP. Other indicators give slightly higher or lower levels of trade integration. For example, for the LDC group as a whole, total trade as a percentage of GDP (in constant 1995 dollars) was 41 per cent in 1997–1998, and total trade as a percentage of GDP (using balance-of-payments estimates of exports and imports of goods and services in current dollars) was 46 per cent.

4. For discussion of the classification, see annex 3.1.

5. In Cape Verde, Maldives and Vanuatu, services exports were important from the outset.

6. These numbers are based on World Bank estimates of exports and imports of goods and services in current dollars.

7. We are grateful to the IMF for furnishing the information on trade restrictiveness.

8. For discussion of the effect of trade liberalization on income inequality, see UNCTAD (1997: Part 2, chapter 4).

9. See Sachs (2000) for a discusssion of the ways in which geography, primary commodity dependence and demographic pressure limit income convergence, and Ghose (2001) for a discussion of the relationship between income convergence and growth of exports of manufactures.

10. For empirical evidence of the fact that primary commodity exports are often less growth-enhancing than exports of manufactured goods, and discussion of the reasons, see Fosu (1996) and Richards (2001).

References

African Development Bank, Asian Development Bank, European Bank for Reconstruction and Development, Inter-American Development Bank, IMF and World Bank (2001). *Global Poverty Report 2001: A Globalized Market — Opportunities and Risks for the Poor*, prepared for the G8 Genoa Summit, July 2001.

Akyüz, Y. and Gore, C.G. (2001). African economic development in a comparative perspective, *Cambridge Journal of Economics*, 25: 265–288.

Auty, R. and Evans, D. (1994). Trade and industrial policy for sustainable resource-based development: policy issues, achievements and prospects, UNCTAD/COM/33, Geneva.

Balassa, B. (1970). Growth strategies in semi-industrial countries, *Quarterly Journal of Economics*, 84: 24–47.

Barham, B., Carter, M.R. and Sigelko, W. (1995). Agro-export production and peasant land access: examining the dynamic between adoption and accumulation, *Journal of Development Economics*, 46: 85–107.

Bhagwati, J.N. (1988) Export-promoting trade strategy: issues and evidence, *World Bank Research Observer*, 3(1): 27–57.

Bhattacharya, D. (2000). New forms of development financing in the LDCs: the case of Bangladesh, background paper for *The Least Developed Countries 2000 Report*, UNCTAD, Geneva.

Carter, M. and Barham, B. (1996). Level playing fields and laissez faire: postliberal development strategy in inegalitarian agrarian economies, *World Development*, 24 (7): 1133–1149.

Cirera, X., McCulloch, N. and Winters, A. (2001). *Trade Liberalization and Poverty: A Handbook*, Centre for Economic Policy Research, London (http://cepr.org/pubs/books/P144.asp).

Dollar, D. and Kraay, A. (2001). Trade, growth and poverty, paper presented at the UNU/WIDER Development Conference on Growth and Poverty, 25–26 May 2001, Helsinki, Finland.

Finance and Development (2002). Globalization: The story behind the numbers, 39(1): 8–9.

Fosu, A. (1996). Primary exports and economic growth in developing countries, *World Economy*, 19 (4): 465–475.

Ghose, A.K. (2001). Global economic inequality and international trade, Employment Paper 2001/12, ILO, Geneva.

Gibbon, P. (2001). Upgrading primary production: a global commodity chain approach, *World Development*, 29 (2): 345–363.

International Monetary Fund (IMF) (1997). *World Economic Outlook, May 1997 — Globalization: Opportunities and Challenges*, IMF, Washington DC.

International Trade Centre UNCTAD/WTO (ITC) (1999). *Export Performance of Least Developed Countries: Country Profiles*, Geneva.

International Trade Centre UNCTAD/WTO (ITC) (2001). *Export Performance of Least Developed Countries: Country Profiles*, technical document prepared for the ITC Business Round Table, Third United Nations Conference on the Least Developed Countries, Brussels, 16 May 2001.

Kirchbach, F. von (2001). An assessment of the LDC export performance from a business and product perspective, paper presented at the ITC Business Round Table, Third United Nations Conference on the Least Developed Countries, Brussels, 16 May 2001, mimeo.

Martin, W. (2001). Trade policy reform in the East Asian transition economies, Working Paper No. 2535, World Bank, Washington DC (http://econ.worldbank.org/view).

Mayer, J. (2000). Globalization, technology transfer and skill accumulation in low-income countries, UNCTAD Discussion Paper No. 150, Geneva.

Mayer, J. (2001). Technology diffusion, human capital and economic growth in developing countries, UNCTAD Discussion Paper No. 154, Geneva.

Mazumdar, J. (2001). Imported machinery and growth in LDCs, *Journal of Development Economics*, 65: 209–224.

Modise, D.M. (2000). Management of mineral revenues: the Botswana experience, paper presented at the UNCTAD Workshop on Growth and Diversification in Mineral Economies, Cape Town, South Africa, 7–9 November 2000.

Richards, P.G. (2001). Exports as a determinant of long-run growth in Paraguay, 1966–1996, *Journal of Development Studies*, 38 (1): 128–146.

Rodriguez, F. and Rodrik, D. (1999). Trade policy and economic growth: a skeptic's guide to the cross-national evidence, NBER Working Paper 7081, National Bureau of Economic Research, Cambridge MA, United States.

Rodrik, D. (1999). *The New Global Economy: Making Openness Work*, Policy Essay No. 24, Overseas Development Council, Washington DC.

Rodrik, D. (2001). Trading in illusions, *Foreign Policy*, 123: 54–62 (http://www.ciaonet.org/olj7fp7fp_MARAPR01ROD01/HTML).

Sachs, J.D. (2000). Globalization and patterns of economic development, Weltwertschaftliches Archiv, Band 136, Heft 4, 579–600.

UNCTAD (1994). *Trade and Development Report, 1994*, United Nations publication, sales no. E.94.II.D.26.

UNCTAD (1995). Recent developments in the diversification of developing countries' commodity exports, UNCTAD/COM/62, Geneva.

UNCTAD (1996). *Trade and Development Report, 1996*, United Nations publication, sales no. E.96.II.D.6.

UNCTAD (1997). *Trade and Development Report, 1997*, United Nations publication, sales no. E.97.II.D.8.

UNCTAD (2000). *The Least Developed Countries Report 2000*, United Nations publication, sales no. E.00.II.D.21.

UNCTAD (2002). Development strategies in a globalizing world, mimeo, Division on Globalization and Development Strategies, Geneva.

Whitehead, A. (2001). Trade, trade liberalization and rural poverty in low-income Africa: a gendered account, background paper prepared for *The Least Developed Countries Report 2002*, UNCTAD, Geneva.

Winters, L.A. (1999). Trade and poverty: is there a connection? In: Bendavid, D., Nordstrom, H. and Winters, L.A. (1999). *Trade, Income Disparity and Poverty*, Special Studies No. 5, WTO, Geneva.

Winters, L.A. (2001). Trade policies for poverty alleviation in developing countries, paper prepared for the Series of Advanced International Policy Seminars on Trade and Development, Brussels, 6 March 2001.

Wood, A. and Mayer, J. (1998). Africa's export structure in a comparative perspective, Study No. 4, African Development in Comparative Perspective, UNCTAD, Geneva.

World Bank (1996). *Global Economic Prospects and the Developing Countries*, World Bank, Washington DC.

World Bank (2001). *Global Economic Prospects and the Developing Countries*, World Bank, Washington DC.

World Bank (2002a). *Global Economic Prospects and the Developing Countries — Making Trade Work for the World's Poor*, World Bank, Washington DC.

World Bank (2002b). *Globalization, Growth and Poverty*, Policy Research Report, Oxford University Press, Oxford.

WTO (2001). *Annual Report 2001*, Geneva.

Commodity export dependence, the international poverty trap and new vulnerabilities

Chapter

4

A. Introduction

The patterns described in the previous chapter show that there is a clear link between dependence on exports of primary commodities and the incidence of extreme poverty. The reasons for this have not featured in current debates on international trade and poverty. Indeed, there does not seem to be an explicit awareness in international policy circles that the commitment to reducing extreme poverty by half by the year 2015 necessarily implies attention to the primary commodity problem.

The present chapter examines some of the mechanisms through which commodity export dependence is related to the poverty trap in which many LDCs are caught, and discusses the vulnerabilities of those LDCs that have begun to shift out of commodities into exports of manufactures and/or services.[1] It begins in section B by considering two purely trade mechanisms through which commodity dependence may be related to poverty, namely the level and volatility of commodity prices, and the productivity, competitiveness and dynamism of the LDC commodity economy. Section C examines how external trade relationships and external finance relationships can interact, both with each other and with the cycle of low domestic investment, savings and productivity which is characteristic of situations of generalized poverty, to reinforce the poverty trap of LDC commodity exporters. This extends the discussion of the poverty trap in chapter 2, and shows how international relationships are integral elements of the poverty trap of commodity-exporting LDCs. Section D discusses the vulnerability of exporters of manufactures and services which are seeking to escape the trap by diversifying out of commodity exports. Section E examines whether globalization is tightening or loosening the poverty trap. The conclusion summarizes the main findings.

There is a clear link between dependence on exports of primary commodities and the incidence of extreme poverty.

B. Commodity export dependence and poverty: trade mechanisms

1. THE LEVEL AND VOLATILITY OF PRIMARY COMMODITY PRICES

The level and volatility of world commodity prices are an important influence on economic growth and the incidence of poverty in LDCs, particularly those that are dependent on primary commodities as their major source of export earnings. Falling real commodity prices result in lower growth rates in commodity-exporting LDCs. This occurs through the direct income losses associated with the price changes. But more important, the deterioration of the terms of trade tightens the foreign exchange constraint, which leads to reduced levels of capacity utilization and reduced efficiency in resource use, owing to a lack of key imports (such as spare parts, intermediate products and replacement equipment), as well as reduced levels of domestic investment. In addition, "commodity-dependent countries often suffer from severe terms of

The level and volatility of world commodity prices are an important influence on economic growth and the incidence of poverty in LDCs.

trade shocks, and this in turn has detrimental effects on their long-term economic growth and investment" (Varangis, Akiyama and Mitchell, 1995: 16). Cross-country regression analysis shows that the adverse effects of negative commodity price shocks work particularly through their effects on investment, and that they are significant even after account has been taken of the quality of government economic policy and institutions. This implies that the adverse effects occur even when what are regarded as "good" policies are in place (Dehn, 2000a, 2000b).[2]

There has been a long-term downward trend in real non-fuel commodity prices since 1960 ... The commodity prices recession of the 1980s was more severe, and considerably more prolonged, than that of the Great Depression of the 1930s.

There has been a long-term downward trend in real non-fuel commodity prices (or in commodity terms of trade)[3] since 1960, with a particularly marked slump in prices in the first part of the 1980s (chart 38). Comparative research shows that "the commodity prices recession of the 1980s has been more severe, and considerably more prolonged, than that of the Great Depression of the 1930s" (Maizels, 1992: 11). In 2001, the UNCTAD combined non-fuel commodity price index, deflated by the price index of manufactured exports of developed countries, was at 55 per cent of its annual average for the period 1979–1981. For some groups of commodities, notably tropical beverages and food, the decline in real world prices has been even steeper, standing at 32 per cent and 53 per cent of the average in 1979–1981 (chart 38). For agricultural raw materials, and minerals, ores and metals, the decline since the start of the 1980s has been less steep, but still significant. Real commodity prices for agricultural raw materials and for minerals, ores and metals in 2001 stood at 65 per cent and 67 per cent respectively of their level in 1979–1981. Real non-fuel

CHART 38. WORLD FREE MARKET PRICES FOR NON-FUEL PRIMARY COMMODITIES AND PRIMARY COMMODITY SUB-GROUPS, 1960–2002[a]

(Index, 1980 =100)

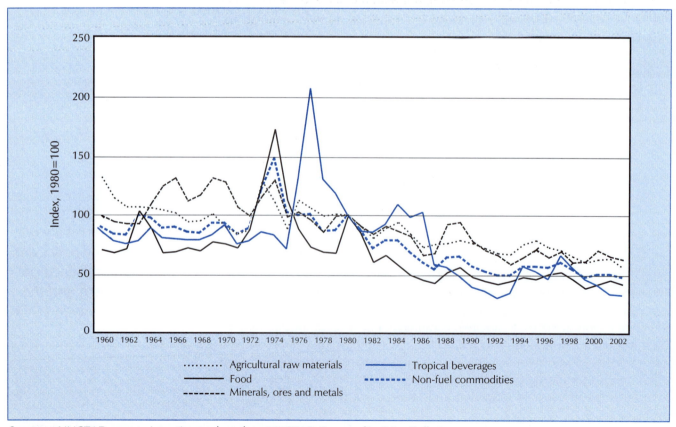

Source: UNCTAD secretariat estimates based on UNCTAD *Commodity Price Bulletin.*

a   Figures for 2002 are based on the first quarter.

commodity prices have also become more volatile than in the period before 1970 (Dehn, 2000a; Cashin and McDermott, 2001).

It is possible to construct estimates of recent movements in the commodity terms of trade of the least developed countries using the IMF index (published in the statistical annex of certain issues of its *World Economic Outlook*) that estimates the world market prices of the non-fuel commodity exports of the least developed countries. On the basis of this index, it is evident that real commodity prices of LDC exports declined by over 30 per cent between 1986 and 1999 (chart 39). But within the overall downward movement, there have been distinct ups and downs. From 1986 to 1992, real commodity prices declined by 33 per cent of their 1986 level. From 1993 to 1997, they improved considerably, standing in 1997 at 44 per cent higher than their level in 1992. But since then, particularly in the wake of the financial crisis in Asia, they have once again declined sharply, in spite of decreases in the unit value of manufactures exported from developed countries.

The volume of commodity exports from LDCs increased by 43 per cent between 1986 and 1999. But the purchasing power of commodity exports increased by only 3 per cent.

Falling real commodity prices mean that a larger volume of exports is required in order to finance a given volume of imports. Using the IMF index as a measure of unit value, it can be estimated that the volume of commodity exports from LDCs increased by 43 per cent between 1986 and 1999 (table 32). But the value of LDC commodity exports increased by only 26 per cent over this period, and the purchasing power of commodity exports[4] increased by only 3 per cent between 1986 and 1999.

Within these overall trends there has been much variability. There were substantial increases in export volumes in 1990–1992, 1994–1995 and 1997–1999. The first and the last of these periods of rapid commodity export growth follow a succession of years (1988–1990 and 1994–1997) in which the export unit value index was above the 1986 level. But both the first and the second of these export volume increases were followed by a sharp downward movement

CHART 39. NON-FUEL COMMODITY TERMS OF TRADE OF LDCS, 1986–1999

(Index, 1986=100)

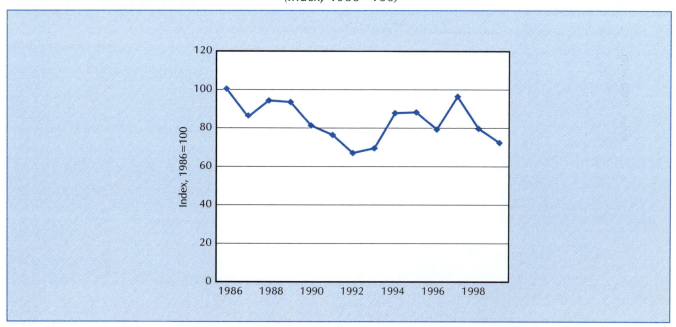

Source: UNCTAD secretariat estimates based on IMF estimates of world market prices of non-fuel primary commodity exports of LDCs (IMF, *World Economic Outlook*, various issues, Statistical Annex) and UN index of unit value of exports of manufactures from developed market-economy countries.

which followed a drop in export prices. The low point in the series with regard to export volume was 1994. Between that date and 1999, the volume of exports from LDCs increased by 54 per cent. The purchasing power of commodity exports from LDCs traced a U-shaped pattern. The purchasing power of commodity exports fell by 20 per cent from 1986 to 1993, but then rose by 28 per cent from 1993 to 1999 (see table 32).

The foreign exchange losses due to the changes in the commodity terms of trade in LDCs have been significant. The annual average foreign exchange losses associated with movements in the commodity terms of trade from 1986 to 1999 were equivalent to $0.68 billion per year (at 1986 prices) during 1987–1989, $2.25 billion per year during 1990–1993, $0.99 billion per year during 1994–1997 and $2.4 billion per year during 1998–1999.[5] The average annual foreign exchange loss in the last period was equivalent to one third of the 1986 value of LDC commodity exports.

As the majority of LDCs are net food and net-oil importers, the effects of deterioration in the commodity terms of trade may be offset partly by trends in food prices and oil prices. The adverse effects of the commodity price declines since 1997 have been dampened somewhat in the LDCs, in the short term at least, owing to lower prices for food imports and until 2000 by lower prices for oil imports (Herrmann and David, 2001). But in LDCs that are highly dependent on primary commodity exports, the trends in real commodity prices remain central to trends in the countries' overall net barter terms of trade.[6] Recent research shows that the decline in the net barter terms of trade is a particular problem for the least developed countries (Mendoza, 2001). Moreover, not only are the net barter terms of trade declining in the world's poorest countries, but there is also strong evidence that the adverse influences on developing countries that Prebisch and Singer warned against 50 years ago are at work in almost all the world's poorest commodity-exporting countries (see box 12). This is creating

Not only are the net barter terms of trade declining in the world's poorest countries, but there is also strong evidence that the adverse influences on developing countries that Prebisch and Singer warned against 50 years ago are at work in almost all the world's poorest commodity-exporting countries

TABLE 32. UNIT VALUE, VOLUME AND PURCHASING POWER OF NON-FUEL COMMODITY EXPORTS OF LDCS, 1986–1999
(Index, 1986=100)

Year	Export unit value[a]	Export volume[b]	Purchasing power of exports[c]
1986	100.0	100.0	100.0
1987	96.5	103.2	88.1
1988	112.7	96.9	91.0
1989	110.8	105.4	98.0
1990	106.0	102.1	82.5
1991	99.4	111.1	84.2
1992	89.8	127.2	84.5
1993	88.4	116.4	80.3
1994	114.7	93.1	81.2
1995	126.7	120.3	105.4
1996	110.1	113.0	88.9
1997	124.6	97.7	93.6
1998	99.8	125.0	98.9
1999	87.9	143.0	102.6

Source: UNCTAD secretariat estimates.

Note:
a The export unit value index is based on IMF estimates of world market prices of LDCs' non-fuel commodity exports (IMF, *World Economic Outlook*, various issues, Statistical Annex).
b The value of LDC commodity exports , based on UN COMTRADE data, divided by their average unit value.
c The value of LDC commodity exports, deflated by the UN index of unit value of exports of manufactures from developed market-economy countries.

an "uphill" external environment that is constantly undermining development and poverty reduction efforts, and inhibiting trade with more prosperous and growing parts of the world from acting as an engine of growth in the LDCs.

The magnitude of the effects of this external environment are worth underlining. World Bank estimates for non-oil-exporting countries in sub-Saharan Africa, most of which are LDCs, suggest that their cumulative terms-of-trade losses over the period from 1970 to 1997 amounted to 119 per cent of regional GDP in 1997 and 51 and 68 per cent of cumulative net resource flows and net resource transfers to the region respectively (World Bank, 2000). It has been estimated that if these resources had been available for domestic uses and invested productively, the annual growth of those countries could have been 1.4 per cent per annum faster. Without these losses, and assuming that resources were invested productively, income per capita could have been 50 per cent higher in those countries and poverty rates would have been concomitantly much lower (UNCTAD, 2000a).

The effects of primary commodity price instability are also particularly significant in the LDCs.

The effects of primary commodity price instability are also particularly significant in the LDCs. As shown in *The Least Developed Countries 2000 Report*, what distinguishes these countries is not necessarily that they are exposed to greater shocks than other developing countries, but rather that the scale of these shocks in relation to domestic resources available to finance investment is extremely large. In a sample of 18 non-fuel commodity-exporting LDCs for which data are available, the maximum two-year terms-of-trade shock over the period 1970–1999 led to income losses of over 100 per cent of the domestic resources available to finance investment in any given year in eight of them, and income losses of over 25 per cent of domestic resources available to finance investment in a further eight (see UNCTAD, 2000b: 38–39).

Commodity price trends also affect the incidence of poverty through their impact on the employment opportunities and earnings of commodity producers. At the household and enterprise level, the impact of price changes depends on whether global and border price trends are passed through to the producer at the local level, and whether improvements in productivity and yields are compensating for falling prices. With regard to price transmission, marketing boards and *caisses de stabilisation* have in the past acted as a buffer between world prices and agricultural producer prices in many commodity-exporting LDCs. As these institutions have been dismantled within the framework of structural adjustment programmes, producers have been more closely exposed to the ups and downs of world commodity markets. Producers have often seen their share of national border prices of commodities increase, although the pattern is mixed (see Boratav, 2001) and has occurred particularly in more accessible and high-population-density areas. But in the face of declining world commodity prices, real producer prices have also declined.

With the dismantling of marketing boards, producers have often seen their share of national border prices of commodities increase, although the pattern is mixed and has occurred particularly in more accessible and high-population-density areas. But in the face of declining world commodity prices, real producer prices have also declined.

The recent example of coffee is a good example of the problems which producers can face. Prices paid to coffee growers have declined between 1995 and 2000 in nominal terms by over 50 per cent in 10 out of 14 LDCs for which data are available (table 33). This implications of this for livelihoods in these countries, particularly in those countries almost completely dependent on coffee exports, cannot be over-emphasized.

BOX 12. THE TERMS OF TRADE OF THE WORLD'S POOREST COMMODITY-EXPORTING COUNTRIES

The Prebisch–Singer hypothesis that there is a long-term decline in the price of primary commodities relative to the price of manufactures continues to be an object of controversy. Most tests of the hypothesis use time series models to estimate trend growth rates in selected relative prices. The focus of concern has been either the net barter terms of trade between producers of primary products (equated with developing countries) and producers of manufactures (equated with industrialized countries), or the prices of a basket of commodities relative to the price of manufactures (the commodity terms of trade). A new approach which has been developed recently is to construct a structural model which seeks to identify different factors which impinge on the prices of manufactured goods and primary commodities (Bloch and Sapsford, 1997).

BOX TABLE 1. TRENDS AND VOLATILITY IN THE NET BARTER TERMS OF TRADE OF THE WORLD'S POOREST[a] COMMODITY-EXPORTING COUNTRIES, 1960–1993[b]

Country	Period 1	Trend	Volatility	Period 2	Trend	Volatility
		Annual average percentage change			Annual average percentage change	
Burkina Faso	1960–1968	0.00	0.127	1969–1991	-3.12	0.059
Burundi[c]	1965–1993	-7.99	-0.307	-	-	-
Chad	1960–1972	12.50	0.034	1973–1993	1.77	0.082
Dem. Republic of the Congo	1960–1984	-9.18	0.110	1985–1993	-6.18	0.037
Ethiopia	1960–1974	0.00	0.063	1975–1993	-10.38	0.192
Guineau-Bissau	1965–1977	-10.72	0.079	1978–1993	0.00	0.216
Madagascar[c]	1960–1991	-1.98	0.128	-	-	-
Malawi	1960–1973	21.95	0.054	1974–1993	-2.86	0.095
Mali	1960–1981	0.00	0.088	1982–1993	-1.47	0.030
Niger	1960–1986	-6.17	0.086	1987–1993	-0.72	0.020
Rwanda	1960–1974	0.00	0.081	1975–1993	-12.30	0.185
Sierra Leone	1960–1977	-2.60	0.072	1978–1993	-3.28	0.065
Sudan	1960–1987	-2.44	0.096	1988–1993	-5.77	0.033
United Rep. of Tanzania	1960–1973	0.00	0.050	1974–1993	-4.16	0.094
Zambia	1960–1979	-21.10	0.124	1980–1993	-7.50	0.099

Source: Sapsford (2001).

Note: A reported trend rate of growth of zero indicates that the relevant estimated coefficient is not significantly different from zero at conventional levels.

a The poorest commodity-exporting countries are identified according to their GNP per capita (World Bank Atlas method) in 1997.

b The net barter term of trade estimates are based on structural model which controls for the influence on the terms of trade of fluctuations in the level of production in the industrialized world.

c Trend and volatility estimates cover the whole data series as there is no structural break in the trend.

Applying this approach, it has been found that the overall trend identified in the time series models is the net effect of separate divergent influences. On the one hand, there are Prebisch and Singer effects that exert a downward pressure on the commodity terms of trade. These effects arise because of differences in market structure (markets for primary products are more perfectly competitive) and differences in the factor bias of technical change (technical change in manufactures is assumed to save raw material inputs and labour). On the other hand, rising industrial output can have a counteracting effect, as primary products used in manufacturing activity experience rising prices when the level of manufacturing activity increases.

Box table 1 above shows estimates of the trend growth rates in the net barter terms of trade (expressed as per cent per annum) of 15 LDCs, which are the world's poorest commodity-exporting countries. The estimates cover the period 1960–1993, for which there is a consistent UNCTAD time series of the terms of trade for those countries. They have been made using a structural model, which controls for the influence on country-specific terms of trade of fluctuations in the level of production in the industrialized world. The OECD's Index of Industrial Production was used as a measure of the level of industrial production in the industrialized world. The table also includes estimates of terms-of-trade volatility for these countries, using the standard error of estimate about the regression line

Box 12 (contd.)

as a measure of volatility. Tests have been carried out to see if there is a structural break in the trend, and if so, this is reported, along with the measure of terms-of-trade volatility in each sub-period.

The table can be read across the rows. It shows for Ethiopia, for example, that, after controlling for the influence on this country's terms of trade of fluctuations in the level of production in the industrialized world, there was a change in the trend growth rate of its terms of trade in 1974, after which date the previous trendless situation was replaced by one in which the terms of trade deteriorated at an annual trend rate of 10.38 per cent. This worsening in trend was accompanied by a trebling of terms-of-trade volatility as between the pre- and post-1974 situations.

The main results of the table can be summarized as follows:

- Of the 15 poorest commodity-exporting countries, all but two experienced a significant change in the trend rate of growth of their terms of trade during the period 1960-1993.
- In 9 out of the 13 cases, the change in the trend occurred between 1972 and 1982.
- Nineteen out of 28 reported trend estimates are negative.
- Only three of the reported trend estimates are positive.
- In 9 out of the 13 countries where there is a trend shift, the pattern shows a worsening of the situation in respect of terms of trade.
- In 6 out of the 13 countries where there is a trend shift, the pattern shows an increase in the volatility of the terms of trade.

These results show that many of the poorest commodity-exporting LDCs in the world have indeed been subject to Prebisch–Singer effects on their terms of trade, which have exerted a continuous downward pressure on economic and export growth, offsetting the positive effects which they might have experienced as a result of the positive effect of expanding industrial output.

Source: Sapsford (2001).

TABLE 33. COFFEE PRICES PAID TO GROWERS IN EXPORTING LDCs, 1995, 1998 AND 2000
(US cents per pound, current terms)

	1995	1998	2000
Colombian milds			
United Rep. of Tanzania	71.32	70.95	64.00[a]
Other milds			
Burundi	53.04	48.94	33.20
Dem. Republic of the Congo	81.65	..	..
Haiti	26.93	..	24.28[a]
Malawi	108.96	67.36	48.99
Madagascar	88.61	52.14	20.82
Rwanda	56.92	46.29	26.38
Uganda	109.80	117.34	76.29
Zambia	107.84	..	..
Brazilian naturals			
Ethiopia	73.32	88.68	49.86
Robustas			
Angola	29.49	49.90	45.36[a]
Burundi	41.11	..	..
Central African Republic	58.31	34.02	16.44
Dem. Republic of the Congo	45.36	..	..
Madagascar	66.46	43.45	17.35
Togo	69.08	48.60	12.40
United Republic of Tanzania	48.14	27.13	17.78[a]
Uganda	94.41	115.02	26.07

Source: International Coffee Organization (2001).

a 1999.

2. Productivity, competitiveness and dynamism of LDC commodity exports

It is possible to offset the consequences of adverse effects of declining terms of trade on material well-being through productivity and quality improvements, and diversification and upgrading within the primary sector. Diversification into more sophisticated primary products can also provide more dynamic growth effects than simple commodities. But within most commodity-exporting least developed countries, the negative effects of terms-of-trade movement on growth and poverty have been exacerbated by a weak primary commodity sector.

The commodity-exporting LDCs generally export a narrow range of primary commodities for which the growth of global demand is slow. Productivity tends to be lower than in other developing countries and productivity growth is slow and certainly insufficient to offset the negative effects of falling commodity prices. In some of their traditional exports, commodity-exporting LDCs are losing market share, and diversification into more dynamic sectors and upgrading into more value-added segments of commodity production are occurring very slowly.

Enterprise-level studies indicate that there are important new developments in the commodity sector within the LDCs (ITC, 2001a, 2001b). But progress is still patchy and small islands of improvement and best practice have not yet been translated into economy-wide and sector-wide structural transformations. Indeed, this dichotomy between pockets of enterprise success at the micro level and a lack of dynamism and diversification at the economy-wide level is a key feature of commodity-exporting LDCs that needs to be addressed in policy terms (see chapter 5).

The productivity gap between LDCs and other developing countries and the rest of the world is discussed extensively in *The Least Developed Countries 1999 Report*. Available evidence on crop yields for seven agricultural exports shows that crop yields were on average lower in LDCs than in other developing countries over the period 1980–1997 in all cases but cocoa. For the two most important agricultural exports of LDCs — coffee and cotton — yields would have to be 10 per cent and 59 per cent higher respectively to reach the average productivity level of other developing countries, and 147 per cent and 219 per cent higher to reach the level of the most advanced producers of these commodities (UNCTAD, 1999: table 23).

The evidence suggests that productivity for these crops is rising in a number of LDCs. But productivity growth on average has not been sufficient to offset the effects of declining commodity prices. For coffee and cotton, yields were 28 per cent and 50 per cent higher respectively, in 2000 than in 1980. But assuming that national prices moved in line with world prices, real returns per hectare would have been 46 per cent lower in 2000 than in 1980 for LDC coffee producers and 5 per cent lower for LDC cotton producers (chart 40). This is, of course, an imperfect measure of profitability as it is necessary also to take account of costs of inputs and labour. But declining real returns imply not only that producers, livelihoods are being squeezed, but also that it is difficult to attract investment and increase productivity. The correction to the oversupply in world commodity markets, which is the cause of low commodity prices, occurs through the market mechanism by the elimination of marginal producers such as those in the LDCs. Such market corrections occur, in real terms, either, as the economics textbooks indicate, through the reallocation of labour and land

Diversification into more sophisticated primary products provide more dynamic growth effects than simple commodities.

Enterprise-level studies indicate that there are important new developments in the commodity sector within the LDCs. But progress is still patchy and small islands of improvement and best practice have not yet been translated into economy-wide and sector-wide structural transformations.

CHART 40. CHANGE IN OUTPUT, YIELDS AND REAL RETURNS PER HECTARE[a]
IN COTTON AND COFFEE PRODUCTION IN LDCS, 1980–2000
(Percentage)

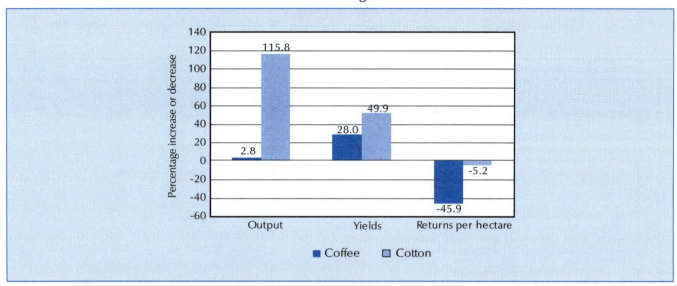

Source: UNCTAD secretariat estimates based on UNCTAD (1999: tables 20 and 21), updated with FAO, FAOSTAT for output and yield changes, and UNCTAD *Commodity Price Bulletin* for estimate of output price changes.

a   The estimates of real returns per hectare assume no change in input prices and labour costs.

resources by switching to more profitable crops or by migrating to work in cities, or through destitution, worsening health and rising death rates.

Not only are the commodity export sectors in LDCs characterized by low productivity, but also their traditional commodities are concentrated in sectors within which world demand is either slower than average or declining, and in a number of these sectors they are actually losing market share. It has been estimated that the LDCs' share in world commodity exports declined from 4.7 per cent in 1970–1972 to 1 per cent in 1998–1999 (Megzari, 2001). If the same share had been maintained as in 1970–1972 (and assuming that this would not have had any impact on prices) LDCs average export earnings would have been $24.9 billion higher than they actually were in 1998–1999. This would have doubled LDC exports. The loss of world market share occurred in food and beverages as well as agricultural raw materials, with LDC market share in those sectors falling between 1970–1972 and 1998–1999 from 3 per cent to 0.9 per cent and from 5 per cent to 1.3 per cent respectively. However, the loss of market share is particularly pronounced for minerals and metals, where the LDC share fell from 8.6 per cent to 1 per cent of the world market.

Table 34 shows the situation in the mid-1990s at a more detailed level of product disaggregation and during a period of relatively good export performance. It is clear that the main products in which LDCs are gaining market share in growing world markets are clothing and textiles. There are only four primary commodity exports in which LDCs are gaining market share and world demand is growing faster than the average — tobacco, leguminous vegetables, fish fillets and tuna. Out of the total LDC non-fuel primary commodity exports recorded in the table of $16.6 billion in 1998, only $3.4 billion (20 per cent) were in products for which world imports were growing during 1994–1998 at above average rates and the LDCs were gaining market share. For agricultural exports, there are gains in market share in a range of commodities, but these are occurring in segments of the global market where growth of world imports is slower than the average or actually declining. For minerals, ores and metals, the picture is more mixed, but once again production is concentrated in products

In 1998, only 20 per cent of the total LDC non-fuel primary commodity exports were in products for which world imports were growing during 1994–1998 at above average rates and the LDCs were gaining market share.

TABLE 34. GROWTH OF WORLD IMPORTS AND CHANGE IN WORLD MARKET SHARE OF MAJOR LDC EXPORTS, 1994–1998

		Change of world market share of LDC exports, 1994–1998				
		Increasing			**Decreasing**	
		Product	Type	1998 export value (million $)	Product	Type	1998 export value (million $)

Growth of world imports, 1994–1998							
	Fast growth rate[a]	T-shirts, singlets and other vests, of cotton, knitted	Manufactures	542	Logs, keruing, ramin, kapur, teak, jongkong, merbau, etc.	Primary commodity	219
		Mens/boys trousers and shorts, of cotton, not knitted	Manufactures	507	Natural uranium & its compounds; mixtures containing natural uranium/its compounds	Primary commodity	152
		Pullovers, cardigans and similar articles of man-made fibres, knitted	Manufactures	453			
		Tobacco, unmanufactured, partly or wholly stemmed or stripped	Primary commodity	335			
		Womens/girls trousers and shorts, of cotton, not knitted	Manufactures	290			
		Pullovers, cardigans and similar articles of cotton, knitted	Manufactures	268			
		Mens/boys anoraks and similar articles, of man-made fibres, not knitted	Manufactures	227			
		Mens/boys shirts, of cotton, knitted	Manufactures	162			
		Womens/girls anoraks & similar article of man-made fibres, not knitted	Manufactures	158			
		Leguminous vegetables dried, shelled, whether or not skinnd or split, nes	Primary commodity	95			
		Mens/boys trousers and shorts, of synthetic fibres, not knitted	Manufactures	93			
		Womens/girls briefs and panties, of cotton, knitted	Manufactures	83			
		Fish fillets frozen	Primary commodity	78			
		Tunas,skipjack&atl bonito,prepared/preserved, whole/in pieces, ex-minced	Primary commodity	76			
		Total	**All goods**	**3367**	**Total**	**All goods**	**371**
		Sub-total	**Manufactures**	**2782**	**Sub-total**	**Primary commodities**	**371**
		Sub-total	**Primary commodities**	**585**	**Sub-total**	**Manufactures**	**-**
	Slow growth rate[b]	Petroleum oils and oils obtained from bituminous minerals, crude	Primary commodity	4988	Copper cathodes and sections of cathodes unwrought	Primary commodity	369
		Diamonds non-industrial unworked or simply sawn, cleaved or bruted	Primary commodity	1777	Cobalt,unwrought, matte & other intermediate products, waste, scrap and powders	Primary commodity	239
		Coffee, not roasted, not decaffeinated	Primary commodity	1186			
		Mens/boys shirts, of cotton, not knitted	Manufactures	589			
		Iron ores&concentrates,oth than roasted iron pyrites, non-agglomerated	Primary commodity	255			
		Hats&other headgear,knitted or made up from lace,or other textile mat	Manufactures	150			
		Cashew nuts, fresh or dried, whether or not shelled or peeled	Primary commodity	147			
		Sesamum seeds, whether or not broken	Primary commodity	139			
		Natural calcium phosphates, aluminum calcium phosphates, etc., unground	Primary commodity	75			
		Total	**All goods**	**9306**	**Total**	**All goods**	**608**
		Sub-total	**Primary commodities**	**8567**	**Sub-total**	**Primary commodities**	**608**
		Sub-total	**Manufactures**	**740**	**Sub-total**	**Manufactures**	**..**
	Negative growth rate[c]	Cotton, not carded or combed	Primary commodity	925	Mens/boys shirts, of man-made fibres, not knitted	Manufactures	219
		Shrimps and prawns, frozen, in shell or not, including boiled in shell	Primary commodity	605	Logs, non-coniferous n.e.s.	Primary commodity	205
		Aluminium ores and concentrates	Primary commodity	418	Carpets of wool or fine animal hair, knotted	Manufactures	158
		Pullovers,cardigans & similar article of wool or fine animal hair,knitted	Manufactures	88	Womens/girls blouses and shirts, of cotton, not knitted	Manufactures	129
					Octopus, frozen, dried, salted or in brine	Primary commodity	122
					Diamonds unsorted whether or not worked	Primary commodity	86
		Total	**All goods**	**2036**	**Grand total**	**All goods**	**919**
		Sub-total	**Primary commodities**	**1948**	**Sub-total**	**Primary commodities**	**505**
		Sub-total	**Manufactures**	**88**	**Sub-total**	**Manufactures**	**413**

Source: UNCTAD secretariat estimates based on ITC (1999).

Note: Product labels correspond with the Harmonized Commodity Description and Coding System (HS), Rev. 0.

a Annual percentage growth of world imports of these products is above the average nominal growth rate of total world imports from 1994–1998 (5.75 per cent per annum).

b Annual percentage growth of world imports of these products is below the average nominal growth rate of total world imports from 1994–1998.

c Annual percentage growth of world imports of these products is negative.

where growth of world imports is slow or declining. From this analysis, it is clear therefore that the problem of export development in the LDCs is not simply a question of competitiveness in traditional sectors. The primary problem now is the failure to diversify into more dynamic sectors.

Comparison between the non-fuel commodity-exporting LDCs and those which have diversified into manufactures and/or services shows that even the primary commodity exports of the latter group are more dynamic than those of the former. As table 35 shows, static unprocessed agricultural products constituted 37 per cent of the primary commodity exports of non-oil commodity exporters in 1981–1983 and 43 per cent in 1997–1999. The share of dynamic agricultural primary commodities, both processed and unprocessed, increased only from 13 to 14 per cent of total primary commodity exports over the period. For the manufactures and/or services exporters, although commodity exports are much less important overall, there is a much greater share of dynamic agricultural products in their commodity exports. Moreover, this share actually increased over the period from 1981–1983 to 1997–1999, from 37 per cent to 48 per cent of their total primary commodity exports.

Commodity-exporting LDCs are also failing to capture more value added through quality improvement, product differentiation and local processing. It is difficult to measure trends in such upgrading in all its aspects. But country-level evidence suggests that decline in quality has been a side effect of agricultural market liberalization in some LDCs (Gibbon, 2001). Moreover, there is clear evidence that there has been a collapse of commodity processing in LDCs over the last 20 years (see table 27, chapter 3). Indeed, the share of processed commodities in total LDC exports fell from 21 to 8 per cent between 1981–1983 and 1997–1999. Thus, in terms of domestic processing, instead of moving up the value chain, the LDCs are sliding down it. This has occurred in both commodity-exporting LDCs and those exporting manufactures and services. The trend is particularly evident in mineral exporters.

The share of processed commodities in total LDC exports fell from 21 to 8 per cent between 1981–1983 and 1997–1999. Thus, in terms of domestic processing, instead of moving up the value chain, the LDCs are sliding down it.

TABLE 35. DIVERSIFICATION WITHIN THE COMMODITY SECTOR IN LDCS AND LDC SUB-GROUPS, 1981–1983, 1987–1989 AND 1997–1999

(Percentage of total primary commodity exports)

	Non-oil commodity exporting LDCs			Oil exporters			Manufactures and/or services exporting LDCs			Total LDCs		
	1981– 1983	1987– 1989	1997– 1999	1981– 1983	1987– 1989	1997– 1999	1981– 1983	1987– 1989	1997– 1999	1981– 1983	1987– 1989	1997– 1999
Unprocessed primary commodities	70.9	69.4	83.9	92.7	96.2	98.0	67.1	72.5	79.6	75.5	77.4	88.9
Static agricultural products	37.4	36.9	42.6	5.7	2.1	2.1	29.5	24.2	27.8	31.9	28.5	28.2
Dynamic agricultural products[a]	9.8	10.6	12.2	0.0	0.3	1.3	27.7	39.2	45.0	10.8	12.0	13.5
Minerals, metals and fuels	23.7	21.9	29.1	86.9	93.8	94.5	9.9	9.1	6.8	32.8	36.9	47.2
Processed primary commodities	29.1	30.6	16.1	7.3	3.8	2.0	32.9	27.5	20.4	24.5	22.6	11.1
Static agricultural products	5.1	4.5	2.6	0.0	0.1	0.0	13.3	8.0	6.2	5.5	3.8	2.3
Dynamic agricultural products[a]	3.2	2.5	1.4	0.0	0.2	0.0	9.4	10.4	3.2	2.3	1.9	1.1
Minerals, metals and fuels	20.8	23.6	12.1	7.3	3.5	1.9	10.2	9.2	10.9	16.7	16.9	7.7
Total	100.0	100.0	100.0	100.0	100.0	100.0	100.0	100.0	100.0	100.0	100.0	100.0

Source: UNCTAD secretariat estimates based on UN COMTRADE data.

Note: The figures are weighted averages. For the countries in each sub-group, see annex table 2 in chapter 3. No data are available for Cambodia, Eritrea, Lao People's Democratic Republic, Lesotho and Yemen.

  a   Dynamic agricultural products include items whose income elasticity of demand is greater than unity and much higher than that of traditional agricultural products. The group includes meat and meat products, fish and fish products, fruits, vegetables, nuts, spices and vegetable oils. For further discussion of this product classification, see Wood and Mayer (1998).

C. Elements of the international poverty trap

Primary commodity dependence is related to poverty not only through trade mechanisms per se, but also through the way in which the growth and composition of trade affect external indebtedness, and how external indebtedness in turn is related to access to external private finance and aid effectiveness. The least developed countries where poverty is greatest are not simply primary commodity exporters focused on a narrow range of low-productivity, weakly competitive, low-value-added commodities. They also tend to have unsustainable external debts and to be enmeshed in an aid/debt service system in which donors, who are also the major creditors, have been allocating aid, explicitly but more often implicitly, so that debts can be serviced. This configuration of external finance and trade relationships can be traced back to the condition of generalized poverty, and these external relationships in turn reinforce the domestic vicious circles which cause generalized poverty to persist. It is the interrelationship between the domestic and external cause-and-effect relationships, together with the interdependence between trade and finance, which creates the international poverty trap.

The main elements and relationships of this international poverty trap are summarized in chart 41. On the left-hand side of the diagram are found the main domestic channels, discussed in the previous chapter, through which generalized poverty acts as a constraint on economic growth. On the right-hand side of the diagram are the external trade and finance relationships which interact with these domestic cycles of stagnation and together cause generalized poverty to persist. The pivot of this complex of interpenetrating external and domestic relationships is low productivity, low physical and human capital investment and low savings.

Five main interrelationships are identified as domestic aspects of the poverty trap. First, domestic resources available to finance physical and human capital investment and productivity growth are low owing to generalized poverty. Second, State capacities are weak as all activities, including administration and law and order, are underfunded. Third, corporate capacities, in business, finance and support services, are weak, even though there may be a thriving informal sector. Fourth, generalized poverty engenders rapid population growth and environmental degradation. Fifth, in a situation of generalized poverty, the probability of political instability and conflict is greater. Low productivity, rapid population growth, environmental degradation, political instability and conflict, weak State capacities and weak corporate capacities all serve to reinforce generalized poverty directly and indirectly. Generalized poverty in turn results in low savings and investment, and low productivity.

Three main interrelationships are identified as international aspects of the poverty trap — the form of primary commodity dependence; the build-up of unsustainable external debt; and the emergence of an aid/debt service system. Each of these is interrelated and each has various cause-and-effect relations with the nexus of generalized poverty and low savings, investment and productivity.

1. THE FORM OF PRIMARY COMMODITY DEPENDENCE

In situations of generalized poverty, poverty itself affects not only economic growth but also the form of a country's trade integration with the global economy. The export structure of primary-commodity-exporting LDCs was in most cases originally established during the colonial period. Those

Primary commodity dependence is related to poverty not only through trade mechanisms per se, but also through the way in which the growth and composition of trade affect external indebtedness, and how external indebtedness in turn is related to access to external private finance and aid effectiveness.

In situations of generalized poverty, poverty itself affects not only economic growth but also the form of a country's trade integration with the global economy.

CHART 41. THE INTERNATIONAL POVERTY TRAP OF COMMODITY-DEPENDENT LDCs

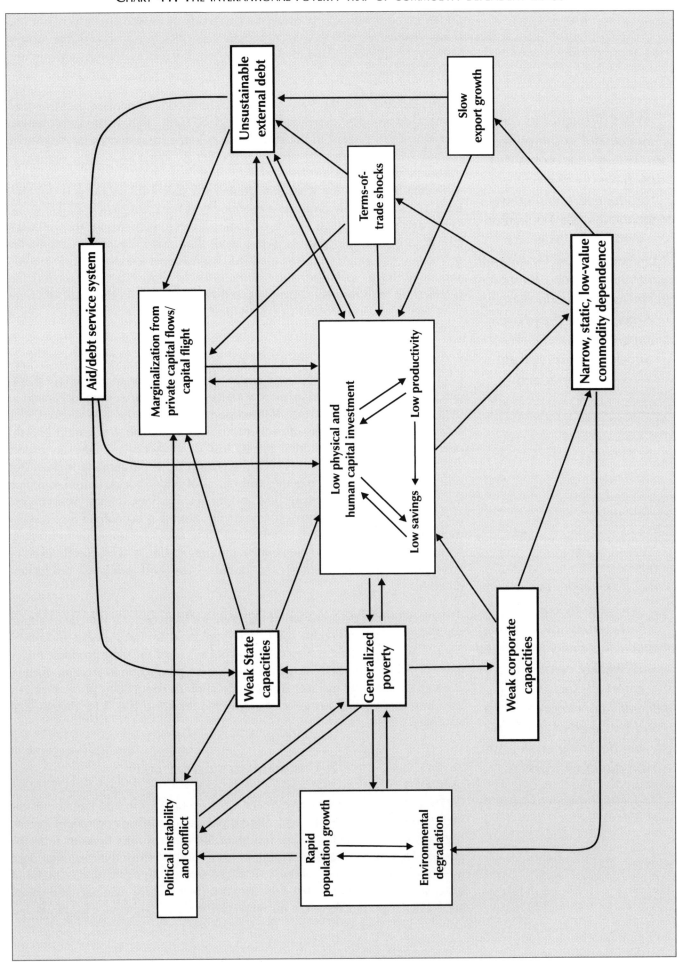

countries continue to depend on a narrow range of undynamic and low-value-added commodity exports owing to low levels of investment in physical and human capital, as well as weak corporate capacities. It is this particular form of primary commodity dependence that then hinders economic growth and poverty reduction.

The fact that it is the form of primary commodity dependence, rather than primary commodity dependence in and of itself, that matters for growth performance is evident in the experience of some more successful developing countries where primary commodity exports have been an integral element in economic growth and sustained development (see World Bank, 1996: chapter 4; Reinhardt, 2000). But what distinguishes the successful countries is that they have developed highly productive commodity sectors and gained market share. They have also diversified into non-traditional commodity exports for which the growth of world demand is faster, and they have upgraded commodity production to capture more value-added. This has enabled faster export growth, and they have sustained the momentum of development founded on productivity improvement, upgrading and diversification in the primary sector by gradually diversifying out of commodity exports into manufacturing and/or service exports.

> *What distinguishes the successful commodity exporting countries is that they have developed highly productive commodity sectors and gained market share. They have also diversified into non-traditional commodity exports for which the growth of world demand is faster, and they have upgraded commodity production to capture more value-added.*

The commodity exporting LDCs are by contrast characterized by a low-productivity, low-value-added and weakly competitive commodity sector that is generally concentrated on a narrow range of products serving declining or sluggish international markets. As discussed in the previous two sections, this form of primary commodity dependence is associated with slow export growth, due to falling real commodity prices, loss of market share, and an export concentration in products for which the growth of world demand is slow. But slow export growth rates, together with terms-of-trade shocks, in turn reinforce the nexus of low productivity, low investment and low savings. Slow export growth implies that most non-oil commodity exporting economies face foreign exchange shortages. Import volumes are low, and low levels of technology imports and lack of complementary imports result in a reduced level of investment, reduced efficiency of resource use and outdated production processes.

> *The commodity exporting LDCs are by contrast characterized by a low-productivity, low-value-added and weakly competitive commodity sector that is generally concentrated on a narrow range of products serving declining or sluggish international markets.*

In situations of declining world real commodity prices, it is difficult to attract investment into commodity production unless there are special incentives created by government. If they can, smallholders react to falling producer prices for export commodities by switching from export production to food production oriented to domestic markets. The deterioration in commodity prices thus can itself lead to a decline in market share, with cumulative effects for the national economy.

2. Unsustainable external debt

The low productivity of investment, slow export growth and large terms-of-trade shocks, together with weak State capacities (including corruption), are all key causes of the build-up of an unsustainable external debt burden. Table 36 groups LDCs on the basis of export structure and whether their external debt was sustainable at the end of the 1990s according to the international criteria of sustainability used in the HIPC Initiative. It is clear that for manufactured goods and service exporters there is a mixed picture in which some have unsustainable external debts and some do not. But for the commodity exporting LDCs there is a remarkable correlation between export structure and external debt. Eighty-five per cent of the LDCs dependent on non-oil primary commodities have an

TABLE 36. EXTERNAL DEBT SUSTAINABILITY IN LDCS GROUPED ACCORDING TO EXPORT COMPOSITION, 1998–2000

(Present value of debt to exports, %)

Sustainable[a]	Unsustainable[a]
Non-oil commodity exporters	
Bhutan (111)	Benin (253)
Eritrea (75)	Burkina Faso (210)
Solomon Islands (53)	Burundi (985)
Uganda (138)	Central African Republic (356)
	Chad (222)
	Dem. Rep. of the Congo (797)
	Ethiopia (343)
	Guinea (286)
	Guinea-Bissau (1321)
	Malawi (314)
	Mali (209)
	Mauritania (319)
	Niger (345)
	Rwanda (628)
	Sao Tome and Principe (1307)
	Sierra Leone (800)
	Sudan (1319)[b]
	Togo (199)
	United Republic of Tanzania (395)
	Zambia (537)
Oil exporters	
Equatorial Guinea (13)	Angola (170)
Yemen (99)	
Manufactures and/or services exporters	
Bangladesh (120)	Cambodia (158)
Cape Verde (128)	Comoros (296)
Djibouti (71)	Gambia (217)
Haiti (132)	Lao PDR (243)
Lesotho (91)	Madagascar (333)
Maldives (32)	Mozambique (187)
Nepal (113)	Myanmar (248)
Samoa (115)	Senegal (151)
Vanuatu (20)	

Source: UNCTAD secretariat estimates based on World Bank, *Global Development Finance, 2002.*

    a   The countries are divided into unsustainable or sustainable on the basis of whether the net present value of debt-to-exports (%) is over 150 or not. The ratio is based on the net present value of debt in the year 2000 and average annual exports of goods and services during 1998–2000. No data available for Afghanistan, Kiribati, Liberia, Somalia and Tuvalu.

    b   Sudan began to export significant quantities of oil in 1999.

unsustainable external debt. The only exceptions are Bhutan, Eritrea, the Solomon Islands and Uganda.

The close association between an export structure focused on non-oil primary commodities and unsustainable external debt suggests that the debt problem of the non-oil commodity exporting LDCs is not purely national, but rather a systemic issue. This is not to say that domestic mismanagement did not play a role in the build-up of debts. Country case studies show that it did, and that domestic mismanagement was reinforced by poor donor policies, particularly export credit granted at the end of the 1970s and 1980s, poor forecasts, and the failure to realize the magnitude and dimensions of the debt problem. However, there is a very high probability that any LDC that exports primary commodities has an unsustainable external debt. This suggests that common factors are at work.[7]

The debt problem of commodity-exporting LDCs is rooted in the low level of domestic resource mobilization, low rates of return on investment, the vulnerability to external shocks and slow export growth. One major condition for debt sustainability is that the rate of growth of exports must be greater than the rate of interest on outstanding debt. As we have seen, what distinguishes the commodity-exporting LDCs from others is that they have had much slower export growth rates. As a result, they have a strong propensity to develop debt problems and also to fall back into debt after debt relief. The commodity price recession of the early 1980s is a root cause of indebtedness in many LDCs, and terms-of-trade shocks associated with movements in primary commodity prices can at all times push poor countries back into unsustainable indebtedness.

Once a country has an unsustainable external debt, this has a number of negative features that further reinforce the trap of generalized poverty. Firstly, as a very large proportion of the debt is owed by Governments rather than by the private sector, debt servicing reduces resources available for public investment in physical and human capital. Secondly, the debt overhang acts as a deterrent to private investment, particularly because of uncertainty. Domestic interest rates may also be very high. Thirdly, debt service payments tighten the foreign exchange constraint. Together, these effects seriously damage growth prospects in poor countries. It is very difficult to establish the kind of investment–export nexus that is at the heart of sustained economic growth. Rather, there is the treadmill of an export–debt repayment nexus, with the return to external viability remaining a perpetual aspiration, as the preconditions for its realization, namely increased productive capacity and efficiency, are never fulfilled.

The probability of this outcome is increased since another important consequence of the build-up of an unsustainable external debt is that it affects the volume, composition and effectiveness of external finance. High levels of external debt deter private capital inflows, contributing to a general perception of risk that discourages lenders and investors. Although highly indebted countries still receive FDI, they have been effectively marginalized from international capital markets. One important consequence of this is that it is difficult to access short-term loans in order to moderate the effects of external and climatic shocks.

3. THE AID/DEBT SERVICE SYSTEM

Unsustainable external debt also undermines aid effectiveness. The importance of the relationships between aid flows and external debt has only recently received attention (Sachs et al., 1999; Kanbur, 2000; Birdsall, Claessens and Diwan, 2001). But there is now clear evidence that the build-up of external debt has influenced donor behaviour. Official donors, who are also the major creditors, have been supplying aid to ensure that official debts can be serviced.

Amongst LDCs this is apparent in the fact that throughout the 1990s gross aid disbursements were strongly correlated with debt service payments (chart 42). Birdsall, Claessens and Diwan (2001), focusing particularly on Africa, have conducted a rigorous econometric analysis to compare the extent to which net transfers are related to GDP per capita (as a proxy for poverty), the quality of policy and external debt during the period 1977–1987 and 1988–1998, under high- and low-debt regimes. They find that donors were much more responsive

There is a very high probability that any LDC that exports primary commodities has an unsustainable external debt.

Unsustainable external debt also undermines aid effectiveness.

CHART 42. GROSS OFFICIAL DISBURSEMENTS TO, AND DEBT SERVICE PAYMENTS OF, LDCs,
1997 AND 1998: ALL OFFICIAL CREDITORS[a] AND MULTILATERAL CREDITORS[a]

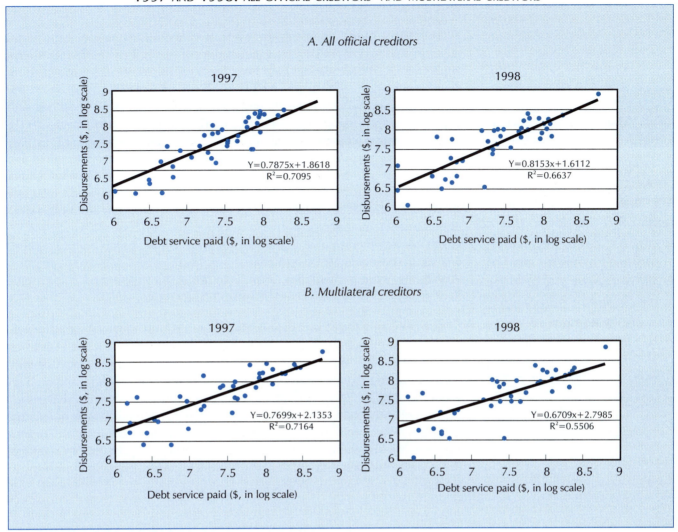

Source: UNCTAD (2000b: chart 42).
a Excluding the IMF.

to the quality of domestic policy and the level of GDP per capita in the low-debt regimes than in the high-debt regimes, and that within the high-debt regimes such responsiveness disappeared in 1988–1998. Within the high multilateral debt regimes, any increase in debt service was being offset by an equivalent increase in aid disbursements. Another study, focusing on 18 sub-Saharan African countries, has estimated that the sum of 31 cents of every additional dollar of grants and concessional loans was used to finance principal repayments of foreign loans, and that as much as 50 cents of every additional dollar of grants was used for the same purpose (Devarajan, Rajkumar and Swaroop, 1999).

The reasons why the "debt-tail" has been wagging the "aid-dog" are various. They include: efforts to mobilize resources to support economic reforms in countries facing debt problems; "defensive lending", i.e. disbursements by official creditors to ensure that debtor countries can continue to service past credits; and "forced lending", which can be attributed to the desire to avoid embarrassing arrears and avert the growing risk of documented development failure (Birdsall, Claessens and Diwan, 2001). But the result is what has been described as "a complex shell game, in which large-scale debt servicing is very imperfectly offset by debt postponements, arrears, new loans and grants from donor governments" (Sachs et al., 1999: 5), a process in which "creditor

The reasons why the "debt-tail" has been wagging the "aid-dog" are various.

governments have been taking away with one hand what they have given with the other" (Killick and Stevens, 1997: 165).

This "debt game" reinforces the cycle of economic stagnation, generalized poverty, slow export growth and external debt. It diminishes the developmental impact of aid, because it subtracts from the level of aid resources available for development purposes. It also adversely affects the quality of aid. From the donors' perspective, it curtails the ability to focus resources on countries with high levels of poverty and good policies (Birdsall, Claessens and Diwan, 2001). From the debtor countries' point of view, the situation is worsened as they become more aid-dependent, in the sense that higher levels of gross aid disbursements are necessary in order to ensure a given positive level of net transfers. Thus, for example in Africa, behind a pattern of high and relatively steady net transfers, there have been large increases in both gross disbursements, increasingly in the form of grants, and debt service payments. Grants have primarily come in the form of projects rather than budget support, and as a consequence Governments have been project-rich and cash-poor. Within this system there has been little room for ownership, and capital formation processes have become dominated by creditor-donors.

In summary, a high level of dependence on a narrow range of unproductive, undynamic and low-value-added commodity exports, an unsustainable external debt burden and enmeshment within the aid/debt service system together characterize the external trade and finance relationships of most commodity-exporting LDCs. These countries are commodity-dependent, debt-relief-dependent and aid-dependent. Each of the elements of this complex of external trade and finance relationships reinforces the other. These external relationships are reinforced by the effects of generalized poverty, and they in turn reinforce the complex of domestic relationships   which cause generalized poverty to persist.

D. The new vulnerabilities of LDCs exporting manufactures and services

Although LDCs which have diversified into manufactures and services are doing better on average than the commodity-exporting LDCs, poverty levels are still unacceptably high when viewed on a global scale. As discussed in the last chapter, poverty levels are still increasing in some. Furthermore, the growth path of these countries remains fragile. The rate of growth of local value-added in production for manufactured exports is much less than the rate of growth of manufactured exports, as production is usually highly dependent on imported inputs (UNCTAD, 2002). Moreover, it is clear that some of the ways in which international primary commodity trade is associated with poverty can also apply to international trade in manufactures and services.

It is apparent that LDCs exporting manufactures have, like those exporting commodities, experienced the adverse effects of falling terms of trade in recent years. The possibility that simultaneous export expansion by developing countries in labour-intensive manufactures, in a situation where industrialized countries continue to protect their own markets and are failing to move out of low-skill products, will drive down the returns from manufactured exports is discussed in depth in UNCTAD (2002). The only study which examines trends in the terms of trade of manufactured goods for LDCs shows that there has been a significant deterioration in the terms of trade of manufactured goods (Maizels et al., 1998).

This "debt game" reinforces the cycle of economic stagnation, generalized poverty, slow export growth and external debt. It diminishes the developmental impact of aid, because it subtracts from the level of aid resources available for development purposes. It also adversely affects the quality of aid.

Although LDCs which have diversified into manufactures and services are doing better on average than the commodity-exporting LDCs, poverty levels are still unacceptably high when viewed on a global scale.

The LDCs exporting manufactures also tend to have a narrow export base which is concentrated in low-skill products, generally clothing and accessories, with few backward linkages within the domestic economy. In Bangladesh, where impressive and sustained falls in the poverty rate have occurred in association with the diversification out of commodities and into manufactures, over 85 per cent of the exports were concentrated in clothing and accessories in 1997–1999. All the LDCs exporting manufactures focus on low-skill activities (see table 26, in chapter 3) and compete mainly on the basis of costs. A particular cause for concern is that imports of machinery and equipment, which are a major channel of technology transfer, are also generally as low as in commodity-exporting LDCs. As table 37 shows, machinery and equipment imports as a percentage of GDP were less than 2 per cent of GDP in the period 1996–1998 in Bangladesh, Haiti, Myanmar and Nepal, and were at levels which were less than half those of other developing countries.

The LDCs exporting manufactures also tend to have a narrow export base which is concentrated in low-skill products, generally clothing and accessories, with few backward linkages within the domestic economy.

All this implies that LDCs exporting manufactures are particularly vulnerable to competition from other low-cost suppliers. A specific issue for LDCs exporting textiles and garments is that exports have traditionally been heavily regulated under the Multi-Fibre Arrangement (MFA), and cost-based competition for simple manufactures will become intense as these regulations are ended. Textiles and garments exports from LDCs have expanded on the basis of quotas within markets of industrialized countries under the MFA. In the Uruguay Round (1994) it was decided to phase out these restrictions by 2005, along with the reduction of non-tariff barriers. The WTO Agreement on Textiles and Clothing stipulates that trade in this sector should be completely free from quantitative restrictions and governed by normal GATT rules. Following the phasing out of the MFA in 2005, the textiles and garments industry in LDCs will face much stiffer competition, greater challenges and more stringent quality requirements.

Competition with producers in China, which currently accounts for over 20 per cent of global market shares, is a major concern of LDC producers. This is heightened by continuing tariff peaks in industrial country markets. While quantitative restrictions on textiles will end on 31 December 2004, there will be a safeguard mechanism in place until the end of 2008 permitting WTO member States to take action to curb imports in the event of market disruptions. But unless the LDC exporters of manufactures can develop and improve their own domestic supply capabilities, upgrade their productive capacities and acquire new skills in textile garments and sustainable economic activities in the future (see Mortimore, 1999), there could well be a reversal of recent progress in poverty reduction.

TABLE 37. MACHINERY AND EQUIPMENT IMPORTS AS A SHARE OF GDP[a]
(Percentage)

	1981–1983	1987–1989	1996–1998
Bangladesh	3.35	1.17	1.55
Haiti	12.69	2.58	1.84
Madagascar	5.91	2.56	2.06
Myanmar	10.54	0.98	0.31
Nepal	3.21	1.69	1.75
LDCs	6.95	2.09	1.23
Other developing countries	8.46	3.05	3.80
Other low-income countries	5.76	1.93	2.60

Source: UNCTAD secretariat estimates, based on Mayer (2001).

a Based on 35 LDCs and 56 other developing countries for which data are available.

For LDCs that export services, the issue of sustainability of recent trends is rather different. For tourism, the key service export for LDCs, the sustainability of the activity depends critically on the quality of natural resources. Destinations are remote, and they are thus subject to cost increases in the airline industry. Moreover, tourist revenues are particularly vulnerable to fluctuations in demand and changes in fashion. The recent reversal of fortunes in some island LDCs indicates the fragility of their progress.

E. Is globalization tightening the international poverty trap?

An important question is whether the current form of globalization is tightening the poverty trap and also increasing the vulnerabilities of those countries that appear to be escaping it. This is a complex issue which requires policy-oriented research in the future. Here the main concern will be to identify the main channels through which globalization can act to either tighten or loosen the poverty trap, and to give some indications of the nature of the relationships. Globalization will be understood as the increasing flow of goods and resources across national borders and as the emergence of a complementary set of organizational and institutional structures to manage the expanding network of international economic activity and transactions. The question of what is the appropriate national policy to harness potential positive effects of globalization and to minimize potential negative effects, including the way in which integration should be managed and the role of economic liberalization, will be deferred until the next chapter.

1. POTENTIAL FORCES LOOSENING THE TRAP

There are four major channels through which international economic relationships can help LDCs to break out of the poverty trap.

Firstly, the expanded access to foreign savings associated with increased international flows of capital provides an opportunity for poor countries to break out of the low-level equilibrium of low incomes, low domestic savings and low investment. Given the resource constraints associated with generalized extreme absolute poverty, an injection of external resources has historically almost invariably been necessary in order to catalyse take-off. Moreover, once growth starts and is sustained, foreign savings permit a faster rate of growth of private consumption without the degree of belt-tightening which would be necessary if growth were financed wholly through domestic savings.

Secondly, generalized poverty implies that national demand is very limited, and national markets tend to be undynamic and usually segmented in ways which enable people to survive. Exporting to international markets enables land and labour resources, hitherto underutilized owing to domestic demand constraints, to be productively mobilized. Local producers in LDCs can also break the constraint of small national markets on the scale of operations, and realize rates of growth far exceeding those possible through domestic demand. The increased participation of countries in international trade should also increase the efficiency of economies through specialization and the furthering of the division of labour. In addition, there will be added benefits from the discipline of increased competition, if domestic producers can survive.

An important question is whether the current form of globalization is tightening the poverty trap and also increasing the vulnerabilities of those countries that appear to be escaping it.

There are four major channels through which international economic relationships can help LDCs to break out of the poverty trap: access to foreign savings, international trade, access to available modern technologies, and international migration.

Thirdly, increased access to available modern technologies enables latecomer economies to realize significant productivity increases without having continually to reinvent. Exporting can facilitate this because a major channel for technology transfer to poor countries is through imports of machinery and transport equipment which are constrained by limited foreign exchange earnings. Foreign direct investment can also serve as an important channel for technology acquisition under the right circumstances.

Fourthly, increased international migration enables poor people in poor countries to find employment even if opportunities are limited in their own country. Emigration can relieve population pressure on scarce resources such as land. Remittances can also provide an important national source of foreign exchange to the countries from which migrants originate, and boost the consumption of household and local community members left behind.

The globalization of production and finance could help to break the poverty trap if it helps LDCs to benefit from these channels of growth and poverty reduction. But globalization is a highly uneven process, both geographically and functionally. Given continued restrictions on international migration, particularly of unskilled labour, individuals exercising the emigration option to escape poverty generally make a choice between poverty at home, and social exclusion, as an illegal immigrant or second-class citizen, abroad. Moreover, many LDCs are marginalized from those aspects of globalization that are potentially beneficial.

The LDCs are generally marginalized from expanding international capital flows and from the diffusion of technology, through FDI and machinery and equipment imports.

We have already seen that primary-commodity-exporting LDCs are increasingly marginalized in international trade. Available evidence also shows that the LDCs are generally marginalized from expanding international capital flows and from the diffusion of technology, through FDI and machinery and equipment imports. The LDC share of total long-term net capital flows to all developing countries fell from 18 per cent in 1987 to about 5 per cent in 2000 (chart 43). The LDC share of net FDI inflows to all developing countries fell from 3.9 per cent in 1975–1982 to 2.1 per cent in 1994–2000. With regard to technology transfer, the evidence for one potential channel shows that the LDC share of total machinery and equipment imports to all developing countries fell from 5 per cent in 1982 to 1.8 per cent in 1998 (chart 44).

CHART 43. LDCs' SHARE OF LONG-TERM NET CAPITAL INFLOWS INTO ALL DEVELOPING COUNTRIES, 1970–2000

(Percentage)

Source: UNCTAD secretariat estimates based on World Bank, *Global Development Finance 2002*, on-line data.

CHART 44. LDCs' SHARE OF TOTAL MACHINERY AND EQUIPMENT IMPORTS BY DEVELOPING COUNTRIES, 1970–1998
(Percentage)

Source: UNCTAD secretariat estimates based on Mayer (2001).

Note: The sample includes 35 LDCs and 56 other developing countries for which data are available.

2. FORCES TIGHTENING THE TRAP: DIRECT EFFECTS

The geographical unevenness of globalization, and the marginalization of many LDCs, particularly commodity-dependent LDCs, from expanding global capital and trade flows and the diffusion of technology, have led some to conclude that LDCs are "outside the globalization process", and that their problem is "not a matter of too much globalisation but too little" (Barnevik, 2001: 37). But this is too simplistic. The current situation of LDCs is best seen as one in which they are marginalized from some potentially positive aspects of globalization and are at the same time experiencing some of the negative aspects.

Two processes, both little understood, are relevant here. The first is the way in which globalization is changing the world commodity economy and the impact of this on the development opportunities of LDCs. The second is the way in which changes in more advanced developing countries associated with globalization are having indirect effects on the development opportunities of LDCs.

With regard to recent changes in the world commodity economy, UNCTAD's work has highlighted a number of changes that have taken place in commodity production and distribution chains, particularly for agricultural products, which are associated with globalization and which are contributing to the diminishing share of LDCs in world commodity exports. What is happening can be reviewed at three levels, namely the international markets, developing commodity-exporting countries and importing countries. But the common denominator of all three is a closer integration of international trade and production through the penetration of large transnationals and distribution companies, such as supermarket chains, into the agricultural supply structures of developing (and developed) countries. A few decades ago, the dominance of large companies in the world commodity economy was principally due to their actions in international markets. Now, increasingly, it is also due to their direct

The current situation of LDCs is best seen as one in which they are marginalized from some potentially positive aspects of globalization and are at the same time experiencing some of the negative aspects.

influence on what is produced, and how. While unprecedented opportunities may be opening up for some producers and exporters, benefiting from this trend and avoiding its negative impacts require that developing country Governments and entrepreneurs have much greater business skills than before.

At the international level, there is a continuing concentration of trade and vertical integration of large firms. Mergers and acquisitions have led to dramatic reductions in the number of firms with significant market shares of commodities such as coffee, cocoa, vegetable oils and grains. Another important change is the disappearance of traders, who once acted as a bridge between buyers and sellers who were largely ignorant of each other and of prices, communications technology, including the Internet, having now closed this gap. Buyers and sellers can find each other much more easily and communicate instantaneously, increasing competition and cutting profit margins for traders. Intensified competition favours those with access to cheaper finance and good logistics. Being big provides advantages on both accounts. With deregulation and the disappearance of marketing boards, large companies with warehousing and shipping facilities in the producing countries are able to exploit their financial and logistical advantages, even buying the produce directly from the farmer.[8] The current setting is characterized by the need for greater capital resources, sophisticated technology, including information technology, and human skills for competing in the more open but more sophisticated markets. Developed country firms are clearly at an advantage in all these respects.

At the level of commodity-exporting developing countries, liberalization, in particular the dismantling of marketing boards, has had three main consequences in terms of market structure. First, large numbers of atomized traders initially emerged but many were later eliminated under intense competition, mainly owing to lack of business skills, but also owing to difficulties with access to finance. Those that survive often have links with foreign firms. This helps them not only in market entry but also with securing finance. Second, the commodity sector was opened up to direct participation by foreign firms that deal with exporters, generally much smaller than themselves, and at times directly with producers. Third, the reduction of import barriers affected local production patterns. Imported processed products, mostly with well-known brand names and often sold through foreign-owned supermarkets, have made important gains in developing countries at the expense of locally produced items (box 13). It should be noted here that agricultural subsidies in developed countries play an important role in bolstering the competitiveness of those countries' agricultural exporters. In 2000, total agricultural support[9] in OECD countries amounted to $327 billion. This is to say that just under two-weeks' worth of total agricultural support in OECD countries was equivalent to the total net ODA disbursements (including imputed multilateral flows) from OECD/DAC members to all the LDCs in the year 2000.

In 2000, total agricultural support in OECD countries amounted to $327 billion. This is to say that just under two-weeks' worth of total agricultural support in OECD countries was equivalent to the total net ODA disbursements from OECD/DAC members to all the LDCs in the year 2000.

Within importing countries, an important development in terms of market structure has been the growth of the modern retailing sector, particularly supermarkets. This has had little effect on bulk products that go through considerable transformation before reaching consumers. But for many dynamic food products, however, there is general agreement that it is the single most influential factor affecting changing conditions of supply and demand. For exporters of such "non-traditional" commodities as fresh fruit and vegetables, large retailers have provided important market access channels. Links with supermarkets provide producers with access to a growing market as well as incentives to improve quality and efficiency. Nevertheless, for many producers and exporters this is obtained at the expense of dependence on a single

Box 13. SUBSIDIZED EXPORTS AND WEST AFRICAN TOMATOES

After the United States and before Turkey, the world's second largest producer of tomato concentrate is the EU. Its tomato farmers are paid a minimum price higher than the world market price, which stimulates production. The processors, in turn, are paid a subsidy to cover the difference between domestic and world prices.

Some of the effects of these subsidies on West African LDCs in the 1990s have been documented. The subsidy is reported to have reached about $300 million in 1997. The processors, then, need to find markets, and about 20 per cent of exports at that time went to West Africa. In the mid-1990s, about 80 per cent of demand in this region was covered by tomato products from the EU, which were cheaper than local supplies. Stiff competition from EU industries led to the closure of tomato-processing plants in several West African countries.

In Senegal, for instance, tomato cultivation was introduced in the 1970s, and progressively acquired an important position for farmers, for whom tomato production was synonymous with a key opportunity to diversify their farming systems and stabilize incomes. In 1990–1991, production of tomato concentrate was 73,000 tons, and Senegal exported concentrate to its neighbours. Over the past seven years, total production has fallen to less than 20,000 tons. One of the main reasons for this dramatic fall was the liberalization of tomato concentrate imports in 1994. Despite the positive impetus provided by the devaluation of the CFA franc, the tomato-processing industry could not compete with EU exporters. Imports of concentrates jumped from 62 tons in 1994 (value: $0.1 million) to 5,130 tons in 1995 (value: $4.8 million) and 5,348 tons in 1996 (value: $3.8 million). SOCAS, the one Senegalese processing firm that has survived, buys imported triple concentrate and processes it into double concentrate. Other West African LDCs — Burkina Faso and Mali — have had similar experience of enormous increases in imports of EU tomato concentrate. Gambia, small as it is, imports even more tomato concentrate than Senegal, and consumption of concentrate is increasingly replacing that of fresh tomatoes.

The lack of credit, and low prices, have contributed to the stagnation of West African tomato-processing industries. If there is to be any hope of competitiveness, factories in the region will need new machines and massive investments. Foreign investment could be one option, but these factories will not interest potential foreign investors as long as the European products dominate the local markets.

Source: EUROSTAT: Eurostep Dossier on CAP and Coherence (www.oneworld.org/eurostep/cap.htm).

Even if LDCs have improved market access (in terms of reduced government restrictions), they will not effectively be able to enter markets if they cannot connect up to global commodity chains.

supermarket or importer in a given country for marketing, product innovation and technical assistance. An important consequence of the growth and internationalization of supermarkets has been increasing global brand-name recognition. As product attributes become more and more psychological, the importance of expenditures on advertising and related activities is increasing. This puts developing country traders at a disadvantage and contributes to concentration in the commodity economy. It is very difficult for developing country exporters to differentiate their products and establish new brand names to compete with the existing globally accepted ones.

The full effects of these trends in the international commodity economy in the LDCs are not well known. But one major danger is the potential for the increasing exclusion of many LDCs from global markets as buyers within commodity chains upgrade their volume and quality criteria for purchasing. Whether or not this phenomenon is occurring is an extremely important issue. Even if LDCs have improved market access (in terms of reduced government restrictions), they will not effectively be able to enter markets if they cannot connect up to global commodity chains.

There is little empirical evidence on this phenomenon; however, to become or remain "interesting" to international buyers, suppliers and supplying locations have to match certain price, volume and reliability criteria over the short to medium term. The reliability criterion has been a particular problem for landlocked LDCs owing to the risks and uncertainties of transit transport systems. Also, it is likely that LDCs may face difficulties because of volume criteria. For example, it has been reported that coffee traders now use a national production level of one million (60 kilogram) bags/year as a world market entry qualification for non-premium suppliers (Economist Intelligence Unit, 1999: 2, reported in Gibbon, 2001). It is also clear that, in general, commodity producers and processors need increasingly large amounts of finance to compete in world markets. Modern technological advances provide considerable economies of scale in processing, but call for large investments in processing plants. For example, large crushing facilities are considered a necessity for competitiveness in the vegetable oils sector. More stringent market requirements call for ever larger investments to meet buyers' quality requirements and specifications.[10] These conditions are, naturally, to the disadvantage of small producers, who need either to organize themselves into larger cooperative entities or to seek links with foreign firms that would extend the necessary finance and know-how. Large investments by Governments are also necessary in order to meet market exigencies. Although such investments often take the form of institutional and technical support, direct investment may be necessary as well.

Another consequence of recent changes in market structure is the increasing gap between international prices and consumer prices. This is associated with the continuing concentration of trade and the vertical integration of large firms. Several recent studies have found that in developed countries the spread between international prices, or import prices, and domestic retail prices first widened in the early 1970s and then widened at an accelerated rate in the 1980s (Morisset, 1998). Since import taxes as well as domestic logistic costs have fallen, the only factors that can explain this tendency are the relative weight and growth of other marketing and distribution costs in the value-adding process beyond the import price, or the market power of intermediary companies. A review of the coffee markets by the UNCTAD secretariat has shown that in countries where concentration in the coffee market is greater, the gap between international and retail prices has increased more than that in countries where the concentration is low. The clear implication of all this is that the producing countries obtain a decreasing proportion of the retail value of the final product. Moreover, this tendency, and the asymmetry just mentioned, have worked against potential increases in consumption that could have been generated had retail prices declined with international prices (United Nations, 2000).

Another effect of recent trends in the structure of the global commodity economy is increasing price instability, which is associated with increasingly close links between financial and commodity markets. The liquidity of commodity futures markets, combined with their large fluctuations, can make them attractive to investors who are drawn by the potentially large gains and not deterred by the correspondingly large risks of losses. The deployment of ever larger amounts of speculative funds has contributed to the increasing instability of commodity prices, although it does not change market fundamentals.

Finally, a number of observers have pointed out that the debt crisis of the 1980s led to supply-side pressures on real commodity prices, including through simultaneous structural adjustment in a large number of producing countries (see, for example, Bleaney, 1993; Spraos, 1993; Lutz and Singer, 1994). As one observer has put it,

> "A global policy shift in the developing world toward greater outward orientation may depress the price of agricultural commodities and hence worsen the terms of trade of developing countries. The direct effects of this are likely to be small, but the indirect effect working through a tightening of the balance-of-payments constraints could be of considerable significance and may entirely offset the expected gains from trade liberalisation...For low-income countries, particularly those heavily

More stringent market requirements call for ever larger investments to meet buyers' quality requirements and specifications.

In countries where concentration in the coffee market is greater, the gap between international and retail prices has increased more than that in countries where the concentration is low.

dependent on agricultural exports, global liberalisation is likely to bring about a tightening of their import capacity constraints. Evidence for SAL [structural adjustment lending] programmes indicates that it is difficult to realise dynamic gains from liberalisation in these circumstances. Even after allowing for the burden of adjustment, countries with SALs do not succeed in raising their growth rates or investment rates above what they would otherwise have been according to the evidence to date. Because of this we should not be too surprised if the gains from global liberalisation are disappointing in many low-income countries" (Bleaney, 1993: 463–464).

The basis of this concern is that if several developing countries expand their exports simultaneously, they will experience a decline in their terms of trade. This is not an academic matter.[11] World Bank research has shown that this adding-up problem (or fallacy of composition) affects a number of agricultural commodities, notably bananas, cocoa, coffee, cotton, tea and tobacco (World Bank, 1996: 50). Moreover, other analysts have added copper, oil and vanilla to this list (Schiff, 1995: 603). Omitting bananas, oil and vanilla, these commodities constituted 42 per cent of the total non-fuel primary commodity exports of LDCs in 1997–1999.

3. Forces tightening the trap: indirect effects

Globalization affects LDCs not simply directly, but also through the way it influences more advanced developing countries, and then in turn has secondary effects on LDCs. The relationships between more advanced developing countries and LDCs are very important to the development prospects of the latter. These relationships can be mutually supportive or competitive.

They can be mutually supportive as the more advanced developing countries could offer an important market for LDC exports. Outward FDI from these countries could, with the appropriate policies, also provide a source of know-how and investment funds for the LDCs, acting at the same time as a mechanism for production upgrading in the more advanced developing countries. Political stability within proximate LDCs is also vital for sustained growth in more advanced developing countries. Economic collapse in the LDCs can precipitate destabilizing regional population movements.

But there are also competitive relationships. In particular, LDCs and other developing countries can be competing in third markets both for commodities and for manufactures. These competitive relationships are heightened if the more advanced developing countries find it difficult to deepen industrialization and move up the technological ladder and out of simpler products being exported by the poorer countries. To the extent that more advanced developing countries meet a "glass ceiling" which blocks their development, there will be increasing competition between LDCs and other developing countries. Globalization tightens the poverty trap within LDCs if it creates such a "glass ceiling" for more advanced developing countries.

Recent trends in global inequality remain a matter of controversy. However, it is generally agreed that only a few developing countries have grown fast enough to substantially reduce the income gap with — and rapidly converge towards — the advanced industrial economies. Moreover, there is increasing polarization in the global economy since the middle strata of developing countries, namely those with incomes between 40 and 80 per cent of the average in the advanced countries, are thinner than in the 1970s (UNCTAD,

It can be estimated that the adding-up problem (or fallacy of composition) affected 42 per cent of the total non-fuel primary commodity exports of LDCs in 1997–1999.

To the extent that more advanced developing countries meet a "glass ceiling" which blocks their development, there will be increasing competition between LDCs and other developing countries. Globalization tightens the poverty trap within LDCs if it creates such a "glass ceiling" for more advanced developing countries.

1997a). This is occurring because at the richer end of international income distribution there is a process of convergence upwards since the relatively poorer countries within the club of industrialized OECD countries (e.g. Ireland) have experienced faster growth rates than the richest countries, whilst at the poorer end of international income distribution there is a process of convergence downwards as some of the richer poor countries experience economic regression. According to the IMF (1997: 78), "the forces of polarization seem to have become stronger since the early 1980s".

These trends imply that many of the more advanced developing countries are facing problems with deepening industrialization and moving up the technological ladder. Various issues of UNCTAD's *Trade and Development Report* in the 1990s showed how asymmetries in the international system, together with global financial instability associated with the globalization of finance, are creating this situation. As a result, it is most likely that this is making the relationship between the more advanced developing countries and the LDCs competitive rather than complementary.

It is highly likely that increasing polarization in the global economy is intensifying the cycle of stagnation and poverty in the poorest countries.

Heightened competition with other exporters of low-skill manufactures is a major process increasing the vulnerability of those LDCs that are seeking to escape the poverty trap by diversification out of commodities. But commodity-exporting LDCs are also affected by what is happening in more advanced developing countries. This is perhaps clearest in the effects of financial crises in emerging markets on the world commodity economy and thus on LDCs. The financial crises of the 1990s, which were associated with the globalization of finance, affected world commodity markets by acting on both the supply and the demand side. Before the Asian crisis in 1997–1998, demand for commodities had been growing rapidly in Asia over the previous two decades, but imports were severely curtailed as a result of the crisis as economic activity declined. At the same time, exports of some products increased, often in response to currency devaluations. The combination of these trends aggravated the cyclical decline in prices which had begun in 1995. This has been particularly difficult for LDCs owing to low productivity and the inability to offset falling prices with increased productivity.

It is thus highly likely that increasing polarization in the global economy is intensifying the cycle of stagnation and poverty in the poorest countries. To the extent that the current form of globalization — uneven, asymmetrical and under-managed — is leading to polarization, it is likely that it is tightening the international poverty trap within which many LDCs are stuck.

F. Conclusion

There is no inevitable relationship between primary commodity dependence and poverty.

This chapter has argued that extreme poverty is persistent and pervasive in non-oil commodity exporting LDCs because they are caught in an international poverty trap. There is no inevitable relationship between primary commodity dependence and poverty. But commodity exporting LDCs have a low-productivity, low-value-added and weakly competitive commodity sector that is generally concentrated on a narrow range of products serving declining or sluggish international markets. The weakness of the primary commodity sector is rooted in the wider problem of low investment and low productivity that is characteristic of situations of generalized poverty. The pattern of export specialization is in turn associated with slow export growth, relatively large terms-of-trade shocks, the build-up of unsustainable external debts, high levels of aid dependence and enmeshment within an aid/debt service system. This

This negative complex of external trade and finance relationships reinforces the domestic vicious circles that cause generalized poverty to persist within many LDCs. Together, these domestic and external relationships create an international poverty trap.

The current form of globalization is tightening the international poverty trap of commodity exporting LDCs and intensifying the vulnerabilities of new exporters of manufactures and services.

negative complex of external trade and finance relationships reinforces the domestic vicious circles that cause generalized poverty to persist within many LDCs. At the same time, the domestic effects of generalized poverty — on savings, investment, productivity, State capacities and corporate capacities — reinforce the negative complex of external trade and finance relationships. Together, these domestic and external relationships create an international poverty trap.

Although LDCs which have diversified out of commodity production generally have a lower incidence of poverty than commodity-dependent LDCs, and in some poverty has been declining, there is no iron law that poor countries which have export specializations in manufacturing and services will be guaranteed income growth and poverty reduction. Poverty levels in LDCs which have managed to diversify out of commodity production are still high by international standards. Moreover, those countries remain vulnerable in that their export success has often been built on low-skill activities in areas where there is intense competition, their export structures are highly dependent on only a few types of product and they face the danger of erosion of special preferences, particularly in the field of textiles and garments.

Finally, it is clear that intensified external relationships of the right kind can have a major role to play in helping LDCs to escape the poverty trap. But it seems likely that the current form of globalization is tightening the international poverty trap of commodity exporting LDCs and intensifying the vulnerabilities of new exporters of manufactures and services. This is happening because LDCs are generally marginalized from aspects of globalization which are potentially beneficial, and are also adversely affected by aspects which may be detrimental. A particularly worrying trend is the association of globalization with the polarization of the world economy. This will make it more difficult to have beneficial subregional and regional relationships which can help countries to break out of the trap. The problem of persistent pervasive poverty in LDCs is not simply a matter of marginalization, but also of the polarization of the world economy.

Notes

1. As in the last chapter, commodity exporting LDCs refer to those countries in which primary commodities constitute over 50 per cent of total exports of goods and services.
2. Resource windfalls associated with commodity price booms have not been well managed in the past, particularly in Africa. But despite this, positive commodity price shocks generally have been found to have positive or neutral effects on growth (Deaton and Miller, 1995; Deaton, 1999). For further discussion of the effects of terms of trade volatility and shocks in Africa, see Bleaney and Greenaway (2001) and Khose and Riezman (2001).
3. The terms "real commodity prices" and "commodity terms of trade" are used interchangeably through this chapter to denote the ratio of non-fuel commodity prices to the prices of manufactured goods.
4. The export value deflated by the unit value of exports of manufactured goods from developing countries.
5. Estimates of the foreign exchange loss resulting from the change in the commodity terms of trade during these periods can by made by deducting the value of commodity exports from developing countries at 1986 prices for any given year from the corresponding value of the purchasing power of these exports in terms of the prices of manufactured goods exported by the industrialized countries.
6. The relative prices of exports and imports for a country.
7. The link between commodity dependence and the debt problem is analysed in further detail in Nissanke and Ferrarini (2001).
8. Improved logistics also allows large firms to buy increasingly on a just-in-time basis, thus reducing the cost of holding stocks and shifting the burden of such finance backwards.

Chocolate companies, for example, which used to hold inventories covering a year or more, have reduced this coverage to as little as four months.

9. Total support estimates (TSE) is "the annual monetary value of all gross transfers from taxpayers and consumers arising from policy measures which support agriculture, net of associated budgetary receipts", and producer support is "the annual monetary value of gross transfers from consumers and taxpayers to agricultural producers, measured at farmgate level, arising from policy measures regardless of their nature, objectives or impacts on farm production and income" (OECD, 2001: 271).

10. For stringent market requirements, see UNCTAD (1997b).

11. For discussion of this issue in relation to commodities, see Akiyama and Larson (1994), Schiff (1995), and Sapsford and Singer (1998), and in relation to exports of manufactures, see UNCTAD (2002).

References

Akiyama, T. and Larson, D.F. (1994). The adding-up problem: strategies of primary commodity exports in sub-Saharan Africa, Policy Research Working Paper No. 1245, World Bank, Washington DC.

Barnevik, P. (2001). Globalisation debate — growth spur, *World Link*, September/ October, 36–38.

Birdsall. N., Claessens, S. and Diwan, I. (2001). Will HIPC matter?: the debt game and donor behaviour in Africa, Carnegie Endowment for International Peace, Discussion Paper No. 3.

Bleaney, M. (1993). Liberalisation and the terms of trade of developing countries: a cause for concern?, *World Economy*, 16 (4): 453–467.

Bleaney, M. and Greenaway, D. (2001). The impact of terms of trade and real exchange rate volatility on investment and growth in sub-Saharan Africa, *Journal of Development Economics*, 65: 491–500.

Bloch, H. and Sapsford, D. (1997). Some estimates of Prebisch and Singer effects on the terms of trade between primary producers and manufacturers, *World Development*, 25 (11): 1873–1884.

Boratav, K. (2001). Movements of relative agricultural prices in sub-Saharan Africa, *Cambridge Journal of Economics*, 25 (3): 395–417.

Cashin, P. and McDermott, C.J. (2001). The long-run behaviour of commodity prices: small trends and big variability, IMF Working Paper WP/01/68, IMF, Washington DC.

Deaton, A. (1999). Commodity prices and growth in Africa, *Journal of Economic Perspectives*, 13 (3): 23–40.

Deaton, A. and Miller, R. (1995). International commodity prices, macroeconomic performance, politics in sub-Saharan Africa, Princeton Studies in International Finance No. 79, Princeton, New Jersey.

Dehn, J. (2000a). The effects on growth of commodity price uncertainty and shocks, Policy Research Working Paper 2455, World Bank, Washington DC.

Dehn, J. (2000b). Private investment in developing countries: the effects of commodity shocks and uncertainty, WPS/2000-11, Centre for the Study of African Economies, Department of Economics, University of Oxford, Oxford.

Devarajan, S., Rajkumar, A.S. and Swaroop, V. (1999). What does aid to African finance? Policy Research Working Paper 2092, World Bank, Washington DC.

Gibbon, P. (2001). Upgrading primary production: a global commodity chain approach, *World Development*, 29 (2): 345–363.

Herrmann, M. and David, M. (2001). Recent price changes in primary commodities, 1998–2000: implications for least developed countries. Background report for *The Least Developed Countries Report 2002*.

International Monetary Fund (IMF) (1997). *World Economic Outlook*, May 1997 — Globalization: Opportunities and Challenges, IMF, Washington, DC.

International Coffee Organization (2001). Review of the coffee market situation, September 2001, International Coffee Council, Eighty-fourth Session, 26–28 September 2001, London.

International Trade Centre UNCTAD/WTO (ITC) (1999). Export Performance of Least Developed Countries: Country Profiles, Geneva.

International Trade Centre UNCTAD/WTO (ITC) (2001a). LDCs' export success stories (summaries), report prepared for the Business Sector Round Table, Third United Nations Conference on the Least Developed Countries, Brussels, 16 May 2001.

International Trade Centre UNCTAD/WTO (ITC) (2001b). *Converting LDC Export Opportunities into Business: A Strategic Response*, United Nations publication, sales no. E.01.III.T.8, Geneva.

Kanbur, R. (2000). Aid, conditionality and debt in Africa. In Tarp, F., ed., *Foreign Aid and Development: Lessons Learnt and Directions for the Future*, Routledge, London.

Khose, M.A. and Riezman, R. (2001). Trade shocks and macroeconomic fluctuations in Africa, *Journal of Development Economics*, 65: 55–80.

Killick, T. and Stevens, S. (1997). Assessing the efficiency of mechanisms for dealing with debt problems of low-income countries. In: Iqbal, Z. and Kanbur, R., eds., *External Finance for Low-income countries*, IMF Institute, Washington DC.

Lutz, M. and Singer, H. (1994). The link between increased trade openness and the terms of trade: an empirical investigation, *World Development*, 22 (11): 1697–1709.

Maizels, A. (1992). *Commodities in Crisis: The Commodity Crisis of the 1980s and the Political Economy of International Commodity Prices*, Clarendon Press, Oxford.

Maizels, A., Berge, K., Crowe, T. and Palaskas, T.B. (1998). Trends in the manufactures terms of trade of developing countries, mimeo, Queen Elizabeth House, University of Oxford, Oxford.

Mayer, J. (2001). Technology diffusion, human capital and economic growth in developing countries, UNCTAD Discussion Paper, No.154, Geneva.

Megzari, A. (2001). Problems and opportunities of commodity diversifcation for the LDCs, paper presented at the joint UNCTAD/CFC workshop on "Enhancing productive capacities and diversification of commodities in LDCs and South-South cooperation", 22–23 March 2001, Geneva.

Mendoza, R. (2001). Terms of trade and inequality in the gains from trade: an empirical analysis, mimeo, UNDP Office of Development Studies, New York.

Morrisset, J. (1998): Unfair trade? The increasing gap between world and domestic prices in commodity markets during the past 25 years. *World Bank Economic Review*, 12 (3) World Bank, Washington DC.

Mortimore, M. (1999). Apparel-based industrialization in the Caribbean Basin: a threadbare garment?, *CEPAL Review*, 67:119–136.

Nissanke, M. and Ferrarini, B. (2001). Debt dynamics and contingency financing: theoretical reappraisal of the HIPC Initiative, paper prepared for the UNU/WIDER Development Conference on Debt Relief, 17–18 August, 2001, Helsinki.

OECD (2001). Agricultural policies in OECD countries: monitoring and evaluation. OECD, Paris.

Reinhardt, N. (2000). Back to basics in Malaysia and Thailand: the role of resource-based exports in their export-led growth, *World Development*, 28 (1): 57–77.

Sachs, J. et al. (1999). Implementing debt relief for HIPCs, Centre for International Development, Harvard University, mimeo.

Sapsford, D. (2001). The terms of trade of the world's poorest countries, mimeo, background note prepared for The Least Developed Countries Report 2002.

Sapsford, D. and Singer, H. (1998). The IMF, the World Bank and commodity prices: a case of shifting sands?, *World Development*, 26 (9): 1653–1660.

Schiff, M. (1995). Commodity exports and the adding-up problem in LDCs: trade, investment and lending policy, *World Development*, 23 (4): 603–615.

Spraos, J. (1993). The terms of trade and the foreign debt of developing countries. Chapter 2 in Nissanke, M. and Hewitt, A., eds., *Economic Crisis in Developing Countries: New Perspectives on Commodities, Trade and Finance*, Pinter Publishers, London and New York.

UNCTAD (1997a). *Trade and Development Report, 1997,* United Nations publication, sales no. E.97.II.D.6, Geneva.

UNCTAD (1997b). Opportunities for vertical diversification in the food processing sector in developing countries, TD/B/COM.1/EM.2/2, 23 June 1997, Geneva.

UNCTAD (1999). *The Least Developed Countries 1999 Report*, United Nations publication, sales no. E.99.II.2, Geneva.

UNCTAD (2000a). Economic Development in Africa: Performance, Prospects and Policy Issues, United Nations, New York and Geneva.

UNCTAD (2000b). *The Least Developed Countries 2000 Report*, United Nations publication, sales no. E.00.II.D.21, Geneva.

UNCTAD (2002). *Trade and Development Report, 2002*, United Nations publication, sales no. E.02.II.D.2, Geneva.

United Nations (2000). World commodity trends and prospects, A/55/332.

Varangis, P. Akiyama, T. and Mitchell, D. (1995). Managing commodity booms and busts, Directions in Development Series, World Bank, Washington DC.

Wood, A. and Mayer, J. (1998). Africa's export structure in a comparative perspective, Study No. 4, African Development in Comparative Perspective, UNCTAD, Geneva.

World Bank (1996). *Global Economic Prospects and the Developing Countries*, World Bank, Washington DC.

National development strategies, the PRSP process and effective poverty reduction

A. Introduction

The point of describing both the incidence and the depth of poverty in the LDCs, and also the main elements of an international poverty trap in which most of them are caught, is not to promote pessimism, but rather to obtain a realistic diagnosis of the policies which are required to reduce poverty in the LDCs. As argued in chapter 2, there are major opportunities for the rapid reduction of poverty in the LDCs through sustained economic growth and development. The critical policy issue is what national and international policies are required in order to enable LDCs to escape the poverty trap and realize those opportunities.

In recent years there has been much greater international recognition that many of the poorest developing countries are trapped in a cycle of stagnation and poverty, and have been unable to benefit from globalization. At the end of the 1990s, there was a radical rethinking by the IMF, the World Bank and the OECD/DAC of the national and international policies needed to tackle the problems of poor countries which were failing to prosper and where poverty rates were persistently high. This rethinking had its origins in the broad consensus that unsustainable external debt was acting as a major impediment to growth and poverty reduction, and in the elaboration of the enhanced HIPC Initiative as a response to this problem. But a new approach has been introduced which has gone far beyond debt relief.

The new approach, which is still evolving, has five key elements. Firstly, poverty reduction has been adopted as a central objective of international development cooperation. Secondly, national Governments will take responsibility for poverty reduction within their countries by developing nationally owned poverty reduction strategies. National ownership means that policies should be domestically formulated and implemented, rather than driven by donors or imposed by the IMF or the World Bank, and that the Government should develop policies through participatory processes which involve national stakeholders and, more generally, civil society. Thirdly, donor countries, which are also the main creditors of indebted poor countries, will selectively focus their aid and debt relief on those countries that have good poverty reduction policies, and good systems of governance for formulating and implementing policies and mobilizing and managing public resources. Donors will work with these countries in a spirit of development partnership. Policy conditionalities — that is, making aid and debt relief conditional on the implementation of particular policy measures — do not disappear with selectivity. But partnership is still possible since conditionalities should be derived from national priorities and strategies, and since aid and debt relief are focused from the start on what are regarded as good policy environments. Fourthly, different donors will increase the coordination of their financial support within countries, reduce the high transaction costs of their activities, and align their support behind national priorities and strategies. Fifthly, rich countries will increase the coherence of

There are major opportunities for the rapid reduction of poverty in the LDCs through sustained economic growth and development. The critical policy issue is what national and international policies are required in order to enable LDCs to escape the poverty trap and realize those opportunities.

international policies to support poverty reduction in the poorest countries by providing greater market access for products from poor countries. Also, although this is much less developed, greater international policy coherence will be provided through efforts to encourage developmental foreign direct investment and other beneficial private capital flows to the poorest countries.

The new approach to national policies and international cooperation underpinned the Programme of Action for the Least Developed Countries for the Decade 2001–2010, which was agreed in Brussels in May 2001. However, for most of the LDCs, the new approach is being put into practice through the preparation and implementation of Poverty Reduction Strategy Papers (PRSPs). The PRSP is, simultaneously, the vehicle through which Governments are expected to elaborate their nationally owned poverty reduction policies, through which the IMF and the World Bank identify satisfactory policy environments, and through which donors are expected to align their assistance for poverty reduction. Effective poverty reduction in many of the LDCs will depend on how this innovative device, which has quite accurately been described, by the Director of the Poverty Reduction Group of the World Bank, as an "experiment", will work (IMF, 2001a: 4)

This chapter examines whether the policy changes that are emerging in the initial stages of the PRSP process are likely to be sufficient to enable them to break out of the poverty trap. The central message of the chapter is that the introduction of the PRSP approach is a major opportunity to achieve greater poverty reduction, but realizing this opportunity will require a real break with the policies of the past. If poverty reduction strategies are simply a matter of integrating pro-poor public expenditure patterns with deeper and broader structural reforms and the macroeconomic policies of the 1990s, they are unlikely to produce the desired results. In situations of generalized poverty, macroeconomic stabilization together with opening the economy to the rest of the world and freeing markets from government interference will not result in rates of economic growth sufficient and sustainable enough to make a significant impact on poverty. It is necessary instead to elaborate development-oriented poverty reduction strategies.

The chapter is organized into four major sections. It begins by considering the current engagement of the LDCs with the PRSP process and some of the achievements and weaknesses which have been identified in the first generation of PRSPs (section B). It goes on to assess the impact of past adjustment policies on poverty in the LDCs (section C). This experience shows why PRSPs are unlikely to result in more effective poverty reduction if they simply add a social dimension to past adjustment policies. Section D identifies some of the key elements which are likely to enter development-oriented poverty reduction strategies. The discussion draws in particular on UNCTAD's analysis of ingredients of East Asian development strategies and their application in Africa (UNCTAD, 1994, 1996, 1998, 2002a), the thinking of the Economic Commission for Latin America and the Caribbean (ECLAC) on ways of achieving development with equity in Latin America (ECLAC, 1990, 1995, 1996, 2000), and elements of a structuralist approach to poverty analysis that has been developed as an alternative to the weak explanatory frameworks that underpinned World Bank country-level Poverty Assessments in the 1990s and that are now being reproduced in the PRSPs (Pyatt, 1999, 2001a, 2001b). Finally, section E discusses the conditions for genuine national ownership and national policy autonomy, which are necessary conditions for the development of poverty reduction strategies that provide a real and improved alternative to past economic reforms and adjustment policies.[1]

The PRSP is, simultaneously, the vehicle through which Governments are expected to elaborate their nationally owned poverty reduction policies, through which the IMF and the World Bank identify satisfactory policy environments, and through which donors are expected to align their assistance for poverty reduction.

The central message of the chapter is that the introduction of the PRSP approach is a major opportunity to achieve greater poverty reduction, but realizing this opportunity will require a real break with the policies of the past.

The discussion does not deal with the difficult problem of countries so affected by conflict that there is a breakdown of internal sovereignty. The international policies which are the necessary complement of national policies are discussed in more detail in the next chapter.

B. LDCs and the PRSP process: achievements and challenges to date[2]

The idea of a Poverty Reduction Strategy Paper was first introduced in late 1999 by the IMF and the World Bank as a new approach to the provision of concessional assistance to low-income countries. Within this new approach, Governments in low-income countries prepare their own PRSP through a participatory process, and this document, after a satisfactory Joint Staff Assessment (JSA) and the endorsement of the Executive Boards of the Bank and the Fund, provides the basis for concessional assistance and debt relief provided to low-income countries by the Fund, the Bank and the international donor community as a whole.[3]

For the IMF, which transformed its Enhanced Structural Adjustment Facility (ESAF) into the Poverty Reduction and Growth Facility (PRGF) in late 1999, the PRSP replaced the Policy Framework Paper (PFP), which had been prepared by the Fund and the Bank and which underpinned the structural adjustment programmes adopted in the LDCs in the 1990s. The production of a satisfactory Interim PRSP (I-PRSP), which is a shorter and less detailed document than a full PRSP, has also been a condition for highly indebted poor countries (HIPCs) to reach decision point (when interim debt relief begins) within the enhanced HIPC Initiative. Moreover, production of a satisfactory full PRSP and its implementation for a year is a condition for reaching HIPC completion point, when debt relief increases and is irrevocably locked in. The PRSP also provides the basis for the World Bank's Poverty Reduction Support Credits (PRSC), which were introduced in 2001 to support low-income countries implementing poverty reduction strategies.

The PRSPs are meant to be country-specific and should vary between countries. However, they are expected to describe the participatory process used in their preparation, and also to include three core elements: (a) a poverty diagnosis; (b) targets, indicators and monitoring systems; and (c) priority public actions over a three-year period. In presenting those public actions, PRSPs are expected to include a country's macroeconomic framework; a summary of the overall public expenditure programme and its allocation among key areas; and a matrix of key policy actions and institutional reforms and target dates for their implementation. The Joint Staff Assessments (JSAs) cover, amongst other things, (a) the adequacy of the poverty diagnosis; (b) the adequacy of the poverty reduction goals, indicators of progress and monitoring systems; (c) the appropriateness of the macroeconomic framework and the financing plan; (d) the adequacy of structural and sectoral policies; and (e) improvements in governance and public sector management.

Thirty-four LDCs are currently engaged in producing or implementing full or interim PRSPs. As of March 2002, six LDCs — Burkina Faso, Mauritania, Mozambique, Niger, Uganda and the United Republic of Tanzania — had produced full PRSPs, and 24 LDCs had produced Interim PRSPs (I-PRSPs). It is expected that as of mid-2002, 17 of those LDCs that have produced I-PRSPs will have completed full PRSPs, and a further 7 LDCs will have completed I-PRSPs

Within this new approach, Governments in low-income countries prepare their own PRSP through a participatory process, and this document provides the basis for concessional assistance and debt relief.

Thirty-four LDCs are currently engaged in producing or implementing full or interim PRSPs.

(table 38). Of the LDCs which are engaged in the process, all except 6 are highly indebted poor countries, and 23 are commodity-exporting economies. Of the 15 LDCs not engaged in the process, six are small island States and six of the others have been externally sanctioned or strongly affected by conflict in the recent past (Afghanistan, Haiti, Liberia, Myanmar, Somalia and Sudan).

There is a large spectrum of views on the achievements of the PRSP approach to date. It is generally agreed that it is too early to assess the impact of the implementation of PRSPs on poverty outcomes. However, many civil society organizations are deeply sceptical that any real change has occurred with the introduction of the PRSP approach.[4]

Of the LDCs which are engaged in the process, all except 6 are highly indebted poor countries, and 23 are commodity-exporting economies.

On balance, it appears that there has been a much more significant break with the past in terms of processes of policy formulation than in the content of policies. The content of I-PRSPs and of the first generation of PRSPs has tended to reaffirm many of the policy directions and policies already in place. In a particularly frank assessment of the achievements and challenges of the PRSP process so far, HIPC Finance Ministers and PRSP Coordinators (2002) note that:

> "in interim PRSPs in particular, where some governments indicated that evidence shows some reforms were exacerbating poverty, their concerns were overruled on the grounds that short-term costs would give way to long-term benefits, or that the costs reflected failure to pursue policies tenaciously. As a result, there has been little evidence of important policy changes on macro or structural policies between PRSPs and PFPs [Policy Framework Papers of the past structural adjustment programmes]" (p. 4).

This, they note, "has begun to change". But many PRSPs have involved "adding large numbers of sectoral actions to structural policies brought forward from PFPs" (p. 4).

Particular weaknesses which other observers have noted in the content of the PRSPs are: the lack of a long-term growth strategy; the weak integration of sector plans into the PRSP; and a tendency to focus on improved and pro-poor public expenditure management rather than private sector investment and employment generation.[5] A general problem is that the PRSPs have a "missing middle" (European Commission, 2001b: 8; ODI, 2001), that is to say the mechanisms which lead from the policies to the outcomes are not elaborated. This is particularly evident in the I-PRSPs, which often have a similar structure (table 39). But the problem is also apparent in the full PRSPs, whose structure does not differ markedly from that of the I-PRSPs, although they all contain a section on costings and financing (Thin, Underwood and Gilling, 2001).

A general problem is that the PRSPs have a "missing middle", that is to say the mechanisms which lead from the policies to the outcomes are not elaborated.

The HIPC Finance Ministers and PRSP Coordinators, who are the ones at the centre of the PRSP process, have pinpointed key features of this problem of the "missing middle". They state that, in many PRSPs (and especially I-PRSPs):

> "the scale of growth planned under the PRSP is frequently adequate to halve poverty by 2015...[but] there is no in depth analysis of how the sectoral and structural measures in the programme will produce the targeted growth rates; nor have programmes examined sufficiently how macro, sectoral and structural measures will translate into changes in the distribution of the benefits of growth. Savings, investment, domestic resource mobilization and employment remain underanalyzed; insufficient attention is being given to social inclusion and equity in many PRSPs. In contrast, a great deal of effort is being expended by governments and the international community to im-

TABLE 38. PROGRESS IN PRSP PREPARATION IN LDCs

	Interim PRSP	PRSP
Afghanistan	-	-
Angola	I	-
Bangladesh	-	-
Benin	June 2000	F
Bhutan	-	-
Burkina Faso	-	May 2000
Burundi	I	-
Cambodia	October 2000	F
Cape Verde	January 2002	-
Central African Republic	December 2000	F
Chad	July 2000	F
Comoros	I	-
Dem. Rep. of the Congo	I	-
Djibouti	November 2001	-
Equatorial Guinea	-	-
Eritrea	I	-
Ethiopia	November 2000	F
Gambia	October 2000	F
Guinea	October 2000	F
Guinea-Bissau	September 2000	F
Haiti	-	-
Kiribati	-	-
Lao PDR	March 2001	-
Lesotho	December 2000	F
Liberia	-	-
Madagascar	November 2000	F
Malawi	August 2000	F
Maldives	-	-
Mali	July 2000	F
Mauritania	-	December 2000
Mozambique	February 2000	April 2001
Myanmar	-	-
Nepal	I	-
Niger	October 2000	January 2002
Rwanda	November 2000	F
Samoa	-	-
Sao Tome and Principe	April 2000	F
Senegal	May 2000	F
Sierra Leone	June 2001	-
Solomon Islands	-	-
Somalia	-	-
Sudan	-	-
Togo	I	-
Tuvalu	-	-
Uganda	-	March 2000
United Republic of Tanzania	March 2000	October 2000
Vanuatu	-	-
Yemen	December 2000	F
Zambia	July 2000	F

Source: IMF, http://www.imf.org/external/np/prsp/prsp.asp; and World Bank, http://poverty.worldbank.org/files/Revised_Country_table_annex_1-sept3.pdf

Note: I and F indicate that countries plan to complete Interim PRSPs and PRSPs respectively before the end of June 2002. This is based on possible country timelines for PRSP preparation indicated by the World Bank in September 2001.

TABLE 39. THE STRUCTURE OF INTERIM PRSPS

1. **General background:** history, changes in policies, events, and structures in the recent past; purpose of drawing up a PRSP; processes involved in drafting the IPRSP.

2. **Poverty profile:** national statistics on income poverty and (usually) "human development" indicators, and how/when these were derived (sometimes involving comparisons across time, and comparisons with aggregate statistics for sub-Saharan Africa or low-income countries; often includes regional and rural–urban comparisons, plus basic information on specific categories of poor people; sometimes includes explicit analysis of causes of poverty, and sometimes assesses deficiencies in available data; occasionally includes sections explicitly on people's perceptions of poverty (but rarely assesses validity and/or policy relevance of these).

3. **Current policies and strategies:** recent history of specific anti-poverty interventions and associated policies and structures; policies on macroeconomic management (inflation, exports, debt, fiscal management), on governance (administrative efficiency, transparency/accountability, corruption, participation), on provision of basic "social services" (health, education, water/sanitation), on infrastructure (energy, transport and communication), on environmental management, on productivity and employment (always includes agriculture, usually also non-agricultural production), and on specific social processes and categories of people (conflict, gender, age, and very occasionally social capital and ethnicity); and on HIV/AIDS.

4. **Poverty reduction objectives and strategic changes:** all the same categories as above under "policies and strategies" (sometimes also includes sections on intersectoral linkages and integration); usually includes sections on major sectors (typically including a "rural sector", which in practice refers to 65–80 per cent of the population).

5. **Plans for development of the full PRSP:** (normally including plans for participatory processes and for costing and financing).

6. **Monitoring and evaluation:** plans (indicators, responsibilities, processes, institutions) for monitoring and evaluation of the PRS.

Source: Thin, Underwood and Gilling (2001: box 1).

In terms of policy processes, the PRSP approach has led to some significant achievements.

prove governance and public sector management, as well as comprehensiveness of expenditure allocation, presentation and tracking" (HIPC Finance Ministers and PRSP Coordinators, 2002: 4).

Turning to macroeconomic policy, the HIPC Ministers and PRSP coordinators state that "our main concern is not realism, but that many programmes continue to be too restrictive...especially for countries which have achieved sustained low inflation. Nor has there been much evidence of exploring possibilities for alternative macroeconomic paths, taking into account non-demand causes of inflation, recovery of demand for money, and private sector credit needs" (ibid.: 4).[6]

In terms of policy processes, country-level analyses reveal more changes than have occurred in policy content.[7] Significant achievements of the PRSP approach include: an increase in country-level leadership in strategy design; greater involvement of civil society in the process of strategy formulation, although according to many NGO participants their involvement has often been tokenistic; increased efforts to improve medium-term public expenditure frameworks and to link budgetary processes to poverty reduction targets; and the mainstreaming of poverty reduction policies through a shift in departmental responsibility for poverty from previously marginalized social welfare departments to Ministries of Finance and of Planning. But a number of countries are also reporting an increase in transaction costs with the new approach, which are particularly related to reporting requirements.

Moreover, increased national ownership, which is a central goal of the PRSP approach, remains constrained in various ways. It is clear that with the introduction of the PRSP approach there is increasing leadership in the technocratic processes of policy formulation. But often this does not extend far outside the central economic ministries, and the degree of political support which the process is receiving is mixed (ODI, 2001). A major flaw in the PRSP process which the HIPC Ministers and PRSP Coordinators (2002) point out is that "it has often bypassed existing parliamentary structures in favour of new and different consultative structures", and thus "parliaments have virtually no involvement except to endorse and debate final versions of PRSPs" (p. 3). Genuine national ownership also involves careful management of the tension between policy conditionality, the building of in-country capacity and changes in behaviour by the donor countries. These issues will be taken up later in section E.

But, increased national ownership, which is a central goal of the PRSP approach, remains constrained in various ways.

C. The need to move beyond adjustment policies

The PRSP process is rightly seen as one which is in evolution, and in which all participants are engaged in learning-by-doing. In order to maximize the effectiveness of the approach in the LDCs as it evolves, it is essential to have a careful and frank assessment now of the impact of past structural adjustment policies on poverty. Many LDCs have been heavily engaged in structural adjustment programmes since the late 1980s, particularly following the introduction by the IMF of the Structural Adjustment Facility and Enhanced Structural Adjustment Facility.[8] Many of these programmes have had intermittent interruptions; some countries have gone further than others; and all policy conditionalities have not been equally met. But in spite of interruptions and policy slippages (which have been generally due to problems of meeting fiscal targets), these programmes have led to significant changes in the policy environment in many LDCs. The impact of these programmes on poverty is a vital issue.

The PRSP approach is founded on the hypothesis that the major weakness of the structural adjustment programmes was that they were not nationally owned, and thus were not well implemented. The expectation is that sustained poverty reduction can follow if national ownership is improved, and if more attention is also paid to social outcomes by integrating a pro-poor and outcome-oriented public expenditure pattern with existing macroeconomic policies and broader and deeper structural reform. However, another interpretation is possible. It is that the policies themselves — in such areas as agriculture, trade, finance, public enterprise, deregulation and privatization — are not the right ones to promote economic growth and reduce poverty in situations of generalized poverty. In these circumstances, different policies are needed to enable countries to break out of a low-level equilibrium economic trap in which productive capacities, markets and the entrepeneurial class are all underdeveloped.

The PRSP approach is founded on the hypothesis that the major weakness of the structural adjustment programmes was that they were not well implemented... However, another interpretation is possible. It is that the policies themselves are not the right ones to promote economic growth and reduce poverty in situations of generalized poverty.

Table 40 shows economic and poverty trends in LDCs before and after the adoption of ESAF-supported structural adjustment programmes. It focuses on 20 LDCs for which data are available. The table compares various indicators of economic performance and poverty trends three years before the year of adoption of an ESAF-funded programme with two three-year periods after that year. For this group of countries, the average real GDP per capita was declining by 1.4 per cent per annum in the three years before the programmes were initiated; they grew by 0.5 per cent per annum in the three years after, and then

TABLE 40. ECONOMIC PERFORMANCE OF THE LDCs, BEFORE AND AFTER THE ADOPTION OF SAF/ESAF PROGRAMMES

	3 years before	1st 3 years after	2nd 3 years after	1997–1999
Average annual real growth rates (%)				
GDP per capita	-1.4	0.5	-1.4	1.4
Exports of goods and services	0.1	6.1	3.4	6.2
Gross capital formation	0.8	2.1	-2.6	7.6
Average per capita private consumption (1985 PPP$)	0.1	-0.1	-2.4	2.0
Average annual ratio (as % of GDP)				
Exports of goods and services	19.6	19.2	18.8	21.0
Gross capital formation	16.1	18.7	18.3	18.5
Gross domestic savings	0.7	2.5	1.1	4.1
Genuine domestic savings	-5.6	-4.1	-5.9	-3.6
Average poverty incidence (% of population)				
Living on less than $1 a day (1985 PPP$)	51.3	52.0	53.3	51.8
Living on less than $2 a day (1985 PPP$)	83.1	83.7	84.1	83.3
Average per capita private consumption (1985 PPP$)	493.2	486.7	477.6	481.2

Source: UNCTAD secretariat estimates based on World Bank, *World Development Indicators 2001,* CD-ROM.

Note: The figures are simple averages. The sample includes all LDCs for which data are available and which are identified by the IMF as ESAF-programme countries, except Equatorial Guinea, Guinea-Bissau, Rwanda and Sierra Leone, which are outliers. The countries are: Bangladesh, Benin, Burkina Faso, Burundi, Central African Republic, Chad, Ethiopia, Gambia, Guinea, Haiti, Lesotho, Madagascar, Malawi, Mali, Mauritania, Mozambique, Nepal, Niger, Togo and Uganda.

declined by 1.4 per cent in the next three years. Average annual private consumption per capita (in 1985 PPP dollars) fell from $493.2 in the three years before to $486.7 in the first three years after and $477.6 in the next three years. The proportion of the total population living below the $1-a-day poverty line rose from 51 per cent to 52 per cent in the first three years after the adoption of the ESAF-funded programme and 53 per cent in the next three years. Moreover, the proportion of the population living below the $2-a-day poverty line rose from 83 per cent in the three years before adoption to 84 per cent in the two three-year periods afterwards.

The main conclusion that can be drawn from this is that ESAF-funded adjustment programmes have not delivered sustainable growth sufficient to make a significant dent in poverty. The main positive effect of these programmes seems to be on the export growth rates. But any growth which is occurring may not be sustainable owing to a weak domestic investment response, the perpetuation of very low domestic savings rates and negative genuine domestic savings (indicating environmental degradation) — see table 40. There is no evidence that these reforms have catalysed private capital flows. For a sample of 29 LDCs undertaking SAF/ESAF-funded reform programmes, the ratio of net FDI to GNP declines between the five years before and after the initiation of reforms in almost half the cases, increasing by over 1 per cent in just five cases (UNCTAD, 2000: 111). Moreover, from the evidence of the composition of exports presented in chapter 3, the reforms have been unable to promote economy-wide structural change towards more dynamic export sectors, although market share is being gained in a number of traditional export sectors. There are indeed examples of domestic business success at the micro level (ITC, 2001), but these islands of success are not yet translating into more widely shared sectoral and economy-wide development.

There are, of course, variations amongst countries around these averages. These differences are due to various factors, including the degree to which programmes were adequately financed, the initial level of external debt, and movements in international commodity prices, as well as the seriousness with

The main conclusion that can be drawn is that ESAF-funded adjustment programmes have not delivered sustainable growth sufficient to make a significant dent in poverty.

which the reform programmes were implemented. The last factor is often singled out as the critical one, and, as noted above, is a central theme underlying the PRSP approach.

Chart 45 seeks to examine this issue by focusing on poverty trends before and after the implementation of adjustment programmes in three groups of countries, which are defined according to the degree of compliance with the policy conditionality of adjustment programmes. The sample is different from the one in table 40, and owing to data constraints is limited to African LDCs. The groups are taken from World Bank (1997), which classifies countries into "strong", "weak" and "poor compliers" on the basis of the degree of compliance with conditionality in relation to: (i) macroeconomic policies (fiscal deficit reduction, public expenditure levels and exchange rates), (ii) public sector management (including civil service reform, public expenditure reform and public enterprise restructuring, and privatization), and (iii) private sector development (financial sector reform, trade policy reform, regulatory environment, and pricing and incentives). The countries which comply the most are defined as "strong compliers"; those which comply the least are "poor compliers"; and those in-between are labelled "weak compliers".

As with all exercises of this nature, the results are dependent on the sample, and there are variations around the average in each group. However, three generalizations can be made from the chart. First, the incidence of poverty clearly increased in countries that are classified as poor compliers. Second,

CHART 45. TRENDS IN THE INCIDENCE OF POVERTY IN AFRICAN ADJUSTING LDCS, CLASSIFIED ACCORDING TO THEIR DEGREE OF COMPLIANCE WITH POLICY CONDITIONALITIES OF STRUCTURAL ADJUSTMENT PROGRAMMES

(Percentage)

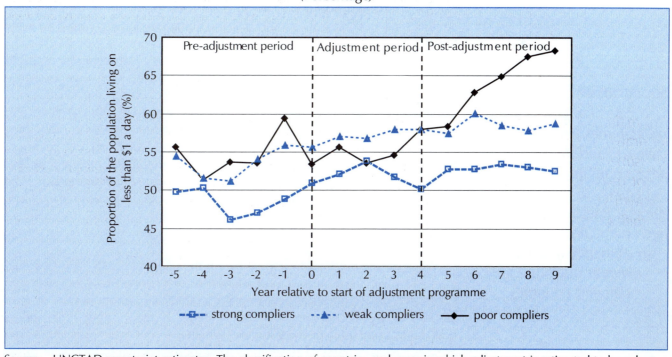

Source: UNCTAD secretariat estimates. The classification of countries and years in which adjustment is estimated to have begun are those of World Bank (1997).

Note: Group averages are unweighted. The countries and the years in which adjustment is estimated to have begun (year 0) are: strong compliers (Benin, 1989; Gambia, 1987; Malawi, 1981; Mali, 1988; Mauritania, 1986; Mozambique, 1988; Sierra Leone, 1992; and United Republic of Tanzania, 1987); weak compliers (Burkina Faso, 1991; Guinea, 1986; Guinea-Bissau, 1985; Madagascar, 1985; Niger, 1986; Senegal, 1986; Togo, 1983; Uganda 1988; and Zambia, 1991); and poor compliers (Burundi, 1986; Central African Republic, 1987; Chad, 1989; Democratic Republic of the Congo, 1986; Rwanda, 1991; Somalia, 1986; and Sudan, 1980).

during the adjustment period, poverty increased by more than two percentage points in the countries classified as weak compliers whilst it fell by more than half a percentage point in those countries classified as strong compliers. Third, after the adjustment period, the downward trend in poverty in the strong adjusters and the upward trend in poverty in the weak adjusters both ceased, leaving both groups of countries with higher poverty incidence than before the adjustment process. On average, 48 per cent of the population were living on less than $1 a day in the strong adjusters during the five-year pre-adjustment period as compared to 53 per cent during the five-year post-adjustment period. Inevitably, this implies that the numbers of poor increased in the strong adjusters.

In short, it would appear that there may be an element of truth in the argument that the degree of compliance with conditionality affected poverty trends in adjusting countries. But the effect is asymmetrical. If you did not comply well, the incidence of poverty increased. However, if you did comply, even strongly, the incidence of poverty did not fall. In each case, given population growth, the numbers of people living in poverty can be expected to have increased, though more steeply in the worst compliers than in the best compliers.

It is difficult to say exactly what mechanisms are responsible for these different outcomes. Many observers have concluded that the elements of adjustment programmes which have contributed most to positive outcomes are the removal of gross macroeconomic imbalances, which were evident in very high rates of inflation and exchange rate misalignment. But there is little evidence that the structural reforms which have been undertaken have had any positive effects on growth. Indeed, one of the IMF's unduly neglected background studies for its own internal evaluation of the ESAF programme finds that the effects of structural policies on growth are "barely discernible when full account is taken of macroeconomic policies, human capital accumulation, initial conditions and exogenous shocks" (Kochhar and Coorey, 1999: 87). Finally, implementation of ESAF-funded programmes acted as a gatekeeper for access to concessional finance. Typically, the increased supplies of foreign exchange associated with the initiation of an ESAF programme enabled the rehabilitation and full utilization of existing capital stock. But expanded official flows also rendered many potential investments remunerative and also led to flourishing informal sector activities. These effects occurred in a wide range of countries. But strong adjusters are less likely to have had underfunded programmes and less likely to have suffered the problems of programme interruptions. The adequacy of the funding of programmes is likely to have been particularly important as an element explaining the different outcomes for different countries.

Whatever the mechanism responsible for the different results, it is clear that even when well implemented, past adjustment programmes have not delivered sustainable growth rates sufficient to make a significant dent in poverty in most LDCs. This result conforms with the findings of many other independent evaluations of adjustment programmes.[9] Whether or not these programmes are actually increasing rates of poverty, as some observers argue, is difficult to say without more detailed analysis of what would have happened without the policies. But the present evidence is sufficient to demonstrate that in general past adjustment policies are not associated with sustained reductions in the incidence of poverty in the LDCs even when they are well implemented. The problem is not that they are excessively focused on economic growth, as is sometimes popularly asserted. The problem is that they cannot deliver

If you did not comply well, the incidence of poverty increased. However, if you did comply, even strongly, the incidence of poverty did not fall.

Strong adjusters are less likely to have had underfunded programmes and less likely to have suffered the problems of programme interruptions. The adequacy of the funding of programmes is likely to have been particularly important as an element explaining the different outcomes for different countries.

accelerated and sustainable economic growth, which is essential for poverty reduction in countries with generalized poverty.

Adjustment programmes have not necessarily been a total failure. They have played an important role in reducing excessively high rates of inflation and correcting overvalued exchange rates. They have also fostered a progressive shift in policy thinking that gives more adequate recognition to the role of market forces and private initiative in the development process, and to the importance of integration with the global economy. But it is necessary to move beyond adjustment now. Getting the Government out of the way and opening up the economy to the rest of the world are not going to achieve the desired results in terms of poverty reduction. The policy model is wrong for this purpose in countries where poverty is generalized.

In moving forward, one must recognize the weak growth results of past adjustment policies, and reject "business as usual" in the content of policies as much as it is rightly being rejected in the processes of policy formulation. On the basis of past experience, we should not expect better results to be achieved if the new policies emerging from the PRSP process differ from those of the past in no other respect than that they are nationally formulated versions of past adjustment programmes. Moreover, although it is true that insufficient attention was given in the past to social outcomes, sustained poverty reduction is not going to follow automatically as the result of the integration of pro-poor public expenditure into traditional macroeconomic policies and structural reforms. Alternative policies need to be explored.

D. Long-term national development strategies and the PRSP process

The core of any PRSP is concerned with policy actions and public expenditure priorities to promote growth and poverty reduction over a three-year period. Although references are generally made to long-term objectives, the link between the PRSP and long-term development strategies is not as yet strong. Poverty reduction strategies will be more effective if they are anchored more firmly in long-term development strategies than if they continue to be dominated by the short-term macoeconomic goals of stabilization together with structural reforms which are geared to improving the efficiency of resource allocation. Long-term national development strategies are not, it must be emphasized, advocated here as a replacement for PRSPs. Rather, they provide the basis on which different policy options within PRSPs can be developed.

A long-term development strategy contains a long-term vision of national objectives; the strategic elements required to achieve these objectives, and their sequencing; and the policy processes to pursue the objectives.[10] Central issues which must be addressed include the following: the nature of the growth mechanism underlying the development process, including accumulation of physical and human capital, and productivity growth through an increasing division of labour, technological progress and structural change, as well the efficiency of resource allocation; the type of structural transformation which may be encouraged as the economy grows; sources of finance for productive investment; the role of trade in the development process; mechanisms for promoting enterprise development and learning; environmental sustainability; and the generation and sustainability of livelihoods for all sections of the population. Creating capable and effective States, and also a dynamic domestic

Adjustment programmes have not necessarily been a total failure... But it is necessary to move beyond adjustment now.

We should not expect better results to be achieved if the new policies emerging from the PRSP process differ from those of the past in no other respect than that they are nationally formulated versions of past adjustment programmes.

Poverty reduction strategies will be more effective if they are anchored more firmly in long-term development strategies.

entrepreneurial class willing to commit its resources to domestic investment rather than to luxury consumption or holding private wealth abroad, is a central institutional issue which also must be addressed in a developmental approach to poverty reduction.

In the approach advocated here priority policy actions within the PRSP would be derived from the overall development strategy. In essence, they would be the steps to be taken in the short term, over a three-year period, in support of long-term goals.

In the approach advocated here priority policy actions within the PRSP would be derived from the overall development strategy. In essence, they would be the steps to be taken in the short term, over a three-year period, in support of long-term goals. Short-term macroeconomic needs would not be ignored. But there would be greater exploration of monetary policy options and fiscal flexibility within the limits of what is prudent, and also analysis of the trade-offs between long-run and short-run objectives. Sectoral policies would be integrated into the PRSP through the analysis of the overall development path. Trade issues are also currently not treated in depth in PRSPs. They are an important aspect of long-term development strategies, and it is from an understanding of the role of trade within the overall development strategy that one can build appropriate trade and complementary policies into the PRSPs.

It is for individual Governments themselves to make their strategic choices. But the analysis of generalized poverty in the present Report suggests four general policy orientations that are likely to have wide, though contextually specific, application. These are: firstly, the central importance of promoting rapid and sustained economic growth; secondly, the establishment of a dynamic investment–export nexus, which, to be sustainable, must be increasingly based on domestic resource mobilization; thirdly, the elaboration of productive development policy options; and fourthly, the adoption of policies to ensure that social groups and regions within a country are not left behind and marginalized as growth takes place (see chart 46). These policy orientations are based on two key insights within the new Programme of Action for the LDCs. The first is that the basic mechanism to reduce poverty in the LDCs is through economic growth and development (United Nations, 2001b: para. 13). The second is that building productive capacities is essential to help LDCs integrate beneficially into the global economy. The overall approach seeks to reduce poverty through sustainable growth and development based on the building of domestic productive capacities.

Trade issues are currently not treated in depth in PRSPs. It is from an understanding of the role of trade within the overall development strategy that one can build appropriate trade policies into the PRSPs.

1. THE IMPORTANCE OF RAPID AND SUSTAINED ECONOMIC GROWTH

In situations of generalized poverty, the most effective mechanism of poverty reduction is rapid and sustained economic growth. As shown in chapter 1, average private consumption per capita in the LDCs during 1995–1999 was equivalent to just 57 cents a day (at current prices and official exchange rates) or $1.39 a day (using 1985 PPP conversion rates). The central task of government in such a situation must be to double average household living standards as quickly as is feasible. A necessary condition for this is growth in GDP per capita.[11] A sufficient condition is that economic growth be of a type that is founded on the accumulation of capital and skills, productivity growth and the expansion of employment opportunities, and which thereby expands the consumption possibilities of households and individuals.

The central task of government in situations of generalized poverty must be to double average household living standards as quickly as is feasible.

Some idea of the likely effects of rapid and sustained economic growth on the incidence of poverty in the LDCs is shown in table 41. One of the forecasts in that table is based on the assumption that a GDP growth rate of 7 per cent per annum is achieved. This is the target growth rate in the Programme of Action for the Least Developed Countries for the Decade 2001–2010, which was agreed at the Third United Nations Conference on the Least Developed Countries in

CHART 46. ELEMENTS OF A DEVELOPMENT-ORIENTED POVERTY REDUCTION STRATEGY IN LDCs

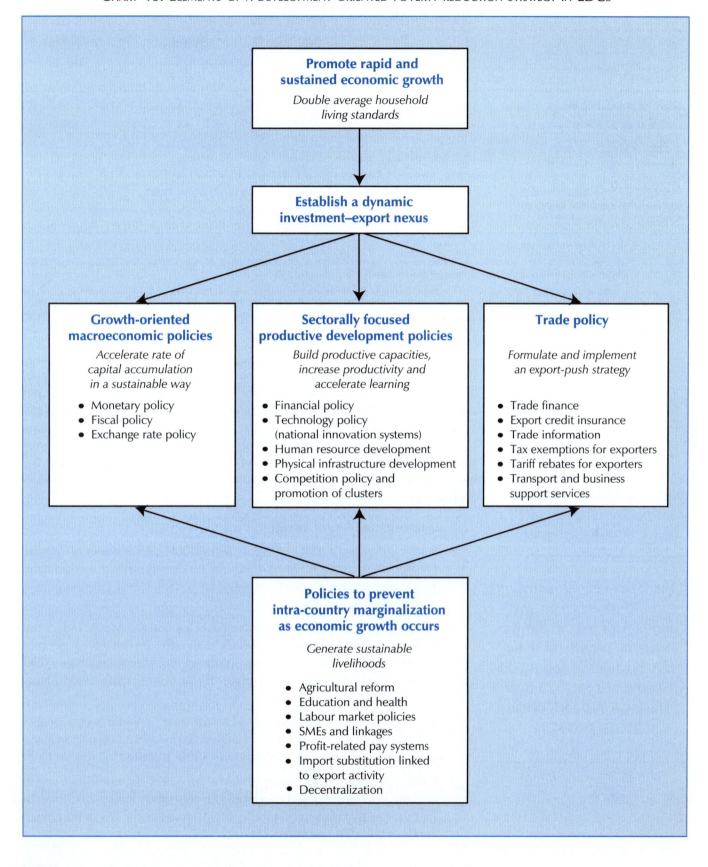

TABLE 41. PROJECTIONS OF THE INCIDENCE OF EXTREME POVERTY AND THE NUMBER OF
EXTREMELY POOR PEOPLE IN LDCs[a] IN 2015: THREE ALTERNATIVE SCENARIOS

	1990	1999	Projection I 2015	Projection II 2015	Projection III 2015
Share of population living on less than $1 a day (%)[b]	49.1	50.5	50.6	43.7	24.0
Number of people living on less than $1 a day (millions)	214.4	270.5	383.6	331.0	181.8
Number of countries on target to halve the incidence of poverty between 1990 and 2015	-	-	7	6	28

Source: UNCTAD secretariat estimates.

Note: Projection I assumes that the trend of the 1990s persists. Projection II assumes that the average annual growth rate is 3.5% starting in 2000. Projection III assumes that the average annual growth rate is 7% starting in 2000.

a   The sample includes 33 LDCs for which the projections can be made: Angola, Bangladesh, Benin, Bhutan, Burkina Faso, Burundi, Cape Verde, Central African Republic, Chad, Comoros, Democratic Republic of the Congo, Ethiopia, Gambia, Guinea, Guinea-Bissau, Haiti, Lesotho, Madagascar, Malawi, Mali, Mauritania, Mozambique, Myanmar, Nepal, Niger, Rwanda, Senegal, Sierra Leone, Togo, Uganda, United Republic of Tanzania, Vanuatu and Zambia.

b   Averages weighted by total population.

Brussels in May 2001. In the light of past experience, this target is no doubt ambitious. But the table shows what the effects on poverty would be if the 7 per cent growth target could be achieved, and if average private consumption per capita grew in line with GDP per capita. The projections assume the incidence of poverty declines in line with the poverty curves which describe the normal relationship between the average private consumption per capita and the incidence of poverty, and also that population growth rates match the UN projections.

From table 41, it is apparent that:

- For the group of LDCs for which data are available, the incidence of extreme poverty will increase between 1990 and 2015 if the growth trends of the 1990s are maintained. However, it will fall by half if the 7 per cent growth target can be achieved.

- Twenty-eight out of 33 LDCs for which data are available would reduce the incidence of extreme poverty between 1990–2015 by half if the 7 per cent growth target could be achieved. By contrast, only seven countries would be able to do so that if the growth trends of the 1990s were simply maintained.

- If the 7 per cent growth target could be achieved, the numbers of people living in extreme poverty in these LDCs would be about 200 million lower in 2015 than if the growth trends of the 1990s persisted.

- If the 7 per cent growth target could be achieved, the numbers living in extreme poverty in these LDCs would be 89 million less in 2015 than in 1999, rather than 113 million more, which would be the case if the growth trends of the 1990s persisted.

If the 7 per cent growth target could be achieved, the numbers of people living in extreme poverty in these LDCs would be about 200 million lower in 2015 than if the growth trends of the 1990s persisted.

The 7 per cent target growth rate of the Brussels Programme of Action is certainly ambitious. But it is only with more rapid and sustained growth that one may expect a significant reduction in the incidence of extreme poverty to be achieved. Moreover, given the high population growth rates in the LDCs, any reduction at all in the numbers of people living in extreme poverty in the LDCs depends on the achievement of such growth rates.

For comparative purposes, table 41 also shows projections of the incidence of poverty based on the assumption that all countries achieved growth rates of only 3.5 per cent per annum, i.e. half the UNLDC III growth targets. Out of the 33 LDCs, only six would reduce the incidence of poverty by half between 1990 and 2015. Moreover, the number of people living in extreme poverty in the LDCs for which we have data would increase by about 61 million between 1999 and 2015. The number of people living in extreme poverty in these 33 LDCs would be 151 million more than if the 7 per cent growth target were met.

2. THE NEED TO ESTABLISH A DYNAMIC INVESTMENT–EXPORT NEXUS[12]

The current PRSPs tend to assume that higher rates of economic growth will occur than in the past. These growth rates are usually included in the PRSPs as an assumed growth rate that is part of the macroeconomic framework. It is unclear how they are derived, and also how they are related to the policies which are proposed. In general, it appears to be assumed that more vigorous implementation of policy reforms, which is expected to stem from national ownership, is the source of the accelerated growth. But, as argued above, this seems to be over-optimistic.

The Programme of Action for the Least Developed Countries for the Decade 2001–2010 envisages increased rates of investment as a basis for higher growth rates. Experience indeed suggests that increasing the rates of investment is the key to promoting rapid and sustained economic growth in developing countries. But it also shows that it is necessary to build a strong investment–export nexus. That is to say, a sustainable growth process requires mutually reinforcing interactions between investment growth and export growth.

A sustainable growth process requires mutually reinforcing interactions between investment growth and export growth.

Exports must play a significant role in output expansion in most LDCs. This is a necessary consequence of the limits of their domestic markets, which are a result of generalized poverty and, in the majority of cases, their relatively small populations. Some export expansion can take place by bringing idle land and underutilized labour into production. But sustained export expansion usually depends on the creation of additional production capacity, as well as on investments to improve productivity through the application of available modern technologies, and investments to diversify into more dynamic market segments. Increased investment — in capital equipment, technical know-how and market knowledge — enables sustained export growth, which in turn enables increased investment. The basic reason for this is that at the early stages of growth the balance-of-payments deficit is a particularly serious constraint on the expansion of economic activity. When investment is growing, imports of capital goods and intermediate goods normally must also grow, and adequate foreign exchange is required to ensure that these are reliably financed.

Establishing a dynamic investment–export nexus requires the creation of profitable investment opportunities, reducing the risks and uncertainty of investment activity, and ensuring the availability of finance so that entrepreneurs are able to invest in expanding production.

Establishing a dynamic investment–export nexus requires the creation of profitable investment opportunities, reducing the risks and uncertainty of investment activity, and ensuring the availability of finance so that entrepreneurs are able to invest in expanding production. Policy intervention of various kinds can play a key role by setting the general conditions for a faster pace of capital accumulation and by correcting specific market failures which impede access to finance, the adoption of technologies and the orientation of domestic production to external markets. Such interventions should be founded upon the recognition that in market-based systems capital accumulation is closely linked to the emergence of a domestic entrepreneurial class willing to commit resources to long-term investment in production and to the reinvestment of their profits in expanding production (UNCTAD, 1998: 212). The combination of public and private initiative that is needed is still best illustrated by the development experience of East Asian newly industrializing economies (UNCTAD, 1994, 1996).

The basis of the whole process is a good general "pro-investment climate" which improves the returns and reduces the risks of private investment. A critical policy issue is: What are the main elements of a pro-investment climate in a situation where over 50 per cent of the population is living in extreme poverty and where there is a poorly developed corporate sector? This requires much more research. But there is a consensus that political stability, a good legal structure and effective contract enforcement are needed to ensure rising levels of private investment. A stable macroeconomic environment is also desirable, although policies to achieve the short-term goal of macroeconomic stability, including the target rate of inflation and the size of the budget and current account deficits, should not be set without consideration of long-term development objectives and, in particular, the need to increase domestic investment. The quality of economic infrastructure, including power, telecommunications, transport and water, is also essential, since deficiencies in this regard can considerably increase transaction costs for business activity (Stern, 2001). Measures to improve health and education, quite apart from their intrinsic value, are critical in increasing the productivity of the working population. Moreover, when the majority of the population is very poor, food constitutes a major share of workers' expenditures on goods and services, and hence the price of food is a major element in the determination of the cost of living for workers. The price of food, which may be locally produced or imported, is thus an important determinant of the competitiveness and profitability of labour-intensive production (Wuyts, 2001) — see box 14. This suggests that measures to increase the productivity of domestic food production are also likely to be an important aspect of a good general pro-investment climate.

Within the general pro-investment climate, special efforts need to be made to ensure the availability of finance for productive investment and also to promote exports. Financial liberalization has been undertaken in many LDCs. It was introduced as a reaction to excessive and often misguided intervention in the financial sector, including public ownership of banks and controls on interest rates and credit allocation, which often resulted in negative real deposit and lending rates and preferential treatment for public entities. But the financial reforms have often resulted in high interest rates and financial instability (UNCTAD, 1998: 214–215). Two important market failures which Governments must now address are the limited access of small and medium-sized domestic enterprises to formal bank credit, and the mismatch between the short-term nature of available financing and the longer-term requirements of productive investment. As argued in UNCTAD (2000), a particular priority is to finance medium-sized domestic businesses which are not commercially bankable but which have the potential to be so if they have access to finance at more normal interest rates. There are no easy solutions to the problem of financing domestic enterprises. But suitable instruments and institutions must be created to provide financial services with different profit, risk and liquidity profiles, to channel resources into long-term productive investment and not simply real-estate development and short-term trading activities, and to ensure that credits reach agricultural smallholders and small and medium-sized domestic industrial enterprises, as well as broadly defined sectors which the Government believes are important for national development. Development banks and venture capital funds may both have a role to play (ECLAC, 1990: 143–148; 2000: 223–

The combination of public and private initiative that is needed is still best illustrated by the development experience of East Asian newly industrializing economies

Two important market failures which Governments must now address are the limited access of small and medium-sized domestic enterprises to formal bank credit, and the mismatch between the short-term nature of available financing and the longer-term requirements of productive investment.

BOX 14. STRATEGIC CHOICES IN CREATING COMPETITIVE LABOUR-INTENSIVE ACTIVITIES IN LATECOMER COUNTRIES

In her analysis of East Asian industrialization, Amsden (1994, 2001) argues that the central challenge which newly industrializing economies such as the Republic of Korea and Taiwan Province of China faced when establishing export-oriented textile industries was how to compete with countries such as Japan, where production was already well established. Wages were higher in the already established production centres, but the latecomer countries could not compete because their labour productivity was lower and thus their unit wage costs were higher. In this situation, Amsden argues, the latecomer countries faced a strategic choice in establishing competitive labour-intensive activities – either they lowered real wages or they raised productivity. She argues that the former approach is typical of structural adjustment policies, whilst the latter was widely used in East Asian newly industrializing economies, whose Governments intervened to subsidize capital investment and learning in order to increase productivity.

Wuyts (2001) extends this analysis in a way that enables it to be applied to least developed countries. He points towards a third route to establishing competitive labour-intensive activities. This involves making cheaper the basic consumer goods that constitute workers' subsistence, particularly food. If this occurs, it is possible for unit wage costs to fall in the latecomer countries without reductions in real wages. From this, Wuyts derives an important conclusion: "If the competitiveness and profitability of labour-intensive production in a newly industrializing country is not to be at the expense of real wages, an important condition is that the expansion of employment outside agriculture should not bring in its wake a rise in the price of basic foodstuffs" (p. 422). He thus argues, following Hayami (1997: 85–90), that agrarian reforms aimed at enhancing productivity in agriculture in general, and in food production in particular, played an important positive role in preventing industrialization processes from being undermined by rising food prices.

Wuyts also extends Amsden's framework in two further ways. The first is by recognizing the varied nature of employment relations, which in an African context for example, can range from protected wage employment, unprotected wage employment, and casual and irregular wage labour, to self-employment and marginal self-employment. Wuyts argues that subsistence costs are as important for the dynamism and competitiveness of informal sector activities as they are for the dynamism and competitiveness of those based on a wage relationship. The second way is by examining the diversified mixture of livelihood strategies that households use in order to secure a living. These involve production for own consumption as well as for the market, and may include "straddling" between agriculture and industry. In some parts of East Asia, the majority of workers in low-wage, labour-intensive rural industries belong to households with access to land, and the economic and social security that this provided effectively subsidized industrial wages. The moderation of the rate of urbanization also kept down the costs of subsistence for society as a whole.

The prices of food and of simple consumer goods, as well as the broader conditions that guarantee economic security for households, are thus essential elements of the competitiveness and viability of labour-intensive production in latecomer countries. The two central ways of making the price of food and simple manufactured goods cheaper are using imports or increasing productivity in the domestic production of food and simple manufactured goods. Making food prices cheaper through imports will give rise to problems of sustainability unless there is sufficient export growth.

Source: Wuyts (2001).

---

228), as well as the various kinds of micro-credit institutions which have sprung up following the pioneering innovation of the Grameen Bank in Bangladesh. National financial policies which create opportunities for "rents", returns in excess of those generated by a competitive market, can also be used to tackle key blockages in financial deepening, deposit mobilization in rural areas and the development of a private long-term credit market (Hellmann, Murdock and Stiglitz, 1996). Donor countries also need to give careful thought to financing domestic enterprise development through such instruments as the Japanese two-step loans (Okuda, 1993).

Promoting exports is also likely to require a special push. The reason for this is that in many of the activities in which the LDCs apparently should have a comparative advantage given their resource endowment, they are quite simply uncompetitive. Historically, this has been a general pattern at early stages of development (Amsden, 2001). In the LDCs, trade liberalization has not been sufficient to reverse the marginalization of commodity exporting LDCs in global trade because the structure of exports remains concentrated in products for which demand is growing slowly or declining in world markets. An export-push strategy, which provides special incentives for exporters, is now necessary.[13] There is a range of well-tried trade policy measures for export promotion, including tariff rebates so that export companies can have access to imported goods at international prices, tax exemptions, preferential credits allowing exporters can have access to finance at internationally competitive rates, export credit insurance, information provision through export promotion agencies, and subsidized infrastructure. The critical priorities for support, as identified by enterprises and business associations in the LDCs themselves, are shown in table 42. Strengthening trade finance and trade promotion institutions emerge as the leading priorities according to business associations and enterprises.

Various difficult strategic decisions must be made by Governments that seek to establish an investment–export nexus. One important strategic choice that

TABLE 42. PRIORITIES FOR TRADE-RELATED TECHNICAL COOPERATION PROGRAMMES
PROPOSED BY ENTERPRISES AND BUSINESS ASSOCIATIONS IN LDCs
*(Percentage of all enterprises and business associations
identifying each priority as a focus for technical cooperation)*

Proposed priorities	Enterprises	Associations
Strengthening trade finance	84	74
Strengthening trade promotion institutions	72	79
Providing up-to-date information on market trends in international markets	64	79
Assistance in developing a national strategy for trade development	61	63
Assistance in improving human resource development facilities	54	65
Assistance in selecting trade and investment partners abroad	57	49
Development of transport services	50	44
Upgrading telecommunications, roads, electricity and water	50	42
Streamlining customs procedures	47	44
Providing up-to-date information on import tariffs and non-tariff barriers	35	47
Assistance in quality control	45	35
Training in international marketing management	30	47
Providing information on market access in the post-Uruguay Round context	24	30
Assistance in product adaptation and development	21	28
Steamlining national taxation	27	21
Training in packaging	21	21
Streamlining bureaucracy	23	14
Guidance in international purchasing and supply management	18	14
Support in acquiring relevant technology	10	16
Streamlining national import tariffs	16	7
Need for recognition of private-sector concerns	10	9
Development of the legal framework for international trade	10	9
Making policies more conducive to international business development	11	9
Reduction of import duties/non-tariff barriers in target markets	10	7
Facilitating access to international markets in general	7	9
Reducing corruption/bribery	7	0
Relaxing foreign exchange controls	7	0
Solutions to problems resulting from difficult geographical access	7	0
Assistance in reducing production costs	4	2
Developing trade support services in general	4	2
Strengthening local enterprises in general	4	2
Facilitating access to raw materials	1	5
Promoting privatization	1	0

Source: WTO (1997: table 1), based on questionnaire surveys.

emerges from the analysis in this Report is whether LDC Governments should seek to increase export growth by upgrading primary commodity exports, or by developing labour-intensive manufactures. The evidence in this Report shows that the latter route may be more effective in poverty reduction. But it is also clear that upgrading primary production exports can be part of a strategy of diversification into labour-intensive manufactures. It has been used in the second-tier newly industrializing economies (Reinhardt, 2000), and also by some of the LDCs which have diversified into textiles and clothing exports. Moreover, the earlier discussion also suggests that the opportunities for upgrading commodity exports have not as yet been properly exploited in the LDCs.[14] Thus the LDCs would be ill-advised to ignore the opportunities within primary commodity production. Export promotion is thus most likely to focus initially on natural-resource-based activities and simple labour-intensive manufactures. The International Trade Centre (ITC) has identified a number of key products which may be particularly promising for export promotion in the LDCs (table 43). These are: cotton fabrics, textiles and clothing; fish products; coffee; cotton and fibres; wood and wood products; oilseed products;

It is clear that upgrading primary production exports can be part of a strategy of diversification into labour-intensive manufactures.

TABLE 43. PRODUCTS WITH EXPORT DEVELOPMENT POTENTIAL IN LDCs

Sectors	All LDCs: average annual exports, 1995–1999 ($ million)	Countries with potential
Goods		
Cotton fabrics, textiles and clothing	2 681	Bangladesh, Nepal, Malawi, Madagascar, Mozambique, Benin, Ethiopia
Fish products	1 800	Bangladesh, Myanmar, Madagascar, Mozambique, Solomon Islands, Equatorial Guinea, Mauritania, Senegal, Maldives
Coffee	1 300	Uganda, Ethiopia, United Republic of Tanzania, Democratic Republic of the Congo, Burundi, Madagascar
Cotton and fibres	1 010	Mali, Benin, Sudan, Chad, Burkina Faso, Togo, Zambia, Madagascar, United Republic of Tanzania
Wood and wood products	856	Myanmar, Solomon Islands, Cambodia, Equatorial Guinea, Democratic Republic of the Congo, Lao People's Democratic Republic, Myanmar, Madagascar
Oilseed products	405	Sudan, Senegal, Solomon Islands, Benin, Myanmar
Vegetables	288	Myanmar, Sudan, Ethiopia, Senegal, Bangladesh, Zambia, Burkina Faso, Gambia, Afghanistan, Madagascar
Fruits and nuts	249	United Republic of Tanzania, Mozambique, Madagascar, Guinea-Bissau, Afghanistan, Somalia, Bhutan, Malawi, Myanmar
Spices	92	Madagascar, Comoros, United Republic of Tanzania, Uganda, Myanmar, Malawi, Lao People's Democratic Republic, Niger, Zambia
Cut flowers and foliage	31	Zambia, United Republic of Tanzania, Uganda, Malawi, Ethiopia, Rwanda, Yemen, Haiti, Madagascar
Medicinal plants	31	Sudan, Democratic Republic of the Congo, Vanuatu, Myanmar, Madagascar, Lao People's Democratic Republic
Services		
Tourism	2 360[a]	United Republic of Tanzania, Maldives, Nepal, Myanmar, Senegal, Uganda, Haiti, Lao People's Democratic Republic
Business-related services	1 254[b]	Myanmar, Nepal, Angola, Madagascar, Ethiopia, Yemen, Senegal, Solomon Islands, Togo, Vanuatu

Source: ITC (2001: table 2).

a   39 LDCs.
b   19 LDCs.

vegetables; fruits and nuts; spices; cut flowers and foliage; medicinal plants; business-related and professional services; and tourism. This, it should be noted, is not a complete list. Petroleum and gemstones play a major part in the economies of several LDCs. Moreover, cultural industries, and particularly music industries, have much potential in the LDCs (see box 15). Within these sectors, particular efforts should be made to upgrade production and capture more value-added.

International competitiveness in some branches of commodity production in LDCs will necessarily start with regaining the national market.

Another strategic issue is the role of import substitution in the development of an investment–export nexus. Historical experience in East Asia shows that exports often developed out of import substitution industries, and it is clear that in Africa as well a major mechanism through which export industries have developed is through expansion from sales in national markets to sales in international markets (Wangwe, 1995). International competitiveness in some branches of commodity production in LDCs will necessarily start with regaining the national market. Moreover, the poverty-reducing effects of export growth are likely to be enhanced if there are backward linkage effects in which local suppliers provide inputs of various types to support export production.

Another strategic issue is the role of domestic and foreign savings in financing the investment-export nexus. External finance is vitally important in the initial stages of building an investment–export nexus, particularly to jump-start this process. But the sustainability of the whole growth process can best be

BOX 15. ECONOMIC OPPORTUNITIES FOR THE MUSIC INDUSTRY IN LDCS

Changing trade patterns in cultural goods and services, especially music, offer new opportunities for least developed countries, rich in cultural assets, which can be transformed into lucrative business opportunities. The tremendously varied and rich store of music in the least developed countries, as witnessed by the growing popularity of World Music in the markets of the North, occupies an increasing place in contemporary popular music. LDCs have vast cultural assets in all arts, especially music, which have so far not been sufficiently exploited in the commercial arena. Not only is the basic resource — musical talent — abundantly available, but also regional musical tastes offer significant opportunities to establish markets for producers in the South.

Global trade trends in the music industry indicate that between 1980 and 2000 exports of recorded music discs and tapes from developed market economies to LDCs grew in nominal terms by 642 per cent, or 10.5 per cent per annum; while imports of developed market economy countries from LDCs rose by 321 per cent — that is to say, 7.4 per cent per annum (see box table 2). LDCs' exports in this sector have been steadily increasing over the last two decades. Despite the dominance of the five major corporations from the developed countries in this field, many LDCs also have internationally recognized brand names — Wyclef Jean, Lauryn Hill, Youssu N'Dour, Salif Keita, Cesaria Evora, Angelique Kidjo, Tabu Ley, Franco Huambo and Kester Emeneya are just some of the world-class musicians from LDCs with a strong presence in Western markets, together with Baba Maal, Kadjia Nin, Lucky Dube, and many others.

Can even the world's poorest countries with their proven excellence in music convert their home-grown talent into export-oriented business opportunities? There are positive signs. The famous Senegalese musician Youssu N'Dour records and exports directly from Dakar, while Salif Keita has set up his own music company in Bamako (Mali) that records young musicians from all over Africa. Both represent relatively successful attempts at starting up domestic music businesses based in LDCs. The efforts of these two internationally acclaimed artists to break free from the major corporations by establishing their own independent record companies in West Africa form part of the attempt by African musicians to change the highly imbalanced situation that currently prevails between African artists and the major media corporations. The popularity of African music in high-information and communication technologies income markets and the increasing use and vast potential of Africa's own largely untapped market are some of the advantages that can be built upon (UNCTAD, 2002b). Some symbolic but supportive international initiatives are taking place in this area; for example, in 2001 the World Bank made available financial support to the music industry in Senegal as a pilot project in its programme to fight poverty.

Ongoing work by UNCTAD on the music industry has shown that many LDCs, despite their strong cultural assets, lack competitive domestic enterprises and business skills to bring musical products to global markets (Andersen, Z. Kozul-Wright and R. Kozul-Wright, 2000). The absence of entrepreneurial and exporting skills poses a serious barrier to exports to high-income markets. But this may be changing with the advent of electronic commerce, which can provide

Box 15 (contd.)

LDCs with new opportunities to reach global markets. Here the digital divide is not only real but may also be bridgeable. A part of this agenda should include the building of the specialized skills for commercializing LDC music products through training and upgrading specifically in business skills, marketing and international partnerships in the export of music products from the LDCs.

Given the objective of increasing the rents earned in the music industry through investment in capacity in all relevant forms, two major policy issues clearly emerge. The first is the critical significance of copyrights and the appropriate regulatory framework (including a pro-local broadcasting media framework). Secondly, a solution should be sought to reduce the various types of market failures that impinge on the development of music and other cultural industries. The most important of these concerns is the lack of access of domestic entrepreneurs to long-term credit and working capital. Private capital markets are unresponsive to music industry participants in most LDCs. The paramount area for policy is the provision of abundant credit, and its provision to local entrepreneurs and music industry participants.

BOX TABLE 2. LDCs IN GLOBAL TRADE IN MUSIC,[a] 1980–2000
(Current $ millions)

Year	Exports from developed market economy countries to:				Imports to developed market economy countries from:			
	World	Developed market-economy countries	Developing countries	LDCs	World	Developed market-economy countries	Developing countries	LDCs
1980	876.0	640.4	91.3	2.8	811.1	788.2	19.9	0.3
1985	1 415.7	1 033.4	160.9	3.1	1 474.0	1 424.6	44.0	0.3
1990	6 809.6	5 820.5	615.9	11.7	6 755.7	6 556.2	173.2	0.2
1995	12 913.5	10 410.2	1 623.7	19.2	12 532.1	11 864.4	601.8	0.4
1996	14 118.8	11 605.2	1 585.5	16.5	13 509.9	12 713.1	731.0	0.4
1997	14 195.3	11 953.8	1 871.1	17.5	13 029.0	12 232.6	703.7	0.6
1998	14 562.9	12 001.5	1 738.9	16.5	14 028.8	13 048.7	862.1	0.6
1999	15 887.1	13 102.4	1 902.9	22.3	14 991.2	13 780.7	1 045.2	0.8
2000	15 510.1	12 405.1	2 179.4	21.0	14 581.5	13 189.6	1 229.9	1.1
Average annual growth rates (%)	15.5	16.0	17.2	10.5	15.5	15.1	22.9	7.4
% change from 1980 to 2000	1 670.7	1 837.2	2 286.1	642.3	1 697.8	1 573.3	6 068.8	320.8

Source: UNCTAD secretariat estimates based on UN COMTRADE data.

a   Recorded discs and tapes.

Policy support is also required for the creation and establishment of effective national copyright regimes and marketing (ibid.). The responsible policy makers may need to assist participants with the development of the capacity to market the product that runs the least risk of piracy. This would include the development of classic venues for the staging of shows and festivals, with adequate arrangements for market differentiation and assistance with innovative forms of Internet marketing. Another relevant support is a taxation regime that targets the users of consumer hardware in the music and entertainment industry and seeks to recoup some of the losses from piracy of intellectual property.

The development of the domestic marketing capacity of the music industry should become a major focus of policy-making. To develop this market, it is necessary that each developing country adopt a package of initiatives, including research, training, apprenticeship, and development of physical and institutional infrastructure, in order to encourage reliance on local knowledge and culture in the marketing of products. Such initiatives would involve market differentiation mechanisms that increase the visibility of products and processes, and thus of artists and festival producers. At the same time, it is necessary to enhance the capacity of the local industry to market its products through the collaborative or commercial use of modern information technology for distribution, particularly marketing-oriented websites, while increasing the use of available means to limit piracy. For example, it might be necessary for incentives to be given to the private sector entities in the music industry to develop Internet malls for the music, entertainment and related industries. Such sites use an appropriate browser (with appropriate search engines) to sell simultaneously a cafeteria of services and products, such as a wide variety of CDs, films, music clips, and other entertainment-related goods and services, to both the consumer and the creator, and therefore bring the latter together for information and distribution purposes. They are widely used by all the major participants in the industry, and are typically not cost-effective for any single artist or operator to develop and use.

ensured if domestic savings start to grow along with investment and exports, and over time increasingly drive the process (Akyüz and Gore, 2001). As a corporate sector expands, corporate profits become increasingly important as a component of domestic savings and their reinvestment becomes a central motor of the accumulation process. But where the majority of the population earn their livelihoods in agriculture, and the main form of production is one in which work is organized by households, increased domestic savings will require increased agricultural productivity. Increasing the overall rate of capital accumulation will depend on the way in which surplus investable resources are channelled into further productive investment both inside and outside agriculture (see Teranishi, 1997). The marketization of agricultural production can be particularly important since it leads to an increasing division of labour and specialization within a country, and also the development of a growing national market. This will contribute to the general pro-investment climate. Recent developments in Vietnam show how a high rate of agricultural growth can provide an important underpinning for export-led growth in low-income countries (Arkadie, 2001).

The sustainability of the whole growth process can best be ensured if domestic savings start to grow along with investment and exports, and over time increasingly drive the process.

In dealing with the agricultural sector, some Governments are likely to face particularly difficult choices in terms of the priority given to the promotion of export crops or staple food crops for home or domestic consumption. Productivity gains in food crops can provide important poverty reduction gains in the early stages of development (Lipton, 2000). If land and labour resources are abundant, there may be no trade-off between export and food crops. Moreover, food can be imported. But in some African LDCs it is clear that the situation is complex and that it is difficult to develop agricultural exports out of local production of staple foods (UNCTAD, 1998).

3. PRODUCTIVE DEVELOPMENT POLICY OPTIONS

Growth-oriented macroeconomic policies are an essential aspect of establishing a dynamic investment–export nexus.

Growth-oriented macroeconomic policies are an essential aspect of establishing a dynamic investment–export nexus in the LDCs. Short-term macroeconomic objectives of internal and external balance should be pursued through means which are consistent with long-term development objectives and which do not require investment levels so low as to compromise future growth. Low and stable interest rates to finance productive investment and competitive exchange rates are ingredients of a growth-oriented approach. But too tight credit ceilings can effectively undermine the ability of local firms to obtain the finance they need to expand production and improve supply capabilities. Fiscal measures, such as tax breaks and special depreciation allowances, can also be used to increase corporate profits and encourage retention in order to accelerate capital accumulation (UNCTAD, 2002a).

Alongside appropriate macroeconomic policies, it is important to adopt mesoeconomic and microeconomic measures that are specifically designed to improve the supply capabilities of the economy.

Experience suggests that, alongside appropriate macroeconomic policies, it is important to adopt mesoeconomic and microeconomic measures that are specifically designed to improve the supply capabilities of the economy.[15] Such measures can enhance macro–micro linkages in a way which supports national development and poverty reduction goals. UNCTAD has identified such measures as an important element of East Asian development strategies. They are also central to the neostructuralist approach which has been elaborated by ECLAC to achieve development with equity whilst integrating into the global economy.[16] The absence of such measures, and of mutually supportive links between macroeconomic, mesoeconomic and microeconomic policies, is a key weakness of the PRSPs at the present time.

Much more is known about the elaboration of productive development policies — which is the term that Latin American economists use to describe these policies — in more advanced developing countries than in the LDCs. However, some general remarks can indicate the types of policy options. Elements of a productive development policy include financial policy, technology policy, human resource development, physical infrastructure development, and industrial organization and competition policy. These elements are coordinated with trade policy. They can form part of, but should not be simply equated with, a selective industrial policy. They are directed at improving productivity and competitiveness in agriculture and natural-resource-based activities as well as in manufacturing.[17] They are designed to accelerate capital accumulation and learning both in specific sectors and throughout the economy, and to manage the complementarities, between enterprises and between productive sectors which can block profitable investment in any single one. These measures should seek to improve the environment within which enterprises operate, both in the economy as a whole and in specific sectors within it, and also help enterprises to identify and acquire competitive advantages through investment and learning. A particular aim is to promote the imitation and adaptation of internationally available technologies in order to reduce costs, improve quality, and introduce goods and services not existing in the country, and to promote the diffusion of best practices from more advanced to less advanced enterprises within the country, including from foreign-owned to locally owned firms.[18]

An important aspect of productive development policies is that they are not simply designed to improve capital accumulation and learning in the economy as a whole, but they also have a sectoral focus. The basis for this approach is the insight that "economic growth is intrinsically tied to the structural context, which is made up of productive and technological apparatuses, the configuration of factor and product markets, the characteristic of entrepreneurial agents, and the way in which these markets and agents relate to the external environment. The leadership exercised by certain sectors and firms is the essential dynamic factor that propels economic growth" (ECLAC, 2000: 219). It is clear that a major aspect of the weak export performance of many LDCs is the composition and concentration of their exports. Also, an important constraint on investment in the early stages of development is that the profitability of investment in one sector is often blocked by conditions in related sectors. Policy needs to tackle these strategic complementarities. In order to ensure that sections of the population are not marginalized as growth occurs, it is also necessary to consider the sectoral pattern of growth and structural heterogeneities such as the divide between the formal and informal sectors.

The sectoral focus of policy may be defined in broad terms. Seventy-five per cent of the LDC population now lives in rural areas, and in most LDCs, most people derive their livelihoods from farming. Thus agriculture is likely to be an initial focus. As agricultural productivity is low and often stagnant, attention must be directed in many countries to promoting agricultural growth by inducing technical change (Mosley, 2001). But it is clear that non-farm rural activities are an important element of the agricultural accumulation process, and these activities should therefore not be ignored. Moreover, certain manufacturing activities and services are also important for some LDCs, and are becoming more important in many LDCs since urbanization is proceeding rapidly (see UNIDO, 2001).

Productive development policies are implemented as far as possible through private or mixed (both public and private) enterprise rather than pure public ownership. The key role of the Government is to harness the entrepreneurial drive, which is the motor of the whole system, to support national development

An important aspect of productive development policies is that they are not simply designed to improve capital accumulation and learning in the economy as a whole, but they also have a sectoral focus.

Agriculture is likely to be an initial sectoral focus. As agricultural productivity is low and often stagnant, attention must be directed in many countries to promoting agricultural growth by inducing technical change.

and poverty reduction. The Government guides the process of capital accumulation and learning, but these policies are best developed and implemented through institutions that enable business perspectives to be incorporated, and through policies which channel activities and energies rather than limit them. Sectoral policies, for example, should arise from joint efforts between the public and private sectors which together formulate a vision and reach a consensus on the way in which support mechanisms should be tailored to particular sectors. These would cover such matters as what institutions are required to support the technological development of a specific sector, what are the collective requirements in terms of labour skills, and how financial resources can be ensured for the expansion of the sector.

This is not a return to the old-style development plans of the past as it is based on plural forms of ownership and entails a developmental partnership between the State and the private sector.

This is not a return to the old-style development plans of the past as it is based on plural forms of ownership and entails a developmental partnership between the State and the private sector. The Government must also ensure that any subsidies or rents which are provided as part of productive development policies are designed to encourage the development of supply capabilities. It is possible to do this by making subsidies or rents conditional on investment, exports, technological learning and productivity targets, by making them temporary, and by establishing "contests" amongst the private sector as an allocation mechanism.[19] The aim is to avoid unproductive rent-seeking by creating rent opportunities that induce economically efficient developmental actions that private markets would not otherwise undertake. Policies should focus on overcoming specific problems which impede the achievement of national development objectives, notably missing markets and the lack of an entrepreneurial base, imperfections in technology and capital markets, and the risks associated with exporting, and on dynamic complementarities between firms and sectors which render competitiveness and productivity systemic rather than merely dependent on firm-level capabilities.

Successful implementation of productive development policies requires enhancement of State capacities. There is a widespread belief that Governments in LDCs, particularly African LDCs, lack the institutional capabilities to manage such policies. State capacities have certainly been eroded over the last 20 years, but experience in other countries shows that, with application, it is possible to learn quickly what does and does not work (Mkandawire, 2001). There is no reason to deny that engagement in a limited number of policies during the initial stages of investment and export promotion will allow Governments in LDCs to learn how to design productive development policies, to find out what incentives are effective and for what purpose, and to learn about the drawbacks that a policy that looks good on paper may have in practice.

Perhaps a greater problem in promoting sustainable growth and building a dynamic investment–export nexus in the LDCs is the weakness of the domestic enterpreneurial class.

Perhaps a greater problem in promoting sustainable growth and building a dynamic investment–export nexus in the LDCs is the weakness of the domestic enterpreneurial class. There are not enough businesses with the capacity and capability to compete internationally, and this is a major constraint on growth in the LDCs. As noted earlier, financing medium-sized domestic businesses is an important issue (see also UNCTAD 2002c). It may be helpful to stimulate local production clusters, to encourage collaborative links with TNCs aimed at encouraging learning and knowledge expansion in domestic enterprises, to expand links with local (and international) universities, technical institutes, research centres and metronomy institutes to guarantee quality, and to provide technical support services to SMEs. Existing entrepreneurial skills may also be focused on short-term trading and housing rather than on long-term production. Particular efforts may be made to ensure that the structure of profitability and the availability of investment funds are biased towards productive investments that can create employment.

4. Policies to prevent marginalization within LDCs

As economic growth occurs, it is highly likely that some groups and regions will be left behind in poverty. A final key element of long-term development strategies is therefore the adoption of policies that prevent marginalization within countries.

The surest way to ensure that economic growth is more inclusive is through the wide distribution of assets, the expansion of productive employment, creating linkages that incorporate marginal sectors into the space of productivity growth, and greater balance between export promotion and import substitution. Particular policies which may be important are the following: agrarian reform and rural development policies (land tenure, agricultural productivity growth, rural industries, rural labour markets); high rates of reinvestment of profits and the establishment of profit-related pay systems; micro-credit; labour market policies; support for small and medium-sized enterprises; promotion of backward linkages from export activity; broad-based human resource development through investment in education and health; and decentralized fiscal systems.[20] Application of principles of good governance can also help to ensure inclusion.

The identification of appropriate policies to prevent marginalization of groups and regions within a country can be aided by the application of an approach to poverty analysis which has been elaborated by Pyatt (1999, 2001a, 2001b). This approach, which he calls a structuralist approach to poverty analysis, can neatly dovetail with the productive development policies. It directs attention to the generation and sustainability of livelihoods, their location within the structure of the economy and the way in which they are affected by the relations of the national economy with the rest of the world (box 16). A particular concern is the vulnerability of people to becoming destitute or dependent on unrequited transfers. It is this focus on vulnerability which is important in understanding how different groups may be marginalized as a national economy grows.

The surest way to ensure that economic growth is more inclusive is through the wide distribution of assets, the expansion of productive employment, creating linkages that incorporate marginal sectors into the space of productivity growth, and greater balance between export promotion and import substitution... Application of principles of good governance can also help to ensure inclusion.

E. Strengthened national ownership and policy autonomy

A necessary condition for the elaboration of alternative poverty reduction strategies that do not reinforce existing adjustment policies but seek to promote poverty reduction through development is strengthened national ownership and policy autonomy. Indeed, enhanced ownership is potentially the most important change which can occur through the PRSP approach (United Nations Development Group, 2001). But enabling genuine national ownership of policies is a complex process. This section focuses on five aspects which require attention: managing the tension between policy ownership and policy conditionality; capacity-building within countries; donor alignment behind PRSPs; joint programming between countries and donors to tackle the poverty reduction financing deficit; and the nature of WTO rights and obligations.

A necessary condition for the elaboration of alternative poverty reduction strategies is strengthened national ownership and policy autonomy.

1. The tension between national ownership and policy conditionality

The basic way in which national ownership is supposed to be strengthened is by international financial institutions (IFIs) and donor countries stepping back

---

BOX 16. GRAHAM PYATT'S STRUCTURALIST APPROACH TO POVERTY ANALYSIS

Pyatt argues that a structuralist approach to poverty analysis should be adopted as the preferred approach to drafting poverty reduction strategies. This approach has three basic features. Firstly, it is founded on the view that household living standards derive from the generation and sustainability of livelihoods. A starting point for developing a poverty reduction strategy should therefore be an understanding of how households in different socioeconomic groups make a living. Secondly, the approach locates the generation and sustainability of livelihoods of different groups within the structure of the economy, which is understood to include both the structure of production and the institutional relationships between households, the corporate sector and government. Locating livelihoods within the structure of the economy focuses attention on the influence on living standards of such factors as the sectoral and regional structure of the economy, the importance of, and connections between, the formal and informal sectors, the division of value added between capital and labour, and the influence of macro policies. On the basis of a mapping of the structure of the economy and interactions between different groups and sectors, it is possible to understand how the level and distribution of living standards are jointly determined. Thirdly, the approach examines the relationships between the structure of the economy and the rest of the world. This brings international aid, private capital flows, debt repayments and trade flows into the analysis of the generation and sustainability of livelihoods at the national level.

The approach involves the adoption of a multi-level framework for locating the causes of poverty, which runs from household characteristics, through the meso structure of the economy, to macroeconomic conditions and the global context. The links between the micro, meso, macro and international levels of analysis are all part of the structuralist approach. Simple social accounting matrices would be constructed on the basis of existing sources to locate livelihoods within the structure of the national economy. Models should then be developed to explore the implications of different strategies, and to develop a range of policy scenarios. For example, the likely impact of different tourist export development policies, with their associated linkages and leakages, could be analysed in this framework.

Pyatt contrasts the structuralist approach with what he calls the "statistical approach" to poverty analysis, which, he argues, was used in the World Bank country-level Poverty Assessments in the 1990s and is now being replicated in the poverty diagnoses of the PRSPs. The statistical approach adopts the household as the basic unit of analysis, divides the population into the poor and the non-poor on the basis of a chosen income or consumption poverty line, and then focuses on the characteristics which distinguish the poor from the non-poor. There is a strong temptation to see these characteristics as important factors which are causing poverty and thus as central ingredients of poverty reduction policy. But various policy errors and biases can result, including a general tendency, which was widespread in World Bank Poverty Assessments and is now being reproduced in the PRSPs, to ignore the critical role of employment generation and labour markets in poverty reduction.

In his own elaboration of the structuralist approach, Pyatt argues that the poor should be identified not through the adoption of an arbitrary national or international poverty line, but as those "individuals who are destitute or otherwise dependent on unrequited transfers" (Pyatt, 2001b: 30). The focus of poverty reduction policies, in his view, should be both these people and also the vulnerable, who are those at risk of becoming destitute or dependent on unrequited transfers. This directs attention to the sustainability of households and their livelihoods, as well as to the generation of the latter. From the perspective of the argument developed in this chapter, it is this focus on vulnerability which is important in understanding how different groups may be marginalized as a national economy grows.

In developing this approach, Pyatt has advocated a holistic approach to monitoring outcomes which may include both monetary and non-monetary measures of living standards. The approach does not need the definition of income/consumption poverty lines. But equally it does not need to reject them. Thus it is possible for the $1-a-day and $2-a-day international poverty lines to enter the policy process, along with other measures of affluence and deprivation, at the monitoring stage.

Source: Pyatt (1999, 2001a, 2001b).

---

from policy formulation processes and not imposing what they consider to be the right policies, but rather allowing countries to which they are supplying concessional aid to establish their own poverty reduction strategies. But there is clearly an inherent tension between country ownership and the need for the international financial institutions and other donors to be assured that their assistance will be well used to support what they regard as credible strategies (Lipumba, 2001). Given the high level of dependence of poor countries on aid and debt relief, there is a danger that country-prepared PRSPs presented to the

Boards of the IMF and the World Bank for endorsement will seek to anticipate what is endorsable. Ownership would actually then be deeper internalization of the norms of the IFIs.

The IMF and the World Bank are certainly signalling that, given the experimental nature of the PRSP approach, there is flexibility in terms of what they expect. Moreover, at the country level their staffs "are widely credited with delicate handling of PRSP processes as such" (ODI, 2001: 60). But the PRSP process remains a compulsory process in which Governments that need concessional assistance and debt relief from the IFIs find out, through the endorsement process, the limits of what is acceptable policy.[21] In such a situation it is very difficult for government officials to take the risks which would enable the full potential of the PRSP approach to be realized. Even if there is no outside interference in the PRSP preparation process, and also no signs of threat to interfere in the process, the mere awareness of dependence on the Joint Staff Assessment and on endorsement by the Boards of the IMF and the World Bank places constraints on the freedom of action of those designing the PRSPs. In effect, the country owns the technical process of policy formulation, but it still lacks the freedom which would release the creative potential of the approach.

In effect, the country owns the technical process of policy formulation, but it still lacks the freedom which would release the creative potential of the approach.

It is widely recognized that the rush to complete Interim PRSPs (I-PRSPs) and PRSPs in order to reach the decision and completion points for the enhanced HIPC Initiative and/or to secure a Poverty Reduction and Growth Facility (PRGF) arrangement has reduced the quality of the PRSPs in terms of country ownership. Some country-level studies also indicate that there has been a degree of "self-censorship" by national authorities, whereby they have held back certain policy ideas which they believed to be heterodox in IMF and World Bank terms, in order to ensure the acceptability of the PRSPs (ODI, 2001).

True country ownership and policy autonomy in the preparation of PRSPs require that the IFIs have total open-mindedness as to what is regarded as a "credible strategy". If this is lacking, the consequences for governance will be adverse, as politicians and policy makers will feel inhibited from saying and doing certains things, and thus the political qualities of a free-thinking society, which are meant to be encouraged through the PRSP process, will atrophy. The nature of policy conditionalities must also be subject to more radical review. The streamlining of conditionality is a welcome trend,[22] but it is not in itself sufficient to enable the development of policy alternatives. There is, rather, a need for both fewer conditions and greater flexibility in their content. Also, as the Co-Chairs of the Special Programme for Africa (SPA) Technical Group have pointed out, donors must "recognize that programmatic support to PRSs [poverty reduction strategies] cannot be based on traditional stop-go mechanisms" (SPA, 2001: 138).

True country ownership and policy autonomy in the preparation of PRSPs require that the IFIs have total open-mindedness as to what is regarded as a "credible strategy".

Even if the PRSP as a document is itself country-owned, a further problem which is emerging is the relationship between the PRSP and the policy conditionalities specified in HIPC decision and completion point documents, PRGF arrangements or Poverty Reduction Support Credits (PRSCs). It is a matter of great concern in this regard that research by the European Commission, covering 10 countries up to November 2000, observed a wide divergence between I-PRSPs and conditionalities for HIPC completion point (European Commission, 2000), and that follow-up research, which extended the coverage by 14 countries, including all countries that reached decision point before September 2001, confirmed the pattern, finding "unclear links between I-PRSP and HIPC documents, with the risk of having parallel (or incoherent) reform tracks" (European Commission, 2001a: 1). This may well reflect the early phases of the application of the PRSP approach. However, it is important that this be continually monitored. The HIPC Finance Ministers and Coordinators of PRSPs (2002) have stated that "countries need to be empowered to verify that conditions spring from the PRSP and to refuse to accept those which do not, in the knowledge that alternative more flexible finance will be available" (p. 5).

2. THE CRUCIAL ROLE OF CAPACITY-BUILDING

Establishing capable States is essential for enhanced national ownership and policy autonomy, and also for the effective implementation of PRSPs. There is excessive pessimism on the potential for doing this, particularly in Sub-Saharan Africa (see Mkandawire, 2001). But nevertheless, a concerted effort and financial resources will be required to build institutional capacities and human resources. Key specific skills required are capacities for: establishing comprehensive and coherent budgets and medium-term expenditure plans (IMF/IDA, 2001a); developing costings for the implementation of PRSPs; economic forecasting; and debt management. Investment in national statistical systems, which allow policy debate to be carried out on the basis of facts, is also vital. Another important technical capacity which requires strengthening in many LDCs is financial auditing and accounting. Technical capacity for auditing and accounting is the backbone of government accountability, but it is extremely weak in many sub-Saharan African LDCs. Enhanced capacity in poverty analysis is also essential. However, weaknesses here may reflect a more general problem in terms of what is known about poverty in poor countries and what responses are possible.

Capacity-building will be enhanced through the institution of learning mechanisms, which should include South–South exchange of experience. But it is also important that the nature of technical assistance be carefully reconsidered. According to HIPC Finance Ministers and PRSP Coordinators (2002), "a huge amount of technical assistance is being provided but much of it is replacing rather than building capacity within our administrations". Past evaluations of the impact of technical cooperation in the LDCs, particularly African LDCs, indicate very poor results in terms of technology transfer and capacity-building (Berg, 1993). According to Berg, multiplicity and duplication, wrong incentives and a lack of integration with domestic structures have all played a role in the failure of technical assistance. In addition, there have been important negative externalities associated with technical assistance, ranging from distorting government pay structures, and discouraging learning and capacity-building in public institutions, to additional monetary costs for recipient Governments.

3. DONOR ALIGNMENT BEHIND NATIONAL PRSPs

A further necessary condition for enhanced country ownership is donor alignment behind the PRSP approach. The importance of this stems from the fact that the accumulation and budgetary processes in most least developed countries are highly dependent on external resources. Without simultaneous support by the donors, and without an effort by them to coordinate their aid with one another and with the domestic economic processes, efforts by the countries themselves to enhance national ownership will necessarily be limited. The internal processes of consultation, transparency and consensus-building around the budget would be rendered futile without timely and accurate financial information from the donors. The lack of synchronization of donors' and recipients' budget cycles, the use of different accounting conventions and classifications, provision of incomplete information on aid disbursement, and

There is excessive pessimism on the potential for establishing capable States... But nevertheless, a concerted effort and financial resources will be required to build institutional capacities and human resources.

A further necessary condition for enhanced country ownership is donor alignment behind the PRSP approach.

Without simultaneous support by the donors, and without an effort by them to coordinate their aid with one another and with the domestic economic processes, efforts by the countries themselves to enhance national ownership will necessarily be limited.

lack of information on aid strategies and future expenditure plans of donors are well-known deficiencies of the aid delivery system which have made the task of financial management in the recipient countries difficult, if not impossible (UNCTAD, 2000).

Quite apart from capacity constraints, a major impediment to comprehensive medium-term public sector expenditure planning and financial management in the LDCs is that a large part of the donor-funded projects and programmes bypass the central government budget. In fiscal year 1999 in the United Republic of Tanzania, for example, only 30 per cent of ODA was estimated to flow through the government budget. In addition, Governments often have little information on aid flows. The OECD's important study of aid in Mali found that the aid flows given in Malian statistics represent only between one and two thirds of the official figures published by the OECD and UNDP in their development cooperation reports.[23] In these circumstances, improved public expenditure management by the national Government will be a necessary, but by no means a sufficient, condition for improved public expenditure.

It is clear that donors are committed to supporting the PRSP process, but "progress in alignment is uneven across partners and countries" (IMF/World Bank, 2002b: 24). As the HIPC Finance Ministers and PRSP Coordinators (2002) put it, "many donors continue to provide off-budget aid, or aid tied to projects which are not essential to the PRSP, and to 'sell' projects to countries which do not have a long-term development or poverty reduction focus, or whose associated financial terms are not sufficiently concessional" (p. 5).

Donors need to end the prevalent practice of parallel staffing and remuneration arrangements for stand-alone projects, which has undermined recipient Governments' ownership, accountability and capacity. Also, donor funds should increasingly take the form of budget support or collaborative sector-side programmes. New forms of aid which bypass the budgetary and monitoring scrutiny of government administration, and are not coordinated with national priorities, need to be restrained. A general principle of partnership, which has been articulated by African countries, is of relevance to LDCs: "Donor assistance should be delivered through government systems unless there are compelling reasons to the contrary; where this is not possible, any alternative mechanisms or safeguards must be time-limited, and develop and build, rather than undermine or by-pass, government systems. This applies to budget processes and procurement systems amongst others" (SPA, 2001: 2). The principle recognizes that some donors and international financial institutions are unlikely to channel assistance through government budgets immediately. Transitional measures are required, and these should be designed in a way that does not undermine government capacity.

Donor assistance should be delivered through government systems unless there are compelling reasons to the contrary.

A concrete proposal to promote partnership is that donor performance monitoring indicators be introduced at the country level. The approach to improving the aid relationship which is being elaborated in the United Republic of Tanzania could serve as a model for this (see box 17).

4. PARTNERSHIP AND THE POVERTY REDUCTION FINANCING GAPS

In developing nationally owned poverty reduction strategies, Governments need to be able to programme future public expenditure jointly with donors. A central thrust of the PRSP process is to ensure that government revenue and aid are used more effectively for poverty reduction, and are shown to be used more

Box 17. Instituting systems for donor performance monitoring at the recipient country level as part of the PRSP process

One practical way to improve aid effectiveness and promote greater partnership in aid relationships is to institute systems for donor performance monitoring at the recipient country level as part of the PRSP process. At the present time, the major official source of aid performance data and performance evaluation is the Development Assistance Committee (DAC) of the OECD. The DAC reports such items as total ODA flows (disbursements and commitments) and flows to principal recipients by donor; total ODA flows as a percentage of donor gross national income by donor country; aggregate composition of aid commitments by major use and purposes, and aggregate technical cooperation commitments; and the tied status of total commitments. Donor performance evaluations are also undertaken through peer reviews by other DAC members.

Instituting donor performance monitoring systems at the national level could complement this activity by gathering and evaluating information in a way which is more closely related to aid recipients' needs. On the basis of close examination of the aid relationship in the United Republic of Tanzania, Helleiner (2000) has suggested various types of indicators which could be useful to recipients. These include the following: the degree to which ODA expenditures flow through the government budget of recipients; the degree to which donor projects and expenditures are coordinated and integrated with national and sectoral plans and are aligned behind the declared priorities of the recipient Governments; the predictability and reliability of aid inflows, including, in particular, the relationships between disbursements and prior commitments; the degree to which the time profile of donor disbursements is responsive to shocks which generate needs for liquidity and increased budget and balance-of-payments support; the degree of tying of procurement; the percentage of aid spent on donor-country-tied technical assistance; the degree to which donors are making long-term commitments; the degree to which donors are enabling national ownership of development programmes; and the extent to which aid is being allocated for development rather than provided as humanitarian assistance or debt relief. For effective partnership, it is also vital that information be provided by donors in the statistical categories of recipient countries and that donors comply with recipient countries' requests for information.

Donor performance monitoring systems at the recipient country level are of particular relevance with the introduction of the PRSP process. They offer a practical method of encouraging and monitoring donor alignment behind individual PRSPs, and of increasing partnership by ensuring that information is available to recipients on a timely basis and in a form which can facilitate national programming and budgeting. This is a practical way to achieve some of the key aims of the PRSP approach.

Such a system has already been set up in the United Republic of Tanzania. Efforts have been made to improve the aid relationship since 1995, when an independent assessment of that relationship, funded by the Danish Government in agreement with the Tanzanian Government, made a number of concrete recommendations for the Tanzanian Government and the donors. Agreement was reached between the Government and the Nordic countries on how the aid relationship could be improved, and this led to a broader discussion with the donor community on concrete steps which needed to be taken. At the meeting of the Consultative Group in 1999, it was agreed in principle that an independent process of monitoring of aid relationships should be instituted. This was followed in 2000 by the preparation of the Tanzanian Assistance Strategy (TAS) to govern the ongoing aid relationship between the Tanzanian Government and its development partners. At the meeting of the Consultative Group in 2000, it was agreed that implementation of the TAS would include independent monitoring and evaluation of donor performance as well as of Tanzanian performance.

Since then the Economic and Social Research Foundation, an independent Tanzanian not-for-profit NGO, has been appointed to work as an honest broker coordinating the independent monitoring with donor funding coordinated by UNDP. The Independent Monitoring Group consists of three Tanzanians, three experts from donor countries and one African non-Tanzanian. All members of the Group were selected on the basis of their independence from the Tanzanian Government and from donor administrations. The work of the Group started in early 2002, and its report will be presented at the Consultative Group meeting in 2002. All parties are committed to supporting the work of the Group up to the end of 2003, after which the situation is to be reviewed in the light of the experience gained.

effectively. However greater poverty reduction can be achieved by enlarging the fiscal space for poverty reduction as well as by improving the poverty-reducing efficiency of public expenditure. The gains from enlarging the fiscal space cannot be realized unless Governments work with donors jointly to examine the trade-offs between different levels of external assistance and poverty reduction, and thus explore the policy options, and poverty-reducing effects, that stem from expanding the resource envelope. Until this happens, the poverty-reducing impact of the PRSP process will necessarily be constrained.

Countries are currently expected to submit PRSPs which are "realistic" in terms of external financing projections. It is hypothetically possible, as the IMF notes, for medium-term projections to be based on "a more normative scenario for grants and concessional loans driven by poverty and growth goals, rather than a continuation of declining trends with unfilled financing gaps" (IMF, 2000). If prior commitments of substantial donor assistance are obtained as programmes are being formulated, higher public spending, compatible with a prudent fiscal stance, can be built in at the outset. But in practice, this is not happening and poverty reduction financing gaps are emerging as Governments prepare their PRSPs. The pace of poverty reduction is then being scaled back to ensure that the PRSP is deemed realistic and thus worthy of donor support.

Examples of this are found in the PRSPs of Uganda and the United Republic of Tanzania. In the latter case, technical studies indicated that the financing of acceptable levels of health care would cost about $9 per head. This would entail a doubling of the present budget allocation for the health care sector. But this was considered unfeasible in view of projections of the overall resource envelope. Therefore, budgetary provision for the sector had to be restricted to available resources, which implied that the delivery of health services under the present circumstances would fall below acceptable levels in the short term (Tanzanian Authorities, 2000). Similarly, in Uganda, discussion with the sector line ministries revealed that there was a gap of the order of 37 per cent between current and required spending levels for full funding of PEAP/PRSP-related programmes.[24] Although such increases were believed by national authorities to be necessary to meet initial PEAP/PRSP targets, the Joint Staff Assessment notes that "Increases of this magnitude are clearly incompatible with macro-economic stability, and accordingly, the government is in the process of refining costing figures, and adjusting and prioritizing activities and targets" (IMF/IDA, 2001b: 5). As the Government paper puts it, the implication is that "the implementation of the PEAP/PRSP will take longer than initially expected and that Government needs to prioritize the different actions to get a more realistic program which can then be used to guide the MTEF" (Uganda, 2001: 12).

A further problem for Governments is the unpredictability of aid flows. This creates major dilemmas for Governments in designing and implementing PRSPs. If a Government takes the commitments at face value and they are surpassed, not only is the resource envelope for poverty reduction underestimated but there are also difficult problems of absorbing unexpected increased flows. If, on the other hand, disbursements fall short of donor commitments, there is a difficult problem of adjusting to the shortfall and redistributing cuts in public expenditure. The overall effect of uncertainty of external financing, together with the supreme requirement for macroeconomic stabilization (small budget deficits and low domestic borrowing by government), implies that Governments have to downscale the public expenditure requirements of poverty reduction. An important feature of HIPC assistance is that Governments know exactly what its time profile is. It would help poverty reduction efforts if ODA flows also had a much higher degree of predictability over a long time horizon.

With greater aid predictability, fiscal flexibility can also be further enhanced through calculating the size of the budget deficit after taking account of grants and the grant element of loans. This can make a great difference to the size of the fiscal deficit. Current practice is to distinguish between the deficit before and after grants, and the deficit after grants has increasingly been seen as more

The gains from enlarging the fiscal space cannot be realized unless Governments work with donors jointly to examine the trade-offs between different levels of external assistance and poverty reduction, and thus explore the policy options, and poverty-reducing effects, that stem from expanding the resource envelope.

It would help poverty reduction efforts if ODA flows had a much higher degree of predictability over a long time horizon.

appropriate for countries which will effectively rely on grants and concessional finance into the long term. However, just as the stock of concessional debt can be split into its implicit grant and market loan components, so can the current flow of loans. A measure of the budget deficit can then be calculated after "augmented" grants, namely grants plus the grant element in soft loans. Failing to account for the grant element in concessional finance "may lead to an inappropriately tight fiscal stance" (Bevan and Adams, 2001: 3). In the United Republic of Tanzania, for example, where this augmented deficit has been applied, the projected deficit before grants was 1 per cent of GDP in 2000–2001, but after grants and concessional loans, the fiscal position was estimated as a surplus of 5 per cent of GDP. This broader concept of the deficit can be more widely applied, and can work if donors increase the predictability of their aid commitments.

5. WTO RIGHTS AND OBLIGATIONS

Many of the financial, fiscal and macroeconomic policies that can help create the basic conditions for faster capital accumulation in LDCs and upgrading through learning are not constrained by WTO obligations.

A final aspect of national ownership and policy autonomy is the nature of WTO rights and obligations. Many of the financial, fiscal and macroeconomic policies that can help create the basic conditions for faster capital accumulation in LDCs and upgrading through learning are not constrained by WTO obligations. Nor to a very large extent are the institutions and informal networks required to support such policies. Various forms of direct and indirect support for export promotion are still allowed for the LDCs, and various forms of protection and other support, especially temporary, are still allowed in order to promote the establishment of particular industries with a view to raising the general living standard of the population.

It is important in this regard that the WTO Agreement on Subsidies and Countervailing Measures recognizes that "subsidies may play an important role in economic development programmes of developing country Members" (GATT secretariat, 1994: Article 27). Least developed countries that are members of the WTO, as well as developing country members with GNP per capita of less than $1,000 per annum, are exempted from the prohibition on export subsidies. Moreover, they are also exempted from the prohibition on subsidies that are contingent upon the use of domestic over imported goods, for eight years from the date of entry into force of the WTO Agreement rather than five years (as is the case for other developing countries). It is also relevant that the contracting parties to the Uruguay Agreement "recognize that the attainment of the objectives of this Agreement will be facilitated by the progressive development of their economies, particularly of those contracting parties the economies of which can only support low standards of living and are in the early stage of development"...[and] recognize further that it may be necessary for those contracting parties, in order to implement programmes and policies of economic development designed to raise the general living standard of their people, to take protective or other measures affecting imports, and that such measures are justified in so far as they facilitate the attainment of the objectives of the Agreement" (GATT secretariat, 1994: Article 18). Furthermore, the Decision on Measures in Favour of Least-Developed Countries states that the least developed countries, while complying with the general rules of the instruments negotiated in the Uruguay Round, "will only be required to undertake commitments consistent with their individual development, financial and trade needs, or their administrative and institutional capabilities" (ibid.: 440). It agrees that "the rules set out in the various agreements and instruments and the transitional provisions in the Uruguay Round should be applied in a flexible and supportive manner for the least-developed countries" (ibid.: 440–441).

It is important that the LDCs familiarize themselves with their rights and that technical assistance helps them to do so.

It is important that the LDCs familiarize themselves with their rights and that technical assistance helps them to do so. It is also important that their effective obligations, as they work out in practice, reflect the spirit of the WTO Agreements. Artificial and arbitrary time frames, such as that regarding subsidies for the use of domestic goods, need to be avoided. WTO rules, as they evolve, must enable the adoption of the type of policies which are necessary to enable the very poor countries to break out of the poverty trap. Implied in what is now being described as the "Doha Development Agenda" is a recognition by the WTO membership of the need to establish an objective link between WTO rules and national policy autonomy to promote development and poverty reduction in countries where living standards are low.

F. Conclusion

There is a strong risk that the policy changes which are emerging in the initial stages of the PRSP process may not be sufficient to promote more effective poverty reduction in the LDCs. The ongoing PRSP process has generated high expectations. It has resulted in significant achievements in terms of policy processes at the country level. In particular, there has been an increase in country leadership in the technical formulation of poverty reduction strategies; major efforts are being made to improve public expenditure and to link budgetary processes to poverty reduction targets; departmental responsibility for the poverty problem has shifted from previously marginalized social welfare ministries to ministries of finance and planning; and there is more involvement of civil society in designing national strategies. But effective poverty reduction in situations of generalized poverty will require a bolder rethinking of policies which moves beyond adjustment policies and anchors the PRSPs, which are three-year plans of action, within long-term development strategies.

Experience shows that adjustment policies can lead to a positive export response. However, the domestic investment and savings response, as well as structural transformation, are weak, and spurts of growth, where they occur, generally prove unsustainable. The first generation of I-PRSPs and PRSPs are tending to build on existing adjustment policies. But integrating pro-poor public expenditure patterns with deeper and broader structural reforms and the macroeconomic policies of the 1990s is not going to produce the expected results in terms of poverty reduction. Rather, there is a danger that countries will end up with the worst of all worlds. The policies adopted in the new poverty reduction strategies will increase exposure to intensely competitive global markets but without facilitating the development of the productive and supply capacities necessary to compete. At the same time, there will be increased institutional dependence and arm's length regulation and administrative guidance of social welfare through international development cooperation.

There is an alternative. This is the elaboration of development-oriented poverty reduction strategies. Such poverty reduction strategies would promote broad-based economic growth and development through less restrictive macroeconomic policies, through active government policies to increase investment, exports and savings, and through sectorally specific measures to enhance production and supply capabilities and to ensure that groups vulnerable to marginalization are not left behind as economic growth takes off. Private enterprise should play the leading role in the achievement of the goals of development-oriented poverty reduction strategies. However, this is not a call for laissez-faire. Rather, the development process should be catalysed and

Implied in what is now being described as the "Doha Development Agenda" is a recognition by the WTO membership of the need to establish an objective link between WTO rules and national policy autonomy to promote development and poverty reduction in countries where living standards are low.

There is a danger that the policies emerging in the first generation of I-PRSPs and PRSPs will increase exposure to intensely competitive global markets, but without facilitating the development of productive capacities necessary to compete. At the same time, there will be increased administrative guidance of social welfare through international development cooperation.

guided by a pragmatic developmental State which, through good governance of markets, harnesses the profit motive for the purposes of national development and poverty reduction.

Particular attention needs to be paid to ensuring that small and medium-sized domestic enterprises have access to finance at interest rates which will enable them to compete internationally, and that internationally available best practices in production and marketing are diffused more widely. Measures to promote supply capabilities must be embedded within a supportive macroeconomic environment that is designed to achieve long-term development objectives rather than simply short-term stabilization. Complementary policies to prevent the marginalization of particular social groups and regions within a country should also be implemented and should pay particular attention to the generation and sustainability of livelihoods within the context of the growth and structure of the economy.

Realizing such an alternative requires enhanced policy autonomy for national Governments. It should be possible, through the PRSP process, to elaborate poverty reduction strategies that provide a real and improved alternative to past economic reforms and adjustment policies. But genuine national ownership, which all participants agree is the bedrock of the whole process, is essential. The rebuilding of State capacities, which have been strongly eroded in the era of adjustment, is essential for the success of any poverty reduction strategy. Governments also need policy autonomy to be able to explore different national policy options and to elaborate, with national stakeholders, poverty reduction strategies which are more closely anchored in long-term development strategies. The ever-present possibility of withdrawal of external concessional assistance is dampening the creativity that could be released through greater national ownership, and inhibiting the political qualities of a free-thinking society. There is a need for less conditionality and more flexible conditionality rather than simply the streamlining of conditionality according to the mandates of international financial institutions. Moreover, policy conditions must be derived from the PRSPs.

Donors should support alternative thinking about how poverty reduction can be achieved through development. Aid inflows need to be coordinated around the policy objectives and actions of the poverty reduction strategies which Governments formulate, and be delivered through government systems as far as possible and provided on a more stable long-term basis. The poverty-reducing impact of expanding the resource envelope through aid inflows should be jointly explored by Governments with donors. Donor performance monitoring systems should also be established at the recipient country level, to encourage, and measure progress towards, partnership in practice.

Finally, it is necessary that further attention be given to the external financial, technology and market constraints that necessarily impinge on what can be achieved through national policy.

Private enterprise should play the leading role in the achievement of the goals of development-oriented poverty reduction strategies. ... The development process should be catalysed and guided by a pragmatic developmental State which, through good governance of markets, harnesses the profit motive for the purposes of national development and poverty reduction.

There is a need for less conditionality and more flexible conditionality rather than simply the streamlining of conditionality according to the mandates of international financial institutions.

Notes

1. The chapter contains a long list of references as it is intended to provide a resource for thinking about national development strategies and poverty reduction.

2. This section draws heavily on discussions at the World Bank International Conference on Poverty Reduction Strategies held in Washington DC from 14 to 17 January 2002, and submissions circulated at the conference. Many of these are reproduced in IMF/ World Bank (2002a), and at the related website, www.imf.org/external/np/prspgen/ review/2002/conf/index.htm

3. For the initial conception of the PRSP approach, see IMF/IDA (1999a, 1999b), IMF/ World Bank (1999) and World Bank Group (2000); for recent progress in the application of the approach, see IMF/IDA (2001c, 2001d), IDA (2001) and IMF/World Bank (2002). The ways in which the PRGF is intended to differ from the ESAF are well summarized in IMF (2000).

4. For some civil society views on the PRSP approach, see EURODAD (2001), Jubilee South (2001), North/South Coalition/IBIS (2001), OXFAM International (2001), Tanzanian Social and Economic Trust (2001) and World Vision (2001). An evaluation of the approach from a human rights perspective is to be found in United Nations (2001a), Hunt, Nowak and Osmani (2002) and Lizin (2002).

5. See, for example, Department for International Development (2001), Kitta (2002), OECD (2001a), ILO (2002) and WHO (2001).

6. For further discussion of the macroeconomic framework of PRSPs, and the need for greater fiscal flexibility, see Adam and Bevan (2001) and Bevan and Adam (2001).

7. For an overview of changes in policy processes, see UNDP (2001). For country-level studies of what is happening in some LDCs in terms of changes in policy processes, see ODI (2001) for sub-Saharan Africa, and Malaluan and Guttal (2002) for some Asian LDCs. Douangdy (2002) gives a summary of views of Asian government officials involved in the PRSP process, and McGee (2001) provides a very detailed desk-based assessment of participation processes associated with the preparation of PRSPs in sub-Saharan Africa.

8. Thirty-four LDCs have been engaged in SAF- or ESAF-financed programmes since 1988, and of those countries, one third were under IMF-supported programmes for over half the total number of months between the beginning of 1988 and the end of 1999, when the ESAF was transformed into the Poverty Reduction and Growth Facility, and 27 countries have been engaged in implementing agreed policies for three or more years in that 12-year period (see UNCTAD, 2000:103–108).

9. Recent assessments of IMF programmes include Przeworski and Vreeland (2000) and Bird (2001). Easterley (2001a) identifies the fact that developing countries continue to stagnate, despite policy reforms which appear to improve what are regarded as the right fundamentals for growth, as a key puzzle of the 1980–2000 period. Examining the economic effects of the number of adjustment loans from the IMF and World Bank received during 1980–1998, he finds 'no systematic effect of adjustment lending on growth' (Easterley, 2001b: 4), and also that the adoption of the adjustment programmes is statistically associated with a lowering of the amount of poverty reduction which follows a given growth rate. EURODAD (2001) includes discussion between the World Bank and NGOs of the findings of the SAPRIN review of adjustment programmes.

10. For a clear statement, made in a different context, of what is meant by a development strategy, see OECD (2001b).

11. The approach advocated here is similar to one of the points in the "Spirit of Monterrey" discussion at the Heads of State retreat at the UN International Conference on Financing for Development, held in Monterrey from 18 to 23 March 2002, which stated: "We undertake to assist the world's poorest countries to double the size of their economies within a decade, in order to achieve the MDGs [Millennium Development Goals]".

12. This section draws in particular on UNCTAD's work on East Asian development strategies and its application in other contexts. See, in particular, UNCTAD (1994, 1996, 1998, 2002a).

13. For a theoretical exposition of the nature of export promotion policies which go beyond the removal of anti-export bias, see Bhagwati (1988). The World Bank (1993) argues that export-push strategies were central to East Asian development success, and puts forward an interpretation of the precise elements of the export-push strategies adopted in East Asia. For a clear view of the precise nature of East Asian export push strategies, see Bradford (1986, 1990, 1994). On export platforms for promoting manufactures exports, see Radelet (1999).

14. For options for upgrading commodity exports in the context of the global organization of production, see Gibbon (2001).

15. For a discussion of the importance of mesoeconomic policies for poverty reduction in adjustment programmes, see World Bank (1990).

16. ECLAC has developed these ideas in a series of publications, particularly notable ones being ECLAC (1990, 1995, 1996, 2000). Some important conceptual foundations are discussed in French-Davis (1988, 1993), and an application to resource-based development is to be found in Ramos (1995). Recent summaries of the approach in the context of elaborating practical alternatives to Washington Consensus policies are contained in Ocampo (1999, 2001).

17. FAO (2001) and UNIDO (2001) argue for the importance of increasing productive capacities, in agriculture and industry respectively, for poverty reduction in LDCs. IFAD (2001) also puts agricultural production improvements as central in its strategy of rural poverty reduction in developing countries notes the importance.

18. This can entail the promotion of national innovation systems. See, for example, UNCTAD (1999) and UNCTAD (2002d) for Ethiopia.

19. For discussion of what has worked and not worked in the context of late industrialization, see Amsden (2001). The way in which now developed countries also actively used 'heterodox' trade and industrial policies in the early stages of their development is discussed in Chang (2002).

20. For discussion of common principles underlying programmes to provide credit and create employment through public works, see Lipton (1996).

21. Some observers would put this in a more extreme form. In the IMF external consultation on conditionality, a World Bank official is quoted as saying that "The PRSP is a compulsory process wherein the people with the money tell the people who want the money what they need to do to get the money" (Alexander, 2001, in IMF, 2001d: 147).

22. For discussion of changes in IMF conditionality, see IMF (2001b, 2001c).

23. For further discussion of these cases see UNCTAD (2000: chapter 6).

24. Uganda's Poverty Eradication Action Plan (PEAP) was formulated in 1997, before the PRSP approach.

References

Adam, C.S. and Bevan, D. L. (2001). PRGF stocktaking exercise on behalf of DFID, November. In: IMF/World Bank (2002a).

Alexander, N. (2001). Short comment on conditionality. In: IMF (2001d).

Akyüz, Y. and Gore, C. (2001). African economic development in a comparative perspective, *Cambridge Journal of Economics*, 25 (3): 265–288.

Amsden, A.H. (1994). Why isn't the whole world experimenting with the East Asian model to develop? Review of the *East Asian Miracle, World Development*, 22 (4): 672–634.

Amsden, A.H. (2001). *The Rise of "The Rest": Challenges to the West from Late-Industrializing Economies,* Oxford University Press, New York and Oxford.

Andersen, B., Kozul-Wright, Z. and Kozul-Wright, R. (2000). Copyrights, competition and development: the case of the music industry, UNCTAD Discussion Paper 145, Geneva.

Arkadie, B. van (2001). Vietnamese growth in the 1990s: lessons to be learnt, background report for *The Least Developed Countries Report 2002*.

Berg, E. (1993). *Rethinking Technical Cooperation: Reforms for Capacity Building in Africa*, UNDP and Development Alternatives, Inc., New York.

Bevan, D.L. and Adam C.S. (2001). Guidance note: poverty reduction strategies and the macroeconomic framework, mimeo, prepared for the Department for International Development, Department of Economics, University of Oxford.

Bhagwati, J. (1988). Export promoting trade strategy: issues and evidence, *World Bank Research Observer*, 3 (1): 27–57.

Bird, G. (2001). IMF programs: do they work? Can they be made to work better?, *World Development*, 29 (11): 1849–1865.

Bradford, C.I. (1986). East Asian "models": myths and lessons. In J.P. Lewis, ed., *Development Strategies Reconsidered*, Overseas Development Council, Washington DC.

Bradford, C.I. (1990). Policy interventions and markets: development strategy typologies and policy options. In Gereffi, G. and Wyman, D.L., eds., *Manufacturing Miracles: Paths to Industrialization in Latin America and East Asia*, Princeton University Press, Princeton, New Jersey.

Bradford, C.I. (1994). From trade-driven growth to growth-driven trade: re-appraising the East Asian development experience, OECD, Paris.

Chang, H-J. (2002). *Kicking Away the Ladder: Development Strategy in Historical Perspective*, Anthem Press, London.

Department for International Development (DFID) (2001). UK DFID contribution to PRSP Review, December. In: IMF/World Bank (2002a).

Douangdy, S. (2002). Report on the Regional Conference on National Poverty Reduction Strategies, held in Hanoi, 4–6 December 2001, presentation at the IMF/World Bank

International Conference on Poverty Reduction Strategies, Washington DC, 14–17 January 2002.

Easterley, W. (2001a). The lost decades: developing countries' stagnation in spite of policy reform 1980–1998, *Journal of Economic Growth*, 6: 137–157.

Easterley, W. (2001b). The effect of IMF and World Bank programmes on poverty, WIDER Discussion Paper No. 2001/102.

ECLAC (1990). *Changing Production Patterns with Social Equity*, United Nations publication, sales no. E.90.IIG.6, Santiago, Chile.

ECLAC (1995). *Latin America and the Caribbean: Policies to Improve Linkages with the Global Economy*, United Nations publication, sales no. E.95.II.G.6, Santiago, Chile.

ECLAC (1996). *Strengthening Development: The Interplay of Macro- and Microeconomics*, United Nations publication, sales no. E.96.II.G.2, Santiago, Chile.

ECLAC (2000). *Equity, Citizenship, Development*, United Nations publication, Santiago, Chile.

EURODAD (2001). Many dollars, any change? Part I: The changing nature of development cooperation: building ownership; Part II: Have structural adjustment policies failed the poor?, October. In: IMF/World Bank (2002). Also available at http://www.worldbank.org/poverty/strategies/review/extrev.htm.

European Commission (2000). Review of conditionalities used for the floating HIPC completion point, SPA task team on contractual relationships and selectivity, 27 November, Brussels.

European Commission (2001a). Comparative review of I-PRSP targets and conditionalities for HIPC completion point, SPA task team on contractual relationships and selectivity, 1 October, Brussels.

European Commission (2001b). PRSP review: key issues, October. In: IMF/World Bank (2002a).

FAO (2001). The role of agriculture in the development of LDCs and their integration into the world economy, paper prepared for the Third United Nations Conference on the Least Developed Countries (Brussels, 14–20 May 2001), Rome.

French-Davis. R. (1988). An outline of a neo-structuralist approach, *CEPAL Review*, 34: 37–44.

French-Davis, R. (1993). Capital formation and the macroeconomic framework: a neostructuralist approach. In: Sunkel, O. *Development from Within: Toward a Neostructuralist Approach for Latin America*, Lynne Rienner Publishers, Boulder and London.

GATT secretariat (1994). *The Results of the Uruguay Round of Multilateral Trade Negotiations*, Geneva.

Gibbon, P. (2001). Upgrading primary production: a global commodity chain approach, *World Development*, 29 (2): 345–363.

Hayami, Y. (1997). *Development Economics: From the Poverty to the Wealth of Nations*, Clarendon Press, Oxford.

Helleiner, G. (2000). Toward balance in aid relationships: donor performance monitoring in low-income coutnries, paper written for a forthcoming Festschrift in honour of Lance Taylor, University of Toronto, Toronto.

Hellmann, T., Murdock, K. and Stiglitz, J. (1997). Financial restraint: toward a new paradigm. In: Aoki, M., Kim, H.-K., and Okuno-Fujiwara, M., eds., *The Role of Government in East Asian Economic Development: Comparative Institutional Analysis*, Clarendon Press, Oxford.

HIPC Finance Ministers and PRSP Coordinators (2002). Reviewing PRSPs: the views of HIPC Ministers and PRSP Coordinators, paper circulated at the IMF/ World Bank International Conference on Poverty Reduction Strategies, Washington DC, 14–17 January 2002.

Hunt, P., Nowak, M. and Osmani, S. (2002). Human rights and poverty reduction strategies: a discussion paper, mimeo, paper prepared for the United Nations Office of the High Commissioner for Human Rights, Geneva.

IDA (2001). Poverty Reduction Strategy Papers and IDA 13, Washington DC.

IFAD (2001). *Rural Poverty Report 2001*, Oxford University Press, New York.

ILO (2002). The decent work agenda and poverty reduction: ILO contribution to IMF/World Bank comprehensive review of the Poverty Reduction Strategy process, paper distributed at the IMF/World Bank International Conference on Poverty Reduction Strategies, 14–17 January 2002, Washington DC.

IMF (2000). Key features of IMF Poverty Reduction and Growth Facility (PRGF) Supported Programs, prepared by the Policy Development and Review Department, 16 August (available at http://www.imf.org/external/np/prgf/2000/eng/key.htm).

IMF (2001a). HIPC debt relief programs and poverty reduction: press conference transcript (available at http://www.imf.org/external/np/tr/2001/tr01043.htm).

IMF (2001b). Structural conditionality in Fund-supported programs, 16 February, Washington DC.

IMF (2001c). Streamlining structural conditionality: review of initial experience, 10 July 2001, Washington DC.

IMF (2001d). External comments and contributions on IMF conditionality, September, Washington DC. (http://www.imf.org/external/np/pdr/cond/2001/eng/collab/comment.pdf).

IMF/IDA (1999a). Poverty Reduction Strategy Papers: status and next steps, 10 November, Washington DC.

IMF/IDA (1999b). Poverty Reduction Strategy Papers: operational issues, 10 December, Washington DC.

IMF/IDA (2001a). Tracking of poverty-reducing public spending in heavily indebted poor countries (HIPCs), 27 March, Washington DC.

IMF/IDA (2001b). Joint Staff Assessment of the Uganda PRSP Progress Report, 9 March, Washington DC.

IMF/IDA (2001c). Poverty Reduction Strategy Papers: progress in implementation, 18 April, Washington DC.

IMF/IDA (2001d) Poverty Reduction Strategy Papers: progress in implementation, 24 September, Washington DC.

IMF/World Bank (1999) Building Poverty Reduction Strategies in developing countries, Development Committee, DC/99-29, 22 September, Washington DC.

IMF/World Bank (2002a). External comments and contributions on the Joint Bank/Fund Staff Review of the PRSP Approach. Volume I: Bilateral agencies and multilateral institutions; Volume II: Civil society organizations and individual contributions, IMF and World Bank, Washington DC (http://www.imf.org/external/np/prsp/review/2001 or http://www.worldbank.org/poverty/strategies/review/extrev.htm).

IMF/World Bank (2002b). Review of the PRSP experience: an issues paper for the January 2002 conference. (http://www.worldbank.org/poverty/strategies/review/index.htm).

ITC (2001). *Converting LDC Export Opportunities into Business: A Strategic Response*, United Nations publication, sales no. E.01.III.T.8, ITC and Odin, Geneva.

Jubilee South (2001). Flawed thinking and failing experiences, November. In: IMF/World Bank (2002a).

Kitta, S. (2002). Japan Bank for International Cooperation (JBIC) views on PRSPs, summary paper distributed at the IMF/World Bank International Conference on Poverty Reduction Strategies, Washington DC, 14–17 January 2002.

Kochhar, K. and Coorey, S. (1999). Economic growth: what has been achieved and how? In Bredenkamp, H. and Schadler, S. (eds.), *Economic Adjustment and Reform in Low-income Countries: Studies by the Staff of the International Monetary Fund*, IMF, Washington DC.

Lipton, M. (1996). Success in anti-poverty, Issues in Development Discussion Paper No. 8, ILO, Geneva.

Lipton, M. (2000). Rural poverty reduction: the neglected priority, mimeo (http://wbln0018.worldbank.org/essd/rdv/vta.nsf/gweb/lipton).

Lipumba, I.H. (2001). Conditionality and ownership: a view from the periphery. In: IMF (2001d).

Lizin, A.-M. (2002). Droits de l'homme et extrême pauvreté, rapport soumis par Mme A.-M. Lizin, Experte indépendante, conformément à la résolution 2000/12 de la Commission des droits de l'homme, E/CN.4/2002/55.

Malaluan, J.J.C., and Guttal, S. (2002). Structural adjustment in the name of the poor: the PRSP experience in the Lao PDR, Cambodia and Vietnam, Focus on the Global South, Thailand (www.focusweb.org).

McGee, R., with Levene, J. and Hughes, A. (2001). Assessing participation in Poverty Reduction Strategy Papers: a desk-based synthesis of experience in sub-Saharan Africa, draft report, October (http://www.worldbank.org/poverty/strategies/review/ids1.pdf).

Mkandawire, T. (2001). Thinking about developmental states in Africa, *Cambridge Journal of Economics*, 25 (3): 289–314.

Mosley, P. (2001). Poverty impact of the green revolution and policies for pro-poor growth in Africa and the least developed countries, background paper prepared for *The Least Developed Countries Report 2002*.

Nissanke, M.K. (2001). Financing enterprise development in sub-Saharan Africa, *Cambridge Journal of Economics*. 25 (3): 343–369.

North/South Coalition/IBIS (2001). Input for the PRSP Review: poverty reduction and participation, November. In: IMF/World Bank (2002a).

Ocampo, J.A. (1999). Beyond the Washington Consensus: an ECLAC perspective, paper presented to the conference on "Beyond the Washington Consensus: Net Assessment and Prospects for a New Approach", organized by the Department of Comparative Research on Development of the Ecole des Hautes Etudes en Sciences Sociales, Paris, and MOST, UNESCO, June, Paris.

Ocampo, J.A. (2001). Rethinking the development agenda, paper presented at the American Economic Association Annual Meeting Panel "Toward a Post-Washington Consensus on Development and Security", New Orleans, 5–7 January 2001.

ODI (2001). PRSP Institutionalisation Study: Final Report, submitted to the Strategic Partnership with Africa, 15 October, London (http://www.odi.org.uk/pppg/institutionalisation.html)

OECD (2001a). OECD/DAC Input into the PRSP Review, November. In: IMF/World Bank (2002a).

OECD (2001b). *The DAC Guidelines: Strategies for Sustainable Development*, OECD, Paris.

Okuda, H (1993). Japanese two-steps loans: the Japanese approach to development finance, *Hitotsubashi Journal of Economics*, 34: 67–85.

OXFAM International (2001). Are PRSPs working? OXFAM contribution to the World Bank/IMF Review Process, December 2001. In: IMF/World Bank (2002a).

Przeworski, A., and Vreeland, J.R. (2000). The effect of IMF programs on economic growth, *Journal of Development Economics*, 62: 385–421.

Pyatt, G. (1999). Poverty versus the poor. In: Pyatt, G.F. and Ward, M. (eds.), *Identifying the Poor*, IOS Press/ISI, Amsterdam/Voorburg.

Pyatt, G. (2001a). An alternative approach to poverty analysis, with particular reference to the Poverty Reduction Strategies being developed in the context of the HIPC Initiative, background paper for *The Least Developed Countries Report 2002*.

Pyatt, G. (2001b). An alternative approach to poverty analysis, mimeo, valedictory address at the Institute of Social Studies, The Hague.

Radelet, S. (1999). Manufactured exports, export platforms and economic growth, CAER Discussion Paper No. 43, Harvard International Institute for Development, Cambridge, MA (http://www.hiid.harvard.edu/projects/caer/index.html).

Ramos, J. (1995). A development strategy founded on natural resource-based production clusters. *CEPAL Review*, 66: 105–127.

Reinhardt, N. (2000). Back to basics in Malaysia and Thailand: the role of resource-based exports in their export-led growth, *World Development*, 28 (1): 57–77.

SPA (2001). SPA's Technical Group input into PRSP Review, with appendices, December 2001. In: IMF/World Bank (2002a).

Stern, N. (2001). *A Strategy for Development*, World Bank, Washington DC.

Tanzanian Authorities (2000). The United Republic of Tanzania: http://www.imf.org/external/NP/prsp/2000/tza/02/index.htm

Tanzanian Social and Economic Trust (TASOET) (2001). Perspectives on the Tanzanian Experience with PRSP-HIPC II, October. In: IMF/World Bank (2002a).

Teranishi, J. (1997). Sectoral resource transfer, conflict, and macrostability in economic development: a comparative analysis. In: Aoki, M., Kim, H.-K., and Okuno-Fujiwara, M., *The Role of Government in East Asian Economic Development: Comparative Institutional Analysis*, Clarendon Press, Oxford.

Thin, N., Underwood, M. and Gilling, J. (2001). Sub-Saharan Africa's Poverty Reduction Strategy Papers from social policy and sustainable livelihoods perspectives, a report for the Department for International Development, Oxford, Oxford Policy Management.

Uganda (2001). Poverty Reduction Paper Progress Report: Uganda Poverty Status Report 2001, Summary, March, Ministry of Finance, Planning and Economic Development, Kampala.

UNCTAD (1994). *Trade and Development Report, 1994*, Part II, chapter 1, The visible hand and the industrialization in East Asia, United Nations publication, sales no. E.94.II.D.2.

UNCTAD (1996). *Trade and Development Report 1996*, Part II, United Nations publication, sales no. E.96.II.D.6.

UNCTAD (1998). *Trade and Development Report*, 1998, Part II, African Development in a Comparative Perspective, United Nations publication, sales no. E.98.II.D.6.

UNCTAD (1999). The Science, Technology and Innovation Policy Review in Colombia, United Nations, New York and Geneva.

UNCTAD (2000). *The Least Developed Countries 2000 Report*, United Nations publication, sales no. E.00.II.D.21, United Nations, Geneva.

UNCTAD (2002a). Development strategies in a globalizing world, mimeo, Division on Globalization and Development Strategies, UNCTAD, Geneva.

UNCTAD (2002b). Youth Forum proceedings: the music industry workshop, UN LDC-III Conference, Brussels, 19 May 2001, United Nations, New York and Geneva. Forthcoming.

UNCTAD (2002c). Growing micro and small enterprises in LDCs. The "missing middle" in LDCs: why micro and small enterprises are not growing, Enterprise Development Series, UNCTAD, Geneva.

UNCTAD (2002d). Investment and Innovation Policy Review in Ethiopia, UNCTAD/ITE/pPC/MISC 4, United Nations, New York/Geneva.

United Nations Development Group (UNDG) (2001). UNDG Guidance Note on the Poverty Reduction Strategy Paper (PRSP), mimeo, United Nations, New York.

UNDP (2001). UNDP: Review of the Poverty Reduction Strategy Paper (PRSP), December. In: IMF/World Bank (2002a).

UNIDO (2001). Building productive capacity for poverty alleviation in least developed countries (LDCs): the role of industry, UNIDO, Vienna.

United Nations (2001a). The Highly Indebted Poor Countries (HIPC) Initiative: a human rights assessment of Poverty Reduction Strategy Papers, E/CN.4/2001/56.

United Nations (2001b). Programme of Action for the Least Developed Countries for the Decade 2001–2010, 8 June, A/CONF.191/11.

Wangwe, S. (1995). (ed.) . *Exporting Africa: Technology, Trade and Industrialization in Sub-Saharan Africa*, UNU/Intech Studies in New Technology, Routledge, London and New York.

WHO (2001). WHO submission to World Bank/IMF Review of PRSPs, "Health in PRSPs", December. In: IMF/World Bank (2002a).

World Bank (1990). *Making Adjustment Work for the Poor: a Framework for Policy Reform in Africa*, World Bank, Washington DC.

World Bank (1993). *The East Asian Miracle: Economic Growth and Public Policy*, World Bank, Washington DC.

World Bank (1997). Adjustment lending in Sub-Saharan Africa: an update, Report No.16594, Washington DC.

World Bank Group (2000). Poverty Reduction Strategy Papers: Internal Guidance Note, Operations Policy and Strategy, January, Washington DC.

World Vision (2001). World Vision submission to the Comprehensive Review of the PRSP Approach, December. In: IMF/World Bank (2002a).

WTO (1997). Principal bottlenecks to international business development and the related technical cooperation needs of least developed countries: a business-sector perspective, WT/LDC/HL/3, Geneva.

Wuyts, M. (2001). Informal economy, wage goods and accumulation under structural adjustment: theoretical reflections based on the Tanzanian experience, *Cambridge Journal of Economics*, 23 (3): 417–438.

International policies for more effective poverty reduction in the LDCs

A. Introduction

Reducing poverty in the LDCs requires action at both the national and the international level. Good national policies are a sine qua non for success in reducing poverty. But good international policies are equally necessary. A good national poverty reduction strategy cannot be fully effective in an adverse international enabling environment. However, significant and sustainable inroads into poverty will certainly follow appropriate and concerted action to tackle both the national and international determinants of poverty in the LDCs. Indeed, joint action is essential to help countries to escape the poverty trap.

This chapter focuses on international policies. The Programme of Action for the Least Developed Countries for the Decade 2001–2010 has the function of providing a common framework for development cooperation between LDCs and their development partners. This chapter therefore seeks to identify aspects of the Programme whose implementation seems particularly important given the analysis of the international poverty trap in this Report. It examines, in particular, the role of debt relief, aid, preferential market access and international commodity policy in supporting the LDCs, as well as the need for increased policy attention to the role of regional dynamics in poverty reduction.

The analysis is founded on the view that the most effective way to reduce poverty in the LDCs is a multi-level approach (see box 18). The discussion of international policies in this chapter thus needs to be seen alongside the national policies discussed in the previous chapter. They are not put forward as "stand-alone" policies; rather, they will work for poverty reduction when they are implemented together with, and in support of, national policies of the type discussed in the previous chapter. Increasing the positive synergies between national and international policy is crucial for effective poverty reduction.

B. The need for re-enhanced debt relief

Unsustainable external debt is a central ingredient of the cycle of economic stagnation and persistent generalized poverty in poor countries. The wide acceptance of this relationship formed the basis of international agreement on the need for comprehensive debt relief for poor countries, which led to the establishment of the HIPC Initiative in 1996 and its enhancement in 1999. A first necessary condition for many LDCs to escape the poverty trap is that there be a durable exit from the debt problem.

Through the enhanced HIPC Initiative, the present value of the stream of future debt service payments, which the LDCs that are also HIPCs (HIPC-LDCs) would have been contractually obliged to make, has been significantly reduced. According to January 2002 estimates, the total reduction in future debt service obligations for all HIPCs thus far is equivalent to around $25 billion in net present value (NPV) terms, and that for HIPC-LDCs can be estimated at around

Good national policies are a sine qua non for success in reducing poverty.

The most effective way to reduce poverty in the LDCs is a multi-level approach.

Unsustainable external debt is a central ingredient of the cycle of economic stagnation and persistent generalized poverty in poor countries.

BOX 18. A MULTI-LEVEL APPROACH TO POVERTY REDUCTION POLICY

The causes of poverty can be identified at different levels of aggregation, running from the local to the global (Pyatt, 1999, 2001). As a corollary, effective poverty reduction requires a multi-level approach in which policies at different levels complement and reinforce each other.

Box table 3 below sets out a policy framework for locating the causes of poverty and for identifying areas of action within a multi-level approach to poverty reduction. The three basic (and most familiar) levels of policy within this framework are local/micro, national/macro and international/global. But the framework also includes the national/meso level and the international/regional level. Elements of the national/meso level are the following: the markets in which households operate (labour markets, credit markets, product markets, insurance markets); the social and economic infrastructure which they use, including health and education services, the transport and communications infrastructure, utilities, irrigation facilities and agricultural extension services; and the regional and sectoral structure of the national economy. These elements are included in the policy framework as various analysts have found that they constitute an important link between macro and micro trends within national economies (World Bank, 1990; Stewart, 1995; ECLAC, 1996; Gore and Figueiredo, 1997). The international/regional level is likewise included as this level is important for understanding links between the global economy and national economy. Elements of the international/regional level include trade, investment and migration linkages, common international transport services and infrastructure structures, and various regional cooperation regimes.

BOX TABLE 3. A MULTI-LEVEL FRAMEWORK FOR EFFECTIVE POVERTY REDUCTION POLICIES

International	(i)	Global markets for goods and services
	(ii)	Financial markets — aid, debt, private capital flows
	(iii)	Technology transfer
	(iv)	Governance and the global economy
	(v)	Global public goods
Regional	(i)	Trade and investment dynamics
	(ii)	Technical cooperation
	(iii)	Transport systems
Macroeconomic	(i)	Monetary policy — the exchange rate and the rate of interest
	(ii)	Fiscal policy: (a) public expenditure and its financing; and (b) the incentive system (including trade policy and the tax system)
	(iii)	Governance of the national economy — role of the executive, legislative and judicial branches of government in relation to each other and the private sector; and the quality of their performance
Mesoeconomic	(i)	Markets for goods and services — commodities and factors of production (land, labour, etc.)
	(ii)	Financial markets (credit)
	(iii)	Inter- and intra-sectoral allocation of public expenditure
	(iv)	Sectoral composition of growth
Microeconomic	(i)	Individuals, households and their micro-enterprises
	(ii)	Communities and non-governmental organizations
	(iii)	Corporate enterprises

Source: Based on Pyatt (1999).

The focus of policy at the micro level is likely to be on the assets of the poor and the productivity and security of those assets. A particular concern may be improving the human capital of the poor, as well as seeking to enhance community development, but enterprise development is also important. Analysis at the national/meso level will suggest that the focus of policy should be on addressing problems associated with non-existent or incomplete markets and imperfections in established markets, on the structure of public expenditure and delivery systems of public services, and on the transformation of national production structures away from activities for which there is low elasticity of demand and few opportunities for productivity growth. At the national/macro level, key aims of poverty reduction will be to promote rapid and sustainable economic and employment growth without excessive inflation. Key policy issues will be fiscal and monetary policy, exchange rate policy and patterns of governance, the latter being understood here to refer to the balance between public action and private enterprise and the degree

Box 18 (contd.)

of decentralization/devolution. Population policy may also be significant. Analysis at the regional/international level may suggest the need for various forms of regional cooperation to provide regional public goods, for example in environmental management or transport services, and to establish regional regimes regulating trade, investment and migration, and reducing vulnerability to instabilities in the global economy. Finally, analysis at the global/international level is likely to focus on debt relief policies, ways of increasing aid flows and aid effectiveness, the promotion of private capital flows and making international trade work for poverty reduction.

Some would argue that the ultimate causes of poverty are to be found at the micro level in the behaviour of individuals. Others suggest that the key cause is national economic growth and macroeconomic policies. Still others argue that the ultimate causes of poverty are found in the international arena, not in the countries themselves, and that particularly with globalization, countries are subject to global forces which are beyond the control of national Governments. These disagreements, which stem from different frames of analysis, are a major source of disagreement in the policy debate about poverty reduction strategies. A balanced view would suggest, however, that the causes of poverty are found at all levels. It follows that the design of a poverty reduction strategy needs to address determinants of poverty at each and every level. There is a need for a comprehensive multi-level approach, which extends from the local/micro level up to the international/global level, if poverty reduction is to be most effective.

Two negative consequences follow if poverty reduction policies are framed only at the local or national level. First, the amount of poverty reduction that can be achieved through policy action is diminished. Second, there can be misleading policy solutions owing to the existence of fallacies of composition. These fallacies occur when relationships in aggregate differ from those observed at the individual level. Thus the efficacy of local poverty reduction projects is constrained by national policies, and the efficacy of national poverty reduction strategies is constrained by international policies. Households will be able to do much more for themselves if markets are functioning, jobs are becoming available and public services are improving. National Governments will be able to do much less for their citizens if global policies constrain export growth, increase the instability of private capital inflows or bias technological development against the very poor.

Equally, however, the efficacy of international policies can be improved by effective national policies, and national macroeconomic policy performance can be improved by good meso-economic policies and by strong local development efforts. Opportunities for poverty reduction will be maximized through a multi-level approach.

$15 billion. But in absolute terms, debt service relief in the near future is less impressive. For the 20 HIPC-LDCs that have reached decision point, debt service due in 2003–2005 (after the full use of traditional debt relief mechanisms and assistance under the enhanced HIPC Initiative) is, in total, $371 million less per year than debt service paid in 1998–2000. Out of 20 LDCs that have reached decision point, debt service payments due in 2003–2005 will be higher than those paid in 1998–2000 in four cases, and for a further six countries, the reduction in debt service payments will be less than $15 million. The reduction of debt service payments exceeds $50 million in only three countries — Madagascar ($53 million), Senegal ($65 million) and the United Republic of Tanzania ($69 million).[1]

These resources can certainly contribute to poverty reduction by enabling Governments to increase social expenditures on health and education, as well as to provide resources for decentralized local initiatives. However, the magnitude of resources released in this way is quite small compared with levels of aid inflows (see OECD, 2000: table 1-23; UNCTAD, 2000a, 151–154). For example, annual debt service relief in 2003–2005 for the 20 HIPC-LDCs that have reached decision point is only 5.5 per cent of net ODA disbursements to those countries in the year 2000. Thus, the way in which the HIPC Initiative can contribute most to poverty reduction is less through the resources released by debt relief than through enabling a durable exit from the debt problem and thus increasing growth prospects, improving private sector investment expectations and enabling aid to be used effectively for development purposes.

Out of 20 LDCs that have reached decision point, debt service payments due in 2003–2005 will be higher than those paid in 1998–2000 in four cases, and for a further six countries, the reduction in debt service payments will be less than $15 million... Annual debt service relief in 2003–2005 for the 20 HIPC-LDCs that have reached decision point is only 5.5 per cent of net ODA disbursements to those countries in the year 2000.

Current expectations that the
enhanced HIPC Initiative will
provide a durable exit from
the debt problem are
unrealistic...

Unfortunately, current expectations that the enhanced HIPC Initiative will provide a durable exit from the debt problem are unrealistic. For HIPC-LDCs two problems are apparent. First, there are 13 HIPC-LDCs that have still not reached decision point, and 11 of these are considered likely to require HIPC assistance to make their debts sustainable.[2] Second, and this will be the focus of attention here, the forecasts that the debt relief which is agreed at HIPC decision and completion points will lead to a durable exit from the debt problem are over-optimistic. This was identified as a central weakness of the enhanced HIPC Initiative in the last *Least Developed Countries Report* (UNCTAD, 2000a: 154– 158). Since then, other evidence and research have confirmed that judgement.

Table 44, based on IMF/World Bank estimates, shows some of the main assumptions that underpin projections of external debt indicators in HIPC-LDCs that had reached decision point by April 2001. Forecasting is, of course, a difficult art. But it is clear that the expectations that current levels of debt relief will lead to future debt sustainability are generally based on the assumption that through the enhanced HIPC Initiative there will be higher economic growth and higher export growth in the period 2000–2010 than in the period 1990–1999, generally with less external finance (grants plus new borrowing) as a ratio of GDP and a higher grant element in loans. More precisely:

- Real GDP growth rates are expected to be higher in 2000–2010 than in 1990–1999 in 15 out of 17 countries.

- Export growth rates are expected to be higher in 2000–2010 than in 1990– 1999 in 14 out of 17 countries.

- New borrowing, as a percentage of GDP, is expected to be lower in 13 out of 17 countries.

- Grants, as a percentage of GDP, are expected to be lower in 13 out of 17 countries.

- External finance, as a percentage of GDP, is expected to be lower in 14 out of 17 countries.

- The grant element in borrowing is expected to be higher in 2000–2010 than in 1990–1999 in all 16 countries for which there are data.

...Real GDP growth rates are
expected to be higher in
2000–2010 than in 1990–
1999 in 15 out of 17
countries. Export growth rates
are expected to be higher in
2000–2010 than in 1990–
1999 in 14 out of 17
countries.

An important question is by how much future trends must deviate from these forecasts before the external debt once again becomes unsustainable. As shown in UNCTAD (2000a), some LDCs would not become sustainable, according to the HIPC criterion of a NPV debt-to-export ratio of 150, before 2005, given current levels of debt relief, even if the optimistic projections were realized. More recent work, which contains a sample of 17 LDCs, shows that 6 out of the 17 will be unsustainable during 2000–2005 even if the optimistic forecasts are realized (Martin, 2001), and it can be estimated that in a further three cases, export growth rates over the period 2000–2005 have to be more than double those of the 1990s for countries to maintain debt sustainability. Close examination of the cases of Burkina Faso and Zambia shows that, in the former case, the NPV debt-to-export ratio will reach 257 per cent in 2010 if export volume growth follows the trend in the 1990s and cotton prices do not recover from their levels in 2001, and in the latter case the NPV debt-to-export ratio will reach 270 per cent if the last decade's trends in the volume and price of copper exports persist (EURODAD, 2001) (chart 47). Future debt sustainability is also quite sensitive to the concessionality of new financing. Scenarios are available in decision point documents for nine LDCs. In four of them the downside scenarios indicate that the NPV debt-to-export ratio would be 40 percentage points higher

TABLE 44. ASSUMPTIONS UNDERLYING MEDIUM-TERM PROJECTIONS IN DEBT SUSTAINABILITY ANALYSIS OF HIPC-LDCS THAT HAVE REACHED DECISION POINT

(Percentage per annum)

	Real GDP growth		Export growthᵃ		Grants % GDP		New borrowings % GDP		% Grant element in borrowing	
									Existing debt at	New borrowing
	1990–1999	2000–2010	1990–1999	2000–2010	1990–1999	2000–2010	1990–1999	2000–2010	End-1999	2000–2010
Benin	4.3	5.5	4.9	7.4	4.0	4.0	3.1	2.0	31.8	52.8
Burkina Faso	3.6	5.9	2.4	9.7	4.7	1.6	4.3	3.3	40.0	55.2
Gambia	3.0	5.6	4.2	6.9	10.1	5.1	7.5	5.5	42.9	52.1
Guinea	3.9	5.3	0.6	7.8	4.0	2.8	4.9	4.7	28.4	70.3
Guinea-Bissau	0.3	7.0	7.3	12.1	10.8	10.3	21.6	3.5	25.0	53.4
Madagascar	1.8	6.2	8.0	8.4	3.0	3.5	3.0	3.0	32.5	51.3
Malawi	4.0	4.4	5.5	4.3	6.8	5.6	10.2	5.2	43.2	71.5
Mali	3.4	5.0	5.8	6.3	7.5	4.1	7.5	4.1	..	55.5
Mauritania	4.3	7.3	2.1	6.0	10.2	8.8	12.0	5.5	24.0	50.6
Mozambique	6.3	5.9	10.1	13.0	15.8	5.5	8.6	4.5	57.1ᵇ	77.5
Niger	2.4	4.4	-3.9	5.4	6.5	4.0	1.5	7.2	32.5	79.5
Rwanda	-1.6	6.1	-2.3	13.7	18.2ᶜ	5.2ᵈ	3.9	15.6	44.8	67.1
Sao Tome and Principe	-0.5	4.1	3.4	9.5	38.9	26.9	40.8	12.8	35.2	70.0
Senegal	3.0	5.0	2.8	6.7	6.0	1.7	5.4	2.3	32.1	63.4
Uganda	6.7	5.6	14.6	10.3	2.6	4.0	12.1	3.1	10.1	69.2
United Rep. of Tanzania	3.1	5.9	10.8	10.3	7.1	7.7	0.9	4.7	27.7	57.9
Zambia	1.0	5.2	-2.3	9.6	10.6ᵉ	5.0	12.7	6.5	22.6	53.6
Simple average	2.9	5.6	4.4	8.7	9.8	6.2	9.4	5.5	33.1	61.8

Source: IMF/World Bank (2001a: table 5, p.24).
   a   Annual average growth rates of goods and non-factor services exports (in nominal $).
   b   End-1998.
   c   1992–1999.
   d   2000–2006.
   e   1990–1998.

over the projection period 2000–2020 if financing terms deteriorated (IMF/World Bank, 2001a).

The enhanced HIPC Initiative is on a knife-edge. The optimistic projections are based on "a policy scenario that assumes a country will strengthen its growth potential by sustaining sound macroeconomic, structural and social policies and that the financial requirements associated with this scenario will materialize on the envisaged terms" (IMF/World Bank, 2001a: 22). However, experience suggests that these policies will not achieve this, particularly if there is an unsustainable external debt. Durable exit from the debt problem is possible if the policies can strengthen economic growth. But the debt problem continually undermines the ability of the policies to have this effect. Thus highly indebted poor countries, as well as creditor countries, can get locked into a repetitive pattern of perpetual economic adjustment to achieve the ever-elusive goal of external viability.[3]

There is some official recognition that the forecasts underlying the expectation that current debt relief is sufficient for a durable exit from the debt problem are over-optimistic. Debt sustainability analyses are re-calculated at HIPC completion point, and additional debt relief is provided if a country's external circumstances have changed significantly (IMF/IDA, 2001). But further and bolder action is necessary to ensure long-term sustainability.

Highly indebted poor countries, as well as creditor countries, can get locked into a repetitive pattern of perpetual economic adjustment to achieve the ever-elusive goal of external viability.

CHART 47. ALTERNATIVE SCENARIOS OF FUTURE EXPORT VALUE IN BURKINA FASO AND ZAMBIA

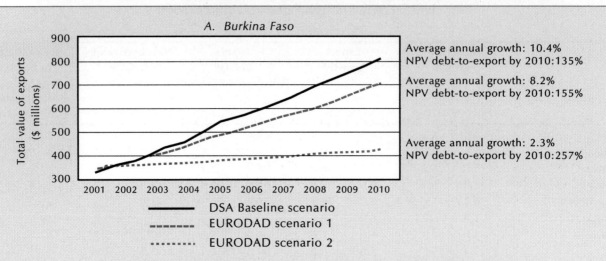

A. Burkina Faso

Average annual growth: 10.4%
NPV debt-to-export by 2010:135%

Average annual growth: 8.2%
NPV debt-to-export by 2010:155%

Average annual growth: 2.3%
NPV debt-to-export by 2010:257%

DSA Baseline scenario
EURODAD scenario 1
EURODAD scenario 2

ASSUMPTIONS UNDERLYING SCENARIOS: BURKINA FASO, 2000–2010

(Average annual percentage growth rate)

	Cotton volume	Cotton price	Gold volume	Gold price	Residual[a] value
DSA baseline scenario	6.0	3.4	9.0	3.0	9.7
EURODAD scenario 1	2.0[b]	0.0	5.0	0.0	9.7
EURODAD scenario 2	2.0	0.0	5.0	0.0	2.4[b]

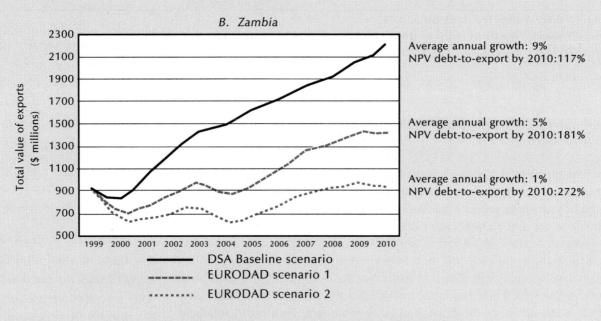

B. Zambia

Average annual growth: 9%
NPV debt-to-export by 2010:117%

Average annual growth: 5%
NPV debt-to-export by 2010:181%

Average annual growth: 1%
NPV debt-to-export by 2010:272%

DSA Baseline scenario
EURODAD scenario 1
EURODAD scenario 2

ASSUMPTIONS UNDERLYING SCENARIOS: ZAMBIA, 2000–2010

(Average annual percentage growth rate)

	Copper volume	Copper price	Residual[a] value
DSA baseline scenario	6.0	4.0	9.0
EURODAD scenario 1	3.0[c]	0.0	9.0
EURODAD scenario 2	7.0[b]	0.0	9.0

Source: EURODAD (2001).
   a   Growth rate of export value of exports of goods and services other than major commodities.
   b   1990–1999 average.
   c   Moderate projection.

At the Fifth HIPC Ministerial Meeting, held in Maputo in November 2001, HIPC Finance Ministers made a number of concrete proposals in this regard. They urged the international financial community:

- To conduct comprehensive assessments of the debt sustainability of all HIPCs, not simply at decision point and completion point, but afterwards as well;

- To aim well below the current HIPC sustainability targets in these assessments in order to ensure long-term sustainability;

- To take account of shocks affecting countries by introducing new measures to combat them, by interpreting policy conditionality more flexibly in the event of shocks, and by factoring shocks more realistically into debt sustainability macroeconomic projections;

- To examine domestic and private sector debt burdens in all future debt sustainability analyses in order to have a picture of total national debt sustainability, and to convene an international forum to examine ways and means of addressing domestic debt problems, which are severely damaging the private sector, growth prospects, government financing, poverty reduction spending, and therefore the sustainability of external debt (HIPC Finance Ministers, 2001: 3).

The HIPC Finance Ministers also urged the international financial community to make more efforts to ensure that countries which have passed decision points are able to reach their completion points rapidly by interpreting with maximum flexibility compliance with existing conditions, reducing conditionality in PRGF and PRSC programmes, not introducing new conditions and providing more predictable and transparent guidelines on compliance and reporting. They also urged all creditors to accelerate and increase debt relief by:

- Front-loading relief more comprehensively both before and after completion points;

- Accelerating the implementation of interim relief agreements to ensure that faster fiscal relief is provided immediately after decision point in line with popular expectations created by HIPC II;

- (For multilateral creditors) Providing interim relief on all loans before the completion point and cancelling 100 per cent of multilateral debt at completion point;

- (For bilateral creditors) Adopting a policy of holding debt service payments in trust for countries which are yet to reach decision points, and cancelling 100 per cent of all bilateral debt service at decision point and 100 per cent of stock at completion point;

- Including all pre-cut-off-date debt in debt for relief, and moving the cut-off-date debt and cancelling post-cut-off-date debt where necessary;

- Maximizing the additionality of all debt relief by reducing diversion of bilateral aid and using more of multilateral organizations' own resources;

- Making more rapid progress on debt relief from non-Paris-Club Governments by convening an international conference of HIPCs, international financial institutions, and non-OECD and other bilateral creditors in order to agree mechanisms for ensuring relief comparable to that provided by the Paris Club, using the IDA buy-back facility, the HIPC Trust Fund or other resources;

- (For those HIPC-LDCs which have not reached decision point) Making increased efforts to reduce the time it takes to reach decision point, by

HIPC Finance Ministers urged the international financial community to take account of shocks affecting countries by introducing new measures to combat them, by interpreting policy conditionality more flexibly in the event of shocks, and by factoring shocks more realistically into debt sustainability macroeconomic projections.

reducing conditionality and being flexible in interpreting track records, and by reintegrating post-conflict countries much more rapidly into the HIPC process (HIPC Finance Ministers, 2001: 3).

These proposals are concrete measures whose implementation in HIPC-LDCs would fulfil key commitments of the Programme of Action for the Least Developed Countries for the Decade 2001–2010 (set out in United Nations, 2001a, paras. 85–87), which are oriented towards a "comprehensive solution to the debt problem, including full, speedy and effective implementation of the enhanced HIPC Initiative and other debt relief measures" (ibid., para. 86). However, it is likely to be necessary to go further. All members of the Panel which prepared the Zedillo Report (United Nations, 2001b) agreed that "a re-enhanced HIPC Initiative, an HIPC3…merits serious consideration" (p. 54). It would obviously be preferable that further writing-off of external debt happens now rather than that highly indebted LDCs and other poor countries remain stuck in a pattern of ever-recurrent debt renegotiation because sustainability targets of the enhanced HIPC Initiative (HIPC II) are unrealistic. The international conferences proposed by the HIPC Finance Ministers could be an important step towards this, as well as UNCTAD's long-standing proposal, first put forward in UNCTAD (1998), for an objective and comprehensive assessment, by an independent panel of experts not unduly influenced by creditor interests, of debt sustainability, eligibility for debt reduction and the amount of debt reduction needed. The close association between falling and volatile commodity prices and unsustainable external debt should be included in discussions, and ways and means of breaking the link, which is central to the international poverty trap, should be explored. Proposals such as state-contingent debt repayment contracts, which link debt service payments to the external environment in terms of world commodity prices, merit some consideration (Nissanke and Ferrarini, 2001).

> *There is a close association between falling and volatile commodity prices and unsustainable external debt. Ways and means of breaking the link, which is central to the international poverty trap, should be explored.*

Whatever debt relief is provided, it is important that it does not subtract from ODA resources, and also does not impose any unfair burdens on less heavily indebted LDCs and other developing countries. Serious attention must thus be given to the issue of financing further debt relief.

Finally, as discussed in earlier Least Developed Countries Reports, and emphasized in the new Programme of Action (United Nations, 2001a: para. 87(ii)(f)), there is a need to continue to review and monitor the debt sustainability situation of LDCs which are not HIPCs. Some of these are considered to be severely and moderately indebted according to the World Bank classification. One of the principles of the HIPC Initiative was that debt relief should be targeted at the poorest member countries for which excessive debt was a particularly formidable obstacle to development. If any LDCs prove to have unsustainable external debts, they should be eligible for treatment comparable to that accorded to the HIPC-LDCs.

C. Aid and its effectiveness

A durable exit from the debt problem cannot be achieved through debt relief alone, but also requires the provision of aid. Aid is essential for the simple reason that in countries where there is generalized poverty, there are limited domestic resources available for financing physical capital formation, the build-up of the human capital base through better health, education and nutrition, the maintenance of environmental resources, and the adequate funding of public services, including administration and law and order. With many people living from hand to mouth, and with a weakly developed domestic corporate sector, domestic savings are necessarily very low. External finance is necessary in order to enable countries to break out of the trap of generalized poverty and to initiate a sustained process of development, with increasing reliance on domestic resources and movement away from aid dependence.

Private capital flows can make a contribution, but this will generally be small in the early stages. Although such flows to the LDCs were increasing in the 1990s, a large share of the increase has been concentrated in a few countries. In spite of extensive efforts to create the right policy environment for private capital inflows from abroad, foreign investors and lenders are generally deterred from placing their money in the LDCs owing to the high costs of asset development, high risks which are rooted in the vulnerability of LDCs to shocks, lack of business support services, weak physical, social and administrative infrastructure, and the small scale of most projects. International capital markets are also characterized by imperfections that limit access to private finance even when projects are financially viable. Thus most LDCs must still rely on official capital flows as their main source of external finance for the immediate future. Aid has a vital role to play in ensuring that countries have access to necessary finance for public sector and private sector development needs when international capital market failures effectively exclude them.

With sustained economic growth there can be a strong domestic savings effort in the LDCs, which could reduce dependence on external finance (UNCTAD, 2000a). Similarly, over time, FDI and international bank loans could increasingly substitute for official grants and loans. But generally private capital inflows are most likely to follow rather than lead economic growth and increased domestic investment. Official development finance is essential to enable countries to break out of the trap of generalized poverty and to initiate a sustained process of development and movement away from aid dependence.

1. The need to implement aid commitments

Although development aid is essential for LDCs in order to enable them to break out of the poverty trap, the actual level of aid inflows was declining in the 1990s. In real per capita terms, net ODA disbursements to the LDCs dropped by 46 per cent between 1990 and 2000. In the latter year, 18 per cent of aid was absorbed in debt relief and emergency assistance. It is also clear that aid inflows have been falling even in LDCs that have what are regarded as a good policy environment. Net ODA per capita to HIPC-LDCs which have reached decision point (which requires a good policy track record in the terms of the IMF and World Bank) has fallen by 35 per cent in real terms from 1990 to 2000, and has fallen by 25 per cent since 1995, the year before the HIPC Initiative was set up.[4]

Effective poverty reduction in the LDCs requires that these trends be reversed, and that there be a substantial increase in aid to the LDCs. The levels of aid inflows that are required in order to promote sustained poverty reduction in the LDCs are best assessed through country-level studies. However, various relevant international estimates have been made of the official finance needed to promote sustainable growth and to achieve international development targets in developing countries or sub-groups amongst them:

- UNCTAD (2000b) suggests that for self-sustained growth rates of 6 per cent a year in sub-Saharan Africa to be achieved, aid will have to double in the short run from about $10 billion to $20 billion a year. This increase is necessary in order to give a big push to development now, so as to initiate

External finance is necessary in order to enable countries to break out of the trap of generalized poverty and to initiate a sustained process of development with increasing reliance on domestic resources and movement away from aid dependence.

Although development aid is essential for LDCs, in real per capita terms, net ODA disbursements to the LDCs dropped by 46 per cent between 1990 and 2000.

Aid inflows have been falling even in LDCs that have what are regarded as a good policy environment.

a virtuous process in which economic growth is increasingly financed by domestic resources and private capital inflows. The precise magnitude of the aid inflows required depends on marginal savings rates and investment efficiency, and a necessary condition for success is the adoption of more growth-oriented policies at the national level.

- World Bank/IMF (2001) has made preliminary estimates of the increased aid that will be required if the international development goal of reducing poverty by half by the year 2015 in 65 low-income countries is to be achieved. These countries — which are designated "uphill" countries, since it will be an uphill struggle to reach the poverty reduction goal — have an average income per capita of below $400 and consist of IDA-only countries plus Pakistan, Nigeria and Zimbabwe. About two thirds of them, 43 countries, are regarded as having good policies in place now. It is estimated that reducing the incidence of extreme poverty by half in these countries will require that annual aid inflows be increased threefold, from $19 billion in 1999 to $58 billion a year in the medium term (additional funding of $39 billion a year). A similar threefold increase, from $5 billion in 1999 to $15 billion a year in the medium term, is also required in the 22 other "uphill" countries, but such inflows are not recommended by the World Bank and IMF unless those countries' domestic policies are changed. For other developing countries, which can be expected to reach the poverty reduction goal if trends manifested in the 1990s continue, it is recommended that net ODA flows, which amounted to $33 billion in 1999, be maintained at the same level.

Earlier UNCTAD research suggests that for self-sustained growth rates of 6 per cent a year in sub-Saharan Africa to be achieved, aid will have to double in the short run from about $10 billion to $20 billion a year.

From these estimates it is clear that a substantial increase in aid inflows is necessary for the purpose of reducing the incidence of extreme poverty by half in the LDCs. Indeed, it is most likely that attaining this goal will require aid inflows to double at least, and, according to the higher World Bank/IMF estimate, to triple.

Some estimates are also available of the additional resources required for the achievement of education and health goals envisaged in the Millennium Development Goals in the LDCs. On the basis of a UNICEF study it can be calculated that there is a need for additional financial resources (from domestic sources and external finance) of $1.8 billion a year (in 1998 prices) for the achievement of the goal of universal primary education in the LDCs by 2015 (Delamonica, Mehrota and Vandemoortele, 2001). The Commission on Globalization and Health of the WHO has also estimated that $17 billion a year up to 2007 (in 2002 prices) will be required from domestic and external sources for the achievement of the targeted health improvements in the LDCs (WHO, 2002).[5]

To achieve the necessary increase in aid inflows, it is essential that donor countries implement, as soon as possible, commitments which they reconfirmed at the Third United Nations Conference on the Least Developed Countries to reach the target of providing 0.15 to 0.20 per cent of their GNP as ODA to the LDCs.

To achieve the necessary increase in aid inflows, it is essential that donor countries implement, as soon as possible, commitments which they reconfirmed at the Third United Nations Conference on the Least Developed Countries to reach the target of providing 0.15 to 0.20 per cent of their GNP as ODA to the LDCs. Some indicative estimates of aid flows to the LDCs that would follow implementation of commitments are shown in table 45. The table contains only indicative estimates as it is not completely clear which donor countries have committed to the 0.20 per cent target, which have committed to 0.15 per cent, and which have not committed to either target.[6] However, it provides an indication of the order of magnitude of aid inflows, it being assumed that the pattern of commitments to the Programme of Action donor targets which prevailed after the Second United Nations Conference on the Least Developed Countries (when the targets were first set) still obtain and are now fulfilled.

TABLE 45. PROJECTED NET ODA DISBURSEMENTS BY OECD/DAC DONORS TO LDCs IN 2005
ACCORDING TO DIFFERENT SCENARIOS[a]
(Constant 2000, $ million)

	2000[b]	2005
Scenario 1:		
If OECD/DAC donors continue the overall ODA trend decrease of the 1990s	12 211	9 862
Scenario 2:		
If OECD/DAC donors maintain their ODA levels of 2000	12 211	13 916
Scenario 3:		
If OECD/DAC donors gradually fulfil their ODA targets by 2010	12 211	17 886
Scenario 4:		
If OECD/ DAC donors gradually fulfil their ODA targets by 2007	12 211	19 915
Scenario 5:		
As scenario 3, and if Japan and the United States increase their ODA to 0.15% of their GNP	12 211	27 037
Scenario 6:		
As scenario 4, and if Japan and the United States increase their ODA to 0.15% of their GNP	12 211	33 641

Source: UNCTAD secretariat estimates based on OECD/DAC Statistical Reporting System, on-line data.
  a For assumptions underlying the projections, see text.
  b Actual net ODA disbursements in 2000.

The table underlines the importance of implementation of the aid targets in the Programme of Action. It shows that net ODA flows to LDCs will fall by 19 per cent in real terms to $10 billion (in 2000 dollars) by 2005 if the trends manifested in the 1990s persist, and they will only rise modestly to about $14 billion if there is no change in ODA/GNP ratios from the 2000 level. However, a 63 per cent increase of aid over 2000 inflows can be achieved by 2005 if all donors except Japan and the United States seek to implement the 0.15 per cent and 0.20 per cent targets by 2007. The level of increased aid inflows which the World Bank and IMF are estimating to be required to achieve the international poverty reduction target in "uphill" countries would be impossible to achieve unless Japan and United States, who are the largest aid donors to LDCs in absolute terms, also undertake to provide at least 0.15 per cent of their GNP as ODA to the LDCs. If they were to adopt this policy, progressively moving to that target by 2007, and other donor countries fulfilled commitments by 2007 as before, it would be possible to increase aid inflows by 176 per cent by 2005.

Such increases in the volume of aid require the rebuilding of political support for aid programmes in donor countries. There were encouraging developments in the Monterrey Conference on Financing for Development.[7] But as the Zedillo Report points out, the public in the donor countries need to be made aware of the stake which they have in sustainable development and poverty reduction in the poorest countries, as well as of the resource costs of development and poverty reduction and the role of aid in their financing (United Nations, 2001b: 54). It is also vital that the LDCs themselves regain donors' confidence and build the support of their own domestic constituencies by increasing transparency and accountability in the use of both internal and external financial resources where possible establishing comprehensive and coherent budgets and medium-term expenditure plans.

It is also vital that the LDCs themselves regain donors' confidence and build the support of their own domestic constituencies by increasing transparency and accountability in the use of both internal and external financial resources where possible establishing comprehensive and coherent budgets and medium-term expenditure plans.

2. MAKING AID MORE EFFECTIVE

There is a need not simply for more aid, but also for more effective aid. Most research actually shows that foreign aid increases investment in recipient

BOX 19. RECENT CONTRIBUTIONS TO THE DEBATE ON AID EFFECTIVENESS

There are many who doubt that aid can work in practice and who argue that empirical evidence shows that it does not work, or that it works only in countries that have undertaken the type of policy reforms advocated by the IMF and the World Bank. However, the weight of evidence does not support either of these contentions (see Beynon, 2001; Hermes and Lensink, 2001).

Econometric studies of aid effectiveness conducted up to the mid-1990s have been reviewed in Hansen and Tarp (2000). They find that:

- Aid increases aggregate savings, though not by as much as the aid flows.

- Aid generally increases investment.

- In all cases where growth is founded on the cumulative expansion of savings and investment, aid has positive effects on growth.

The majority of recent studies have also confirmed that foreign aid has a positive effect of aid on growth, and that this occurs through increasing physical and human capital accumulation. But no link has been found between aid inflows and growth in factor productivity (World Bank, 2001). One result which is particularly important for the LDCs suggests that, all other things being equal, aid is more effective in countries subject to high external and climatic shocks (Guillaumont and Chauvet, 2001). The result implies that aid may be particularly important in lessening the negative effects of high vulnerability. Recent research also shows that high levels of external debt can reduce the positive effects of aid inflows on growth and investment (Hansen, 2001).

Donors have been particularly influenced by econometric work which purportedly shows that aid has a positive impact on growth only if a certain type of national policy environment is present, one in which the economy is open and government intervention is limited (Burnside and Dollar, 1997, 2000). This work has provided the basis for some of the conclusions in the key World Bank report on aid (World Bank, 1998). The consequence is that aid is seen as helping poverty reduction best through strengthening the policy environment for poverty reduction. But close scrutiny of the Burnside and Dollar studies has shown that their findings are not econometrically robust (Hansen and Tarp, 2000, 2001; Dalgaard and Hansen, 2001). What is perhaps more important is that in recent work increasing attention is being given to the proposition that although the impact of aid on growth is generally positive, there are decreasing marginal returns to aid inflows owing to such factors as absorptive capacity constraints, institutional destruction caused by aid inflows, and negative effects on exchange rates. Given diminishing marginal returns, the question has arisen whether the effects of aid become negative, and if so, at what point. Estimates vary, but most have suggested that aid can have a negative impact on growth once it exceeds 25–50 per cent of GNP (Lensink and White, 2001). One would expect that where the turning point lies depends on the aid delivery system; and given a very uncoordinated aid delivery system in which multiple donors are pursuing their own agenda, it could be reached quite quickly.

It is certainly necessary to have a realistic view of how aid works in practice. Moreover, one must recognize a central dilemma of aid is that "Aid is likely to be most effective in countries which need it least, and least effective in countries that need it most" (Ehrenpreis, 2001). However, the ineffectiveness of aid has been exaggerated. The central policy issue is not whether aid works, but how to make it work better.

Aid effectiveness depends on both aid recipients' policies and aid donors' policies.

countries (see box 19). However, in the past aid was not yielding as much value for money as it could. The current conventional wisdom suggests that the major reason for this was that it was allocated to countries where the national policy environment was not right and national policies were weakly owned. However, this is a "one-eyed" explanation. Aid effectiveness depends on both aid recipients' policies and aid donors' policies. It is certainly true that the nature of aid recipients' policies affects aid effectiveness. However, the finding that it works only within open economies with limited government is not econometrically robust (see box 19). Increased selectivity, in which aid flows are focused on what are regarded as the right national policy environments, will not make aid work better unless there are also improvements in donors' policies. Moreover, if what are regarded as the right national policies are actually not those that are appropriate in countries in which there is generalized poverty, one should not expect that increased selectivity will increase aid effectiveness.

As argued in *The Least Developed Countries 2000 Report*, the process of structural adjustment in the 1980s and 1990s itself undermined aid effectiveness. In that period, relatively strong coordination of policy conditionality around IMF and World Bank structural adjustment programmes tied aid disbursements to what we have argued in the last chapter was an inappropriate policy model for national development and poverty reduction. At the same time, there was no mechanism for coordinating aid inflows and thus the aid delivery system was characterized by a multiplicity of fragmented aid-funded programmes and projects that generated high transaction costs for recipient countries and were weakly integrated into national economic and administrative structures. The combination of (i) the drive to reduce the budget deficit (excluding grants), (ii) interruptions of aid flows when fiscal targets were not met or other policy slippages occurred, (iii) rising debt service obligations and (iv) the proliferation of donor projects that were increasingly managed through parallel government structures, disrupted development processes and eroded State capacities (UNCTAD, 2000a: 175–192). One of the reasons why the introduction of the PRSP approach is so important is that it should enable greater coordination of aid inflows around a common objective and a common nationally defined strategy. The approach thus has much potential to increase aid effectiveness. However, as discussed in the last chapter, important changes in donor behaviour are required in order to achieve those gains, notably in policy conditionality and donor alignment behind national strategies. To achieve this, it would be helpful if practical experiences in building a genuine partnership through new institutional mechanisms for donor performance monitoring at the recipient country level, such as that which is evolving in the United Republic of Tanzania (see box 17, chapter 5), are generalized amongst the LDCs.

One of the reasons why the introduction of the PRSP approach is so important is that it should enable greater coordination of aid inflows around a common objective and a common nationally defined strategy. The approach thus has much potential to increase aid effectiveness.

Apart from conditionality, coordination and ownership issues which the PRSP approach is expected to deal with, there are four other important shifts in donor policies which are necessary for increased aid effectiveness. Firstly, it is necessary that the donor-driven aid/debt service system, which was outlined in chapter 4, be ended. In the 1990s, the donor community "was stuck in a dance of new rounds of transfers to finance debt service, avoid embarrassing arrears, and stave off growing risks of documented development failures" (Birdsall, Claessens and Diwan, 2001: 21). Aid will not effectively promote development until it is used for development purposes rather than as part of this "debt game". It is for this reason that increased and accelerated debt relief is so important, as the 'debt-tail' will not stop wagging the 'aid-dog' until there is a sustainable exit from the debt problem.

Aid effectiveness will be enhanced if aid is concentrated in major under-funded activities that can provide high developmental returns in terms of sustained growth and poverty reduction in the long run.

Secondly, donor countries must implement in an expeditious manner the OECD/DAC recommendation to untie aid to the LDCs, which was agreed in May 2001 and included as a commitment in the Programme of Action for the Least Developed Countries for the Decade 2001–2010. It has been estimated that the tying of aid to procurement from donor countries has reduced the value of aid by as much as 20–25 per cent. Increased international competition in procurement should increase aid effectiveness. However, it is unfortunate that both food aid and technical assistance were excluded from the agreement to untie aid, in the latter case because some donor countries believed that their own consultancy services sector was "too weak to face world competition" (*Financial Times*, 2001). The implications of these exclusions for aid effectiveness should be monitored.

Thirdly, aid effectiveness will be enhanced if aid is concentrated in major under-funded activities that can provide high developmental returns in terms of

Box 20. The MISA Initiative

In some Latin American countries, an innovative approach has been introduced to reduce poverty, to enhance the human capital of the poor and to combat child labour. The approach involves providing a minimum income to the poorest and most vulnerable families, conditional on regular school attendance by all their children of school-going age. It has been implemented in the Bolsa-Escola Programme in Brazil, and in a different form in the Progresa Programme in Mexico. As a deliverable for the Third United Nations Conference on the Least Developed Countries, the ILO and UNCTAD brought together an Advisory Group to prepare a report on the desirability and feasibility of applying this approach in African least developed countries.

The report argues that there is a strong justification for applying the Minimum Income for School Attendance (MISA) approach in African least developed countries in order to achieve both education and poverty reduction objectives. Direct private costs of school attendance for a sample of African LDCs are, on average, slightly more than twice the level of public recurrent expenditures per pupil in the 1990s. Moreover, households sending their children to school have to bear significant opportunity costs, in terms of the income forgone arising from the reduced availability of child labour. These can be estimated as about 35 per cent of average rural incomes and are generally more than twice the level of public recurrent expenditure per pupil in African LDCs. Poor households are not sending their children to school as they cannot meet these costs. Measures are required to reduce the costs of educating children incurred by poor households, so as to ensure that the benefits of the necessary supply-side policies to improve education reach the poor, and thus to achieve schooling for all. This is what MISA programmes do.

MISA programmes not only support the achievement of educational objectives, but also can make a major contribution to poverty reduction. They contribute to poverty reduction through: (i) the immediate poverty-alleviating effect on the household budget; (ii) the long-term effect on building up the assets of poor households in terms of human capital, which is important for both poverty reduction and growth enhancement; and (iii) the wider short-term poverty reduction effects of the cash transfer which occur through the direct effects of the income and security provided by the cash transfer, the multiplier effects of the cash injection on the local community, changes in the sense of citizenship of poor and excluded groups, increased social policy coordination and enhanced gender balance. The last effect occurs when mothers are the recipients of the cash transfers.

MISA programmes give poor and vulnerable households more room for manoeuvre in their livelihood strategies. They help to prevent households and communities from becoming enmeshed in clientelistic and paternalistic practices, strengthening their autonomy. The poor are usually excluded from formal credit and insurance markets and informal safety nets are imperfect, particularly in the face of common risks. Moreover, the poor can face labour market exclusion owing to malnutrition. In this situation, the MISA approach can enable household members to get out of counter-productive risk-management strategies which lock them into low-risk/low-return activities, diminish specialization and lower the degree of marketization of the economy.

In short, MISA programmes offer an approach to promote economic opportunity, to facilitate empowerment, and to enhance the security and dignity of poor households at one and the same time. As such, they provide a powerful and innovative approach which can be integrated within poverty reduction strategies to help achieve their goals.

The cost of implementing a MISA programme in an African LDC will depend on the design chosen and the scope. The ILO/UNCTAD report estimates that the total costs per country of a "bare-bones" programme, which merely seeks to close the gap between the gross enrolment rate and the net enrolment rate, are generally under $50 million a year.

Given present constraints on domestic financing, MISA programmes must largely be funded, at least in the initial stages, through international sources of finance. Debt relief offers one possible source, but the enhanced HIPC Initiative opens up insufficient fiscal space to provide a viable source of finance. Thus MISA programmes must largely be funded by international aid, probably through a multi-donor funding process. Aid has not traditionally been used to provide cash transfers to households. But the benefits are likely to be substantial and, as the Progresa experience in particular has shown, justify this kind of innovative approach to aid. International social funds to support Africa are currently being proposed and MISA programmes could fit logically within this framework.

As a follow-up to the ILO/UNCTAD report, and following the high level of interest expressed in the approach by the Government of Mozambique, work is under way to establish a pilot project in Mozambique. This is being supported by the Ford Foundation.

Source: ILO/UNCTAD (2001).

TABLE 46. EXTERNAL ASSISTANCE TO AGRICULTURE (EAA) IN LDCS, 1981–1999

Year	External assistance to agriculture (current $, million)	External assistance to agriculture (1998 $, million)[a]	Share of EAA in total ODA (%)
1981	2 173	3 890.8	21.1
1982	2 317	4 287.6	22.0
1983	2 214	4 124.4	21.5
1984	1 808	3 444.5	17.0
1985	2 228	4 211.7	20.5
1986	2 329	3 501.7	17.8
1987	2 845	3 696.7	17.9
1988	3 354	4 028.8	21.0
1989	2 826	3 477.0	18.2
1990	3 090	3 381.1	19.3
1991	1 881	1 981.7	10.7
1992	2 505	2 487.3	14.7
1993	1 708	1 724.6	11.0
1994	1 520	1 468.0	9.3
1995	1 798	1 586.8	11.5
1996	2 185	1 988.5	15.0
1997	2 205	2 161.6	15.7
1998	2 270	2 270.0	16.0
1999	2 145	2 105.6	14.3
Average 1981–1990	2 518	3 804.4	19.6
Average 1991–1999	2 014	1 974.9	13.1

Source: UNCTAD secretariat estimates based on FAO (2001).

a   Real external assistance for agriculture is estimated using the DAC deflator.

sustained growth and poverty reduction in the long run. What this implies is using aid not simply to promote the establishment of policy frameworks that are expected to support poverty reduction, but also using it selectively within countries to finance essential missing ingredients for a sustained process of development and poverty reduction. Such selectivity within countries is particularly important if aid inflows increase, as there is otherwise a danger that there will be diminishing returns to aid. Major under-funded activities should be identified by Governments as part of their PRSPs. Investment in education and health are certainly important, and there is scope here for innovative approaches to aid that could have multiple beneficial effects (box 20). But aid should not be concerned only with social sectors on the ground that these are easily monitorable as being pro-poor. In the last two decades, there has been a tendency to focus aid to the LDCs increasingly on social sectors, and in the context of declining total aid flows this shift in priorities has implied that the allocation of aid to productive sectors and economic infrastructure has been neglected. These areas can provide important developmental returns. Indeed, they are fundamental to a long-term transition in which the growth process increasingly relies on exports, domestic savings and private capital inflows.

A particularly stark example is that of agriculture, from which the majority of people in the LDCs earn their livelihood. In real terms external assistance to agriculture in the LDCs in the 1990s was half the level it was in the 1980s (table 46). However, there are major opportunities for productivity growth and poverty reduction through increased public investment in agricultural research and development, rural infrastructure and also agricultural extension, which requires official external finance. A Green Revolution in certain minor cereals and also cassava can play a key role in rural poverty reduction in many LDCs, and aid could effectively support this process (Mosley, 2000).

Investment in education and health are certainly important... But aid should not be concerned only with social sectors on the ground that these are easily monitorable as being pro-poor... The allocation of aid to productive sectors and economic infrastructure has been neglected.

It is important, therefore, that donor and recipient countries explore possibilities for investment in production as well as in social sectors. Given past experience, it is likely to be important to focus on how aid can facilitate productivity growth as well as increased investment, and also export development. Major gains may also come from improvements in technical assistance, which absorbs an important part of aid flows, but which, evaluations suggests has not contributed much to building domestic capability (Arndt, 2000). Renewed attention also needs to be given to the way in which aid can facilitate the transfer of technology to the LDCs and can help finance enterprise development within them, as well as to the links between ODA and developmental FDI.

Finally, the effectiveness of aid can be increased if donors deliver it in a way which contributes to economic stability rather than acts as a source of shocks. Available evidence shows that foreign aid flows are both very variable and unpredictable for the LDCs. In the majority of cases for which data are available, annual variations in aid are actually higher than annual variations in export revenues, and fluctuations in aid inflows have served to reinforce, rather than dampen, external shocks (UNCTAD, 2000a: Part II, chapter 5). Comparisons of donor aid projections with donor aid disbursements also show that "aid cannot be reliably predicted on the basis of donors' commitments" (Bulir and Hamann, 2001: 18) and that "the predictive power of donors' commitments tends to be lower in poorer and in more aid-dependent countries" (ibid.: 12). Bulir and Hamann's analysis of official projections of aid made by both national authorities and the IMF in ESAF-funded programmes in 37 countries, including 14 LDCs, shows that:

- For project aid, and focusing on authorities' projections at the time of budget presentation (which usually take updated commitments by donors at face value), the average errors in projections vis-à-vis disbursements is 15 per cent, which is equivalent to about 1.5 per cent of GDP. On average, disbursements were overestimated, but there were a fair number of cases in which aid disbursements were underestimated.

- For programme aid, and focusing on IMF-programme projections (the numbers used in IMF Board meeting documents, which are based on updated commitments of donors), the average errors between projections and disbursements vary between countries where programmes are interrupted owing to breaches of conditionality (which will necessarily lead to lower disbursements than projected) and those without interruption. There is, nevertheless, a general pattern in which projections overestimate aid actually received. Countries with programme interruptions received on average only about one third of programme aid commitments (equivalent to 3.3 per cent of GDP). But countries with uninterrupted programmes received only three quarters of programme aid commitments even though they remained officially on track. Disbursements exceeded IMF programme projections in only four out of 28 countries in all.

- The quarterly distribution of programme aid also falls considerably short of the programmed path. On average, actual quarterly out-turns deviate by about 50 per cent from the quarterly path estimated at the beginning of the programme period (i.e. if the country expected $10 million it receives on average either $5 million or $15 million), and out of 23 countries for which quarterly data are available, only two countries receive programme aid with prediction errors lower than 20 per cent.

Renewed attention also needs to be given to the way in which aid can facilitate the transfer of technology to the LDCs and can help finance enterprise development within them, as well as to the links between ODA and developmental FDI.

In short, "official projections of aid (including those of the IMF) are subject to large errors and... particularly in the case of program aid, they seem to exhibit a substantial upward bias" (Bulir and Hamann, 2001: 28).

Given the importance of aid for investment and resource allocation in most LDCs, the unpredictability of aid can have major adverse consequences in reducing the effectiveness of aid in poverty reduction. More stable and more predictable aid inflows are therefore essential for increased aid effectiveness.

D. Market access and its effectiveness

At the same time as foreign aid has been declining, there have been increasing efforts to support the LDCs by providing them with preferential market access for their exports. The need for specific market access advantages for developing countries was first noted more than three decades ago, at UNCTAD II in 1968, and special treatment for the LDCs has been provided by developed countries through the Generalized System of Preferences (GSP) schemes, and by developing countries through the Global System of Trade Preferences among Developing Countries (GSTP). In the Singapore Ministerial Declaration in 1996 WTO members agreed to take measures in favour of LDCs, "including provision for taking positive measures, for example, duty-free access on an autonomous basis, aiming at improving their overall capacity to respond to the opportunities offered by the trading system".

Following this Declaration, several WTO members provided details of existing or planned measures of enhanced market access for the LDCs at the High-level Meeting on Integrated Initiatives for LDCs' Trade Development in 1997. At an Ad Hoc Expert Group meeting, convened by the Secretary-General of UNCTAD in 1998, on GSP, GSTP and the new initiatives for LDCs, experts reported on new initiatives taken by a number of developing countries — India, Indonesia, Morocco, the Republic of Korea, South Africa, Thailand and Turkey — pursuant to their announcements at the High-level Meeting. In 1999, in the preparations for the Third WTO Ministerial Conference in Seattle, the European Union launched a proposal directed at "entering into a commitment to ensure duty-free market access not later than at the end of the new round of negotiations for essentially all products exported by the LDCs". In May 2000, a number of developed and developing countries announced further tariff preferences for the LDCs. The Quad countries (Canada, the EU, Japan and the United States), which import about three quarters of total LDC exports, also proposed to implement both tariff-free and quota-free treatment, "consistent with domestic requirements and international agreements", under their preferential schemes for "essentially all" products originating in the LDCs. Arguably, the "essentially all" qualification of the offer was designed to cover the respective concerns of the Quad countries in agriculture (the European Union), textiles and clothing (the United States and Canada) and fish (Japan). Moreover, the use of the word "consistent" with the existing requirements suggests that current rules of origin and administrative procedures will not be modified.

Most of the Quad countries have recently undertaken concrete action to provide more favourable market access conditions to LDCs and sub-Saharan African countries. In May 2000, the United States enacted the African Growth and Opportunity Act (AGOA), by which the basic United States GSP scheme was amended in favour of designated sub-Saharan African countries to include a larger range of products. In particular, preferential treatment was granted to

At the same time as foreign aid has been declining, there have been increasing efforts to support the LDCs by providing them with preferential market access for their exports.

Most of the Quad countries have recently undertaken concrete action to provide more favourable market access conditions to LDCs and sub-Saharan African countries.

selected apparel articles subject to special provisions, rules of origin and customs requirements. In September 2000, the Canadian Government enlarged the product coverage of its GSP scheme to allow 570 products originating in LDCs to enter its market duty-free. On 5 March 2001, as a major deliverable prepared for the Third United Nations Conference on the Least Developed Countries, the "Everything but Arms" (EBA) proposal of the European Union Commission, granting unrestricted duty-free access to all LDCs products, excluding arms, was approved and entered into effect. The original proposal was amended to provide longer transition periods for the phasing-out of customs duties on three very sensitive products, namely bananas, rice and sugar. Following a review of the GSP scheme of Japan, conducted in December 2000, that scheme was revised and extended for 10 years until 31 March 2011. The revised scheme introduced, as of 1 April 2001, an additional list of industrial products originating in LDC beneficiaries that are granted duty- and quota-free entry.

In theory, preferential market access provided through these initiatives can enhance the competitive advantage of the LDC exporters and thus promote faster export growth in the LDCs... However, improved market access is commercially meaningless if the LDCs cannot produce in the sectors in which they have preferential treatment and lack the marketing skills, information and connections to convert market access into market entry.

In theory, preferential market access provided through these initiatives can enhance the competitive advantage of the LDC exporters and thus promote faster export growth in the LDCs.[8] However, in practice realizing this competitive advantage depends critically on supply capabilities. Improved market access is commercially meaningless if the LDCs cannot produce in the sectors in which they have preferential treatment and they lack the marketing skills, information and connections to convert market access into market entry. In assessing the potential effects of recent market access initiatives for growth and poverty reduction in the LDCs, it is also important to be cognizant of past experience with unilateral trade preferences. This shows that the mere granting of tariff preferences or duty-free market access to exports originating in LDCs does not ensure that the trade preferences can be effectively utilized by them. Indeed, available estimates suggest that in the late 1990s about half of LDC exports to Quad markets which were potentially eligible for GSP preferential treatment in reality did not (and still largely do not) qualify for the preferential tariff rates, thus causing unnecessary payment of most-favoured-nation (MFN) customs duties, rejected imports, unnecessary testing, spoilage, legal fees and forgone opportunities in general (UNCTAD, 2001a).

In 1999, 99 per cent of total imports into the EU from non-ACP LDCs were eligible for GSP treatment, but only 34 per cent of the imports eligible for preferential treatment actually received it.

The utilization ratio, defined as the ratio between total imports actually receiving preferences and the total imports eligible for preferences in any given market, was better for the United States (77 per cent), Japan (73 per cent) and Canada (59 per cent). But just 34 per cent of exports from non-ACP (African, Caribbean and Pacific) LDCs potentially eligible for GSP preferential treatment in the EU were receiving this treatment in 1999 (table 47). In effect, although the EU preferential scheme covered about 99 per cent of products, more than two thirds of non-ACP LDC exports (more than $2 billion) paid MFN duties rather than receiving the preferences. Data are unavailable for ACP LDCs, but there is no reason to assume that similar patterns did not prevail.[9]

It is also worth noting that relatively high utilization rates (for instance, in the case of the United States and Canada) do not guarantee that market access at preferential rates exists and has been effective. This holds particularly true where important sectors of interest to LDC exporters (processed food, garments and footwear, to mention just a few) may be excluded by a preferential arrangement. In this case, the lack of product coverage is the main problem affecting the value of trade preferences rather than the utilization of the few preferences available. It remains to be seen whether the recent initiatives expanding product coverage in new sectors will result in utilization rates higher than those recorded under other schemes traditionally providing preferences to those sectors.

TABLE 47. EFFECTIVE BENEFITS OF QUAD COUNTRIES' GENERALIZED SYSTEM OF PREFERENCES (GSP) FOR LDCs, LATE 1990s

	Imports from LDCs							
	Total imports 1	Dutiable imports 2	Covered by GSP scheme 3	Receiving preferential treatment 4	Total/ dutiable imports (2/1)	GSP-eligible/ dutiable imports (3/2)	Utilization rate (4/3)	Utility rate (4/2)
	$ millions				Percentage			
Canada[a]	256	92	10	6	36	11	59	6
EU[b]	3 562	3 101	3 075	1 035	87	99	34	33
Japan[c]	1 248	765	314	229	61	41	73	30
USA[a]	4 975	4 247	2 282	1 747	85	54	77	41
USA, excl. minerals	2 613	2 078	113	89	80	5	79	4
Total	10 041	8 205	5 681	3 017	82	69	53	37
Total, excl. USA minerals	7 679	6 036	3 512	1 359	79	58	39	23

Source: UNCTAD (2001a).

Note: EU excludes ACP LDCs and USA excludes Haiti, a beneficiary of the Caribbean Basin Initiative.
  a   1998.
  b   1999.
  c   1997.

Utilization rates also vary amongst LDCs. In 1997, Bangladesh supplied more than half of the preferential exports of all LDCs to the EU, Norway and Canada, while Angola supplied the United States with more than 80 per cent of the latter's preferential imports from the LDCs. Mauritania and Bangladesh accounted for 75 per cent of total preferential imports from LDCs into Japan, while Nepal, Bangladesh and Sierra Leone supplied Switzerland with about 85 per cent of its preferential imports from LDCs (UNCTAD, 2001b: 8–9).

The reasons for the low and uneven levels of utilization are various. They include: the lack of security of market access, which is due to the autonomous and unilateral character of the GSP; rules of origin which, amongst other things, restrict the use of imported materials and components and which are overly restrictive given the level of productive development in the LDCs; and lack of technical knowledge, human resources and institutional capacity to take advantage of preferential arrangements which require in-depth knowledge of national tariff systems in various preference-giving countries (UNCTAD, 2001a).

The reasons for the low and uneven levels of utilization of trade preferences include: the lack of security of market access, rules of origin, and lack of technical knowledge, human resources and institutional capacity.

Non-tariff barriers also pose serious impediments to the realization of trading opportunities for LDCs. These barriers include quotas as well as technical and product standards, and sanitary and phytosanitary measures. Non-tariff barriers appear to be applied particularly to agricultural goods and textiles. It has been estimated that as regards LDC exports of agricultural and fishery products, 42 per cent of the product lines estimated at the HS 06-digit level face non-tariff barriers in Quad country markets, and that as regards LDC exports of textiles and clothing, 66–69 per cent of the product lines face non-tariff barriers in Quad country markets (Bacchetta and Bora, 2001: table 21). A particular problem is phytosanitary measures. Thirty per cent of LDC exports are affected by environment-related trade barriers, and the figure is particularly high for a number of Asian LDCs (Fontagne, Kirchbach and Mimouni, 2001).

Thirty per cent of LDC exports are affected by environment-related trade barriers.

The basic potential value-added of the recent initiatives to grant duty-free and quota-free market access to the LDCs lies in the enhancement of preference margins on tariff peak products (see table 48), and the expansion of product coverage, in addition to existing GSP and GSTP preferences. Amongst the Quad countries, expansion of product coverage would be particularly desirable in the cases of Canada, Japan and the United States. It is estimated that in the later 1990s the percentage of dutiable exports excluded from preferences was as high as 90 per cent in Canada, 59 per cent in Japan and 47 per cent in the United States (95 per cent, excluding oils and minerals). Product coverage was much wider in the EU. For example, in 1997, before the "Everything but Arms" initiative, only 11 out of 502 items exported to the EU from all LDCs as a group with a value of more than $500,000 were not eligible for duty- and quota-free access (Stevens and Kennan, 2001).

TABLE 48. AVERAGE TARIFF RATES ON TARIFF PEAK PRODUCTS AND ALL GOODS IMPORTED BY QUAD COUNTRIES, 1999
(Average tariff rates, unweighted in percentage)

	Number of countries	All goods imports	Tariff peak products
Canada			
MFN rate		8.3	30.5
Preferential rate			
LDCs	47	4.4	22.8
GSP-only beneficiaries	108	6.2	28.2
Other preferential arrangements[a]			
Caribbean community	18	4.3	23.3
Australia	1	7.8	28.2
Chile	1	2.4	12.2
Israel	1	2.5	11.8
Mexico	1	3.1	15.9
New Zealand	1	7.8	28.2
USA	1	1.6	7.1
EU			
MFN rate		7.4	40.3
Preferential rates			
ACP LDCs	37	0.8	11.9
Non-ACP LDCs	11	0.9	12.6
GSP-only beneficiaries	42	3.6	19.8
Other preferential arrangements[a]			
Non-LDC ACP countries	32	0.9	12.4
Eastern Europe and Middle East	30	1.8	20.1
Japan			
MFN rate		4.3	27.8
Preferential rate			
LDCs	42	1.7	19.0
GSP-only beneficiaries	127	2.3	22.7
USA			
MFN rate		5.0	20.8
Preferential rate			
LDCs	38	1.8	14.4
GSP-only beneficiaries	80	2.4	16.0
Other preferential arrangements[a]			
Caribbean community	22	1.6	13.5
ANDEAN	4	1.7	14.0
Canada	1	0.1	0.6
Israel	1	0.1	0.6
Mexico	1	0.3	1.6

Source: Hoekman, Ng and Olarreaga (2001: table 3), reproduced in IMF/World Bank (2001b).

Note: Tariff peak products are products facing import tariffs of 15 per cent or more. In 1996–1998, as a percentage of total imports from LDCs, such products constituted: Canada, 30.2%; EU, 2.8%; Japan, 2.1%; and USA, 15%.

   a   For a detailed explanation of the sample compositions in the different country groups, see Hoekman, Ng and Olarreaga (2001: 11, footnote to table 3).

It has been estimated that if the EU initiative were extended and all Quad members were to grant duty-free access for tariff peak products (products with tariff rate of over 15 per cent), LDC exports would increase by 11 per cent (Hoekman, Ng and Olarreaga, 2001).[10] However, gains are concentrated in only a few countries, particularly exporters of manufactures. Bangladesh is the major beneficiary in absolute terms, accounting for 60 per cent of the total increase in LDC exports which would follow from duty-free access of tariff-peak products to the Canadian market, 47 per cent of the total increase in LDC exports which would follow from duty-free access to the Japanese market, and 67 per cent of the total increase which would follow from duty-free access to the United States market. Other countries exporting manufactures would also benefit significantly in relative terms, with Cambodia, Haiti and the Lao People's Democratic Republic, as well as Cape Verde and Maldives, all expected to witness an increase in exports of more than 20 per cent, and Madagascar, Myanmar and Nepal also seeing gains. The exports of three primary commodity exporters — Liberia, Malawi and Somalia — are expected to increase by 20 per cent or more, and other countries expected to see relatively important export increases are Gambia, Kiribati, Sudan and Togo.

Actual gains may well be smaller than these simulated estimates. The other major study of the impact of duty- and quota-free market access for LDCs to Quad countries suggests that LDC exports will not increase by 11 per cent, but rather by just 3 per cent (UNCTAD/Commonwealth Secretariat, 2001). Moreover, both simulations, as they themselves stress, ignore the problem of low utilization rates, as well as the weak export capacity and supply constraints, which mean that the effective benefits are lower than those simulated.

It is certainly desirable that developed countries that have not already done so work towards the objective of duty-free and quota-free access for all least developed countries' exports, as envisaged in the Programme of Action for the Least Developed Countries for the Decade 2001–2010 adopted in Brussels. But various measures are also required in order to improve the effectiveness of trade preferences for the LDCs in the context of recent proposals for duty-free and quota-free market access. These are:

- An increase in the stability and predictability of trade preferences through a set of multilaterally agreed criteria to be adhered to by all preference-giving countries in the operation of their preferential schemes (see box 21);

- Expansion of product coverage to include excluded products;

- Development of a harmonized and updated set of rules of origin to be applied in the context of the initiative for duty-free and quota-free market access in favour of the LDCs, taking into account the industrial reality of those countries;

- Technical assistance activities aimed at providing information services and training courses to local producers and exporters, strengthening human resources and institutional capacities to comply with administrative and customs procedures under different GSP schemes and preferential arrangements, and establishing a network of cooperating institutions. UNCTAD has particular expertise in this area.

In the end, the ultimate constraint on realizing the benefits of trade preferences is weak supply capabilities. In this regard, increased aid flows to promote exports, investment and increased domestic resource mobilization remain essential, as well as the national policy autonomy to enable LDC

LDC Governments should strengthen the productivity and competitiveness of activities which are of strategic importance to trade and development.

Box 21. Binding trade preferences for LDCs

Binding trade preferences is one mechanism that can be used to increase the commercial benefits of trade preferences for LDCs. Such binding would enhance the benefits of new initiatives to provide quota- and duty-free access for LDCs by increasing their predictability and increasing the security of preferential market access.

Binding trade preferences could be ensured through the negotiation of a new multilateral (WTO) legal instrument, (a) imparting stability and predictability to the duty-free treatment granted to LDCs, while (b) ensuring the maximum contractual security of preferences since any temporary withdrawal of duty-free treatment would be subject to the disciplines of the relevant WTO Agreements, and (c) harmonizing and matching rules-of-origin requirements with the actual industrial capacity of LDCs to increase utilization of trade preferences.

A WTO-compatible instrument might also include other aspects of market access, beyond tariff and origin, by making reference to other specific proposals on market access made by LDCs in recent years, for example with respect to S&D provisions.

The issue of "binding" was raised by the LDCs in the preparations for the Seattle Ministerial Conference in 1999. The Programme of Action for the Least Developed Countries for the Decade 2001–2010, in its paragraph 68(h), contains a commitment that "improvements in market access for LDCs should be granted on a secure and predictable basis". The LDCs' Ministerial Declaration of Zanzibar (July 2002) called upon the fourth WTO Ministerial Conference to agree on: "A binding commitment on duty free and quota free market access for all products from LDCs on a secure, long term and predictable basis with realistic and flexible Rules of Origin to match the industrial capacity of the LDCs" (para. 4). The outcome of the Doha WTO Ministerial Conference, however, did not reflect this proposal in that in the final Declaration, where Ministers committed themselves to working towards the objective of quota- and duty-free market access as well as to considering additional measures for progressive improvements in market access for LDCs (para. 42), the word "binding" was again omitted from the text. This is reflected in the current WTO work programme on market access for the LDCs, as adopted by the Sub-Committee on Least Developed Countries on 12 February 2002. In the wording of this work programme, however, the "examination of possible additional measures for progressive and predictable improvements in market access…and further improvement of the preferential access schemes such as the GSP schemes" (para. 7) might still leave some room for consideration of the issue of binding preferences. Furthermore, in the Doha Declaration Ministers "reaffirm the commitments we undertook at LDC III and agree that the WTO should take into account in designing its work programme for LDCs, the trade related elements of the Brussels Declaration and Programme of Action".

The single undertaking to emerge from the Doha Development Round should contain a contractual instrument providing "binding" status for duty-free access to LDCs, accompanied by supportive provisions on rules of origin and other matters of relevance to effective access market and utilization of these preferences. Without secure access and the assurance that duty-free access will actually be achieved, the possibility of attracting the necessary investment to meet the supply-side problems would seem rather slim for most LDCs.

Governments to strengthen the productivity and competitiveness of activities which are of strategic importance to trade and development.[11]

E. The Integrated Framework to support LDCs in their trade and trade-related activities

One recent initiative which is an opportunity to improve supply capabilities is the Integrated Framework for Trade-related Technical Assistance (IF). The basic objective of the IF, which was introduced in 1997, was to increase the benefits from trade-related technical assistance being provided by six core agencies,[12] by ensuring that trade-related technical assistance was demand-driven, that it matched the specific needs of each LDC, and that it enhanced rather than undermined each LDC's ownership of trade-related technical assistance. Trade-related technical assistance activities were broadly defined as:

- Establishing institutions to handle trade policy issues;

- Strengthening export supply capabilities;

- Strengthening trade support services;

- Strengthening trade facilitation capabilities;

- Training and human resource development for these four areas;

- Assistance in the creation of a supportive trade-related regulatory and policy framework that will encourage trade and investment.

The introduction of the IF was a response to the Uruguay Round Decision on Measures in Favour of Least Developed Countries, which called for "substantially increased technical assistance in the development, strengthening and diversification of their production and export bases including those of services, as well as in trade promotion, to enable them to maximize the benefits from liberalized access to markets" (GATT secretariat, 1994: 441). In the initial phase of the implementation of the IF, 40 LDCs were able to specify their needs for technical assistance, and 37 designated national focal points to coordinate IF implementation. But round-table meetings with potential donor countries were held only in Bangladesh, Gambia, Haiti, Uganda and the United Republic of Tanzania, and modest resources were generated only in the case of Uganda. From the LDCs' point of view, these outcomes fell far short of expectations.

An evaluation of this phase of the IF concluded that the main reason for the poor performance was that trade-related proposals were not mainstreamed into the broader development strategy of a country. New arrangements for enhancing the implementation of the IF were thus proposed and it was agreed to implement the new approach on a pilot basis — the IF Pilot Scheme (PS) — in three PS countries (Cambodia, Madagascar and Mauritania), the Governments of which all demonstrated a strong interest in integrating trade priorities into their national development strategies, and a strong commitment to do so. The central focus of the pilot scheme is what is called "trade mainstreaming", a process which is designed to ensure that trade policy, trade-related technical assistance and capacity-building needs are articulated in a broad development context. For this purpose, "trade integration studies" are being carried out on a country-by-country basis. The studies, which are led by the World Bank, are intended to provide the basis for identification of trade priorities and needs for trade-related capacity building which are to be incorporated into individual least developed countries' development plans and strategies expressed through the PRSPs. This will occur through consideration of the findings and recommendations of the studies in national trade integration strategy workshops/PRSP Committees, which involve all stakeholders. Agencies will indicate their role in responding to these needs and how to meet them, and trade priorities identified in the studies will be presented to World Bank Consultative Group Meetings or UNDP Round Tables, as the case may be, for bilateral donor financing.[13]

The pilot scheme is still evolving, and individual country studies will no doubt produce various results. However, the comparative analysis of the relationship between poverty, trade and development in earlier chapters of this Report provides some important general insights that can help to improve the IF process as it advances. Our analysis underlines the importance of integrating trade into PRSPs, and also the wisdom of the judgement that this should be done through an examination of how trade can fit into the overall national development strategy. But it indicates strongly that integration studies must see integration as a means to beneficial development and poverty reduction rather than as an end in itself. It should not be assumed from the outset that the goal is to strengthen the policy environment for trade liberalization; rather, the objective should be to promote trade in a way which supports development and poverty reduction.

The central focus of the pilot scheme is what is called "trade mainstreaming", a process which is designed to ensure that trade policy, trade-related technical assistance and capacity-building needs are articulated in a broad development context.

Integration studies must see integration as a means to beneficial development and poverty reduction rather than as an end in itself.

The principle of ownership, which has underpinned the IF from the outset, needs to be fully respected. This will require great sensitivity, since the capacity to undertake strategic analysis of trade issues is, by definition, limited. This is particularly important because when trade policy conclusions are mainstreamed into PRSPs, they will become the basis for policy conditionalities whose fulfilment will be required in order to ensure access to concessional assistance of all kinds, not simply access to trade-related technical assistance. If the principle of ownership is not respected, a process which was originally envisaged for the purpose of meeting the special needs of the LDCs will be transformed into an obligation which reduces the policy autonomy of the LDCs in the interests of other agendas. Ideally, the trade integration studies will themselves be a process through which national capacities are strengthened.

For the IF to make a significant contribution, the IF must now move speedily to implementing concrete capacity-building projects which bring tangible benefits for the LDCs.

Donor countries may face particularly difficult choices in financing trade-related technical assistance. One reason is that, relative to the usual development budgets of the LDCs, the costs of fully implementing WTO obligations are very high. It has been estimated, for example, that the average costs per country of implementing Uruguay Round commitments regarding customs valuation, sanitary and phytosanitary standards and intellectual property rights were $130 million in the late 1990s, which was more than the annual central government capital expenditure budget in seven out of 12 LDCs, and more than the annual gross domestic fixed capital in three of them (Finger and Schuler, 2000). As the IF process advances, it will be important that donors ensure an appropriate balance between different aspects of trade-related technical assistance which deserve attention, as they are put forward by the strategy workshops.

Finally, after five years of existence, the IF must now move speedily to implementing concrete capacity-building projects which bring tangible benefits for the LDCs. For the IF to make a significant contribution to the LDCs' capacity-building challenge, there must be a serious commitment to follow up on studies and workshops by donors and agencies, and to support the development of export supply capabilities through financial assistance as well as technical assistance.

F. International commodity policy

Improved market access is a necessary but not a sufficient condition for making international trade a tool for development. Given the overwhelming importance of primary commodities for the economies of many LDCs, and also the relationship between primary commodity dependence and extreme poverty, a review and recasting of international commodity policy are also of paramount importance.

A review and recasting of international commodity policy are of paramount importance.

For more than a decade after 1974, price-stabilizing international commodity agreements were the focus of international commodity policy. The success of this approach has been mixed at best, and its revival appears unlikely. The need to address the specific problems faced by commodity-exporting countries, however, is evident. This section attempts to provide some ideas about a framework for concerted and cooperative action by primary commodity exporters and importers that would aim to enhance the potential of commodity production and exports as a basis for development and poverty reduction, particularly for the LDCs. This framework for international commodity policy covers actions complementary to WTO negotiations, including in particular negotiations on the subsidies to agriculture in OECD countries, whose reduction is of paramount importance for increasing agricultural exports by developing countries.

In order to promote development and poverty reduction in producing countries, an international commodity policy must address three issues. The first is the availability in producing countries of exportable products in sufficient volumes that would interest buyers and that meet the consumers' increasingly stringent requirements. Second, exporting countries need to enter supply chains for these products at points where higher degrees of value added are generated. The third issue is world primary commodity prices. Excessive instability in primary commodity prices, at least its negative impacts, needs to be mitigated and the problem of a continual downward trend of these prices must be addressed.

The first two of these issues can be considered primarily the responsibility of the LDCs themselves. But international support in these areas is an indispensable aspect of international commodity policy. With regard to the third issue, international cooperation is indispensable, including for the application of market-based price risk management instruments within producing countries.

The implementation of international commodity policy requires cooperation and, where possible, coordination between three pillars, namely international organizations within the UN system, providers of bilateral assistance and NGOs, and international commodity bodies (ICBs), as well as the Common Fund for Commodities (CFC). Each of these has a particular role to play in addressing the three issues mentioned above, based on expertise and comparative advantage. Cooperation and coordination are indispensable in order to generate synergies, prevent duplication or contradiction, and to place the actions in a global developmental perspective so as to avoid or mitigate undesirable impacts on vulnerable countries and producers. The provision of reliable information and analysis is also crucial for the success of international commodity policy.

At the present time, there is a disconnection between the accumulated knowledge about how to enhance supply capabilities in commodity-dependent countries and the activities of the IF.

Regarding the first issue, namely enhancing supply capacities through improved availability of exportable products in sufficient volumes that would interest buyers and that meet the consumers' increasingly stringent requirements, technical assistance needs to be provided by international organizations in their respective areas of competence and by ICBs for their specific commodities. Priority should be given to countries with the greatest need for such assistance, and in this regard LDCs that are highly dependent on a single primary commodity for their export earnings and in which there is generalized poverty merit close attention. Financing can be mobilized by increasing the resources available through the CFC or directly through the relevant international organizations. It is clear that the Integrated Framework can have a role to play. But at the present time, there is a disconnection between the accumulated knowledge about how to enhance supply capabilities in commodity-dependent countries and the activities of the IF. In areas such as research and development, quality control and assurance, a subregional approach may be adopted. Regarding the question of the availability of quantities sufficient to interest important buyers, organizational arrangements within countries appear to be crucial and NGOs working in the field, in conjunction with local producers' groupings, seem best placed to provide effective assistance. Given the abundance of supplies in world markets of many commodities of interest to LDCs, improvement of supply capacities should be interpreted to mean provision of better-quality and higher-valued products, possibly in their processed forms, rather than an outright increase in the quantities put on world markets.

As argued in chapter 4, the changing structure of world commodity markets (with liberalization in developing exporting countries and, on the buyers' side, increasing concentration and the importance of supermarket chains) requires developing country Governments and entrepreneurs to have much greater business skills than before. The new structure of supply chains leads to the generation of increasingly high proportions of value added at the marketing and distribution stages. The new approach to international commodity policy must include measures that would enable developing countries, in particular LDCs, to participate more fully at these stages of the supply chain. Research by international organizations, in cooperation with ICBs, is required in order to understand better the structure of supply chains, identify the specific stages of high-value-added generation and assess the potential for exporting countries to enter these activities. This would also include the identification of constraints that may be eliminated through negotiations or overcome by technical and financial assistance and those that may be impossible to deal with in the current context. This identification would then lead to concerted action by the organizations and Governments concerned, and in cooperation with large transnationals where possible, to assist exporters through financial, technical and managerial assistance in their attempts to capture a higher proportion of the value added of the final products.

The new approach to international commodity policy must include measures that would enable developing countries, in particular LDCs, to participate more fully at higher value-added stages of the supply chain.

Mitigating excessive instability in world primary commodity prices, at least its negative impacts, and dealing with the problem of the continual downward trend of these prices also require concerted action by ICBs and international organizations, supported by governmental policies. Past efforts to mitigate excessive instability through economic measures in international commodity agreements (ICAs) have been successful only for limited periods of time. In view of this mixed record and the current lack of political will to implement such economic measures, their reintroduction into ICAs appears unlikely. One possible approach in this respect seems to be the promotion of arrangements between buyers and sellers that are based on longer-term commitments rather than on daily dealings. All parties must accept, however, that attaining some degree of stability may mean forgoing short-term gains. The introduction of at least some aspects of "fair trade" principles into mainstream trade may be an avenue to explore in this connection. For this to happen, incentives need to be provided by Governments and there needs to be cooperation between the NGO community and large business concerns. A joint UNCTAD/International Development Research Centre project is exploring modalities in this regard, with an initial focus on coffee. Some firms, such as Starbucks, have already decided to procure part of their supplies under "fair trade" arrangements, and the marketing of Max Havelaar products through the Migros supermarket chain in Switzerland has been a determining factor in achieving significant market shares, notably in bananas.

Mitigating excessive instability in world primary commodity prices, at least its negative impacts, and dealing with the problem of the continual downward trend of these prices also require concerted action

Since instability is inherent in commodity markets, price risk management instruments are a way to limit the incidence of instability for producers and traders. But for risk management instruments to be used successfully in the LDCs, innovative organizational forms will be needed to reach small farmers. A considerable investment in training will also be required and there is a need to establish the requisite institutional and legal frameworks. Ongoing application of these instruments in some LDCs is likely to reveal both the problems and the potential of this approach.

Compensatory financing is another means of mitigating some of the negative impacts of instability in prices and earnings. The international community, in discussing a new developmental approach to international commodity policy, must reconsider the use of compensatory financing for export earnings shortfalls. This is particularly important as an aspect of addressing what the new Programme of Action for the Least Developed Countries calls the "structural causes of indebtedness" (United Nations, 2001a, para. 86). The IMF contingency credit line is not available to a country which is borrowing from any other IMF facility and the IMF Compensatory Financing Facility (CFF) is so expensive that it would breach the concessional borrowing ceilings which are standard in Poverty Reduction Growth Facility (PRGF) programmes (Martin, 2001). The EU's "B envelope" funding, designed in part to replace its STABEX and SYSMIN export shortfall compensation windows, is more flexible. It introduces contingency financing for export and budget shortfalls, based on indices of vulnerability to economic and climatic shocks. Unfortunately, the terms governing access to this finance are very restrictive, requiring shocks which are equivalent to a 10 per cent drop in export earnings as well as a 10 per cent worsening of the budget deficit (ibid.). The design of appropriate contingency financing facilities for LDCs and other low-income countries is urgent. Also, donors can seek to ensure that the volume of aid inflows is anti-cyclical, and does not reinforce the effects of a sudden decline in the prices of key commodity exports.

There is increasing recognition that there has been a long-term decline in world primary commodity prices. The reasons are disputed, but they include improvements in yields and productivity, the benefits of which have largely accrued to buyers, and the entry of new producers into primary commodity markets. It would naturally be unreasonable to suggest that productivity improvements be limited. The elements of international commodity policy mentioned above, however, could help producers in capturing more of the benefits of such improvements. The entry of new producers into already crowded markets is a more contentious issue. Increases in supplies in one country can result in a decline in prices that may have significant negative effects on other producers. International commodity policy should include modalities whereby regular consultations among international organizations, ICBs and Governments, as well as improved transparency, would help in directing efforts to increase production away from crowded markets to more dynamic products. In this connection, support is needed to assist high-cost producers in overcoming exit barriers that may prevent them from reacting rationally to declining prices, and to help those producers for whom the exit barriers cannot be eliminated. International commodity policy should also consider mechanisms for voluntary supply management schemes. In considering such mechanisms it is necessary to evaluate carefully the different objectives (elimination of accumulated stocks and reduction of production) and different instances of supply control (discouragement of new entrants, of increased production or of exports, and encouraging exit from production), as well as what is expected of consumers. In relation to declining prices, international commodity policy must also accord sufficient importance to increasing consumption of commodities, both through generic promotion and through new and innovative uses.

One key to the future behaviour of the international commodity economy is the position of more advanced developing countries. If they are able to move up the ladder of development and export increasingly sophisticated manufacturing products, it will be much easier for the less developed developing countries, including the LDCs, to expand commodity exports without saturating markets.

The international community, in discussing a new developmental approach to international commodity policy, must reconsider the use of compensatory financing for export earnings shortfalls.

One key to the future behaviour of the international commodity economy is the position of more advanced developing countries. If they are able to move up the ladder of development, it will be much easier for the less developed developing countries, including the LDCs, to expand commodity exports without saturating markets.

Accelerated growth in middle-income countries will also ultimately be an important source of increased demand for primary commodities.

Accelerated growth in middle-income countries will also ultimately be an important source of increased demand for primary commodities.

Finally, the opportunity of using the WTO negotiations in support of the design and implementation of international commodity policy, and diversification efforts of commodity-dependent countries should be seriously considered. In this respect, it is noteworthy that small island developing States and a group of "single commodity exporters" have made proposals in the WTO in the context of the negotiations relating to the Agreement on Agriculture.

G. South–South cooperation and the problem of polarization

South–South cooperation including the encouragement of regional trade and investment dynamics, can be an important element in the development of new export capacities in the LDCs.

Another area of international policies for effective poverty reduction in the LDCs is enhanced South–South cooperation. This is generally a neglected part of analyses of how to reduce poverty in poor countries, and has not yet been adequately addressed in the PRSP approach. However, it is an essential part of the multi-level approach to poverty reduction which is being advocated here. Moreover, the Programme of Action for the Least Developed Countries for the Decade 2001–2010 recognized that it could play an important role in the development of the LDCs, and encouraged the use of "triangular mechanisms", through which "successful South–South cooperation may be attained using financial contributions from one or more donors, and taking advantage of economic complementarities among developing countries" (United Nations, 2001a, para. 19).

Possible areas for South–South cooperation noted in the Programme of Action include the encouragement of regional trade and investment dynamics, which, as is evident in this Report, can be an important element in the development of new export capacities in the LDCs, as well as technical assistance and exchange of best practices in a range of areas (such as the MISA Initiative). A number of LDCs are landlocked or transit countries, and for these countries a regional approach to transport infrastructure financing and to the development and management of transit systems is likely to be a particularly important aspect of the building of a dynamic investment–export nexus (UNCTAD, 1999b). Within sub-Saharan Africa, the corridor development approach, pioneered in the Southern African Development Community, is likely to be particularly promising. This seeks to concentrate viable productive investment projects within selected corridors connecting inland production areas to ports at the same time as infrastructure investment takes place. The synchronous development of directly productive activity and infrastructure ensures a revenue stream which renders the infrastructure investment attractive to private business. At the same time, infrastructure investments attract economic activity and help to promote the agglomeration process. Government policy aims to attract "anchor investments" which ensure the basic viability of infrastructure, and then to seek to attract other investment, a process called "densification". Performance-related incentives are geared towards encouraging domestic and foreign investment in internationally competitive and labour-absorbing projects, and are targeted to specific locations. They include tax holidays, grants to small and medium-sized enterprises, and grants to foreign investors to reimburse costs of shipping machinery and equipment to the corridor. Firms can also avail themselves of accelerated depreciation allowances, schemes to help manufacturers facing tariff reduction to modernize their plant and equipment, low interest schemes, support for basic research and

It is important that South–South cooperation be a complement to, and not a substitute for, North–South cooperation.

development, and venture capital finance. Special attention is paid to small and medium-sized enterprises.

It is important that South–South cooperation be a complement to, and not a substitute for, North–South cooperation. It is also important that enhanced South–South cooperation takes place in a context in which the various asymmetries in the international system that are making it difficult for the more advanced developing countries to deepen industrialization and move up the technological ladder are addressed. It will be difficult for the LDCs to get on and move up the ladder of development if the more advanced developing countries face a "glass ceiling" which blocks their development. Policies to counter the increasing polarization in the global economy are thus also necessary for poverty reduction in the LDCs.

H. Conclusion

In countries where there is generalized poverty, poverty reduction requires effective national policies which promote sustained growth and development. Through the PRSP process and related initiatives, Governments in LDCs are taking responsibility for poverty reduction within their national territories. However, success cannot be ensured unless sufficient resources are provided so that Governments committed to achieve the goal of poverty reduction and sustained development are not thwarted owing to lack of resources. It is also essential that national policy autonomy goes hand in hand with national responsibility.

In countries where there is generalized poverty, poverty reduction requires effective national policies which promote sustained growth and development. However, success cannot be ensured unless sufficient resources are provided so that Governments committed to achieve the goal of poverty reduction and sustained development are not thwarted owing to lack of resources. It is also essential that national policy autonomy goes hand in hand with national responsibility.

Drawing from the array of measures listed in the Programme of Action for the Least Developed Countries for the Decade 2001–2010, this chapter has identified important elements that should be part of a supportive international environment for poverty reduction in LDCs. These elements follow from the analysis of the nature and dynamics of poverty in the LDCs, and in particular the cause-and-effect relationship, which cause generalized poverty to persist. They are not stand-alone policies, but rather should be keyed into domestic policies designed to promote private investment, increased domestic resource mobilization and increased exports, and designed to ensure that, as economic growth takes place, specific groups and regions within countries are not left behind and marginalized.

The analysis confirms the importance of a number of the directions of the Programme of Action, in particular the need substantially to increase aid flows to the LDCs by implementing donor commitments and the need for more effective aid. More stable and predictable aid inflows are essential for increased aid effectiveness. Donor countries must implement in an expeditious manner the OECD/DAC recommendations to untie aid to the LDCs, which were included as a comment in the Programme of Action. Aid effectiveness will also be enhanced if productive sectors, notable agriculture, and economic infrastructure, which both have been relatively neglected in the context of declining total aid flows, receive greater attention.

Improving market access for the LDCs is shown to be not simply a matter of providing quota- and duty-free access, but also of making trade preferences commercially meaningful for exporters in the LDCs. Trade preferences should also not be seen as a substitute for aid inflows when supply capacities are weak. The Integrated Framework (IF) can help if trade-related technical assistance activities are broadly defined and focused on strengthening export supply capacities, if the principle of ownership is fully respected in the mainstreaming of trade issues into PRSPs, and if financial assistance and technical assistance are provided to increase supply capabilities. The disconnect between the IF and the accumulated knowledge on upgrading primary commodity exports, also needs to be speedily bridged.

The analysis identifies increased and accelerated debt relief as an important requirement for effective poverty reduction in many LDCs. The debt issue has received much less international attention recently as non-governmental organizations have shifted their attention to trade issues. However, an unsustainable debt burden is still central to the international poverty trap in which many LDCs are caught. The Programme of Action does not go far enough in this area, though it must be said that the over-optimism of expectations of a sustainable exit from the debt problem has become clearer and clearer with the passing of time.

In the end, addressing the socio-economic marginalization of the LDCs will require addressing the polarization in the global economy.

The analysis also shows that much more attention should be given by the international community to two areas within the Programme of Action that are currently under-emphasized in the international support for poverty reduction, namely, international primary commodity policy and South–South cooperation. The former is the most glaring missing link in the current approach to poverty reduction, as the incidence of extreme poverty is closely related to primary commodity dependence. The latter is important because regional trade and investment linkages, as well as learning based on more successful development experiences, offer an important strand for effective development within the LDCs.

South–South cooperation needs to be developed within the context of the creation of a more supportive global environment that reduces the polarization of the global economy and the marginalization of the poorest countries at the same time. In the end, addressing the socio-economic marginalization of the LDCs will require addressing the polarization in the global economy. Gains from differentiated treatment will be particularly strong for LDCs if an approach is adopted which enables all developing countries to advance. Indeed, this may very well be essential in order to prevent more developing countries from slipping into the LDC category.

Notes

1. These are UNCTAD secretariat estimates based on IMF/IDA (2002a).

2. The eleven countries are: Burundi, the Central African Republic, Comoros, the Democratic Republic of the Congo, the Lao People's Democratic Republic, Liberia, Myanmar, Sierra Leone, Somalia, Sudan and Togo. The external debts of Angola and Yemen are considered sustainable without HIPC assistance.

3. For country case studies of what is happening on the ground in Mali, Ethiopia and Uganda, and an empirical evaluation of the adequacy of the HIPC Initiative, see Serieux and Samy (2001). For latest IMF/IDA views on the issue of long-term external debt sustainability, see IMF/IDA (2002a).

4. These are UNCTAD secretariat estimates based on OECD/DAC Statistical Reporting System, on-line databases. The percentage change of net ODA per capita in real terms (1999 $) is weighted by the population.

5. The Zedillo Report (United Nations, 2001b), prepared for the International Conference on Financing for Development in Monterrey, has estimated that meeting all the International Development Goals will require an extra $50 billion a year of ODA, almost double what is currently provided.

6. For precise definition of the options open to donors in terms of their aid commitments, see Part One, chapter 2, section F.

7. In particular, the United States announced that it would increase its bilateral development assistance by more, and more rapidly, than the increase originally announced, and would seek to initiate an increase in aid in the next 12 months, and that aid would be doubled, reaching an increase of $5 billion in the third year. The EU announced that it had agreed to increase its development aid to 0.39 per cent of GNI by 2006 as a first step towards the 0.7 per cent target. Japan promised an increase in aid as soon as domestic conditions improved.

8. For a general discussion of how tariff barriers in rich countries affect poverty, see World Bank (2002).

9. Both the EU's GSP scheme and the EU–ACP arrangement have similar requirements and a similar basic structure in terms of tariff preferences.

10. If all Quad members were to grant duty-free access for tariff peak products to both LDCs and other developing countries, it is estimated that LDC exports will increase by 6 per cent. This estimate does not include the possibility of increased exports from LDCs to other developing countries, which could arise because of the trade expansion in other developing countries which would follow their improved access to developed country markets. Unfortunately, no research has yet been undertaken on how LDCs might benefit from market access concessions from developed countries for all developing countries (LDCs and other developing countries), coupled with improved access for LDCs to developing country markets through regional integration arrangements.

11. The importance of national policy autonomy and the development of supply capabilities is emphasized in UNCTAD (1999a). Significantly, one study of the impact of improved market access in Quad countries on 37 sub-Saharan African countries finds that if total factor productivity increased by 1.5 per cent, gains in welfare would be comparable to the gains from completely unrestricted market access (Ianchovichina, Mattoo and Olarreaga, 2000).

12. The six core agencies are the IMF, ITC, UNCTAD, UNDP, World Bank and WTO.

13. An IF Trust Fund, managed by UNDP on behalf of the six core agencies, has been established to finance the "mainstreaming process". As of February 2002, 18 donors had made pledges to the Trust Fund totalling approximately $9.1 million. The overall process is guided by the IF Steering Committee (IFSC) and the Inter-agency Working Group (IAWG). The IFSC has a tripartite structure comprising donors, LDC representatives and representatives of the core agencies. Its functions are policy guidance and oversight, coordination, monitoring and assessment of IF progress. The IAWG's functions are exchange of information, coordination of events, preparation of the work programme and budget, and sequencing of activities.

References

Arndt, C. (2000). Technical cooperation. In Tarp, F. (ed.), *Foreign Aid and Development: Lessons Learnt and Directions for the Future*, Routledge Studies in Development Economics 17, Routledge, London.

Bacchetta, M. and Bora, B. (2001). Post-Uruguay Round market access barriers for industrial products, UNCTAD Policy Issues in International Trade and Commodities Study Series No. 12, Geneva.

Beynon, J. (2001). Policy implications for aid allocations of recent research on aid effectiveness and selectivity, paper presented at the Joint Development Centre/DAC Experts Seminar on "Aid effectiveness, selectivity and poor performance", 16 January 2001.

Birdsall, N., Claessens, S. and Diwan, I. (2001). Will HIPC matter? The debt game and donor behaviour in Africa, Carnegie Endowment for International Peace, Economic Reform Project Discussion Paper No. 3, March.

Bulir, A. and Hamann, J. (2001). How volatile and predictable are aid flows, and what are the policy implications?, revised version (25 July 2001) of paper presented at the IMF Workshop on Macroeconomic Policies and Poverty Reduction, 12–13 April 2001, Washington DC.

Burnside, C. and Dollar, D. (1997). Aid, policies and growth, Policy Research Working Paper 1777, World Bank, Development Research Group, Washington DC.

Burnside, C. and Dollar, D. (2000). Aid, policies and growth, *American Economic Review*, 90 (4): 847–868.

Dalgaard, C.-J. and Hansen, H. (2001). On aid, growth and good policies, *Journal of Development Studies*, 37: 17–41.

Delamonica, E., Mehrota, S. and Vandemoortele, J. (2001). Is EFA affordable?, UNICEF Staff Working Paper, Evaluation, Policy and Planning Series, EPP-01-001, New York.

ECLAC (1996). *Strengthening Development: The Interplay of Macro- and Microeconomics*, United Nations sales no. E.96.II.G.2, Santiago, Chile.

Ehrenpreis, D. (2001). Introductory remarks on policy issues, OECD/DAC Seminar on Aid Effectiveness, Growth and Policy, 10 July, OECD, Paris.

EURODAD (2001). What goes down might not come up: how declining commodity prices could undermine the HIPC Initiative, paper available at www.eurodad.org

FAO (2001). The Role of Agriculture in the Development of LDCs and their Integration into the World Economy, paper prepared for the Third United Nations Conference on the Least Developed Countries (Brussels, 14–20 May 2001), Rome.

Financial Times (2001). Japan opens way for OECD deal to untie $2 bn aid, 15 May, London.

Fontagne, L., von Kirchbach, F. and Mimouni, M. (2001): A first assessment of environment-related trade barriers, CEPII Working Paper, No. 2001-10, October, Paris.

Finger, M. and Schuler, P. (2000). Implementation of Uruguay Round commitments: the development challenge, *World Economy*, 24 (4): 511–525. Also available as a World Bank Policy Research Working Paper No. 2215 at www.worldbank.org/research/trade.

GATT secretariat (1994). The results of the Uruguay Round of Multilateral Trade Negotiations, Geneva.

Gore, C.G. and Figueiredo, J. B. (eds.) (1997). *Social Exclusion and Anti-Poverty Strategy: A Debate*, International Institute for Labour Studies, Research Series No.110, ILO, Geneva.

Guillaumont, P. and Chauvet, L. (2001). Aid and performance: a reassessment, *Journal of Development Studies*, 37 (6): 66–92.

Hansen, H. (2001). The impact of aid and external debt on growth and investment: insights from cross-country regression analysis, background note prepared for *The Least Developed Countries Report 2002*, Geneva.

Hansen, H. and Tarp, F. (2000). Aid effectiveness disputed, *Journal of International Development*, 12 (3): 375–398.

Hansen, H. and Tarp, F. (2001). Aid and growth regressions, *Journal of Development Economics*, 64 (2): 547–570.

Hermes, N. and Lensink, R. (2001). Guest editors of Special Issue of *Journal of Development Studies* on "Changing the Conditions for Development Aid: A New Paradigm?", 64: 2.

HIPC Finance Ministers (2001). Declaration of the 5th HIPC Ministerial Meeting. Implementing HIPC II, Maputo, 21 November.

Hoekman, B., Ng, F. and Olarreaga, M. (2001). Eliminating excessive tariffs on exports of least developed countries, mimeo, World Bank, Washington DC.

Ianchovichina, E., Mattoo, A. and Olarreaga, M. (2000). Unrestricted market access for sub-Saharan Africa: how much is it worth and who pays?, mimeo, World Bank, Washington DC.

ILO/UNCTAD (2001). The Minimum Income for School Attendance (MISA) Initiative: Achieving International Development Goals in African Least Developed Countries, Report of the ILO/UNCTAD Advisory Group, May 2001, Geneva.

IMF/IDA (2001). Enhanced HIPC Initiative: completion point considerations, 17 August, Washington DC.

IMF/IDA (2002a). Heavily Indebted Poor Countries (HIPC) Initiative: status of implementation, 12 April, Washington DC.

IMF/IDA (2002b). The Enhanced HIPC Initiative and the achievement of long-term external debt sustainability, 15 April, Washington, DC.

IMF/World Bank (2001a). The challenge of maintaining long-term external debt sustainability, Development Committee, DC2001-0013, 20 April, Washington DC.

IMF/World Bank (2001b). Market access for developing countries' exports, 27 April, Washington DC.

Lensink, R. and White, H. (2001). Are there negative returns to aid? *Journal of Development Studies*, 64 (2): 42–65.

Martin, M. (2001). Long-term sustainability for HIPCs: how to respond to shocks, mimeo, Development Finance International, London.

Mosley, P. (2000). Overseas aid, technical change in agriculture and national economic strategy in Africa and the least developed countries, background report for *The Least Developed Countries 2000 Report*, Geneva.

Nissanke, M. and Ferrarini, B. (2001). Debt dynamics and contingency financing: theoretical reappraisal of the HIPC Initiative, mimeo (October 2001), revised version of paper presented at the UNU/WIDER Development Conference on Debt Relief, 17–18 August 2001, Helsinki.

OECD (2000). *Development Cooperation 1999 Report*, OECD, Paris.

Pyatt, G. (1999). Poverty versus the poor. In: Pyatt, G.F. and Ward, M. (eds.), *Identifying the Poor*, IOS Press/ISI, Amsterdam/Voorburg.

Pyatt, G. (2001). An alternative approach to poverty analysis, with particular reference to the Poverty Reduction Strategies being developed in the context of the HIPC Initiative, background paper for *The Least Developed Countries Report 2002*.

Serieux, J.E. and Samy, Y. (2001) Guest editors of special issue of *Canadian Journal of Economics* on "Debt Relief for the Poorest Countries, 21: 2.

Stevens, C. and Kennan, J. (2001). The impact of the EU's "Everything but Arms" Proposal: a report to OXFAM, mimeo, Institute for Development Studies at the University of Sussex, Brighton, UK.

Stewart, F. (1995). *Adjustment and Poverty: Options and Choices*, Routledge, London and New York.

UNCTAD (1998). *Trade and Development Report, 1998. Part II*, African Development in a Comparative Perspective, United Nations publication, sales no. E.94.II.D.2., Geneva.

UNCTAD (1999a). Integrating least developed countries into the global economy: proposals for a comprehensive new plan of action in the context of the Third WTO Ministerial Conference, adopted in the final plenary of the Coordinating Workshop for Senior Advisors to Ministers of Trade in LDCs in preparation for the Third WTO Ministerial Conference, Sun City, South Africa, 21–25 June 1999, LDC/CW/SA/6.

UNCTAD (1999b). African transport infrastructure, trade and competitiveness, TD/B/4/10, 20 August.

UNCTAD (2000a). *The Least Developed Countries 2000 Report*, United Nations publication, sales no. E.00.II.D.21, United Nations, Geneva.

UNCTAD (2000b). *Economic Development in Africa: Performance, Prospects and Policy Issues*, United Nations, New York and Geneva.

UNCTAD (2001a). Improving market access for least developed countries, UNCTAD/DITC/TNCD/4.

UNCTAD (2001b). The benefits associated with the least developed country status and the question of graduation, E/2001/CRP.5, 17 July, Geneva.

UNCTAD/Commonwealth Secretariat (2001). Duty and quota free market access for LDCs: an analysis of Quad initiatives, UNCTAD/DITC/TAB/Misc.7, London and Geneva.

United Nations (2001a). Programme of Action for the Least Developed Countries for the Decade 2001–2010, 8 June, A/CONF.191/11.

United Nations (2001b). Technical Report of a High-level Panel on Financing for Development (Zedillo Report), 26 June, A/55/1000.

WHO (2002). *Macroeconomics and Health: Investing in Health for Economic Development*, Report of the Commission of Macroeconomics and Health, 20 December, Geneva.

World Bank (1990). *Making Adjustment Work for the Poor: A Framework for Policy Reform in Africa*, World Bank, Washington D.C.

World Bank (1998). *Assessing Aid: What Works, What Doesn't and Why*, World Bank, Washington DC.

World Bank (2001). *Global Development Finance: Building Coalitions for Effective Development Finance*, World Bank, Washington DC.

World Bank (2002). *Global Economic Prospects and the Developing Countries: Making Trade Work for the Poor*, World Bank, Washington DC.

World Bank/IMF (2001). Financing for development, Development Committee, DC 2001-0024, 18 September.

Statistical Annex

BASIC DATA ON THE
LEAST DEVELOPED COUNTRIES

The Statistical Annex has been prepared using the same data sources as recent Least Developed Countries Reports. This is to ensure continuity. Tables 19 to 29, on financial flows, net ODA and debt, are based on OECD/DAC sources. These diverge somewhat from the World Bank data on capital flows, which are used in main text of this Report.

Contents

Explanatory Notes

Definition of country groupings

Least developed countries

The United Nations has designated 49 countries as least developed: Afghanistan, Angola, Bangladesh, Benin, Bhutan, Burkina Faso, Burundi, Cambodia, Cape Verde, the Central African Republic, Chad, the Comoros, the Democratic Republic of the Congo, Djibouti, Equatorial Guinea, Eritrea, Ethiopia, Gambia, Guinea, Guinea-Bissau, Haiti, Kiribati, the Lao People's Democratic Republic, Lesotho, Liberia, Madagascar, Malawi, Maldives, Mali, Mauritania, Mozambique, Myanmar, Nepal, Niger, Rwanda, Samoa, Sao Tome and Principe, Senegal, Sierra Leone, Solomon Islands, Somalia, Sudan, Togo, Tuvalu, Uganda, the United Republic of Tanzania, Vanuatu, Yemen and Zambia. Except where otherwise indicated, the totals for least developed countries refer to these 49 countries.

Major economic areas

The classification of countries and territories according to main economic areas used in this document has been adopted for purposes of statistical convenience only and follows that in the UNCTAD *Handbook of International Trade and Development Statistics 2001*.[1] Countries and territories are classified according to main economic areas as follows:

Developed market economy countries: Australia, Canada, the European Union (Austria, Belgium, Denmark, Finland, France, Germany, Greece, Ireland, Italy, Luxembourg, the Netherlands, Portugal, Spain, Sweden and the United Kingdom), Faeroe Islands, Gibraltar, Iceland, Israel, Japan, New Zealand, Norway, South Africa, Switzerland and the United States.

Countries in Eastern Europe: Albania, Belarus, Bulgaria, the Czech Republic, Estonia, Hungary, Latvia, Lithuania, Poland, the Republic of Moldova, Romania, the Russian Federation, Slovakia and Ukraine.

Developing countries and territories: All other countries, territories and areas in Africa, Asia, America, Europe and Oceania not specified above.

Other country groupings

DAC member countries: The countries members of the OECD Development Assistance Committee are Australia, Austria, Belgium, Canada, Denmark, Finland, France, Germany, Greece, Ireland, Italy, Japan, Luxembourg, the Netherlands, New Zealand, Norway, Portugal, Spain, Sweden, Switzerland, the United Kingdom and the United States.

OPEC member countries: The countries members of the Organization of Petroleum Exporting Countries are Algeria, Ecuador, Gabon, Indonesia, the Islamic Republic of Iran, Iraq, Kuwait, the Libyan Arab Jamahiriya, Nigeria, Qatar, Saudi Arabia, the United Arab Emirates and Venezuela.

Other notes

Calculation of annual average growth rates. In general, they are defined as the coefficient b in the exponential trend function $y^t = ae^{bt}$ where t stands for time. This method takes all observations in a period into account. Therefore, the resulting growth rates reflect trends that are not unduly influenced by exceptional values.

Population growth rates are calculated as exponential growth rates.

The term "dollars" ($) refers to United States dollars, unless otherwise stated.

Details and percentages in tables do not necessarily add up to totals, because of rounding.

The following symbols have been used:
   A hyphen (-) indicates that the amount is nil or negligible.
   Two dots (..) indicate that the data are not available or are not separately reported.
   A dot (.) indicates that the item is not applicable.
   Use of a dash (–) between dates representing years, e.g. 1980–1990, signifies the full period involved, including the initial and final years.

[1]   United Nations Publication, Sales No. E/F.01.II.D.24.

Abbreviations

ACBF	African Capacity Building Foundation
ADF	African Development Fund
AfDB	African Development Bank
AFESD	Arab Fund for Economic and Social Development
AsDB	Asian Development Bank
BADEA	Arab Bank for Economic Development in Africa
BDEAC	Banque de Développement des Etats de l'Afrique Centrale
BITS	Swedish Agency for International Technical and Economic Cooperation
BOAD	West African Development Bank
CCCE	Caisse centrale de coopération économique
CEC	Commission of the European Communities
CIDA	Canadian International Development Agency
DAC	Development Assistance Committee
DANIDA	Danish International Development Agency
DCD	Development Cooperation Department
EC	European Community
ECA	Economic Commission for Africa
EDF	European Development Fund
EEC	European Economic Community
ESAF	Enhanced Structural Adjustment Facility
ESCAP	Economic and Social Commission for Asia and the Pacific
FAC	Fonds d'aide et de coopération
FAO	Food and Agriculture Organization of the United Nations
GDP	gross domestic product
GNI	gross national income
GNP	gross national product
GTZ	German Technical Assistance Corporation
IBRD	International Bank for Reconstruction and Development
IDA	International Development Association
IDB	Inter-American Development Bank
IFAD	International Fund for Agricultural Development
ILO	International Labour Organization
IMF	International Monetary Fund
IRF	International Road Federation
IRU	International Road Transport Union
IsDB	Islamic Development Bank

ITU	International Telecommunication Union
KFAED	Kuwait Fund for Arab Economic Development
KfW	Kreditanstalt für Wiederaufbau
LDC	least developed country
ODA	official development assistance
OECD	Organisation for Economic Co-operation and Development
OECF	Overseas Economic Co-operation Fund
OPEC	Organization of Petroleum Exporting Countries
PRGF	Poverty Reduction and Growth Facility
SAF	Structural Adjustment Facility
SDC	Swiss Development Corporation
SDR	special drawing rights
SFD	Saudi Fund for Development
SITC	Standard International Trade Classification (Revision I)
UNDP	United Nations Development Programme
UNESCO	United Nations Educational, Scientific and Cultural Organization
UNFPA	United Nations Population Fund
UNHCR	United Nations High Commissioner for Refugees
UNICEF	United Nations Children's Fund
UNTA	United Nations Technical Assistance
USAID	United States Agency for International Development
WFP	World Food Programme
WHO	World Health Organization

1. Per capita GDP and population: Levels and growth

Country	Per capita GDP (in 1999 dollars)		Annual average growth rates of per capita real GDP (%)		Population		
					Level (millions)	Annual average growth rates (%)	
	1980	1999	1980–1990	1990–1999	1999	1980–1990	1990–1999
Afghanistan	..	..	..	..	21.9	-1.2	4.6
Angola	909	685	0.8	-3.0	12.5	2.7	3.4
Bangladesh	228	361	1.9	3.1	126.9	2.2	1.6
Benin	354	405	-0.5	1.9	5.9	3.0	2.7
Bhutan	434	733	4.6	4.0	0.6	2.6	2.2
Burkina Faso	189	228	0.8	1.0	11.6	2.8	2.8
Burundi	131	107	1.4	-4.9	6.6	2.8	2.1
Cambodia	..	285	..	2.1	10.9	3.1	2.7
Cape Verde	774	1389	3.6	3.0	0.4	1.7	2.3
Central African Republic	357	297	-1.0	-0.3	3.5	2.4	2.1
Chad	179	211	3.4	-1.3	7.5	2.5	3.0
Comoros	401	291	-0.3	-3.3	0.7	3.1	2.8
Dem. Rep. of the Congo	350	115	-1.6	-8.3	50.3	3.3	3.4
Djibouti	..	..	..	..	0.6	6.4	2.1
Equatorial Guinea	..	1575	-2.9	-1.2	0.4	5.1	2.6
Eritrea	..	180	..	1.6[a]	3.7	1.9	2.9
Ethiopia	97	107	0.1	1.9	61.1	2.8	2.7
Gambia	360	345	-0.1	-0.8	1.3	3.7	3.6
Guinea	481	502	-0.5	1.3	7.4	2.5	2.8
Guinea-Bissau	202	186	1.2	-1.8	1.2	2.0	2.2
Haiti	808	485	-2.6	-2.8	8.1	2.4	1.7
Kiribati	679	732	-1.0	1.8	0.1	1.7	1.4
Lao PDR	147	259	2.0	3.7	5.3	2.7	2.7
Lesotho	309	415	1.8	2.0	2.1	2.5	2.3
Liberia	..	..	..	..	2.9	3.6	1.0
Madagascar	353	241	-1.6	-1.6	15.5	2.7	3.3
Malawi	168	171	-1.8	2.6	10.6	4.4	1.3
Maldives	481	1359	6.3	4.4	0.3	3.2	2.9
Mali	235	248	0.2	1.0	11.0	2.6	2.4
Mauritania	371	369	-0.8	1.3	2.6	2.7	2.8
Mozambique	196	209	-1.5	2.5	19.3	1.5	3.6
Myanmar	..	..	..	..	45.1	1.8	1.2
Nepal	142	210	1.9	2.2	23.4	2.6	2.5
Niger	309	199	-3.3	-0.9	10.4	3.3	3.4
Rwanda	322	270	-1.2	-1.3	7.2	3.4	-0.1
Samoa	1 264	1 250	0.7	0.8	0.2	0.3	1.1
Sao Tome and Principe	..	328	-4.4	-0.4	0.1	2.4	2.2
Senegal	482	519	0.2	0.7	9.2	2.8	2.6
Sierra Leone	314	142	-1.8	-6.4	4.7	2.2	1.8
Solomon Islands	602	806	2.9	0.3	0.4	3.6	3.3
Somalia	..	..	..	..	9.7	2.9	2.3
Sudan	249	345	-2.1	6.1	28.9	2.6	2.0
Togo	453	334	-1.3	-0.4	4.5	3.0	2.8
Tuvalu[b]	..	1931	..	2.2	0.0	1.3	2.8
Uganda	185	300	0.7	4.3	21.1	2.2	2.8
United Rep. of Tanzania	307	268	-0.5	-0.9	32.8	3.2	2.9
Vanuatu	1 328	1 327	0.6	-0.3	0.2	2.5	2.5
Yemen	..	387	..	-0.7	17.5	3.4	4.7
Zambia	505	370	-1.3	-2.1	9.0	2.3	2.4
All LDCs	284	288	-0.2	1.1	637.4	2.5	2.5
All developing countries	893	1 326	1.9	3.0	4 770.7	2.1	1.7
Developed market economy countries	18 491	26 692	2.5	1.6	889.5	0.7	0.6
Countries in Eastern Europe	2 881	2 405	2.0	-3.6	318.2	0.6	-0.2

Source: UNCTAD, *Handbook of Statistics 2001*; World Bank, *World Development Indicators 2001*, CD-ROM.

Note: Data for Ethiopia prior to 1992 include Eritrea. Population data for Bhutan is from national sources.

a 1993–1999.
b Population 11,000 and area 30 km^2.

2. REAL GDP, TOTAL AND PER CAPITA: ANNUAL AVERAGE GROWTH RATES
(Percentage)

Country	Total real product					Per capita real product				
	1980–1990	1990–1999	1997	1998	1999	1980–1990	1990–1999	1997	1998	1999
Afghanistan	..	..	..			..	..	..		
Angola	3.5	0.4	6.2	3.2	2.7	0.8	-3.0	2.8	0.0	-0.5
Bangladesh	4.1	4.8	5.9	5.7	5.2	1.9	3.1	4.1	3.9	3.4
Benin	2.5	4.6	5.7	4.5	5.0	-0.5	1.9	2.9	1.8	2.2
Bhutan	7.3	6.3	7.8	6.6	5.7	4.6	4.0	4.9	3.5	2.6
Burkina Faso	3.6	3.8	4.7	6.2	5.2	0.8	1.0	1.9	3.3	2.4
Burundi	4.3	-2.9	0.4	4.8	-1.0	1.4	-4.9	-1.2	3.2	-2.6
Cambodia	..	4.8	1.0	1.0	4.5	..	2.1	-1.3	-1.2	2.3
Cape Verde	5.4	5.4	5.2	5.0	6.0	3.6	3.0	2.8	2.6	3.5
Central African Republic	1.4	1.8	5.3	4.7	3.4	-1.0	-0.3	3.3	2.7	1.5
Chad	6.0	1.7	4.5	6.7	-0.7	3.4	-1.3	1.7	4.0	-3.2
Comoros	2.8	-0.6	0.5	-0.5	-1.4	-0.3	-3.3	-2.2	-3.1	-4.1
Dem. Rep. of the Congo	1.6	-5.2	-5.7	3.0	-15.0	-1.6	-8.3	-8.1	0.6	-17.0
Djibouti	..	..	..	..	..	..	..	..	..	..
Equatorial Guinea	2.0	1.3	1.7	1.6	0.0	-2.9	-1.2	-0.9	-0.9	-2.5
Eritrea	..	5.0[a]	7.9	3.9	0.8	..	1.6[a]	3.7	-0.3	-3.1
Ethiopia	2.9	4.6	5.2	-1.4	6.2	0.1	1.9	2.6	-3.7	3.7
Gambia	3.6	2.8	4.9	4.9	6.4	-0.1	-0.8	1.4	1.5	3.1
Guinea	2.0	4.2	4.8	4.5	3.3	-0.5	1.3	4.1	4.3	3.0
Guinea-Bissau	3.2	0.3	5.9	-28.1	7.9	1.2	-1.8	3.5	-29.7	5.5
Haiti	-0.2	-1.1	1.4	3.1	2.2	-2.6	-2.8	-0.3	1.4	0.5
Kiribati	0.7	3.2	3.3	6.1	2.5	-1.0	1.8	1.8	4.6	1.0
Lao People's Dem. Rep.	4.7	6.6	6.9	4.0	7.3	2.0	3.7	4.2	1.3	4.6
Lesotho	4.4	4.3	8.1	-4.6	2.8	1.8	2.0	5.7	-6.8	0.6
Liberia	..	..	..	..	..	..	..	..	..	..
Madagascar	1.1	1.7	3.6	3.9	4.7	-1.6	-1.6	0.5	0.9	1.7
Malawi	2.5	4.0	4.9	3.1	4.2	-1.8	2.6	2.5	0.3	1.3
Maldives	9.7	7.4	7.8	8.9	8.8	6.3	4.4	4.9	5.9	5.8
Mali	2.8	3.5	6.8	3.4	5.5	0.2	1.0	4.2	0.9	2.9
Mauritania	1.8	4.2	3.2	3.7	4.1	-0.8	1.3	0.4	0.9	1.3
Mozambique	-0.1	6.2	11.1	11.9	7.3	-1.5	2.5	8.1	9.3	5.0
Myanmar	..	..	..	..	..	..	..	..	..	..
Nepal	4.6	4.8	5.0	2.3	3.3	1.9	2.2	2.5	-0.1	0.9
Niger	-0.1	2.4	2.8	10.4	-0.6	-3.3	-0.9	-0.5	7.0	-3.6
Rwanda	2.2	-1.5	12.8	9.5	6.1	-1.2	-1.3	3.6	-1.2	-3.2
Samoa	1.0	2.0	1.6	1.3	1.0	0.7	0.8	0.3	-0.1	-0.5
Sao Tome and Principe	-2.2	1.7	1.0	2.5	2.5	-4.4	-0.4	-1.1	0.4	0.5
Senegal	3.1	3.3	5.0	5.7	5.1	0.2	0.7	2.3	3.0	2.4
Sierra Leone	0.3	-4.7	-17.6	-0.8	-8.1	-1.8	-6.4	-20.0	-4.0	-11.0
Solomon Islands	6.6	3.6	-0.5	0.4	-0.5	2.9	0.3	-3.6	-2.7	-3.5
Somalia	..	..	..	..	..	..	..	..	..	..
Sudan	0.4	8.2	9.7	6.1	5.2	-2.1	6.1	7.5	3.9	3.0
Togo	1.7	2.4	4.2	-2.2	2.1	-1.3	-0.4	1.5	-4.8	-0.5
Tuvalu	..	5.1	3.5	14.9	3.0	..	2.2	0.7	11.9	0.3
Uganda	3.0	7.2	4.7	5.6	7.4	0.7	4.3	1.9	2.8	4.4
United Rep. of Tanzania	2.7	2.0	3.5	4.0	4.7	-0.5	-0.9	1.2	1.8	2.5
Vanuatu	3.1	2.2	2.7	6.0	-2.5	0.6	-0.3	0.3	3.5	-4.8
Yemen	..	4.0	8.1	4.8	2.2	..	-0.7	4.0	1.1	-1.3
Zambia	1.0	0.2	3.3	-1.9	2.4	-1.3	-2.1	0.9	-4.1	0.2
All LDCs	2.3	3.6	5.0	4.4	4.3	-0.2	1.1	2.6	2.0	1.9
All developing countries	4.0	4.7	5.3	1.3	3.7	1.9	3.0	3.6	-0.2	2.1
Developed market economy countries	3.2	2.3	2.8	2.1	2.6	2.5	1.6	2.3	1.5	2.1
Countries in Eastern Europe	2.6	-3.8	1.8	-1.0	2.4	2.0	-3.6	2.0	-0.7	2.6

Source: UNCTAD, Handbook of Statistics 2001; World Bank, World Development Indicators 2001, CD-ROM.
Note: Data for Ethiopia prior to 1992 include Eritrea.
a   1993–1999.

3. Agricultural production, total and per capita: Annual average growth rates

Country	Percentage share of agriculture in:				Annual average growth rates (%) Total agricultural production					Annual average growth rates (%) Per capita agricultural production				
	Total labour force		GDP											
	1980	1999*	1980	1999	1980–1990	1990–1999	1997	1998	1999	1980–1990	1990–1999	1997	1998	1999
Afghanistan	61	68	..	..	-2.6	6.4	9.7	8.3	4.0	-1.4	1.7	7.0	6.1	1.2
Angola	74	72	14[a]	7	0.8	4.2	0.5	14.7	-5.0	-1.9	0.7	-2.7	11.2	-7.9
Bangladesh	75	63	40	25	2.1	2.4	2.0	3.2	13.1	0.0	0.7	0.3	1.4	11.2
Benin	70	56	35	38	6.6	6.4	7.7	-1.9	0.7	3.4	3.6	4.9	-4.5	-2.0
Bhutan	93	94	57	38	1.6	1.9	1.2	0.0	-1.9	-0.9	-0.3	-1.5	-3.0	-4.8
Burkina Faso	87	92	33	31	6.4	4.0	4.8	8.6	-3.7	3.5	1.1	2.1	5.7	-6.3
Burundi	93	91	62	52	2.8	-1.9	-1.8	-5.2	2.1	-0.1	-3.8	-3.3	-6.6	0.5
Cambodia	75	71	43[b]	51	6.3	4.9	2.8	1.7	9.5	3.2	2.2	0.5	-0.6	7.2
Cape Verde	52	24	16[c]	12	11.3	4.2	-11.8	19.1	8.0	9.5	1.8	-14.1	16.4	5.4
Central African Rep.	72	74	40	55	2.3	3.5	-2.1	1.2	-1.2	-0.1	1.3	-4.0	-0.8	-3.0
Chad	83	77	45	36	2.5	5.2	8.3	21.1	-12.2	0.0	2.1	5.4	18.1	-14.5
Comoros	83	74	34	39	2.5	2.6	1.6	8.0	5.5	-0.6	-0.2	-1.1	5.0	2.7
Dem. Rep. of the Congo	72	64	25	58[d]	3.1	-1.5	-0.7	-0.3	-3.2	-0.2	-4.7	-3.2	-2.7	-5.6
Djibouti	..	..	3[e]	4[d]	8.8	-0.2	0.8	0.8	1.3	2.3	-2.3	-0.4	-0.1	0.3
Equatorial Guinea	66	71	69[a]	16	1.3	-2.3	-9.9	2.8	6.4	-3.6	-4.8	-12.0	0.0	3.7
Eritrea	..	78	..	17	..	7.2[f]	-0.5	44.9	-7.4	..	3.5[f]	-4.4	39.2	-11.0
Ethiopia	80[g]	83	56[h]	52	..	4.2[f]	1.1	-7.3	5.9	..	1.6[f]	-1.4	-9.5	3.3
Gambia	84	80	31	31	0.7	2.1	30.4	-2.3	43.1	-2.9	-1.4	26.0	-5.4	38.5
Guinea	81	85	24[c]	24	-0.4	3.9	4.5	5.5	1.8	-2.9	1.1	3.7	5.4	1.4
Guinea-Bissau	82	83	44	62	3.8	2.7	3.7	2.3	4.1	1.8	0.4	1.5	0.1	1.9
Haiti	70	63	33[i]	29	-0.1	-0.5	3.1	-0.7	1.8	-2.5	-2.2	1.5	-2.4	0.0
Kiribati	..	..	21	21	0.5	3.3	0.0	4.6	-13.1	-1.2	1.8	-1.3	3.4	-14.2
Lao People's Dem.Rep.	76	77	61[e]	53	3.2	3.7	11.9	3.4	16.6	0.5	0.9	9.0	0.8	13.5
Lesotho	86	38	25	18	1.8	0.3	4.3	-16.9	-1.5	-0.7	-1.9	1.9	-18.7	-3.7
Liberia	74	69	36	..	0.2	3.3	28.3	14.8	5.0	-3.3	2.3	17.5	3.3	-4.5
Madagascar	81	77	30	30	1.7	1.3	1.5	-0.5	3.2	-1.0	-1.9	-1.5	-3.3	0.2
Malawi	83	84	44	38	1.4	4.6	-1.0	10.7	7.6	-2.9	3.3	-3.3	7.7	4.6
Maldives	..	24	..	16	2.1	2.3	2.1	4.3	8.5	-1.1	-0.5	-0.6	1.3	5.8
Mali	86	82	48	47	3.0	3.5	3.4	5.2	2.5	0.4	1.1	1.0	2.7	0.0
Mauritania	69	53	30	25	1.3	0.9	-2.1	-0.9	-0.2	-1.4	-1.9	-4.6	-3.6	-2.9
Mozambique	84	81	37	33	-0.6	5.4	6.9	7.1	1.5	-2.0	1.8	4.0	4.5	-0.6
Myanmar	53	63	47	60	0.7	4.7	0.4	1.7	11.3	-1.1	3.5	-0.7	0.4	9.9
Nepal	93	79	62	42	4.2	2.5	3.0	0.3	1.8	1.5	0.0	0.5	-2.0	-0.6
Niger	91	88	43	41	-0.3	3.2	-19.3	51.0	-3.9	-3.5	-0.1	-21.8	46.2	-6.9
Rwanda	93	91	50	46	1.2	-2.4	3.9	8.0	7.1	-2.2	-2.3	-4.6	-2.5	-2.2
Samoa	..	..	46	42[i]	0.2	0.3	0.0	0.0	0.0	-0.1	-0.8	-1.2	-1.1	-1.7
Sao Tome and Principe	..	..	28	21	-1.3	5.3	2.9	7.6	7.3	-3.5	3.1	0.7	5.4	5.0
Senegal	81	77	19	18	3.8	1.6	-5.2	-1.3	18.9	1.0	-1.0	-7.6	-3.9	15.9
Sierra Leone	70	63	33	43	2.3	-0.9	6.1	-7.8	-12.8	0.1	-2.6	2.9	-10.8	-15.6
Solomon Islands	30	27	..	..	-0.4	4.0	4.4	2.7	2.6	-3.8	0.7	1.3	-0.4	-0.6
Somalia	78	75	68	65[i]	1.8	1.9	4.3	-6.0	-2.5	-1.0	-0.4	0.2	-10.3	-6.9
Sudan	71	63	33	40	-0.7	5.6	0.7	1.6	-1.0	-3.2	3.5	-1.4	-0.4	-3.1
Togo	73	61	27	41	4.6	3.9	5.7	-2.1	5.6	1.5	1.1	3.0	-4.7	3.0
Tuvalu	..	..	..	..	-4.1	-1.0	0.0	0.0	0.0	-5.0	-3.7	0.0	0.0	0.0
Uganda	86	81	72	44	3.1	1.8	-0.3	7.0	3.4	0.8	-1.0	-2.9	4.1	0.5
United Rep. of Tanzania	86	81	..	45	2.7	0.8	-5.0	4.6	1.8	-0.5	-2.0	-7.1	2.2	-0.2
Vanuatu	..	..	19	25[d]	1.2	1.6	16.5	3.4	-15.2	-1.2	-0.9	13.9	0.7	-17.1
Yemen	62	53	..	17	3.9	3.6	6.2	9.0	-2.0	0.4	-1.1	2.1	5.2	-5.4
Zambia	73	71	15	25[d]	4.3	1.2	-10.9	-5.1	12.9	1.9	-1.2	-12.9	-7.2	10.6
All LDCs	77	74	35	30	1.7	2.9	1.4	2.9	4.7	-0.7	0.4	-1.1	0.6	2.2
All developing countries	66	57	17	14	3.7	3.9	3.1	2.8	3.2	1.5	2.1	1.4	1.2	1.5

Source: UNCTAD secretariat calculations based on data from FAO; the Economic Commission for Africa; the World Bank (*World Development Indicators 2001*, CD-ROM; UNDP, *Human Development Report 2001;* and other international and national sources.

a 1985. b 1987. c 1986. d 1997. e 1989. f 1993–1999. g Includes Eritrea. h 1981. i 1990. * Or latest year available.

4. Food production, total and per capita: Annual average growth rates
(Percentage)

Country	Total food production					Per capita food production				
	1980–1990	*1990–1999*	*1997*	*1998*	*1999*	*1980–1990*	*1990–1999*	*1997*	*1998*	*1999*
Afghanistan	-2.4	6.5	10.0	8.5	3.9	-1.2	1.8	7.3	6.1	1.2
Angola	1.1	4.4	0.4	15.0	-4.6	-1.6	0.9	-2.9	11.4	-7.5
Bangladesh	2.2	2.3	1.4	3.5	11.3	0.1	0.6	-0.3	1.7	9.4
Benin	5.4	5.3	12.5	-1.7	0.9	2.3	2.5	9.5	-4.2	-1.7
Bhutan	1.6	1.9	1.3	0.0	-2.0	-1.0	-0.3	-1.6	-3.0	-4.8
Burkina Faso	5.7	3.3	-3.1	11.7	-2.8	2.8	0.5	-5.7	8.8	-5.4
Burundi	2.7	-1.6	-0.5	-5.8	0.1	-0.1	-3.6	-2.1	-7.1	-1.6
Cambodia	6.2	5.0	3.0	1.7	9.8	3.0	2.3	0.6	-0.5	7.6
Cape Verde	11.4	4.2	-11.9	19.0	8.1	9.5	1.9	-14.0	16.3	5.4
Central African Republic	2.4	3.6	-2.9	3.4	1.7	-0.1	1.4	-4.8	1.5	-0.2
Chad	2.1	4.9	9.7	21.2	-12.1	-0.4	1.9	6.7	18.2	-14.4
Comoros	2.4	2.7	2.0	7.1	6.3	-0.7	-0.1	-0.7	4.2	3.5
Dem. Rep. of the Congo	3.3	-1.3	-0.6	0.1	-3.0	0.0	-4.6	-3.2	-2.3	-5.3
Djibouti	8.8	-0.2	0.8	0.8	1.3	2.3	-2.3	-0.4	-0.1	0.3
Equatorial Guinea	1.5	-0.7	-8.7	4.1	6.6	-3.3	-3.2	-10.8	1.4	3.9
Eritrea	..	7.3[a]	-0.6	45.9	-7.5	..	3.6[a]	-4.5	40.0	-11.0
Ethiopia	..	4.3[a]	1.1	-7.9	6.2	..	1.7[a]	-1.3	-10.1	3.7
Gambia	0.7	2.3	31.4	-1.9	43.1	-2.9	-1.3	27.1	-5.1	38.8
Guinea	-0.8	4.1	4.1	4.7	0.8	-3.2	1.2	3.4	4.5	0.5
Guinea-Bissau	3.9	2.7	3.8	2.4	3.8	1.9	0.4	1.6	0.2	1.6
Haiti	0.0	-0.3	3.3	-0.8	1.7	-2.4	-2.0	1.6	-2.5	0.0
Kiribati	0.5	3.3	0.0	4.6	-13.1	-1.2	1.8	-1.3	3.4	-14.2
Lao People's Dem. Rep.	3.1	4.2	12.3	3.5	19.9	0.4	1.4	9.3	0.9	16.9
Lesotho	1.9	0.8	4.1	-15.4	-1.7	-0.6	-1.4	1.8	-17.3	-3.8
Liberia	0.9	2.0	19.8	9.1	2.9	-2.6	0.9	9.7	-1.7	-6.4
Madagascar	1.7	1.5	2.0	-0.8	3.2	-1.0	-1.7	-0.9	-3.7	0.2
Malawi	0.6	5.5	-4.2	23.9	11.5	-3.7	4.2	-6.4	20.6	8.5
Maldives	2.1	2.3	2.1	4.3	8.5	-1.1	-0.5	-0.6	1.3	5.8
Mali	2.1	2.6	0.8	7.5	4.2	-0.4	0.2	-1.6	5.0	1.6
Mauritania	1.3	0.9	-2.1	-0.9	-0.2	-1.4	-1.9	-4.6	-3.6	-2.9
Mozambique	0.1	5.4	6.2	6.5	1.6	-1.3	1.7	3.3	4.1	-0.6
Myanmar	0.8	4.7	0.4	1.5	12.1	-1.0	3.5	-0.9	0.2	10.7
Nepal	4.3	2.5	3.0	0.3	1.8	1.7	0.1	0.6	-2.0	-0.6
Niger	-0.3	3.2	-19.3	51.5	-4.1	-3.5	-0.2	-21.8	46.8	-7.1
Rwanda	0.8	-2.2	3.2	8.2	7.4	-2.5	-2.1	-5.3	-2.3	-1.9
Samoa	0.2	0.3	0.0	0.0	0.0	-0.1	-0.8	-1.2	-1.1	-1.6
Sao Tome and Principe	-1.2	5.3	2.8	7.7	7.2	-3.5	3.0	0.7	5.3	5.0
Senegal	3.9	1.8	-5.9	-0.9	20.0	1.0	-0.8	-8.3	-3.4	17.0
Sierra Leone	1.7	-0.7	4.8	-7.1	-9.9	-0.5	-2.5	1.8	-10.0	-12.8
Solomon Islands	-0.4	4.0	4.4	2.7	2.6	-3.8	0.7	1.3	-0.4	-0.6
Somalia	1.8	1.9	4.2	-6.0	-2.5	-1.0	-0.4	0.1	-10.2	-7.0
Sudan	-0.7	5.8	1.4	2.0	-0.9	-3.2	3.7	-0.7	0.0	-3.0
Togo	3.2	3.7	3.5	-5.0	7.9	0.2	0.9	0.8	-7.4	5.1
Tuvalu	-4.1	-1.0	0.0	0.0	0.0	-5.0	-3.7	0.0	0.0	0.0
Uganda	3.1	1.1	2.7	7.7	2.4	0.9	-1.6	0.0	4.8	-0.5
United Rep. of Tanzania	3.0	0.8	-5.3	7.6	2.0	-0.2	-2.0	-7.5	5.3	-0.2
Vanuatu	1.2	1.6	16.5	3.5	-15.3	-1.2	-0.9	13.9	0.7	-17.1
Yemen	4.1	3.4	5.9	9.0	-2.1	0.7	-1.3	1.9	5.1	-5.6
Zambia	4.1	0.9	-13.3	-5.3	13.4	1.8	-1.4	-15.2	-7.5	10.9
All LDCs	1.7	2.8	1.1	3.4	4.8	-0.7	0.3	-1.3	1.0	2.3
All developing countries	3.7	4.1	3.2	3.2	3.4	1.6	2.4	1.5	1.6	1.8

Source: UNCTAD secretariat calculations, based on data from FAO.

a Average 1993–1999.

5. The manufacturing sector: Annual average growth rates and shares in GDP
(Percentage)

Country	Share in GDP		Annual average growth rates				
	1980	1999	1980–1990	1990–1999	1997	1998	1999
Afghanistan	..	..	..[b]	..	..	..	..
Angola	10[a]	4	-11.1[b]	-1.4	9.3	4.9	7.1
Bangladesh	16	15	3.0	7.5	5.1	8.5	3.2
Benin	8	8	5.1	5.6	5.6	3.0	6.5
Bhutan	3	12	13.0	10.7	3.6	13.0	12.0
Burkina Faso	16	22	2.0	4.2	11.2	12.4	12.9
Burundi	7	9	5.7	8.0	-2.8	2.0	12.3
Cambodia	11[d]	6	8.7[e]	8.2	7.6	6.4	..
Cape Verde	7[f]	8	8.6[g]	4.5	-3.5	1.6	4.0
Central African Republic	7	9	5.0	-0.4	-7.9	4.7	6.4
Chad	11[h]	12	..	..	..	..	..
Comoros	4	5	4.9	-0.3	0.5	0.2	-1.4
Dem. Republic of the Congo	14	7[i]	..	..	..	..	
Djibouti	6[j]	6[k]	..	..	..	..	
Equatorial Guinea	..	2[i]	..	..	..	..	
Eritrea	..[j]	15	..	..	..	..	
Ethiopia	8[l]	7	-0.9	5.8	6.2	-3.5	7.0
Gambia	6	6	7.8	0.8	1.5	1.5	3.0
Guinea	5[m]	4	4.0[n]	3.7	4.5	5.0	5.5
Guinea-Bissau	14[f]	10	9.2[g]	4.1	3.3	-40.0	164.7
Haiti	..	7	..	..	..	..	..
Kiribati	2	1	-0.9	1.9	..	..	..
Lao People's Dem. Republic	9[j]	17	8.9[o]	12.6	8.5	9.7	12.6
Lesotho	7	17[k]	13.7	9.4[p]	..	..	..
Liberia	8[a]	..[i]	..[b]	..	..	..	..
Madagascar	11[a]	11[k]	2.1[b]	0.6	2.4	..	..
Malawi	14	14	3.6	-2.7	3.8	2.0	4.0
Maldives	..	6	10.5	8.5	9.8	5.0	..
Mali	7	4	6.8	3.2	7.2	1.2	-2.1
Mauritania	13[a]	10	-2.1[b]	-0.9	-22.0	4.8	12.2
Mozambique	..	13	..	17.6[q]	34.0	15.9	4.5
Myanmar	..	..	..	..	..	..	
Nepal	4	9	9.3	9.5	7.1	3.4	5.7
Niger	4	6	-2.7[b]	2.3	4.6	3.7	4.5
Rwanda	17	12	2.6	6.1	16.6	10.4	8.4
Samoa	5	11[r]	..	..	..		
Sao Tome and Principe	9[f]	5	0.5[g]	1.4	1.1	2.0	2.2
Senegal	11	17	4.6	3.7	3.3	7.8	4.9
Sierra Leone	5	4	..	5.0[p]	..	..	
Solomon Islands	..	..	..	..	..	..	
Somalia	5	..	..	..	..	..	
Sudan	7	9	..	..	..	..	
Togo	8	9	1.7	2.4	2.9	6.1	1.5
Tuvalu	..	..	..	..	..	..	
Uganda	4	9	3.7	14.2	13.4	14.4	11.3
United Republic of Tanzania	..	7	..	2.3	5.0	8.0	4.9
Vanuatu	4	5[k]	..	..	..		
Yemen	..	11	..	4.5	1.1	3.8	0.7
Zambia	8	12	4.0	0.7	5.1	1.8	2.8
All LDCs[s]	10	11	..	..	..	..	..

Source: UNCTAD secretariat calculations, based on data from the World Bank (*World Development Indicators 2001*), CD-ROM.

a 1985. b 1985–1990. c 1988. d 1987. e 1987–1990. f 1986. g 1986–1990. h 1983. i 1993. j 1989.
k 1997. l 1981. m 1988. n 1988–1990. o 1984–1990. p 1990–1996. q 1994–1999. r 1991.
s Average of countries for which data are available.

6. INVESTMENT: ANNUAL AVERAGE GROWTH RATES AND SHARES IN GDP
(Percentage)

Country	Share in GDP		Annual average growth rates				
	1980	1999	1980–1990	1990–1999	1997	1998	1999
Afghanistan	..	..	..	..	..	..	..
Angola	18[a]	..	..	..	..	..	..
Bangladesh	22	22	1.4	9.1	11.1	12.1	9.8
Benin	15	18	-5.3	5.0	15.0	3.3	6.7
Bhutan	31	47	4.4	9.5	0.3	7.5	..
Burkina Faso	17	28	8.6	5.9	0.8	23.5	-5.8
Burundi	14	9	6.9	-1.8	-32.7	45.8	10.9
Cambodia	9[c]	15		..	..	..	..
Cape Verde	33[d]	38	-4.7[e]	9.1	3.4	6.8	9.7
Central African Republic	7	14		..	..	..	..
Chad	3[f]	10		..	..	..	..
Comoros	33	15	-4.2	-1.8	1.0	-2.6	1.5
Dem. Rep. of the Congo	10	8	-5.1	-2.8	-1.0	16.9	..
Djibouti	..	..	..	..	..	..	..
Equatorial Guinea	..	41	..	39.9	-0.9	70.1	-48.0
Eritrea	..	47	..	..	..	..	..
Ethiopia	13[g]	18	2.1[h]	12.1	5.9	-0.2	11.7
Gambia	27	18	0.0	5.8	-15.7	14.0	38.4
Guinea	15[d]	17	3.3[e]	2.4	7.5	2.7	4.5
Guinea-Bissau	28	16	12.9	-13.0	-19.9	-41.3	-30.6
Haiti	17	11	-0.6	2.2	8.9	8.1	5.1
Kiribati	33	56[i]	..	..	..	..	..
Lao People's Dem. Republic	6[j]	25	..	..	..	..	..
Lesotho	37	47	5.3	2.3	0.9	-13.6	1.5
Liberia	27	..	..	..	..	..	..
Madagascar	15	13	4.9	1.1	-0.6	9.0	8.7
Malawi	25	15	-2.8	-8.9	9.4	-7.3	11.5
Maldives	..	..	..	..	..	..	..
Mali	15	21	3.6	-1.4	-10.6	6.1	4.5
Mauritania	26	18	6.9	7.8	15.9	0.0	-8.9
Mozambique	6	33	3.8	10.7	1.9	41.1	47.1
Myanmar	..	..		..	..	..	..
Nepal	18	22	6.0	7.2	-2.6	0.9	-15.4
Niger	28	10	-7.1	3.9	10.4	13.7	-8.6
Rwanda	16	14	4.3	2.1	38.9	26.4	-12.6
Samoa	33	52[i]	..	..	..	..	..
Sao Tome and Principe	17	40	-0.8	-0.9	-8.8	10.0	4.4
Senegal	12	19	5.2	4.5	4.3	17.6	1.7
Sierra Leone	18	5[k]	..	..	..	..	..
Solomon Islands	36	29[l]	..	..	..	..	..
Somalia	42	16[l]	..	..	..	..	..
Sudan	15	..	..	..	..	..	..
Togo	28	13	2.7	-2.0	-0.4	-11.3	1.5
Tuvalu	..	..					
Uganda	6	16	8.0[m]	9.0	-2.7	3.7	9.0
United Rep. of Tanzania	..	17	..	-2.8	-5.3	14.3	4.8
Vanuatu	26[n]	44[l]	..	..	..	..	..
Yemen	..	22	..	7.7	18.6	10.9	-4.4
Zambia	23	17	-4.3	4.5	14.0	9.3	8.7
All LDCs	17	20	1.4	6.0	6.1	9.8	3.5

Source: UNCTAD, *Handbook of Statistics 2001;* and the World Bank, *World Development Indicators 2001,* CD-ROM.

Note: Aggregate figures based on countries for which data are available.

a 1985. b 1985–1990. c 1988. d 1986. e 1986–1990. f 1982. g 1981. h 1981–1990. i 1992. j 1984. k 1998. l 1990. m 1982–1990. n 1983.

7. INDICATORS ON AREA AND POPULATION

Country	Area		Population					
	Total	% of arable land and land under permanent crops	Density	Total	Urban	Activity rate[a]		
	(000 km²)	1999	Pop./km² 1999	(mill.) 1999	% 1999	M	F 2000	T
Afghanistan	652.1	12.4	34	21.9	22	88	50	69
Angola	1 246.7	2.8	10	12.5	34	90	75	83
Bangladesh	144.0	64.0	882	126.9	24	87	68	78
Benin	112.6	16.7	53	5.9	42	83	76	79
Bhutan	47.0	3.4	13	0.6	7	91	60	76
Burkina Faso	274.0	12.6	42	11.6	18	90	78	84
Burundi	27.8	42.8	236	6.6	9	94	86	90
Cambodia	181.0	21.6	60	10.9	16	86	85	86
Cape Verde	4.0	10.2	104	0.4	61	90	50	68
Central African Republic	623.0	3.2	6	3.5	41	87	68	77
Chad	1 284.0	2.8	6	7.5	24	90	70	80
Comoros	2.2	52.9	303	0.7	33	86	64	75
Dem. Rep. of the Congo	2 344.9	3.5	21	50.3	30	85	63	74
Djibouti	23.2	..	27	0.6	83	..	..	..
Equatorial Guinea	28.1	8.2	16	0.4	47	91	48	69
Eritrea	117.6	5.0	32	3.7	18	87	77	82
Ethiopia	1 104.3	10.7	55	61.1	17	86	59	73
Gambia	11.3	20.0	112	1.3	32	90	70	80
Guinea	245.9	6.0	30	7.4	32	87	80	84
Guinea-Bissau	36.1	12.4	33	1.2	23	91	60	75
Haiti	27.8	33.0	291	8.1	35	82	58	70
Kiribati	0.7	50.7	113	0.1	39	..	..	..
Lao People's Dem. Rep.	236.8	4.1	22	5.3	23	90	78	84
Lesotho	30.4	10.7	69	2.1	27	85	50	67
Liberia	111.4	4.0	26	2.9	45	83	56	70
Madagascar	587.0	5.3	26	15.5	29	89	71	80
Malawi	118.5	21.3	90	10.6	24	87	79	83
Maldives	0.3	10.0	928	0.3	26	86	68	77
Mali	1 240.2	3.8	9	11.0	30	90	74	82
Mauritania	1 025.5	0.5	3	2.6	57	87	65	76
Mozambique	801.6	4.3	24	19.3	39	91	83	87
Myanmar	676.6	15.4	67	45.1	27	90	68	79
Nepal	140.8	20.8	166	23.4	12	86	58	72
Niger	1 267.0	3.9	8	10.4	20	93	71	82
Rwanda	26.3	43.4	275	7.2	6	94	86	90
Samoa	2.8	43.1	62	0.2	22	..	..	..
Sao Tome and Principe	1.0	42.7	150	0.1	46	..	..	..
Senegal	196.7	11.8	47	9.2	47	87	63	75
Sierra Leone	71.7	7.5	66	4.7	36	85	46	65
Solomon Islands	28.9	2.1	15	0.4	19	89	82	86
Somalia	637.7	1.7	15	9.7	27	87	65	76
Sudan	2 505.8	7.1	12	28.9	35	86	35	61
Togo	56.8	42.3	79	4.5	33	87	55	71
Tuvalu[b]	..	..	380	..	53	..	..	..
Uganda	241.0	34.6	88	21.1	14	91	81	86
United Rep. of Tanzania	883.7	5.3	37	32.8	26	88	83	86
Vanuatu	12.2	9.8	15	0.2	20	..	..	..
Yemen	528.0	3.2	33	17.5	25	84	32	58
Zambia	752.6	7.1	12	9.0	40	87	67	77
ALL LDCs	20 719.7	6.7	31	637.4	28	88	66	77
All developing countries	83 890.7	11.3	57	4 770.7	48	87[c]	60[c]	73[c]

Source: UNCTAD, *Handbook of Statistics 2001*; FAO, *Production Yearbook 1998*; ILO, *World Labour Report 2000*; and UNICEF, *The State of the World's Children 2001*.

a   Economically active population, labour force participation rates calculated as a percentage of those in the labour force at age 15–64 to total population at age 15–64.   b Population 11,000 and area 30 km².   c Includes South Africa.

8. Indicators on demography

Country	Infant mortality rate (per 1,000 live births)		Average life expectancy at birth (years)						Crude birth rate (per 1,000 people)		Crude death rate (per 1,000 people)	
	1985–1990	1995–2000[a]	1985–1990 M	F	T	1995–2000[a] M	F	T	1985–1990	1995–2000[a]	1985–1990	1995–2000[a]
Afghanistan	173	165	41	41	41	42	43	43	49	48	24	22
Angola	139	126	42	45	44	43	46	45	52	51	20	20
Bangladesh	105	79	53	53	53	58	58	58	38	31	13	10
Benin	104	88	49	53	51	52	55	54	49	43	16	13
Bhutan	96	63	52	54	53	60	62	61	41	36	14	10
Burkina Faso	114	99	46	49	48	44	46	45	48	47	18	18
Burundi	119	120	46	49	47	40	42	41	47	43	18	21
Cambodia	100	83	52	55	54	54	59	57	47	38	14	11
Cape Verde	74	56	62	67	64	66	71	69	36	32	9	6
Central African Republic	105	101	45	50	47	43	46	44	42	40	18	19
Chad	133	123	43	46	44	44	46	45	48	48	21	20
Comoros	95	76	53	57	55	57	60	59	42	39	12	10
Dem. Rep. of the Congo	99	91	50	53	51	49	52	51	48	48	15	15
Djibouti	122	117	45	49	47	44	47	46	47	41	18	18
Equatorial Guinea	127	108	44	48	46	48	52	50	44	43	20	16
Eritrea	114	89	46	49	48	50	53	52	45	41	17	14
Ethiopia	132	115	44	47	45	44	45	45	47	45	19	19
Gambia	144	125	41	44	43	44	47	45	46	40	21	18
Guinea	146	124	42	43	43	46	47	47	47	46	21	18
Guinea-Bissau	151	131	40	43	42	43	46	44	45	45	23	20
Haiti	106	68	50	54	52	49	55	52	42	32	15	13
Kiribati	69	53	52[b]	52[b]	52[b]	56	60	58	26[c]	32	9[c]	..
Lao People's Dem. Rep.	116	97	47	50	48	51	54	53	45	38	18	14
Lesotho	107	108	55	58	56	51	52	51	38	35	13	15
Liberia	108	111	51	54	53	47	49	48	44	50	14	17
Madagascar	116	100	47	49	48	51	53	54	45	44	17	15
Malawi	155	140	45	47	46	41	41	41	52	47	21	22
Maldives	82	46	61	58	60	66	64	65	42	37	10	7
Mali	142	130	47	50	48	50	52	51	51	50	20	19
Mauritania	115	106	47	50	48	49	52	51	44	44	17	15
Mozambique	137	137	42	45	44	39	42	41	45	45	21	22
Myanmar	104	92	52	56	54	54	58	56	31	27	13	12
Nepal	110	83	53	51	52	58	57	57	39	36	14	11
Niger	153	136	41	41	41	44	44	44	56	55	24	21
Rwanda	123	122	44	47	46	39	40	39	44	42	18	22
Samoa	44	30	61	67	64	65	72	69	38	29	7	6
Sao Tome and Principe	..	59	..	..	..	..	..	..	..	..	..	..
Senegal	76	62	46	50	48	50	54	52	46	40	18	13
Sierra Leone	183	165	35	38	37	36	39	37	49	50	27	26
Solomon Islands	33	24	62	64	63	66	69	67	39	40	8	5
Somalia	132	122	43	47	45	45	49	47	52	52	20	19
Sudan	103	86	50	52	51	54	56	55	40	36	15	12
Togo	97	83	50	54	52	50	53	51	44	41	14	14
Tuvalu	..	..	..	..	..	..	..	..	..	..	..	..
Uganda	124	106	43	46	45	41	42	42	51	50	20	20
United Rep. of Tanzania	92	81	51	54	53	50	52	51	45	40	13	13
Vanuatu	57	32	61	65	63	66	69	67	37	34	8	6
Yemen	105	74	52	53	53	58	60	59	49	51	14	10
Zambia	98	94	50	52	51	41	40	41	45	44	15	21
ALL LDCs	117	102	48	50	49	49	51	50	43	40	16	15
All developing countries	77	65	59	62	60	61	65	63	30	25	10	9

Source: United Nations, *World Population Prospects 2000 Revision*; UNICEF, *The State of the World's Children 2001*; ESCAP, *Statistical Yearbook for Asia and the Pacific 1992*; World Bank, *World Development Indicators 2001*; and AsDB, *Key Indicators of Developing Asian and Pacific Countries 1995*.

a   Or latest year available. b 1988. c 1985.

9. INDICATORS ON HEALTH

Country	Low birth-weight infants (percentage) 1995–1999[b]	Percentage of women attended during childbirth by trained personnel 1995–2000[b]	Percentage of 1-year-old child immunized against DPT[a] (3 doses) 1997–1999[b]
Afghanistan	20[c]	8[c]	37
Angola	19[c]	..	29
Bangladesh	30	13	69
Benin	..	60	90
Bhutan	..	15[c]	88
Burkina Faso	21[c]	27	37
Burundi	..	24[c]	63
Cambodia	..	34	64
Cape Verde	9[c]	54	69
Central African Republic	15[c]	46[c]	28
Chad	..	15	33
Comoros	8[c]	52	75
Dem. Rep. of the Congo	15[c]	..	15
Djibouti	11[c]	79[c]	23
Equatorial Guinea	..	5[c]	81
Eritrea	13[c]	21	56
Ethiopia	16[c]	10	64
Gambia	..	44[c]	87
Guinea	13	35	46
Guinea-Bissau	20[c]	25	63
Haiti	15[c]	21	61
Kiribati	3[c]	72[c]	78
Lao People's Dem. Rep.	18[c]	14[c]	56
Lesotho	11[c]	50[c]	64
Liberia	..	58[c]	23
Madagascar	5	47	48
Malawi	20[c]	55[c]	94
Maldives	13	90[c]	97
Mali	16	24	52
Mauritania	11[c]	40[c]	19
Mozambique	12	44	81
Myanmar	24[c]	56	75
Nepal	..	9	76
Niger	15[c]	18	21
Rwanda	17[c]	26[c]	85
Samoa	6[c]	76[c]	98
Sao Tome and Principe	7[c]	86[c]	73
Senegal	4	47	60
Sierra Leone	11[c]	..	22
Solomon Islands	20[c]	85[c]	86
Somalia	16[c]	2[c]	18
Sudan	15[c]	86[c]	88
Togo	20[c]	51	48
Tuvalu	3[c]	100[c]	84
Uganda	13	38	54
United Rep. of Tanzania	14[c]	35	82
Vanuatu	7[c]	79[c]	93
Yemen	19[c]	22	72
Zambia	13[c]	47	92
All LDCs	18	28	58
All developing countries	17	52	72

Source: UNICEF, *The State of the World's Children 2001*; World Bank, *World Development Indicators 2001*; and WHO, *The World Health Report 1998*.

a   Diphtheria, pertussis and tetanus.

b   Data refer to the most recent year available during the period specified in the column heading.

c   Indicates data that refers to years or periods other than those specified in the column heading, differ from the standard definition, or refer to only part of the country.

10. INDICATORS ON NUTRITION AND SANITATION

Country	Total food supply (daily calories intake per capita)		Percentage of population with access to safe water or adequate sanitation							
			Urban				**Rural**			
			Water		Sanitation		Water		Sanitation	
	1980	1999	1980	1999[a]	1980	1999[a]	1980	1999[a]	1980	1999[a]
Afghanistan	2085	1755	28	19	..	25	8	11	..	8
Angola	2134	1873	85	34	40	70	10	40	15	30
Bangladesh	1965	2201	26	99	21	82	40	97	1	44
Benin	2023	2489	26	74	48	46	15	55	4	6
Bhutan	..	..	50	86	..	65	5	60	..	70
Burkina Faso	1671	2376	27	84	38	88	31	37	5	16
Burundi	2022	1628	90	96	40	79	20	49	..	50
Cambodia	1702	2000	..	53	..	58	..	25	..	10
Cape Verde	2556	3166	100	64	34	95	21	89	10	32
Central African Republic	2301	1978	..	80	..	43	..	46	..	23
Chad	1646	2230	..	31	..	81	..	26	..	13
Comoros	1784	1800	..	98	..	98	..	95	..	98
Dem. Rep. of the Congo	2086	1637	43	89	..	53	5	26	10	6
Djibouti	1733	2129	50	100	43	99	20	100	20	50
Equatorial Guinea	..	..	47	45	99	60	..	42	..	46
Eritrea	..	1646	..	63	..	66	..	42	..	1
Ethiopia	..	1803	..	77	..	58	..	13	..	6
Gambia	1644	2598	85	80	..	41	..	53	..	35
Guinea	2269	2133	69	72	54	94	2	36	1	41
Guinea-Bissau	1898	2245	18	29	21	88	8	55	13	34
Haiti	2025	1977	48	49	39	50	8	45	10	16
Kiribati	2617	2982	93	82	87	54	25	25	80	44
Lao People's Dem. Rep.	2084	2152	21	59	..	84	12	100	..	34
Lesotho	2179	2300	37	98	13	93	11	88	14	92
Liberia	2504	2089	..	79	..	56	..	13	..	4
Madagascar	2374	1994	80	85	9	70	7	31	..	30
Malawi	2246	2164	77	95	100	96	37	44	81	70
Maldives	2160	2298	11	100	60	100	3	100	1	41
Mali	1746	2314	37	74	79	93	0	61	0	58
Mauritania	2118	2702	80	34	5	44	85	40	..	19
Mozambique	1940	1939	..	86	..	69	..	43	..	26
Myanmar	2326	2803	38	88	38	65	15	60	15	39
Nepal	1878	2264	83	85	16	75	7	80	1	20
Niger	2139	2064	41	70	36	79	32	56	3	5
Rwanda	2292	2011	48	60	60	12	55	40	50	8
Samoa	2495	..	97	95	86	95	94	100	83	100
Sao Tome and Principe	2103	2269	..	..	..	..	..	..	..	..
Senegal	2207	2 307	77	92	100	94	25	65	2	48
Sierra Leone	2087	2016	50	23	31	23	2	31	6	31
Solomon Islands	2203	2222	91	94	82	98	20	65	10	18
Somalia	1735	1555	60	46	45	69	20	28	5	35
Sudan	2201	2360	100	86	63	87	31	69	0	48
Togo	2281	2527	70	85	24	69	31	38	0	17
Tuvalu	..	..	..	100	..	100	..	100	..	100
Uganda	2056	2238	45	72	40	96	8	46	10	72
United Rep. of Tanzania	2252	1940	88	80	83	98	39	42	47	86
Vanuatu	2526	2 766	65	63	95	100	53	94	68	100
Yemen	1937	2 087	93	85	60	87	19	64	..	31
Zambia	2273	1934	65	88	100	99	32	48	48	64
All LDCs	1888	2018	51	80	44	73	24	54	12	33
All developing countries[b]	2288	2 684	73	91	50	81	32	70	13	34

Source: FAO, *Production Yearbook 1994*; WHO/UNICEF, *Water Supply and Sanitation Sector Monitoring Report 1993* and *1996*; WHO, *The International Drinking Water Supply and Sanitation Decade: End of Decade Review* (as at December 1990), *Review of National Progress* (various issues); and UNICEF, *The State of the World's Children 2001*.

a   Or latest year available.   b   Average of countries for which data are available.

11. INDICATORS ON EDUCATION AND LITERACY

Country	Adult literacy rate (%)			School enrolment ratio (% of relevant age group)											
				Primary						Secondary					
	Estimated year 2000			1980			1997[a]			1980			1997[a]		
	M	F	T	M	F	T	M	F	T	M	F	T	M	F	T
Afghanistan	51	21	36	54	12	34	64	32	49	16	4	10	32	11	22
Angola	56	29	42	187	163	175	95	88	92	32	9	20	15	10	12
Bangladesh	52	30	41	75	46	61	74	66	72	26	9	18	25	13	19
Benin	52	34	38	91	43	67	98	57	78	24	8	16	26	11	18
Bhutan	61	34	47	23	10	17	34	22	28	3	1	2	7	2	5
Burkina Faso	33	13	23	22	13	17	48	31	40	4	2	3	11	6	8
Burundi	56	41	48	32	21	26	55	46	51	4	2	3	8	5	7
Cambodia	48	22	35	..	..	..	123	104	113	..	..	..	31	17	24
Cape Verde	84	65	74	119	110	114	150	147	148	9	7	8	54	56	55
Central African Republic	60	35	47	92	51	71	69	45	57	21	7	14	15	6	10
Chad	67	41	54	52	19	36	76	39	57	9	1	5	15	4	9
Comoros	64	49	56	100	72	86	84	69	77	30	15	22	24	19	21
Dem. Rep. of the Congo	88	74	81	108	77	92	86	59	72	35	13	24	32	19	26
Djibouti	65	38	51	44	26	35	44	33	39	15	9	12	17	12	14
Equatorial Guinea	93	75	83	153	120	136	..	..	..	20	4	12	..	..	..
Eritrea	..	..	..	..	..	..	59	48	53	..	..	..	24	17	20
Ethiopia	44	33	39	48	27	37	55	30	43	12	7	9	14	10	12
Gambia	44	30	37	70	36	53	87	67	77	16	7	11	30	19	25
Guinea	55	27	41	48	25	36	68	41	54	24	10	17	20	7	14
Guinea-Bissau	53	21	37	94	43	68	79	45	62	10	2	6	14	4	9
Haiti	51	47	49	83	71	77	49	46	48	14	13	14	21	20	21
Kiribati	..	..	..	..	..	..	..	..	..	..	..	..	..	..	..
Lao People's Dem. Rep.	74	51	62	123	104	113	123	101	112	25	16	21	34	23	28
Lesotho	74	94	84	85	122	103	102	114	108	14	21	18	25	36	31
Liberia	70	37	53	61	34	48	..	..	..	31	12	22	..	..	..
Madagascar	60	32	46	131	129	130	92	91	92	15	11	13	16	16	16
Malawi	75	47	60	72	48	60	140	127	134	7	3	5	21	12	17
Maldives	96	96	96	153	139	146	130	127	128	..	..	..	67	71	69
Mali	48	33	40	34	19	26	58	40	49	12	5	8	17	8	13
Mauritania	51	30	40	47	26	37	84	75	79	17	4	11	21	11	16
Mozambique	60	28	44	99	76	87	70	50	60	8	3	5	9	5	7
Myanmar	89	81	85	93	89	91	122	117	120	25	19	22	29	30	30
Nepal	59	24	41	119	50	86	129	96	113	33	9	22	51	33	42
Niger	24	8	16	33	18	25	36	23	29	7	3	5	9	5	7
Rwanda	74	61	67	66	60	63	82	80	81	4	3	3	12	9	11
Samoa	..	..	..	..	..	..	100	101	100	..	..	..	59	66	62
Sao Tome and Principe	..	..	..	..	..	..	..	..	..	..	..	..	..	..	..
Senegal	47	28	37	55	37	46	78	65	71	15	7	11	20	12	16
Sierra Leone	51	23	36	61	43	52	60	41	50	20	8	14	22	13	17
Solomon Islands	..	..	..	85	65	76	89	103	97	22	9	16	21	14	17
Somalia	36	14	24	28	15	21	9	5	7	13	5	9	..	..	..
Sudan	68	46	57	59	41	50	55	47	51	20	12	16	23	20	21
Togo	72	43	57	144	93	118	140	99	120	50	16	33	40	14	27
Tuvalu	..	..	..	..	..	..	..	..	..	..	..	..	..	..	..
Uganda	78	57	67	56	43	50	68	81	74	7	3	5	15	9	12
United Rep. of Tanzania	84	67	75	99	86	93	67	66	66	4	2	3	6	5	6
Vanuatu	..	..	..	..	..	..	94	101	98	..	..	..	23	18	20
Yemen	67	25	46	72	16	45	100	40	70	11	3	7	53	14	34
Zambia	85	71	78	97	83	90	91	86	89	22	11	16	34	21	27
All LDCs[b]	61	41	51	77	54	66	81	62	72	21	9	15	24	15	19
All developing countries[b]	81	66	74	103	85	95	108	95	102	42	28	35	57	46	52

Source: UNESCO, Compendium of Statistics on Illiteracy (1990 and 1995 editions), Statistical Yearbook (1999), Trends and Projections of Enrolment by Level of Education and by Age, 1960–2025 (as assessed in 1993); World Culture Report 2000; and ECA, African Socio-economic Indicators, 1990–91.

a   Or latest year available.   b   Average of countries for which data are available.

12. INDICATORS ON COMMUNICATIONS AND MEDIA

Country	Post offices open to the public (per 100,000 inhabitants) 1980	1999[a]	Telephones 1980	1999[a]	Radio receivers (per 1,000 inhabitants) 1980	1999[a]	Circulation of daily newspapers 1980	1999[a]
Afghanistan	..	2.0	2.0	1.3	75	132	6.0	5.6
Angola	1.4	0.5	5.1	7.7	21	54	20.0	11.0
Bangladesh	8.2	7.1	1.1	3.4	17	50	3.0	9.3
Benin	..	2.7	5.0[c]	6.6	66	110	0.3	2.2
Bhutan	6.3	6.0	..	17.9	12	19	..	..
Burkina Faso	1.2	0.7	1.5[c]	4.0	18	33	0.2	1.3
Burundi	0.4[d]	0.4	1.3[e]	2.8	39	152	0.2	3.2
Cambodia	..	0.5	..	2.5	92	128	..	1.7
Cape Verde	18.7[d]	12.8	5.7[f]	112.1	142	183	..	..
Central African Republic	3.1[e]	1.0	2.1[f]	2.7	52	83	..	1.8
Chad	0.5[e]	0.5	1.5[g]	1.3	168	242	0.2	0.2
Comoros	..	5.6	5.0[c]	9.6	119	141	..	..
Democratic Rep. of the Congo	1.4	1.0	0.8	0.3	193	376	2.0	2.7
Djibouti	1.6	1.9	16.8	14.0	75	84	..	..
Equatorial Guinea	4.6[d]	5.9	..	12.9	401	428	7.0	4.9
Eritrea	..	1.5	..	7.3	..	484	..	..
Ethiopia	1.1[f]	0.9	2.3	3.1	168	196	1.0	1.5
Gambia	..	..	5.4[h]	23.0	114	394	..	1.7
Guinea	..	1.3	1.9[g]	5.9	30	49	..	..
Guinea-Bissau	..	2.2	..	7.0	31	44	8.0	5.4
Haiti	..	1.1	..	8.6	19	55	7.0	2.5
Kiribati	42.4	31.2	12.3	42.6	193	212	..	..
Lao People's Dem. Rep.	2.1	1.9	2.1[g]	6.5	109	143	4.0	3.7
Lesotho	9.2	7.6	..	9.7	25	49	3.2	7.6
Liberia	2.6	1.2	..	2.4	179	329	6.0	16.0
Madagascar	5.8	6.1	4.3	3.2	180	198	6.0	4.6
Malawi	3.9	3.0	5.2	3.8	186	250	3.0	2.6
Maldives	85.6	85.4	6.8	79.6	82	129	6.0	19.0
Mali	1.9[d]	1.2	..	2.5	15	54	1.0	1.2
Mauritania	3.7	2.3	2.5[d]	6.4	129	151	..	0.5
Mozambique	4.8	2.1	4.5[f]	4.0	21	40	4.0	2.7
Myanmar	3.3	2.8	1.1[h]	5.5	23	70	10.0	10.0
Nepal	9.6	21.4	1.0[c]	11.3	21	39	8.0	11.0
Niger	2.7	0.6	1.7	1.7	45	66	0.5	0.2
Rwanda	..	1.8	0.9	1.7	34	102	0.1	0.1
Samoa	..	22.4	36.9	48.7	644	1035	..	..
Sao Tome and Principe	55.9	9.3	15.1[f]	31.4	245	272	..	..
Senegal	..	1.5		17.9	99	142	6.0	5.0
Sierra Leone	3.3[d]	1.3	..	3.8	176	274	3.0	4.7
Solomon Islands	..	31.8	..	18.8	88	141	..	..
Somalia	..	..	..	1.5	19	53	1.0	1.2
Sudan	4.0	1.7	3.4	8.7	225	271	6.0	27.0
Togo	15.2	1.0	3.8	8.4	203	227	6.0	3.6
Tuvalu	..	..	..	11.5	215	384	..	..
Uganda	..	1.5	3.6	2.6	100	127	2.0	2.1
United Republic of Tanzania	3.2	1.8	5.0	4.5	81	279	11.0	3.9
Vanuatu	5.3	..	23.2[c]	28.4	196	350	..	..
Yemen	2.4	1.5	..	16.6	28	64	12.0	15.0
Zambia	7.0[f]	1.8	10.7	9.2	56	160	19.0	4.0
All LDCs[b]	6.7	2.8	2.3	5.0	79	185	5.0	8.0
All developing countries[b]	13.1[i]	10.1	15.5	69.0	117	244	35.0	40.0

Source: UNCTAD, *Handbook of Statistics 2001*; UNESCO, *Statistical Yearbook 1999* and *World Culture Report 2000*; Universal Postal Union, *Postal Statistics 1999*.

a Or latest year available.   b Average of countries for which data are available.
c 1978. d 1982. e 1983. f 1981. g 1977. h 1979. i Excluding China.

13. INDICATORS ON TRANSPORT AND TRANSPORT NETWORKS[a]

Country	Road networks			Railways				Civil aviation			
	Total	Paved	Density	Network	Density	Freight	Passenger	Freight		Passenger	
								Total	Inter-national	Total	Inter-national
	km	%	km/1,000 km²	km	km/1,000 km²	mill. ton km	mill. pass. km	mill. tons.	km	thousands	
Afghanistan	21 000	13.3	32.2	..	..	..	..	7.4	7.3	140	36
Angola	51 429	10.4	41.0	2 523	2.0	1 890	360	36.5	35.0	531	120
Bangladesh	201 182	9.5	1 360.0	2 746	19.1	718	5 348	143.1	143.0	1 215	892
Benin	6787	20.0	60.3	579	5.1	220	230	13.7	13.7	84	84
Bhutan	3 285	60.7	50.0	..	..	..	..	..	..	31	31
Burkina Faso	12 100	16.0	44.2	607	2.2	72	152	13.7	13.7	147	132
Burundi	14 480	7.1	520.9	..	..	..	..	..	..	12	12
Cambodia	35 769	7.5	190.0	601	3.3	34	80	..	..	..	..
Cape Verde	1 100	78.0	272.7	..	..	..	..	0.6	0.5	252	114
Central African Republic	24 307	2.7	38.5	..	..	..	..	13.7	13.7	84	84
Chad	33 400	0.8	26.0	..	..	..	..	13.7	13.7	84	84
Comoros	900	76.5	409.1	..	..	..	..	..	..	..	..
Dem. Rep. of the Congo	157 000	..	67.0	5 088	2.2	1 836	580	1.6	..	59	..
Djibouti	2 890	12.6	124.6	100	4.3	..	..	..	..	..	..
Equatorial Guinea	2 880	..	102.5	..	..	..	..	-	-	21	8
Eritrea	4 010	21.8	34.1	..	..	..	..	..	..	..	..
Ethiopia	28 652	13.3	25.9	781	0.7	103	185	101.5	101.2	861	617
Gambia	2 700	35.4	238.9	..	..	..	..	..	..	..	..
Guinea	30 500	16.5	124.0	940	3.8	660	116	1.4	1.4	59	59
Guinea-Bissau	4 400	10.3	130.0	..	..	..	..	..	..	13	..
Haiti	4 160	24.3	160.0	100	3.6	..	..	..	..	..	..
Kiribati	670	..	920.0	..	..	..	..	0.8	0.8	3	3
Lao People's Dem. Rep.	22 321	13.8	94.3	..	..	..	..	1.5	0.9	197	54
Lesotho	5 940	17.9	195.7	16	0.5	..	..	..	..	1	1
Liberia	10 600	6.2	95.2	493	4.4	..	..	..	..	..	..
Madagascar	30 623	11.6	52.2	1 030	1.8	93	46	32.4	31.3	635	168
Malawi	16 451	19.0	..	789	6.7	48	40	0.8	0.5	112	63
Maldives	..	..	..	..	..	..	..	17.0	16.9	344	273
Mali	15 100	12.1	20.0	642	0.5	4	9	13.7	13.7	84	84
Mauritania	7 660	11.3	7.5	650	0.6	16 623	7	13.9	13.7	187	103
Mozambique	30 400	18.7	37.9	3 150	3.9	1 420	500	6.6	4.9	235	87
Myanmar	28 200	12.2	50.0	2 775	4.1	648	4 675	6.2	5.4	537	145
Nepal	7 700	41.5	60.0	52	0.4	..	..	16.0	15.9	583	452
Niger	10 100	7.9	8.0	..	..	..	..	13.7	13.7	84	84
Rwanda	14 900	9.1	566.5	2 652	100.7	2 140	2 700	..	..	..	..
Samoa	790	42.0	260.0	..	..	..	..	0.8	..	92	..
Sao Tome and Principe	320	68.1	330.0	..	..	..	..	..	..	34	20
Senegal	14 576	29.3	74.1	906	4.6	386	179	13.7	13.7	103	84
Sierra Leone	11 300	8.0	163.2	84	1.2	..	..	0.4	0.4	19	19
Solomon Islands	1 360	2.5	60.0	..	..	..	..	1.3	1.3	98	23
Somalia	22 100	11.8	34.7	..	..	..	..	..	..	..	..
Sudan	11 900	36.3	4.7	4 756	1.9	1 970	985	33.9	29.5	390	245
Togo	7 520	31.6	132.4	514	9.1	17	132	13.7	13.7	84	84
Tuvalu	8	..	40.0	..	..	..	..	..	..	..	..
Uganda	..	..	..	1 100	4.6	82	315	21.7	19.0	179	36
United Rep. of Tanzania	88 200	4.2	99.8	3 575	4.0	523	935	2.3	1.3	190	75
Vanuatu	1 070	23.9	87.7	..	..	..	..	1.9	1.9	86	86
Yemen	64 725	8.1	122.6	..	..	..	..	21.4	16.0	731	480
Zambia	66 781	18.0	52.8	1 924	2.6	1 625	547	0.4	0.4	42	42

Source: IRU, *World Transport Statistics 1996*; IRF, *World Road Statistics 2001*; ICAO, Statistical Year Book, *Civil Aviation Statistics of the World 1999*.

a   Data refer to 1999 for road network and 1999 for civil aviation or latest year available.

14. INDICATORS ON ENERGY

Country	Coal, oil, gas and electricity		Fuelwood, charcoal and bagasse		Installed electricity capacity	
	Consumption per capita in kg of coal equivalent				kW/1,000 inhabitants	
	1980	1998	1980	1998	1980	1998
Afghanistan	48	26	99	99	25	23
Angola	135	171	362	183	85	38
Bangladesh	45	111	23	24	11	28
Benin	51	45	347	344	4	3
Bhutan	9	93	777	262	8	178
Burkina Faso	33	44	277	312	6	7
Burundi	14	19	252	255	2	7
Cambodia	22	24	213	218	6	3
Cape Verde	194	141	..	..	21	17
Central African Republic	26	37	358	335	13	12
Chad	22	7	206	208	8	4
Comoros	48	52	..	..	10	8
Democratic Rep. of the Congo	75	32	298	335	64	65
Djibouti	326	278	..	..	124	137
Equatorial Guinea	124	153	645	383	32	12
Eritrea	..	..	..	..	..	..
Ethiopia	21[a]	14[a]	296[a]	285[a]	9[a]	7[a]
Gambia	128	89	452	338	17	24
Guinea	85	74	246	221	39	25
Guinea-Bissau	81	94	177	134	9	9
Haiti	56	80	322	288	22	33
Kiribati	220	126	..	..	33	25
Lao People's Dem. Republic	30	45	354	308	78	50
Lesotho	..	..	..	..	..	..
Liberia	480	70	709	589	163	125
Madagascar	86	47	194	242	11	15
Malawi	58	40	288	314	24	18
Maldives	129	574	..	..	13	92
Mali	27	24	196	191	6	11
Mauritania	178	544	1	1	35	42
Mozambique	151	39	351	323	156	126
Myanmar	65	101	143	149	19	32
Nepal	18	63	305	282	5	14
Niger	50	49	191	200	6	10
Rwanda	28	40	292	232	8	5
Samoa	310	382	145	149	84	109
Sao Tome and Principe	213	266	..	..	43	43
Senegal	214	148	..	..	30	26
Sierra Leone	79	42	709	237	29	28
Solomon Islands	212	182	..	126	53	29
Somalia	108	..	192	315	5	9
Sudan	81	61	282	289	16	21
Togo	72	74	66	94	13	8
Tuvalu	..	..	..	..	..	0
Uganda	29	34	235	236	12	9
United Republic of Tanzania	44	36	331	392	14	17
Vanuatu	248	161	68	48	85	61
Yemen	92	375	45	8	20	48
Zambia	403	166	496	502	301	259
All LDCs	66	76	212	210	28	32
All developing countries	521	904	125	135	88	213

Source: United Nations, *Energy Statistics Yearbook 1983, 1998* and *Statistical Yearbook 1985/86.*

a   Includes Eritrea.

15. INDICATORS ON THE STATUS OF WOMEN IN LDCs

Country	Education, training and literacy: Female–male gaps[a]				Health, fertility and mortality			Economic activity, employment					Political participation	
	Adult literacy rate	School enrolment ratio			Average age at first marriage (years)	Total fertility rate (births per woman)	Maternal mortality (per 100,000 births)	Women as a percentage of total:				Female labour force: Agriculture/ total	Legis-lators	Decision makers in all ministries
		Primary	Second-ary	Post-secondary				Labour force	Employ-ees	Self-employed	Unpaid family	(%)	(%)	(%)
	1999[b]		1997[c]		1997[c]	1995-2000[c]	1999[c]	1999[c]	1998[c]	1998[c]	1998[c]	1997[c]	1999[c]	1999[c]
Afghanistan	35	50	34	46	18	7	..	35	..	..	..	85	..	-
Angola	52	97	82	23	18	7	..	46	..	..	..	86	..	14
Bangladesh	57	87	58	20	17	3	440	42	9	8	77	76	5	5
Benin	43	59	48	23	18	6	500[d]	48	3	64	29	65	..	13
Bhutan	50	88	..	..	..	6	380	40	..	..	..	98	..	..
Burkina Faso	40	64	58	29	17	7	..	47	13	16	66	94	..	10
Burundi	70	86	70	34	22	6	..	50	13	53	60	98	..	8
Cambodia	35	100	66	23	21	5	470	52	46	..	..	78	..	..
Cape Verde	77	100	95	..	25	4	55	39	46	30	3	32	..	13
Central African Republic	57	69	50	16	19	5	1100	47	10	52	55	87	..	4
Chad	65	58	37	14	17	6	830	44	..	..	..	91	..	0
Comoros	79	83	81	..	22	5	500	42	24	25	..	91	..	7
Dem. Rep. of the Congo	67	70	63	20	20	6	..	43	..	..	..	81	..	..
Djibouti	71	75	66	77	19	5	..	40	33	28	22	..	..	..
Equatorial Guinea	80	102	90	15	..	6	..	36	..	..	74	91	..	4
Eritrea	59	91	83	15	..	6	1 000[d]	47	..	..	..	85	17	5
Ethiopia	74	62	55	25	18	6	..	40	5	28	65	86	..	5
Gambia	66	79	60	55	..	5	..	44	..	..	64	92	..	29
Guinea	..	58	31	12	16	5	670	47	..	..	60	92	..	8
Guinea-Bissau	31	59	51	11	18	6	910	40	..	..	4	96	..	18
Haiti	92	105	95	38	24	4	..	43	18	57	10	57	..	..
Kiribati	..	..	..	..	..	..	..	..	..	..	..	..	..	..
Lao People's Dem. Rep.	50	90	72	44	..	6	650	..	..	..	..	81	..	..
Lesotho	130	118	122	115	21	5	..	37	38	24	39	59	..	6
Liberia	46	..	..	..	19	6	560	39	..	..	..	84	..	8
Madagascar	81	102	100	80	20	5	490	44	..	..	..	88	..	19
Malawi	61	102	59	42	18	7	620[d]	49	13	57	58	96	..	4
Maldives	100	97	..	..	19	5	350	35	43	44	7	28	..	6
Mali	69	69	56	24	16	7	580[b]	46	17	15	53	89	..	21
Mauritania	60	91	52	21	19	6	550	44	15	23	38	63	..	4
Mozambique	47	76	62	31	18	6	1 100[d]	49	..	..	82	96	..	..
Myanmar	90	99	96	156	22	2	230	43	..	..	..	78	..	..
Nepal	39	67	58	32	18	5	540	41	15	36	61	98	..	3
Niger	34	61	53	17	16	7	590[b]	44	8	17	24	97	..	10
Rwanda	81	101	78	22	21	6	..	56	15	33	53	98	..	5
Samoa	97	101	112	..	25	4	..	37	37	9	8	..	..	7
Sao Tome and Principe	..	..	..	..	18	5	..	..	32	26	54	..	..	..
Senegal	57	83	67	40	18	6	560	42	..	..	..	..	..	7
Sierra Leone	..	79	59	21	..	..	1800	36	20	24	72	81	..	10
Solomon Islands	..	85	66	..	21	5	550	50	20	39	..	85	..	6
Somalia	39	53	56	24	20	7	1600	43	..	..	..	88	..	..
Sudan	65	84	90	88	19	5	550	28	..	..	..	84	..	..
Togo	54	74	52	21	19	6	480	39	15	48	54	65	..	9
Tuvalu	..	..	..	..	..	..	..	..	..	..	..	..	..	..
Uganda	72	85	60	49	18	7	510	48	7	39	54	88	..	13
United Rep. of Tanzania	78	102	83	24	19	6	530[b]	49	..	..	88	91	..	13
Vanuatu	..	95	78	..	23	4	..	..	..	..	..	..	..	..
Yemen	36	40	26	14	18	8	350	28	8	13	69	88	..	..
Zambia	83	98	71	39	19	6	650[d]	45	16	55	54	83	..	3
All LDCs	68	83	66	36	19	5	..	43	..	..	..	83	..	9

Source: UNDP, *Human Development Report 2001*; United Nations, *The World's Women 2000: Trends and Statistics*; *Women's Indicators and Statistics* (Wistat); UNESCO, *Statistical Yearbook* 1999 and *World Culture Report 2001*; UNICEF, *The State of the World's Children 2001*; and estimates by the Bureau of Statistics of the ILO.

Note: Data for female legislators include senior officials and managers as percentage of total.

a Females as percentage of males. b Estimates. c Or latest year available. d UNICEF-WHO estimate based on statistical modelling.

16. Leading exports of all LDCs in 1999–2000

SITC	Item	Value[a] ($ millions)	As percentage of		
			LDCs	Developing countries	World
	All commodities	25 464.2	100.00	1.51	0.44
333	Petroleum oils, crude and crude oils obtained from bituminous minerals	7 528.1	29.56	3.27	2.50
842	Outer garments, men's, of textile fabrics	1 434.5	5.63	7.00	4.37
667	Pearls, precious and semi-precious stones unworked or worked	1 365.8	5.36	11.44	3.01
263	Cotton	1 166.9	4.58	24.33	14.83
845	Outergarments and other articles, knitted	1 112.8	4.37	4.23	2.65
844	Undergarments of textile fabrics	990.8	3.89	10.46	7.25
843	Outergarments, women's, of textile fabrics	944.3	3.71	3.59	2.17
071	Coffee and coffee substitutes	802.4	3.15	8.61	6.46
846	Undergarments knitted or crocheted	682.7	2.68	3.77	2.23
036	Crustaceans and molluscs, fresh, chilled, frozen, salted, in brine or dried	676.0	2.65	6.32	4.22
247	Other wood rough, squared	527.6	2.07	22.13	6.82
034	Fish, fresh, chilled, frozen	486.5	1.91	5.94	2.29
287	Ores and Concentrates of base metals, n.e.s	443.8	1.74	4.83	2.44
334	Petroleum products, refined	370.8	1.46	0.57	0.28
121	Tobacco, unmanufactd	359.1	1.41	10.35	5.97
682	Copper	299.4	1.18	2.52	1.02
057	Fruit and nuts (not including oil nuts), fresh or dried	261.4	1.03	2.27	0.96
222	Oil-seeds and oleaginous fruit, whole or broken excluding flours and meals	233.6	0.92	5.49	1.80
971	Gold, non-monetary	229.5	0.90	3.00	1.09
281	Iron ore and concentrates	215.9	0.85	5.38	2.54

Source: UNCTAD secretariat computations based on data from the United Nations Statistics Division.

a   Annual average 1999–2000.

17. MAIN MARKETS FOR EXPORTS OF LDCs: PERCENTAGE SHARES IN 2000 (OR LATEST YEAR AVAILABLE)

Country	Developed market economy countries					Countries in Eastern Europe	Developing countries			Other and unallocated
	Total	European Union	Japan	USA and Canada	Others		Total	OPEC	Other	
Afghanistan	32.9	29.6	0.3	2.4	0.5	9.7	57.4	4.5	52.9	0.0
Angola	68.9	18.6	0.0	49.9	0.3	0.0	26.3	0.0	26.3	4.8
Bangladesh	76.4	38.8	1.3	35.2	1.1	0.5	8.8	2.0	6.8	14.3
Benin	33.2	27.7	0.0	3.8	1.6	0.2	64.8	13.1	51.7	1.8
Bhutan	-	-	-	-	-	-	-	-	-	-
Burkina Faso	32.4	27.3	2.2	1.4	1.5	0.9	51.3	19.9	31.4	15.5
Burundi	74.1	50.7	0.9	8.3	14.1	0.0	5.5	0.1	5.4	20.4
Cambodia	54.7	12.2	2.2	39.8	0.4	0.0	29.6	0.1	29.6	15.7
Cape Verde	90.5	68.5	0.0	21.8	0.3	0.3	5.3	0.2	5.1	3.9
Central African Republic	79.7	77.7	0.3	1.5	0.2	0.6	16.5	4.4	12.1	3.1
Chad	65.1	57.9	1.0	6.1	0.1	6.4	18.3	6.1	12.1	10.2
Comoros	69.9	47.8	2.1	19.0	1.0	0.7	28.7	0.1	28.6	0.7
Dem. Republic of the Congo	94.5	75.1	1.5	17.4	0.5	0.2	5.2	0.1	5.1	0.1
Djibouti	9.3	9.0	0.0	0.3	0.0	0.4	90.2	5.1	85.1	0.0
Equatorial Guinea	73.0	55.3	4.2	13.0	0.5	0.0	26.9	0.0	26.9	0.0
Eritrea	-	-	-	-	-	-	-	-	-	-
Ethiopia	60.6	39.4	11.1	6.1	4.0	1.6	36.2	9.4	26.8	1.6
Gambia	71.8	53.8	14.9	2.9	0.2	1.8	26.4	1.2	25.2	0.1
Guinea	64.3	48.4	0.4	15.2	0.3	16.6	18.5	1.4	17.1	0.7
Guinea-Bissau	9.4	8.6	0.0	0.7	0.0	0.2	90.5	0.0	90.5	0.0
Haiti	98.6	5.5	0.2	92.4	0.5	0.1	1.2	0.6	0.6	0.0
Kiribati	67.5	2.1	57.9	6.3	1.2	8.8	23.7	0.0	23.7	0.0
Lao People's Dem. Rep.	43.6	34.9	3.7	3.3	1.6	1.0	26.9	0.0	26.9	28.4
Lesotho	-	-	-	-	-	-	-	-	-	-
Liberia	85.1	69.6	0.0	6.0	9.5	0.9	13.9	0.6	13.3	0.0
Madagascar	84.4	58.4	3.7	21.7	0.7	1.2	10.2	0.3	9.9	4.2
Malawi	72.4	31.4	7.4	12.6	21.0	13.3	11.0	1.0	10.0	3.3
Maldives	86.7	32.7	1.4	35.1	17.5	0.1	12.8	0.1	12.7	0.4
Mali	43.4	30.1	0.5	10.7	2.1	2.1	41.1	5.7	35.3	13.5
Mauritania	77.9	61.1	16.1	0.1	0.6	3.7	17.1	0.1	17.0	1.3
Mozambique	63.8	31.1	4.7	6.4	21.6	1.3	33.9	0.1	33.8	1.0
Myanmar	49.0	16.2	5.9	26.2	0.7	0.2	48.3	1.4	46.8	2.4
Nepal	61.2	23.0	3.1	33.7	1.4	0.2	37.0	0.0	37.0	1.6
Niger	57.3	50.3	1.9	4.7	0.4	0.0	42.7	35.4	7.3	0.1
Rwanda	46.0	38.2	0.4	5.1	2.3	2.3	17.4	0.3	17.1	34.3
Samoa	91.2	5.3	0.2	13.1	72.5	0.3	6.9	0.0	6.9	1.6
Sao Tome and Principe	93.4	69.5	3.3	8.1	12.5	1.0	5.5	0.0	5.5	0.0
Senegal	41.4	38.5	1.3	1.5	0.2	0.0	49.8	0.5	49.3	8.8
Sierra Leone	92.6	46.3	1.0	11.5	33.9	0.0	4.5	0.0	4.5	2.9
Solomon Islands	39.4	14.4	21.8	0.6	2.7	0.2	60.1	2.3	57.8	0.2
Somalia	1.3	0.7	0.2	0.3	0.1	0.0	98.6	58.8	39.9	0.0
Sudan	46.1	13.7	25.1	0.2	7.1	1.1	52.7	15.0	37.8	0.2
Togo	20.5	14.0	0.0	1.9	4.5	5.0	63.2	12.8	50.4	11.3
Tuvalu	35.3	26.9	0.0	0.0	8.4	11.8	52.9	33.6	19.3	0.0
Uganda	72.6	54.9	3.5	8.2	6.0	18.2	7.7	1.4	6.2	1.5
United Rep. of Tanzania	45.8	31.7	6.6	4.9	2.6	3.0	50.0	2.7	47.4	1.2
Vanuatu	79.1	28.5	31.4	17.4	1.7	0.2	17.0	0.0	17.0	3.8
Yemen	21.2	3.6	1.8	12.8	3.0	0.0	74.8	4.7	70.1	4.0
Zambia	49.9	29.2	11.9	2.6	6.2	0.5	44.5	6.6	37.9	5.1
All LDCs	62.5	30.7	3.4	26.0	2.4	1.3	29.8	2.7	27.1	6.3
All developing countries	70.2	29.2	10.0	28.2	2.8	1.1	26.3	2.9	23.4	2.3

Source: UNCTAD secretariat calculations based on data from IMF, *Direction of Trade Statistics,* CD-ROM.

18. Main sources of imports of LDCs: Percentage shares in 2000 (or latest year available)

Country	Developed market economy countries					Countries in Eastern Europe	Developing countries			Other and unallocated
	Total	European Union	Japan	USA and Canada	Others		Total	OPEC	Other	
Afghanistan	23.2	8.4	12.1	2.3	0.3	6.7	70.0	3.4	66.7	0.0
Angola	65.3	41.5	1.1	10.5	12.2	5.7	28.8	0.8	28.0	0.1
Bangladesh	27.3	9.9	9.3	3.8	4.3	0.8	50.7	7.3	43.5	21.2
Benin	48.0	43.1	1.4	2.7	0.8	4.4	47.2	2.2	45.0	0.4
Bhutan	-	-	-	-	-	-	-	-	-	-
Burkina Faso	31.7	27.8	1.3	2.3	0.3	2.1	61.7	27.5	34.1	4.6
Burundi	36.1	25.5	2.3	2.4	6.0	0.4	59.3	17.7	41.6	4.1
Cambodia	12.1	6.0	3.1	1.7	1.3	0.3	79.0	3.2	75.8	8.6
Cape Verde	84.6	80.2	0.0	2.6	1.8	1.2	8.8	0.1	8.7	5.4
Central African Republic	53.3	45.5	3.2	1.7	2.8	1.9	26.3	1.1	25.2	18.5
Chad	57.4	49.0	1.0	6.2	1.2	0.6	42.0	16.2	25.8	0.0
Comoros	68.4	44.5	0.6	1.5	21.8	0.2	30.2	8.5	21.7	1.2
Dem. Republic of the Congo	57.6	32.2	1.3	1.8	22.3	0.2	39.3	11.0	28.3	2.9
Djibouti	37.5	30.2	3.7	2.8	0.8	0.7	58.7	20.5	38.3	3.0
Equatorial Guinea	90.3	43.3	4.8	38.1	4.1	0.4	8.9	0.0	8.9	0.4
Eritrea										
Ethiopia	43.8	27.1	4.3	9.6	2.8	7.0	48.5	24.9	23.5	0.8
Gambia	53.0	45.4	2.6	3.6	1.5	1.0	45.1	3.5	41.6	0.8
Guinea	62.7	46.9	2.0	10.5	3.3	1.2	34.9	2.9	32.0	1.2
Guinea-Bissau	53.4	49.5	1.5	0.8	1.7	1.5	36.7	0.2	36.4	8.3
Haiti	72.6	9.8	2.9	58.9	1.0	0.3	25.5	2.1	23.4	1.6
Kiribati	53.2	4.2	10.6	7.4	30.9	16.8	28.8	0.2	28.7	1.1
Lao People's Dem. Republic	13.9	7.9	4.3	0.7	1.0	0.4	83.5	0.4	83.1	2.2
Lesotho	-	-	-	-	-	-	-	-	-	-
Liberia	60.8	40.3	15.8	1.0	3.8	2.8	36.3	0.1	36.2	0.1
Madagascar	61.4	50.5	3.0	2.6	5.3	0.3	31.9	2.1	29.7	6.5
Malawi	63.8	12.4	2.3	2.7	46.4	0.0	32.5	0.2	32.4	3.7
Maldives	16.0	9.7	1.4	2.0	2.8	0.1	83.6	33.2	50.4	0.3
Mali	31.4	26.1	0.6	3.1	1.6	0.3	61.1	0.8	60.3	7.1
Mauritania	61.3	55.3	2.6	2.8	0.6	6.1	24.1	13.0	11.1	8.5
Mozambique	48.2	13.0	2.3	5.2	27.7	0.0	11.2	1.5	9.7	40.6
Myanmar	15.8	4.9	8.8	0.8	1.3	0.5	78.7	9.4	69.3	5.0
Nepal	11.8	5.6	2.3	2.0	2.0	0.4	86.1	10.9	75.1	1.8
Niger	49.3	37.1	1.8	10.0	0.4	1.3	45.7	9.7	36.0	3.6
Rwanda	39.2	23.0	3.5	7.8	4.9	1.9	37.2	2.6	34.6	21.7
Samoa	79.4	0.7	9.0	26.9	42.9	0.3	18.1	0.3	17.8	2.2
Sao Tome and Principe	92.6	83.7	1.4	2.3	5.2	2.4	4.9	0.2	4.7	0.0
Senegal	61.0	51.1	2.3	5.8	1.9	2.9	35.7	9.0	26.6	0.4
Sierra Leone	53.6	44.4	1.2	5.2	2.8	28.7	14.6	4.0	10.6	3.1
Solomon Islands	46.6	5.1	6.3	4.8	30.5	0.0	50.9	2.0	48.9	2.5
Somalia	11.8	9.6	0.1	1.8	0.2	0.1	77.1	5.7	71.4	11.0
Sudan	45.7	34.4	2.4	2.5	6.4	3.9	49.8	13.0	36.8	0.7
Togo	32.9	27.9	2.0	1.7	1.2	0.5	65.7	3.8	61.9	0.9
Tuvalu	38.9	12.2	3.1	0.0	23.6	0.2	60.5	0.3	60.2	0.3
Uganda	38.5	23.0	3.2	3.4	8.9	3.8	56.9	2.9	54.0	0.8
United Republic of Tanzania	47.0	23.1	5.0	3.8	15.0	0.6	49.7	12.4	37.2	2.7
Vanuatu	48.9	7.2	3.8	1.4	36.5	0.5	32.6	0.4	32.2	18.0
Yemen	40.5	24.3	3.5	8.1	4.6	3.0	53.2	22.1	31.1	3.2
Zambia	70.7	14.6	2.2	2.7	51.2	0.2	25.4	0.4	25.0	3.7
All LDCs	42.1	24.5	5.6	5.4	6.7	2.1	48.6	7.6	41.0	7.2
All developing countries	54.8	18.8	12.9	19.1	4.0	2.1	40.2	5.6	34.6	2.9

Source: UNCTAD secretariat calculations based on data from IMF, *Direction of Trade Statistics,* CD-ROM.

19. COMPOSITION OF TOTAL FINANCIAL FLOWS TO ALL LDCs
IN CURRENT AND IN CONSTANT DOLLARS
(Net disbursements)

	Millions of current dollars						Millions of 1990 dollars[f]					
	1985	1990	1997	1998	1999	2000	1985	1990	1997	1998	1999	2000
Concessional loans & grants	9 493	16 752	13 036	12 806	12 325	12 476	12 328	16 752	12 534	12 314	11 627	11 769
Of which:												
DAC	8 754	16 166	12 926	12 701	12 153	12 277	11 370	16 166	12 429	12 213	11 465	11 582
Bilateral	5 484	9 889	7 638	7 633	7 244	7 734	7 123	9 889	7 345	7 340	6 834	7 296
Multilateral[a]	3 270	6 277	5 288	5 068	4 909	4 543	4 247	6 277	5 084	4 873	4 631	4 286
Grants	6 399	11 826	9 965	10 234	10 431	10 314	8 311	11 826	9 582	9 840	9 841	9 730
Loans	2 355	4 340	2 961	2 467	1 722	1 963	3 059	4 340	2 847	2 373	1 624	1 852
Technical assistance	2 221	3 375	3 112	2 778	2 614	2 706	2 885	3 375	2 992	2 671	2 466	2 553
Other[b]	6 533	12 791	9 814	9 923	9 539	9 571	8 485	12 791	9 437	9 542	8 999	9 029
OPEC	729	580	75	53	130	156	946	580	72	51	123	147
Bilateral	648	571	76	53	107	149	841	571	73	51	101	141
Multilateral[c]	81	9	-1	0	23	7	105	9	-1	0	22	6
Grants	434	520	10	25	55	78	564	520	9	24	52	74
Loans	295	60	65	28	75	78	382	60	63	27	71	73
Non-concessional flows	**435**	**742**	**1 617**	**2 486**	**2 433**	**759**	**565**	**743**	**1 555**	**2 390**	**2 295**	**716**
Of which:												
DAC	397	797	1 616	2 443	2 388	737	515	797	1 554	2 348	2 253	695
Bilateral official	497	689	281	37	208	-79	645	688	270	36	196	-75
Multilateral[a]	238	29	-63	-95	-2	-4	309	29	-60	-92	-2	-4
Export credits[d]	-324	-522	219	236	209	60	-421	-522	211	227	197	56
Direct investment	-64	307	1 223	1 139	1 903	-9	-83	307	1 176	1 095	1 796	-8
Other[e]	50	295	-44	1 126	70	769	65	295	-43	1 082	66	726
Total financial flows	**9 928**	**17 494**	**14 653**	**15 292**	**14 758**	**13 235**	**12 893**	**17 495**	**14 089**	**14 704**	**13 922**	**12 485**

Source: UNCTAD secretariat calculations based on OECD; *Geographical Distribution of Financial Flows to Aid Recipients, 1996-2000* and *International Development Statistics 2001* CD-ROM.

a From multilateral agencies mainly financed by DAC member countries.
b Grants (excluding technical assistance grants) and loans.
c From multilateral agencies mainly financed by OPEC member countries.
d Guaranteed private.
e Bilateral financial flows originating in DAC countries and their capital markets in the form of bond lending and bank lending (either directly or through syndicated "Eurocurrency credits"). Excludes flows that could not be allocated by recipient country.
f The deflator used is the unit value index of imports.

20. DISTRIBUTION OF FINANCIAL FLOWS TO LDCS AND TO ALL DEVELOPING COUNTRIES, BY TYPE OF FLOW
(Percentage)

	To least developed countries						To all developing countries					
	1985	*1990*	*1997*	*1998*	*1999*	*2000*	*1985*	*1990*	*1997*	*1998*	*1999*	*2000*
Concessional loans & grants	**95.6**	**95.8**	**89.0**	**83.7**	**83.5**	**94.3**	**69.8**	**69.2**	**20.8**	**21.1**	**20.0**	**26.9**
Of which:												
DAC	88.2	92.4	88.2	83.0	82.4	92.7	62.7	61.9	20.5	20.8	19.8	26.5
Bilateral	55.3	56.5	52.1	49.9	49.1	58.4	44.3	45.7	13.8	14.6	14.4	19.4
Multilateral[a]	32.9	35.9	36.1	33.1	33.3	34.3	18.4	16.2	6.7	6.2	5.4	7.1
Grants	64.5	67.6	68.0	66.9	70.6	77.9	44.8	46.3	16.6	16.6	16.0	22.0
Loans	23.7	24.8	20.2	16.1	11.7	14.8	17.9	15.6	3.9	4.2	3.8	4.5
Technical assistance	22.4	19.3	21.2	18.1	17.7	20.4	18.7	17.8	6.2	6.0	5.6	7.8
Other[b]	65.8	73.1	67.0	64.9	64.7	72.3	44.0	44.1	14.3	14.8	14.2	18.7
OPEC	7.3	3.3	0.5	0.3	0.9	1.2	7.2	7.2	0.2	0.2	0.1	0.2
Bilateral	6.5	3.2	0.5	0.3	0.7	1.1	6.9	7.1	0.2	0.2	0.1	0.2
Multilateral[c]	0.8	0.1	0.0	0.0	0.2	0.1	0.3	0.1	0.0	0.0	0.0	0.0
Grants	4.3	3.0	0.1	0.1	0.4	0.6	6.0	7.1	0.1	0.1	0.1	0.2
Loans	3.0	0.3	0.4	0.2	0.5	0.6	1.2	0.1	0.1	0.1	0.0	0.0
Non-concessional flows	**4.4**	**4.2**	**11.0**	**16.3**	**16.5**	**5.7**	**30.2**	**30.8**	**79.2**	**78.9**	**80.0**	**73.1**
Of which:												
DAC	4.0	4.6	11.0	16.0	16.2	5.6	31.2	30.5	79.0	78.2	79.7	72.3
Bilateral official	5.0	3.9	1.9	0.2	1.4	-0.6	8.2	9.8	2.8	5.3	6.3	-1.2
Multilateral[a]	2.4	0.2	-0.4	-0.6	0.0	0.0	17.8	12.4	4.8	6.7	5.2	4.5
Export credits[d]	-3.3	-3.0	1.5	1.5	1.4	0.5	2.2	-1.5	0.6	0.9	1.2	3.5
Direct investment	-0.6	1.8	8.3	7.4	12.9	-0.1	14.3	32.7	40.3	42.4	48.9	54.3
Other[e]	0.5	1.7	-0.3	7.5	0.5	5.8	-11.3	-22.9	30.5	22.9	18.1	11.2
Total financial flows	**100.0**	**100.0**	**100.0**	**100.0**	**100.0**	**100.0**	**100.0**	**100.0**	**100.0**	**100.0**	**100.0**	**100.0**

For source and note, see table 19.

21. SHARE OF LDCS IN FINANCIAL FLOWS TO ALL DEVELOPING COUNTRIES, BY TYPE OF FLOW
(Percentage)

	1985	1990	1997	1998	1999	2000
Concessional loans & grants	**31.4**	**29.7**	**27.1**	**25.5**	**23.8**	**24.8**
Of which:						
DAC	32.3	32.0	27.4	25.6	23.8	24.8
Bilateral	28.6	26.5	24.0	22.0	19.5	21.3
Multilateral[a]	41.1	47.5	34.5	34.3	35.3	34.4
Grants	33.0	31.3	26.1	25.9	25.2	25.1
Loans	30.5	34.2	32.9	24.6	17.6	23.5
Technical assistance	27.5	23.3	21.7	19.5	18.3	18.5
Other[b]	34.3	35.5	29.9	28.1	25.9	27.4
OPEC	23.5	9.8	14.7	12.7	49.1	33.0
Bilateral	21.8	9.8	13.9	12.3	46.2	34.0
Multilateral[c]	65.0	13.3	2.9	-	69.2	19.4
Grants	16.6	8.9	3.1	7.5	28.0	21.3
Loans	60.6	68.0	33.6	34.3	110.7	73.2
Non-concessional flows	**3.3**	**3.0**	**0.9**	**1.3**	**1.2**	**0.6**
Of which:						
DAC	2.9	3.2	0.9	1.3	1.2	0.5
Bilateral official	14.0	8.6	4.3	0.3	1.3	3.4
Multilateral[a]	3.1	0.3	-0.6	-0.6	0.0	-0.1
Export credits[d]	-34.2	43.3	17.2	10.6	7.0	0.9
Direct investment	-1.0	1.2	1.3	1.1	1.5	0.0
Other[e]	-1.0	-1.6	-0.1	2.1	0.1	3.7
Total financial flows	**22.9**	**21.4**	**6.4**	**6.4**	**5.7**	**7.1**

Note: No percentage is shown when either the net flow to all LDCs or the net flow to all developing countries in a particular year is negative.
For other notes and sources, see table 19.

22. Net ODA[a] from individual DAC member countries to LDCs as a group

Donor country[b]	% of GNI					Millions of dollars					% change from
	1990	1997	1998	1999	2000	1990	1997	1998	1999	2000	1990 to 2000
Denmark	0.37	0.29	0.33	0.35	0.34	462	496	563	549	537	16.2
Norway	0.52	0.34	0.34	0.26	0.27	532	525	497	455	424	-20.3
Luxembourg	0.08	0.17	0.19	0.19	0.25	10	30	32	33	45	350.0
Sweden	0.35	0.24	0.20	0.13	0.24	775	522	451	409	528	-31.9
Netherlands	0.30	0.22	0.22	0.13	0.21	834	820	822	632	793	-4.9
Ireland	0.06	0.15	0.14	0.12	0.14	21	90	91	92	113	438.1
Portugal	0.17	0.16	0.13	0.08	0.11	100	166	142	124	118	18.0
Switzerland	0.14	0.11	0.09	0.08	0.10	325	314	268	268	269	-17.2
United Kingdom	0.09	0.06	0.07	0.04	0.10	834	843	1 009	718	1 406	68.6
Belgium	0.19	0.08	0.11	0.06	0.09	367	217	256	177	213	-42.0
Finland	0.24	0.08	0.08	0.09	0.09	317	93	106	105	109	-65.6
France	0.19	0.11	0.08	0.05	0.09	2 286	1 540	1 156	1 132	1 141	-50.1
Germany	0.12	0.05	0.05	0.05	0.06	1 769	1 193	1 212	1 133	1 206	-31.8
New Zealand	0.04	0.06	0.06	0.05	0.06	18	36	28	32	27	50.0
Australia	0.06	0.05	0.04	0.04	0.06	171	197	159	172	211	23.4
Austria	0.07	0.05	0.04	0.02	0.05	110	96	89	74	102	-7.3
Total DAC	**0.09**	**0.05**	**0.05**	**0.04**	**0.05**	**15 199**	**11 405**	**11 181**	**11 122**	**12 211**	**-19.7**
Canada	0.13	0.08	0.06	0.03	0.04	740	489	354	328	307	-58.5
Japan	0.06	0.04	0.04	0.09	0.04	1 753	1 830	1 599	2 619	2 127	21.3
Italy	0.13	0.03	0.00	0.04	0.04	1 382	335	840	400	388	-71.9
Spain	0.04	0.04	0.02	0.02	0.03	194	202	129	187	142	-26.8
United States	0.04	0.02	0.02	0.02	0.02	2 199	1 362	1 371	1 479	1 987	-9.6
Greece	-	-	-	0.00	0.02	-	9	7	4	18	..

Source: UNCTAD secretariat calculations based on OECD, *Development Co-operation Report*, various issues, and *International Development Statistics 2001*, CD-ROM.

a Including imputed flows through multilateral channels.
b Ranked in descending order of the ODA/GNP ratio in 2000.

23. BILATERAL ODA FROM DAC MEMBER COUNTRIES AND TOTAL FINANCIAL FLOWS FROM MULTILATERAL AGENCIES[a] TO ALL LDCs

(Millions of dollars)

	Net disbursements						Commitments					
	1985	*1990*	*1997*	*1998*	*1999*	*2000*	*1985*	*1990*	*1997*	*1998*	*1999*	*2000*
A. Bilateral donors												
Australia	58.2	104.5	125.7	111.4	90.4	123.4	59.1	97.0	104.6	122.9	161.1	139.0
Austria	12.1	62.1	53.8	64.3	55.1	59.2	11.9	132.4	105.3	81.6	81.3	54.7
Belgium	179.1	273.5	167.9	192.7	130.2	147.5	83.5	273.5	176.3	198.7	136.0	152.6
Canada	329.7	391.6	276.1	220.2	208.8	194.4	352.1	353.9	293.7	266.6	205.5	263.3
Denmark	126.0	295.1	335.8	402.0	412.2	373.5	148.6	269.2	360.5	218.1	359.8	598.4
Finland	60.6	194.6	54.1	68.0	64.8	62.8	127.7	129.7	54.3	74.7	73.7	37.1
France	723.9	1 857.1	1 269.2	910.5	896.7	845.5	901.7	1 480.4	1 391.1	1 055.6	1 115.6	887.3
Germany	584.9	1 160.6	807.1	892	793.7	663.3	843.7	1 323.2	771.8	1 014.6	939.4	494.2
Greece	-	-	0.3	1.5	0.6	1.7	-	-	0.3	1.5	0.6	1.8
Ireland	10.4	13.9	80.2	82.1	82.4	96.7	10.4	13.9	80.2	82.1	82.4	96.7
Italy	420.1	968.8	247.7	481.0	171.9	240.1	530.7	846.0	217.4	432.0	145.3	269.0
Japan	562.9	1 067.2	1 012.8	1 163.5	1 158.8	1 290.2	633.2	1 144.7	1 435.8	1 226.2	1 384.5	1 237.5
Luxembourg	-	7.9	26.0	28.0	29.1	39.3	-	-	19.0	22.7	32.7	39.4
Netherlands	256.2	592.7	627.3	622.2	430.5	559.9	251.9	681.7	521.9	434.2	442.0	607.9
New Zealand	7	13.3	26.7	23.2	24.8	22.9	12.2	9.7	0	23.2	23.9	22.9
Norway	156.8	356.7	380.4	362.6	333.7	307.3	151.1	187.0	255.8	218.9	413.5	245.5
Portugal	-	99.6	159.1	130.4	120.5	95.2	-	-	108.4	131.8	196.8	240.4
Spain	-	96.7	150.2	70.1	107.2	66.1	-	-	137.4	106.3	107.2	90.9
Sweden	200.8	530.2	363.4	301.1	288.2	335.7	210.5	332.4	157.8	437.2	465.7	292.1
Switzerland	87.2	232.1	178.9	183.8	177.2	165.7	137.4	215.0	186.2	123.6	148.5	203.2
United Kingdom	281.5	472.9	558.8	686.9	628.2	998.9	232.3	480.0	565.1	752.5	616.8	1 010.3
United States	1 427.0	1 098.0	737.0	635.7	1 038.7	1 045.0	1 362.4	1 152.1	845.8	949.2	1 344.1	1 222.2
Total bilateral concessional	5 484.4	9 889.1	7 638.5	7 633.2	7 243.7	7 734.3	6 060.4	9 121.8	7 788.7	7 974.2	8 476.4	8 206.4
B. Multilateral donors												
1. Concessional												
AfDF	173.5	561.4	448.1	420.4	332.0	206.6	344.4	864.4	660.7	647.9	494.4	398.5
AsDB	229.6	448.1	329.2	401.2	349.4	388.4	383.7	536.4	556.3	437.3	470.3	589.5
CEC	554.8	1 168.3	1 332.8	1 447.4	1 273.3	996.2	579.0	790.8	1 100.9	2 558.2	2 264.2	2 021.7
IBRD	0.7	-	-	-	-	-	-	-	-	-	-	-
IDA	1 178.8	2 138.0	2 010.2	1 680.0	1 875.6	1 847.8	1 584.4	2 986.0	2 291.2	2 958.8	2 549.0	2 270.4
IDB	10.7	11.7	44.2	56.2	49.2	26.4	24.7	56.0	51.1	97.5	2.0	1.8
IFAD	108	120.5	44.8	71.9	53.5	78.6	83.2	72.1	117.8	152.5	201.2	152.1
IMF Trust fund	-108.8	-	-	-	-	-	-	-	-	-	-	-
IMF (SAF/ESAF)	-	297.8	106.0	126.4	47.8	-5.7	-	-	-	-	-	-
Others:	1 123.1	1 531.8	972.6	864.5	928.3	1 004.7	1 123.1	1 531.7	1 004.2	844.6	907.4	30.2
Of which:												
UNDP	276.2	366.6	338.5	301.8	263.3	186.8						
UNHCR	201.8	197.7	119.7	102.8	104.8	172.1						
UNICEF	126.6	232.7	164.7	150.0	160.6	170.6						
UNTA	62.0	59.0	97.0	63.6	103.0	113.4						
WFP	346.3	501.3	151.5	141.5	206.3	216.6						
Total	3 270.4	6 277.6	5 287.9	5 068.0	4 909.1	4 543.0	4 122.5	6 837.4	5 782.2	7 696.8	6 888.5	5 464.2
2. Non-concessional												
AfDB	142.9	106.9	-30.5	-108.3	-85.9	-100.1						
AsDB	-0.8	-0.5	4.1	14.7	18.2	10.2						
EC	20.0	-14.0	-2.8	-2.4	11.9	46.3						
IBRD	55.0	-82.0	-71.9	-57.9	-42.6	-26.2						
IFC	20.5	18.4	37.0	58.5	96.3	63.8						
Other	-	-	1.4	-	-	1.6						
Total	237.6	28.8	-62.7	-95.4	-2.1	-4.4						
Total concessional (A+B.1)	8 754.8	16 166.7	12 926.4	12 701.2	12 152.8	12 277.3						
Grand total	8 992.4	16 195.5	12 863.7	12 605.8	12 150.7	12 272.9	10 182.9	15 959.2	13 570.9	15 671.0	15 364.9	13 670.6

Source: UNCTAD secretariat calculations based on *International Development Statistics 2001*, CD-ROM.

a   Multilateral agencies mainly financed by DAC countries.

24. ODA TO LDCS FROM DAC MEMBER COUNTRIES AND MULTILATERAL AGENCIES MAINLY FINANCED BY THEM:
DISTRIBUTION BY DONOR AND SHARES ALLOCATED TO LDCS IN TOTAL ODA FLOWS TO ALL DEVELOPING COUNTRIES
(Percentage)

	Distribution by donor						Share of LDCs in ODA flows to all developing countries					
	1985	1990	1997	1998	1999	2000	1985	1990	1997	1998	1999	2000
Bilateral donors												
Australia	0.7	0.6	1.0	0.9	0.7	1.0	10.9	13.9	16.4	14.9	12.5	16.4
Austria	0.1	0.4	0.4	0.5	0.5	0.5	6.9	20.8	17.9	22.6	16.9	23.6
Belgium	2.0	1.7	1.3	1.5	1.1	1.2	65.1	49.9	39.0	36.1	30.3	31.3
Canada	3.7	2.4	2.2	1.7	1.7	1.7	33.1	23.2	22.0	18.2	18.0	16.9
Denmark	1.4	1.8	2.6	3.2	3.4	3.0	55.2	42.5	34.5	41.0	41.0	37.2
Finland	0.7	1.2	0.4	0.5	0.5	0.5	47.5	39.1	27.6	33.2	27.3	29.3
France	8.2	11.5	9.8	7.2	7.4	6.9	30.2	33.1	26.8	21.7	21.8	23.6
Germany	6.6	7.2	6.2	7.0	6.5	5.4	29.9	26.2	22.6	26.0	24.7	25.1
Greece	-	-	0.0	0.0	0.0	0.0	-	-	1.4	3.2	1.2	2.1
Ireland	0.1	0.1	0.6	0.6	0.7	0.8	60.5	60.7	69.3	69.1	57.1	64.0
Italy	4.8	6.0	1.9	3.8	1.4	2.0	53.9	46.3	58.8	70.5	46.1	65.6
Japan	6.4	6.6	7.9	9.2	9.5	10.5	22.0	15.7	15.5	13.6	11.1	13.5
Luxembourg	0.0	0.0	0.2	0.2	0.2	0.3	-	53.0	39.8	37.1	34.4	43.1
Netherlands	2.9	3.7	4.9	4.9	3.5	4.6	33.6	32.5	30.0	30.0	20.2	23.6
New Zealand	0.1	0.1	0.2	0.2	0.2	0.2	16.3	16.4	23.9	23.7	24.7	27.0
Norway	1.8	2.2	2.9	2.9	2.7	2.5	47.8	47.2	42.5	39.2	33.9	33.6
Portugal	-	0.6	1.2	1.0	1.0	0.8	-	96.4	97.5	73.9	58.2	53.4
Spain	-	0.6	1.2	0.6	0.9	0.5	-	15.3	19.7	8.4	13.1	9.2
Sweden	2.3	3.3	2.8	2.4	2.4	2.7	34.6	38.6	31.2	29.9	26.2	27.8
Switzerland	1.0	1.4	1.4	1.4	1.5	1.3	38.4	42.3	31.9	29.8	25.5	27.0
United Kingdom	3.2	2.9	4.3	5.4	5.2	8.1	33.9	32.1	28.9	33.1	29.0	37.6
United States	16.1	6.8	5.7	5.0	8.5	8.5	22.9	15.5	15.3	10.8	15.5	14.5
Total	62.1	61.1	59.1	60.1	59.5	63.0	28.6	26.5	24.0	22.0	19.5	21.3
Multilateral donors												
AfDF	2.0	3.5	3.5	3.3	2.7	1.7	82.6	93.1	76.0	73.0	72.4	68.8
AsDB	2.6	2.8	2.6	3.2	2.9	3.2	58.4	40.7	32.6	40.1	37.3	41.9
CEC	6.3	7.2	10.3	11.4	10.5	8.1	42.0	45.6	26.1	29.0	27.0	23.4
IBRD	-	-	-	-	-	-	2.1	-	-	-	-	-
IDA	13.3	13.2	15.6	13.2	15.4	15.0	45.4	54.7	38.7	35.3	42.7	45.2
IDB	0.1	0.1	0.3	0.4	0.4	0.2	3.0	7.6	15.2	17.1	22.0	17.3
IFAD	1.2	0.7	0.3	0.6	0.4	0.6	40.0	49.2	41.4	54.1	42.6	55.5
IMF	-1.2	1.8	0.8	1.0	0.4	0.0	36.5	92.7	59.6	70.0	26.6	5.1
UN	12.7	9.5	7.4	6.6	7.4	7.9	36.9	35.8	35.4	33.7	33.3	29.8
Other	0.9	0.1	0.1	0.2	0.4	0.3	51.7	8.4	11.3	7.3	21.6	16.8
Total	37.9	38.9	40.9	39.9	40.5	37.0	41.5	47.3	34.5	34.4	35.3	34.3
Grand total	100.0	100.0	100.0	100.0	100.0	100.0	32.4	32.0	27.4	25.6	23.8	24.8

Source: UNCTAD secretariat calculation based on OECD, *Geographical Distribution of Financial Flows to Aid Recipients, 1996–2000* and *International Development Statistics 2002, CD-ROM.*

25. TOTAL FINANCIAL FLOWS AND ODA FROM ALL SOURCES TO INDIVIDUAL LDCs
(Net disbursements in millions of dollars)

Country	Total financial flows						Of which: ODA					
	1985	1990	1997	1998	1999	2000	1985	1990	1997	1998	1999	2000
Afghanistan	-6	129	219	148	149	162	17	131	230	154	143	141
Angola	258	92	882	1 180	1 409	135	91	269	355	335	388	307
Bangladesh	1 107	2 167	1 058	1 425	1 191	1 223	1 131	2 095	1 011	1 263	1 215	1 172
Benin	97	243	270	173	225	226	95	268	221	211	211	239
Bhutan	24	50	104	53	65	51	24	47	69	56	67	53
Burkina Faso	190	347	388	392	435	343	195	331	368	400	398	336
Burundi	154	254	52	86	64	79	139	264	56	77	74	93
Cambodia	13	42	340	345	283	407	13	42	335	337	279	399
Cape Verde	71	107	144	162	179	119	70	108	111	130	137	94
Central African Rep.	112	254	99	118	158	51	104	250	91	120	117	76
Chad	179	315	265	235	207	-137	181	314	228	168	188	131
Comoros	51	45	27	100	139	-2	47	45	27	35	21	19
Dem. Rep. of the Congo	462	1 410	163	576	-336	198	306	897	158	126	132	184
Djibouti	103	192	109	100	271	91	81	194	85	81	75	71
Equatorial Guinea	28	62	26	34	9	22	17	61	24	25	20	21
Eritrea	0	0	117	167	149	184	0	0	123	167	149	176
Ethiopia	788	988	639	791	656	688	719	1 016	579	660	643	693
Gambia	48	108	39	37	33	45	50	99	39	39	33	49
Guinea	108	284	424	317	235	331	115	293	381	359	238	153
Guinea-Bissau	63	135	134	96	53	84	58	129	124	96	52	80
Haiti	142	154	273	348	262	176	150	168	325	407	263	208
Kiribati	12	20	16	17	28	18	12	20	16	17	21	18
Lao People's Dem. Rep.	64	150	388	294	304	286	37	150	329	283	295	281
Lesotho	118	148	136	14	18	15	93	142	92	66	31	42
Liberia	-294	519	-17	527	682	688	91	114	76	73	94	68
Madagascar	210	430	1 188	408	356	319	186	398	834	495	359	322
Malawi	118	518	367	460	437	427	113	503	343	434	446	445
Maldives	11	38	42	33	32	12	9	21	26	25	31	19
Mali	377	474	439	408	470	385	376	482	429	347	354	360
Mauritania	224	219	249	126	263	209	207	237	238	172	219	212
Mozambique	330	1 051	1 065	1 280	1 150	1 146	300	1 002	948	1 040	804	876
Myanmar	311	117	245	173	150	58	346	164	50	72	81	107
Nepal	244	429	474	444	370	409	234	426	402	408	351	390
Niger	285	382	304	245	189	185	303	396	333	292	187	211
Rwanda	184	286	229	352	375	319	180	291	230	350	373	322
Samoa	20	54	48	35	24	29	19	48	27	37	23	27
Sao Tome and Principe	12	54	34	27	28	36	12	55	33	28	28	35
Senegal	306	759	566	555	657	474	289	818	423	501	536	423
Sierra Leone	56	64	130	70	76	187	65	61	119	106	74	182
Solomon Islands	22	58	133	55	40	55	21	46	42	43	40	68
Somalia	380	488	81	84	120	103	353	494	81	80	115	104
Sudan	1 117	740	88	211	230	317	1 129	822	139	209	243	225
Togo	556	1 128	977	995	904	1 194	484	1 173	945	1 000	990	1 045
Tuvalu	91	257	116	268	-31	60	111	260	125	129	71	70
Uganda	3	5	-1	4	7	0	3	5	10	5	7	4
United Rep. of Tanzania	220	665	764	699	592	786	180	668	813	647	591	819
Vanuatu	39	149	-66	0	72	71	22	50	27	41	37	46
Yemen	397	331	318	294	770	290	392	405	356	311	458	265
Zambia	523	583	568	329	609	680	322	480	610	349	623	795
All LDCs	9 928	17 494	14 653	15 292	14 758	13 234	9 492	16 752	13 036	12 806	12 325	12 476
All developing countries	43 325	81 616	230 461	238 162	258 920	186 781	30 255	56 471	48 041	50 247	51 677	50 310
Memo items:												
In current dollars per capita:												
All LDCs	22	34	24	25	23	20	21	33	21	21	19	19
All developing countries	12	20	50	51	54	39	8	14	10	11	11	10
In constant 1990 dollars[a] (million):												
All LDCs	12 893	17 494	14 089	14 704	13 922	12 485	12 328	16 752	12 534	12 314	11 627	11 769
All developing countries	54 157	81 616	213 390	224 681	248 961	179 597	37 805	56 471	44 483	47 403	49 690	48 375
In constant 1990 dollars[a] per capita:												
All LDCs	28	34	23	24	22	19	27	33	21	20	18	18
All developing countries	15	20	46	48	52	37	10	14	10	10	10	10

Source: UNCTAD secretariat estimates based on OECD, *Geographical Distribution of Financial Flows to Aid Recipients, 1996-2000* and *International Development Statistics,* CD-ROM.

a The deflator used is the unit value index of imports.

26. ODA FROM DAC MEMBER COUNTRIES AND MULTILATERAL AGENCIES MAINLY FINANCED BY THEM, TO INDIVIDUAL LDCs

Country[a]	Average: 1980–1989						Average: 1990–2000					
	Per capita ODA $	Total ODA $ mill.	Of which: Technical assistance	Bilateral ODA	Of which: Grants	Multi-lateral ODA	Of which: Grants	Per capita ODA $	Total ODA $ mill.	Of which: Technical assistance	Bilateral ODA	Of which: Grants	Multi-lateral ODA	Of which: Grants
				As percentage of total ODA							As percentage of total ODA		
Bangladesh	13.6	1330.5	12.6	58.7	49.0	41.3	10.9	12.2	1447.1	17.4	50.8	53.6	49.2	12.4
Mozambique	30.7	406.3	15.0	76.7	61.1	23.3	15.8	61.1	1047.9	16.9	68.3	66.2	31.7	20.6
United Rep. of Tanzania	32.9	707.5	24.7	76.6	72.1	23.4	9.7	34.4	1021.0	20.6	67.4	69.3	32.6	10.9
Ethiopia	12.1	494.2	22.3	52.4	48.4	47.6	34.2	15.8	873.0	18.7	50.3	48.8	49.7	30.3
Zambia	51.4	327.5	27.7	79.3	58.8	20.7	9.9	99.9	819.0	15.9	54.2	56.1	45.8	9.4
Uganda	14.8	216.4	21.1	38.0	37.8	62.0	25.9	36.6	695.4	17.7	52.7	49.6	47.3	18.9
Senegal	66.0	416.2	28.0	67.7	49.4	32.3	11.8	68.5	573.0	28.0	69.5	75.3	30.5	13.0
Malawi	28.5	209.3	25.8	47.9	43.8	52.1	21.8	47.2	467.7	20.6	46.7	43.9	53.3	25.5
Mali	38.9	302.8	23.9	63.4	49.8	36.6	18.5	43.0	428.9	27.4	61.6	58.8	38.4	17.7
Madagascar	24.3	243.7	20.8	57.6	35.0	42.4	13.5	30.0	412.6	23.8	62.0	69.5	38.0	15.1
Rwanda	30.6	184.8	35.1	60.8	56.3	39.2	20.1	64.9	408.9	19.9	58.4	58.6	41.6	27.4
Nepal	16.6	271.2	27.1	53.4	50.1	46.6	13.4	19.1	407.9	31.1	60.3	55.7	39.7	11.4
Burkina Faso	29.3	229.1	35.6	70.6	62.6	29.4	17.3	38.6	403.3	26.5	61.4	61.0	38.6	22.0
Sudan	31.2	660.5	22.4	63.1	58.1	36.9	21.7	14.3	381.9	22.2	48.8	50.6	51.2	38.5
Angola	12.9	102.2	27.8	67.5	51.0	32.5	31.0	32.2	354.3	18.6	59.3	50.5	40.7	33.9
Guinea	30.2	149.6	17.4	52.6	31.3	47.4	17.3	48.1	330.3	19.2	48.2	45.6	51.8	21.6
Haiti	24.5	149.0	28.8	65.6	58.2	34.4	12.4	41.7	315.5	25.4	69.9	70.2	30.1	15.9
Niger	37.7	245.7	30.9	65.4	58.9	34.6	17.2	33.5	307.1	29.9	65.3	69.1	34.7	20.9
Somalia	58.4	386.0	30.9	58.5	50.5	41.5	29.0	35.2	301.1	14.5	72.1	72.6	27.9	26.3
Cambodia	8.2	59.7	58.3	24.4	24.4	75.6	75.6	30.1	299.4	34.9	61.3	62.2	38.7	23.3
Yemen	24.0	229.6	35.8	50.7	44.4	49.3	19.2	18.7	279.3	25.4	56.9	51.8	43.1	13.1
Dem.Rep.of the Congo	14.2	444.4	32.2	65.9	45.0	34.1	11.1	5.9	266.7	25.7	65.9	64.8	34.1	25.6
Benin	29.9	118.9	28.9	54.0	47.7	46.0	20.6	47.3	253.5	24.2	60.6	58.7	39.4	16.1
Lao People's Dem. Rep.	14.9	53.4	32.2	42.3	45.2	57.7	28.1	51.3	245.4	24.1	54.2	55.2	45.8	10.5
Mauritania	86.3	151.1	25.6	59.7	52.6	40.3	19.6	102.3	239.1	18.5	46.1	42.9	53.9	31.2
Chad	28.4	143.2	23.2	55.2	51.1	44.8	34.7	33.6	224.7	23.9	50.8	49.9	49.2	20.3
Burundi	32.3	151.8	31.8	50.5	42.2	49.5	19.5	30.8	188.6	22.1	48.9	50.0	51.1	33.4
Afghanistan	2.5	37.7	70.5	53.2	71.5	46.8	47.1	9.4	179.4	31.0	59.0	59.8	41.0	41.0
Central African Rep.	51.3	132.5	30.1	61.3	50.9	38.7	17.6	46.2	151.6	27.5	59.3	63.3	40.7	22.6
Togo	41.3	123.5	29.2	57.3	53.2	42.7	14.5	36.9	149.9	23.9	61.3	60.1	38.7	14.7
Sierra Leone	20.9	74.4	33.0	61.1	50.1	38.9	24.0	34.7	149.4	15.6	44.9	41.6	55.1	21.6
Eritrea	-	-	-	-	-	-	-	40.1	131.3	24.2	70.1	67.4	29.9	20.0
Cape Verde	235.0	72.6	26.7	69.5	68.6	30.5	23.1	302.9	115.7	30.2	67.8	64.4	32.2	17.9
Guinea-Bissau	83.9	73.2	26.2	55.0	54.4	45.0	21.8	104.4	113.7	29.1	61.8	50.7	38.2	19.6
Myanmar	8.6	319.4	13.4	69.9	27.0	30.1	7.1	2.5	107.6	33.7	69.9	72.3	30.1	27.5
Liberia	42.9	94.0	31.3	74.4	56.3	25.6	11.4	43.2	106.8	16.3	39.1	35.8	60.9	58.3
Lesotho	68.0	102.7	36.5	61.1	60.2	38.9	22.6	52.1	100.7	31.1	52.6	50.4	47.4	27.3
Djibouti	175.7	67.2	49.7	75.6	74.1	24.4	14.2	162.3	95.8	40.2	78.2	73.8	21.8	13.0
Gambia	90.9	67.7	29.2	53.9	52.4	46.1	24.1	58.3	64.8	29.8	49.3	50.5	50.7	24.2
Bhutan	15.5	22.9	45.2	37.4	38.2	62.6	48.8	33.0	62.0	37.7	67.9	66.0	32.1	23.3
Sao Tome and Principe	147.8	15.5	21.6	38.4	34.6	61.6	35.7	353.0	46.8	29.1	58.7	51.5	41.3	17.0
Solomon Islands	135.7	36.2	35.5	65.5	59.0	34.5	19.6	121.2	46.1	44.7	67.7	63.6	32.3	22.2
Vanuatu	250.1	32.8	50.6	82.4	81.3	17.6	14.7	239.8	40.6	55.6	78.3	77.9	21.7	9.9
Samoa	161.6	25.4	37.3	65.6	65.5	34.4	21.7	239.7	40.4	42.8	69.8	69.7	30.2	12.6
Comoros	87.9	39.5	31.7	54.8	48.0	45.2	27.4	64.0	38.9	36.5	54.3	56.7	45.7	31.9
Equatorial Guinea	87.5	25.5	25.5	52.4	43.4	47.6	26.6	94.6	37.9	42.3	65.5	65.4	34.5	22.4
Maldives	74.6	13.6	36.7	64.9	65.7	35.1	22.7	122.7	30.7	26.9	58.8	56.9	41.2	14.7
Kiribati	235.7	15.6	37.6	87.3	87.3	12.7	11.8	231.1	18.0	46.4	84.4	84.4	15.6	14.3
Tuvalu	1003.3	8.0	24.3	92.4	92.4	7.6	7.4	654.2	6.7	48.0	84.4	84.4	15.6	11.0
All LDCs	21.8	9784.6	25.0	62.1	51.9	37.9	17.8	25.4	14791.5	22.4	58.6	58.3	41.4	20.0
All developing countries	8.3	30430.2	29.9	70.9	53.5	29.1	15.1	11.9	53188.9	29.2	70.5	61.8	29.5	16.0

Source: UNCTAD secretariat estimates, mainly based on data from the OECD/DAC secretariat.
a   Ranked in descending order of total ODA received in 1990–2000.

27. EXTERNAL DEBT (AT YEAR END) AND DEBT SERVICE, BY SOURCE OF LENDING
($ millions)

	External debt (at year end)					% of total		Debt service[a]					% of total	
	1985	1990	1997	1998	1999	1985	1999	1985	1990	1996	1997	1998	1985	1998
I. Long-term	**68 426**	**111 234**	**128 460**	**133 626**	**133 056**	**91.3**	**94.8**	**4292**	**4495**	**4470**	**4247**	**4017**	**90.1**	**90.7**
A. Concessional	39 179	59 016	81 285	86 116	82 690	52.3	59.0	1037	1536	2137	2018	2105	21.8	47.5
(a) OECD countries	10 168	18 899	17 711	16 820	16 370	13.5	11.7	270	495	557	460	474	5.7	10.7
(b) Other countries	14 951	8 031	10 580	11 067	6 574	20.0	4.7	346	421	216	178	208	7.3	4.7
(c) Multilateral agencies	14 060	32 086	52 994	58 229	59 746	18.8	42.6	421	620	1364	1380	1423	8.8	32.1
B. Non-concessional	29 247	52 218	47 175	47 510	50 366	39.0	35.8	3255	2959	2333	2229	1912	68.3	43.2
(a) OECD countries	13 952	15 360	19 986	20 807	20 511	18.6	14.6	1976	1379	1558	1518	1253	41.5	28.3
(i) official/officially guaranteed	10 495	13 498	17 034	17 274	16 975	14.0	12.1	1473	892	1300	1333	928	30.9	21.0
(ii) financial markets	3 457	1 862	2 952	3 533	3 536	4.6	2.5	503	487	258	185	325	10.6	7.3
(b) Other countries	8 484	29 463	22 313	22 396	25 880	11.3	18.4	201	245	236	178	120	4.2	2.7
(c) Multilateral agencies	6 811	7 395	4 876	4 307	3 975	9.1	2.8	1078	1335	539	533	539	22.6	12.2
II. Short-term	**6 498**	**11 637**	**7 324**	**8 589**	**7 267**	**8.7**	**5.2**	**471**	**443**	**318**	**355**	**412**	**9.9**	**9.3**
Total	74 924	122 871	135 784	142 215	140 323	100.0	100.0	4 763	4 938	4 788	4 602	4 429	100.0	100.0
Of which: use of IMF credit	5 284	5 378	6 142	6 496	6 319	7.1	4.5	904	910	496	526	554	19.0	12.5

Source: UNCTAD secretariat calculations, based on information from the OECD secretariat.

Note: Figures for total debt and total debt service cover both long-term and short-term debt as well as the use of IMF credit.

a Data are not available for 1999.

28. TOTAL EXTERNAL DEBT AND DEBT SERVICE PAYMENTS OF INDIVIDUAL LDCs
($ millions)

Country	Debt (at year end)					Debt service[a]				
	1985	1990	1997	1998	1999	1985	1990	1996	1997	1998
Afghanistan	2 275	5 086	5 584	5 587	5 546	47	115	3	4	3
Angola	3 045	8 348	7 488	8 361	8 314	372	328	684	703	588
Bangladesh	6 831	12 299	14 794	16 150	17 315	396	634	819	782	726
Benin	774	1 394	1 745	1 667	1 701	38	48	50	54	54
Bhutan	9	82	140	124	125	0	6	18	19	13
Burkina Faso	574	1 094	1 540	1 468	1 539	32	36	61	54	56
Burundi	476	1 017	1 155	1 165	1 115	26	54	32	32	34
Cambodia	715	1 733	2 120	2 197	2 043	14	37	37	12	17
Cape Verde	108	139	210	255	366	6	7	10	15	17
Central African Republic	354	861	923	840	855	30	36	17	17	40
Chad	172	593	1 063	1 056	1 092	15	15	28	33	36
Comoros	135	211	229	212	199	2	3	3	4	7
Dem. Republic of the Congo	5 795	10 318	10 864	11 614	9 094	654	555	138	88	124
Djibouti	305	210	315	340	350	40	28	14	13	10
Equatorial Guinea	111	196	250	238	226	12	7	6	8	8
Eritrea	..	..	76	161	220	-	-	-	-	4
Ethiopia	4 135	8 441	9 454	9 515	9 205	153	189	355	106	112
Gambia	241	390	485	527	514	13	35	27	29	28
Guinea	1 355	2 596	3 341	3 418	3 259	82	174	118	153	148
Guinea-Bissau	380	626	810	871	822	17	8	23	13	7
Haiti	732	873	1 089	1 155	1 204	45	34	34	38	54
Kiribati	..	..	..	..	..	..	..	..	..	..
Lao People's Dem. Republic	1 142	1 755	2 433	2 545	2 655	14	10	27	31	36
Lesotho	169	469	1 099	988	999	22	29	85	93	122
Liberia	1 400	1 731	1 727	1 635	1 507	87	71	56	245	30
Madagascar	2 139	3 538	3 920	3 926	3 977	145	265	106	215	153
Malawi	1 034	1 557	2 322	2 570	2 594	120	116	98	94	108
Maldives	59	74	202	194	206	12	10	13	30	16
Mali	1 463	2 548	3 273	3 036	3 109	56	80	117	81	95
Mauritania	1 469	2 041	2 333	2 374	2 285	115	151	126	112	106
Mozambique	2 276	4 168	5 937	6 244	7 001	184	125	146	120	123
Myanmar	3 716	4 638	5 175	6 159	5 761	274	105	195	164	202
Nepal	631	1 687	2 472	2 716	3 057	24	75	86	82	82
Niger	1 239	1 796	1 665	1 607	1 497	124	136	45	51	53
Rwanda	374	806	1 142	1 224	1 275	27	32	21	25	24
Samoa	74	93	169	189	193	7	6	6	6	7
Sao Tome and Principe	86	128	252	271	253	4	2	4	4	5
Senegal	2 467	4 362	3 893	3 833	4 286	176	391	243	231	267
Sierra Leone	632	657	1 013	1 061	1 067	43	28	17	17	37
Solomon Islands	294	135	164	211	182	16	12	10	6	13
Somalia	1 884	2 165	2 169	2 275	2 005	56	35	7	3	9
Sudan	8 346	11 139	9 490	10 392	9 288	281	25	48	57	61
Togo	984	1 460	1 351	1 610	1 605	78	124	57	55	46
Tuvalu	..	..	..	..	..	..	..	..	..	..
Uganda	1 156	2 406	3 513	3 632	3 622	150	121	143	169	165
United Republic of Tanzania	3 393	5 420	6 069	6 000	6 043	112	177	278	220	269
Vanuatu	128	353	91	108	119	17	26	32	3	4
Yemen	5 315	5 776	3 824	4 090	4 480	406	191	123	108	148
Zambia	4 532	5 462	6 411	6 404	6 153	219	246	222	203	162
Total LDCs	74 924	122 871	135 784	142 215	140 323	4 763	4 938	4 788	4 602	4 429

Source: UNCTAD secretariat calculations, based on information from the OECD secretariat.

Note: Figures for total debt and total debt service cover both long-term and short-term debt as well as the use of IMF credit.
     a   Data are not available for 1999.

29. DEBT AND DEBT SERVICE RATIOS
(Percentage)

Country	Debt/GDP					Debt service/exports[a]				
	1985	1990	1997	1998	1999	1985	1990	1996	1997	1998
Afghanistan	..	..	..	..	..	..	..	..	..	..
Angola	45	81	97	130	97	15	8	..	..	16
Bangladesh	32	41	35	37	38	34	34	18	15	12
Benin	74	76	82	72	72	15	18	14	16	14
Bhutan	5	29	35	31	28	..	8	16	15	10
Burkina Faso	40	40	65	57	60	21	10	22	20	16
Burundi	41	90	121	133	156	20	61	63	33	48
Cambodia	..	155	69	77	66	..	54	5	1	2
Cape Verde	..	41	42	47	63	..	16	9	11	14
Central African Republic	41	58	93	80	81	17	16	9	9	24
Chad	17	34	70	63	71	12	6	10	12	11
Comoros	118	84	118	108	103	11	8	7	11	14
Dem. Rep. of the Congo	81	110	188	208	..	33	20	8	6	..
Djibouti	89	49	63	66	..	..	..	7	6	..
Equatorial Guinea	139	148	50	52	32	50	17	3	2	2
Eritrea	..	..	12	24	34	-	-	-	-	4
Ethiopia	62	123	148	145	143	28	35	45	10	11
Gambia	107	123	118	126	131	13	18	15	16	13
Guinea	..	92	88	95	94	..	20	16	20	18
Guinea-Bissau	264	257	301	423	377	121	33	82	23	23
Haiti	36	29	39	30	28	14	7	13	16	12
Kiribati	..	..	..	..	..	..	..	..	..	..
Lao People's Dem. Rep.	48	203	141	202	185	15	10	6	7	8
Lesotho	58	75	107	113	114	54	28	37	33	51
Liberia	128	..	..	..	..	19	..	..	..	..
Madagascar	75	115	111	105	107	41	52	13	28	19
Malawi	91	86	92	148	143	44	26	19	16	19
Maldives	69	51	59	53	..	53	18	..	..	..
Mali	111	105	132	117	121	25	19	22	13	15
Mauritania	215	200	213	237	239	28	32	25	26	27
Mozambique	51	166	169	160	176	145	61	42	31	30
Myanmar	..	..	..	..	..	..	..	..	..	..
Nepal	24	46	50	56	61	8	20	9	6	7
Niger	86	72	90	77	74	42	37	13	17	14
Rwanda	22	31	61	60	65	14	22	25	17	22
Samoa	84	64	88	108	109	28	13	..	..	..
Sao Tome and Principe	165	221	573	661	538	44	25	36	33	42
Senegal	96	77	89	82	90	24	13	10	15	39
Sierra Leone	53	73	119	158	159	24	13	10	15	39
Solomon Islands	184	64	44	70	60	19	12	..	..	..
Somalia	215	236	..	..	..	102	39	..	..	..
Sudan	67	85	92	104	96	39	..	..	..	..
Togo	129	90	90	114	114	21	23	13	11	10
Tuvalu	..	..	..	..	..	..	..	..	..	..
Uganda	33	56	56	54	56	31	39	20	20	24
United Rep. of Tanzania	..	127	79	70	69	..	33	21	18	24
Vanuatu	108	231	36	44	48	28	37	..	..	..
Yemen	..	124	58	65	66	..	25	6	4	9
Zambia	201	166	164	198	195	27	21	22	17	19
All LDCs	64	86	84	87	81	27	22	16	14	15

Source: UNCTAD secretariat, mainly based on information from the OECD secretariat, the World Bank and the IMF.

Note: Debt and debt service are defined as in table 27.

a Exports of goods and services (including non-factor services); data are not available for debt service in 1999.

30. LDCs' DEBT RESCHEDULINGS WITH OFFICIAL CREDITORS, 1990–2001

Country		Date of meeting	Cut-off date	Consolidation period (months)	Percentage of principal and interest consolidated[a]	Terms	Arrears	Rescheduling of previously rescheduled debt	Goodwill clause	Estimated amounts rescheduled ($ million)
Benin	II	Dec. 1991	31/3/89	15	100	London terms	Yes	Yes	Yes	160
	III	June 1993	31/3/89	29	100	London terms	Yes	No	Yes	25
	IV[b]	Oct. 1996	31/3/89	-	-	Naples terms (67%)[c]	Yes	Yes	No	209
	V	Oct. 2000	31/3/89	12	100	Cologne terms	No	Yes	Yes	5
Burkina Faso	I	Mar. 1991	1/1/91	15	100	Toronto terms	Yes	No	Yes	63
	II	May 1993	1/1/91	32	100	London terms	Yes	No	No	36
	III[b]	June 1996	1/1/91	-	-	Naples terms (67%)[c]	No	Yes	Yes	64
	IV	Oct. 2000	1/1/91	12	100	Cologne terms	No	Yes	Yes	1
Cambodia	III[b]	Jan. 1995[d]	31/12/85	30	100	Naples terms (67%)	No	Yes	No	249
Central African Republic	V	June 1990	1/1/83	12	100	Toronto terms	No	Yes	No	4
	VI	Apr. 1994	1/1/83	12	100	London terms	Yes	Yes	Yes	33
	VII[b]	Sep 1998	1/1/83	34	100	Naples terms (67%)	Yes	Yes	Yes	26
Chad	II[b]	Feb. 1995[d]	30/6/89	..	100	Naples terms (67%)	..	..	No	24
	III[b]	June 1996[d]	30/6/89	32	100	Naples terms (67%)	Yes	Yes	Yes	..
	IV	June 2001	30/6/89	23	100	Cologne terms	No	Yes	Yes	15
Djibouti	I	May 2000	31/3/98	32	100	Non-concessional	Yes	-	Yes	16
Equatorial Guinea	III	Apr. 1992[d]	..	..	..	London terms	Yes	Yes	Yes	32
	IV	Feb. 1994[d]	..	..	..	London terms	Yes	-	Yes	51
Ethiopia	I	Dec. 1992	31/12/89	37	100	London terms	Yes	No	Yes	441
	II[b]	Jan. 1997	31/12/89	34	100	Naples terms (67%)	Yes	Yes	Yes	184
	III[b]	Apr. 2001	31/12/89	37	100	Naple terms (67%)	Yes	-	Yes	430
Guinea	III	Nov. 1992	1/1/86	..	100	London terms	Yes	Yes	Yes	203
	IV[b]	Jan. 1995	1/1/86	12	100	Naples terms (50%)	Yes	Yes	Yes	156
	V[b]	Feb. 1997	1/1/86	36	100	Naples terms (50%)	Yes	Yes	..	..
	VI	May 2001	1/1/86	40	100	Cologne terms	Yes	Yes	Yes	151
Guinea-Bissau	III[b]	Feb. 1995	31/12/86	36	100	Naples terms (67%)	No	No	Yes	195
	IV	Jan. 2001	31/12/86	37	100	Cologne terms	Yes	Yes	Yes	141
Haiti	I[b]	May 1995	1/10/93	13	100	Naples terms (67%)	No	No	Yes	117
Madagascar	VII	July 1990	1/7/83	13	100	Toronto terms	Yes	Yes	Yes	139
	VIII[b]	Mar. 1997	1/7/83	35	100	Naples terms (67%)	No	Yes	Yes	247
	IX	Mar. 2001	1/7/83	39	100	Cologne terms	Yes	Yes	Yes	254
Malawi	IV	Jan. 2001	1/1/97	37	100	Cologne terms	Yes	No	Yes	..
Mali	III	Oct. 1992	1/1/88	35	100	London terms	Yes	Yes	Yes	20
	IV[b]	May 1996	1/1/88	-	-	Naples terms (67%)[c]	Yes	Yes	No	33
	V	Oct. 2000	1/1/88	10	100	Cologne terms	No	No	Yes	4
Mauritania	V	Jan. 1993	31/12/84	24	100	London terms	No	Yes	Yes	218
	VI[b]	June 1995	31/12/84	36	100	Naples terms (67%)	Yes	Yes	Yes	66
	VII	Mar. 2000	31/12/84	36	100	Cologne terms	Yes	Yes	Yes	80
Mozambique	III	June 1990	1/2/84	30	100	Toronto terms	Yes	Yes	Yes	719
	IV	Mar. 1993	1/2/84	24	100	London terms	Yes	Yes	Yes	440
	V[b]	Nov. 1996	1/2/84	32	100	Naples terms (67%)	Yes	Yes	Yes	664
	VI[e]	May 1998	1/2/84	32	100	Lyon terms	Yes	Yes	Yes	n.a.
	VII	July 1999	1/2/84	-	100	90% NPV reduction	yes	yes	yes	1860

Table 30 (cont.)

Country		Date of meeting	Cut-off date	Consolidation period (months)	Percentage of principal and interest consolidated[a]	Terms	Arrears	Rescheduling of previously rescheduled debt	Goodwill clause	Estimated amounts rescheduled ($ million)
Niger	VII	Sep. 1990	1/7/83	28	100	Toronto terms	Yes	Yes	Yes	116
	VIII	Mar. 1994	1/7/83	15	100	London terms	Yes	Yes	Yes	160
	IX[b]	Dec. 1996	1/7/83	31	100	Naples terms (67%)	Yes	Yes	Yes	128
	X	Jan. 2001	1/7/83	37	100	Cologne terms	Yes	Yes	Yes	115
Rwanda	I[b]	July 1998	31/12/94	35	100	Naples terms (67%)	Yes	-	Yes	64
Sao Tome & Principe	I[b]	May 2000	1/4/99	37	100	Naples terms (67%)	Yes	-	Yes	26
Senegal	VIII	Feb. 1990	1/1/83	12	100	Toronto terms	Yes	Yes	Yes	107
	IX	June 1991	1/1/83	12	100	Toronto terms	Yes	Yes	No	114
	X	Mar. 1994	1/1/83	15	100	London terms	Yes	Yes	Yes	237
	XI[b]	Apr. 1995	1/1/83	29	100	Naples terms (67%)	Yes	Yes	Yes	169
	XII[b]	June 1998	..	-	100	Naples terms (67%)[c]	Yes	Yes	No	428
	XIII	Oct. 2000	1/1/83	18	100	Cologne terms	No	Yes	Yes	21
Sierra Leone	V	Nov. 1992	1/7/83	16	100	London terms	Yes	Yes	Yes	164
	VI	July 1994	1/7/83	17	100	London terms	Yes	Yes	Yes	42
	VII[b]	Mar. 1996	1/7/83	24	100	Naples terms (67%)	No	Yes	Yes	39
	VIII[b]	Oct. 2000	1/7/83	36	100	Naples terms (67%)	Yes	Yes	No	180
Togo	VIII	July 1990	1/1/83	24	100	Toronto terms	No	Yes	No	88
	IX	June 1992	1/1/83	24	100	London terms	No	Yes	Yes	52
	X[b]	Feb. 1995	1/1/83	33	100	Naples terms (67%)	No	Yes	Yes	239
Uganda	V	June 1992	1/7/81	18	100	London terms	Yes	Yes	Yes	39
	VI[b]	Feb. 1995[d]	-	-	-	Naples terms (67%)[c]	No	Yes	No	110
	VII	Apr. 1998	1/7/81	-	-	Lyon terms (80%)[f]	No	Yes	No	110
	VIII	Sep. 2000	1/7/81	-	100[g]	Cologne terms[c]	-	-	-	145
United Rep. of Tanzania	III	Mar. 1990	30/6/86	12	100	Toronto terms	Yes	Yes	Yes	200
	IV	Jan. 1992	30/6/86	30	100	London terms	Yes	Yes	Yes	691
	V[b]	Jan. 1997	30/6/86	36	100	Naples terms (67%)	Yes	Yes	Yes	608
	VI	Apr. 2000	30/6/86	36	100	Cologne terms	Yes	Yes	Yes	390
Yemen	I[b]	Sep. 1996	1/1/93	10	100	Naples terms (67%)	Yes	..	Yes	113
	II[b]	Nov. 1997	1/1/93	36	100	Naples terms (67%)	Yes	No	No	..
	III[b]	June 2001	1/1/93	-	-	Naples terms (67%)[c]	-	No	No	420
Zambia	IV	July 1990	1/1/83	18	100	Toronto terms	Yes	Yes	Yes	963
	V	July 1992	1/1/83	33	100	London terms	Yes	Yes	Yes	917
	VI[b]	Feb. 1996	1/1/83	36	100	Naples terms (67%)	Yes	Yes	Yes	566
	VII[b]	Apr. 1999	1/1/83	36	100	Naples terms (67%)	Yes	Yes	Yes	1063

Source: Paris Club Agreed Minutes.
Note: Roman numerals indicate the number of debt reschedulings for the country since 1976.
a   Terms of current maturities.
b   Naples terms; number in brackets indicates the percentage of reduction applied.
c   Stock reduction.
d   Dates of informal meeting of creditors on the terms to be applied in the bilateral agreements, as creditors did not call for a full Paris Club meeting.
e   Amendment to the November 1996 agreement.
f   Additional stock reduction ("Topping up") on previously rescheduled debt.
g   In addition to pre cut-off date debts, part of post cut-off date debt was also cancelled.

31. ARRANGEMENTS IN SUPPORT OF STRUCTURAL ADJUSTMENT IN LDCs
(As of December 2000)
Millions of SDRs (except where otherwise indicated)

Country	IMF — Stand-by/Extended Facility — Period	Amount	SAF/ESAF/PRGF — Period	Amount	Structural adjustment — Date of approval	IDA	African Facility[1]	Co-financing[2]	Sector and other adjustment — Date of approval	IDA	African Facility[1]	Co-financing[2]	Purpose
Bangladesh	July 1979 - July 1980	85.0	Feb. 1987 - Feb. 1990	201.3					June 1987	147.8			Industrial policy reform
	Dec. 1980 - Dec. 1983[3]	800.0[4]	Aug. 1990 - Sep. 1993	345[5]					Apr. 1989	137.0			Energy sector
	March 1983 - Aug. 1983	68.4							Oct. 1989	1.8[6]			
	Dec. 1985 - June 1987	180.0							June 1990	132.7		Germany (DM 26m)	Financial sector
									Nov. 1990	2.5[6]			"
									Nov. 1991	2.2[6]			"
									May 1992	109.3		USAID (18.2)	Public resource management
									Oct. 1992	72.2			Industry
									Dec. 1992	2.5[6]			"
									Feb. 1994	175.0			Jute sector
									May 1994	2.4[6]			"
									Dec. 1994	2.3[70]			"
									Dec. 1995	2.3[70]			"
									Nov. 1996	2.0			"
Benin			June 1989 - June 1992	21.9[7]	May 1989	33.5			Nov. 1993	3.7		DANIDA (4); ACBF (2)	Economic management
			Jan. 1993 - May 1996	51.9[5]	June 1991	41.3							
					May 1995	25.8							
Burkina Faso			Aug. 1996 - Jan. 2000	27.2[71]	June 1991	60.0		EC (30); AfDB (20); France (17); Canada (13); Germany (12)	Feb. 1985	13.8		France/CCCE (3.2); Netherlands (2.1); Germany/GTZ (2); France/FAC (1.7);	Fertilizers
			Mar. 1991 - Mar. 1993	22.1[8]					Feb. 1992	49.6		EDF (99); AfDB (60.6); CIDA (29.8); Germany (28.6); West African Development Fund (10.2); BADEA (8.5); CCCE & FAC (7.8); IsDB (5.5); BOAD (3.1); UNDP (0.6); France (21); EC (20); AfDB (13)	Transport sector
Burundi	Aug. 1986 - March 1988	21.0	Mar. 1993 - May 1996	53.0[5]	Nov. 1998	11.0			June 1992	20.6			Agriculture
			June 1996 - Sep. 1999	39.8[5]	Dec. 1999	18.0	14.3		Mar. 1994	18.0			Economic recovery
			Sep. 1999 - Sep. 2002	39.1[71]	May 1986	13.2					(16.2)		Economic management
			Aug. 1986 - Aug. 1989	29.9	June 1988	64.9		Japan (11); Switzerland (7.7); Japan (18.1); Germany (6); Saudi Arabia (2.9)					Structural adjustment credit III
			Nov. 1991 - Nov. 1994	42.7[5]									
Cambodia			May 1994 - Aug. 1997	84.0[5]	June 1992	22.0			July 1988	11.9			Economic rehabilitation
			Oct. 1999 - Oct. 2002	58.5[71]					Sep. 1995	25.4			Structural adjustment credit
Cape Verde	Feb. 1998 - May 1999	2.1			Feb. 2000	21.9			Dec. 1997	21.8			Economic reforms support
	Feb. 1998 - Mar. 2000	2.1											
Central African Republic	Feb. 1980 - Feb. 1981	4.0[9]	June 1987 - May 1990	21.3	Sep. 1986	12.3			July 1987	11.5		Saudi Arabia (2); Japan (6)	Cotton sector
	April 1981 - Dec. 1981	10.4[10]	July 1998 - July 2001	49.4[71]	June 1988	28.9			Dec. 1999	14.4			Fiscal consolidation credit
	April 1983 - April 1984	18.0[10]			June 1990	34.5	14	ADF (25)					
	July 1984 - July 1985	15.0											
	Sep. 1985 - March 1987	15.0[11]											
	June 1987 - May 1988	8.0											
	Mar. 1994 - Mar. 1995	16.5											

Table 31 (cont.)

Country	IMF arrangements — Stand-by/Extended Facility: Period	Amount	SAF/ESAF/PRGF: Period	Amount	World Bank loans and credits — Structural adjustment: Date of approval	IDA	African Facility[1]	Co-financing[2]	Sector and other adjustment: Date of approval	IDA	African Facility[1]	Co-financing[2]	Purpose
Chad			Oct. 1987 - Oct. 1990	21.4					July 1988 April 1989	11.9 45.4	(16.2)	USAID (23); Germany (22.7); CCCE (13.1); ADF (11.3); BDEAC (10.6); EDF (4.8); OPEC Fund for Int.Dev.(4.5); FAC (3.3); UNDP (0.5)	Public finance and cotton sector Transport sector
Comoros	Mar. 1994 - Mar. 1995	16.5	Sep. 1995 - Apr. 1999 Jan. 2000 - Jan. 2003 June 1991 - June 1994	49.6[5] 36.4[71] 3.2	Feb. 1996 June 1997 May 1999	20.2 18.0 22.2			Mar. 1994 June 1991	14.4 6.0	ADF (17); UNDP (1)		Economic recovery Public sector structural adjustment credit III Macroeconomic reform and capacity-building
Dem. Republic of the Congo	Aug. 1979 - Feb. 1981 June 1981 - June 1984[27] Dec. 1983 - March 1985 April 1985 - April 1986 May 1986 - Mar. 1988 May 1987 - May 1988 June 1989 - June 1990	118.0[59] 912.0[60] 228.0[61] 162.0 214.2[62] 100.0[64] 116.4[65]	May 1987 - May 1990 June 1996 - June 1999	203.7[63] 69.5[5]					June 1986 June 1987	17.6 42.2	(60) (94.3)	Japan (15.7)	Industrial sector Agricultural and rural dev.
Djibouti	April 1996 - June 1997	4.6	Oct. 1999 - Oct. 2002	19.1[71]									
Equatorial Guinea	July 1980 - June 1981 June 1985 - June 1986	5.5 9.2[12]	Dec. 1988 - Dec. 1992 Feb. 1993 - Feb. 1996	12.9[13] 12.9[5]									
Ethiopia	May 1981 - June 1982	67.5	Oct. 1992 - Nov. 1995 Oct. 1996 - Oct. 1999	49.4 88.5[5]	June 1993 Jan. 1994 Dec. 1994	176.5 0.3[6] 0.16							
Gambia	Nov. 1979 - Nov. 1980 Feb. 1982 - Feb. 1983 April 1984 - July 1985[15] Sep.1986 - Oct. 1987	1.6 16.9 12.8[14] 5.1	Sep.1986 - Nov. 1988 Nov. 1988 - Nov. 1991 June 1998 - June 2001	12.0[16] 20.5[5] 20.6[71]	Aug. 1986 June 1989	4.3 17.9	9.9	United Kingdom (4.5); ADF (9); ADF (6); Netherlands (2.5)					
Guinea	Dec. 1982 - Nov. 1983 Feb. 1986 - March 1987 July 1987 - Aug. 1988	25.0[17] 33.0[18] 11.6	July 1987 - July 1990 Nov. 1991 - Dec. 1996 Jan. 1997 - Jan. 2000 Jan. 1997 - Jan. 2001	40.5[19] 57.9[5] 70.8[5] 70.8[71]	Feb. 1986 June 1988 Dec. 1992 Dec. 1997	22.9 47.0 0.16 50.8	15.6	France (26.7); Germany (9.4); Japan (27.8); Switzerland (4.8); ADF (12); Japan (11.2)	June 1990	15.4			Education sector Public sector

Table 31 (cont.)

	IMF arrangements – Stand-by/Extended Facility Period	Stand-by Amount	SAF/ESAF/PRGF Period	SAF/ESAF/PRGF Amount	Structural adjustment – Date of approval	Structural adj. IDA	Structural adj. African Facility[1]	Structural adj. Co-financing[2]	Sector & other adj. – Date of approval	Sector IDA	Sector African Facility[1]	Sector Co-financing[2]	Purpose
Guinea-Bissau			Oct. 1987 - Oct. 1990	5.3[20]	May 1987	8.0	4	Switzerland (5.2); Saudi Arabia (3.2); ADF (11.3); IFAD (5.3); Netherlands (4.8); USAID (4.5); ADF (12.0)[22]	Dec.1984	10.1		Switzerland (SwF 4.5 m)	Economic recovery programme[21]
Haiti	Oct. 1978 - Oct. 1981[24]	32.2[23]	Jan. 1995 - July 1998	11.0[5]	May 1989	18.0			Mar.1987	32.8			Economic recovery
	Aug. 1982 - Sep. 1983	34.5							Dec. 1994	26.8			"
	Nov. 1983 - Sep. 1985	60.0[25]											
	Sep.1989 - Dec.1990	21.0[18]											
	Mar. 1995 - Mar.1996	20.0											
Lao People's Dem. Republic	Aug. 1980 - Aug. 1981	14.0	Dec.1986 - Dec. 1989	30.9[26]	May 2000	18.0							
			Oct.1996 - Oct. 1999	91.1[5]									
Lesotho	Sep.1994 - Sep. 1995	8.4	Sep.1989 - Sep. 1992	20.5	June 1989	30.8							
	July 1995 - July 1996	7.2	June 1993 - May 1997	35.2[5]	Oct. 1991	30.0							
			June 1988 - June 1991	10.6	Feb. 1996	26.9							
			May 1991 - Aug. 1994	18.1[5]									
			Sep.1996 - Sep. 1997	7.2[5]									
Madagascar	June 1980 - June 1982	64.5[27]	Aug. 1987 - May 1989	46.5[29]	Mar. 1997	48.6			May 1986	19	(33)	KfW (4); Japan (3); ADF (40); Switzerland (8)	Agricultural sector
	April 1981 - June 1982	76.2[28]	May 1989 - May 1992	76.9[5]	Mar. 1997	0.4			June 1988	90.5			Public sector
	July 1982 - July 1983	51.0[14]	Nov. 1996 - Nov. 1999	81.4[5]	May 1999	73.5			Mar.1989	1.1[6]			Public sector
	April 1984 - Mar. 1985	33.0	Nov. 1996 - July 2000	81.4[7]					Oct.1989	0.9[6]			"
	April 1985 - April 1986	29.5							Nov.1990	1.2[6]			"
	Sep.1986 - Feb. 1988	30.0							Nov.1991	1[6]			Multisector rehabilitation
	Sep.1988 - July 1989	13.3[30]							Dec.1992	1[6]			Structural adjustment credit II
Malawi	Oct. 1979 - Dec. 1981[31]	26.3	July 1988 - Mar. 1994	67.0[5]	June 1981	36.7[33]	37.3	Germany/KfW (6.4); Japan/OECF (22.6); USAID (15); Japan (17.7); United Kingdom (7.5); Germany (5)	April 1983	4.6		IFAD (10.3)	Smallholder fertilizers
	May 1980 - March 1982	49.9[32]	Oct.1995 - Dec. 1999	51.0[5]	Dec. 1983	51.9			June 1988	50.6		OECF (30); USAID (25); ADF (19.5); EEC (16)	Industrial and trade policy adjustment
	Aug. 1982 - Aug. 1983	22.0			Dec. 1985	28.0			Mar. 1989	4.0[6]			"
	Sep.1983 - Sep. 1986	81.0[34]			Jan. 1987		8.4		Oct. 1989	3.8[6]			"
	March 1988 - May 1989	13.0							April 1990	52.6		USAID (25); United Kingdom (16.5); Netherlands (5); Germany, EEC and Japan (6.1)	Agriculture
									Nov. 1990	5.1[6]			Industry and trade

Table 31 (cont.)

	IMF arrangements				World Bank loans and credits								
	Stand-by/Extended Facility		SAF/ESAF/PRGF		Structural adjustment				Sector and other adjustment				
						Amount				Amount			
Country	Period	Amount	Period	Amount	Date of approval	IDA	African Facility[1]	Co-financing[2]	Date of approval	IDA	African Facility[1]	Co-financing[2]	Purpose
Malawi (cont.)	Nov. 1994 - June 1995	15.0							Nov. 1991	4.0[6]		AfDB (13.4)	Agriculture
									June 1992	85.4			Entrepreneurship dev. & drought recovery
									Dec. 1992	4.3[6]			"
			Nov. 1996	2.4[70]					Nov. 1994	27.6[6]			"
			Dec. 1998	67.2					Dec. 1994	3.2[6]			"
									April 1996	70.3			Fiscal restructuring & deregulation programme
									April 1996	2.9[70]			Fiscal restructuring and and de-regulation program. II
Mali	May 1982 - May 1993	30.4	Aug. 1988 - Aug. 1991	35.6[14]	Dec. 1990	50.3		EC (20); AfDB (18)	June 1988	29.4		Japan (38.7); Saudi Arabia (5.9); ADF (45)	Public enterprise sector
	Dec. 1983 - May 1985	40.5	Aug. 1992 - April 1996	79.2[5]					June 1990	40.7		FAC/CCCE (50.8); SDC (6.9); Netherlands (5.2); Germany (2.9)	Agricultural sector/ investment
	Nov. 1985 - March 1987	22.9[36]	April 1996 - Aug. 1999	62.0[5]					Mar. 1994	18.2			Economic recovery
	Aug. 1988 - June 1990	12.7	Aug. 1999 - Aug. 2002	46.7[71]					Jan. 1995	34.3			Education
									June 1996	41.6			Economic management
Mauritania	July 1980 - March 1982[38]	29.7[37]	Sep.1986 - May 1989	23.7[39]	June 1987	11.7	21.4	Saudi Arabia (4.8); Germany (2.8)	Feb. 1990	19.4			Agricultural sector/ investment
	June 1981 - March 1982	25.8	May 1989 - Jan. 1995	50.9[5]					June 1990	30.7		CCCE (8); Germany (2); WFP (1); Japan (50); SFD (19.8); KFAED (13.7); AFESD (10.3); Abu Dhabi Fund (6.1); Spain (5); Germany (4)	Public enterprises
	April 1985 - April 1986	12.0	Jan. 1995 - July 1998	42.8[5]	Feb. 1999	0.1			Nov. 1990	2.9[6]			Public enterprises
	April 1986 - April 1987	12.0	July 1999 - July 2002	42.5[71]	Nov. 1999	0.1			Nov. 1991	1.9[6]			"
	May 1987 - May 1988	10.0			May 2000	22.4			Dec. 1992	1.6[6]			"
									Jan. 1994	1.0[6]			"
									Nov. 1996	0.4[6]			Public resource management
									Dec. 1997	0.3			Public resource management / Fiscal reform
Mozambique			June 1987 - June 1990	42.7	Feb. 1997	69.1			May 1985	45.5	(18.6)	Switzerland (11.2)	Economic rehabilitation programme I
			June 1990 - Dec. 1995	130.1[5]					Aug. 1987	54.5		United Kingdom (17.5); Switzerland (12.8); Germany (10.9); Sweden (9.4); Finland (8.9)	Economic rehabilitation programme II
			June 1996 - Aug. 1999	75.6[5]					May 1989	68.2			Economic rehabilitation programme III
			June 1999 - June 2002	87.2[71]					June 1992	132		Switzerland (6)	Economic recovery
									June 1994	141.7			Economic recovery II

Table 31 (cont.)

| Country | IMF arrangements | | | | World Bank loans and credits | | | | | | | | |
| | Stand-by/Extended Facility | | SAF/ESAF/PRGF | | Structural adjustment | | | | Sector and other adjustment | | | | Purpose |
	Period	Amount	Period	Amount	Date of approval	IDA	African Facility[1]	Co-financing[2]	Date of approval	IDA	African Facility[1]	Co-financing[2]	
Nepal	Dec. 1985 - April 1987	18.7			Mar. 1987	40.9							
			Oct. 1987 - Oct. 1990	26.1	June 1989	46.2							
			Oct. 1992 - Oct. 1995	33.6[5]									
Niger	Oct. 1983 - Dec. 1984	18.0	Nov. 1986 - Nov. 1988	23.6[40]	Feb. 1986	18.3	36.6	KfW (5)	June 1987	46			Public enterprises
	Dec. 1984 - Dec. 1985	16.0											
	Dec. 1985 - Dec. 1986	13.5											
	Dec. 1986 - Dec. 1987	10.1											
	Mar. 1994 - Mar. 1995	18.6	Dec. 1988 - Dec. 1991	47.2[5]	Mar. 1997	21.6			Mar. 1994	18.2	15.4		Economic recovery
			June 1996 - Aug. 1999	58.0[5]	Oct. 1998	48.0							Public sector
													Public finance reform
Rwanda	Oct. 1979 - Oct. 1980	5.0[42]	April 1991 - April 1994	30.7[26]	June 1991	67.5		Switzerland (SwF 10m); Belgium (BF 400m)	Jan. 1995	34.3			Emergency recovery
			June 1998 - June 2001	71.4[71]	Mar. 1999	53.0							
Samoa	Aug. 1979 - Aug. 1980	0.7[42]											
	June 1983 - June 1984	3.4											
	July 1984 - July 1985	3.4											
Sao Tome and Principe			June 1989 - June 1992	2.8[43]	June 1987	3.1	2.3	ADF (8.5); ADF(12); IMF (2.6)					
			Apr. 2000 - Apr. 2003	6.7[71]	June 1990	7.5							
Senegal	Oct. 1987 - Oct. 1988	21.3	Nov. 1986	43.0	Feb. 1986	18.3							
			Nov. 1986 - Nov. 1988	59.6	May 1987	35.0	31.4	7.1	Dec. 1989	35.3			Str.adjustment credit III (supplement)
				144.7	Mar. 1989	4.2							Structural credit IV
Sierra Leone	Mar. 1994 - Aug. 1994	48.0	Nov. 1988 - June 1992	131.0	Feb. 1990	62.4			Dec. 1995	1.8			Agricultural sector
	Nov. 1979 - Nov. 1980	17.0	Aug. 1994 - Jan. 1998		May 1990	3.5			Nov. 1996	1.3			Energy sector
	March 1981 - Feb. 1984[45]	186.0[44]	Apr. 1998 - Apr. 2001	107.0[71]	Nov. 1990	5.1			June 1984	20.3		IFAD (5.4)	Agriculture
	Feb. 1984 - Feb. 1985	50.2[46]	Nov. 1986 - Nov. 1989	40.5[47]	Apr. 1992	3.5			April 1992	31.4			Reconstruction
	Nov. 1986 - Nov. 1987	23.2			May 1998	74.0			April 1992	0.2[6]			Imports
					Oct. 1993	35.9			Dec. 1992	0.2[6]			
					Jan. 1994	0.16							
					Dec. 1995	0.2[6]							
					Nov.1996	0.2[70]							
						0.1							
					Feb. 2000	21.9							
Solomon Islands													
Somalia	Feb. 1980 - Feb. 1981	11.5[48]	June 1987 - June 1990	30.9[26]	June 1999	8.9			June 1989	54.2		ADF (25); BITS (0.5)	Agriculture
	July 1981 - July 1982	43.1											
	July 1982 - Jan. 1984	60.0											
	Feb. 1985 - Sep.1986	22.1											
	June 1987 - Feb.1989	33.2											
Sudan	May 1979 - May 1982[49]	427.0							June 1983	46.4			Agricultural rehabilitation
	Feb. 1982 - Feb. 1983	198.0[50]											
	Feb. 1983 - March 1984	170.0											
	June 1984 - June 1985	90.0[51]											

Table 31 (cont.)

Country	IMF arrangements — Stand-by/Extended Facility Period	Amount	IMF arrangements — SAF/ESAF/PRGF Period	Amount	World Bank loans and credits — Structural adjustment Date of approval	IDA	African Facility[1]	Co-financing[2]	Sector and other adjustment Date of approval	IDA	African Facility[1]	Co-financing[2]	Purpose
Togo	June 1979 - Dec. 1980	15.0[52]			May 1983	36.9							
	Feb. 1981 - Feb. 1983	47.5[53]											
	March 1983 - April 1984	21.4			May 1985	28.1							
	May 1984 - May 1985	19.0			Aug. 1985		9.7						
	May 1985 - May 1986	15.4											
	June 1986 - April 1988	23.0	Mar. 1988 - May 1989	26.9[54]	Mar. 1988	33.0		ADF (17.3); Japan (20.8)					
	Mar. 1988 - April 1989	13.0	May 1989 - May 1993	46.1[5]	Mar. 1989	0.1[6]							
					Oct. 1989	0.2[6]							
			Sep.1994 - June 1998	65.2[5]	Dec. 1990	39.6			Feb. 1991	10.2			Population and health
									April 1996	32.2			Economic recovery and adjustment
Uganda	Jan. 1980 - Dec. 1980	12.5							Feb. 1983	63.5			Agricultural rehabilitation
	June 1981 - June 1982	112.5							May 1984	47.2	18.8	Italy/DCD (10)	Reconstruction
	Aug. 1982 - Aug. 1983	112.5							Sep. 1987	50.9		United Kingdom/ODA (16)	Economic recovery
	Sep.1983 - Sep. 1984	95.0[55]	June 1987 - April 1989	69.7[56]					Mar. 1989	1.3[6]			......
			April 1989 - June 1994	219.2[57]					April 1989	19[6]			......
									Oct. 1989	1.2[6]			......
									Feb. 1990	98.1	(12.8)		......
			Sep. 1994 - Nov. 1997	120.5[5]					Nov. 1990	1.5[6]			......
									Dec. 1990	69.5			Agriculture
									Nov. 1991	1.2[6]			Economic recovery
									May 1993	72.8			Finance
			Nov. 1997 - Nov. 2000	100.4[71]					Jan. 1994	0.8[6]			"
									Mar. 1998	59.2			Education sector
United Republic of Tanzania	Sep. 1980 - June 1982	179.6[58]							Nov. 1986	41.3	38.2	Germany (17.3); Switzerland (9.2); United Kingdom (7.3); Saudi Arabia (4); ADF (24);	Multisector rehabilitation
	Aug. 1986 - Feb. 1988	64.2	Oct. 1987 - Oct. 1990	74.9					Jan. 1988	22.5	(26.0)	United Kingdom (15); Switzerland (14); Netherlands (10)	Industrial rehabilitation and trade adjustment
									Dec. 1988	97.6			Multisector rehabilitation
									Mar. 1989	9.7[6]			Industrial rehabilitation
									Oct. 1989	8.3[6]			Industry and trade adjustment
			July 1991 - July 1994	181.9[5]					Mar. 1990	150.4		Netherlands (40); United Kingdom (20)	Agriculture
									Dec. 1990	11.5[6]			Finance
			Nov. 1996 - Feb. 2000	181.6[5]	June 1997	93.2[70]			Nov. 1991	8.6[6]			"
					Dec. 1997	1.8			Nov. 1991	150.2		United Kingdom (16.8); Switzerland (6.6)	"
			Mar. 2000 - Mar. 2003	135.0[71]	Dec. 1999	0.8			Dec. 1992	8.2[6]			Stru.adjustment credit
					June 2000	141.8							
Yemen	Mar. 1996 - June 1997	132.4	Oct. 1997 - Oct. 2000	264.8[5]	Nov. 1997	58.9			April 1996	53.7			Economic recovery
	Oct. 1997 - Oct. 2000	105.9	Oct. 1997 - Oct. 2000	264.8[71]	Mar. 1999	35.8							Financial sector
	Oct. 1997 - Mar. 2001	105.9											Public sec. mgmt. adj. credit

Table 31 (cont.)

	IMF arrangements				World Bank loans and credits								
	Stand-by/Extended Facility		SAF/ESAF/PRGF		Structural adjustment				Sector and other adjustment				
						Amount				Amount			
Country	Period	Amount	Period	Amount	Date of approval	IDA	African Facility[1]	Co-financing[2]	Date of approval	IDA	African Facility[1]	Co-financing[2]	Purpose
Zambia	April 1978 - April 1980	250.0							Jan. 1985	24.7	(10)	AfDB (23.4); CIDA (6.8); USAID (5); Switzerland (4.8); Germany (18.8)	Agricultural rehabilitation
	May 1981 - May 1984[24]	800.0[66]											
	April 1983 - April 1984	211.5[67]							Mar. 1991	149.6			Economic recovery
	July 1984 - April 1986	225[68]							Mar. 1991	19.4[6]			
	Feb. 1986 - Feb. 1988	229.8[69]							May 1992	7.6[6]			Privatization and industry
									June 1992	146			
									Dec. 1992	15.1[6]			
									June 1993	72.1			
									Aug. 1993	7.0[6]			
									Jan. 1994	12.1[6]			Economic and social adjustment
			Dec. 1995-Dec. 1998	701.7[5]					Mar. 1994	108.9			
									Dec. 1994	9.7[6]			
					Aug. 1996	62.4			June 1995	19.1			Economic recovery and investment promotion
			Mar. 1999 - Mar. 2002	254.5[5]	Nov. 1996	5.4			July 1995	90.0			
					Jan. 1999	122.7							
						2.0			Dec. 1995	8[70]			Economic and social adjustment
			Mar. 1999 - Mar. 2002	254.5	June 2000	105.5			June 1996	16.0			Public sector reform and export promotion Fiscal sustainability credit.

Sources: IMF, *Annual Report, 2000* and various issues; *IMF Survey* (various issues); World Bank, *Annual Report, 2000* and various issues; *World Bank News* (various issues).

m = million

1. Special Facility for Sub-Saharan Africa; amounts in parentheses are expressed in millions of dollars.
2. Including special joint financing and bilateral support; amounts are in millions of dollars unless stated otherwise.
3. Extended Facility arrangement, cancelled as of June 1982.
4. SDR 580 m not purchased.
5. ESAF.
6. Supplemental credit.
7. SDR 6.3 m not purchased.
8. SDR 15.8 m not purchased.
9. SDR 2.4 m not purchased.
10. SDR 13.5 m not purchased.
11. SDR 7.5 m not purchased.
12. SDR 3.8 m not purchased.
13. SDR 3.7 m not purchased.
14. SDR 10.2 m not purchased.
15. Cancelled as of April 1985.
16. SDR 3.4 m not purchased.
17. SDR 13.5 m not purchased.
18. SDR 6.0 m not purchased.
19. SDR 11.6 m not purchased.
20. SDR 1.5 m not purchased.
21. Supported by IMF; (SDR 1.88 m purchased in first credit tranche).
22. Additional financing.
23. SDR 21.4 m not purchased.
24. Extended Facility arrangement.
25. SDR 39 m not purchased.
26. SDR 22.1 m not purchased.
27. Cancelled as of April 1981; SDR 54.5 m not purchased.
28. Augmented in June 1981 with SDR 32.3 m; SDR 70 m not purchased at expiration of arrangement.
29. SDR 33.2 m not purchased.
30. Cancelled as of May 1989; SDR 10.5 m not purchased.
31. Cancelled as of May 1980; SDR 20.9 m not purchased.
32. SDR 9.9 m not purchased.
33. IBRD loan.
34. Original amount decreased from SDR 100 m; SDR 24 m not purchased.
35. Extended Facility arrangement; cancelled as of August 1986.
36. SDR 6.6 m not purchased.
37. SDR 20.8 m not purchased.
38. Cancelled as of May 1981.
39. SDR 6.8 m not purchased.
40. SDR 6.7 m not purchased.
41. ESAF; original amount decreased from SDR 50.6 m.
42. Not purchased.
43. SDR 2 m not purchased.
44. Including an increase of SDR 22.3 m in June 1981. SDR 152 m not purchased.
45. Extended Facility arrangement; cancelled as of April 1982.
46. SDR 31.2 m not purchased.
47. SDR 29 m not purchased.
48. SDR 5.5 m not purchased.
49. Extended Facility arrangement; cancelled as of February 1982; SDR 176 m not purchased.
50. SDR 128 m not purchased.
51. SDR 70 m not purchased.
52. SDR 1.75 m not purchased.
53. SDR 40.3 m not purchased.
54. SDR 19.2 m not purchased.
55. SDR 30.0 m not purchased.
56. SDR 19.9 m not purchased.
57. ESAF; original amount increased from SDR 179.3 m.
58. SDR 154.6 m not purchased.
59. SDR 9.0 m not purchased.
60. Cancelled as of June 1982; SDR 737 m not purchased.
61. SDR 30 m not purchased.
62. Cancelled as of April 1987; SDR 166.6 m not purchased.
63. SDR 58.2 m not purchased.
64. SDR 75.5 m not purchased.
65. SDR 41.4 m not purchased.
66. Cancelled as of July 1982; SDR 500 m not purchased.
67. SDR 67.5 m not purchased.
68. Cancelled as of February 1986; SDR 145 m not purchased.
69. Cancelled as of May 1987; SDR 194.8 m not purchased.
70. From IDA reflows.
71. PRGF, Poverty Reduction and Growth Facility Trust, formerly Enhanced Structural Adjustment Facility.

Printed in Switzerland
GE.02-50980–May 2002–7,825

UNCTAD/LDC/2002

United Nations publication
Sales No. E.02.II.D.13

ISBN 92-1-112562-6
ISSN 0257-7550